THE
GREAT
WORLD
ATLAS

List of Credits

An Insight to Our World & The World in Maps. Designed and produced by Engineering Surveys Reproduction (ESR) Ltd. Cartographic Design and Production Manager, Keith Brook. Senior Cartographic Editor, Zoë Goodwin. Cartographic Editor, Lindsay Evans. Cartographers: Nicky Chapman, Mike Larby, Gill Dalton, David Handley-Clarke, Chris Major. Cartographic Consultant, Allan Marles. Cartographic Illustrator, Janos Marffy. Illustrator, Tom McArthur.

Continents and Countries. Text by Rupert O Matthews. Designed by Philip D Clucas, MSIAD. Edited by Joseph F Ryan, PhD. The following flags are copyright by and used with permission from The Flag Research Center, Winchester, Mass. 01890: Afghanistan, Albania, Andorra, Azerbaijan, Bahrain, Bangladesh, Bermuda, Bosnia-Herzegovina, Brazil, Bulgaria, Cape Verde, Congo, Croatia, Czech Republic, Djibouti, Dominica, El Salvador, Equatorial Guinea, Estonia, Finland, Georgia, Haiti, Iraq, Kazakhstan, Kiribati, Kyrgyzstan, Latvia, Lithuania, Marshall Islands, Micronesia, Mongolia, Nepal, Nicaragua, Russia, San Marino, Saudi Arabia, Slovak Republic, Slovenia, Spain, Tajikistan, Tuvalu, United Arab Emirates, Uzbekistan, Yugoslavia, Zimbabwe.

The World from Space. Text by Jo Francis. Designed by Philip D Clucas, MSIAD. Edited by Joseph F Ryan, PhD. The publishers wish to thank all those involved in the production of this section and, in particular, the photo technicians at ESR Ltd, Richard Ross, John Gill, Michael Hodson Designs, Apollo Colour Repro Ltd, E. S. Computing Ltd, Typogram Ltd, Link-Line Ltd and Jos Poels at The Flag Institute which provided flags for the Democratic Republic of the Congo, Belarus, Cambodia, Comoros, Ethiopia, Macedonia, Oman, Palau, Seychelles and Turkmenistan. Acknowledgments also to Yoyo Platt for her contribution, J H for his suggestions, Andy Clarke at the Science Photo Library, and Teddy Hartshorn and Mark Austin of Digital Vision for providing the photographic images from the National Aeronautics and Space Administration (NASA). The publishers would also like to thank Digital Vision for their kind permission to reproduce the illustrations in this book, except for the following images supplied by the Science Photo Library (picture numbers in brackets): page 89 (5, 6) Robert M Carey, NOAA, 90 (1) Julian Baum & David Angus, 90 (2) NASA, 90 (3) NOAA, 90 (4) European Space Agency (ESA), 94 (2) ESA, Eurimage, 94 (3) National Remote Sensing Centre (NRSC) Ltd, 94 (4) NRSC Ltd, 95 (6) NRSC Ltd, 97 Geospace, 98 (3) Geospace, 101 (6) BP/NRSC, 102-103 (4) J Knighton, 104 (1) J Knighton, 105 (7) Earth Satellite Corporation, 108 (1) NRSC Ltd, 109 (6) Earth Satellite Corporation, 110 (1) CNES, 1986 Distribution SPOT Image, 110 (3) copyright 1995, Worldsat International & J Knighton, 110 (4) BP/NRSC, 124 (1) Gene Feldman, NASA GSFC, 124 (2) BP/NRSC.

5052 The Great World Atlas
This updated edition published in 1999 by CLB,
A division of Quadrillion Publishing Ltd,
Distributed in the USA by Quadrillion Publishing Inc.,
230 Fifth Avenue, New York, NY 10001

Copyright © 1989, 1991, 1992, 1993, 1995, 1996, 1998, 1999
Quadrillion Publishing Ltd, Godalming Business Centre
Woolsack Way, Godalming, Surrey, England GU7 1XW

Printed in Spain

This edition revised and edited by Joseph F Ryan, PhD

THE
GREAT
WORLD
ATLAS

FOREWORD BY

William R. Mead

Professor Emeritus of Geography
University College London

CLB

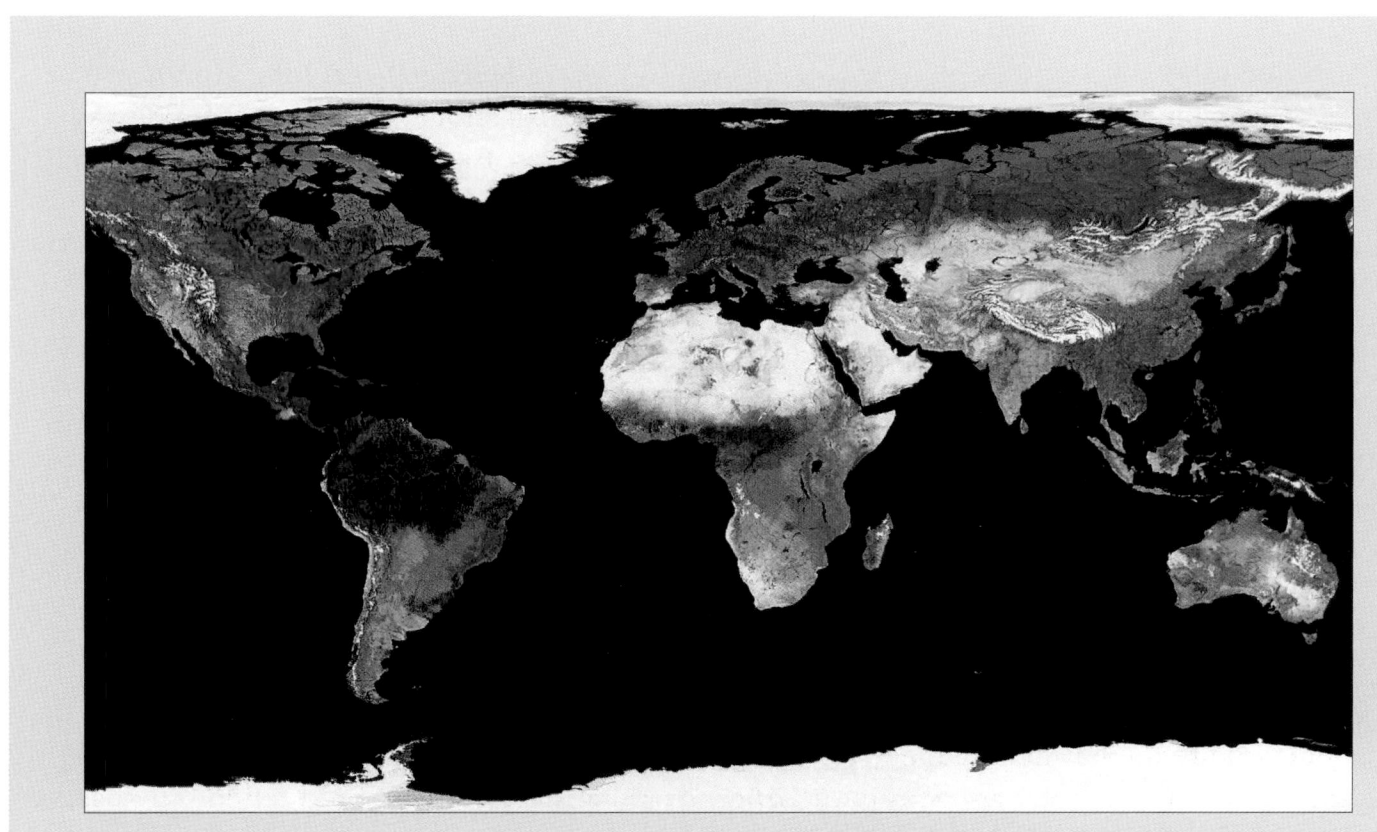

The world revealed with the accuracy of satellite imagery

FOREWORD

In 1636 a bound collection of maps was published by Gerard Mercator and John Hondt with a frontispiece illustrating the titan Atlas bearing the world on his shoulders. As a result, the word 'atlas' entered the vocabulary as a synonym for a book of maps. In the seventeenth century only the very rich could afford the luxury of an atlas. Cartographic masterpieces by Dutch map engravers offered their patrons the first view of a world the horizons of which were being swiftly broadened by maritime discovery.

Today, most households can afford an atlas even if they do not own one. Certainly, the need for and the attraction of the atlas have never been greater. Never have so many people been on the move around the world. Never have so many been concerned with the impact of world events. 'Atlas-eaters', Dylan Thomas called those who were hungry for world news. The atlas, through its co-ordinates of latitude and longitude, can answer the question 'Where?'. Or, perhaps, more precisely, the index to the atlas provides the answer – hence the importance of the extended index to this volume.

In an atlas, the science of map-making is married to the art of map presentation. Techniques of production are increasingly refined; sources of information are increasingly precise. Satellite imagery, photogrammetry and computerisation have transformed map production. An atlas, however, is no substitute for a globe. The two are complementary, for not even the larger globes can include a fraction of the information that is packed into an atlas. The task of projecting the globe onto a flat surface has taxed the ingenuity of mathematicians since the Greeks first attempted to measure the circumference of the Earth. The variety of formidably-named projections employed in this book illustrates the extended range of options available to present-day cartographers.

Atlases have a romantic appeal as well as a utilitarian value. The novelist Alan Sillitoe, in a memorable essay on maps, recalls the flights of fancy set in motion by his 'first cheap layer-tinted atlas'. To turn the pages which follow – to contemplate the controlling features of land and sea, to reflect upon the boundaries that define the outlines and shape the destinies of countries, and to respond to the magic of the infinity of place names – is to experience a stimulus to the imagination as well as to the intellect.

William R. Mead
PROFESSOR EMERITUS OF GEOGRAPHY, UNIVERSITY COLLEGE LONDON

CONTENTS

Planet Earth viewed from above the Moon's surface, set against the vastness of space

AN
INSIGHT
TO OUR
WORLD

Once it was possible to live unaffected by the world at large. But, as the poet John Donne recognised over three and a half centuries ago, 'No man is an Island, entire of it self'. Swift travel, globe-spanning communications and intense media coverage underscore our interdependence. This section, therefore, considers the planet from a macro perspective while also examining some of the major patterns of human interaction. Earth is an incomparable but fragile world. Enjoined to 'think globally, act locally', the following pages set the wider stage, allowing us to reflect upon our relationships with other peoples and the environment.

*Rampant economic growth is possible only at the Earth's expense **Above:** iron-ore mine **Above right:** oil-rig flare **Right:** mass production of cars*

THE SOLAR SYSTEM

Modern scientific and astronomical studies have increased our knowledge of the universe and the Earth's place within it immensely. Space exploration has solved many mysteries, but there is still much to be learnt.

The Earth is one of nine planets and numerous smaller bodies that orbit the Sun. The Sun is part of a much larger group of perhaps 100 billion stars that make up the Milky Way. This in turn is only one of the billions of galaxies in an incomprehensibly large universe.

Orbiting the Sun

Under the control of the Sun's gravitational force each planet maintains an elliptical orbit. Except for Mercury and Pluto, which are inclined 7° and 17° respectively, the orbits of the other planets lie within 3° of the plane of the Sun's equator.

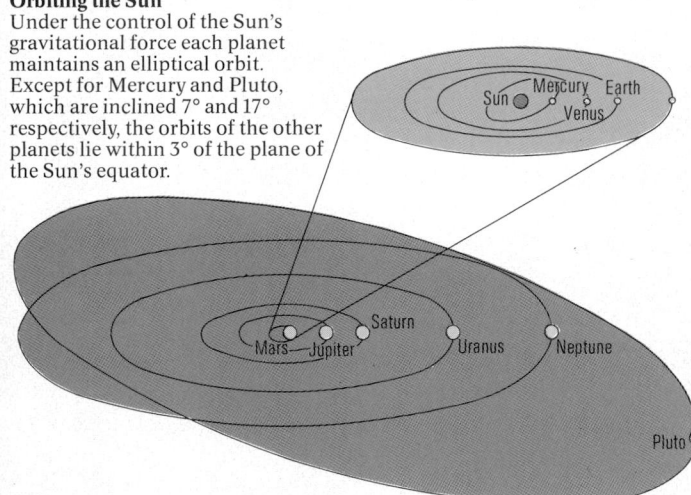

	Sun	Mercury	Venus	Earth	Mars	Jupiter	Saturn
Distance from the Sun (mean) millions of km	-	57·9	108·2	149·6	227·9	778·3	1427
Orbit (sidereal period) days	-	88	224·7	365·25	687	4332·5	10759·2
Rotation d—days hr—hours	24·6d	58·65d	243d	23·93hr	24·62hr	9·8hr	10·2hr
Orbital inclination	-	7°	3°23'	0°	1°52'	1°18'	2°29'
Equatorial diameter km	1392530	4878	12104	12756	6787	142800	120600
Mass (Earth—1)	333000	0·055	0·815	1 5·97x10²⁴kg	0·012	317·8	92·2
Density (water—1)	1·41	5·43	5·24	5·52	3·94	1·32	0·7
Number of satellites	-	0	0	1	2	16	17

The Sun is a huge, brilliant star at the centre of the Solar System. It is thought to be about five billion years old; halfway through its stable period of existence. The source of the Sun's immense energy is the continuous fusion of hydrogen into helium. Temperatures in the photosphere can reach 5500°C. Above the photosphere lies the chromosphere, the top layer of which contains numerous spicules that reach into the lower corona. The corona extends far beyond the Sun and produces a bright glow. Solar prominences often appear as great arches extending into the corona. The most conspicuous features on the surface of the Sun are dark blemishes called sunspots. These groups may be associated with violent solar flares.

Mercury is the smallest of the terrestrial planets and the closest to the Sun. The surface is distinctly lunar in appearance, extensively cratered, with smoother volcanic plains. Long lines of cliffs and scarps cut across the plains and craters alike. These probably resulted from crustal shortening as the planet cooled and shrank. Mercury has the greatest temperature extremes of any planet, rising to 480°C during daylight and falling to −180°C at night. This, as well as the virtual lack of atmosphere, indicates that no known form of life could survive there.

Venus is the planet most similar to Earth in both size and mass. However, it is altogether a more hostile world. A dense atmosphere (96 per cent carbon dioxide) obscures the surface under permanent cloud whilst maintaining a temperature of about 480°C. Radar mapping has revealed a landscape of highland 'continents', 'lowlands' and undulating plains. There are also shallow craters, large volcanoes and some rift valleys and trenches. Space probes have shown that the surface is strewn with smooth rocks.

Earth is the largest of the inner planets. The lower atmosphere consists mainly of nitrogen and oxygen. Ozone in the upper layers protects the Earth from the Sun's harmful radiation. The Earth is unique in having a surface largely covered with water (70 per cent), the remainder by continental land masses. Plate tectonics is the dominant process responsible for the structure of the surface, which is then subjected to erosional forces, creating a changing landscape.

Mars has a thin atmosphere which is mainly carbon dioxide (95 per cent). The mean surface temperature is about −40°C, ranging from −138°C at the winter pole to 27°C at the equator, causing strong atmospheric circulation. Dust storms can occur, enveloping the planet, and may take months to settle. Surface features include craters that are often filled with dust, lava plains and giant volcanoes such as Olympus Mons (25km high and 500km across its base), immense canyons, winding river-like valleys, the formation of which is subject to speculation, and polar ice caps which expand and contract with the seasons.

Asteroids are probably the remains of the debris from which the planets formed. They range in diameter from 1000km (the largest, Ceres), to less than 1km. The orbits of most asteroids lie between Mars and Jupiter.

Jupiter is the largest and most massive of the planets. It rotates faster than any other planet. This causes the equatorial region to bulge and the poles to flatten. The atmosphere is composed primarily of hydrogen and helium. The immense heat emanating from the planet's interior produces huge convection currents in the atmosphere. This drives strong wind systems that generate the alternate light- and dark-coloured bands of cloud that encircle the planet. A prominent feature is the Great Red Spot, which was first seen in the 17th century. It is thought to be a huge storm. Other storms have been observed, but none have survived for more than a few days. Jupiter's ring system appears to consist of particles temporarily entrapped by the planet's intense magnetic field. Its satellite system has at least 16 moons.

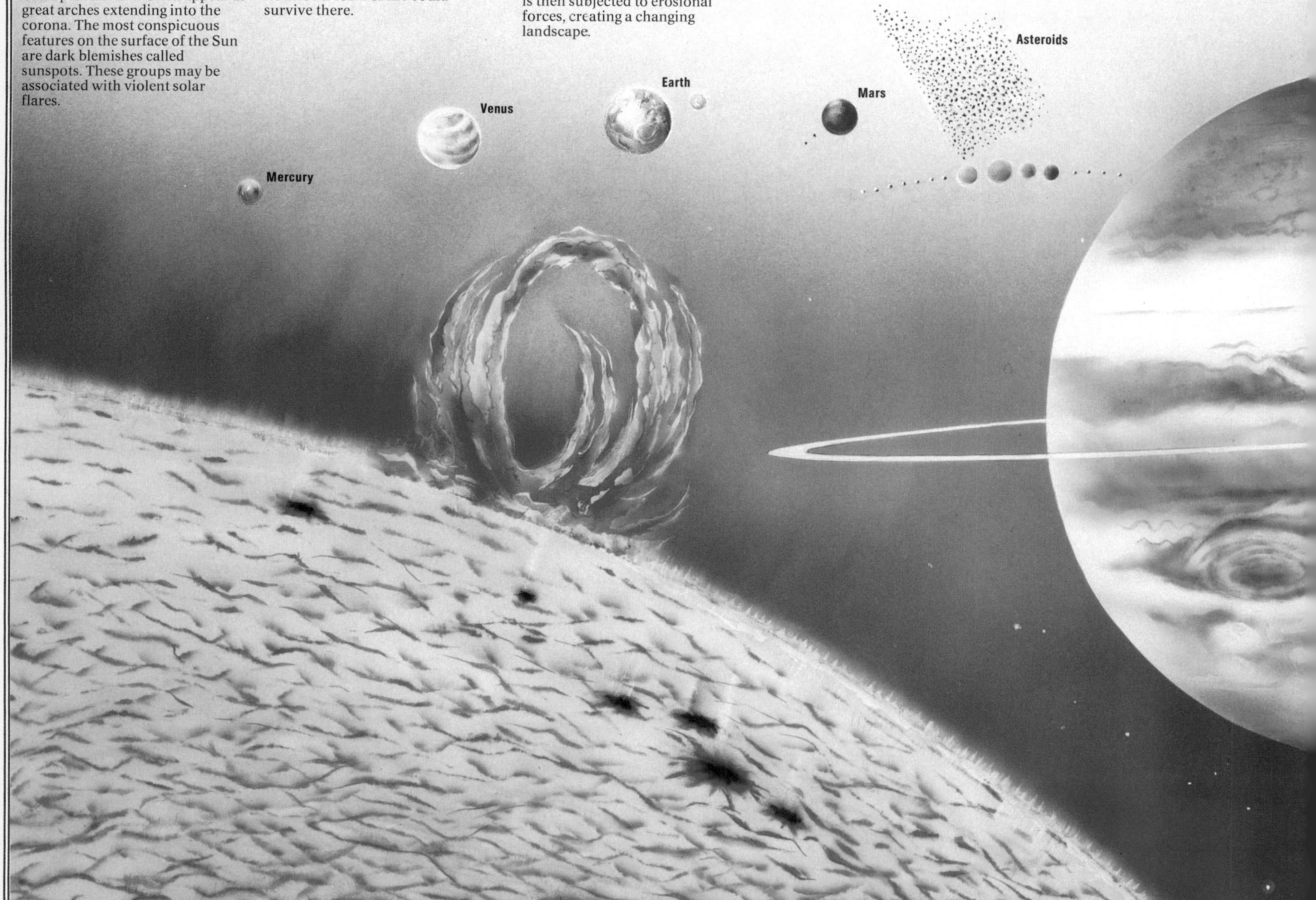

Mercury

Venus

Earth

Mars

Asteroids

Uranus	Neptune	Pluto
1870	4497	5900
30684·8	60190·5	90465
16·3hr	18·2hr	6·38d
0°46′	1°46′	17°12′
51800	48600	3000
14·5	17·2	0·002
1·27	1·76	1·1?
5	2	1

Saturn, broadly similar in structure and composition to Jupiter, has a significantly lower mean density, and a greater degree of polar flattening. The atmosphere consists mainly of hydrogen, with some helium. It is thought that droplets of helium formed in Saturn's upper atmosphere sink towards the core, heating the interior as they descend. This may explain why the planet emits over twice as much heat as it receives. Saturn's belt-zone pattern is less conspicuous, and large cloud features are scarce. Strong zonal winds are symmetrical about the equator. The equatorial jet can blow at a speed of 1800km per hour. The most prominent feature of Saturn is its ring system, which is composed of small particles coated with water ice orbiting the planet in nearly circular paths. Seventeen satellites have so far been detected.

Uranus is thought to have a rocky, metallic core surrounded by a deep envelope of water, methane and ammonia 'ices', with a deep atmosphere composed mainly of hydrogen, helium and methane. Its axis is inclined by 98°, causing strong seasonal effects. The poles receive more solar radiation during each orbit than the equator. This, coupled with the lack of an internal heat source, suggests that atmospheric circulation is weak. Uranus has nine slightly elliptical rings of debris orbiting its equatorial region. It is also known to have five satellites.

Neptune was discovered due to the irregularities in the motion of Uranus's orbit which indicated the existence of another planet. Its composition is thought to be very similar to that of Uranus. However, as it emits twice as much heat as it receives, an internal heat source is thought to be responsible. Neptune has a 'bluish' appearance that has been attributed to the methane in the atmosphere. It has two satellites: Triton and Nereid.

Pluto lies on the fringe of the Solar System. Although a planet was believed to exist beyond the orbit of Neptune, Pluto was not found until 1930. Its satellite, Charon, was not discovered until 1978. The planet is thought to be made up of a mixture of frozen gases and rock. It has an eccentric orbit, which is presently inside the orbit of Neptune, where it will remain until the end of the century.

Pluto

Neptune

Uranus

Saturn

Jupiter

11

Designed and produced by E.S.R.

EARTH AND MOON

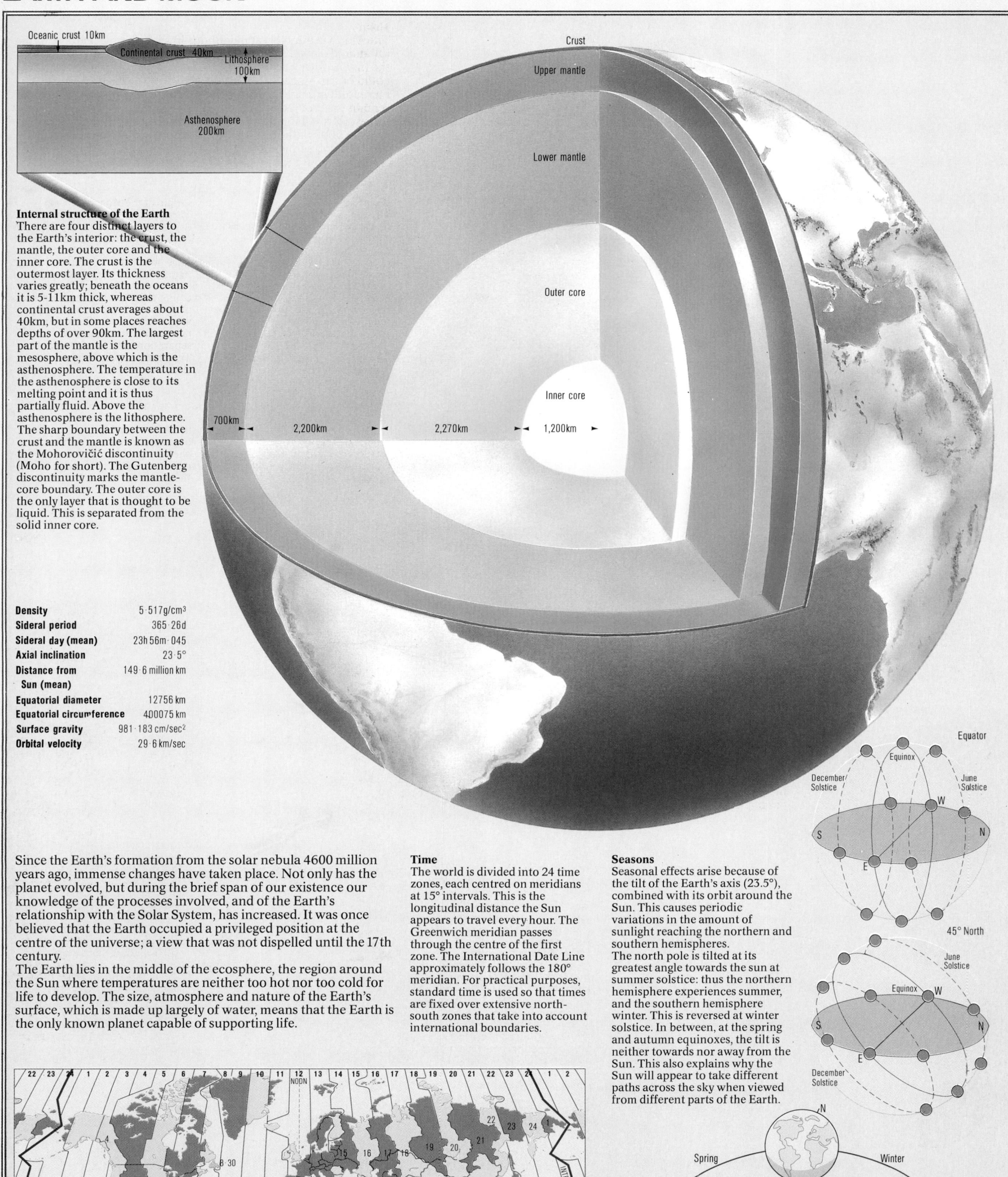

Internal structure of the Earth

There are four distinct layers to the Earth's interior: the crust, the mantle, the outer core and the inner core. The crust is the outermost layer. Its thickness varies greatly; beneath the oceans it is 5-11km thick, whereas continental crust averages about 40km, but in some places reaches depths of over 90km. The largest part of the mantle is the mesosphere, above which is the asthenosphere. The temperature in the asthenosphere is close to its melting point and it is thus partially fluid. Above the asthenosphere is the lithosphere. The sharp boundary between the crust and the mantle is known as the Mohorovičić discontinuity (Moho for short). The Gutenberg discontinuity marks the mantle-core boundary. The outer core is the only layer that is thought to be liquid. This is separated from the solid inner core.

Density	5·517g/cm³
Sideral period	365·26d
Sideral day (mean)	23h 56m·04s
Axial inclination	23·5°
Distance from Sun (mean)	149·6 million km
Equatorial diameter	12756 km
Equatorial circumference	400075 km
Surface gravity	981·183 cm/sec²
Orbital velocity	29·6 km/sec

Labels in diagram: Oceanic crust 10km, Continental crust 40km, Lithosphere 100km, Asthenosphere 200km. Crust, Upper mantle, Lower mantle, Outer core, Inner core. 700km, 2,200km, 2,270km, 1,200km.

Since the Earth's formation from the solar nebula 4600 million years ago, immense changes have taken place. Not only has the planet evolved, but during the brief span of our existence our knowledge of the processes involved, and of the Earth's relationship with the Solar System, has increased. It was once believed that the Earth occupied a privileged position at the centre of the universe; a view that was not dispelled until the 17th century.

The Earth lies in the middle of the ecosphere, the region around the Sun where temperatures are neither too hot nor too cold for life to develop. The size, atmosphere and nature of the Earth's surface, which is made up largely of water, means that the Earth is the only known planet capable of supporting life.

Time

The world is divided into 24 time zones, each centred on meridians at 15° intervals. This is the longitudinal distance the Sun appears to travel every hour. The Greenwich meridian passes through the centre of the first zone. The International Date Line approximately follows the 180° meridian. For practical purposes, standard time is used so that times are fixed over extensive north-south zones that take into account international boundaries.

Seasons

Seasonal effects arise because of the tilt of the Earth's axis (23.5°), combined with its orbit around the Sun. This causes periodic variations in the amount of sunlight reaching the northern and southern hemispheres.

The north pole is tilted at its greatest angle towards the sun at summer solstice: thus the northern hemisphere experiences summer, and the southern hemisphere winter. This is reversed at winter solstice. In between, at the spring and autumn equinoxes, the tilt is neither towards nor away from the Sun. This also explains why the Sun will appear to take different paths across the sky when viewed from different parts of the Earth.

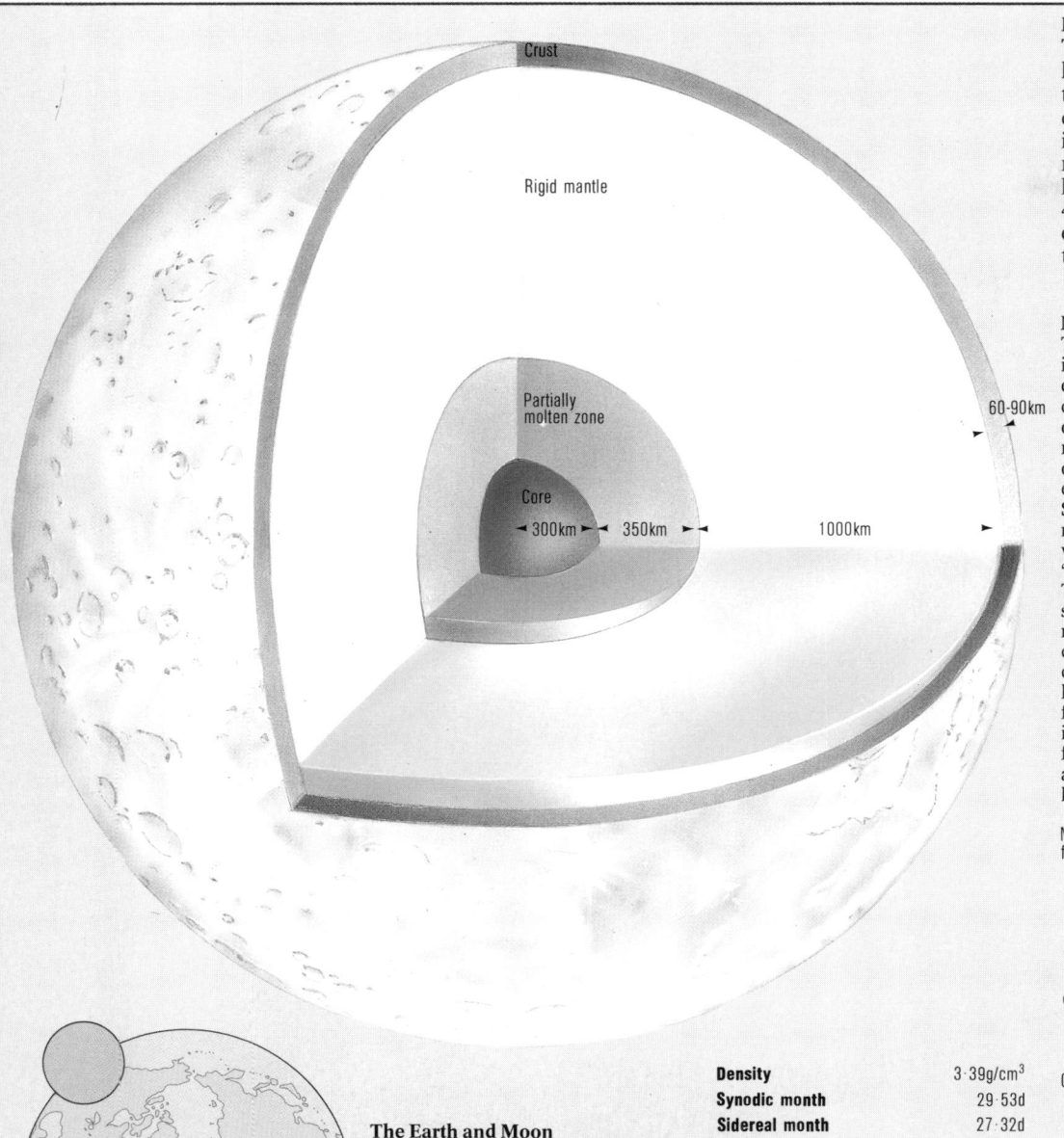

Crust

Rigid mantle

Partially
molten zone

Core

◄ 300km ► ◄ 350km ► ◄ 1000km ►

60–90km

Moon

The Moon is our closest neighbour in space. Some features of the lunar landscape can be seen with the naked eye. It was not until the invention of the telescope, however, that serious observation could begin. Since then our knowledge of the Moon has increased; man has even walked on its surface. Yet some theories remain unresolved and exploration continues. Scientific analysis has established that the Earth and Moon are about the same age – 4500 to 5000 million years, yet they have undergone different evolutionary sequences. There is no atmosphere or weather on the Moon as its gravity is insufficient to hold any gases.

Moon

The lunar interior has been investigated by means of heat flow experiments and seismometers during Apollo missions. The core of the Moon appears to be relatively much smaller than that of the Earth, and it is probably extremely rich in iron. Surrounding the core is the lunar mantle overlaid by the crust, which is covered by a rocky 'topsoil' known as the regolith. The surface of the Moon has several distinctive features. The maria or 'seas' were probably created by vast lava flows. The craters which dominate the landscape are thought to originate from volcanic activity and the impact of vast meteorites. Other features are narrow trenches, rilles and mountain ranges reaching heights over 4500m.

Origin of the Moon

Various theories have been suggested as to how the Moon originated, and it is still a matter of conjecture. It might originally have been part of the Earth's mantle that became unstable and broke away. However, the Moon's composition is different from that of the Earth's mantle and neither appears to have sufficient angular momentum to enable the separation to have taken place. The Moon may have formed elsewhere and been subsequently 'captured' by the Earth, though this is thought to be a statistically unlikely event. Another possibility is that the Moon condensed from the solar nebula close to the Earth, but independently of it. The Moon could have formed from a cloud of material which once surrounded the Earth.

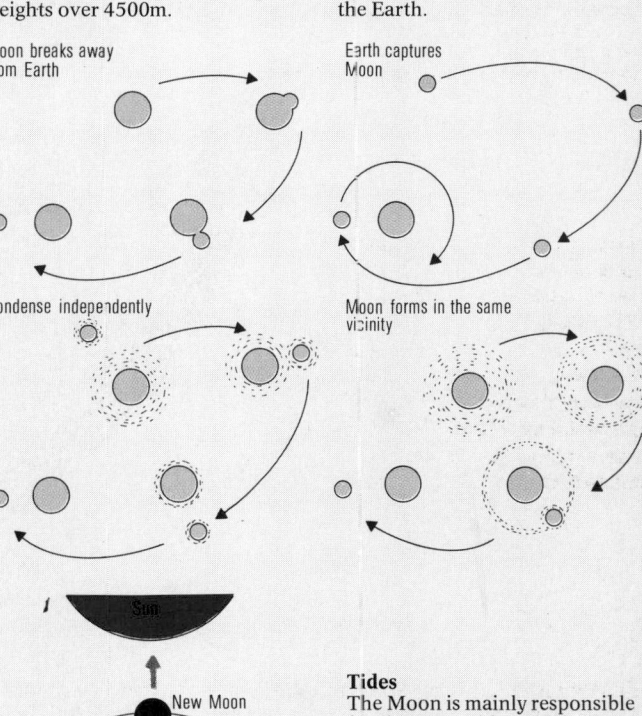

Moon breaks away from Earth

Earth captures Moon

Condense independently

Moon forms in the same vicinity

The Earth and Moon

The relative sizes of the Moon and the Earth are compared in the diagram. The mass of the Moon is much lower than that of the Earth, as is its specific gravity. Discrepancies between the Earth and Moon are much less marked than those between other planets and their satellites. The Earth-Moon system is regarded by some as a double planet.

Density	3·39g/cm³
Synodic month	29·53d
Sidereal month	27·32d
Inclination of Lunar orbit to ecliptic	5° 8′
Distance from Moon to Earth (mean)	384 400 km
Diameter	3476km
Temperature	−150°C to ±130°C
Surface gravity	162·2 cm/sec²
Orbital velocity	1·024 km/sec
Escape velocity	2·4 km/sec

Eclipses

When the Sun, Moon and Earth are in exact alignment, the Moon covers the whole disk of the Sun. A total eclipse is seen within the umbra (the area of deepest shadow) and a partial eclipse from the penumbra. If the Moon is near apogee (farthest point from Earth) the Sun is not completely covered and a ring of sunlight remains around the dark lunar disk. This is known as an annular eclipse. A lunar eclipse takes place when the Full Moon passes into the shadow cast by the Earth instead of passing above or below the shadow. If the Moon brushes the umbra it will be partially eclipsed; a total eclipse occurs when the Moon lies completely within the Earth's umbra.

Tides

The Moon is mainly responsible for the ocean tides, which rise and fall twice daily on Earth. The Moon's gravitational pull distorts the ocean surface into an ellipsoidal shape. When the Sun and Moon are aligned (New and Full Moon), higher 'spring' tides occur. When they are pulling at right angles (first and last quarter), lesser 'neap' tides arise. Although the height of the rise in mid-ocean is approximately a metre, the effect in coastal waters is complicated by local factors, and a much greater tidal range can occur.

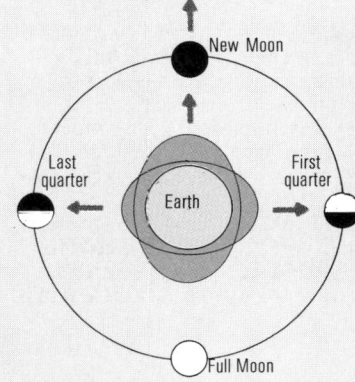

Sun

New Moon

Last quarter

First quarter

Earth

Full Moon

Phases of the Moon

The Moon completes a cycle of phases every 29.5 days. The Moon shines by reflecting sunlight; at any moment one hemisphere is lit while the other is dark. When a New Moon lies directly in line with the Sun, the hemisphere that faces the Earth is dark. The Moon then moves to the east of the Sun. More of the illuminated hemisphere becomes visible as the angle between the Sun and Moon increases, from a thin crescent to a fully illuminated disk when opposite the Sun, eventually returning to a New Moon.

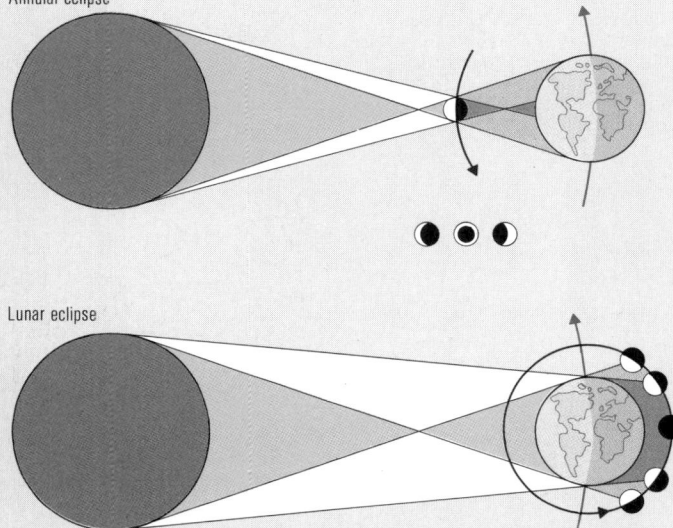

Solar eclipse

Annular eclipse

Lunar eclipse

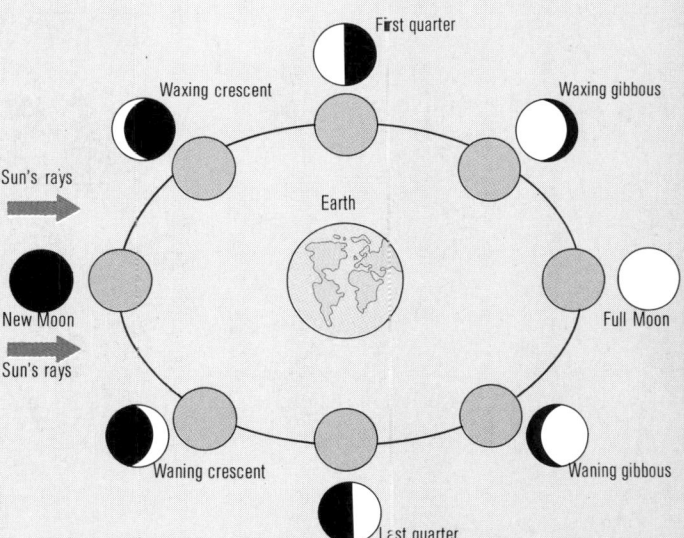

First quarter

Waxing crescent

Waxing gibbous

Sun's rays

Earth

New Moon

Full Moon

Sun's rays

Waning crescent

Waning gibbous

Last quarter

Designed and produced by E.S.R.

MOVING CONTINENTS

The Earth's development is still a matter of much conjecture and debate. Until comparatively recently the view that the structure of the Earth has remained essentially fixed throughout geological time was common. The matching of many pairs of coastlines (strictly, continental shelves) led to the first detailed geological and structural comparisons. Palaeomagnetism has probably proved to be the most influential proof of continental drift, in conjunction with palaeontology, palaeoclimatology and other geological evidence.

Plate tectonics, the field of Earth studies which encompasses the theory of continental drift, offers an explanation for many of the Earth's varied structural and geophysical phenomena. According to theory, the lithosphere consists of rigid segments called plates. These can contain both oceanic and continental crust, which 'float' across the more mobile asthenosphere. Major interactions occur along the plate margins.

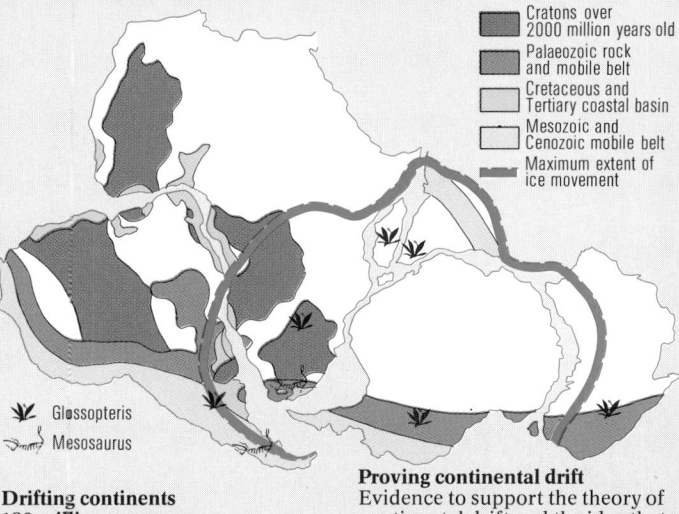

Cratons over 2000 million years old
Palaeozoic rock and mobile belt
Cretaceous and Tertiary coastal basin
Mesozoic and Cenozoic mobile belt
Maximum extent of ice movement

Glossopteris
Mesosaurus

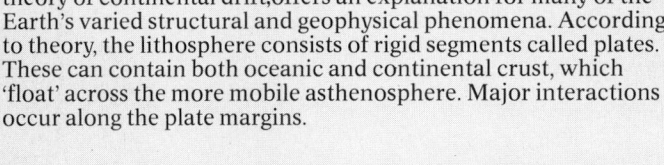

180 Million years ago

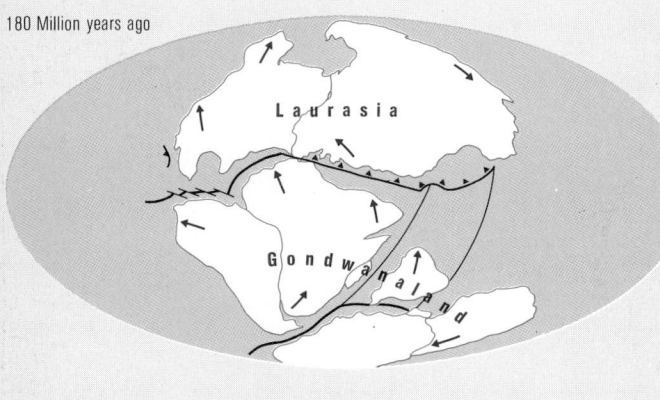

135 Million years ago

65 Million years ago

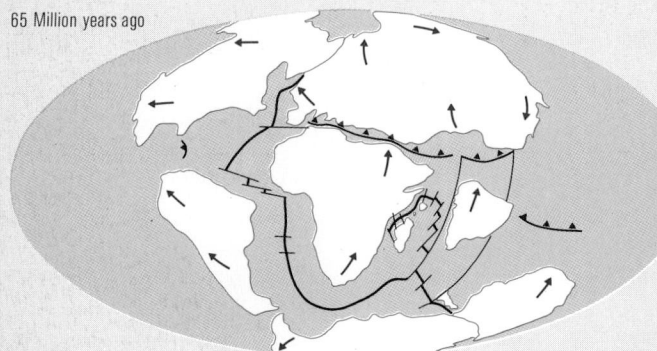

Present

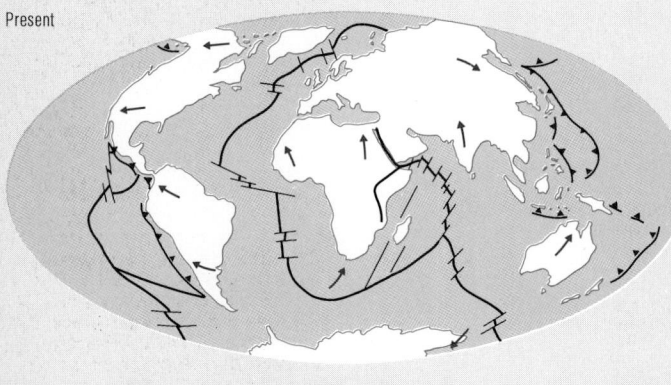

50 Million years ahead

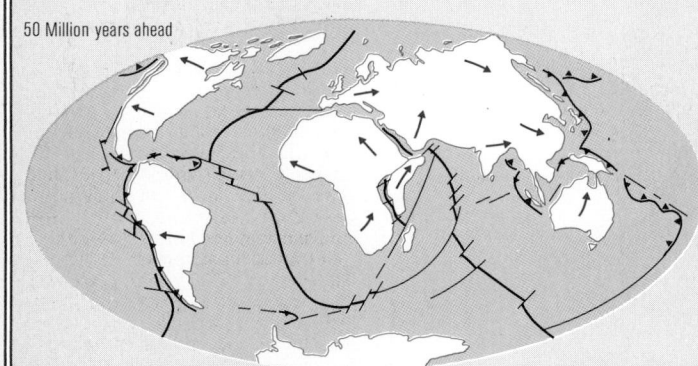

Drifting continents
180 million years ago
The fragmentation of the supercontinent Pangaea began about 200 million years ago. Two major rifts initiated the breakup. The rift zone between North America and Africa generated a northern continental group, Laurasia. The rift that separated the southern landmass of Gondwanaland sent India in a northward direction and simultaneously split South America and Africa from Australia and Antarctica.

135 million years ago
Both Gondwanaland and Laurasia continued to drift northwards. Africa and South America began splitting apart to form the origins of the South Atlantic. India continued heading northwards to Asia. The southern part of the North Atlantic had widened considerably.

65 million years ago
South America had completely separated from Africa and the South Atlantic emerged as a full-fledged ocean. Madagascar had broken away from Africa. In the south, Australia was still connected to Antarctica.

Present
The northward movement of India has led to a collision with Asia, from which the Himalayas resulted. The separation of Greenland from Eurasia is also a recent event in geological time. South America has connected with North America, whilst Australia has drifted north away from Antarctica. Africa is moving away from the Arabian peninsula as the Red Sea rift widens.

50 million years ahead
By extrapolating plate movements into the future, important changes can be seen. A new sea emerges as East Africa parts company with the mainland. Australia and Papua New Guinea migrate north. The Baja peninsula slides past the North American plate along the San Andreas Fault. The continents will undoubtedly continue to change shape and position: exactly how must still be speculative.

Proving continental drift
Evidence to support the theory of continental drift and the idea that today's continents were once joined comes from various geological and geophysical investigations. Rocks from 'matching coastlines' such as South America and Africa, are often similar in age, type and structure. Fossil remains of the reptile *Mesosaurus* have been found on both sides of the South Atlantic. Similarly the remains of the fossil fern *Glossopteris* also indicates that the continents were once joined. Comparisons of palaeomagnetism in rocks of various ages and the Earth's changing magnetic field seems to confirm continental movement.

Plate tectonics
The mobile behaviour of the material within the asthenosphere allows the motion of lithospheric plates, which form a rigid outer shell to the Earth. Each plate moves as a distinct unit. Most earthquakes, volcanoes and mountain building occur along the plate margins.

There are three types of plate boundary: Divergent (constructive) where plates move apart and upwelling of material from the mantle creates oceanic ridges; Convergent (destructive) where plates collide, causing the lithosphere of one plate to be consumed along a subduction zone; Transform margin, along which plates slide, neither creating nor destroying the lithosphere.

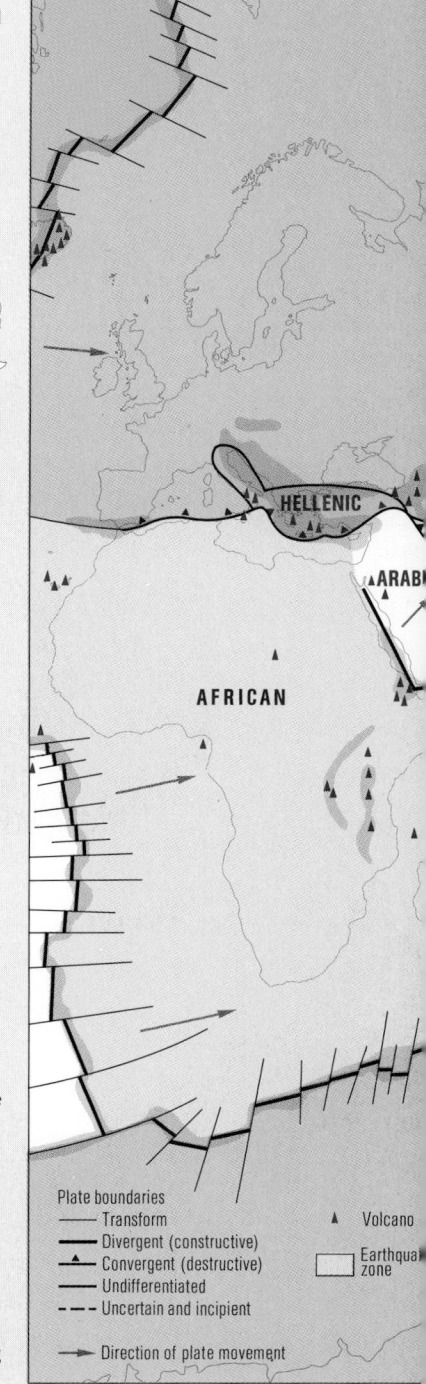

HELLENIC
ARAB
AFRICAN

Plate boundaries
Transform
Divergent (constructive)
Convergent (destructive)
Undifferentiated
Uncertain and incipient
Direction of plate movement
Volcano
Earthquake zone

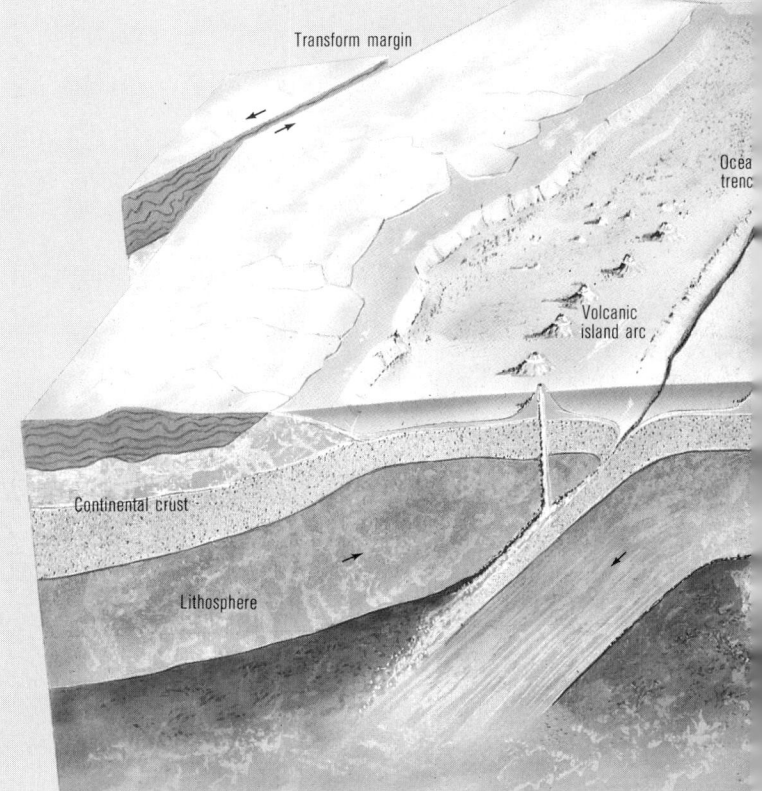

Transform margin
Ocean trench
Volcanic island arc
Continental crust
Lithosphere

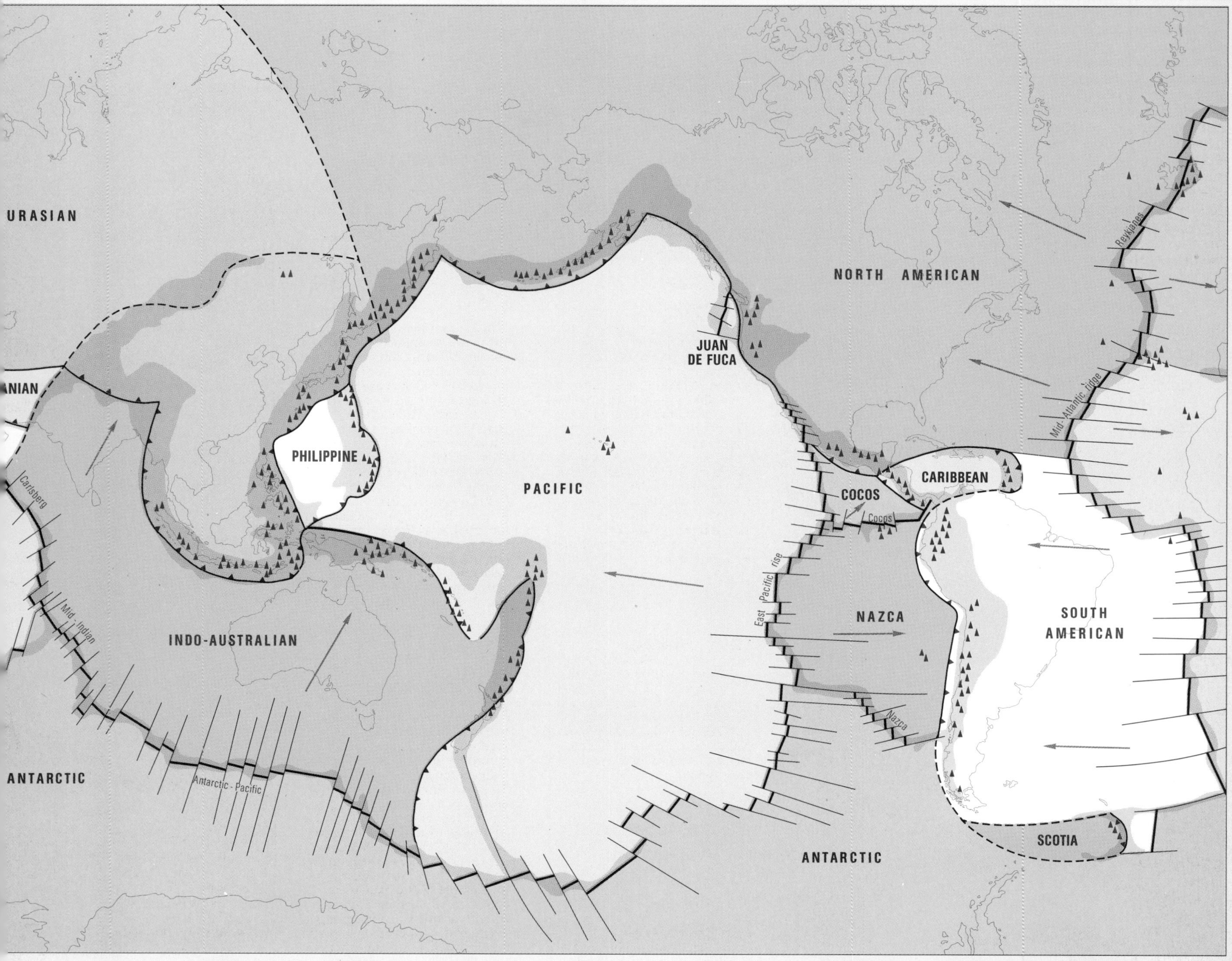

URASIAN

ANIAN

NORTH AMERICAN

JUAN
DE FUCA

PHILIPPINE

Carlsberg

Mid. Indian

PACIFIC

East Pacific rise

Mid-Atlantic Ridge

Reykjanes

COCOS

Cocos

CARIBBEAN

NAZCA

Nazca

SOUTH
AMERICAN

INDO-AUSTRALIAN

ANTARCTIC

Antarctic-Pacific

ANTARCTIC

SCOTIA

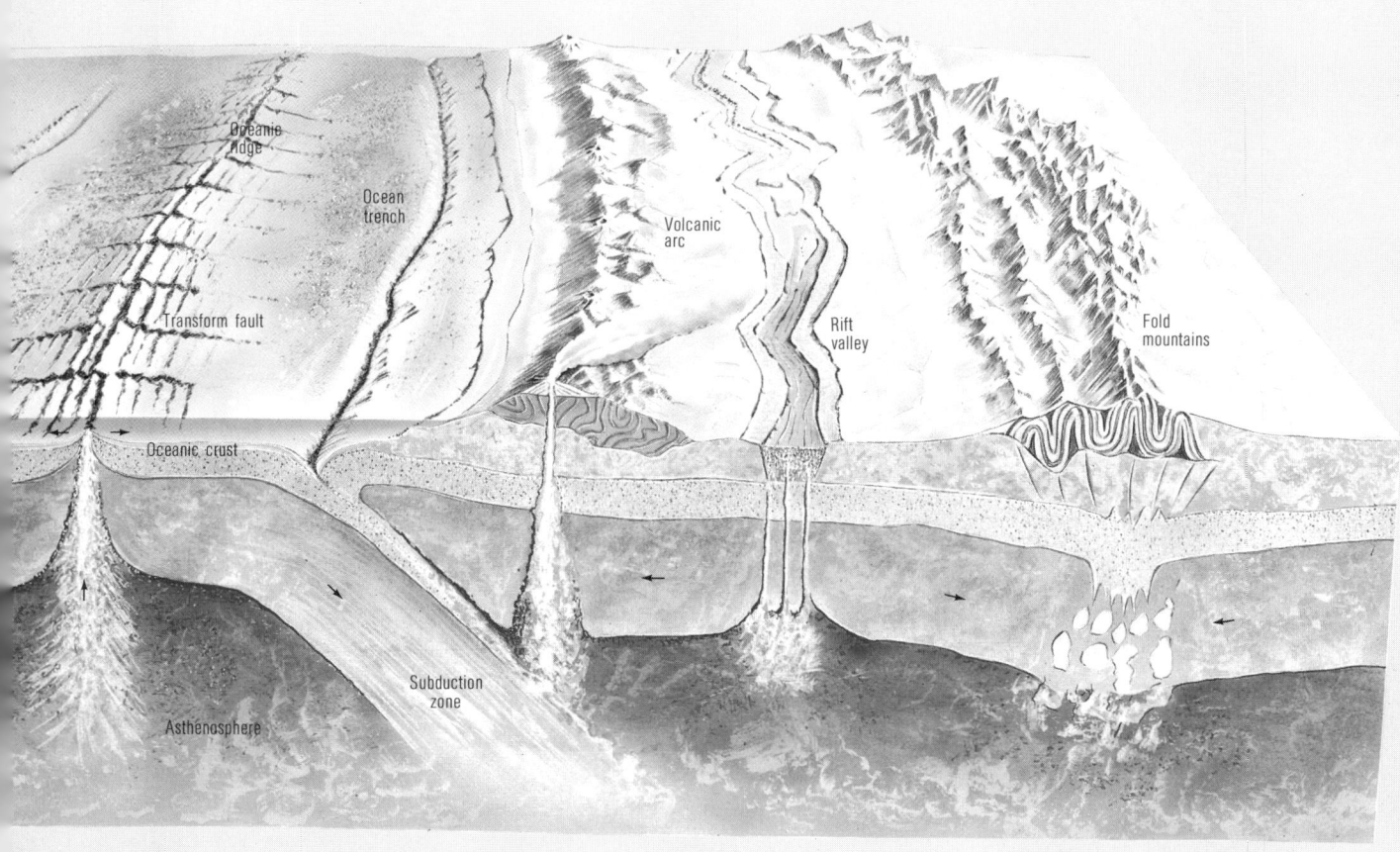

Oceanic
ridge

Ocean
trench

Volcanic
arc

Rift
valley

Fold
mountains

Transform fault

Oceanic crust

Subduction
zone

Asthenosphere

Tectonic features
At a divergent plate margin molten material rises to form new lithosphere. When the magma reaches the surface it cools, solidifies and continues to diverge. The ocean floors are thus in a state of continuous creation and spreading. The Red Sea is believed to be the site of a recently formed divergent boundary. Lateral spreading within a continent can generate large down-faulted valleys, or rifts, like the Great Rift Valley of East Africa.

Plate destruction occurs along subduction zones, often indicated by seismic activity. Continents will remain at the surface while the denser oceanic lithosphere is consumed in an ocean trench. The subducting lithosphere re-enters the Earth's interior, slowly melts and becomes reassimilated. Some magma may eventually migrate to the surface producing volcanic arcs, of which the Andes are an example. Island arcs, such as the Aleutian Islands, are often associated with descending oceanic plates.

If continental plates converge new mountain ranges will result. These are composed of deformed sedimentary rocks and fragments of volcanic arc compressed together. The most recently formed are the Himalayas, but the Alps and the Urals are also thought to have originated in this manner. At transform margins tectonic effects are less dramatic as plates slide against one another. However, as in southern California increased seismic and volcanic activity occurs.

Designed and produced by E.S.R.

THE EARTH'S LANDSCAPE

The landscape around us is the result of a complex system of natural processes. Different rocks of igneous, sedimentary or metamorphic origin comprise the underlying structure. These can be brought to the surface of the Earth by various forces. When exposed to the elements of nature they are slowly weathered, leading to the disintegration and decomposition of the rock. The debris is then carried away and deposited elsewhere. In turn this may be acted upon by other agents. The Earth's surface reflects the processes at work at any given time. Although the forces which shape the landscape appear to act very slowly, in geological terms the alterations are very swift.

The number of people inhabiting the Earth has risen exponentially, and technology has expanded in conjunction with this growth. The human impact on the landscape has thus become increasingly significant. Construction, excavation, reclamation, hydrological work and farming create the most visible features of this changing environment.

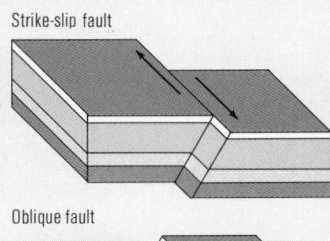

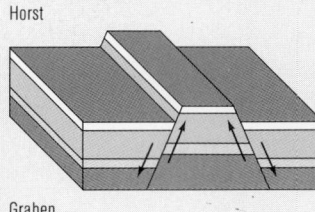

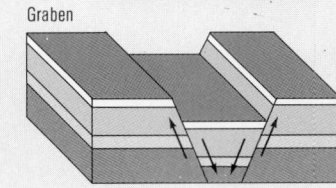

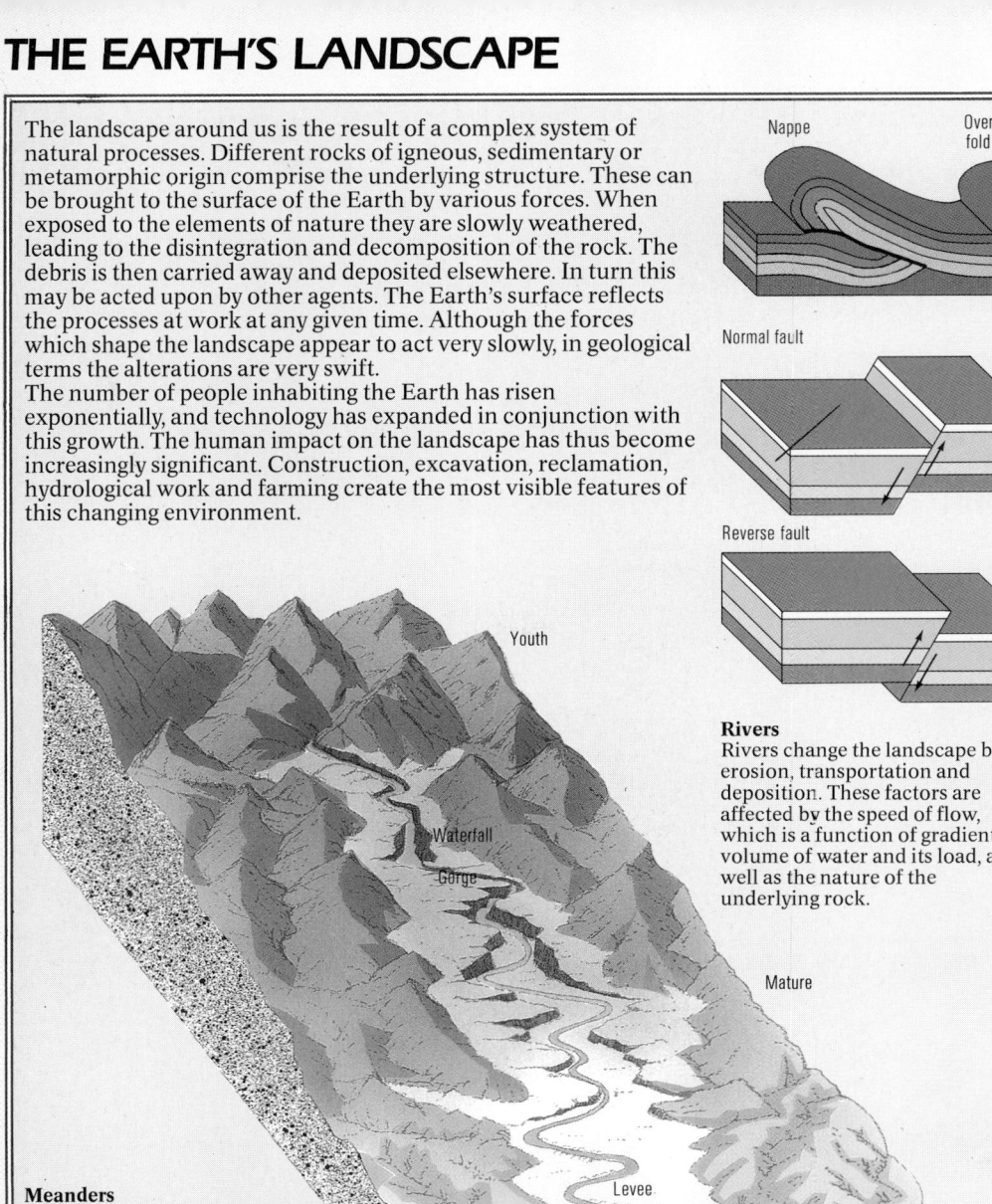

Meanders

Sweeping bends are known as meanders; these continually change position. The maximum velocity of the river occurs on the outside bend, causing erosion of the bank, while the reduced current on the inside bend results in the deposition of sediment. As the meander accentuates, the two arms eventually meet and the river abandons the loop as an oxbow lake.

Rivers

Rivers change the landscape by erosion, transportation and deposition. These factors are affected by the speed of flow, which is a function of gradient, the volume of water and its load, as well as the nature of the underlying rock.

Erosion is most active in the upper tract of a river. Vertical corrosion is great, cutting steep 'V-shaped' valleys between interlocking spurs. In this stage waterfalls and rapids are common. Downstream, the valley widens as a flood plain develops across which the river begins to meander. During its final stage, the river will meander across a wide alluvial plain bordered on either side by levees and bluffs. Braiding may occur when the river divides into intertwining channels. The water transports a large sediment load and on reaching the coast this may be deposited as a delta or swept away by strong sea currents. A river constantly tries to reach a graded profile. If there is a change in base level it will be forced to regrade its course.

Folds and faults

In response to pressure, the strata of the Earth's crust may be bent or warped into a fold. Folds range in intensity from broad and gentle undulations to tightly compressed plications in which the dips of the beds are parallel on either side of the fold. A fault is a fracture in the Earth's crust along which displacement has taken, or is taking, place. It is possible to classify faults according to the nature of the relative displacement between the two crustal blocks involved. In general, thrust and reverse faults result from compressional forces, whereas normal faults are a consequence of tensional stresses trying to pull the crust apart.

Some regions have undergone several phases of deformation resulting in very complex structures.

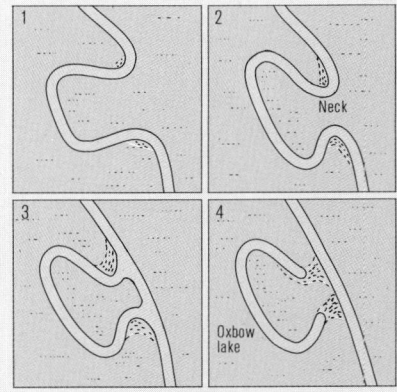

Underground water

Some rocks are eroded by carbonation, caused by the chemical reaction of the rock with rainwater, which contains carbon dioxide. When limestone is exposed at the surface, a well-defined pavement develops, consisting of clints separated by grikes. Large caverns are created at or below the water table. Groundwater follows lines of weakness along joints and bedding planes, slowly forming large cavities. When the water table lowers, a gallery may be left abandoned. A gorge is formed when the roof collapses. Surface streams flow into dissolved sink or swallow holes and down deep chimneys. Gours occur where the water flows over an irregular surface, the turbulence depositing calcite, which builds up into ridges. Underground streams flow along the water table; if part of the roof is below the water, it is known as a siphon. Eventually, the stream will emerge at a resurgence. Groundwater containing dissolved carbonates dripping from the ceiling may evaporate to form a stalactite. Stalagmites appear on the floor where the carbonate is deposited by the shock of the dripping. A great variety of stalactites and stalagmites occur; sometimes they meet to form a continuous pillar or column.

Volcanoes and igneous activity

Volcanoes that eject ash form cinder cones comprising layers of cinder and dust from successive eruptions. More commonly, a volcano will produce alternate layers of lava and cinder. If the lava is plentiful, a shield volcano can occur, built up from many lava flows and covering a large area. Fissure eruptions release flows of very fluid lava that can extend over great distances. Magma does not always reach the surface and often cools at depth to form batholiths, laccoliths that arch the overlying strata upward, dykes that cut through strata, and sills injected between strata. Hot springs, gas vents and geysers may also occur. When igneous rocks are exposed, they form distinctive scenery as they are more resistant to erosion than the surrounding rocks.

Composite volcano

Cinder cone

Shield volcano

Fissure eruption

Volcanic plug or neck

Laccolith exposed by erosion

Lava flow

Vent

Volcano

Caldera

Geyser

Hot spring

Exposed dike

Sill

Pipe

Laccolith

Dyke

Batholith

Magma

Wind

Wind action is most effective in arid and semi-arid regions. Accumulations of sand as dunes can assume surprisingly consistent patterns. Crescent shaped Barchan dunes slowly migrate downwind. Transverse dunes form a series of long ridges that are separated by troughs, orientated at right angles to the prevailing wind. Seif or longitudinal dunes form parallel to the prevailing wind on bare rock surfaces. Where wind direction is variable, irregular star-shaped dunes may develop.
Exposed rock surfaces are eroded by abrasion, often causing strange shapes and effects. Fine particles seldom travel more than a metre above the surface. The wind's sandblasting effect is thus limited in vertical extent. Continued erosion at the base of a rock, however, may leave it precariously balanced.

Irregular dunes

Seif dunes

Wind

Transverse dunes

Wind

Barchan dunes

Wind

Wind direction

Movement of sand particles

Ice – a valley glacier

Glaciers cover nearly ten per cent of the Earth's land surface. However, in the recent geological past ice sheets extended over vast areas. Many present-day landscapes resulted from the action of these glaciers.
There are three main types of glaciers: valley glaciers, which originate above the snow line in mountain areas; piedmont glaciers, formed when valley glaciers join and spread out at the foot of mountains; and ice caps or sheets, which spread out laterally from their source area.
The immense abrasive power of debris caught in the ice erodes 'U' shaped valleys. Interlocking spurs are truncated and tributary valleys left hanging above the deepened main valley.
Sediments within the ice and moraine carried along the surface are deposited ungraded as till at the glacier snout. Meltwater carries deposits over the outwash plain where kettleholes and drumlins can be seen. Eskers are deposits from streams which were once under the ice.

Waves

Coastlines are continually changing: they may have resulted from land emergence or submergence and are shaped by erosional and depositional activities of waves, currents and tides.
Material transported by longshore drift may be deposited as a spit across a bay. This can develop into a baymouth bar which seals off the bay, completely enclosing a lagoon. A tombolo, a form of spit, links an island to the mainland. Caves caused by wave erosion on either side of a headland may unite to form a natural arch. When the arch collapses, sea stacks remain.

Wave deposition

Lagoon

Beach

Spit

Tombolo

Baymouth bar

Wave erosion

Headland

Cliff

Arch

Cave

Stack

Pyramidal peak

Bergschrund

Firn (compacted snow)

Corrie

Marginal crevasses

Arête

'U' shaped valley

Lateral moraine

Ice dammed lake

Truncated spur

Hanging valley

Transverse crevasses

Medial moraine

Glacial table

Sérac

Icefall

Englacial moraine

Subglacial moraine

Striations

Roche moutonnée

Ice cave

Meltwater tunnel

Snout

Meltwater

End moraine

Esker

Outwash fan

Drumlins

Kettleholes

Outwash plain

Designed and produced by E.S.R.

THE ATMOSPHERE

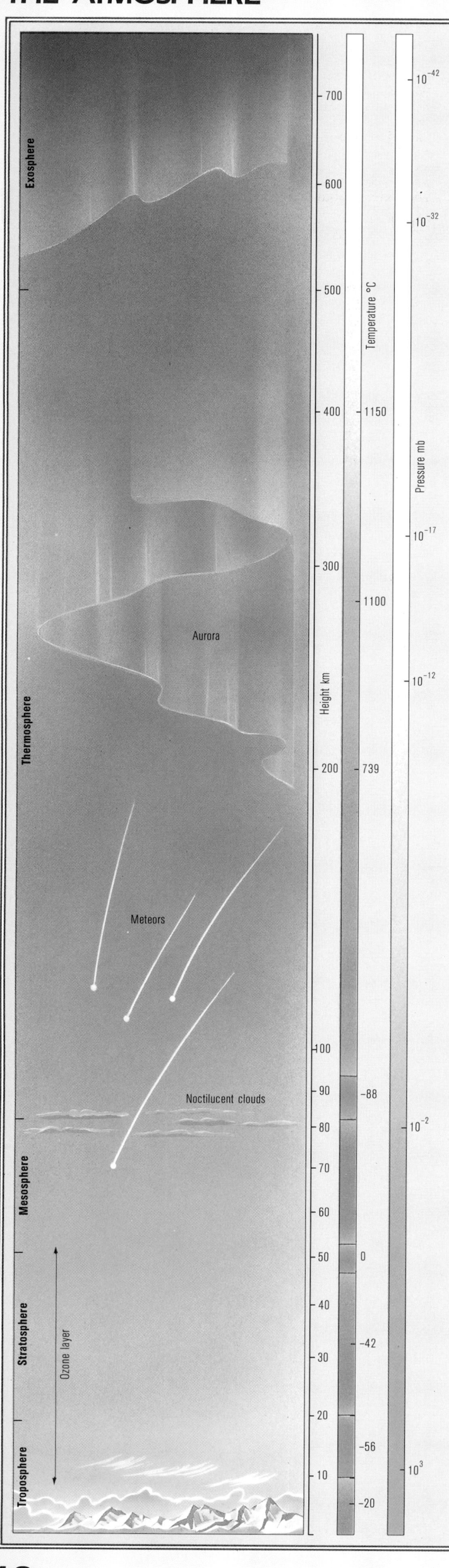

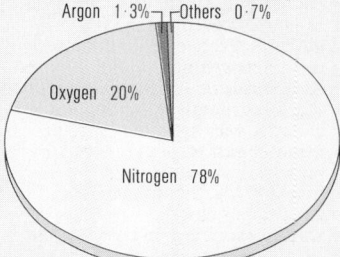

Exosphere, Thermosphere
and Mesosphere
Stratosphere
Troposphere

Earth

The atmosphere, which is unlike that of any other planet, encircles and protects the Earth. Changes in the composition of the atmosphere are closely associated with the evolution of the Earth. One of the most important transitions was the increase in oxygen when photosynthetic plants evolved.

The atmosphere is a mixture of gases, the largest proportion of which is nitrogen. The most important is oxygen, without which life could not be sustained; other gases are present in quite small quantities.

Near the Earth's surface, gravitational pull increases the density of the atmosphere. We do not feel this air pressure because of the equal air pressure inside our bodies. Variation in air pressure has a major influence on weather, as does the amount of water vapour in the atmosphere. These elements are in turn affected by a number of factors such as the evaporation of water from the oceans, wind movements and the topography of the Earth.

Structure of the atmosphere
The atmosphere can be divided into various layers, depending on its physical properties. Variations in temperature and pressure result from the distribution of solar heating and help to distinguish the different zones.

Atmospheric composition
The composition of the Earth's atmosphere has changed as the planet has evolved. At present the largest proportion is formed of nitrogen followed by oxygen. Argon and carbon dioxide can also be found, as well as other inert gases such as neon and helium. The atmosphere also contains variable amounts of water vapour, up to three per cent, and small quantities of sulphur dioxide.

Argon 1·3% — Others 0·7%
Oxygen 20%
Nitrogen 78%

Exosphere merges into the vacuum of space. It is extremely rarefied and is composed mainly of hydrogen and helium.

Thermosphere absorbs ultraviolet radiation. Temperatures rise steeply with height to several thousand degrees. This region is the source of the ionosphere; disturbances in this region appear as glowing lights of varying colours – aurorae. They occur primarily over the poles because the charged particles from the Sun are channelled there by the Earth's magnetic field. Short-wave and long-wave radio transmissions are also reflected at various layers within the ionosphere.

It would appear that human activities are altering the natural atmospheric conditions of the planet. To what extent this is happening is still a matter of great debate.

The ozone (a form of oxygen), in the upper atmosphere, screens the Earth from the Sun's ultraviolet rays and is deteriorating. The use of man-made refrigerant gases such as chlorofluorocarbons (CFCs) are a contributing factor. Conversely, other pollutants, such as methane, are by a complex set of chemical reactions increasing ozone levels nearer the ground, which may be adding to the 'greenhouse effect', a phrase which has been used to describe a general warming of the atmosphere.

Since the industrial revolution, carbon dioxide levels have increased by 30 per cent. This is a direct result of burning fossil fuel and destroying vast tracts of forest. The carbon dioxide traps outgoing radiation, which leads to an increase in temperatures. It has been predicted that an average rise of 3°C is possible, and as much as 8-10°C at the poles. Sea levels would rise as a result of melting ice and thermal expansion of the oceans. Many areas of low-lying land would then be flooded and island nations swamped. Accompanying these temperature rises would be changes in rainfall patterns which could affect agricultural productivity. In general it is also thought that tropical conditions would gradually extend northwards.

Mesosphere extends to a height of about 80km and in it there is a marked fall in temperature to −120°C. Meteors from space tend to burn out in this region as they meet increased air resistance.

Other forms of atmospheric pollution are also causing concern. Industrial emissions of sulphur oxide and nitrogen oxide dissolve in rain, which is often transported great distances before returning to Earth as sulphuric and nitric acids. Their deposition as 'acid rain' can have dire effects on ecosystems. Forests are affected, soils leached and water supplies contaminated. Exhaust-caused smogs and lead emitted from vehicles also have a detrimental effect on the atmosphere.

It is known that the atmosphere and climate of the planet have changed with time. Our knowledge, however, is far from complete in many areas. Whether changes in atmospheric conditions are natural or man-made is to some degree still a matter of speculation and controversy.

Stratosphere contains the ozone layer, which absorbs the Sun's harmful ultraviolet light. As a result, the temperature rises to about 10°C before decreasing again in the stratopause. Noctilucent clouds may form from compressed meteoric dust in this region.

Troposphere is the lowest layer of the atmosphere and contains all the climatic activities that affect us. It reaches about 8km above the poles and 15km above the equator. Pressure is at its greatest due to the weight of the layers above, and 80 per cent of the mass of the atmosphere is found here. Near ground level, visible and infrared radiation is absorbed. Temperature decreases with height until the tropopause is reached.

Greenhouse effect
The balance of the incoming and outgoing solar radiation is disturbed by the increased amount of carbon dioxide which traps infrared radiation. This causes a general warming of the atmosphere known as the greenhouse effect.

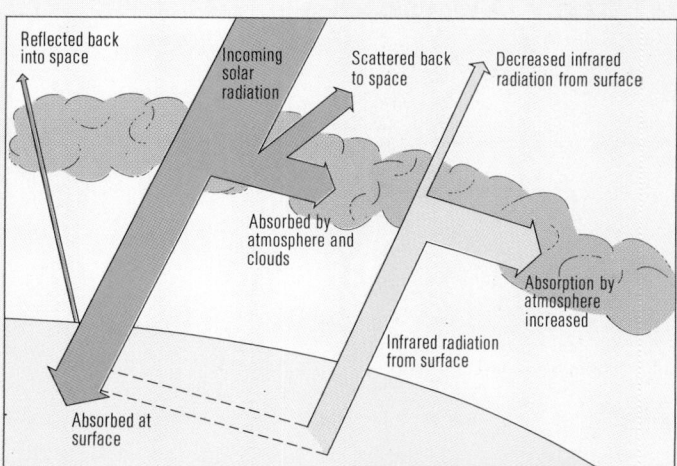

Reflected back into space
Incoming solar radiation
Scattered back to space
Decreased infrared radiation from surface
Absorbed by atmosphere and clouds
Absorption by atmosphere increased
Infrared radiation from surface
Absorbed at surface

Clouds

Clouds can be classified on the basis of their appearance and height. The basic forms are cirrus, stratus and cumulus. Other clouds reflect one of these forms or are combinations or modifications of them.

Cirrus thin, delicate, fibrous ice-crystal clouds. Sometimes appear as hooked filaments called 'mares-tails', often the first sign of an approaching depression.

Cirrocumulus thin, white ice-crystal clouds in the form of ripples, waves or globular masses all in a row. May produce a 'mackerel sky'.

Cirrostratus thin sheet of white ice-crystal clouds that may give the sky a milky look. Sometimes produce haloes around the Sun or Moon.

Altocumulus white to grey clouds often composed of separate globules. Frequently indicates unsettled weather.

Altostratus stratified veil of clouds that are generally thin and may produce very light precipitation.

Stratocumulus soft, grey clouds in globular patches or rolls. Rolls may join together to make a continuous cloud.

Stratus low uniform layer, forms dull, overcast skies. Associated with depressions, may often produce drizzle and rain.

Nimbostratus amorphous layer of dark grey clouds. One of the chief precipitation-producing clouds.

Cumulus dense, billowy clouds often characterised by flat bases. May occur as isolated clouds or closely packed.

Cumulonimbus towering cloud sometimes spreading out on top to form an 'anvil head'. Associated with heavy rainfall, thunder, lightning, hail and tornadoes.

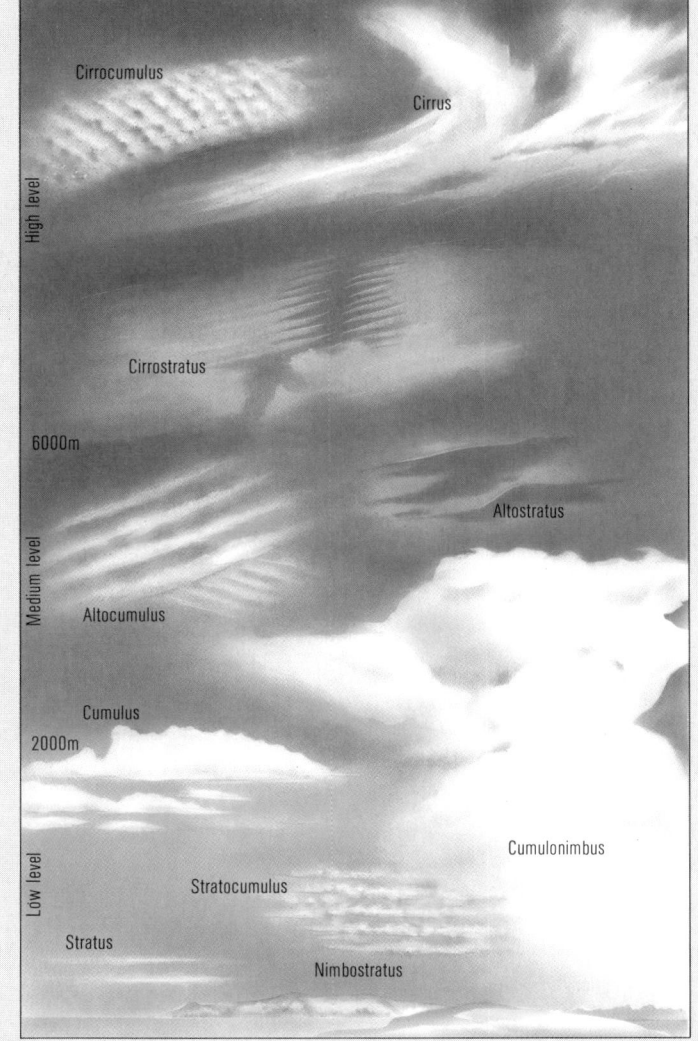

Clouds

Without clouds there would be no precipitation. Variations in the amount of precipitation from place to place as well as local differences from time to time have a significant impact not only on the nature of the physical landscape but also on people's lifestyles.

Clouds consist of microscopic drops of water or ice crystals suspended in the atmosphere. Formation occurs when air that contains water vapour becomes saturated and reaches its dew point. This is usually the result of the air rising and thus cooling. The water vapour then condenses around dust particles.

Wind

The unequal heating of the Earth by solar radiation generates pressure differences. These inequalities cause the movement of air from areas of higher pressure to areas of lower pressure. A system of general circulation is thus generated by semipermanent cells of high and low pressure over the oceans. Wind direction is then subject to deflection by the Coriolis effect, to the right in the northern hemisphere, to the left in the southern hemisphere. This is complicated by seasonal pressure changes over land, which can give rise to seasonal reversals of wind known as monsoons.

Circulation of the air

The temperature differences between the poles and the equator provide the thermal energy to drive atmospheric circulation. Warm air at the equator rises and flows towards the poles at high levels. Cold polar air moves towards the equator at low levels to replace it. Once the effect of rotation is added, the Coriolis effect, this simple convection system breaks down into smaller cells.

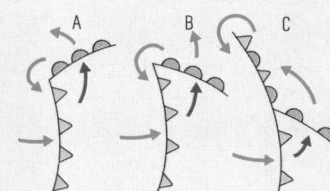

A Depression

Variable weather in the middle latitudes often results from the development of low pressure areas known as depressions, a common feature of which is the formation of warm and cold fronts. The warm, light air rises above the cool air along the warm front. Behind, the cold air forces its way under the warm air along the cold front. Gradually, the cold front catches up with the warm front and the warm air is pushed above the cold in an occlusion. In the northern hemisphere, the air circulates in an anticlockwise direction and in the southern, it circulates clockwise.

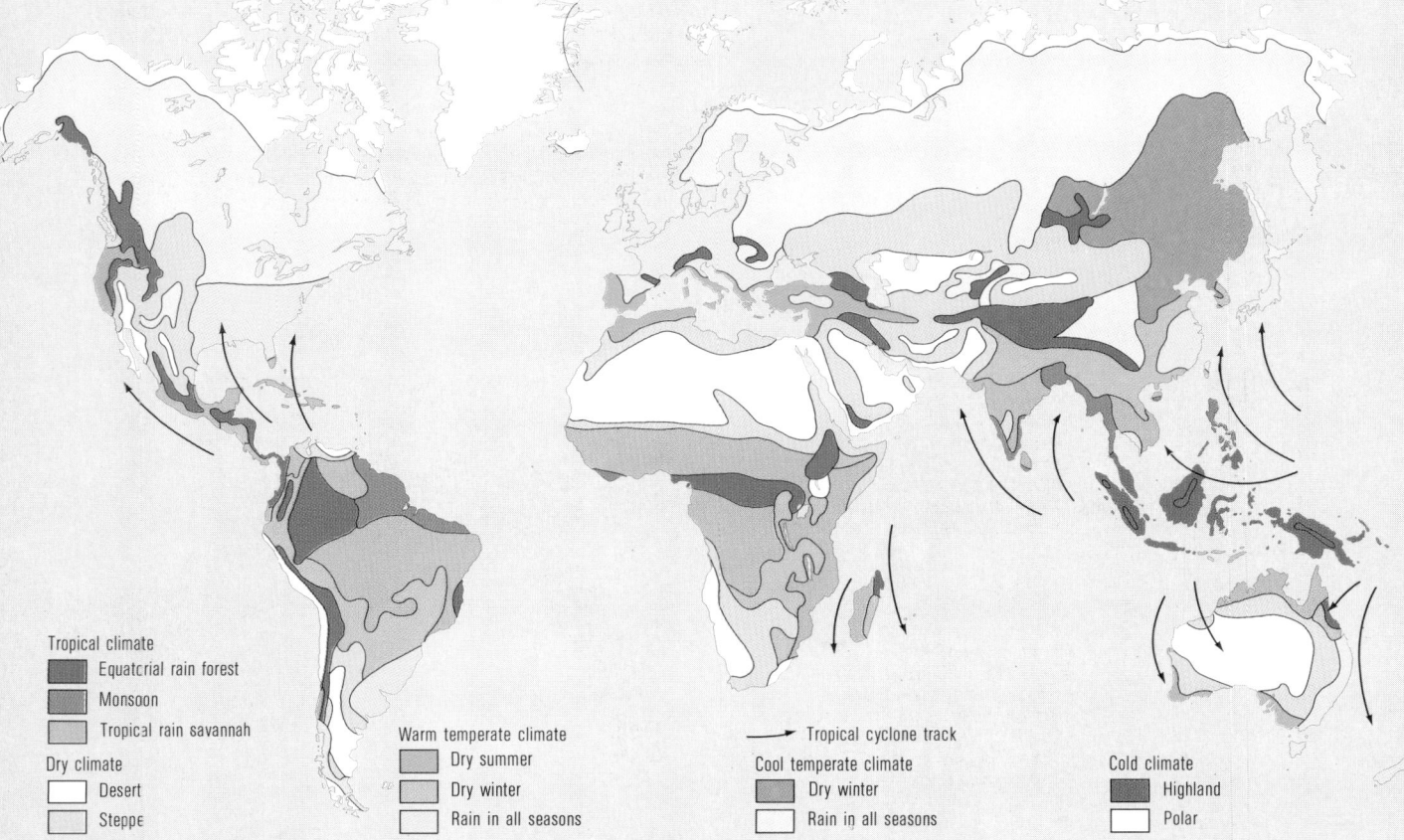

Climate

The climate of an area is its characteristic weather considered over a long period of time. Differences in latitude, prevailing air masses, either local or regional, the relative distribution of land and sea, as well as the topography, will all have an effect on the climatic conditions experienced. The most popular climatic classification is that devised by Wladimir Köppen. It is based on the seasonal variations of temperature and rainfall and their effect on vegetation growth. The range of climates can broadly be defined according to latitude. Hot, tropical climates are dominated by equatorial air masses throughout the year. Temperate climates of the mid-latitudes are very variable, subjected alternately to subpolar and subtropical air masses as well as seasonal shifts. Polar climates of high latitudes are strongly seasonal, influenced by subpolar and polar air masses.

Geological evidence suggests that during other periods the planet experienced a more uniform climate. The present variable pattern may be due, in part, to the fact that the Earth is still recovering from the last Ice Age, although opinion varies as to whether fluctuations in climate should be regarded as abnormal.

Tropical climate
- Equatorial rain forest
- Monsoon
- Tropical rain savannah

Dry climate
- Desert
- Steppe

Warm temperate climate
- Dry summer
- Dry winter
- Rain in all seasons

→ Tropical cyclone track

Cool temperate climate
- Dry winter
- Rain in all seasons

Cold climate
- Highland
- Polar

Designed and produced by E.S.R.

EVOLUTION OF LIFE

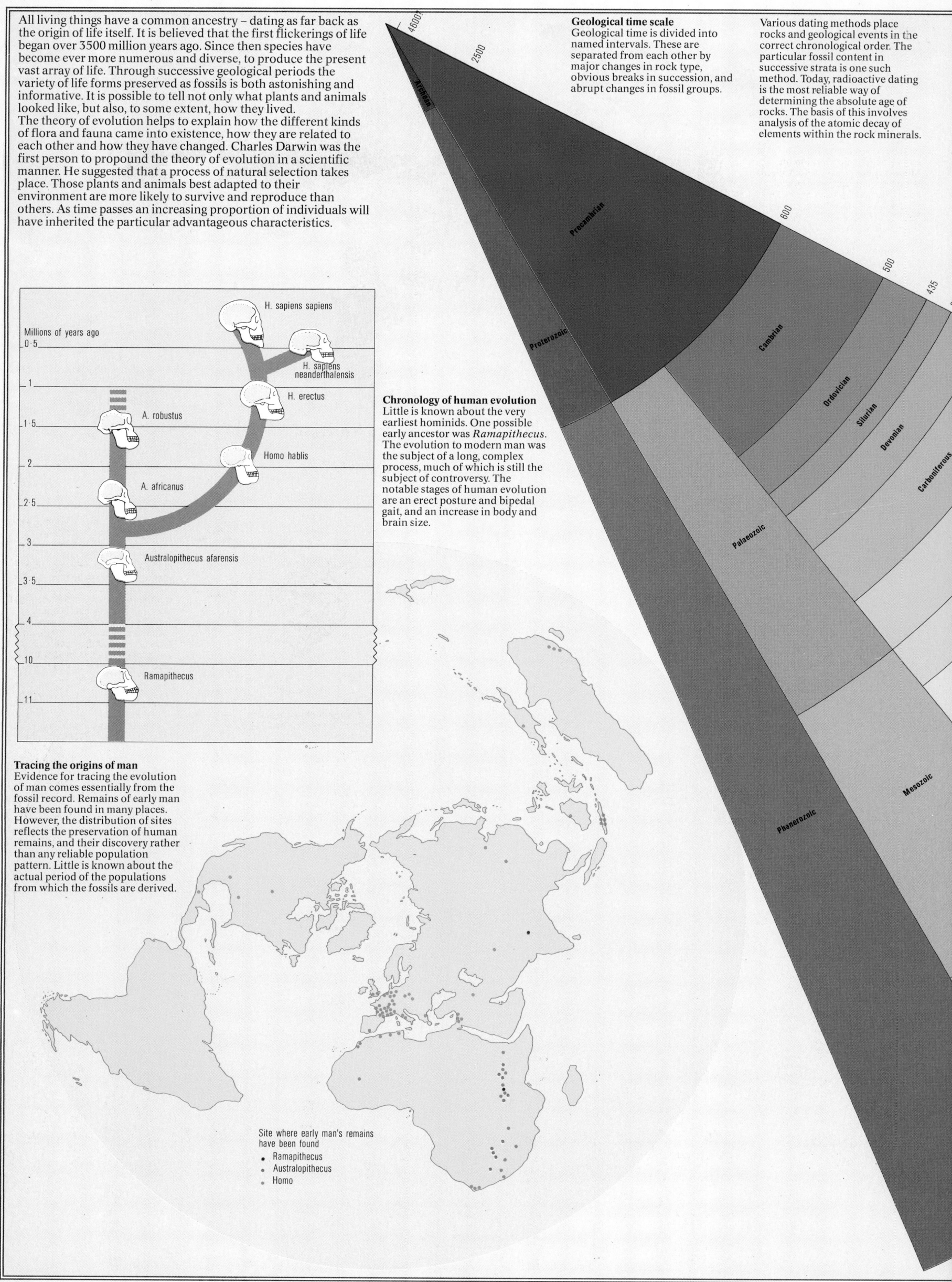

All living things have a common ancestry – dating as far back as the origin of life itself. It is believed that the first flickerings of life began over 3500 million years ago. Since then species have become ever more numerous and diverse, to produce the present vast array of life. Through successive geological periods the variety of life forms preserved as fossils is both astonishing and informative. It is possible to tell not only what plants and animals looked like, but also, to some extent, how they lived.

The theory of evolution helps to explain how the different kinds of flora and fauna came into existence, how they are related to each other and how they have changed. Charles Darwin was the first person to propound the theory of evolution in a scientific manner. He suggested that a process of natural selection takes place. Those plants and animals best adapted to their environment are more likely to survive and reproduce than others. As time passes an increasing proportion of individuals will have inherited the particular advantageous characteristics.

Geological time scale
Geological time is divided into named intervals. These are separated from each other by major changes in rock type, obvious breaks in succession, and abrupt changes in fossil groups.

Various dating methods place rocks and geological events in the correct chronological order. The particular fossil content in successive strata is one such method. Today, radioactive dating is the most reliable way of determining the absolute age of rocks. The basis of this involves analysis of the atomic decay of elements within the rock minerals.

Chronology of human evolution
Little is known about the very earliest hominids. One possible early ancestor was *Ramapithecus*. The evolution to modern man was the subject of a long, complex process, much of which is still the subject of controversy. The notable stages of human evolution are an erect posture and bipedal gait, and an increase in body and brain size.

Tracing the origins of man
Evidence for tracing the evolution of man comes essentially from the fossil record. Remains of early man have been found in many places. However, the distribution of sites reflects the preservation of human remains, and their discovery rather than any reliable population pattern. Little is known about the actual period of the populations from which the fossils are derived.

Millions of years ago

H. sapiens sapiens
H. sapiens neanderthalensis
H. erectus
A. robustus
Homo hablis
A. africanus
Australopithecus afarensis
Ramapithecus

Site where early man's remains have been found
- Ramapithecus
- Australopithecus
- Homo

4600
2500
Archean
Precambrian
Proterozoic
600
500
435
395
Cambrian
Ordovician
Silurian
Devonian
Carboniferous
Palaeozoic
Mesozoic
Phanerozoic

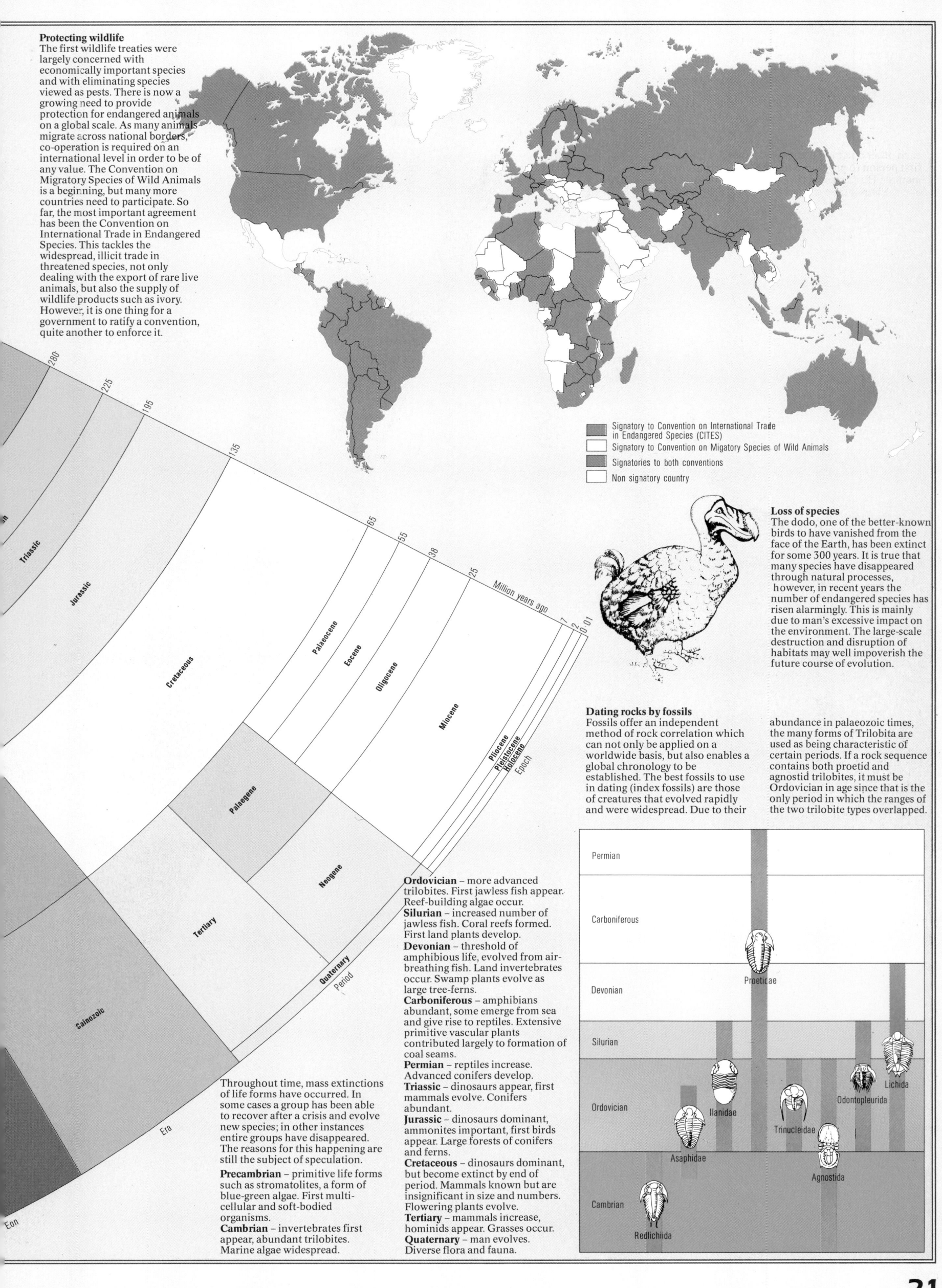

Protecting wildlife
The first wildlife treaties were largely concerned with economically important species and with eliminating species viewed as pests. There is now a growing need to provide protection for endangered animals on a global scale. As many animals migrate across national borders, co-operation is required on an international level in order to be of any value. The Convention on Migratory Species of Wild Animals is a beginning, but many more countries need to participate. So far, the most important agreement has been the Convention on International Trade in Endangered Species. This tackles the widespread, illicit trade in threatened species, not only dealing with the export of rare live animals, but also the supply of wildlife products such as ivory. However, it is one thing for a government to ratify a convention, quite another to enforce it.

Signatory to Convention on International Trade in Endangered Species (CITES)

Signatory to Convention on Migatory Species of Wild Animals

Signatories to both conventions

Non signatory country

Loss of species
The dodo, one of the better-known birds to have vanished from the face of the Earth, has been extinct for some 300 years. It is true that many species have disappeared through natural processes, however, in recent years the number of endangered species has risen alarmingly. This is mainly due to man's excessive impact on the environment. The large-scale destruction and disruption of habitats may well impoverish the future course of evolution.

Dating rocks by fossils
Fossils offer an independent method of rock correlation which can not only be applied on a worldwide basis, but also enables a global chronology to be established. The best fossils to use in dating (index fossils) are those of creatures that evolved rapidly and were widespread. Due to their abundance in palaeozoic times, the many forms of Trilobita are used as being characteristic of certain periods. If a rock sequence contains both proetid and agnostid trilobites, it must be Ordovician in age since that is the only period in which the ranges of the two trilobite types overlapped.

Throughout time, mass extinctions of life forms have occurred. In some cases a group has been able to recover after a crisis and evolve new species; in other instances entire groups have disappeared. The reasons for this happening are still the subject of speculation.

Precambrian – primitive life forms such as stromatolites, a form of blue-green algae. First multi-cellular and soft-bodied organisms.
Cambrian – invertebrates first appear, abundant trilobites. Marine algae widespread.

Ordovician – more advanced trilobites. First jawless fish appear. Reef-building algae occur.
Silurian – increased number of jawless fish. Coral reefs formed. First land plants develop.
Devonian – threshold of amphibious life, evolved from air-breathing fish. Land invertebrates occur. Swamp plants evolve as large tree-ferns.
Carboniferous – amphibians abundant, some emerge from sea and give rise to reptiles. Extensive primitive vascular plants contributed largely to formation of coal seams.
Permian – reptiles increase. Advanced conifers develop.
Triassic – dinosaurs appear, first mammals evolve. Conifers abundant.
Jurassic – dinosaurs dominant, ammonites important, first birds appear. Large forests of conifers and ferns.
Cretaceous – dinosaurs dominant, but become extinct by end of period. Mammals known but are insignificant in size and numbers. Flowering plants evolve.
Tertiary – mammals increase, hominids appear. Grasses occur.
Quaternary – man evolves. Diverse flora and fauna.

Designed and produced by E.S.R.

EXPLORATION AND DISCOVERY

The early explorers who travelled beyond their own shores were accomplished shipbuilders and seamen. The Vikings, Chinese and Arabs were among those who first reached distant lands. Some merchants and missionaries reached remote inland areas. Within a relatively short space of time the great voyages of discovery had charted the vast expanses of sea and largely determined the extent and shape of the continental landmasses. These geographical explorations were later expanded and consolidated by expeditions of a more scientific nature.

Antarctic explorers

- – – – Belingshausen 1819-21
- –·–·– Weddell 1820-24
- ——— Biscoe 1831-32
- –··–·· Wilkes 1839-40
- –·–·– Ross 1840-43
- ——— Shackleton 1907-9
- – – – Scott 1910-12
- ——— Amundsen 1911-12
- ········ Hillary-Fuchs 1955-58

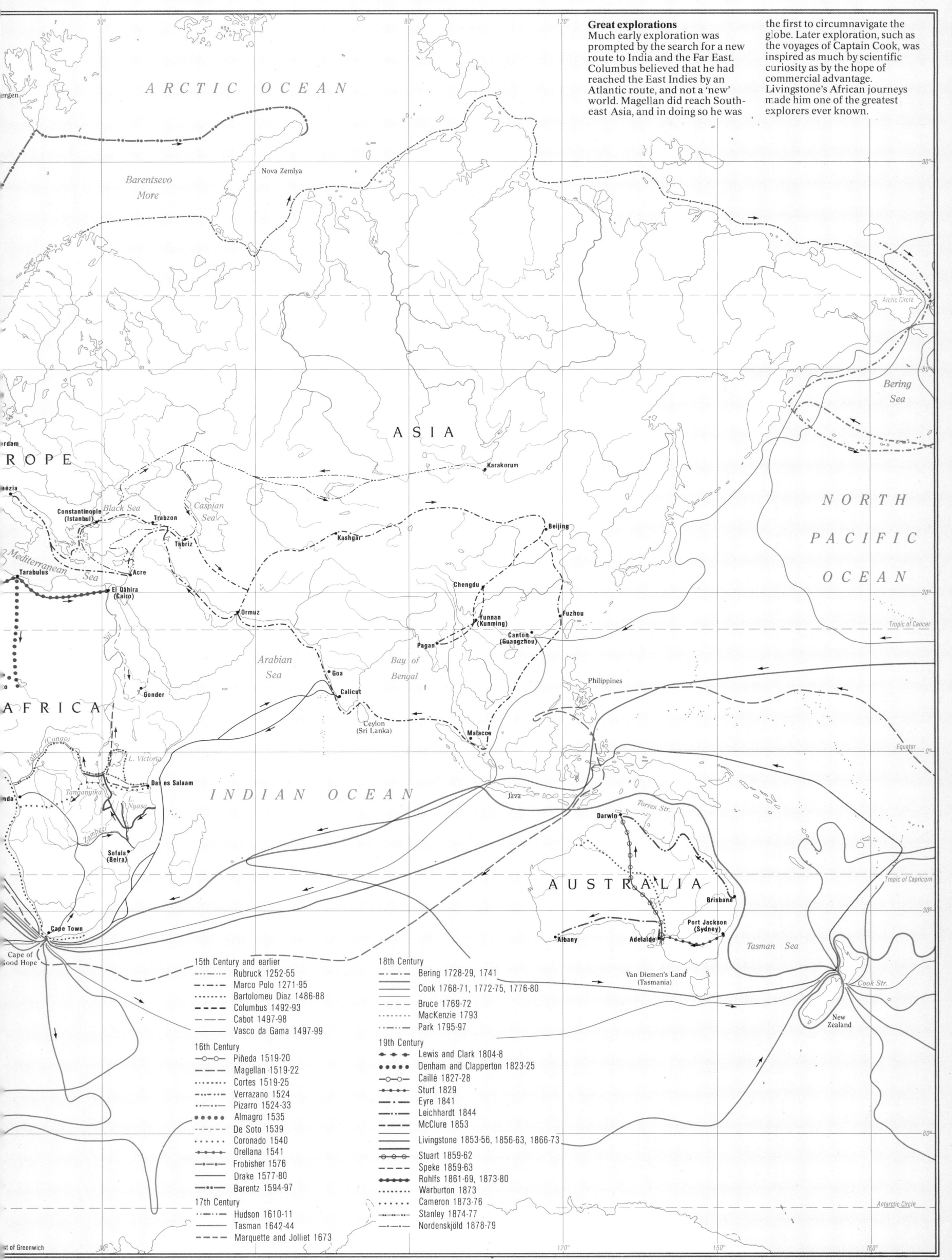

ARCTIC OCEAN

Great explorations
Much early exploration was prompted by the search for a new route to India and the Far East. Columbus believed that he had reached the East Indies by an Atlantic route, and not a 'new' world. Magellan did reach Southeast Asia, and in doing so he was the first to circumnavigate the globe. Later exploration, such as the voyages of Captain Cook, was inspired as much by scientific curiosity as by the hope of commercial advantage. Livingstone's African journeys made him one of the greatest explorers ever known.

Barentsevo More

Nova Zemlya

Arctic Circle

Bering Sea

ASIA

Karakorum

NORTH PACIFIC OCEAN

ROPE

Black Sea
Constantinople (Istanbul)
Trabzon
Caspian Sea
Tabriz
Kashgar
Beijing

Mediterranean Sea
Tarabulus
Acre
El Qâhira (Cairo)
Ormuz

Chengdu
Yunnan (Kunming)
Fuzhou

Tropic of Cancer

Pagan
Canton (Guangzhou)

AFRICA

Gonder

Arabian Sea
Goa
Calicut

Bay of Bengal

Philippines

Ceylon (Sri Lanka)
Malacca

(Congo)
L. Victoria
Dar es Salaam
Tanganyika
L. Nyasa
Zambezi

INDIAN OCEAN

Java

Equator

Darwin
Torres Str.

Sofala (Beira)

AUSTRALIA

Tropic of Capricorn

Brisbane

Cape Town

Albany
Adelaide
Port Jackson (Sydney)

Tasman Sea

Cape of Good Hope

Van Diemen's Land (Tasmania)

Cook Str.

New Zealand

15th Century and earlier
–··–··– Rubruck 1252-55
–·–·–·– Marco Polo 1271-95
·········· Bartolomeu Diaz 1486-88
– – – – Columbus 1492-93
———— Cabot 1497-98
———— Vasco da Gama 1497-99

16th Century
–o–o–o– Piñeda 1519-20
———— Magellan 1519-22
– · – · – Cortes 1519-25
– – – – Verrazano 1524
–·–·–·– Pizarro 1524-33
•••••• Almagro 1535
– – – – De Soto 1539
·········· Coronado 1540
•••••• Orellana 1541
–·–·–·– Frobisher 1576
———— Drake 1577-80
———— Barentz 1594-97

17th Century
– – – – Hudson 1610-11
———— Tasman 1642-44
– – – – Marquette and Jolliet 1673

18th Century
–·–·–·– Bering 1728-29, 1741
———— Cook 1768-71, 1772-75, 1776-80
– – – – Bruce 1769-72
·········· MacKenzie 1793
·········· Park 1795-97

19th Century
–◆–◆–◆– Lewis and Clark 1804-8
•••••• Denham and Clapperton 1823-25
–o–o–o– Caillé 1827-28
–◆–◆–◆– Sturt 1829
–·–·–·– Eyre 1841
–◆–◆–◆– Leichhardt 1844
———— McClure 1853
———— Livingstone 1853-56, 1856-63, 1866-73
–o–o–o– Stuart 1859-62
–◆–◆–◆– Speke 1859-63
•••••• Rohlfs 1861-69, 1873-80
– – – – Warburton 1873
·········· Cameron 1873-76
·········· Stanley 1874-77
–·–·–·– Nordenskjöld 1878-79

Antarctic Circle

st of Greenwich

23

Designed and produced by E.S.R.

ORGANISATIONS AND AFFILIATIONS

Today's large number of nations is a relatively recent phenomenon. As colonialism declined, the number of independent nations grew. Some of the recently established national boundaries have created artificial divisions which often divide tribal lands and separate ethnic communities. Many newly emergent countries have been beset by instability, civil war and other turbulent events. The outcome of disputes within and between nations is now often dependent upon global opinion or intervention.

Nations are becoming more involved in each other's affairs by virtue of trade, technology and aid. Also, problems such as terrorism, pollution, ecological issues and many more may be tackled more effectively through collaborative effort. An array of international and regional bodies, consultative agencies and other cohesive groupings reflect this growing interdependence of nations. There has been a rapid growth in recent years in the number of non-governmental organisations. They range from development groups like OXFAM to conservation groups such as Greenpeace and Friends of the Earth. These and other pressure groups seek to influence governments and international agencies. Some highly effective campaigns have increased world awareness of the disasters and problems faced in other parts of the globe as well as bringing to the fore many environmental issues.

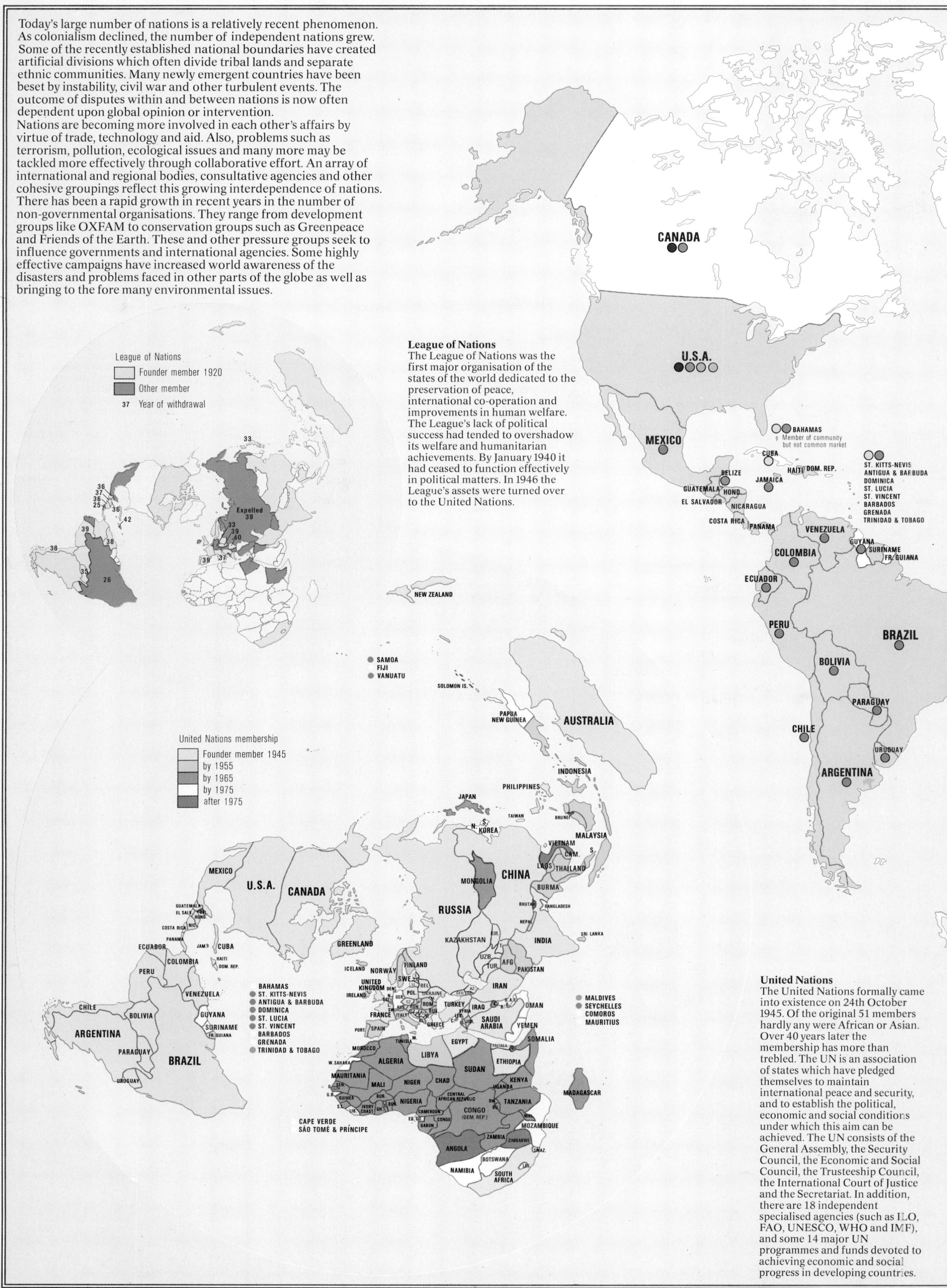

League of Nations
- Founder member 1920
- Other member
- 37 Year of withdrawal

League of Nations
The League of Nations was the first major organisation of the states of the world dedicated to the preservation of peace, international co-operation and improvements in human welfare. The League's lack of political success had tended to overshadow its welfare and humanitarian achievements. By January 1940 it had ceased to function effectively in political matters. In 1946 the League's assets were turned over to the United Nations.

United Nations membership
- Founder member 1945
- by 1955
- by 1965
- by 1975
- after 1975

United Nations
The United Nations formally came into existence on 24th October 1945. Of the original 51 members hardly any were African or Asian. Over 40 years later the membership has more than trebled. The UN is an association of states which have pledged themselves to maintain international peace and security, and to establish the political, economic and social conditions under which this aim can be achieved. The UN consists of the General Assembly, the Security Council, the Economic and Social Council, the Trusteeship Council, the International Court of Justice and the Secretariat. In addition, there are 18 independent specialised agencies (such as ILO, FAO, UNESCO, WHO and IMF), and some 14 major UN programmes and funds devoted to achieving economic and social progress in developing countries.

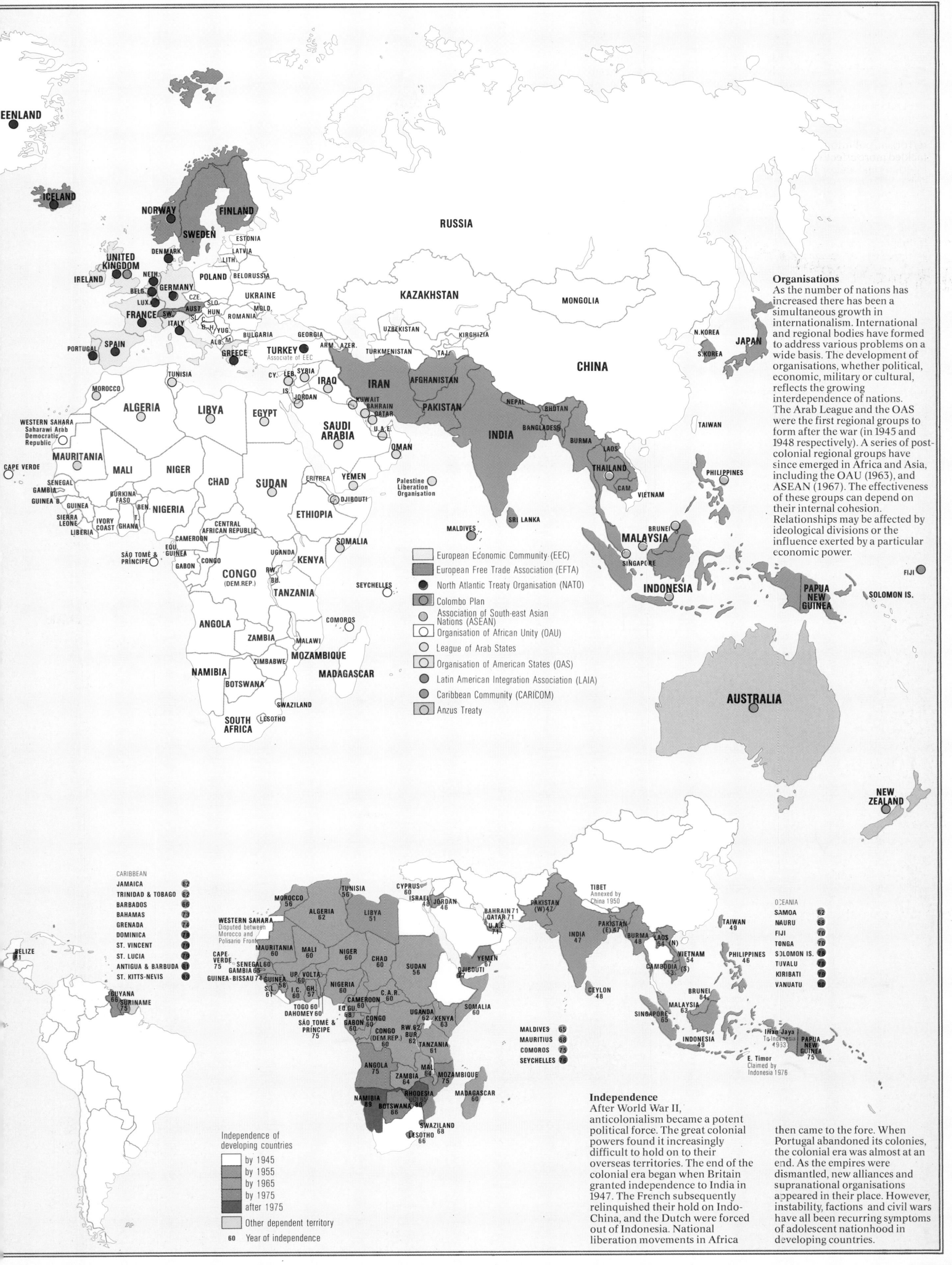

Organisations

As the number of nations has increased there has been a simultaneous growth in internationalism. International and regional bodies have formed to address various problems on a wide basis. The development of organisations, whether political, economic, military or cultural, reflects the growing interdependence of nations. The Arab League and the OAS were the first regional groups to form after the war (in 1945 and 1948 respectively). A series of post-colonial regional groups have since emerged in Africa and Asia, including the OAU (1963), and ASEAN (1967). The effectiveness of these groups can depend on their internal cohesion. Relationships may be affected by ideological divisions or the influence exerted by a particular economic power.

Legend:
- European Economic Community (EEC)
- European Free Trade Association (EFTA)
- North Atlantic Treaty Organisation (NATO)
- Colombo Plan
- Association of South-east Asian Nations (ASEAN)
- Organisation of African Unity (OAU)
- League of Arab States
- Organisation of American States (OAS)
- Latin American Integration Association (LAIA)
- Caribbean Community (CARICOM)
- Anzus Treaty

Independence

After World War II, anticolonialism became a potent political force. The great colonial powers found it increasingly difficult to hold on to their overseas territories. The end of the colonial era began when Britain granted independence to India in 1947. The French subsequently relinquished their hold on Indo-China, and the Dutch were forced out of Indonesia. National liberation movements in Africa then came to the fore. When Portugal abandoned its colonies, the colonial era was almost at an end. As the empires were dismantled, new alliances and supranational organisations appeared in their place. However, instability, factions and civil wars have all been recurring symptoms of adolescent nationhood in developing countries.

Independence of developing countries:
- by 1945
- by 1955
- by 1965
- by 1975
- after 1975
- Other dependent territory
- 60 Year of independence

CARIBBEAN
JAMAICA	62
TRINIDAD & TOBAGO	62
BARBADOS	66
BAHAMAS	73
GRENADA	74
DOMINICA	78
ST. VINCENT	79
ST. LUCIA	79
ANTIGUA & BARBUDA	81
ST. KITTS-NEVIS	83

OCEANIA
SAMOA	62
NAURU	68
FIJI	70
TONGA	70
SOLOMON IS.	78
TUVALU	78
KIRIBATI	79
VANUATU	80

Designed and produced by E.S.R.

25

POPULATION

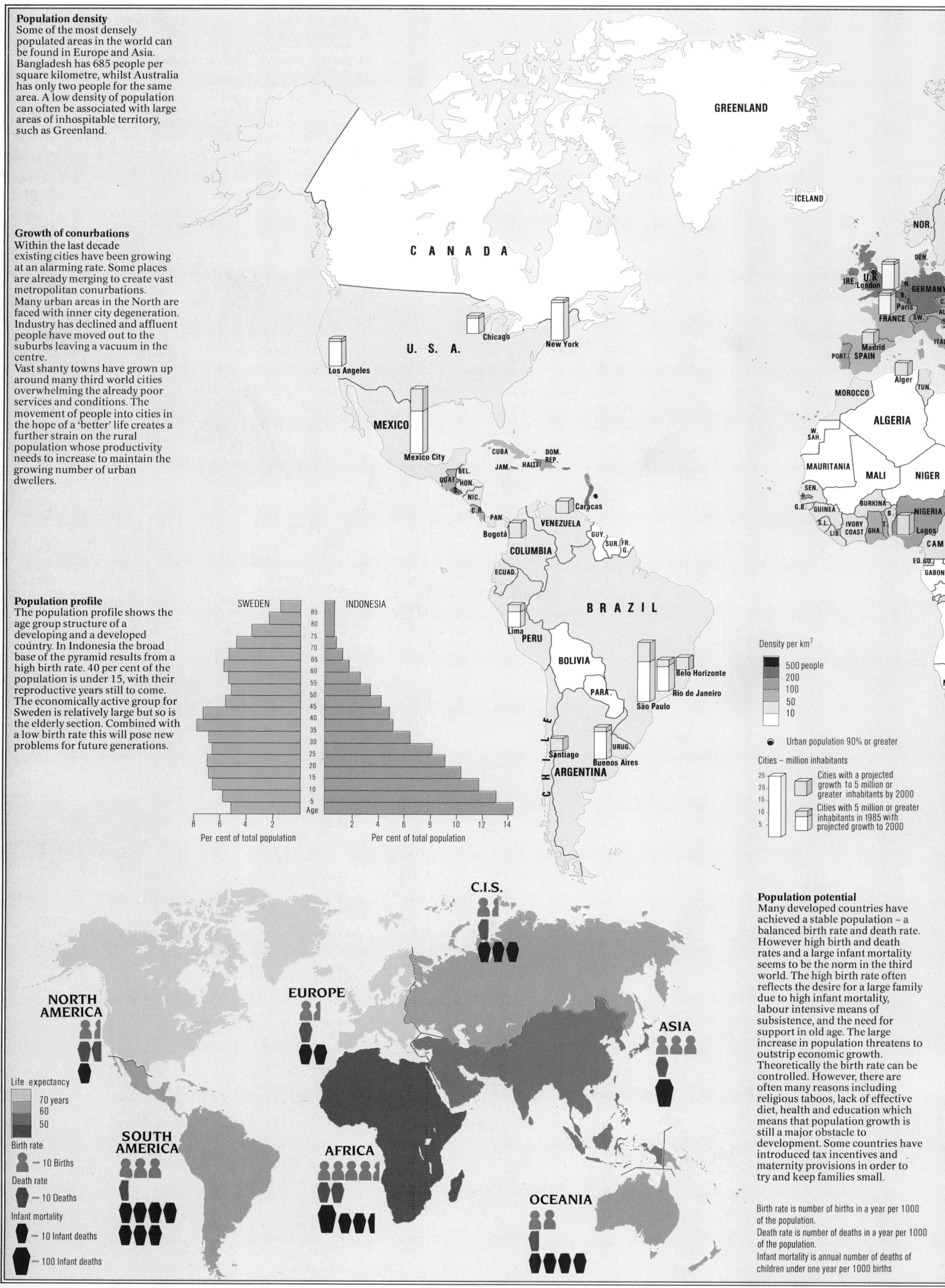

Population density
Some of the most densely populated areas in the world can be found in Europe and Asia. Bangladesh has 685 people per square kilometre, whilst Australia has only two people for the same area. A low density of population can often be associated with large areas of inhospitable territory, such as Greenland.

Growth of conurbations
Within the last decade existing cities have been growing at an alarming rate. Some places are already merging to create vast metropolitan conurbations. Many urban areas in the North are faced with inner city degeneration. Industry has declined and affluent people have moved out to the suburbs leaving a vacuum in the centre.
Vast shanty towns have grown up around many third world cities overwhelming the already poor services and conditions. The movement of people into cities in the hope of a 'better' life creates a further strain on the rural population whose productivity needs to increase to maintain the growing number of urban dwellers.

Population profile
The population profile shows the age group structure of a developing and a developed country. In Indonesia the broad base of the pyramid results from a high birth rate. 40 per cent of the population is under 15, with their reproductive years still to come. The economically active group for Sweden is relatively large but so is the elderly section. Combined with a low birth rate this will pose new problems for future generations.

Population profile chart
SWEDEN | INDONESIA
Age: 85, 80, 75, 70, 65, 60, 55, 50, 45, 40, 35, 30, 25, 20, 15, 10, 5
8 6 4 2 — Per cent of total population
2 4 6 8 10 12 14 — Per cent of total population

Density per km²
- 500 people
- 200
- 100
- 50
- 10

● Urban population 90% or greater

Cities – million inhabitants
25, 20, 15, 10, 5

Cities with a projected growth to 5 million or greater inhabitants by 2000

Cities with 5 million or greater inhabitants in 1985 with projected growth to 2000

Population potential
Many developed countries have achieved a stable population – a balanced birth rate and death rate. However high birth and death rates and a large infant mortality seems to be the norm in the third world. The high birth rate often reflects the desire for a large family due to high infant mortality, labour intensive means of subsistence, and the need for support in old age. The large increase in population threatens to outstrip economic growth. Theoretically the birth rate can be controlled. However, there are often many reasons including religious taboos, lack of effective diet, health and education which means that population growth is still a major obstacle to development. Some countries have introduced tax incentives and maternity provisions in order to try and keep families small.

Birth rate is number of births in a year per 1000 of the population.

Death rate is number of deaths in a year per 1000 of the population.

Infant mortality is annual number of deaths of children under one year per 1000 births

Legend (bottom left)
Life expectancy
- 70 years
- 60
- 50

Birth rate
👤 = 10 Births

Death rate
= 10 Deaths

Infant mortality
= 10 Infant deaths
= 100 Infant deaths

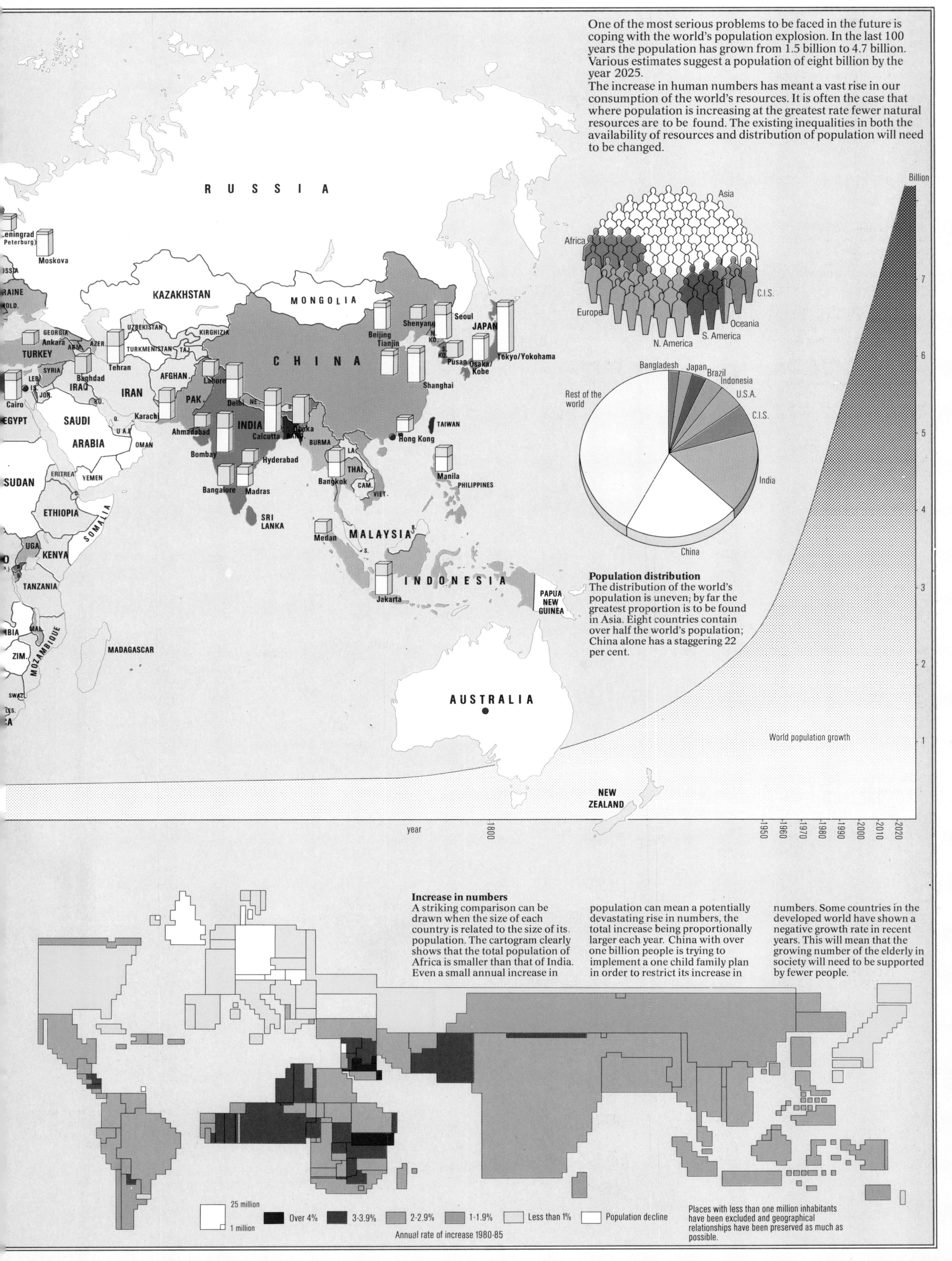

One of the most serious problems to be faced in the future is coping with the world's population explosion. In the last 100 years the population has grown from 1.5 billion to 4.7 billion. Various estimates suggest a population of eight billion by the year 2025.

The increase in human numbers has meant a vast rise in our consumption of the world's resources. It is often the case that where population is increasing at the greatest rate fewer natural resources are to be found. The existing inequalities in both the availability of resources and distribution of population will need to be changed.

Population distribution
The distribution of the world's population is uneven; by far the greatest proportion is to be found in Asia. Eight countries contain over half the world's population; China alone has a staggering 22 per cent.

World population growth

Increase in numbers
A striking comparison can be drawn when the size of each country is related to the size of its population. The cartogram clearly shows that the total population of Africa is smaller than that of India. Even a small annual increase in population can mean a potentially devastating rise in numbers, the total increase being proportionally larger each year. China with over one billion people is trying to implement a one child family plan in order to restrict its increase in numbers. Some countries in the developed world have shown a negative growth rate in recent years. This will mean that the growing number of the elderly in society will need to be supported by fewer people.

25 million
1 million

Over 4% | 3-3.9% | 2-2.9% | 1-1.9% | Less than 1% | Population decline

Annual rate of increase 1980-85

Places with less than one million inhabitants have been excluded and geographical relationships have been preserved as much as possible.

27

Designed and produced by E.S.R.

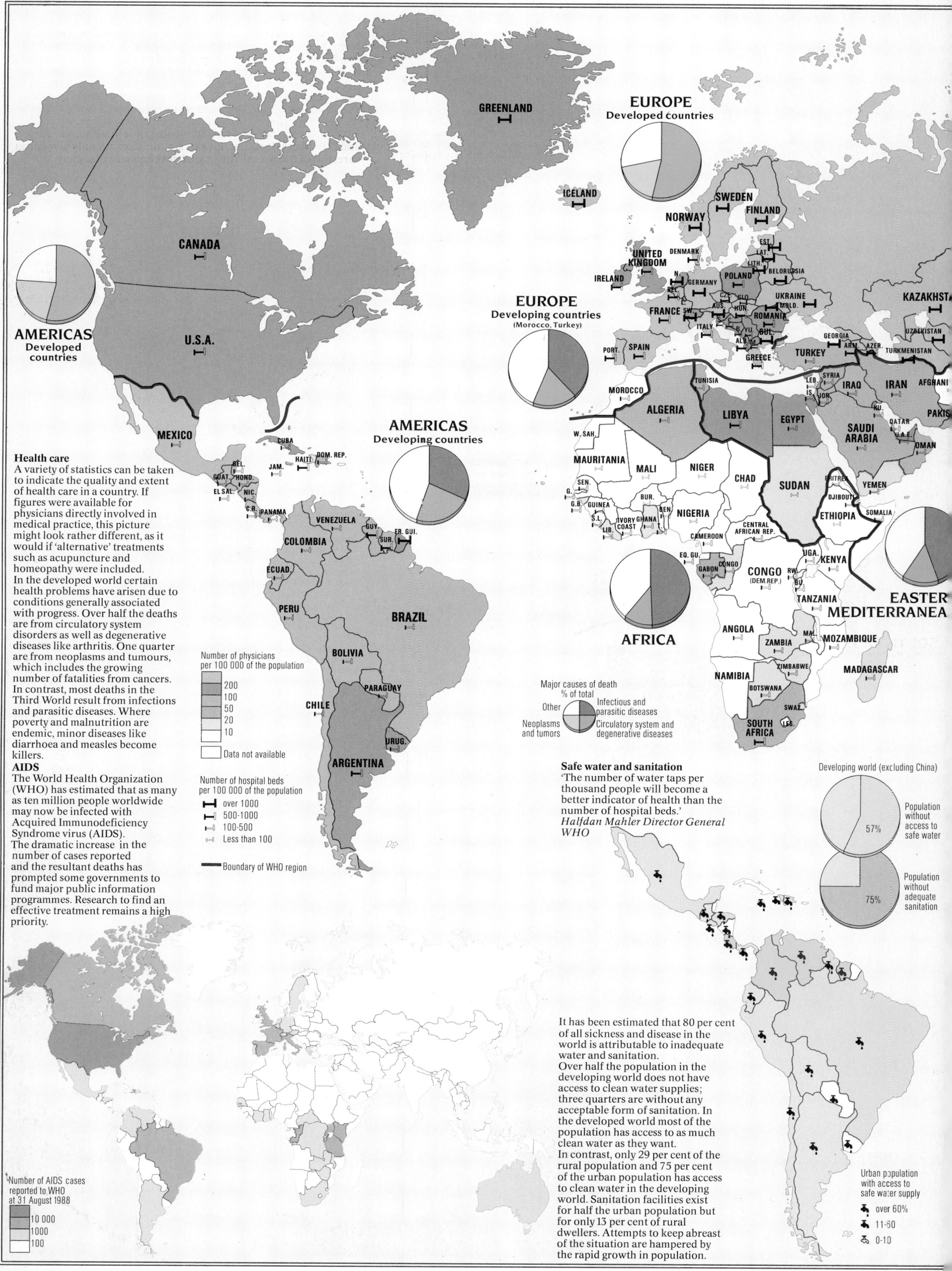

EUROPE Developed countries

EUROPE Developing countries (Morocco, Turkey)

AMERICAS Developed countries

AMERICAS Developing countries

AFRICA

EASTER MEDITERRANEA

Health care

A variety of statistics can be taken to indicate the quality and extent of health care in a country. If figures were available for physicians directly involved in medical practice, this picture might look rather different, as it would if 'alternative' treatments such as acupuncture and homeopathy were included.
In the developed world certain health problems have arisen due to conditions generally associated with progress. Over half the deaths are from circulatory system disorders as well as degenerative diseases like arthritis. One quarter are from neoplasms and tumours, which includes the growing number of fatalities from cancers. In contrast, most deaths in the Third World result from infections and parasitic diseases. Where poverty and malnutrition are endemic, minor diseases like diarrhoea and measles become killers.

AIDS

The World Health Organization (WHO) has estimated that as many as ten million people worldwide may now be infected with Acquired Immunodeficiency Syndrome virus (AIDS).
The dramatic increase in the number of cases reported and the resultant deaths has prompted some governments to fund major public information programmes. Research to find an effective treatment remains a high priority.

Number of physicians per 100 000 of the population

- 200
- 100
- 50
- 20
- 10

Data not available

Number of hospital beds per 100 000 of the population

- over 1000
- 500-1000
- 100-500
- Less than 100

— Boundary of WHO region

Major causes of death % of total

- Other
- Infectious and parasitic diseases
- Neoplasms and tumors
- Circulatory system and degenerative diseases

Safe water and sanitation

'The number of water taps per thousand people will become a better indicator of health than the number of hospital beds.'
Halfdan Mahler Director General WHO

Developing world (excluding China)

57% — Population without access to safe water

75% — Population without adequate sanitation

It has been estimated that 80 per cent of all sickness and disease in the world is attributable to inadequate water and sanitation.
Over half the population in the developing world does not have access to clean water supplies; three quarters are without any acceptable form of sanitation. In the developed world most of the population has access to as much clean water as they want.
In contrast, only 29 per cent of the rural population and 75 per cent of the urban population has access to clean water in the developing world. Sanitation facilities exist for half the urban population but for only 13 per cent of rural dwellers. Attempts to keep abreast of the situation are hampered by the rapid growth in population.

Number of AIDS cases reported to WHO at 31 August 1988

- 10 000
- 1000
- 100

Urban population with access to safe water supply

- over 60%
- 11-60
- 0-10

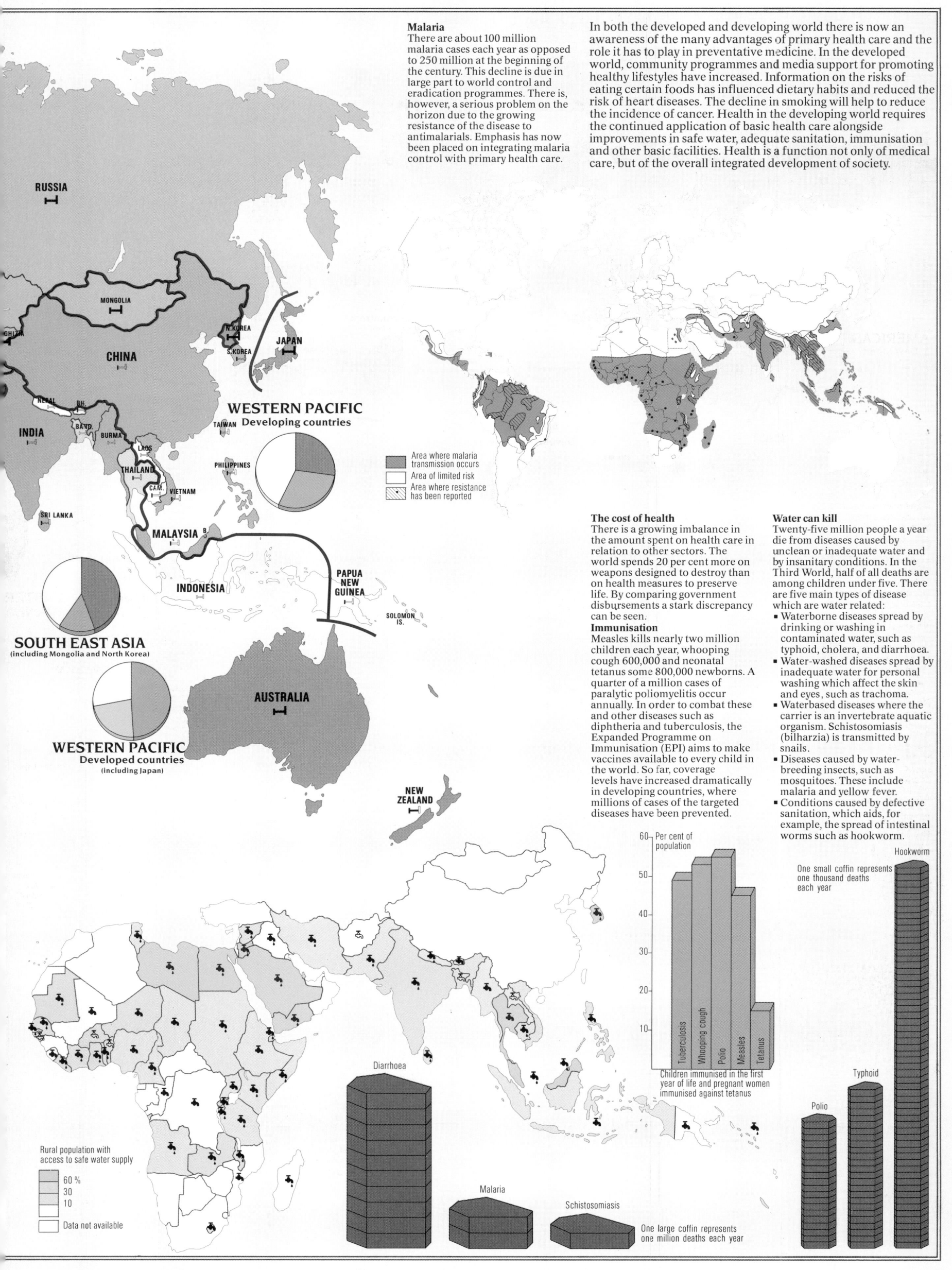

Malaria
There are about 100 million malaria cases each year as opposed to 250 million at the beginning of the century. This decline is due in large part to world control and eradication programmes. There is, however, a serious problem on the horizon due to the growing resistance of the disease to antimalarials. Emphasis has now been placed on integrating malaria control with primary health care.

In both the developed and developing world there is now an awareness of the many advantages of primary health care and the role it has to play in preventative medicine. In the developed world, community programmes and media support for promoting healthy lifestyles have increased. Information on the risks of eating certain foods has influenced dietary habits and reduced the risk of heart diseases. The decline in smoking will help to reduce the incidence of cancer. Health in the developing world requires the continued application of basic health care alongside improvements in safe water, adequate sanitation, immunisation and other basic facilities. Health is a function not only of medical care, but of the overall integrated development of society.

RUSSIA

MONGOLIA

CHINA

N.KOREA

S.KOREA

JAPAN

NEPAL

BH.

INDIA

BANG.

BURMA

LAOS

THAILAND

CAM.

VIETNAM

SRI LANKA

WESTERN PACIFIC
Developing countries

TAIWAN

PHILIPPINES

MALAYSIA

Area where malaria transmission occurs

Area of limited risk

Area where resistance has been reported

SOUTH EAST ASIA
(including Mongolia and North Korea)

INDONESIA

PAPUA NEW GUINEA

SOLOMON IS.

AUSTRALIA

WESTERN PACIFIC
Developed countries
(including Japan)

NEW ZEALAND

The cost of health
There is a growing imbalance in the amount spent on health care in relation to other sectors. The world spends 20 per cent more on weapons designed to destroy than on health measures to preserve life. By comparing government disbursements a stark discrepancy can be seen.

Immunisation
Measles kills nearly two million children each year, whooping cough 600,000 and neonatal tetanus some 800,000 newborns. A quarter of a million cases of paralytic poliomyelitis occur annually. In order to combat these and other diseases such as diphtheria and tuberculosis, the Expanded Programme on Immunisation (EPI) aims to make vaccines available to every child in the world. So far, coverage levels have increased dramatically in developing countries, where millions of cases of the targeted diseases have been prevented.

Water can kill
Twenty-five million people a year die from diseases caused by unclean or inadequate water and by insanitary conditions. In the Third World, half of all deaths are among children under five. There are five main types of disease which are water related:
- Waterborne diseases spread by drinking or washing in contaminated water, such as typhoid, cholera, and diarrhoea.
- Water-washed diseases spread by inadequate water for personal washing which affect the skin and eyes, such as trachoma.
- Waterbased diseases where the carrier is an invertebrate aquatic organism. Schistosomiasis (bilharzia) is transmitted by snails.
- Diseases caused by water-breeding insects, such as mosquitoes. These include malaria and yellow fever.
- Conditions caused by defective sanitation, which aids, for example, the spread of intestinal worms such as hookworm.

60 Per cent of population
50
40
30
20
10

Tuberculosis
Whooping cough
Polio
Measles
Tetanus

Children immunised in the first year of life and pregnant women immunised against tetanus

Hookworm

One small coffin represents one thousand deaths each year

Diarrhoea

Typhoid

Polio

Malaria

Schistosomiasis

Rural population with access to safe water supply

60 %
30
10
Data not available

One large coffin represents one million deaths each year

29

EDUCATION AND WORK

It has been argued that the kind of education provided by schools may be less important than 'traditional' wisdom derived from experience, especially in cultures other than those in the industrialised world. Education in the Third World has often been modelled on imported curricula which reflect the needs and conditions of a different society. Though newly independent nations introduce more suitable subjects, they may often lack the resources for relevant teaching materials.

Illiteracy

An illiterate person, one who is unable to read or write, is at a basic disadvantage in a world where literacy is an increasingly critical skill. Despite many literacy programmes, the total number of illiterates – over 800 million people, most of them in developing countries – continues to grow. These nations have only 12 per cent of the world's education budget. Most African countries spend less than ten per cent of GNP on education. There is a noticeable gap between the levels of male and female illiteracy, the latter being higher. This is often due to cultural differences and religious attitudes.

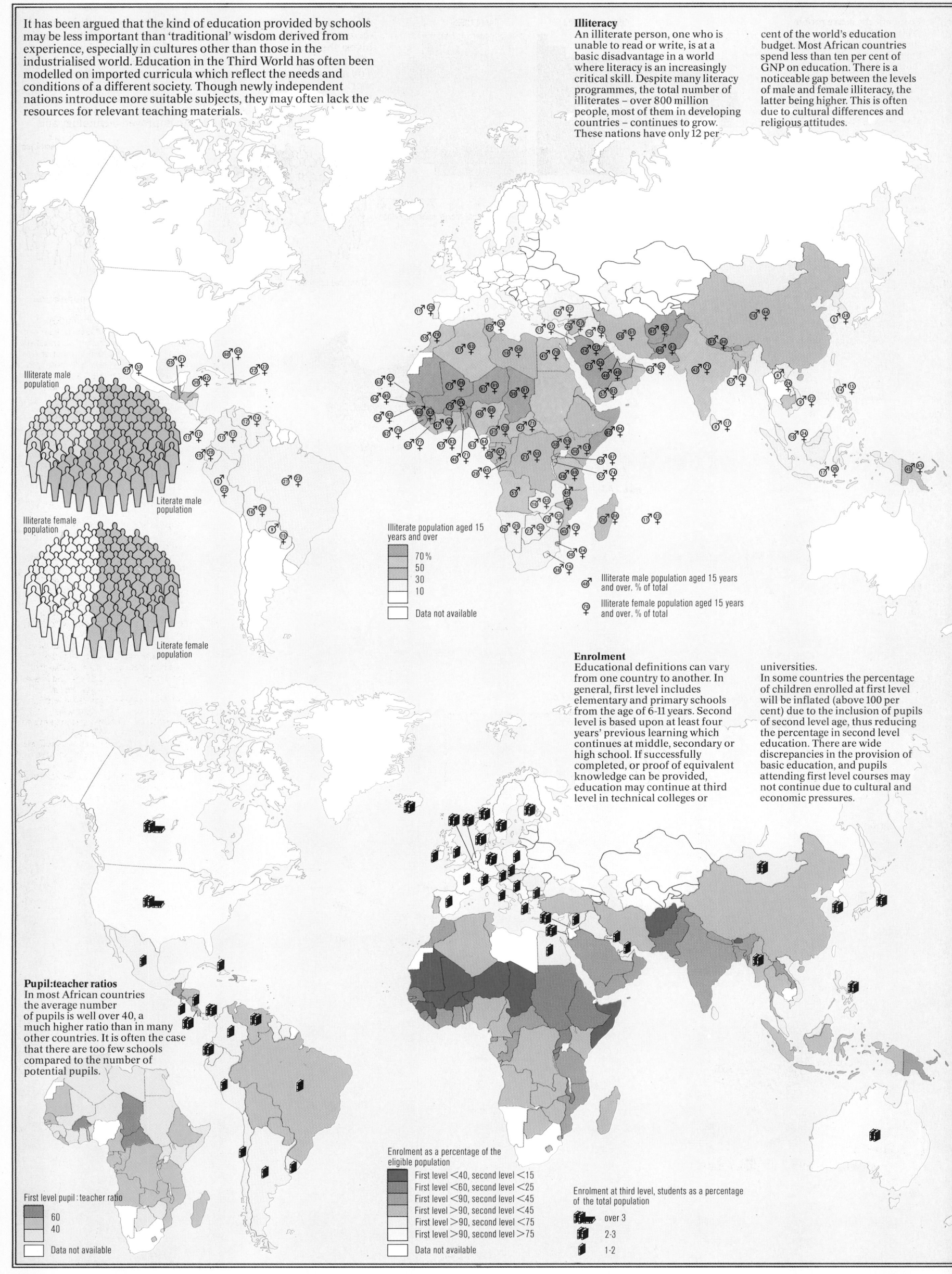

Illiterate male population

Literate male population

Illiterate female population

Literate female population

Illiterate population aged 15 years and over

- 70 %
- 50
- 30
- 10

Data not available

♂ 49   Illiterate male population aged 15 years and over. % of total

♀ 70   Illiterate female population aged 15 years and over. % of total

Enrolment

Educational definitions can vary from one country to another. In general, first level includes elementary and primary schools from the age of 6-11 years. Second level is based upon at least four years' previous learning which continues at middle, secondary or high school. If successfully completed, or proof of equivalent knowledge can be provided, education may continue at third level in technical colleges or universities.

In some countries the percentage of children enrolled at first level will be inflated (above 100 per cent) due to the inclusion of pupils of second level age, thus reducing the percentage in second level education. There are wide discrepancies in the provision of basic education, and pupils attending first level courses may not continue due to cultural and economic pressures.

Pupil:teacher ratios

In most African countries the average number of pupils is well over 40, a much higher ratio than in many other countries. It is often the case that there are too few schools compared to the number of potential pupils.

First level pupil : teacher ratio
- 60
- 40

Data not available

Enrolment as a percentage of the eligible population
- First level <40, second level <15
- First level <60, second level <25
- First level <90, second level <45
- First level >90, second level <45
- First level >90, second level <75
- First level >90, second level >75

Data not available

Enrolment at third level, students as a percentage of the total population
- over 3
- 2-3
- 1-2

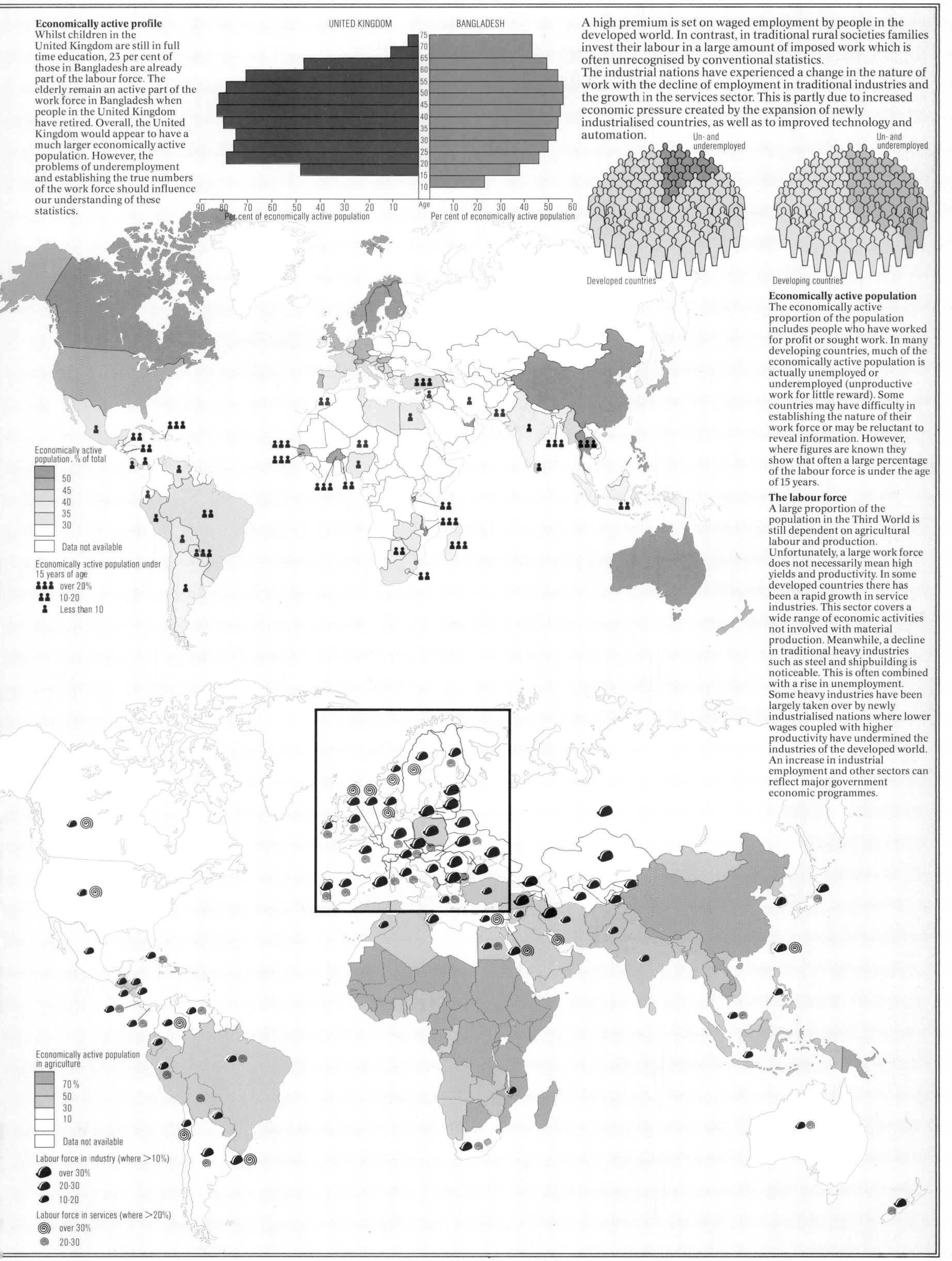

Economically active profile
Whilst children in the
United Kingdom are still in full
time education, 23 per cent of
those in Bangladesh are already
part of the labour force. The
elderly remain an active part of the
work force in Bangladesh when
people in the United Kingdom
have retired. Overall, the United
Kingdom would appear to have a
much larger economically
active population. However, the
problems of underemployment
and establishing the true numbers
of the work force should influence
our understanding of these
statistics.

UNITED KINGDOM   BANGLADESH

Per cent of economically active population   Per cent of economically active population

A high premium is set on waged employment by people in the
developed world. In contrast, in traditional rural societies families
invest their labour in a large amount of imposed work which is
often unrecognised by conventional statistics.
The industrial nations have experienced a change in the nature of
work with the decline of employment in traditional industries and
the growth in the services sector. This is partly due to increased
economic pressure created by the expansion of newly
industrialised countries, as well as to improved technology and
automation.

Un- and underemployed   Un- and underemployed

Developed countries   Developing countries

Economically active population
The economically active
proportion of the population
includes people who have worked
for profit or sought work. In many
developing countries, much of the
economically active population is
actually unemployed or
underemployed (unproductive
work for little reward). Some
countries may have difficulty in
establishing the nature of their
work force or may be reluctant to
reveal information. However,
where figures are known they
show that often a large percentage
of the labour force is under the age
of 15 years.

The labour force
A large proportion of the
population in the Third World is
still dependent on agricultural
labour and production.
Unfortunately, a large work force
does not necessarily mean high
yields and productivity. In some
developed countries there has
been a rapid growth in service
industries. This sector covers a
wide range of economic activities
not involved with material
production. Meanwhile, a decline
in traditional heavy industries
such as steel and shipbuilding is
noticeable. This is often combined
with a rise in unemployment.
Some heavy industries have been
largely taken over by newly
industrialised nations where lower
wages coupled with higher
productivity have undermined the
industries of the developed world.
An increase in industrial
employment and other sectors can
reflect major government
economic programmes.

Economically active
population . % of total

50
45
40
35
30

Data not available

Economically active population under
15 years of age
over 20%
10-20
Less than 10

Economically active population
in agriculture

70 %
50
30
10

Data not available

Labour force in industry (where >10%)
over 30%
20-30
10-20

Labour force in services (where >20%)
over 30%
20-30

31

Designed and produced by E.S.R.

LAND USE

Over the millenia the earth's landscape has changed significantly, due in no small part to man. The population explosion has put vegetation at risk as the need for agricultural land has increased. In order to meet the demand, forests have been cleared and degraded and marginal lands exhausted. Once fertile soils are rapidly becoming mineral-stressed. The requirement for forest products has risen, leading to even greater demolition of our woodlands. Man's expansion and construction has put all land uses under pressure.

The advancing desert
Over one quarter of land is now affected by rapidly encroaching deserts. 'Desertization' refers to instances in which the process is natural. Desertification usually occurs in arid and semi-arid areas and involves additional human factors. Expanding populations move onto marginal lands, where deforestation, over-cultivation and over-grazing occur, often accompanied by drought. This reduces the productivity of the land, which quickly degrades under stress.

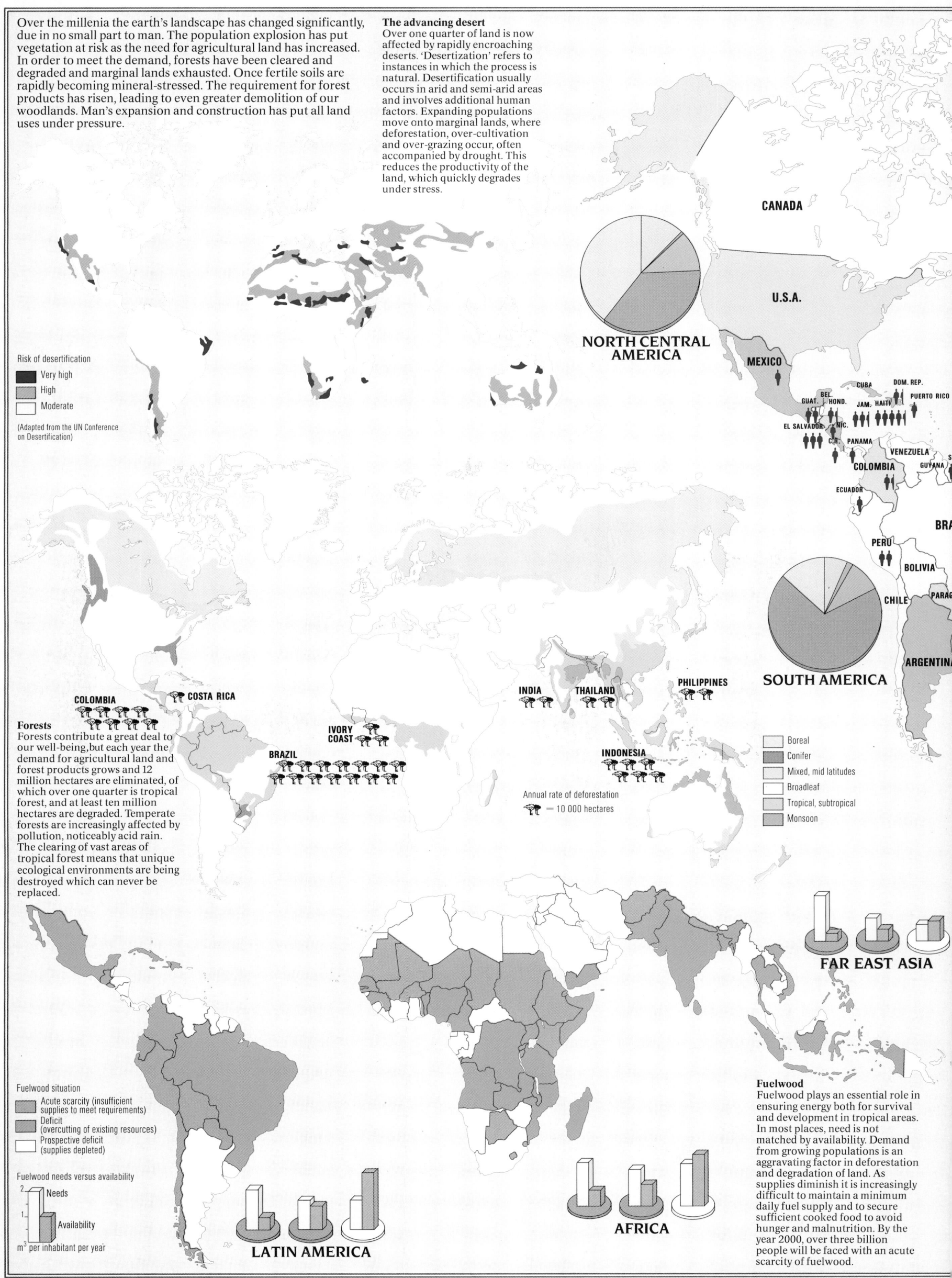

Risk of desertification
- Very high
- High
- Moderate

(Adapted from the UN Conference on Desertification)

CANADA

U.S.A.

NORTH CENTRAL AMERICA

MEXICO

DOM. REP.
BEL. CUBA
GUAT. HOND. JAM. HAITI PUERTO RICO
EL SALVADOR NIC.
C.R. PANAMA
VENEZUELA
COLOMBIA GUYANA
ECUADOR
BRA
PERU
BOLIVIA
CHILE PARAG
ARGENTINA

SOUTH AMERICA

Forests
Forests contribute a great deal to our well-being, but each year the demand for agricultural land and forest products grows and 12 million hectares are eliminated, of which over one quarter is tropical forest, and at least ten million hectares are degraded. Temperate forests are increasingly affected by pollution, noticeably acid rain. The clearing of vast areas of tropical forest means that unique ecological environments are being destroyed which can never be replaced.

COLOMBIA   COSTA RICA

BRAZIL   IVORY COAST

INDIA   THAILAND   PHILIPPINES

INDONESIA

Annual rate of deforestation
— 10 000 hectares

- Boreal
- Conifer
- Mixed, mid latitudes
- Broadleaf
- Tropical, subtropical
- Monsoon

FAR EAST ASIA

Fuelwood situation
- Acute scarcity (insufficient supplies to meet requirements)
- Deficit (overcutting of existing resources)
- Prospective deficit (supplies depleted)

Fuelwood needs versus availability
- 2
- Needs
- 1
- Availability
- m³ per inhabitant per year

LATIN AMERICA

AFRICA

Fuelwood
Fuelwood plays an essential role in ensuring energy both for survival and development in tropical areas. In most places, need is not matched by availability. Demand from growing populations is an aggravating factor in deforestation and degradation of land. As supplies diminish it is increasingly difficult to maintain a minimum daily fuel supply and to secure sufficient cooked food to avoid hunger and malnutrition. By the year 2000, over three billion people will be faced with an acute scarcity of fuelwood.

32

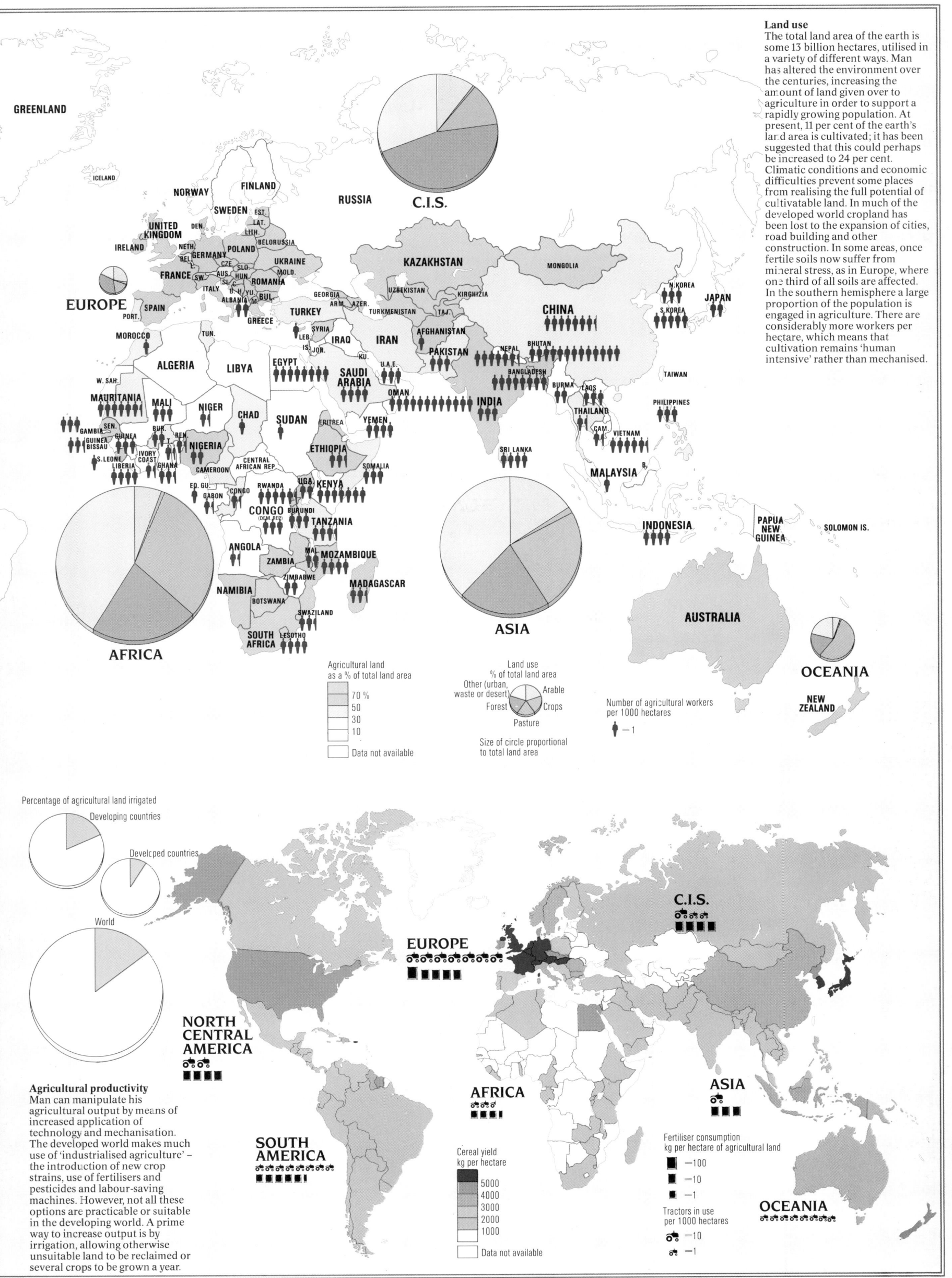

Land use

The total land area of the earth is some 13 billion hectares, utilised in a variety of different ways. Man has altered the environment over the centuries, increasing the amount of land given over to agriculture in order to support a rapidly growing population. At present, 11 per cent of the earth's land area is cultivated; it has been suggested that this could perhaps be increased to 24 per cent. Climatic conditions and economic difficulties prevent some places from realising the full potential of cultivatable land. In much of the developed world cropland has been lost to the expansion of cities, road building and other construction. In some areas, once fertile soils now suffer from mineral stress, as in Europe, where one third of all soils are affected. In the southern hemisphere a large proportion of the population is engaged in agriculture. There are considerably more workers per hectare, which means that cultivation remains 'human intensive' rather than mechanised.

Agricultural land as a % of total land area
70 %
50
30
10
Data not available

Land use % of total land area
Other (urban, waste or desert)
Forest
Arable
Crops
Pasture
Size of circle proportional to total land area

Number of agricultural workers per 1000 hectares
— 1

Percentage of agricultural land irrigated
Developing countries
Developed countries
World

Agricultural productivity

Man can manipulate his agricultural output by means of increased application of technology and mechanisation. The developed world makes much use of 'industrialised agriculture' – the introduction of new crop strains, use of fertilisers and pesticides and labour-saving machines. However, not all these options are practicable or suitable in the developing world. A prime way to increase output is by irrigation, allowing otherwise unsuitable land to be reclaimed or several crops to be grown a year.

Cereal yield kg per hectare
5000
4000
3000
2000
1000
Data not available

Fertiliser consumption kg per hectare of agricultural land
—100
—10
—1

Tractors in use per 1000 hectares
—10
—1

33

Designed and produced by E.S.R.

FOOD

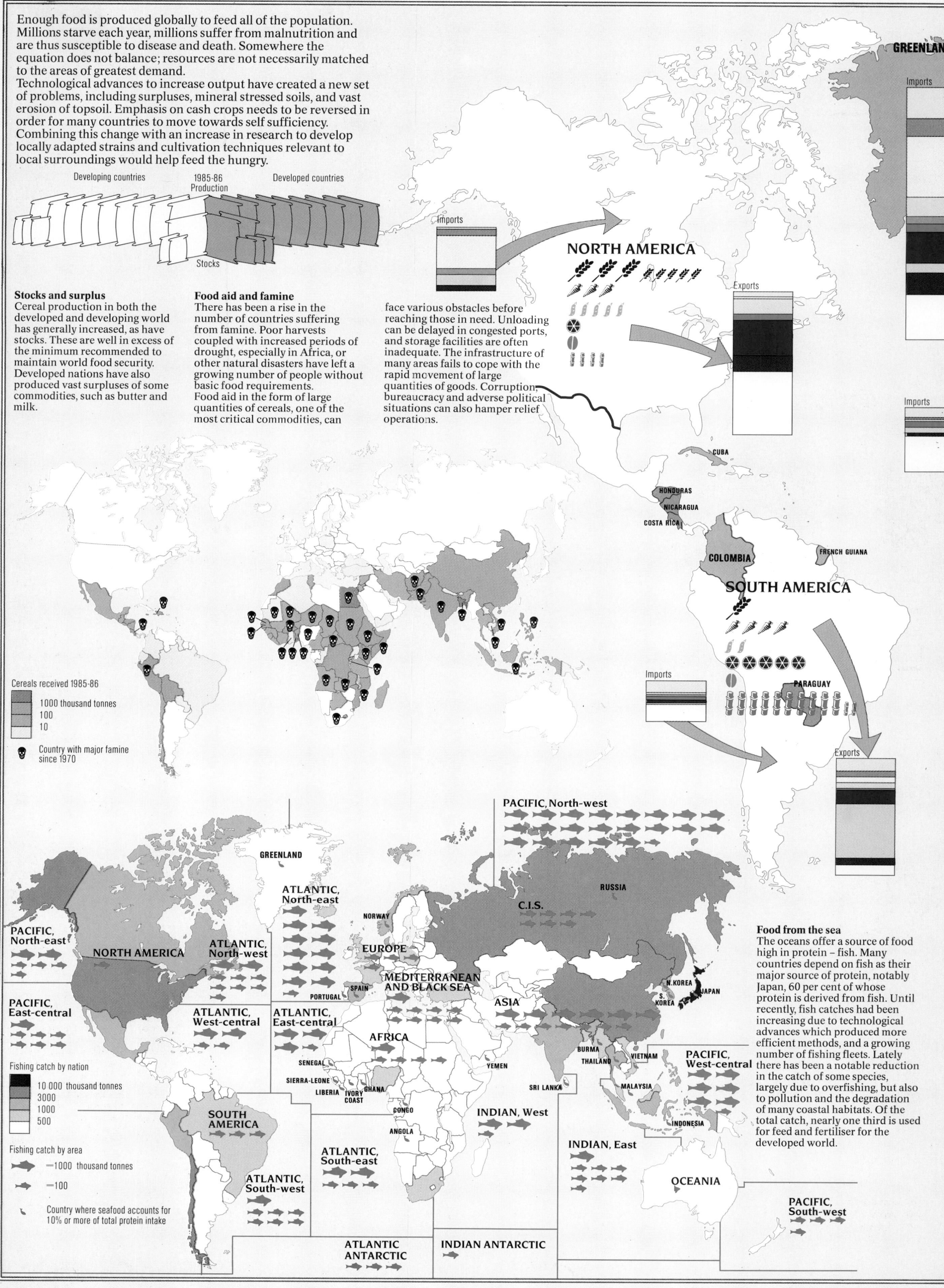

Enough food is produced globally to feed all of the population. Millions starve each year, millions suffer from malnutrition and are thus susceptible to disease and death. Somewhere the equation does not balance; resources are not necessarily matched to the areas of greatest demand.
Technological advances to increase output have created a new set of problems, including surpluses, mineral stressed soils, and vast erosion of topsoil. Emphasis on cash crops needs to be reversed in order for many countries to move towards self sufficiency. Combining this change with an increase in research to develop locally adapted strains and cultivation techniques relevant to local surroundings would help feed the hungry.

Developing countries
1985-86 Production
Developed countries
Stocks

Stocks and surplus

Cereal production in both the developed and developing world has generally increased, as have stocks. These are well in excess of the minimum recommended to maintain world food security. Developed nations have also produced vast surpluses of some commodities, such as butter and milk.

Food aid and famine

There has been a rise in the number of countries suffering from famine. Poor harvests coupled with increased periods of drought, especially in Africa, or other natural disasters have left a growing number of people without basic food requirements.
Food aid in the form of large quantities of cereals, one of the most critical commodities, can face various obstacles before reaching those in need. Unloading can be delayed in congested ports, and storage facilities are often inadequate. The infrastructure of many areas fails to cope with the rapid movement of large quantities of goods. Corruption, bureaucracy and adverse political situations can also hamper relief operations.

GREENLAND
Imports

NORTH AMERICA
Imports
Exports

Imports

CUBA
HONDURAS
NICARAGUA
COSTA RICA
COLOMBIA
FRENCH GUIANA
SOUTH AMERICA
Imports
PARAGUAY
Exports

Cereals received 1985-86

1000 thousand tonnes
100
10

Country with major famine since 1970

Food from the sea

The oceans offer a source of food high in protein – fish. Many countries depend on fish as their major source of protein, notably Japan, 60 per cent of whose protein is derived from fish. Until recently, fish catches had been increasing due to technological advances which produced more efficient methods, and a growing number of fishing fleets. Lately there has been a notable reduction in the catch of some species, largely due to overfishing, but also to pollution and the degradation of many coastal habitats. Of the total catch, nearly one third is used for feed and fertiliser for the developed world.

PACIFIC, North-west
PACIFIC, North-east
NORTH AMERICA
ATLANTIC, North-west
ATLANTIC, North-east
GREENLAND
NORWAY
C.I.S.
RUSSIA
EUROPE
MEDITERRANEAN AND BLACK SEA
SPAIN
PORTUGAL
ATLANTIC, East-central
ASIA
N. KOREA
S. KOREA
JAPAN
PACIFIC, East-central
ATLANTIC, West-central
AFRICA
SENEGAL
SIERRA-LEONE
LIBERIA
IVORY COAST
GHANA
CONGO
ANGOLA
YEMEN
SRI LANKA
BURMA
THAILAND
VIETNAM
MALAYSIA
PACIFIC, West-central
INDIAN, West
INDONESIA
INDIAN, East
OCEANIA
PACIFIC, South-west

Fishing catch by nation

10 000 thousand tonnes
3000
1000
500

Fishing catch by area

−1000 thousand tonnes
−100

Country where seafood accounts for 10% or more of total protein intake

SOUTH AMERICA
ATLANTIC, South-east
ATLANTIC, South-west
ATLANTIC ANTARCTIC
INDIAN ANTARCTIC

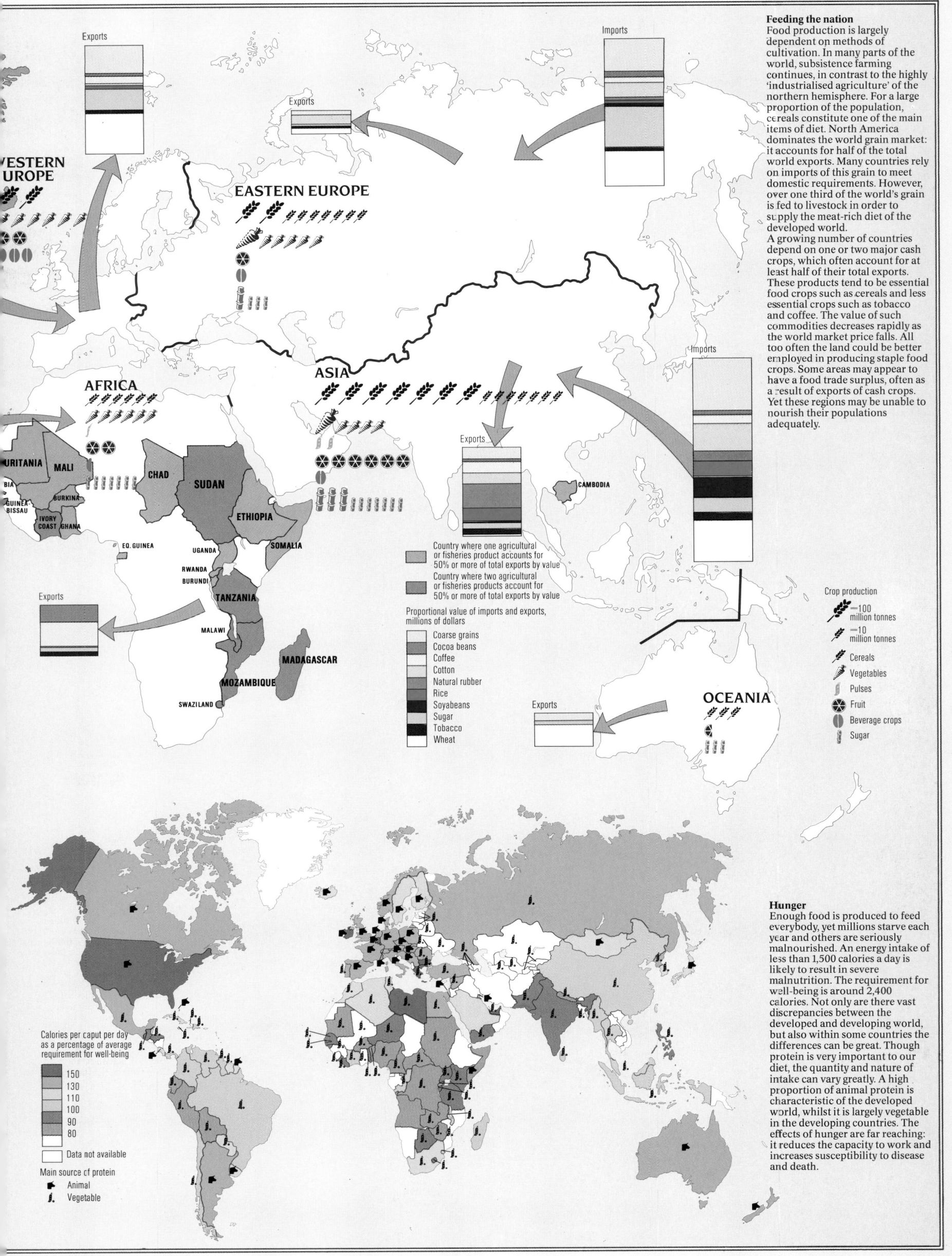

Feeding the nation
Food production is largely dependent on methods of cultivation. In many parts of the world, subsistence farming continues, in contrast to the highly 'industrialised agriculture' of the northern hemisphere. For a large proportion of the population, cereals constitute one of the main items of diet. North America dominates the world grain market: it accounts for half of the total world exports. Many countries rely on imports of this grain to meet domestic requirements. However, over one third of the world's grain is fed to livestock in order to supply the meat-rich diet of the developed world.
A growing number of countries depend on one or two major cash crops, which often account for at least half of their total exports. These products tend to be essential food crops such as cereals and less essential crops such as tobacco and coffee. The value of such commodities decreases rapidly as the world market price falls. All too often the land could be better employed in producing staple food crops. Some areas may appear to have a food trade surplus, often as a result of exports of cash crops. Yet these regions may be unable to nourish their populations adequately.

Exports

Imports

WESTERN EUROPE

EASTERN EUROPE

ASIA

AFRICA

URITANIA MALI CHAD SUDAN ETHIOPIA SOMALIA UGANDA RWANDA BURUNDI TANZANIA MALAWI MOZAMBIQUE MADAGASCAR SWAZILAND BIA GUINEA-BISSAU BURKINA IVORY COAST GHANA EQ. GUINEA

CAMBODIA

OCEANIA

Exports

Imports

Exports

Exports

Country where one agricultural or fisheries product accounts for 50% or more of total exports by value
Country where two agricultural or fisheries products account for 50% or more of total exports by value

Proportional value of imports and exports, millions of dollars
Coarse grains
Cocoa beans
Coffee
Cotton
Natural rubber
Rice
Soyabeans
Sugar
Tobacco
Wheat

Crop production
=100 million tonnes
=10 million tonnes
Cereals
Vegetables
Pulses
Fruit
Beverage crops
Sugar

Hunger
Enough food is produced to feed everybody, yet millions starve each year and others are seriously malnourished. An energy intake of less than 1,500 calories a day is likely to result in severe malnutrition. The requirement for well-being is around 2,400 calories. Not only are there vast discrepancies between the developed and developing world, but also within some countries the differences can be great. Though protein is very important to our diet, the quantity and nature of intake can vary greatly. A high proportion of animal protein is characteristic of the developed world, whilst it is largely vegetable in the developing countries. The effects of hunger are far reaching: it reduces the capacity to work and increases susceptibility to disease and death.

Calories per caput per day as a percentage of average requirement for well-being
150
130
110
100
90
80
Data not available

Main source of protein
Animal
Vegetable

Designed and produced by E.S.R.

Energy from fossil fuels is limited by geology, and supplies are being exhausted. Even if new discoveries are made and extraction is viable there is still a limit to how long these will last. There is a growing awareness of the environmental damage caused by the increased use of coal. The many problems of nuclear power have made it a high risk option, and not the energy panacea envisaged by many. As a result, interest in renewable sources of energy has grown: wind, geothermal, power from the sea, hydro and solar are all possible alternatives for the production of energy.

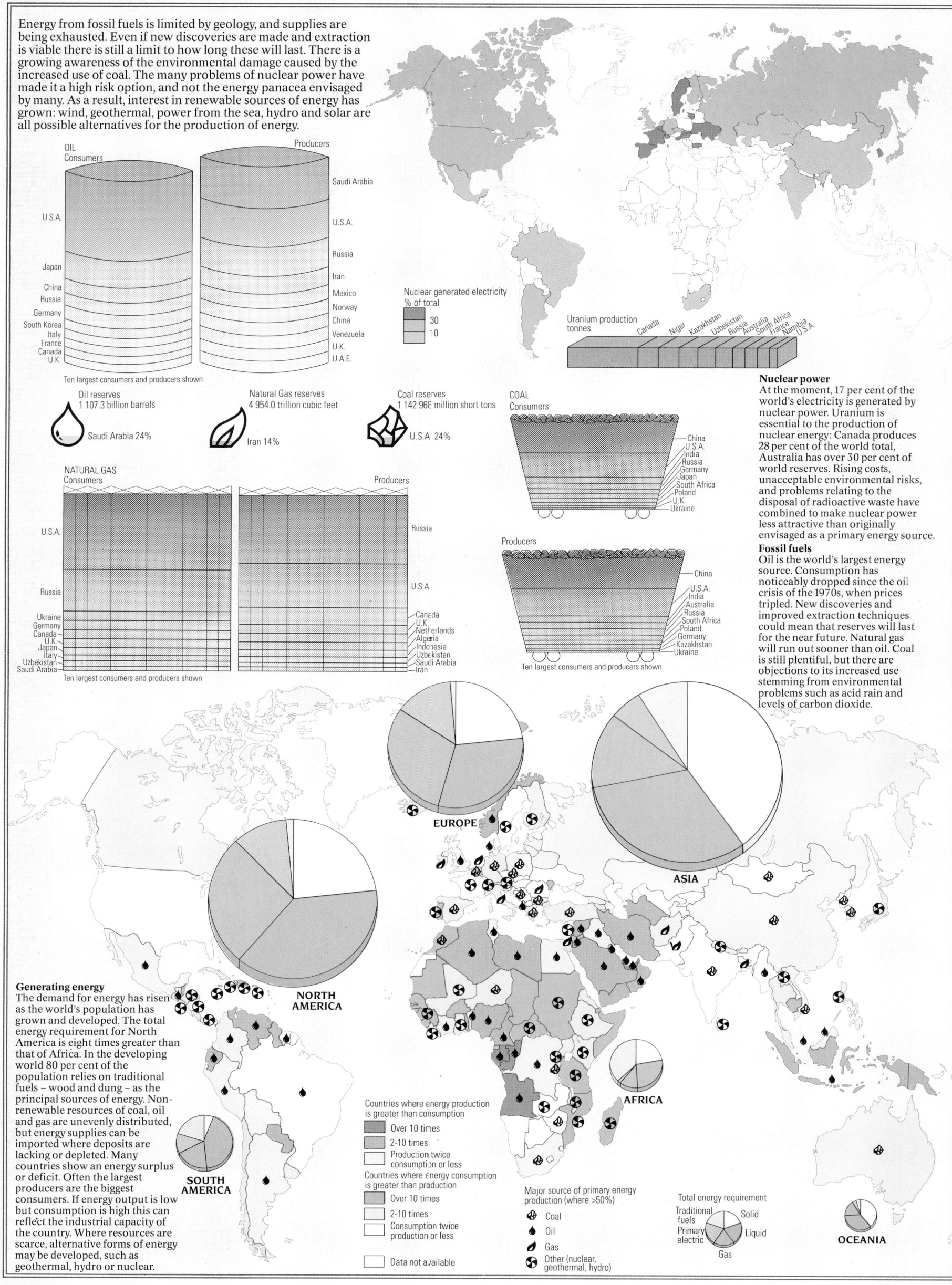

OIL
Consumers
Producers

U.S.A.
Japan
China
Russia
Germany
South Korea
Italy
France
Canada
U.K.

Saudi Arabia
U.S.A.
Russia
Iran
Mexico
Norway
China
Venezuela
U.K.
U.A.E.

Ten largest consumers and producers shown

Oil reserves
1 107.3 billion barrels
Saudi Arabia 24%

Natural Gas reserves
4 954.0 trillion cubic feet
Iran 14%

Coal reserves
1 142 968 million short tons
U.S.A 24%

Nuclear generated electricity
% of total
30
10

Uranium production
tonnes

Canada Niger Kazakhstan Uzbekistan Russia Australia South Africa France Namibia U.S.A.

NATURAL GAS
Consumers
Producers

U.S.A.
Russia
Ukraine
Germany
Canada
U.K.
Japan
Italy
Uzbekistan
Saudi Arabia

Russia
U.S.A.
Canada
U.K.
Netherlands
Algeria
Indonesia
Uzbekistan
Saudi Arabia
Iran

Ten largest consumers and producers shown

COAL
Consumers

China
U.S.A.
India
Russia
Germany
Japan
South Africa
Poland
U.K.
Ukraine

Producers

China
U.S.A.
India
Australia
Russia
South Africa
Poland
Germany
Kazakhstan
Ukraine

Ten largest consumers and producers shown

Nuclear power

At the moment, 17 per cent of the world's electricity is generated by nuclear power. Uranium is essential to the production of nuclear energy: Canada produces 28 per cent of the world total, Australia has over 30 per cent of world reserves. Rising costs, unacceptable environmental risks, and problems relating to the disposal of radioactive waste have combined to make nuclear power less attractive than originally envisaged as a primary energy source.

Fossil fuels

Oil is the world's largest energy source. Consumption has noticeably dropped since the oil crisis of the 1970s, when prices tripled. New discoveries and improved extraction techniques could mean that reserves will last for the near future. Natural gas will run out sooner than oil. Coal is still plentiful, but there are objections to its increased use stemming from environmental problems such as acid rain and levels of carbon dioxide.

EUROPE

ASIA

NORTH AMERICA

AFRICA

Generating energy

The demand for energy has risen as the world's population has grown and developed. The total energy requirement for North America is eight times greater than that of Africa. In the developing world 80 per cent of the population relies on traditional fuels – wood and dung – as the principal sources of energy. Non-renewable resources of coal, oil and gas are unevenly distributed, but energy supplies can be imported where deposits are lacking or depleted. Many countries show an energy surplus or deficit. Often the largest producers are the biggest consumers. If energy output is low but consumption is high this can reflect the industrial capacity of the country. Where resources are scarce, alternative forms of energy may be developed, such as geothermal, hydro or nuclear.

SOUTH AMERICA

Countries where energy production is greater than consumption
Over 10 times
2-10 times
Production twice consumption or less

Countries where energy consumption is greater than production
Over 10 times
2-10 times
Consumption twice production or less

Data not available

Major source of primary energy production (where >50%)
Coal
Oil
Gas
Other (nuclear, geothermal, hydro)

Total energy requirement
Traditional fuels
Solid
Primary electric
Liquid
Gas

OCEANIA

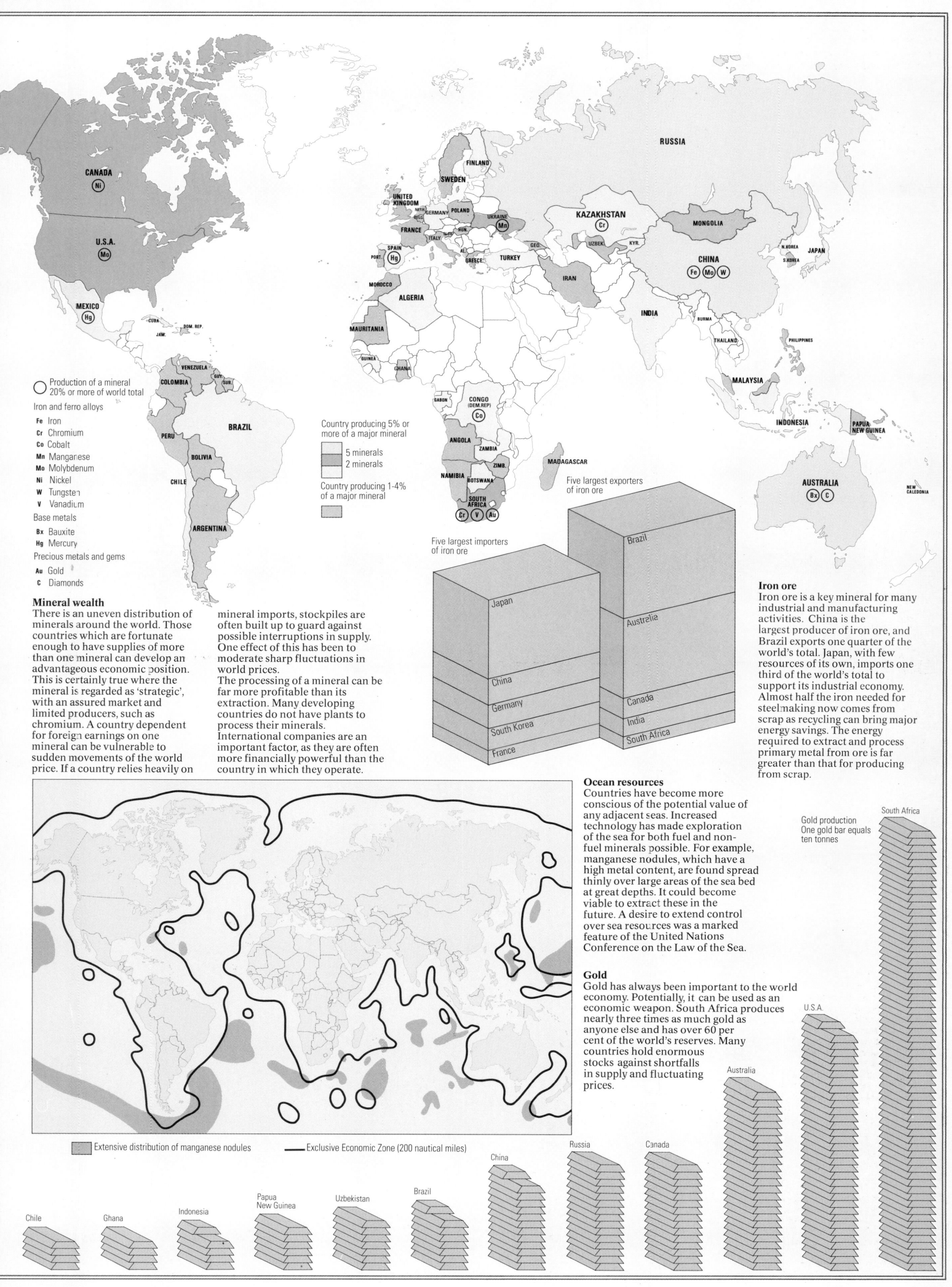

Mineral wealth

There is an uneven distribution of minerals around the world. Those countries which are fortunate enough to have supplies of more than one mineral can develop an advantageous economic position. This is certainly true where the mineral is regarded as 'strategic', with an assured market and limited producers, such as chromium. A country dependent for foreign earnings on one mineral can be vulnerable to sudden movements of the world price. If a country relies heavily on mineral imports, stockpiles are often built up to guard against possible interruptions in supply. One effect of this has been to moderate sharp fluctuations in world prices.

The processing of a mineral can be far more profitable than its extraction. Many developing countries do not have plants to process their minerals. International companies are an important factor, as they are often more financially powerful than the country in which they operate.

Production of a mineral
20% or more of world total

Iron and ferro alloys
Fe Iron
Cr Chromium
Co Cobalt
Mn Manganese
Mo Molybdenum
Ni Nickel
W Tungsten
V Vanadium

Base metals
Bx Bauxite
Hg Mercury

Precious metals and gems
Au Gold
C Diamonds

Country producing 5% or more of a major mineral

5 minerals
2 minerals

Country producing 1-4% of a major mineral

Five largest importers of iron ore

Five largest exporters of iron ore

Iron ore

Iron ore is a key mineral for many industrial and manufacturing activities. China is the largest producer of iron ore, and Brazil exports one quarter of the world's total. Japan, with few resources of its own, imports one third of the world's total to support its industrial economy. Almost half the iron needed for steelmaking now comes from scrap as recycling can bring major energy savings. The energy required to extract and process primary metal from ore is far greater than that for producing from scrap.

Ocean resources

Countries have become more conscious of the potential value of any adjacent seas. Increased technology has made exploration of the sea for both fuel and non-fuel minerals possible. For example, manganese nodules, which have a high metal content, are found spread thinly over large areas of the sea bed at great depths. It could become viable to extract these in the future. A desire to extend control over sea resources was a marked feature of the United Nations Conference on the Law of the Sea.

Gold

Gold has always been important to the world economy. Potentially, it can be used as an economic weapon. South Africa produces nearly three times as much gold as anyone else and has over 60 per cent of the world's reserves. Many countries hold enormous stocks against shortfalls in supply and fluctuating prices.

Extensive distribution of manganese nodules — Exclusive Economic Zone (200 nautical miles)

Gold production
One gold bar equals ten tonnes

Designed and produced by E.S.R.

TRADE

As trade has expanded, the production of goods has become increasingly specialised – components and raw materials from one country are shipped overseas for assembly or processing, then returned to their country of origin, or re-exported elsewhere. The dominance of established industrial countries is under threat from rapidly expanding industrial nations. Multinational corporations also play a large part in trade flows: they are mainly based in the developed world, which has a commanding influence on markets. Many developing countries, in order to achieve economic growth, face the dilemma between gearing production to satisfy overseas demands, while importing goods needed at home, or orientating production to domestic needs and increasing infrastructure at home. If trade is to prosper, the mutual interdependence of the developed and developing world both in demand and supply of goods needs to be recognised.

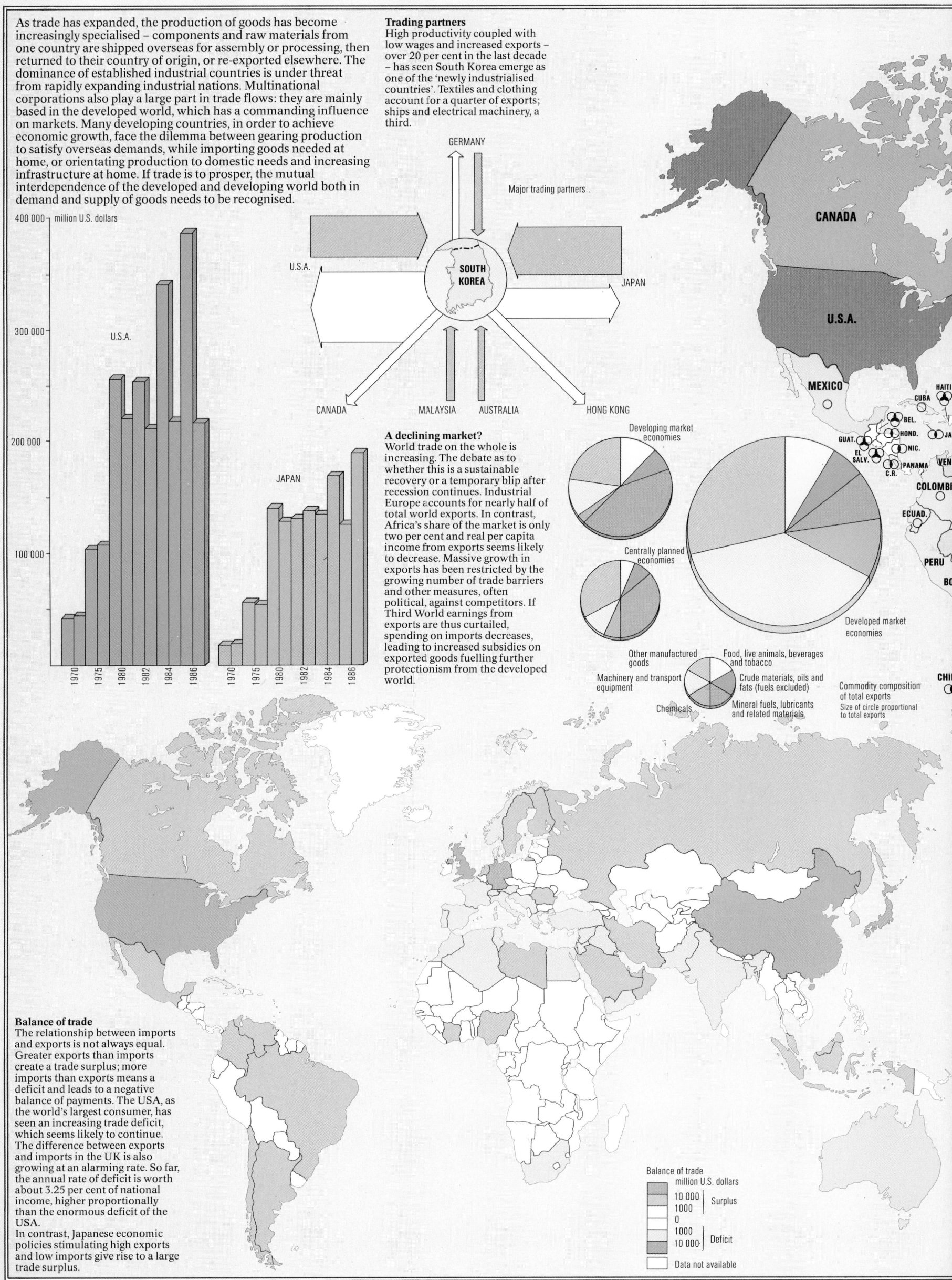

Trading partners
High productivity coupled with low wages and increased exports – over 20 per cent in the last decade – has seen South Korea emerge as one of the 'newly industrialised countries'. Textiles and clothing account for a quarter of exports; ships and electrical machinery, a third.

GERMANY

Major trading partners

U.S.A.

SOUTH KOREA

JAPAN

CANADA   MALAYSIA   AUSTRALIA   HONG KONG

A declining market?
World trade on the whole is increasing. The debate as to whether this is a sustainable recovery or a temporary blip after recession continues. Industrial Europe accounts for nearly half of total world exports. In contrast, Africa's share of the market is only two per cent and real per capita income from exports seems likely to decrease. Massive growth in exports has been restricted by the growing number of trade barriers and other measures, often political, against competitors. If Third World earnings from exports are thus curtailed, spending on imports decreases, leading to increased subsidies on exported goods fuelling further protectionism from the developed world.

Developing market economies

Centrally planned economies

Developed market economies

Other manufactured goods

Machinery and transport equipment

Chemicals

Food, live animals, beverages and tobacco

Crude materials, oils and fats (fuels excluded)

Mineral fuels, lubricants and related materials

Commodity composition of total exports
Size of circle proportional to total exports

Balance of trade
The relationship between imports and exports is not always equal. Greater exports than imports create a trade surplus; more imports than exports means a deficit and leads to a negative balance of payments. The USA, as the world's largest consumer, has seen an increasing trade deficit, which seems likely to continue. The difference between exports and imports in the UK is also growing at an alarming rate. So far, the annual rate of deficit is worth about 3.25 per cent of national income, higher proportionally than the enormous deficit of the USA.
In contrast, Japanese economic policies stimulating high exports and low imports give rise to a large trade surplus.

CANADA

U.S.A.

MEXICO   HAITI   CUBA   BEL.   HOND.   JAM
GUAT.   NIC.   EL SALV.   C.R.   PANAMA   VENE
COLOMBIA
ECUAD.
PERU   BO
CHIL

400 000 — million U.S. dollars

U.S.A.

JAPAN

300 000

200 000

100 000

1970 1975 1980 1982 1984 1986   1970 1975 1980 1982 1984 1986

Balance of trade
million U.S. dollars
10 000 ⎫
1000 ⎬ Surplus
0
1000 ⎫
10 000 ⎭ Deficit
Data not available

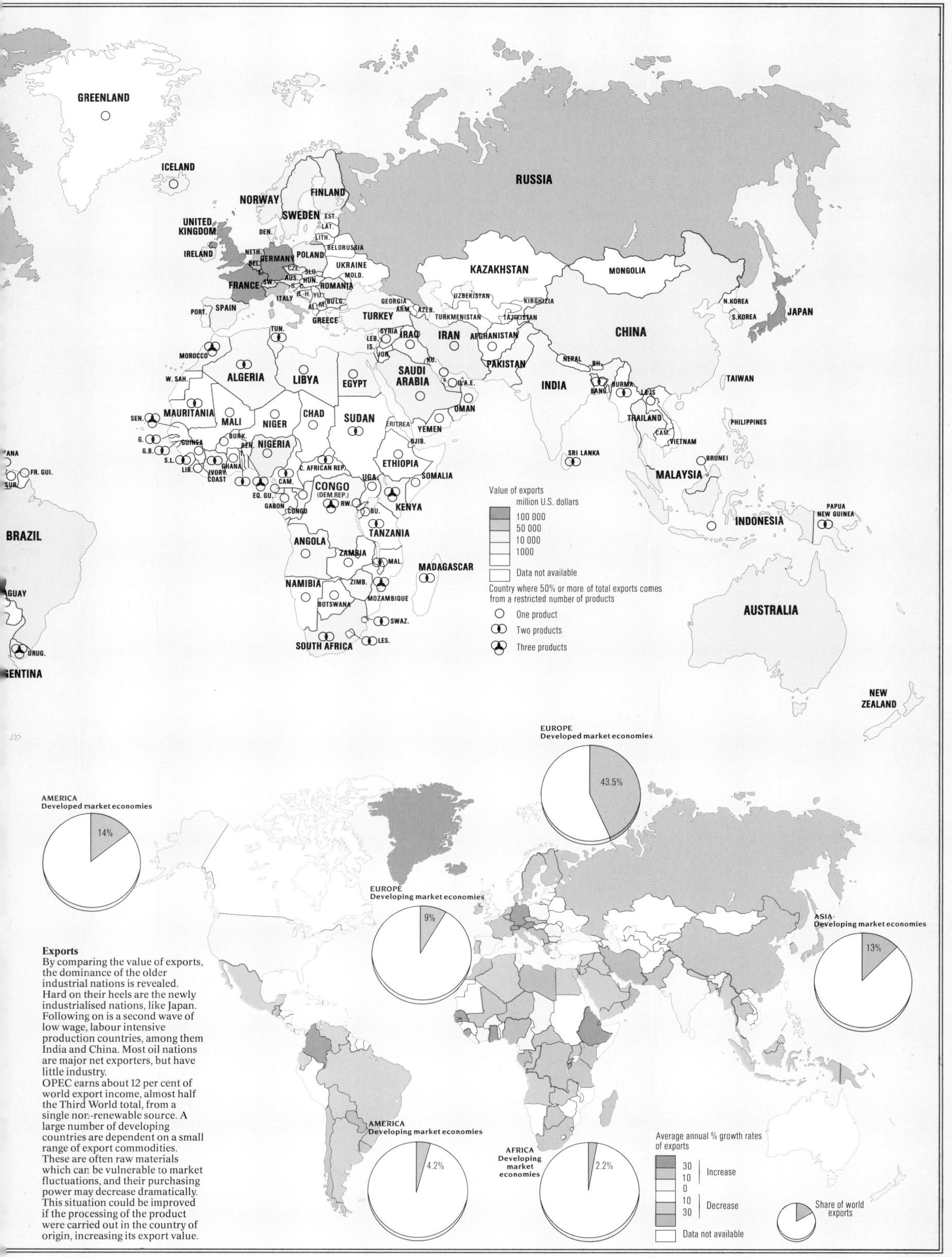

Value of exports
million U.S. dollars

100 000
50 000
10 000
1000

Data not available

Country where 50% or more of total exports comes
from a restricted number of products

○ One product
◑ Two products
◕ Three products

EUROPE
Developed market economies

43.5%

AMERICA
Developed market economies

14%

EUROPE
Developing market economies

9%

ASIA
Developing market economies

13%

AMERICA
Developing market economies

4.2%

AFRICA
Developing
market
economies

2.2%

Average annual % growth rates
of exports

30
10 } Increase
0
10
30 } Decrease

Data not available

Share of world
exports

Exports

By comparing the value of exports,
the dominance of the older
industrial nations is revealed.
Hard on their heels are the newly
industrialised nations, like Japan.
Following on is a second wave of
low wage, labour intensive
production countries, among them
India and China. Most oil nations
are major net exporters, but have
little industry.

OPEC earns about 12 per cent of
world export income, almost half
the Third World total, from a
single non-renewable source. A
large number of developing
countries are dependent on a small
range of export commodities.
These are often raw materials
which can be vulnerable to market
fluctuations, and their purchasing
power may decrease dramatically.
This situation could be improved
if the processing of the product
were carried out in the country of
origin, increasing its export value.

39

WEALTH AND DEBT

The chasm between the rich and poor nations of the world is widening. Existing methods of reducing the difference involve loans and aid from governments, UN organisations and aid agencies. In the future the international economic system needs to be redesigned to finance and invest in sustainable development of national resources and programmes to combat poverty.

Aid donors
Aid has mostly been provided by the developed nations, particularly members of the Development Assistance Committee (DAC) of the Organisations of Economic Cooperation and Development (OECD). However, in recent years a growing proportion has come from the major oil producing nations. The total amount of aid donated by a country can seem enormous, but as a proportion of GNP a rather different view of the nation's generosity emerges.

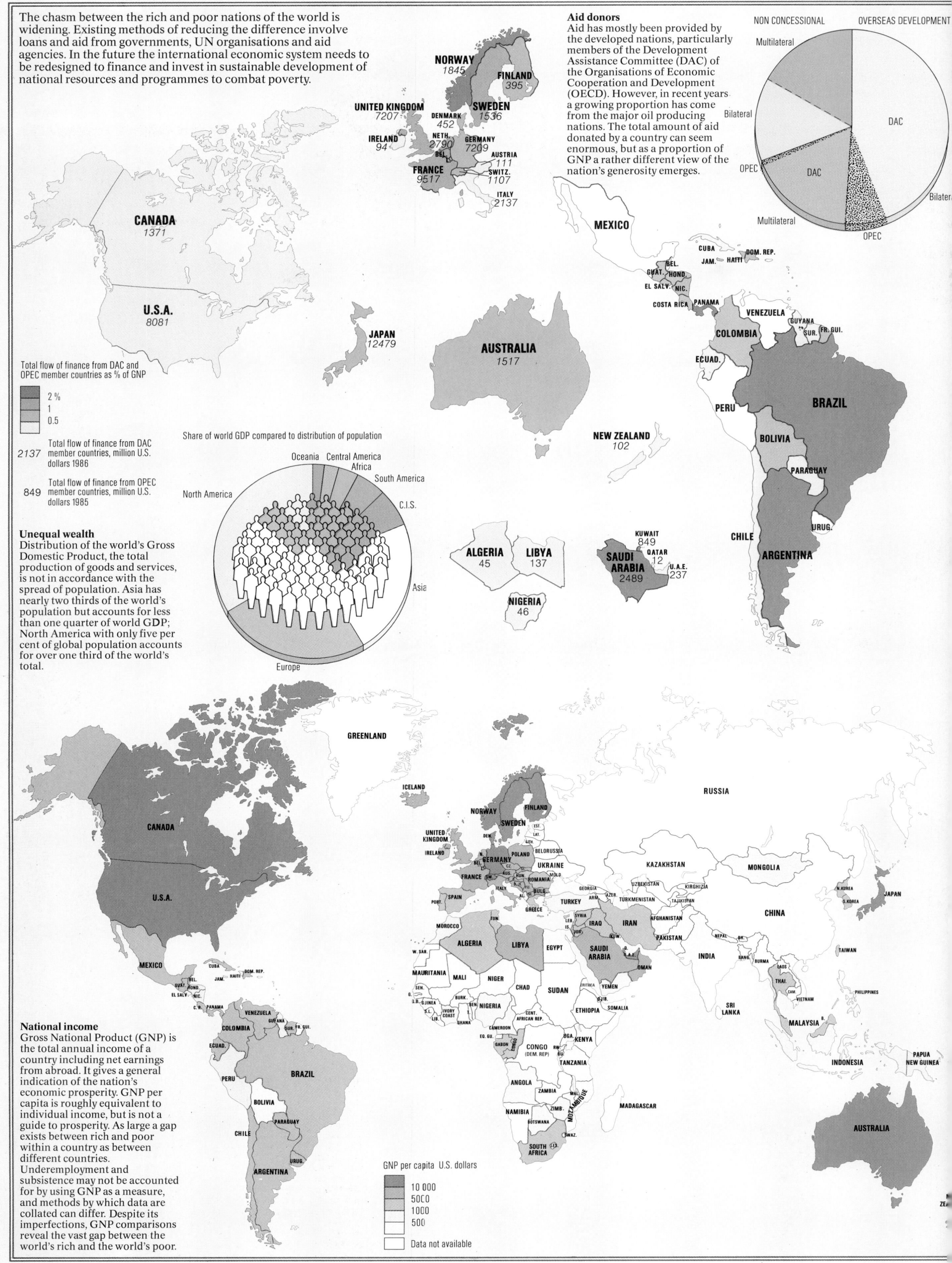

NON CONCESSIONAL   OVERSEAS DEVELOPMENT

Multilateral

Bilateral

DAC

OPEC

DAC

Multilateral

Bilateral

OPEC

NORWAY *1845*

FINLAND *395*

SWEDEN *1536*

UNITED KINGDOM *7207*

DENMARK *452*

IRELAND *94*

NETH. *2790*

GERMANY *7209*

BEL.

FRANCE *9517*

AUSTRIA *111*

SWITZ. *1107*

ITALY *2137*

CANADA *1371*

U.S.A. *8081*

JAPAN *12479*

MEXICO

CUBA   DOM. REP.

JAM.   HAITI

BEL.

GUAT.   HOND.

EL SALV.   NIC.

COSTA RICA   PANAMA

VENEZUELA

GUYANA

SUR.   FR. GUI.

COLOMBIA

ECUAD.

PERU

BRAZIL

BOLIVIA

PARAGUAY

CHILE

URUG.

ARGENTINA

AUSTRALIA *1517*

NEW ZEALAND *102*

ALGERIA *45*   LIBYA *137*

KUWAIT *849*

QATAR *12*

SAUDI ARABIA *2489*

U.A.E. *237*

NIGERIA *46*

Total flow of finance from DAC and OPEC member countries as % of GNP

- 2 %
- 1
- 0.5

2137 Total flow of finance from DAC member countries, million U.S. dollars 1986

849 Total flow of finance from OPEC member countries, million U.S. dollars 1985

Share of world GDP compared to distribution of population

North America

Oceania   Central America   Africa

South America

C.I.S.

Asia

Europe

Unequal wealth
Distribution of the world's Gross Domestic Product, the total production of goods and services, is not in accordance with the spread of population. Asia has nearly two thirds of the world's population but accounts for less than one quarter of world GDP; North America with only five per cent of global population accounts for over one third of the world's total.

National income
Gross National Product (GNP) is the total annual income of a country including net earnings from abroad. It gives a general indication of the nation's economic prosperity. GNP per capita is roughly equivalent to individual income, but is not a guide to prosperity. As large a gap exists between rich and poor within a country as between different countries. Underemployment and subsistence may not be accounted for by using GNP as a measure, and methods by which data are collated can differ. Despite its imperfections, GNP comparisons reveal the vast gap between the world's rich and the world's poor.

GREENLAND

ICELAND

RUSSIA

CANADA

NORWAY   FINLAND   SWEDEN   EST.   LAT.

UNITED KINGDOM   DEN.   LITH.

IRELAND   BELORUSSIA

NETH.   POLAND

GERMANY   UKRAINE

FRANCE   ITALY   ROMANIA   MOLD.

SPAIN   PORT.   BULG.

GREECE   TURKEY   GEORGIA   ARM.   AZER.

KAZAKHSTAN   MONGOLIA

UZBEKISTAN   KIRGHIZIA

TURKMENISTAN   TAJIKISTAN

N. KOREA   JAPAN

S. KOREA

U.S.A.

MOROCCO   SYRIA   IRAQ   IRAN   AFGHANISTAN   CHINA   TAIWAN

W. SAH.   ALGERIA   LIBYA   EGYPT   SAUDI ARABIA   PAKISTAN   NEPAL   BHU.

MEXICO   MAURITANIA   MALI   NIGER   CHAD   SUDAN   YEMEN   OMAN   INDIA   BANG.   BURMA   LAOS   THAI.   VIETNAM   PHILIPPINES

CUBA   DOM. REP.

GUAT.   HOND.   HAITI   JAM.

EL SALV.   NIC.   SEN.   GAMBIA   GUINEA   NIGERIA   ERITREA   DJIB.

C.R.   PANAMA   S.L.   IVORY COAST   GHANA   CENT. AFRICAN REP.   ETHIOPIA   SOMALIA   SRI LANKA   CAM.   MALAYSIA

VENEZUELA   GUYANA   GABON   CONGO   KENYA   PAPUA NEW GUINEA

COLOMBIA   FR. GUI.   EQ. GU.   CONGO (DEM. REP)   TANZANIA   INDONESIA

ECUAD.

PERU   BRAZIL   ANGOLA   ZAMBIA   MOZAMBIQUE   MADAGASCAR

BOLIVIA   NAMIBIA   ZIMB.   BOTSWANA

PARAGUAY   SWAZ.   AUSTRALIA

CHILE   SOUTH AFRICA

URUG.

ARGENTINA

GNP per capita U.S. dollars

- 10 000
- 5000
- 1000
- 500
- Data not available

40

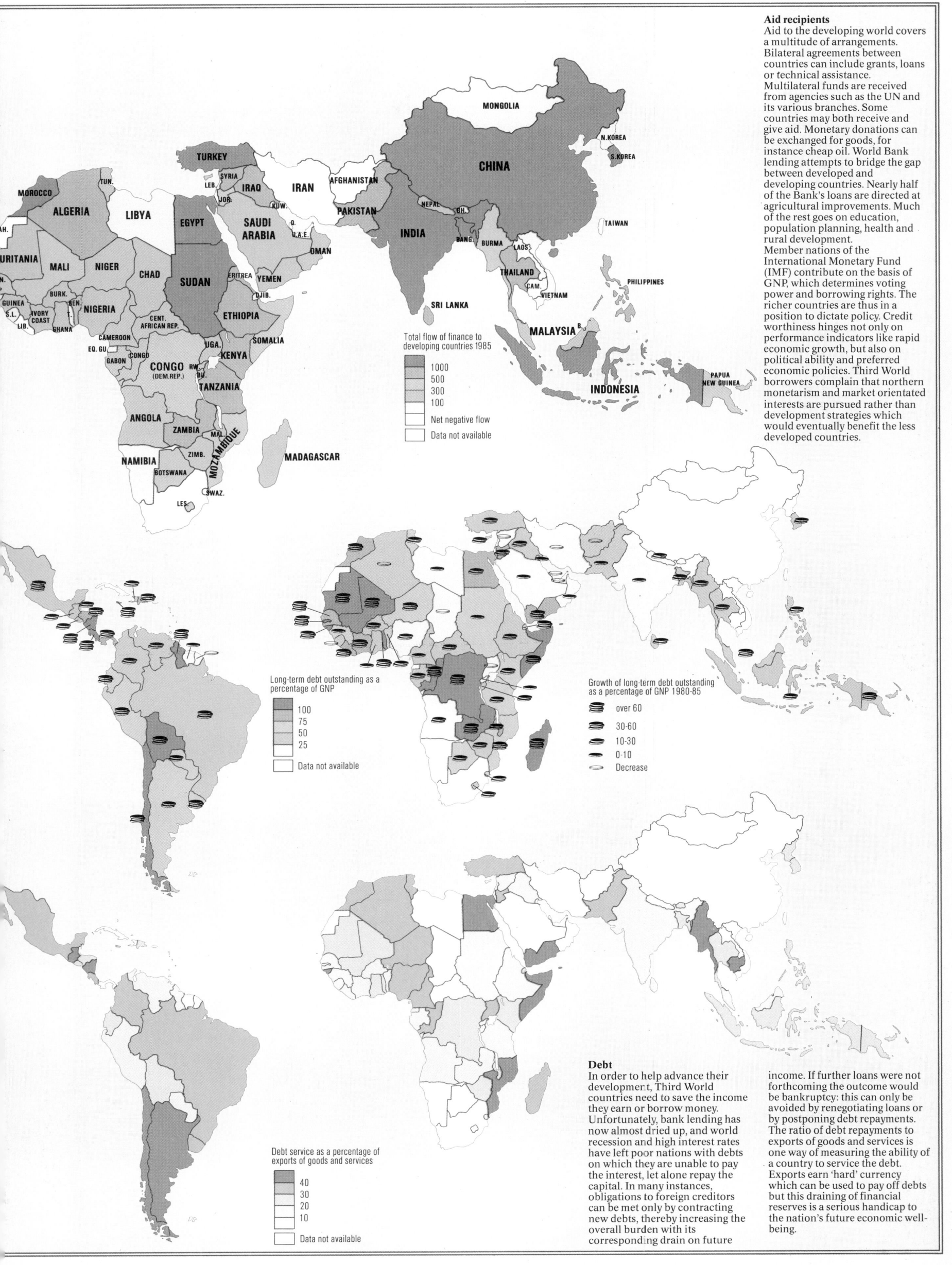

Aid recipients

Aid to the developing world covers a multitude of arrangements. Bilateral agreements between countries can include grants, loans or technical assistance. Multilateral funds are received from agencies such as the UN and its various branches. Some countries may both receive and give aid. Monetary donations can be exchanged for goods, for instance cheap oil. World Bank lending attempts to bridge the gap between developed and developing countries. Nearly half of the Bank's loans are directed at agricultural improvements. Much of the rest goes on education, population planning, health and rural development.

Member nations of the International Monetary Fund (IMF) contribute on the basis of GNP, which determines voting power and borrowing rights. The richer countries are thus in a position to dictate policy. Credit worthiness hinges not only on performance indicators like rapid economic growth, but also on political ability and preferred economic policies. Third World borrowers complain that northern monetarism and market orientated interests are pursued rather than development strategies which would eventually benefit the less developed countries.

Total flow of finance to developing countries 1985

- 1000
- 500
- 300
- 100
- Net negative flow
- Data not available

Long-term debt outstanding as a percentage of GNP

- 100
- 75
- 50
- 25
- Data not available

Growth of long-term debt outstanding as a percentage of GNP 1980-85

- over 60
- 30-60
- 10-30
- 0-10
- Decrease

Debt

In order to help advance their development, Third World countries need to save the income they earn or borrow money. Unfortunately, bank lending has now almost dried up, and world recession and high interest rates have left poor nations with debts on which they are unable to pay the interest, let alone repay the capital. In many instances, obligations to foreign creditors can be met only by contracting new debts, thereby increasing the overall burden with its corresponding drain on future income. If further loans were not forthcoming the outcome would be bankruptcy: this can only be avoided by renegotiating loans or by postponing debt repayments. The ratio of debt repayments to exports of goods and services is one way of measuring the ability of a country to service the debt. Exports earn 'hard' currency which can be used to pay off debts but this draining of financial reserves is a serious handicap to the nation's future economic well-being.

Debt service as a percentage of exports of goods and services

- 40
- 30
- 20
- 10
- Data not available

Designed and produced by E.S.R.

Grand Tetons, Wyoming, United States of America

CONTINENTS
AND
COUNTRIES

One of the most noteworthy post-1945 trends has been the fragmentation of empires, whether colonial or communist, and the emergence of numerous new countries. There is, therefore, an underlying tendency away from remote centralised control towards regional or local autonomy, despite the simultaneous existence of many supranational organisations. The sheer variety of nations, however, can sometimes disguise our essential common humanity, so it is necessary to guard against parochialism and seek to embrace all peoples. As such, the following section examines every country across all the continents in a celebration of diversity.

Right: Face-paint decoration of a native of Papua New Guinea

Above: A Senegalese tribesman
Right: Amid the sandy wastes of the Namib Desert in southwestern Africa

EUROPE

*A*s the cradle of industrialisation and the Western civilisation which now dominates the world's economies, Europe may justly claim to be the historical heart of the modern world. It was in Europe that technological advances made industrial mass production possible for the first time. This led to an economic ascendancy over the rest of the world, which continued until the same processes were taken up by the booming population of North America and the industrial lead crossed the Atlantic.

Geographically, Europe is a highly diverse and fragmented continent without any of the vast plains, mountain ranges or deserts which characterise other landmasses. In Europe, everything is on a much smaller scale. The greatest mountain chain is the Alps. Its peaks stretch across northern Italy and on into eastern Europe, but they are dwarfed by the Asian Himalayas or the South American Andes. The largest plain is that of the Ukraine, much of it devoted to the production of grain crops, but again this is far smaller than the North American prairies or the Mongolian grasslands.

Europe is, however, immensely diverse, with a wide variety of landscape forms being found in relatively small areas. Fertile plains jostle with mountain ranges and dense forests with productive meadows. It is the sheer diversity of the geological make-up that gives the continent its characteristic appearance. Nowhere is it possible to travel far without coming across a change in scenery.

Hidden beneath this fragmented landscape is a wide variety of mineral wealth. Pockets of almost every conceivable metal ore are to be found scattered across Europe. Though none occurs in the kind of mass deposit encountered on other continents, these ores have provided the raw materials for European industry for many centuries, and only now are being surpassed by bulk ores from elsewhere.

Until the immigration of racial groups from other continents in large numbers during the late 20th century, the population of Europe was remarkably homogeneous. Almost the entire population was descended from Indo-Europeans, who spread across the continent in antiquity. Earlier peoples were swamped by these new cultures, only surviving in isolated pockets, such as that of the Basques of northern Spain.

The populations of Europe, however, have strong historic cultures and concepts of nationhood which transcend the rather academic classification of Indo-European. These nationalist identities are a powerful cultural impetus within Europe and sources of much pride. They may also lead to factional violence, and attempts at supranational states have rarely survived. Among the relatively recent to fall before nationalist feelings is the former Yugoslavia, where civil war raged after the secession of Croatia, Slovenia, Bosnia-Hercegovina and Macedonia. The colossal Soviet Union, too, crumbled following severe economic difficulties and political unrest. The Baltic States took the opportunity of leaving the union first, followed by the other republics, which remained bound together, however, within the hastily created Commonwealth of Independent States.

The keynote of Europe is diversity. There is diversity in landscape, in geology and in human culture. Packed into the second smallest of the continents are over thirty countries based around identifiable national groupings. But even within countries nationalist divisions can be found. The state of Italy was united a little over a century ago and strong regional differences of culture, language and lifestyle are still apparent. Europe is nothing if not a continent of contrasts.

◄ Iceland - 'Land of Fire and Ice'.   ▲ Traditional costume, Bulgaria.

▲ Dubrovnik, Croatia.   ▼ Pünderich, overlooking the Mosel, Germany.

ALBANIA

Population: 3.4 million
Area: 28,748 square kilometres
Capital: Tirana
Language: Albanian and Greek
Currency: Lek

The mountain state of Albania was virtually cut off from the rest of Europe for decades. A province of first the Byzantine and later the Ottoman Empires, Albania gained independence as a kingdom in 1912 and as a Communist republic in 1946. Until the early 1990s, the old-style Stalinist regime retained a tight grip on running the country. In 1992, however, a non-communist regime was elected. Under Communism, the nation tried to revolutionise its economy by abandoning the traditional agricultural techniques which formerly employed the population and today less than half the workforce is in farming. The country has a rich potential for hydroelectric power.

ANDORRA

Population: 62,500
Area: 468 square kilometres
Capital: Andorra-la-Vella
Language: Catalan, Spanish and French
Currency: French Franc and Spanish Peseta

The independent mountain state of Andorra has retained its freedom unchanged since 1278, when the rival powers of the region agreed on a compromise. The country was to be ruled jointly by Spain's Bishop of Urgel and the Comte de Foix, although the rights of the latter subsequently passed to the President of the French Republic. In everyday practice, however, Andorrans govern themselves and a new democratic constitution was adopted in 1993. Tourism and duty-free shopping bolster the modern prosperity.

AUSTRIA

Population: 8.05 million
Area: 83,858 square kilometres
Capital: Vienna
Language: German
Currency: Schilling

Until 1918 the heart of the vast Hapsburg Empire, which encompassed the Danube Basin and much of the Balkans, Austria is now a democratic republic based upon the German-speaking parts of that Empire. The capital, Vienna, has a long tradition of sophisticated culture and excellence in the arts. The economy of Austria is broadly based, though agriculture is limited by the terrain. The mountains attract large numbers of tourists who come to enjoy winter skiing and summer walking.

BELGIUM

Population: 10.14 million
Area: 30,528 square kilometres
Capital: Brussels
Language: Flemish, French and German
Currency: Belgian Franc

The present constitutional monarchy dates back to 1830, when the Belgian people rebelled against Dutch rule and invited a German prince to become their king. The country is governed by a two-chamber Parliament acting under the monarch. The Flemish- and French-speaking areas each enjoy a degree of regional self-government. The nation is predominantly urban, with industry and services leading the economy. The coal, steel and other metal industries dominate the scene. Agriculture contributes only a small proportion to the economy, but Belgium is now almost self-sufficient in foods.

▲ *An open-air restaurant, Brussels, Belgium.*

BOSNIA-HERCEGOVINA

Population: 4.37 million
Area: 51,129 square kilometres
Capital: Sarajevo
Language: Serbo-Croat
Currency: Dinar

Bosnia-Hercegovina, part of the former Yugoslavia, declared independence in April 1992 and, thereafter, was deeply divided by civil war. Bosnia's Serbian minority, the largest ethnic Serbian group in any of the breakaway republics, boycotted the 1992 referendum on independence, with the two Serbian members of the Bosnian collective presidency resigning when the result was made known. Ancient religious and ethnic tensions soon erupted into open conflict. Despite the presence of a UN peacekeeping force, and numerous peace initiatives, war continued for some time. Manufacturing industries include steel, aluminium and textiles.

▲ *Tranquil countryside, Finland.*

Above right: *The Schonbrunn Palace, Vienna, Austria.*

▼ *Old-world charm, Czech Republic.*

▼ *Nyhavn, in Copenhagen, Denmark.*

▲ *Corn harvest, Albania.*

▼ *An Orthodox priest, Cyprus.*

▲ *The Orthodox Cathedral, Tallinn, Estonia.*

▲ *Vineyards, Santenay, France.*

▲ *The mountain state of Andorra.*

BULGARIA

Population: 8.43 million
Area: 110,994 square kilometres
Capital: Sofia
Language: Bulgarian
Currency: Lev

Bulgaria became independent of the Ottoman Empire in 1908 and was made a Communist republic following the Russian occupation in 1946. In 1989 street protests and demands for reform led the National Assembly to approve a multi-party democracy and free elections. In 1990 the Communist government resigned and a new constitution was drawn up in 1991. The river valleys have fertile soils and a climate conducive to heavy grain crops and livestock rearing. The traditional dominance of agriculture has been overtaken by a growing industrial sector.

CROATIA

Population: 4.84 million
Area: 56,538 square kilometres
Capital: Zagreb
Language: Croatian
Currency: Kuna

One of the six former Yugoslav republics, Croatia seceded from the Yugoslav federation in October 1991. Violent internal conflict arose as long-standing tensions between Croats and ethnic Serbs erupted. Helped by Yugoslav troops, the Serbian minority tried to seize power by force. Fighting continued throughout 1991 and at the beginning of 1992 UN peace-keeping troops intervened, establishing four peacekeeping zones. Key industries include steel, cement, cotton and wool, wine and beer.

CYPRUS

Population: 729,800
Area: 9,251 square kilometres
Capital: Nicosia
Language: Greek and Turkish
Currency: Cypriot Pound

Settled by Greek-speakers during the Iron Age, Cyprus has during its history been ruled by the Persians, Romans, Venetians, Turks and British. In 1960 it gained its independence from Britain, but strife between Greek and Turkish communities led to the arrival of UN peacekeepers. Despite their presence, a threatened coup by the Greeks resulted in invasion in 1974 by Turkish forces. The occupied north declared itself a republic in 1983, although this has gained only Turkish recognition. Tourism and light industry play a prime economic role, although traditional agriculture remains important.

CZECH REPUBLIC

Population: 10.33 million
Area: 78,864 square kilometres
Capital: Prague
Language: Czech
Currency: Koruna

The Czech Republic occupies the western regions of what was formerly Czechoslovakia and has a predominantly urban culture with strong German influences. Once part of the Hapsburg Empire, Czechoslovakia became independent in 1918. Communists took power with Soviet aid in 1948, and an attempt at liberalisation in 1968, known as the Prague Spring, was crushed by Russian tanks. In November 1989 mass public demonstrations led to the resignation of the Communist government and the legalisation of opposition parties. Ethnic and economic tensions between Czechs and Slovaks led to the separation of the two regions in 1993. The Czech Republic is a heavily industrialised nation.

DENMARK

Population: 5.3 million
Area: 43,094 square kilometres
Capital: Copenhagen
Language: Danish
Currency: Krone

The rich soil and temperate climate of Denmark have aided the traditionally-strong agricultural sector. Grains, potatoes and vegetables are grown in quantities, but it is livestock which dominates. Recently the industrial sector has grown significantly and manufacturing now outstrips agriculture in terms of economic value. The constitution is based on the monarch, who cannot act without the consent of the democratically-elected parliament.

ESTONIA

Population: 1.6 million
Area: 45,100 square kilometres
Capital: Tallinn
Language: Estonian
Currency: Kroon

In September 1991 Estonia was accepted as an independent nation for the first time since its annexation by the Soviet Union in 1939. The republic has been dominated by economic central planning from Moscow for over five decades and relies heavily on agriculture for employment and prosperity. Gas-rich shale and phosphates represent the only mineral wealth and industrial base for this small nation. Co-operation with the other Baltic states is already established and other foreign economic links are being vigorously pursued.

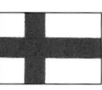

FINLAND

Population: 5.12 million
Area: 338,144 square kilometres
Capital: Helsinki
Language: Finnish and Swedish
Currency: Markka

Ruled in turn by Denmark, Sweden and Russia, Finland gained independence in 1917, when the people took advantage of the chaos following the Russian Revolution to seize power. In 1940, war with Russia resulted in Finland losing much territory around Lake Ladoga to the Soviets. Modern foreign policy emphasises the need for friendly relations with Russia and with Scandinavian nations. The economy of the nation is broadly based. The vast forests provide raw material for a lumber trade. The small area of land suitable for agriculture is heavily used for raising livestock, particularly cattle in the south and reindeer in the north. Industry is concentrated on the extraction and processing of iron deposits.

FRANCE

Population: 58 million
Area: 543,965 square kilometres
Capital: Paris
Language: French
Currency: French Franc

The modern state of France is generally traced back to the accession of the Capetian dynasty to the throne of the Western Franks in 987, though Frankish power was established in the region as early as A.D. 500. The monarchy was overthrown in the Revolution of 1789, after which France was ruled by republics, emperors and kings. The Fifth Republic was established in 1958. The present constitution allows for a democratically-elected parliament, which operates under the guidance of a President. The economy of the nation is highly developed, with industry and services being dominant employers. Agriculture remains largely in the hands of small-scale farmers and produces quantities of grain and fruits, most notably grapes, from which the famous French wines are produced.

GEORGIA

Population: 5.43 million
Area: 69,700 square kilometres
Capital: Tbilisi
Language: Russian
Currency: Lari

In April 1991, Georgia became an independent state, with a remarkable 98.9 per cent popular vote in favour of independence. A period of political instability followed.

Vast manganese deposits form the basis for the prosperous mining industry, though coal is also found in quantity and other minerals are exploited on a smaller scale.

GERMANY

Population: 81.54 million
Area: 356,978 square kilometres
Capital: Berlin
Language: German
Currency: Mark

Unity and division have been the hallmarks of German history. The disparate German tribes were united under the Frankish Empire in the 9th century, but this fell apart, to be replaced by the Holy Roman Empire of the Middle Ages. Initially strong, the Empire broke up into dozens of small states and city republics. This pattern persisted until 1871 when the German states were united under Prussian rule as the German Empire. This nation remained together until 1945, when Germany lost much territory and was divided as Communist East and Democratic West Germany. In 1990 the overthrow of the Communist regime in East Germany led to reunification. The stronger West German economy is concentrating on raising the prosperity of East Germany.

GREECE

Population: 10.4 million
Area: 131,957 square kilometres
Capital: Athens
Language: Greek
Currency: Drachma

Home of the ancient civilisation which has had such a profound influence on all Western culture, Greece is today working to join the front runners in European economies. The magnificent history, fine climate and attractive beaches have made Greece a favourite tourist resort for generations. Tourism is now the largest single industry in terms of foreign earnings. The mountainous terrain limits agriculture, but there are extensive olive groves and citrus orchards. Industry is concentrated on food processing, textiles and leatherwork. After a period of military rule in the 1970s, Greece reverted to a democratic system of government.

HUNGARY

Population: 10.21 million
Area: 93,032 square kilometres
Capital: Budapest
Language: Hungarian
Currency: Forint

Formerly a dominant state within the Hapsburg Empire, which ruled the Danube Basin from the Alps to the Black Sea, Hungary became independent in 1918. In 1949 a Communist government was imposed, and the 1956 nationalist rising was put down by Soviet tanks and troops. After popular protests and demands for reform, the Communist Party was disbanded in 1989, opening the way for democratic elections. Wheat, maize and potatoes are the main crops, and large numbers of cattle and pigs are raised. In recent years the role of industry in the economy has increased in importance, with metallurgy, chemicals and electronics predominating.

ICELAND

Population: 267,806
Area: 102,819 square kilometres
Capital: Reykjavik
Language: Icelandic
Currency: Icelandic Krona

Viking settlers began arriving in Iceland in the 9th century, ousting the few Irish monks already there. An independent society based on Viking social rules existed until 1264, when factional violence led to Norwegian control. In 1381, Iceland passed to the Danish crown. It recovered full self-government in 1918 and severance from Denmark in 1946. The present republic operates with two chambers under an elected President. Only two per cent of land is farmed and livestock is kept in small numbers. Fishing provides the basis of the economy. Industry is very limited.

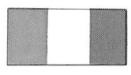

IRELAND

Population: 3.62 million
Area: 70,000 square kilometres
Capital: Dublin
Language: Gaelic and English
Currency: Irish Pound

In 1801, after centuries of growing British influence, the Irish Parliament was dissolved and the country was governed from Westminster. In 1921 the Catholic southern counties of Ireland gained independence after an armed uprising, becoming the Republic of Ireland in 1949, while the largely Protestant counties of Ulster remained part of Britain. Ongoing civil violence and terrorist activities have disrupted life in border counties and dominate Irish relations with Britain. The economy has traditionally been agricultural, although industrial activity has grown rapidly in recent years, and is now more important to the economy than farming. Food processing, textiles and electrical engineering are dominant.

ITALY

Population: 57.27 million
Area: 301,308 square kilometres
Capital: Rome
Language: Italian
Currency: Italian Lira

The various city states, kingdoms and duchies of Italy were not united until 1861, and the republic was established in 1946. The present constitution allows for two chambers, the lower elected directly and the upper elected by the historic regions. The President is elected by the two houses of parliament. There are numerous political parties representing many shades of opinion, though fascism is banned. Southern parts of the country are generally less well developed than the north. Grapes are widely grown for wine production. Industry is concentrated in northern cities where textiles, food processing and the manufacture of machinery lead the sector.

LATVIA

Population: 2.49 million
Area: 64,600 square kilometres
Capital: Riga
Language: Latvian
Currency: Lats

The troubled history of Latvia as an independent nation began with a democratic government being installed with British military support in 1919. In 1940 Soviet power was imposed. Together with Lithuania and Estonia, Latvia became independent once again in 1991. Five decades of economic central planning has given Latvia a heritage of heavy industry, with steel, railway equipment and textiles dominating. The previous agricultural economic base has been greatly reduced.

LIECHTENSTEIN

Population: 30,923
Area: 160 square kilometres
Capital: Vaduz
Language: German
Currency: Swiss Franc

The tiny Principality of Liechtenstein dates back to 1434. In 1712 the principality passed to the Liechtenstein family, which held it from the Holy Roman Emperor. When that empire collapsed in 1806, the family retained their domains and in 1923 joined Switzerland in a customs and currency union. The present constitution places power in the hands of the Prince, though legislation needs approval of the democratically-elected parliament. The economy is based on a mixture of agriculture, light industry and commerce.

▲ *Dusk in Mykonos, Greece.*

▲ *A round tower, Co. Wicklow, Ireland.*

▼ *Luxembourg, one of Europe's smallest nations.*

▲ *The Principality of Monaco.*

▼ *The Principality of Liechtenstein.*

▲ *The Danube River, Budapest, Hungary.*

◄ *Heavy industry, Lithuania.*

▲ *A characteristic view of Malta.*

▼ *The Old City, Riga, Latvia.*

◄ *The Colosseum, Rome, Italy.*

▲ *Kinderdijk, east of Rotterdam, Netherlands.*

LITHUANIA

Population: 3.8 million
Area: 65,300 square kilometres
Capital: Vilnius
Language: Lithuanian
Currency: Litas

With a population composed of some 80 per cent ethnic Lithuanians, the republic long desired independence. In the spring of 1991 an overwhelming majority voted for separation from the then Soviet Union, but it was not until September 1991 that this became a reality. Traditionally an agricultural nation, Lithuania is now dominated by industry, particularly heavy engineering and textiles.

LUXEMBOURG

Population: 412,800
Area: 2,586 square kilometres
Capital: Luxembourg
Language: French, German, Letzebuergesch
Currency: Luxembourg Franc

The tiny state of Luxembourg enjoyed varying degrees of self government until being conquered by France in 1795. In 1815 the current Grand Duchy came into being under the Dutch monarchy, and in 1890 full independence came. The Grand Duke is closely involved in administration with the democratically-elected parliament. The nation is part of a customs union with Belgium and Belgian currency can be used within Luxembourg. Industry is based on a thriving iron and steel business. Agriculture plays a minor role in national life.

MACEDONIA

Population: 1.95 million
Area: 25,713 square kilometres
Capital: Skopje
Language: Macedonian
Currency: Denar

Though Macedonia declared its independence from the former Yugoslavia in 1992, it was not recognised as an independent state by the international community until 1993 because of Greek objections to the use of the name 'Macedonia'. The state is landlocked, surrounded by Greece to the south, Serbia to the north, Albania to the west, and Bulgaria to the east, and throughout its history has been threatened by claims on its borders. Agriculture, particularly wheat, grapes and corn, are important to the economy.

MALTA

Population: 376,335

Area: 316 square kilometres
Capital: Valletta
Language: Maltese and English
Currency: Maltese Lira

During World War II Malta was a vital British naval base and came under attack by German and Italian forces. In 1942, King George VI awarded the George Cross to the people of Malta. This medal is featured on·the Maltese flag, together with the colours of the Knights of Malta, who ruled between 1530 and 1798. Malta gained independence from Britain in 1964, though economic ties remain close. Malta's strategic position in the Mediterranean makes commerce, trade and ship-building lucrative industries. Tourism is the biggest single earner of foreign currency for Malta. The constitution is a multi-party democracy in which two major parties dominate.

MONACO

Population: 30,000
Area: 1.5 square kilometres
Capital: Monaco
Language: Monegasque and French
Currency: French Franc

The small Principality of Monaco has been the domain of the Grimaldi family since 1297, placing itself under French protection in 1861. The constitution allows for democratic government though the Prince retains much influence. The main economic base of Monaco is tourism, with nearly ten times as many visitors as residents in the course of a year. The scenic coastline and fine beach delight many tourists, but it is the famous casino which is the major attraction. Agriculture is virtually non-existent but the industrial sector is growing in importance.

NETHERLANDS

Population: 15,424,122
Area: 33,811 square kilometres
Capital: Amsterdam and The Hague
Language: Dutch
Currency: Dutch Guilder

The nation came into being in the late 16th century, when the prosperous Protestant cities rebelled against oppressive Catholic rule from Spain. Much of the Netherlands has been reclaimed from the sea by massive projects. Much of this land is devoted to agriculture, with potatoes, sugar beet and grain being major crops. Cut flowers and flower bulbs are produced in large quantities for export, while dairy cattle graze on meadows to produce milk from which famous Dutch cheeses are made. The nation's position at the mouth of the Rhine has long ensured lucrative trade connections.

NORWAY

Population: 4.4 million
Area: 323,878 square kilometres
Capital: Oslo
Language: Norwegian
Currency: Norwegian Krone

In 1905 Norway gained independence from Sweden. The country's constitution places power in the hands of a democratically-elected parliament, though the monarch retains control of the armed forces. The mountainous terrain makes agriculture difficult and much food needs to be imported. Hydro-electric power is produced in quantity and supplies ninety-nine percent of domestic needs. Offshore oil and gas have added to the energy self-reliance of Norway. Industry is prosperous and is based on the processing of domestic metals, agricultural products and timber from the vast upland forests.

▲ *The Lofoton Islands, Norway.*

POLAND

Population: 38.61 million
Area: 312,685 square kilometres
Capital: Warsaw
Language: Polish
Currency: Zloty

The powerful kingdom of Poland collapsed in the late 18th century and was divided between the Prussian, Hapsburg and Russian empires. Reconstitution and independence did not occur until 1918. The German invasion of Poland in 1939 sparked World War II, and following liberation in 1945 Poland was ruled by a Communist regime imposed by the Soviet Union. Communist rule ended in 1989 after several years of opposition from the trade union Solidarity. Free elections were called for 1991, with opposition parties campaigning for the first time in decades. The Polish economy is industrially based, with iron and steel, textiles and machine manufacture being the most important. The agricultural

sector is still important, producing wheat, rye and potatoes, together with large quantities of dairy produce.

PORTUGAL

Population: 9.9 million
Area: 91,905 square kilometres
Capital: Lisbon
Language: Portuguese
Currency: Escudo

A coup in 1974 overthrew the dictatorship which had governed Portugal since 1933. In 1976, constitutional government was resumed. The present constitution, adopted in 1982, allows for an elected President who chooses the Prime Minister from the Assembly, which is elected by universal adult suffrage. Manufacturing is based on textiles and leather goods. Agriculture is based on grains and potatoes, and wine, cork and olives are important export earners.

ROMANIA

Population: 22.73 million
Area: 237,500 square kilometres
Capital: Bucharest
Language: Romanian and Hungarian
Currency: Leu

The overthrow of the Communist regime of President Ceausescu in 1989 was attended by street fighting and great confusion. Subsequently, in December 1991, a new democratic constitution was approved. Until the Communist takeover in 1947 Romania was a traditionally agricultural kingdom with little industry. The past decades have seen massive government encouragement of industry, which today is concentrated on iron and steel, chemicals and textiles. The farms continue to produce large quantities of wheat and maize, and sheep-rearing remains important.

SAN MARINO

Population: 24,003
Area: 61.19 square kilometres
Capital: San Marino
Language: Italian
Currency: Italian Lira

Legend has it that the 4th-century Saint Marinus founded the republic as a self-governing Christian community to escape persecution. The republic won full independence from the Pope in 1631, and in 1862 concluded a treaty with the newly-created Italian nation, securing continued independence. Agriculture is an important source of employment and wine is exported. Small scale industrial activity includes

chemicals, ceramics and paints. Much economic wealth comes from tourism and the sale of unique coins and stamps.

SLOVAK REPUBLIC OR SLOVAKIA

Population: 5.37 million
Area: 49,039 square kilometres
Capital: Bratislava
Language: Slovak, Czech
Currency: Slovak Koruna

The Czech and Slovak states had been joined in 1918, following the collapse of the Austro-Hungarian Empire. The Slovak people, however, were proud of their heritage and determined to assert their sovereignty eventually. As such, Slovakia separated from the former Czechoslovakia in January 1993, forming an independent state. The abandonment of the union has dislocated the development of the country's economy, and agriculture and industry are underdeveloped.

SLOVENIA

Population: 1.98 million
Area: 20,253 square kilometres
Capital: Ljubljana
Language: Slovene
Currency: Tolar

Slovenia, formerly one of the Yugoslav republics, declared its independence in October 1991 and was recognised as an independent state by Germany later that year, with other powers following suit in 1992. The population of Slovenia is not as ethnically diverse as that of Croatia and Bosnia-Hercegovina. It is unified both by religion and by language, and consequently has not suffered the violence that has marked the recent history of the other former Yugoslav republics. Metallurgy and furniture-making are the traditional industries.

SPAIN

Population: 40.46 million
Area: 492,592 square kilometres
Capital: Madrid
Language: Spanish and regional
Currency: Peseta

Spain regained its monarchy in 1975 after an interruption of forty-four years with the accession of King Juan Carlos. The constitution vests power in a parliament named the *Cortes*, with a lower house elected by proportional representation and a senate elected by province. The traditional agricultural economic base has now been overtaken by industry, but remains important. Wheat and barley are the major crops. Industry is dominated by motor vehicles, textiles, paper, and iron

and steel, which together account for the majority of exports.

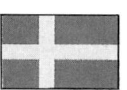

SWEDEN

Population: 8.84 million
Area: 449,964 square kilometres
Capital: Stockholm
Language: Swedish
Currency: Swedish Krona

Sweden acquired approximately its present boundaries a thousand years ago, but has since been united with other Scandinavian nations and in the 17th century enjoyed Baltic hegemony. The present monarchy dates from 1809, when the French general Jean Bernadotte was chosen to become king on the extinction of the native line. The constitution introduced in 1975 reduced the role of monarch to ceremonial and gave power to the democratic parliament. The highly-prosperous economy is based on iron ore deposits. Over half of all manufacturing is made up of metal smelting, metal machinery and other metal products. A further quarter of the sector is composed of timber, plywood and other wood products. Agriculture is well developed, but on a small scale.

SWITZERLAND

Population: 7.02 million
Area: 41,129 square kilometres
Capital: Berne
Language: German, French, Italian, Romansch
Currency: Swiss Franc

A confederation of twenty-three cantons, Switzerland is famous for its neutrality. But the state had its origins in a defensive alliance in 1291, and saw many wars in its early centuries of existence. The constitution vests supreme power in the electorate which can demand laws and changes to the constitution. Each canton is self-governing, with its own parliament; the federal government being responsible for war, peace and treaties. Most crops are grown on the fertile central plain. Manufacturing is a major activity and is based on textiles, chemicals and the processing of agricultural produce. Banking and finance is a well-established sector of the economy.

COMMONWEALTH OF INDEPENDENT STATES

The Commonwealth of Independent States (CIS) came into being in 1991 when the regime that had controlled the former USSR collapsed. This loose structure handles only major central issues, while the individual nations assume other powers. There are separate listings for those republics that did not join the CIS: Estonia, Georgia, Latvia and Lithuania.

ARMENIA

Population: 3.7 million
Area: 29,800 square kilometres
Capital: Yerevan
Language: Armenian, Russian, Kurdish
Currency: Dram

Armenia's rugged terrain allows only limited agriculture based on olive groves, cotton and sub-tropical fruits. Wide ranging mineral deposits are more promising for the economy and efficient exploitation of these in the wake of freedom from central Soviet planning may lead to prosperity.

AZERBAIJAN

Population: 7.5 million
Area: 86,600 square kilometres
Capital: Baku
Language: Azeri, Armenian, Russian
Currency: Manat

Recently the scene of ethnic violence between the Azerbaijani majority and the Armenian minority, this republic is rich in natural resources. Industry is based on reserves of oil, iron ore, bauxite and various precious metals. Agriculturally, the republic produces grapes and tobacco.

BELARUS

Population: 10.4 million
Area: 207,600 square kilometres
Capital: Minsk
Language: Russian, Polish and other languages
Currency: Rouble

Belarus is hilly and contains large tracts of marshland, particularly to the southwest. The economy of the republic is based on its rich pasture land and pockets of agricultural land. The processing of the farm output accounts for much of the industry, but there are also large chemical and steel concerns.

KAZAKHSTAN

Population: 16.5 million
Area: 2,717,300 square kilometres
Capital: Akmola
Language: Kazakh, Russian
Currency: Tenge

The Central Asian republic of Kazakhstan declared independence from the former USSR in December 1991. Formerly a pastoral economy, agriculture and the mineral wealth are now exploited on a large scale.

KYRGYZSTAN

Population: 4.46 million
Area: 199,900 square kilometres
Capital: Bishkek
Language: Kyrgyz, Russian, Jagatai
Currency: Som

Traditionally a pastoral region, the economy of Kyrgyzstan remains firmly based on livestock. Agriculture has also become important. Much of the industry is based on processing agricultural products, though mining contributes to the economy.

MOLDOVA

Population: 4.4 million
Area: 33,700 square kilometres
Capital: Chisinau
Language: Romanian, Russian, Gagauz
Currency: Leu

Populated mainly with ethnic Romanians, Moldova is economically dominated by agriculture and the processing of farm products. Another major output is the production of concrete and other building materials.

RUSSIA

Population: 147.5 million
Area: 17,075,400 square kilometres
Capital: Moscow
Language: Russian, numerous other languages
Currency: Rouble

Russia is the largest country in the world. Industry is well developed and is a major employer. The transition from central state control to a free market has been fraught with difficulties, and internal political and social unrest exacerbates the situation.

▲ *The golden domes of the Kremlin, Moscow, Russia.*

TAJIKISTAN

Population: 5.7 million
Area: 143,100 square kilometres
Capital: Dushanbe
Language: Tajik, Jagatai, Russian
Currency: Tajik Rouble

Following independence from the former Soviet Union, Tajikistan suffered some years of civil war. The republic is largely dependent on agriculture, with coal, lead and zinc mining accounting for most of the country's industrial activity.

TURKMENISTAN

Population: 4.5 million
Area: 448,100 square kilometres
Capital: Ashgabat
Language: Turkish, Russian, Jagatai
Currency: Manat

Rich oil, coal and sulphur deposits form the basis for an industrial economy, although agriculture, notably cotton, maize, fruit and vegetables, provides the majority of the employment. Turkmenistan was the first of the Central Asian Republics to declare itself free of Moscow, in August 1990.

UKRAINE

Population: 52.14 million
Area: 603,700 square kilometres
Capital: Kiev
Language: Ukrainian, Russian
Currency: Hryvna

The traditional grain basket of eastern Europe, the Ukraine is still a highly productive agricultural region, its output including: wheat, buckwheat, beet, sunflower, cotton, flax, tobacco, soys, hops, fruit and vegetables.

UZBEKISTAN

Population: 22.2 million
Area: 447,400 square kilometres
Capital: Tashkent
Language: Jagatai, Russian, Tatar
Currency: Som

The Uzbek economy is based on intensive agriculture producing silk, rice, sub-tropical fruits and grapes with mineral exploitation on a modest scale. Industry is limited and is largely based on the rich deposits of oil, coal and copper.

UNITED KINGDOM

Population: 58.78 million
Area: 243,000 square kilometres
Capital: London
Language: English, Welsh, Gaelic
Currency: Pound Sterling

The United Kingdom is a constitutional monarchy governing Britain, the northern counties of Ireland and neighbouring islands. The kingdoms of England and Scotland were united in 1603 when King James VI of Scotland inherited the English throne. The constitution allows for a single elected chamber together with a part-appointed, part-

▲ *The interior of St Peter's, the Vatican.*

inherited House of Lords. Agriculture is well developed and produces about half the nation's requirements. Industry and commerce are the basis of the economic wealth.

VATICAN

Population: 1,000
Area: 0.3 square kilometres
Capital: Vatican City
Language: Italian, Latin
Currency: Italian Lira

The Vatican is the smallest independent state in the world and exists solely as the residence of the Pope, the head of the Roman Catholic Church. Until 1860 the Pope ruled areas of central Italy, but these were incorporated to the Kingdom of Italy, which in 1870 invaded Rome and confined the Pope to the Vatican complex. In 1929 the Vatican was recognised as an independent state in return for the Pope relinquishing claims over Rome and surrounding territory. The Vatican is the administrative headquarters of the Catholic Church.

YUGOSLAVIA, FEDERAL REPUBLIC OF

Population: 10.54 million
Area: 102,173 square kilometres
Capital: Belgrade
Language: Serbian, Albanian, Hungarian and others
Currency: Dinar

Yugoslavia came into being in 1918 as a confederation of southern Slavonic peoples newly independent of the Hapsburg Empire. The new constitution of 1946 made the nation a grouping of six republics, in which the Communist was the only legal political party. Attempts in 1989-90 by the central government to curb the internal government of the republics led to widespread protest. When the Serbian-dominated former Yugoslavia dissolved into civil war, Bosnia-Hercegovina, Croatia, Macedonia and Slovenia formed independent republics. The self-proclaimed Federal Republic of Yugoslavia, formed from Serbia and Montenegro, emerged from the rump territory of the earlier Communist state.

ASIA

*A*sia is the largest and most populated continent on Earth. Just two nations, China and India, between them account for nearly two billion inhabitants. An Asian country, Bangladesh is the most densely populated on Earth, with around 730 people to each square kilometre. This compares to a mere twenty-five per square kilometre in the United States.

The incredible population statistics are made possible by the remarkably fertile soils and productive climates of Asia. Bangladesh, for example, is almost ideal for rice cultivation. The monsoon climate provides the alternate wet and dry season needed by the cereal, while the flat landscape makes the flooding and draining of fields easy to accomplish. Massive crops are produced each year. Similar conditions prevail in eastern China, where rural populations have reached saturation point in some areas.

But if Asia has been endowed with vast, life-giving resources, it also has its share of natural disasters. Earthquakes, floods and typhoons are common. Given the concentrated populations, these calamities claim horrendous death tolls among the local peoples. Many regions of Asia have a history scattered with the records of bumper crops leading to population booms, the children of which are then wiped out by disaster and famine.

Not only does Asia contain some of the densest populations in the world, it also boasts some of the emptiest regions anywhere. The vast expanses of Siberia consist of open tundra bordering the Arctic Ocean and, further south, extensive boreal forests. These great coniferous forests cover a staggering 1,100,000,000 hectares and are thought to contain about one-quarter of all the world's trees.

In central eastern Asia there are extensive grasslands on which pastoralist peoples lead traditional lives which have scarcely changed in centuries. Mongolia and neighbouring sections of both China and and the former Soviet Union are the home of ethnic Mongols, who herd cattle and horses on the open plains as their ancestors have done for millenia.

Ethnically, the population of Asia is incredibly diverse. In addition to recent immigrations of Europeans and Africans there is a wide range of indigenous peoples. In the far east, Mongoloid races form the vast majority. In the subcontinent of India Indo-Europeans and Dravidians constitute the bulk of the population. Here, as elsewhere in Asia, there are remnant populations of far older peoples. The inland uplands of Sri Lanka are home to the Veddah, who are apparently unrelated to the majority population but have affinities with the Aboriginals of Australia. Similarly enigmatic are the Ainu of Japan.

Culturally, too, the Asians present a bewildering picture to the world. Asia has been the cradle of major world religions: Buddhism, Hinduism, Confucianism and Taoism all originated in Asia, and continue to find the bulk of their adherents on that continent. Islam, originating on the Arabian peninsula, has spread across much of southern Asia as far as the Pacific Ocean.

The vast continent of Asia is rich in both agricultural and human resources. However, much of the population continues to live at subsistence level. Increases in population have kept pace with farming technology and crop increases and the per capita wealth remains low. National prosperity in most nations is devoted to finding food for their growing populations rather than in improving the standard of living. So long as this cycle of improved food production and increased population continues, the traditional lifestyles and general impoverishment of Asia looks likely to continue.

▲ *The Himalayas, Nepal.*

▼ *Temple dancers, Bali, Indonesia.*

◀ *Lake Kawaguchi and Mount Fujiyama, Japan.*

▼ *A natural rock formation in Dukhan, Qatar.*

◀ *The back-breaking task of planting rice, Laos.*

▼ *The bustling city of Taipei, Taiwan.*

AFGHANISTAN

Population: 20.5 million
Area: 652,090 square kilometres
Capital: Kabul
Language: Pashto, Dari
Currency: Afghani

Afghanistan is a country in turmoil and has been for generations. The Soviet invasion in 1979 led to the various factions uniting against the aggressor. After the withdrawal of Soviet forces, however, internal disputes re-emerged. The mountainous republic has a long tradition of tribal independence and weak government control. The social structure remains fragmented, with most of the population belonging to distinctly different ethnic groups linked by the Islamic religion. The bulk of the population are subsistence farmers or nomadic herdsmen, the latter mainly in the south. Fruit, bread and mutton are the basis of the nation's self-produced food supply. Gas is found in the far north.

BAHRAIN

Population: 586,109
Area: 706.6 square kilometres
Capital: Manama
Language: Arabic
Currency: Bahraini Dinar

In 1882 the Emirate of Bahrain handed control of its foreign affairs to Britain. In 1971 the arrangement was ended and the Emir proclaimed his nation's independence and soon after dismissed Parliament to rule the nation himself. In 1992 the Emir set up a Consultative Council. Until 1931 Bahrain was an impoverished state subsisting on pearl fishing, small scale agriculture and the profits of trade. The discovery of oil changed everything and vast wealth poured into the nation. The thirty-three islands that make up the state now support a flourishing manufacturing economy, including the production of aluminium alloys, ships and medical equipment. So many people now live in Bahrain that ninety percent of food needs to be imported and water supply is a chronic problem.

BANGLADESH

Population: 118.7 million
Area: 148,393 square kilometres
Capital: Dhaka
Language: Bengali, English
Currency: Taka

In a good year Bangladesh is almost ideally suited to intensive cultivation of rice. As many as three crops can be grown on the rich soils within just twelve months. As a consequence the nation is extremely densely populated by peasant farmers growing vast crops for their own consumption and for sale. Unfortunately, recurrent natural disasters, such as floods and cyclones, take a heavy toll in human life and destroy crops. The extremely high birth rate means that the agricultural wealth is fully used feeding the people rather than in improving their living conditions. Other than glass sand, mineral deposits and industry are negligible. Government of the country has been unstable, with a number of coups and military takeovers since independence from Pakistan in 1971.

BHUTAN

Population: 0.6 million
Area: 46,500 square kilometres
Capital: Thimphu
Language: Dzongkha, Nepalese, English
Currency: Ngultrum

The mountain kingdom of Bhutan is an anomaly in India, having managed to retain its quasi-independence when Britain withdrew from the subcontinent, while other kingdoms became merged into the new state of India. Bhutan receives an annual subsidy from India in return for abiding by that country's foreign policy. Internal government is conducted by the king, with the advice of an elected assembly. The electoral system is unusual in that each family has one vote regardless of its number, and monks are separately represented. Bhutan is made up of a number of valleys isolated from each other by precipitous mountains and sheer cliffs. The different ethnic groups have scarcely mixed and they retain their identities. The basis of the economy is agriculture, with many hill tribes surviving at subsistence level. Large mineral deposits have been found but the difficult terrain has hampered exploitation.

BRUNEI

Population: 276,300
Area: 5,765 square kilometres
Capital: Bandar Seri Begawan
Language: Malay, English
Currency: Brunei Dollar or Ringgit

The Sultan of Brunei is reputed to be the richest man on earth, with a personal fortune in the region of twenty-six billion US Dollars. This massive wealth is based on the oilfields of Brunei and on the fact that all national finance is conducted through the Sultan. The first oil well was drilled in 1929, and since that time fresh reserves have been continually identified. Oil production remains high and is the basis of the nation's wealth. The Sultan is currently encouraging the growth of other businesses in order to limit his people's reliance on international oil prices. The traditional industries of boat-building, silver-smithing and weaving remain in operation, and the agriculture of the tropical country continues to produce rubber, fruits and rice.

CAMBODIA

Population: 9.86 million
Area: 181,035 square kilometres
Capital: Phnom Penh
Language: Khmer, Chinese
Currency: Riel

The once-wealthy Kingdom of Cambodia, or Kampuchea, is trying to emerge from its recent history of violence and poverty. In 1970 Prince Sihanouk was ousted from power by a republican movement. When the war in Vietnam spilled into Cambodia in 1975 the Communist Khmer Rouge took power. This new regime abolished money, expelled foreigners, and forced city dwellers to move to the countryside. Mass executions followed any attempt at protest, and it is thought that some fifteen per cent of the population died in these years. Vietnamese troops imposed a new government in 1979. Nationalist resistance under Prince Sihanouk and the Khmer Rouge began a civil war interrupted by fragile peace agreements. A new constitution was promulgated in 1993 restoring parliamentary monarchy. There is little industry and the population relies on subsistence agriculture.

CHINA (PEOPLE'S REPUBLIC OF)

Population: 1,199 million
Area: 9,572,000 square kilometres
Capital: Beijing
Language: Mandarin and numerous dialects
Currency: Renminbi Yuan

With a civilisation dating back at least 3,500 years, China has one of the oldest cultures on Earth. Despite periods of civil war and instability, there has been a constant pressure for unity among the Chinese, principally to resist the incursions of foreign 'barbarians'. The Empire collapsed in 1912, to be replaced by the rule of several warlords. The Communist Party restored unity in 1949 under Chairman Mao and has held power since. In 1989, the pro-democracy movement was brutally suppressed by the Chinese government, an action that was condemned internationally. There is intensive cultivation of rice, wheat and beans together with the raising of cattle, pigs and sheep. Small-scale, traditional industries are carried on within villages but large, state-run factories in the cities produce silk, cotton and heavy industrial goods. Special economic zones have helped China's economy expand very rapidly. Hong Kong reverted to Chinese control in 1997.

▲ *Tianzi Mountains, China.*

▼ *The ancient town of Dalï, China.*

INDIA

Population: 913.2 million
Area: 3,165,596 square kilometres
Capital: New Delhi
Language: Hindi, English, regional languages
Currency: Rupee

India is the most populous democracy in the world, but suffers from periods of political unrest and demands for independence by ethnic minorities. Despite this, however, the polyglot nation remains intact and the processes of democracy have not been overthrown. The present Indian state originated in 1947, when the provinces of British India gained independence and joined with several semi-independent monarchies to form a federal union. The economic base of the nation is agriculture, with almost 70 percent of the population dependent on the land for their living. Rice and wheat are the main crops, though beans and sugar are also produced. Tea is grown in large quantities for export, and coffee production is increasing. Small industries are important, and there is expansion in petro-chemicals based on oil and gas production.

▲ *Dusty hill-country Afghanistan.*

▶ *Tropical rain forest, Brunei.*

▲ *Zhang Jia Khou Pass, Great Wall, China.*

▲ *Ceremonial costumes, Bhutan.*

▼ *The 'Wailing Wall', Jerusalem, Israel.*

▲ *New development in oil-rich Bahrain.*

▼ *In the Golden Temple of Amritsar, India.*

▲ *Low-lying Bangladesh, veined by rivers.*

▼ *14th Ramadhan Mosque, Baghdad, Iraq.*

◀ *Tehran, capital of Iran.*

INDONESIA

Population: 191.36 million
Area: 1,919,443 square kilometres
Capital: Jakarta
Language: Malay, Indonesian, English and Dutch
Currency: Rupiah

The East Indies, of which area Indonesia occupies a large percentage, were previously famous as the Spice Islands, supplying mace, nutmeg, cinnamon and pepper to grace the cuisines of the world. So valuable was this trade that fierce battles were fought along the trade routes and for control of the islands themselves. In the early 17th century the Dutch gained dominance of the islands and remained the ruling power until the Japanese invasion of 1941. Independence came in 1949, since when the islands have experienced periods of both democracy and dictatorship. Spices are now negligible in the Indonesian economy. Oilfields are dominant, producing most of southern Asia's oil, backed by copper and manufactured goods. Agriculture employs many people in the production of rice, cassava and sweet potatoes for local consumption, and coffee, rubber and coconuts for export.

IRAN

Population: 63.2 million
Area: 1,648,000 square kilometres
Capital: Tehran
Language: Farsi, Kurdish, Arabic
Currency: Rial

In 1979 a popular revolution overthrew the monarchy and established an Islamic Republic under the control of the Ayatollah Khomeni. This event marked a revival of fundamentalist Islam, which has been felt elsewhere throughout the Islamic world. The basis of the modern Iranian economy is oil, which was discovered in 1908. The industry has suffered several setbacks with the destruction of refineries and ports during the Iran-Iraq War of 1980-88, but oil remains the chief export and currency earner. Other minerals exist in some quantity but are exploited on only a modest scale. Most of the country is unsuited to agriculture due to the lack of rain, but crops include wheat and barley. Millions of sheep, cattle and goats are grazed on the sparse grasslands.

IRAQ

Population: 19 million
Area: 435,000 square kilometres
Capital: Baghdad
Language: Arabic and Kurdish
Currency: Iraqi Dinar

The economy of Iraq was severely disrupted by the Gulf War of 1990-91. The war began in August 1990 when Iraq invaded Kuwait without warning and announced the annexation of that state. International forces gathered in Saudi Arabia while attempts were made to persuade Iraq to withdraw. On 16th January allied air strikes on Iraqi positions began and in February a campaign crushed the Iraqi army and liberated Kuwait. International sanctions on Iraq crippled its economy, which before the war was based on oil exports. Internally agriculture is a major employer and large crops can be raised in the fertile Tigris-Euphrates Valley. Industry was poorly developed before hostilities. The nation is ruled by the Ba'th Party led by Saddam Hussein, the country's President.

ISRAEL

Population: 5.71 million
Area: 21,946 square kilometres
Capital: Jerusalem
Language: Hebrew, Arabic, English
Currency: Shekel

The six pointed Star of David dominates the flag of Israel, symbolising the overwhelming Jewish heritage of the nation. The state of Israel came into being in 1948 as a homeland for Jews from around the world. The demand for a Jewish state became especially strong after the persecution at the hands of the Nazis. Its creation antagonised neighbouring Arab states and the nation's history has been dominated by intermittent warfare and constant terrorist activities. Israel currently occupies large areas of territory which officially belong to neighbouring states. The nation has few mineral resources and agriculture is only possible in irrigated areas. Israel produces much of its own food and its manufacturing industries are healthy.

JAPAN

Population: 125.57 million
Area: 377,812 square kilometres
Capital: Tokyo
Language: Japanese
Currency: Yen

The Emperor of Japan belongs to a family that has occupied the throne for many centuries, reputedly since the sun goddess began the dynasty in around 600 BC. For many years the nation was actually ruled by powerful noblemen known as Shogun, but the Emperor regained power in 1867, and in 1947 the present democratic constitution was introduced. Since the devastation of World War II, Japan has fully revitalised its industry and is now a major economic world power. The most important industries are iron and steel, car manufacture, electronics and chemicals, in which Japan leads the world in technical expertise as well as profitable productivity. The small area of land suitable for agriculture is intensively worked to produce rice, fruit and livestock, but the nation needs to import most of its foods.

JORDAN

Population: 4.1 million
Area: 91,860 square kilometres
Capital: Amman
Language: Arabic
Currency: Jordan Dinar

The Kingdom of Jordan is ruled by the last surviving monarch of the four Arab kingdoms established following the collapse of the Ottoman Empire in 1918. In 1991, political parties in the kingdom were legalised and martial law, imposed in 1967, was lifted. During the 1967 war with Israel, Jordan lost control of the West Bank of the River Jordan which remained under Israeli rule. This entailed the loss of nearly half of the kingdom's fertile land, a serious blow to an economy dependent on agriculture. The farmland of Jordan produces large quantities of tomatoes, olives and citrus fruits. Livestock is grazed on the arid grasslands and near desert of the east. Industry is dependent on the mining and processing of phosphates and potash.

KOREA (NORTH)

Population: 23.26 million
Area: 122,762 square kilometres
Capital: Pyongyang
Language: Korean
Currency: Won

In 1945 the defeat of Japan in World War II led to a joint occupation of Korea by Russian and American forces. In 1948 the Russian zone declared itself the People's Democratic Republic of Korea and established a Communist state under Kim Il Sung, who ruled until his death in 1994. He was succeeded by his son Kim Jong Il, under whom the country remains a closed society. Industry was intensively developed during the Japanese occupation and North Korea today produces steel in quantity and is also a shipbuilding power. Cotton spinning, hydro-electricity, and cotton, silk and rayon weaving are also important. Agriculture is run by the state and rice, maize and potatoes are produced in large quantities, although famine is not unknown.

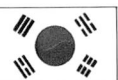

KOREA (SOUTH)

Population: 44.61 million
Area: 99,263 square kilometres
Capital: Seoul
Language: Korean
Currency: Won

Following liberation from Japan, Korea was divided into Russian and American areas. In 1948 the American zone became the Republic of Korea, with a democratic constitution. In 1950 North Korea invaded in an attempt to reunite the nation under Communism. International forces backed the South, while China supported the Communist forces. In 1953 a ceasefire was agreed but no peace treaty has ever been signed. Political life in South Korea has been unstable, with periods of military control. The 1988 Constitution, however, provides for presidential rule. Agriculture remains important in the South Korean economy, with large quantities of rice, radishes and fruits being produced. Industry has increased dramatically and includes production of ships, textiles, motor vehicles and electronics.

KUWAIT

Population: 2.02 million
Area: 17,818 square kilometres
Capital: Kuwait City
Language: Arabic, English
Currency: Kuwaiti Dinar

Kuwait is an hereditary emirate on the Arabian Gulf that has been ruled by the same family since 1756. In 1899 the Emirate placed itself under British protection, only becoming fully independent again in 1961. In 1990 Kuwait was invaded and overrun by Iraqi forces which annexed the nation. American, British and Allied troops under United Nations approval liberated Kuwait in 1991. Kuwait's oil wells were left flaming by the war and months later many were still on fire. The economy of Kuwait is almost entirely dependent on its vast oil reserves, which bring in large quantities of foreign currency.

LAOS

Population: 4.58 million
Area: 236,800 square kilometres
Capital: Vientiane
Language: Lao, French, English
Currency: Kip

The modern state of Laos is unusual in having been founded by a Communist movement led by a royal prince. When the

▲ *Wadi Kum, Jordan.*

Above right: *The volcanic island of Mauritius.*

▲ *Stormy skies over the Maldives.*

▲ *A children's orchestra, North Korea.*

▼ *Waiting for petrol, Kuwait.*

▲ *Angkor Wat, Cambodia.*

▼ *Rice field, Malaysia.*

▼ *Misfat Oasis, Oman.*

▶ *Beirut, capital of Lebanon.*

▲ *On the grass plains of Mongolia.*

▶ *Agriculture in South Korea.*

French relinquished colonial control of the Lao people in 1947, a constitutional monarchy was established. The Pathet Lao rebel movement headed by Prince Souphanouvong and allied Communists from North Vietnam, began a rebellion. This culminated in 1975 with the collapse of the Royal government and the installation of a Communist state under the Pathet Lao party. The nation is predominantly agricultural, with many of the Lao raising rice in the valleys of the various rivers of Laos. The mountainous interior and poor communications have made exploitation of mineral deposits difficult and industry is at only a rudimentary level.

LEBANON

Population: 2.84 million
Area: 10,452 square kilometres
Capital: Beirut
Language: Arabic, French, English
Currency: Lebanese Pound

Lebanon is well known for the factional violence that tore this previously prosperous nation apart. During the 1960s the Palestine Liberation Organization began using bases in southern Lebanon to attack Israel. This led to great tension between the Christians and Moslems within Lebanon and civil war broke out in 1975. Israel invaded in 1982, occupying much of the south. Syrian troops have also intervened in an attempt to enforce a ceasefire among the factions. Lebanon has a constitution with an elected National Assembly and a President, but power has often remained in the hands of radical groups. Lebanon is now engaged in reconstruction but is largely agricultural, having lost its main banking, manufacturing and tourist industries during the years of conflict.

MALAYSIA

Population: 21.3 million
Area: 329,758 square kilometres
Capital: Kuala Lumpur
Language: Malay, Chinese, English
Currency: Ringgit

The government of Malaysia is unique in that the rulers of the nine states meet every five years to elect one of their number to be the supreme ruler, or Yang de-Pertuan Agong. Operating under the head of state is a Parliament elected from the states, in which political power is vested. The nation is among the most prosperous of Southeast Asia, having a highly diversified economy. Exports are dominated in value by manufactured goods, though agri-

culture provides employment for most people. The lush farmland not only produces food for internal consumption but also exports cash crops such as rubber, cocoa, tobacco, sugar cane and tea. There are substantial deposits of tin in the country, together with oilfields, which add to the national wealth.

MALDIVES

Population: 253,298
Area: 298 square kilometres
Capital: Malé
Language: Divehi
Currency: Rufiyaa

Scattered across the Indian Ocean, southwest of India, the Maldives number around 1,200 islands, but only 202 are inhabited. The islands were dominated by the Arabs from around 1100 and Islam is the dominant religion among the mixed population. Britain established a protectorate over the islands in 1887 and returned full independence in 1965. The Sultan was overthrown and a republic established in 1968. The stability of the islands was threatened by an attempted coup in 1988. The coral islands lack mineral wealth and only small patches of land are suitable for farming. The economy is based on fishing, tourism and the processing of coconuts and reeds into craftwork for sale abroad.

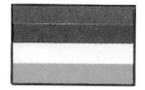

MAURITIUS

Population: 1.13 million
Area: 2,040 square kilometres
Capital: Port Louis
Language: English
Currency: Mauritius Rupee

Mauritius is composed of a number of islands in the Indian Ocean. The two largest islands, Mauritius itself and Rodrigues, are separated by over 500 kilometres of open ocean. The islands have an economy based on the production of sugar. Sugar cane covers most of the arable land and industry is dominated by sugar refineries. Tobacco and tea are also grown for export, while maize, beef and goat meat are produced for internal consumption. The government is a democracy based on universal suffrage, producing an assembly which elects a prime minister who appoints a cabinet.

MONGOLIA

Population: 2.3 million
Area: 1,566,500 square kilometres
Capital: Ulan Bator
Language: Mongol
Currency: Tugrik

During the early 13th century the Mongols, under the leadership of

Genghis Khan, conquered many peoples, creating a massive empire encompassing China, Central Asia and parts of eastern Europe. By the late 17th century, however, the Mongols had fallen under Chinese control. In 1924 the Mongols, with Soviet support, drove the Chinese out and declared an independent Mongolian nation. The new Communist government suppressed traditional Buddhist and Shamanist religions and pursued a policy of farm collectivisation and industrialisation, which has been partially successful. However, many of the people still lead a traditional nomadic lifestyle, caring for herds of livestock. Millions of cattle, horses, sheep and goats are driven across the vast grasslands by expert horsemen. The 1992 Constitution introduced democratic institutions and a market economy.

MYANMAR (UNION OF)

Population: 44.74 million
Area: 676,577 square kilometres
Capital: Yangon (Rangoon)
Language: Burmese, Thai, English
Currency: Kyat

The history of Myanmar (formerly Burma) has been one of upheaval, fragmentation and unification. Since it was granted its freedom from Britain in 1947 there have been numerous coups and attempted coups. The military junta which seized control in 1988 held democratic elections, but then held on to the reins of power. The army currently numbers some 300,000 troops. Myanmar's economy is dominated by traditional agriculture, based on rice, cattle and pigs, and flourishes in the wet tropical climate of the region. Industrial activity is mainly concerned with processing cash crops of sugar and cotton, or with manufacturing fertiliser and agricultural tools. Timber, rubber and rice are the main exchange earners.

NEPAL

Population: 19.28 million
Area: 147,181 square kilometres
Capital: Kathmandu
Language: Nepalese
Currency: Nepalese Rupee

The mountain kingdom of Nepal is unique in having the only flag which is not rectangular in shape. The traditional triangular banner carries a sun to represent the ruling Maharaja and a moon to symbolise the prime minister, until 1951 an hereditary post. Nepal pursued a policy of isolation until the mid 1950s, since when the economy has been slowly modernised. Many

Nepalese live in inaccessible mountain valleys where they continue to practise traditional farming techniques. Others produce cash crops of herbs and potatoes or keep cattle to produce ghee, a form of clarified butter. A valuable source of foreign currency comes from the Gurkha troops recruited in Nepal to serve in the British army. Under a constitution introduced in 1990 the Maharaja permits political parties and free elections.

OMAN

Population: 2.14 million
Area: 309,500 square kilometres
Capital: Muscat
Language: Arabic, English
Currency: Rial

Until 1937 the Sultanate of Oman was a somewhat impoverished Moslem state relying upon fishing and date production for its livelihood. However, in that year oil was discovered and, although reserves are not vast, Oman's petrochemical industry now dominates the economy. Attempts are being made to diversify by improving agriculture and the fishing industry. Copper mining in the interior is being encouraged. Agreements with Yemen and Saudi Arabia in 1995 completed the demarcation of Oman's borders with its neighbours. According to its Constitution of 1996, Oman is a hereditary absolute monarchy and is ruled by decrees issued by the Sultan. There is, however, a Cabinet of prominent citizens to assist the Sultan.

▲ *Honeymoon Lake, Pakistan.*

PAKISTAN

Population: 130.2 million
Area: 796,095 square kilometres
Capital: Islamabad
Language: Urdu, Punjabi, Sindi, English
Currency: Pakistan Rupee

The nation of Pakistan was created in 1947 by the British as an Islamic homeland after fears were expressed by the Moslems about joining a Hindu-dominated India. The population is united by its religion, but otherwise is very diverse, with occasional calls for independence by various ethnic groups. Periods of democracy have alternated with military rule, and there have been frequent charges of corruption in both types of government. The economy is based upon agriculture, which employs over half the workforce. The irrigated plains around the Indus and its tributaries produce large quantities of rice, wheat and sugar for domestic consumption and some cotton for export. Tax and economy laws favour the peasant smallholder.

PHILIPPINES

Population: 69.8 million
Area: 300,000 square kilometres
Capital: Manila
Language: Filipino, Spanish, English, tribal languages
Currency: Piso

The Philippines is composed of 7,100 islands and islets, but few of these are inhabited and most do not even have names. From about 1550 Spain gradually acquired control over the profitable Spice Islands of the Philippines and ruled until 1898, when the United States took over. Independence was achieved in 1946, and since that time a fragile democracy has been interrupted by military coups, fraudulent elections and corruption. The Philippines is an agricultural nation with rice, maize and coconuts as the main crops. Many coastal villages depend on fishing for income. The mining of nickel, zinc and copper lead the mining industry, while manufacturing is rapidly gaining in importance. The nation remains dependent on imported food and materials.

▲ Banaue rice terraces, Philippines.

QATAR

Population: 539,000
Area: 11,437 square kilometres
Capital: Doha
Language: Arabic
Currency: Qatari Riyal

The long, streaming banner of the Emirate of Qatar is based upon the red and white banner imposed by Britain in the 19th century on all Gulf states which were party to an anti-pirate agreement. Britain controlled foreign policy until 1971, when Qatar was granted full independence. The Emir is an absolute monarch who rules by decree, but an Advisory Council of prominent citizens is consulted on major issues. Oil was first exploited during the 1950s and since then has come to dominate the economy. Oil revenue is being used to improve agriculture and fishing, with the long term aim of the country becoming self-sufficient. Industry is also being encouraged. Most of Qatar is desert, thinly populated by nomadic Bedouin tribes. Lack of water is a perennial problem.

SAUDI ARABIA

Population: 16.9 million
Area: 2,200,000 square kilometres
Capital: Riyadh
Language: Arabic
Currency: Rial

The religious kingdom of Saudi Arabia was carved out of the deserts by the aristocratic Saud family of the Wahhabi Islamic sect earlier this century, and was internationally recognised as recently as 1927. The king is also custodian of the holy mosques and the power structure is based upon Koranic law, though an assembly may be consulted by the king if he wishes. The desert kingdom began producing oil in 1937, and the economy rapidly shifted away from traditional reliance on dates and nomadic herds to concentrate on petrochemicals. There has also been some diversification into light industry and the production of plastics as a by-product of oil refining. In 1990-91 Saudi Arabia was used as a base for forces fighting to liberate Kuwait from Iraqi occupation.

SEYCHELLES

Population: 73,850
Area: 455 square kilometres
Capital: Victoria
Language: Creole, English, French
Currency: Seychelles Rupee

When Portuguese sailors discovered the Seychelles in the 16th century they were uninhabited, and not until the 1770s was permanent colonisation begun by France. Britain acquired the islands in 1810 and independence was granted in 1976. A coup took place within a year of independence, and the Seychelles became a one-party state until other parties were legalised in 1991. The idyllic coral islands and tropical climate make the Seychelles a popular holiday resort, and tourism is the major industry. The large fishing fleet catches tuna for

▲ Istanbul, Turkey, at dusk.

▶ Abu Dhabi, United Arab Emirates.

▲ La Digue, Seychelles.

▲ The Singapore River, Singapore.

▼ Mecca, Saudi Arabia.

▶ Abu Dhabi, United Arab Emirates.

▲ Sailing junks, Vietnam.

◀ Stilt fisherman, Sri Lanka.

▲ A Yemeni landscape.

▼ Damascus, Syria.

canning and export, while coconuts, cinnamon bark and copra are the main cash crops.

SINGAPORE

Population: 2.9 million
Area: 647.5 square kilometres
Capital: Singapore
Language: Malay, Mandarin, Tamil, English
Currency: Singapore Dollar

The city state of Singapore was founded by Sir Stamford Raffles in 1819 as a trading port of the British East India Company. Since then the city has flourished as a trading and manufacturing centre. Singapore passed from the Company to the British Government in the 19th century before acquiring independence in 1965. Though it has no mineral resources and virtually no farmland, Singapore is a leading economic power in Asia. Commercial and merchant banks number almost 200, and together provide the economic mainspring for much of Southeast Asia. The manufacturing base is diverse, including the processing of chemicals, foods, rubber and textiles. The state is a democracy with free elections though power is almost monopolised by a single party.

SRI LANKA

Population: 17.9 million
Area: 65,610 square kilometres
Capital: Colombo
Language: Sinhala, Tamil, English
Currency: Sri Lankan Rupee

Sri Lankan politics are dominated by ethnic violence between the majority Sinhalese and the Tamils, the largest minority. Many Tamils wish to form their own nation in the north of the island, and extremists undertake periodic terrorist action. Other minority groups include Europeans, Malays and the Veddah tribesmen who inhabit the forested mountains and are probably descendants of the original inhabitants. Agriculture dominates the economy, with rubber, coconuts and especially tea being grown as cash crops for export. Efforts are being made to improve rice production to reduce reliance on imported food. Industry centres on the processing of agricultural products, while precious stones are the only mineral resources of note.

SYRIA

Population: 14.62 million
Area: 185,180 square kilometres
Capital: Damascus
Language: Arabic, Kurdish, Armenian
Currency: Syrian Pound

Arabs form the overwhelming bulk of the Syrian population and the Islamic religion is a strong unifying force. Government is by a democratically-elected Parliament, and the Arab Socialist Party has formed a majority since 1963, with President Assad holding executive power. Syria has been a major power in the Middle East, taking part in wars against Israel and maintaining a peace-keeping force in Lebanon. The economy is based on oil and textiles, which together make up about three-quarters of exports. Irrigated farmland in the Euphrates Valley and in the west produces quantities of wheat, and barley for domestic consumption. The southern deserts are sparsely populated by nomadic pastoralists raising livestock at subsistence level.

TAIWAN

Population: 21.5 million
Area: 36,182 square kilometres
Capital: Taipei
Language: Chinese dialects and Japanese
Currency: New Taiwan Dollar

When the Communist Party gained control of mainland China in 1949 the surviving nationalists fled to the island of Taiwan and set up a rival Republic of China, which is now usually referred to as Taiwan. Neither regime recognises the other as legitimate, and a continual propaganda war has been carried on. Until the Nationalist takeover, Taiwan was an agricultural island with intensively-farmed pockets of fertile land. Rice, pineapples and bananas are still produced in quantity on the few areas suitable for agriculture amid the mountainous terrain. Industrial development has been the keynote of Taiwan's economy since 1949. Light industry was encouraged first, but iron, steel and shipbuilding are now well established, together with electronics.

THAILAND

Population: 58.34 million
Area: 513,115 square kilometres
Capital: Bangkok
Language: Thai, Lao, Chinese, Malay, Khmer
Currency: Baht

The kingdom of Thailand dates back many centuries, but the present dynasty came to power in 1782, when the founder threw off Burmese control. The kingdom never succumbed to European colonialism but was overrun by Japan in World War II. The royal dynasty remains on the throne, but political power has changed hands rapidly between Parliament and army factions as coups have been common in recent years. The majority of the population lives in rural areas, where the fertile soil and ideal climate allow Thailand to produce far more food than it needs. Rice is a substantial export. The beautiful old temples and notorious nightlife of Bangkok make Thailand a popular tourist resort attracting many visitors.

▲ *Buddhist priests, Bangkok Thailand.*

TURKEY

Population: 62.53 million
Area: 779,452 square kilometres
Capital: Ankara
Language: Turkish
Currency: Turkish Lira

The Turks formerly ruled the vast Ottoman Empire, embracing the Balkans, the Near East and much of North Africa, and modern Turkey has a flag derived from that of the Empire. The modern republic was founded in 1923, when the last emperor was deposed. Democratic government has been interrupted by periods of military control, most recently in 1980-83. The interior plateau has a fertile soil and produces large quantities of grain, while the warmer coast produces heavy crops of olives, figs and citrus fruits. Flax and cotton form the basis of a flourishing textile industry. Agriculture employs over half the work-force, some at little above subsistence level. Industry is dominated by the production of iron and steel, motor vehicles and cement, and is growing under state encouragement.

UNITED ARAB EMIRATES

Population: 2.4 million
Area: 83,657 square kilometres
Capital: Abu Dhabi
Language: Arabic, English
Currency: Dirham

As the name suggests, the United Arab Emirates is a confederation of seven independent nations: Abu Dhabi, Dubai, Ash Shariqah, Ajman, Umm al Qaywayn, Al Fujayrah and Ras al Khaymah. The federation is ruled jointly by the seven Emirs, who appoint ministers to legislate and agree upon a joint budget. The federation came into being when Britain gave the Emirs full independence after a period when Britain controlled foreign policy in return for giving military protection. The bulk of the territory is desert, with little opportunity for agriculture, though fishing has potential and there is a large export trade. The economy is basically dependent on oil, which is produced in large quantities. Oil revenues are used to promote a more diversified economy and to improve living conditions.

VIETNAM

Population: 74 million
Area: 329,566 square kilometres
Capital: Hanoi
Language: Vietnamese
Currency: Dong

Vietnam formally came into being on 2nd July 1976 with the union of the former nations of North and South Vietnam following the Vietnam War. Just two years later Vietnam invaded Cambodia, finally withdrawing in 1988. The constitution claims that Vietnam is a proletarian dictatorship under Marxism-Leninism. In effect all power is in the hands of the Communist Party, which has followed a consistently pro-Russian stance, thus angering its neighbour China. This has led to border skirmishes in recent years. Well over half the population is directly dependent on agriculture. Over fifteen million tonnes of sweet potatoes are produced each year, but Vietnam still needs to import food. There is little heavy industry and light industry is localised and small-scale.

YEMEN

Population: 15.8 million
Area: 555,000 square kilometres
Capital: Sana'a
Language: Arabic
Currency: Riyal

In May 1990 the former states of Yemen and the People's Democratic Republic of Yemen merged to form a single nation. The new constitution of the united Republic of Yemen allowed for free, multi-party elections after an interim period of two years, during which complicated arrangements for fusing the armies, administrations and economies would be put into effect. There was a period of civil war in 1994 and, in the same year, a constitution founded on Islamic law was adopted. The new nation has very little industry and most of the population is engaged in agriculture, usually at subsistence level. The arid nature of much of Yemen restricts agriculture to river valleys. Coastal villages supplement farming with fishing, much of the catch being dried and exported.

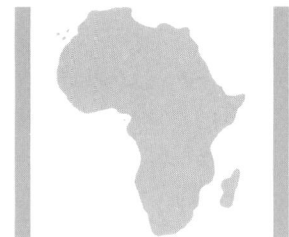

AFRICA

*A*frica is, in general, an underdeveloped continent, where political violence and dictatorships are common. It is also, however, a continent of great potential, with a magnificent environmental heritage and the possibility of significant improvements.

Africa may be divided, for cultural and geographical reasons, into two distinct regions. The first includes the Islamic states that fringe the Mediterranean and northern Atlantic coasts. These countries are united by a common language and religion which is the result of their Islamic past. Most have fertile coastal areas backed by vast desert interiors inhabited only by nomadic tribesmen. Oilfields are present in most of these states, ensuring a national wealth that pays for schemes to improve the quality of life.

The second region stretches from the Sahara Desert to the Cape of Good Hope. This is a more diverse area, ranging from dense rainforest through open savannah to desert conditions, but united by having a mainly Negro population and having gained independence from European colonial rule. There are, however, distinct differences within this region.

West Africa is characterised by settled farming communities of great tribal diversity, where mineral exploitation and industry is well developed compared to elsewhere in Africa. East Africa is dominated by plains originally populated by semi-nomadic pastoral tribes, where minerals are less common and farming plays a more dominant role in the economy. Southern Africa is as diverse as the entire continent, with areas of fertile farmland, dense forests and open plains to be found within a relatively short distance of each other.

Countries bordering the Sahara are subject to periodic droughts, which bring great misery in their wake. Population booms over the past decades have led to a reliance on good crops and when these fail famine follows. Famines, like those in Ethiopia and neighbouring countries such as Somalia, have killed millions of people. Elsewhere in Africa famine is not such a constant threat, but chronic poverty and poor medical services cause a low life expectancy.

Though the age of European colonisation in Africa is now over, the signs of those times are still evident. The official language of the majority of states is still that of the colonising power. The diverse tribal tongues of most countries – some have over 200 languages – make a lingua franca essential, and it has been found convenient to maintain that of the former ruling European power.

Former French colonies in Africa often share a common currency: the Franc CFA. This currency is issued by the Banque Centrale des Etats de l'Afrique de l'Ouest and is locked into the French Franc at a set rate. This arrangement has advantages for those countries within it, but also has the effect of robbing them of total discretion over their own economies which, to some extent, remain vulnerable to outside control.

Many African states abandoned democracy following independence. In some cases this was due to the total dominance of a single party, which then outlawed opposition, but has frequently been the result of a military coup. Also, many African countries have experienced dictatorship at some stage and are still ruled without democracy, though several nations have returned to multi-party civilian rule. There have been numerous accusations of human rights violations in some African states.

Much attention has been focused on South Africa since the abandonment of the apartheid system and the introduction of a multi-racial parliament. Nelson Mandela was elected President in May 1994.

The mineral wealth of Africa is vast and largely unexplored. Effective capital investment and improved communications would bring this wealth into the economy, but international companies are unwilling to invest heavily in countries subject to civil war or frequent coups.

Africa is undoubtedly a beautiful and potentially wealthy continent, but its endemic problems and recurring violence have locked it into a cycle of poverty which will prove difficult to break.

◀ *Sierra Leone beaches.*　　　▲ *People of Ethiopia.*

▲ A village in Mozambique.

► A waterfall in Cameroon.

▼ Harare, Zimbabwe.

ALGERIA

Population: 28.58 million
Area: 2,381,741 square kilometres
Capital: Algiers
Language: Arabic, Berber, French
Currency: Algerian Dinar

Algeria gained its independence from France in 1962 after nearly a decade of guerrilla warfare. The bulk of the population lives along the Mediterranean coast and in the adjacent mountains, where the climate is milder and the land more fertile than in the arid Sahara which makes up most of the country. The discovery of large natural gas fields has made Algeria relatively wealthy, and some of these resources are spent on free health treatment and high-quality education. Although European influences are strong in coastal towns, many people continue to lead a traditional Islamic lifestyle. A new constitution in 1996 defines the fundamental components of the Algerian people as Islam, and Arab and Berber identity.

ANGOLA

Population: 11.5 million
Area: 1,246,700 square kilometres
Capital: Luanda
Language: Portuguese, tribal languages
Currency: Kwanza

For most of its independent existence Angola has been racked by civil war between the communist MPLA party, which forms the central government, and the rebel UNITA organisation, which controls much of southern Angola. The long years of warfare caused much hardship and seriously disrupted the economy, making this one of the poorer African nations. However, oil production in the north and diamond mining provide a source of foreign capital which may lead to economic revival. The coastal region is the centre for industrialisation and urban lifestyles. The high plateau of the interior is heavily forested and inhabited by tribes which live in a traditional way with their own languages and religions.

BENIN

Population: 5.46 million
Area: 112,622 square kilometres
Capital: Porto-Novo
Language: French, tribal languages
Currency: Franc CFA

In December 1989, the leadership abandoned Marxism-Leninism and called for a national conference to steer the country towards pluralist democracy. Traditional agricultural lifestyles and tribal culture dominate in the interior. It is thought that about ninety per cent of the population practise subsistence farming. In the mountainous far north, Islamic culture has filtered down from the desert regions. Only on the coast is industry to be found, and even this is heavily based on the agricultural produce of the interior, particularly sugar and palm oil. The Semé oilfield, located ten miles offshore, helps to boost the economy.

BOTSWANA

Population: 1.4 million
Area: 581,730 square kilometres
Capital: Gaborone
Language: English, Setswana, Sishona, San, Hottentot
Currency: Pula

Botswana is rare among African states in having maintained its democratic constitution since independence in 1966. There is an elected National Assembly, to which the President is responsible, and a House of Chiefs to advise the government. The vast majority of the population live in traditional villages, where cattle farming is the main activity, though some crops are also sown. Diamond and copper mining are major industries. In addition, many young people work in South Africa for some years in order to earn money for their families at home. The vast Kalahari Desert in the southwest of the country is inhabited by nomadic tribes.

BURKINA FASO

Population: 10 million
Area: 274,122 square kilometres
Capital: Ouagadougou
Language: French, tribal languages
Currency: Franc CFA

As one of the poorest and most unstable countries in Africa, Burkina Faso has experienced much hardship. Numerous coups and government changes have occurred. A new constitution was approved in 1991. The state is largely an artificial creation, being a former French administrative district covering the territory of several indigenous tribes. The vast majority of the population are engaged in subsistence farming in traditional tribal society. The country is periodically struck by drought and famine, being on the southern fringe of the Sahara. The exploitation of recently discovered gold and manganese deposits is hampered by a poor transportation system and lack of capital. The state depends largely on foreign aid and remains chronically depressed.

BURUNDI

Population: 5.36 million
Area: 27,834 square kilometres
Capital: Bujumbura
Language: Kirundi, French, Kiswahili
Currency: Burundi Franc

Sometime in the 16th century Tutsi tribes invaded the area and conquered the Hutu peoples. Following a period of German and Belgian rule, Burundi became independent in 1962 under a Tutsi monarch. In 1966, however, he was overthrown by the Tutsi-dominated army, which subsequently suppressed Hutu unrest and dismissed Presidents at will. Even today, the country remains dangerously split between the two main ethnic groups, with violence occurring all too easily. Tea and coffee plantations are the mainstays of both industry and the export economy. The majority of the population, however, remains dependent on subsistence agriculture based on bananas, maize and cattle.

CAMEROON

Population: 12.2 million
Area: 475,442 square kilometres
Capital: Yaoundé
Language: French, English, tribal languages
Currency: Franc CFA

Much of the interior of Cameroon is virtually inaccessible during the rainy season, when torrential downpours wash away roads and flood large areas. This isolation is emphasised by ethnic diversity, with twenty-four languages and as many as 200 tribes. The fragmentation has slowed economic development, though the nation is relatively wealthy by African standards. The economy is based largely on agriculture, with coffee, cocoa and palm oil forming the bulk of export crops. The majority of farmland is, however, devoted to producing foods such as cassava, maize and groundnuts for local consumption. Industry is concentrated on aluminium smelting and the processing of agricultural products. Oil revenue has helped the government to invest in new projects.

CAPE VERDE

Population: 417,000
Area: 4,033 square kilometres
Capital: Praia
Language: Portuguese, Crioulo
Currency: Cape Verde Escudo

The Cape Verde Islands have been independent only since 1975, when Portugal relinquished. Once a single-party state, the ruling elite joined several other African

▲ *Farm workers in Angola.*

▲ *A scene on the Chobe River, Botswana.*

▲ *Celebrations on the anniversary of the Algerian Revolution.*

▲ *A village in Chad.*

▼ *A domestic scene in Burkina Faso.*

▲ *Barren, drought-scarred landscape, Cape Verde.*

▲ *Riverboat merchant, Benin.*

▼ *The Central African Republic.*

▲ *Bathers in the Comoros.*

countries in 1990 by announcing an intention to allow democracy. The present constitution was adopted in 1992. Cape Verde has strong historical links with Guinea-Bissau. The islands are small, rugged and arid, with little opportunity for farming. Coconuts, coffee and sugar are produced in small quantities on irrigated land. Fishing is far more productive for the local population with large numbers of tuna being landed each year. The climate and scenic coastline hold out the promise of an increase in tourism.

CENTRAL AFRICAN REPUBLIC

Population: 3.07 million
Area: 622,436 square kilometres
Capital: Bangui
Language: French, Sango, tribal languages
Currency: Franc CFA

For thirteen years until 1979 this country was ruled by Jean-Bedel Bokassa, who proclaimed himself Emperor and staged a lavish coronation ceremony. He was eventually overthrown by the army. In 1992, the Constitution was revised to allow multi-party democracy. Though potentially rich in minerals and agriculture, the economy has been held back by political instability, poor communications and, in particular, by the lack of a coastline. Diamond, gold and uranium mining lead the small industrial sector, while the majority of the population remain employed in subsistence agriculture.

CHAD

Population: 6.28 million
Area: 1,284,000 square kilometres
Capital: N'Djaména
Language: French, Arabic, tribal languages
Currency: Franc CFA

Endemic civil war marked the history of Chad following independence from France in 1960. The fighting between various ethnic factions was based upon a struggle between the nomadic, Moslem north and the agricultural and animist south. The situation was confused by shifting alliances and foreign intervention, including by French troops trying to restore order. Exploitation of gold deposits and oil remains minimal. The population remains desperately poor and depends on subsistence agriculture.

COMOROS

Population: 490,000
Area: 1,862 square kilometres
Capital: Moroni
Language: Comorian, Makua, French, Arabic
Currency: Comorian Franc

When the three Comoros islands declared themselves to be independent of France in 1975, a fourth island, Mayotte, refused to follow them. The state has suffered a number of coups and has chronic problems of disease and poverty. The islands have, over the centuries, received influxes of African, Indonesian, Arabic and European peoples and today have a mixed population. The majority of the population engages in subsistence farming. In recent years commercial production of vanilla, cloves and coffee has been undertaken and these now account for much of the country's exports. Though independent, the Comoros remain economically linked with France.

▲ *The Congo's Sangha River.*

CONGO

Population: 2.94 million
Area: 341,821 square kilometres
Capital: Brazzaville
Language: French, tribal languages
Currency: Franc CFA

Formerly a French colony, the Congo was a single-party, Marxist-Leninist state until 1992 when multi-party democracy was restored. The nation is relatively wealthy by African standards, with oil reserves offshore and productive gold mines. It is also rich in minerals particularly lead, copper and zinc and there are reserves of phosphates and iron. Industry is well established around the capital and produces cement and textiles among other products. However, more than three-quarters of the population remains engaged in farming, much of it at subsistence level. The vast bulk of the population is found in the southern parts of the country, for the northern regions are covered by dense forests and unfertile land.

CONGO, DEMOCRATIC REPUBLIC

Population: 45.26 million
Area: 2,344,885 square kilometres
Capital: Kinshasa
Language: French, Lingala, Kiswahili, Tshiluba, Kikongo, tribal languages
Currency: Zaire

In late 1996 secessionist forces of the Alliance of Democratic Forces for the Liberation of Congo-Zaire (ADFL) began to drive the regular Zairean army before them. By early 1997 President Mobutu was forced from power and the new regime took control. The vast interior of the country is largely covered by the Congo Basin, in which flourishes dense rainforest. Much of this area has never been properly explored and remains home to tribes leading traditional lifestyles. Best known are the pygmies, but several hundred other peoples maintain their own language and culture. Government control is limited to regions along the Congo River and the more open regions. Here mineral mining is the mainstay of the economy, with exploitation of rich deposits of copper, oil and cobalt being predominant.

DJIBOUTI

Population: 586,000
Area: 23,200 square kilometres
Capital: Djibouti
Language: Somali, Afar, French
Currency: Djibouti Franc

The state of Djibouti is dominated by disputes between Somalis and Afars. The hinterland is composed of arid grazing lands, although the bulk of the population lives in or around Djibouti City. The city has a long history as a trading centre and the economy is largely dependent on the port. Djibouti was a one-party state until 1992, when a constitution paved the way for democracy.

EGYPT

Population: 60.24 million
Area: 997,739 square kilometres
Capital: Cairo
Language: Arabic, French, English
Currency: Egyptian Pound

Egypt was conquered by the Arabs in the 7th century, and today the nation is firmly Moslem in culture and outlook. People and prosperity are concentrated in the Nile Valley, as they have been since recorded history began here in 3,000 BC. The waters of the Nile allow irrigation of the farmland which produces the bulk of the nation's food as well as export crops. Industry is well advanced in the major towns and cities. Tourism plays a major role in the economy. Egypt has a relatively stable political system though it is coming under increasing pressure from Islamic fundamentalists.

EQUATORIAL GUINEA

Population: 420,000
Area: 28,051 square kilometres
Capital: Malabo
Language: Spanish, Portuguese patois
Currency: Franc CFA

Equatorial Guinea is divided between the mainland territory on the Mbini River and the islands of Bioko and Annobon. Cocoa and coffee remain important export crops, although the majority of farmland is used for subsistence agriculture, with cassava and sweet potatoes being the chief products. The wet, hot tropical climate produces vast forests in the interior and these are now exploited for their timber, which provides the largest proportion of the country's exports. Although over half the population live in towns, there is virtually no industry in the country.

ERITREA

Population: 3.53 million
Area: 93,679 square kilometres
Capital: Asmara
Language: Tigrinya, Arabic, Tigré, English
Currency: Birr

Eritrea, a country with a diverse climate and geography, has been under Italian, British and Ethiopian rule. In 1991, after thirty years of armed struggle by the Eritrean People's Liberation Front, the country won its right to self-determination. Two years of provisional government followed, and after an internationally monitored referendum in April 1993, full independence was achieved.

ETHIOPIA

Population: 55 million
Area: 1,098,000 square kilometres
Capital: Addis Ababa
Language: Amharic, Oromo
Currency: Birr

Drought, famine and civil war dogged Ethiopia for many years. Famine claimed hundreds of thousands of lives and the internal political unrest worsened the situation. In 1993, however, Eritrea seceded and the fighting ceased, although there remain many ethnic groups within the country which desire freedom from strong central rule. About 80 per cent of the work force are employed in agriculture which, in productive years, accounts for valuable exports of coffee and sugar. Industry is centred around the capital and primarily produces textiles, processed food and drinks.

▲ *Thatched huts in Equatorial Guinea.*

Above right: *Children in Guinea-Bissau.*

▼ *Filling water pots, Ghana.*

▲ *Women at work in Gambia.*

▲ *The mountain village of Ha Thuhlo, Lesotho.*

▶ *Landscape of Gabon.*

▼ *Kenyatta Centre, Nairobi, Kenya.*

▶ *Abidjan, Ivory Coast.*

GABON

Population: 1.01 million
Area: 267,667 square kilometres
Capital: Libreville
Language: French, tribal languages
Currency: Franc CFA

Made up largely of the drainage basin of the Ogooue River, Gabon has numerous natural resources but lacks the finance and population to take best advantage of them. Offshore oil is being exploited, as are deposits of uranium and manganese, but the economy remains based chiefly on agriculture. The Equator runs through the centre of Gabon, and this dictates the climate and range of crops which can be produced. Most agriculture is subsistence, though sugar cane is grown in large quantities near the coast for export. The government of Gabon under a single-party state was stable from 1967 until 1990, when free elections were held and the existing system dismantled amid allegations of ballot-rigging.

GAMBIA

Population: 1.09 million
Area: 10,689 square kilometres
Capital: Banjul
Language: English, tribal languages
Currency: Dalasi

The Gambia exists because of the river from which it takes its name. The nation is made up of a narrow strip of land which follows the twists and turns of the river from Koina to the ocean. Several tribes have their territories along the river and their chiefs have an established position within the constitution. The nation is basically agricultural and has only one export of any importance. This is the groundnut, thousands of tons of which are shipped out each year. More recently the government has tried to break this hazardous dependence on a single crop. In 1982 Gambia joined with Senegal, which virtually surrounds it, to form the Confederation of Senegambia but this was dissolved in 1989.

GHANA

Population: 16.47 million
Area: 238,537 square kilometres
Capital: Accra
Language: English, tribal languages
Currency: Cedi

As the first black African state to become independent of a European colonial power, in 1957, Ghana has set several trends in African history. The colours of the Ghanaian flag – red, green and yellow – have been adopted by several other colonies on achieving independence, while the black star of African freedom has also become a popular motif. Ghana has experienced several coups and was ruled for many years by a Provisional Council led by Flight Lieutenant Jerry Rawlings. In 1992, democratic elections were held and Rawlings was elected President. The economy is based on cash crop agriculture, with cocoa the most important crop, though tobacco, coffee and tropical fruits are catching up. Industrial activities are based around the mining of gold, diamonds and, more recently, oil.

GUINEA

Population: 6.5 million
Area: 245,857 square kilometres
Capital: Conakry
Language: French, tribal languages
Currency: Guinean Franc

Guinea followed Ghana to independence one year later and adopted the same colours for its flag, though they are arranged in vertical rather than horizontal stripes. Several tribal groupings are included within Guinea, with the Fulani being the largest at around forty percent of the population. From 1984 until 1991 power rested with a military junta. Military rule was replaced by a Transitional Committee for National Rectification. The nation has a tropical climate, with a summer monsoon which brings heavy rain and high temperatures. Combined with fertile soils this climate creates ideal conditions for a variety of crops including rice, sugar cane and tropical fruits. Vast reserves of bauxite are now being mined as are iron ore deposits and diamonds.

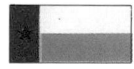

GUINEA-BISSAU

Population: 1.06 million
Area: 36,125 square kilometres
Capital: Bissau
Language: Portuguese, Crioulo
Currency: Franc CFA

For many years a one-party state, Guinea-Bissau became a multi-party democracy in 1991. The fertile soil and tropical climate allow the production of large quantities of rice, rubber and groundnuts, much of which is exported. Most of the population remains dependent on subsistence agriculture and industry is virtually non-existent. Guinea-Bissau has a crushing foreign debt more than one hundred times the size of the government's annual budget. Ethnically the population is divided between the coastal Balante and the Muslim Fulani of the inland regions, though there are several smaller tribes.

IVORY COAST

Population: 13.72 million
Area: 320,783 square kilometres
Capital: Yamoussoukro
Language: French, tribal languages
Currency: Franc CFA

The Ivory Coast, or Cote d'Ivoire, takes its name from the early trade in ivory that dominated the region when it was first discovered by Europeans in the 15th century. Thereafter slavery, and more recently coffee, were mainstays of the economy. Today, the rich soil of the coastal regions has been turned to support a wide variety of crops including yams, cassava and a number of tropical fruits for export. Despite this fertility the economy of the Ivory Coast is held back by massive foreign debts and limited mineral resources. Opposition parties were legalised in 1990, but the former sole party still retained power having won the vast majority of seats in the National Assembly.

KENYA

Population: 26.44 million
Area: 582,646 square kilometres
Capital: Nairobi
Language: Swahili, Kikuyu, English tribal languages
Currency: Kenya Shilling

Committed until 1990 to the concept of 'democracy with one party', the state of Kenya has enjoyed more stability than many other African nations since it achieved independence in 1963. This has combined with rich natural resources and a long history of international trade to make it economically viable, though not particularly wealthy. Most of the population inhabits the interior highlands, where coffee, tea and sugar are grown in large quantities for export, or the lower hills, where maize, cassava and sweet potatoes are produced for local consumption. The vast semi-arid plains are the home of gazelles, zebra and lions, which attract over half a million tourists each year, boosting the economy. The coastal towns have thriving commercial centres.

LESOTHO

Population: 2.11 million
Area: 30,355 square kilometres
Capital: Maseru
Language: Sesotho, English
Currency: Loti

Lesotho is one of the few African tribal kingdoms to survive into modern times. Following a coup in 1986 the king had to act on the advice of the army, but a democratic constitution was promulgated in 1993 and replaced military rule. In the early 19th century refugees from vicious warfare in the north fled to the mountains of Lesotho and became welded into a kingdom under Moshoeshoe I, who placed himself under British protection. This wise move ensured the Sotho clans retained some form of self-government throughout the colonial era, and in 1966 became independent outside the Union of South Africa. The country has few natural resources and little agricultural land. Young people work in South Africa for long periods of time, earning enough money to support their families and keep the fragile economy of the kingdom in balance.

LIBERIA

Population: 2.83 million
Area: 99,067 square kilometres
Capital: Monrovia
Language: English, tribal languages
Currency: Liberian Dollar

The flag of Liberia is similar to that of the United States of America, indicating the origins of the nation. In 1822 an American society landed a party of freed slaves on the coast in Monrovia in an attempt to establish a haven for such people. In 1847 the nation declared itself independent and adopted a constitution similar to that of the United States. Recent years have witnessed violent upheavals, with coups and civil war raging fiercely. The situation is not yet completely stable. Liberia has rich mineral resources, in particular massive iron ore deposits, which make up seventy percent of exports, together with gold and diamonds. The vast bulk of the population is engaged in farming, with numerous commercial farms growing coffee, rice and sugar cane.

LIBYA

Population: 5.59 million
Area: 1,759,540 square kilometres
Capital: Tripoli
Language: Arabic
Currency: Libyan Dinar

Until recently one of the poorest Mediterranean nations, Libya is now one of the richest, following the discovery of massive oilfields in 1959. In 1969 King Idris was overthrown by Colonel Muammar Qadhafi, who established Libya as an Arab republic. The country has since vociferously supported Arab unity and nationalism, and has often incurred Western enmity. The economy is based on natural oil and gas, which account for nearly all exports. Internally, however, agriculture dominates,

▲ *A lake in the Fezzan dessert, Libya.*

with the most fertile lands of North Africa producing rich harvests of dates, citrus fruits and cereals. Ambitious irrigation projects are under way which aim to add to the land under cultivation.

MADAGASCAR

Population: 13.5 million
Area: 587,041 square kilometres
Capital: Antananarivo
Language: Malagasy, French
Currency: Malagasy Franc

The original kingdom, comprising a mixed population of Malayo-Polynesian and African stock, was overrun by the French in 1897. In 1960 the island became independent as a republic, and subsequently suffered several coups. The country was ruled by the Supreme Revolutionary Council and the President from 1975-1991, when anti-government unrest led to political changes. A new constitution instituted the Third Republic in 1992. The economy is based on agriculture and forestry, but some diversification is taking place. The fertile soils produce heavy crops of coffee, tobacco and tropical fruits, the processing of which forms the basis of the island's small-scale industries.

MALAWI

Population: 11 million
Area: 118,484 square kilometres
Capital: Lilongwe
Language: Chichewa, English
Currency: Kwacha

Ruled for many years as a one-party state, a new constitution in 1994 provided for the holding of multi-party elections. The country is landlocked with few resources. Agriculture is the basic activity, with most of the population relying on subsistence farming for a livelihood. Tobacco and tea are grown for export, but occupy only a small part of the total agricultural land. Marble is the only major quarrying material and industry is restricted to local consumer goods. As a mountainous state, however, Malawi has massive potential for hydroelectricity and this is now being exploited. The economy remains reliant on its migrant workers, who leave the country for South Africa or Zambia to work in mines and factories.

MALI

Population: 9.2 million
Area: 1,248,574 square kilometres
Capital: Bamako
Language: French, Bambara, tribal languages
Currency: Franc CFA

Mali is one of the world's poorest nations, being dependent on an agriculture at the mercy of drought and semi-desert conditions. The majority of the diverse population is concentrated in the southwest, where the Senegal and Niger rivers give a semblance of reliability to the water supply for irrigation. Millet, cassava and sweet potatoes are the chief crops for local consumption, while cotton is produced for export. The northern and eastern regions are covered by desert and are virtually uninhabited. Mineral wealth remains untapped due to poor transport and a lack of capital. In 1992, following years of military rule, the country held its first democratic elections.

MAURITANIA

Population: 2.33 million
Area: 1,030,700 square kilometres
Capital: Nouakchott
Language: Arabic, French, Pulaar, Soninke, Wolof
Currency: Ouguiya

The crescent and star on Mauritania's green flag indicates its Islamic heritage. The vast desert region of the north and east is the home of nomadic herdsmen, but the majority of the population inhabits the Senegal Valley in the southwest. In this region millet, rice and dates are produced in large quantities for local consumption. Coastal villages land large catches of Atlantic fish, which are dried or salted locally to form a large proportion of exports by value. A long-running conflict with Morocco over the Western Sahara territory, which ended in 1979, proved to be a constant drain on the economy. Industry today remains extremely limited, being mostly restricted to food processing or iron-ore production. In 1992 the country held its first multi-party elections.

MOROCCO

Population: 26.1 million
Area: 458,730 square kilometres
Capital: Rabat
Language: Arabic, Berber, French, Spanish
Currency: Dirham

The Islamic kingdom of Morocco became independent of France in 1956, though the Sultan had always enjoyed some degree of control. The sultanate became a kingdom in 1957. The king holds supreme authority over both secular and religious life, though the government is actually carried out by a democratically-elected parliament. The bulk of the state's wealth is based on its rich mineral deposits, particularly phosphates and lead ore, which are extensively mined. Most of the population remains dependent on agriculture, however, and traditional crops of cereals, fruits and tomatoes are prominent. Neighbouring Mauritania renounced its claim to the Western Sahara in 1979, although Saharawi guerrillas seeking independence maintained an armed struggle.

MOZAMBIQUE

Population: 16 million
Area: 799,380 square kilometres
Capital: Maputo
Language: Portuguese, tribal languages
Currency: Metical

The national flag of Mozambique features a book, a hoe and a rifle; symbols which are apt for this poverty-ridden state in southern Africa. From 1977 the Marxist FRELIMO party was the only legal political party in Mozambique. Armed insurgency led by RENAMO continued until an agreement was reached in 1992 ending the civil war. The hoe symbolises the agricultural base of the national economy, which relies on cereals, bananas and various types of nut. There is some relatively substantial industry in the area of Maputo, including steel, engineering, docks and railways, textiles and processing. The long coastline on the Indian Ocean offers fine fishing opportunities.

NAMIBIA

Population: 1.51 million
Area: 826,704 square kilometres
Capital: Windhoek
Language: English, Afrikaans, German
Currency: Namibia Dollar, South African Rand

▲ *A typical Senegalese, Senegal.*

▲ *Fertile river banks, Morocco.*

▼ *Terraced hillsides, Rwanda.*

▲ *Tanandava, Madagascar.*

▲ *Djenné, Mali.*

▲ *A young girl, Mauritania.*

◄ *Lumber workers, Lagos, Nigeria.*   ▼ *A village in Malawi.*

▲ *Refugees in Niger.*

▲ *Oranjemund, Nambia.*

The vast desert state of Namibia gained independence in 1990, after many years of political instability. Cuban troops from Communist Angola backed the SWAPO guerrilla movement, while South Africa attempted to maintain its influence by enforcing a constitution. The independence elections resulted in victory for SWAPO, but not by the margin needed to fulfil its goal of one-party rule. Instead, a multi-party republic was approved. The political struggle was made more bitter by the vast mineral wealth of Namibia, which helps provide one of the highest average incomes on the continent. Diamonds and uranium form the basis of the mineral industry. Most of the people are engaged in stock ranching of either cattle or sheep.

NIGER

Population: 9.46 million
Area: 1,186,408 square kilometres
Capital: Niamey
Language: French, Hausa, Djerma, Fulani
Currency: Franc CFA

In 1996, the president was deposed and parliament dissolved in a bloodless coup. The state was then ruled by a military council. Only around the southwestern borders is Niger a productive agricultural country. Here the Niger River provides water for irrigation and drinking. The bulk of the population is concentrated in this region, where they farm at a subsistence level. The capital, Niamey, stands on the banks of the Niger River and has some small-scale industry. Elsewhere through southern Niger a number of oases permit farming, but away from the Niger River the land is generally devoted to grazing livestock. In the north, which has been subject to Tuareg guerrilla activity, the Sahara makes even grazing virtually impossible.

NIGERIA

Population: 97.22 million
Area: 923,773 square kilometres
Capital: Abuja
Language: English, French, various tribal languages
Currency: Naira

Details regarding Nigeria are somewhat unclear due to years of political instability, marked by coups and civil war. In 1963 the population was reckoned to be 55,670,000, but recent massive growth is known to have taken place. The country's economic figures are equally uncertain. The rich agricultural soil supports thriving farming communities, which produce crops of millet, cassava and yams for local consumption. Export crops include cocoa and groundnuts. Industrial activity has been boosted by rich oil reserves. Nigeria was suspended from the Commonwealth following the execution in 1995 of Ogoni separatist Ken Saro-Wiwa and eight other civil rights activists.

RWANDA

Population: 7.46 million
Area: 26,338 square kilometres
Capital: Kigali
Language: Kinyarwanda, French, English, Swahili
Currency: Rwanda Franc

The Republic of Rwanda became independent in 1962. Independence from Belgium came in the wake of a savage internal struggle between the agricultural Hutu majority and the pastoral Tutsi, who had held power for centuries. More recently, in 1990, rebel Tutsi forces of the Rwandan Patriotic Front invaded from Uganda. The ensuing civil war was marked by genocide, and UN personnel were deployed in an attempt to separate the warring factions. Rwanda is a densely-populated agricultural country producing sweet potatoes and cassava for local use and coffee for sale abroad. The constitution of 1991 permits multi-party democracy.

▲ *Sao Tome, capital of Sao Tome and Principe.*

SAO TOME AND PRINCIPE

Population: 131,100 million
Area: 845 square kilometres
Capital: Sao Tome
Language: Portuguese, Lungwa Sao Tome, Fang
Currency: Dobra

The 1990 constitution established the monopoly of one party, the MLSTP, although a move to democracy was agreed. The economy of the islands is heavily dependent on two agricultural crops: cocoa and copra, and fluctuations in the international markets have great effects upon the country. Attempts have been made to diversify crop production. More success, however, has been achieved in expanding a fishing industry to exploit the vast tuna shoals of the Gulf of Guinea. The flag of the republic features two black stars to symbolise the two islands and carries the green and yellow colours common to many African states.

SENEGAL

Population: 7.97 million
Area: 197,161 square kilometres
Capital: Dakar
Language: French, Wolof, tribal languages
Currency: Franc CFA

In 1960 Senegal became independent of France as part of the Mali Confederacy. After only a few months Senegal withdrew, adding a green star to the Mali flag to proclaim its independence. The nation was a one-party state for some years, but is now a democracy despite several coup attempts. The groundnut, or peanut, was introduced in the 1600s as a cheap food for slaves being transported to the Caribbean, and it remains the country's most important crop. Cotton is also grown for export and attempts at diversifying into other areas have been made. The nation has a good transportation system and this has encouraged modest industrialisation, though this is still largely confined to the capital, Dakar.

SIERRA LEONE

Population: 4.46 million
Area: 73,326 square kilometres
Capital: Freetown
Language: English, Krio, tribal languages
Currency: Leone

Freetown was founded as a settlement for freed slaves by the British in 1787, but the area was not formally taken over as a colony until 1808. When independence came in 1961 Sierra Leone adopted a flag showing blue for the ocean, white for unity and green for agriculture. Military coups occurred in 1992 and 1996. Following the latter, however, presidential and parliamentary elections were held and a new government formed. The vast majority of the population engages in subsistence farming. A small amount of coffee and cocoa is exported, but the country's economy depends mainly on the mining of bauxite, diamonds and molybdenite. Local government is based on tribal units. Each chief is supported by a Council of Elders which is responsible for law and order in the area and which has powers to raise and spend taxes.

SOMALIA

Population: 9.2 million
Area: 637,657 square kilometres
Capital: Mogadishu
Language: Somali, Arabic, English, Italian
Currency: Somali Shilling

Somalia has been plagued by inter-factional fighting, with settled government replaced by anarchy. The Somali people are a widely-scattered nation of herdsmen who range far across the arid grazing lands of the Horn of Africa. Somalia came into being in 1960 when British Somaliland merged with Italian Somalia and became independent. In 1969 General Barre seized power in a coup. A long-running civil war caused him to flee the country in 1991. Severe famine and continuing conflict left the state in crisis. The internal troubles have prevented exploitation of Somalia's iron ore and gypsum, and the development of industry in general. Over three-quarters of the Somalis lead a traditional lifestyle based on cattle, goats, sheep and camels. A few engage in agriculture along the river banks, but this activity is continually under threat from drought.

SOUTH AFRICA

Population: 41.54 million
Area: 1,224,691 square kilometres
Capital: Pretoria
Language: Afrikaans, English, tribal languages
Currency: Rand

Conflict between the white minority and various factions among the black majority overshadowed South African history for many years. In 1991 the government announced the end of the apartheid system, a policy of separate racial development. In 1994 the country held its first non-racial elections, with the African National Congress winning the largest proportion of the vote. South Africa is the wealthiest state in Africa. Its prosperity is founded on the efficient exploitation of a

▲ *A Sudanese group, near Jonglei Canal, Sudan.*

vast mineral wealth and large agricultural potential. Gold is mined in staggering quantity and is the most valuable of several mining exports. Industry is well developed, with food processing, metal smelting and machinery manufacture being the most productive. The massive economic base of South Africa makes several neighbouring countries dependent upon it and attracts large numbers of migrant workers.

SUDAN

Population: 28.9 million
Area: 2,505,813 square kilometres
Capital: Khartoum
Language: Arabic, English, tribal languages
Currency: Sudanese Pound

In 1989 the army overthrew the government and pledged itself to ending the bitter civil war between the Arabic and Islamic north, and the south, where black Africans practising tribal religions form the majority. Despite this pledge armed conflict continues to bring misery to millions of Sudanese. The war, combined with government control of the economy, led to drastic food shortages in 1991-92. The country consists mainly of desert or arid grassland, where cattle, goats and sheep are grazed. Agriculture is concentrated along the Nile and in the south, where irrigation is possible. Cotton and sugar are grown for export, as is gum arabic in the forested southwest. Land devoted to producing food is vulnerable to the periodic droughts of the region. The large mineral reserves are undeveloped due to political instability.

SWAZILAND

Population: 850,628
Area: 17,400 square kilometres
Capital: Mbabane
Language: Swazi, English
Currency: Lilangeni

Sandwiched between Mozambique and South Africa, the Kingdom of Swaziland gained independence from Britain in 1968. There is a House of Assembly and a House of Senators, but also a Swazi National Council at which all Swazi men are entitled to be heard. The flag depicts the traditional shield and spears with which the Swazi successfully defended themselves against Zulu aggression in the early 19th century. Today, Swaziland is a predominantly agricultural country with the bulk of the population being engaged in subsistence farming. European settlers operate large-scale enter-

▲ *The coronation of Mswati III, Swaziland.*

prises producing sugar cane, cirus fruits and cotton for export. Industry is mainly limited to the mining of asbestos, coal and iron ore, chiefly for export.

TANZANIA

Population: 29.7 million
Area: 945,037 square kilometres
Capital: Dodoma
Language: English, Swahili, tribal languages
Currency: Tanzanian Shilling

The republic of Tanzania is made up of over 100 tribes, each with its own language and customs. From 1977 this diverse population was kept together by a government based on a single political party, the leader of which, Ali Mwinyi, won the 1990 presidential election. In 1992 a law was passed introducing multi-party democracy. The nation came into being in 1964, when the African majority on Zanzibar overthrew the Islamic Sultan and joined mainland Tanganyika to form a new republic. Most of the population is engaged in agriculture. Crops such as coconuts, cardamoms and cocoa have been introduced in an attempt to gain export sales. Deposits of several metal ores have recently been found but remain unexploited.

TOGO

Population: 3.5 million
Area: 56,785 square kilometres
Capital: Lomé
Language: French, Ewe, Kabre
Currency: Franc CFA

A white star for hope dominates the flag of Togo. This former German colony passed through French control after World War I before achieving independence in 1960. The first decade of freedom was marred by internal violence and power was eventually seized by the military. A new constitution, however, was approved in 1992. Vast reserves of phosphates, bauxite and iron ore have provided a base for the Togo

▲ *A crowded market, Togo.*

▲ *Mogadishu, Somalia.*

▼ *Ngorongoro Conservation Area, Tanzania.*

▲ *Typical Tunisian architecture.*

▲ *Kampala, Uganda's capital.*

▼ *Vineyards, South Africa.*

economy since exploitation began in 1953. Most of the population is engaged in agriculture on the pockets of fertile land among the inland hills. Maize and cassava are the bulk crops for local consumption, though coffee, cocoa and cotton are produced for export. The short coastline is dotted with fishing villages which reap rich harvests in the tropical waters.

TUNISIA

Population: 8.8 million
Area: 164,150 square kilometres
Capital: Tunis
Language: Arabic, French
Currency: Tunisian Dinar

The Tunisian flag has been in use since 1835 when this was a province of the Turkish Empire, and it retains the crescent, star and red field of the Turkish flag. After a period as a French protectorate, Tunisia became an independent kingdom in 1956 and a republic the following year. Oil fields exist in Tunisia, but are not rich enough to dominate the economy in the same way as in other Arab countries. Mining of lead, iron and zinc ores is also an important source of mineral wealth. Tunisia remains, however, an agricultural nation, with nearly half the working population occupied on farms, mostly in the northern half of the country. Tomatoes, olives and citrus fruits are among the most important crops. Fishing is an important employment along the coast.

UGANDA

Population: 16.67 million
Area: 241,038 square kilometres
Capital: Kampala
Language: English, Kiswahili, tribal languages
Currency: Uganda Shilling

Uganda has experienced several coups and foreign invasions since independence, giving rise to numerous regimes, the most notorious being that of Idi Amin in the 1970s. The nation is made up of numerous tribes, each with its own language and culture. The political troubles have prevented the development of an industrial economy, though there is some copper mining. By contrast, agriculture is well developed and Uganda can feed itself while still producing cotton, sugar cane and coffee for export. Fishing on Lake Victoria is also a major occupation. Uganda was a British protectorate from 1894 to 1961. English is still widely spoken and the bulk of the population is Christian.

▲ *Kapenta drying racks, Zambia.*

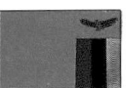

ZAMBIA

Population: 8.94 million
Area: 752,614 square kilometres
Capital: Lusaka
Language: English, tribal languages
Currency: Kwacha

The Zambian economy is almost entirely dependent on copper, thousand of tonnes of which are produced each year. The country is therefore vulnerable to changes on the international commodities market. The bulk of the population is employed in farming, much of it subsistence. Maize and livestock are the main agricultural products, though some sugar cane is produced for export. The development of more sophisticated agriculture is hampered by the tsetse fly and occasional droughts. Independence came to Zambia in 1964, and it was ruled by the United National Independence Party of Kenneth Kaunda until 1991, when multi-party elections were held.

ZIMBABWE

Population: 11.5 million
Area: 390,759 square kilometres
Capital: Harare
Language: English, tribal languages
Currency: Zimbabwe Dollar

Zimbabwe came into being in 1980, when the former white-ruled Rhodesia became a democracy under black rule. President Mugabe moved the nation towards Marxism. The new nation was named after enigmatic stone ruins discovered in the region, which indicated an advanced civilisation that had vanished some centuries earlier. The country has a balanced economy, with mining, industry and agriculture all playing their part. Mining is based on the exploitation of gold, nickel and coal deposits. Agriculture is largely conducted by subsistence farmers producing maize and sorghum. Larger scale farms produce tobacco for export and fruits. The extensive industrial scene is dominated by the processing of mining and agricultural products.

The AMERICAS

*T*he Americas are continents of contrast, where wealth and poverty, wilderness and man-made landscapes can be found in the greatest diversity and extremes.

Stretching from the Arctic Ocean to the chill, stormy waters off Cape Horn, the Americas embrace the full range of climatic zones, from frozen tundra to tropical heat and then to bare, frozen plains again. Nor is the physical geology any less diverse. The vast prairies of Central North America are flat and featureless and the Amazon Basin is a vast, alluvial depression where no land is more than a few metres above sea level. But in the Andes and Rockies the Americas can also boast one of the longest and most rugged mountain chains in the world.

Associated with climatic and geographical variation are those of ecology and habitat. The tropical regions of South and Central America are the site of the largest and most diverse rainforests in the world. These forests cover vast areas of land and contain more species of plants and animals than the rest of the world put together. The sheer beauty and diversity of the rainforests are staggering. Yet it is in the Americas that destruction of the rainforests is at its most widespread. The vast boreal forests of the far north are less under threat, though they are heavily exploited for timber and pulp. Elsewhere, a combination of semi-aridity and suitable temperature produces vast grasslands on which graze huge herds of animals.

The human impact on the Americas has been immense. North America is generally more prosperous and has felt the influence of man more widely than either Central or South America. The open prairies have been emptied of the millions of bison and are now ploughed to produce massive crops of grain to feed the world. Those areas unsuited to grain agriculture are grazed by cattle and sheep, banishing the native fauna to special reserves.

The mineral wealth of the north has been exploited and is still being extracted on a massive scale. Gold, silver, copper and other metals are gouged from the ground in huge quantities by large international companies.

These changes have resulted in a highly developed and prosperous economy for the peoples of North America. Large cities have sprung up across the United States and Canada, with populations numbering into the millions. Roads, railways and flightpaths provide good communications across the northern continent, allowing free trade and transport links further to aid prosperity.

By contrast, much of Central and South America is relatively untouched by human progress and living conditions are generally poorer. Though large areas of rainforest are being destroyed, areas still stand untouched by anything except the activities of hunter-gatherer societies which have co-existed with the forests for millennia. Industry and mining are poorly developed and the bulk of the population relies on farming for a livelihood. Often the farmers operate at subsistence level, barely producing enough for their own needs. Many of the peoples of the interior have little contact with Western-style civilisation. Both in the high Andes and in the dense forests there exist settlements whose inhabitants continue to live as their ancestors have done for generations. Technology and beliefs are much as they have always been, preserving cultures in tune with their surroundings, but giving poor life expectancy and low standards of living.

Many of the nations are poverty stricken and have fragile economies. Though the dominant and more prosperous nations provide aid, the tiny island republics of the Caribbean remain devoid of natural resources and have economies based on the growing of bananas or coconuts and on tourism.

Taken together the Americas provide a startling contrast of landscapes, natural ecologies and human activities. If they are continents of wealth, plenty and beauty, they are also lands where poverty, deprivation and squalor are equally common.

◀ *A hillside dwelling, Colombia.*

▲ Lake and mountain scenery, Colorado, USA.

▶ Prickly Bay Beach, Grenada.

▲ Caracas, capital of Venezuela.

ANTIGUA AND BARBUDA

Population: 63,900
Area: 442 square kilometres
Capital: St John's
Language: English
Currency: Eastern Caribbean Dollar

This nation of three islands takes its name from the two populated islands, the third being Redonda. The islands were discovered by Christopher Columbus in 1493 but Spanish attempts at colonisation failed, as did those of France. Only when British settlers arrived to grow sugar cane in the late 17th century did a permanent settlement result. The sugar crop was abandoned in the 1970s in favour of more diversified agriculture, with cotton and fruit ranking high. The wealth of the nation, however, lies in tourism. This is a paradise for those seeking a relaxing holiday. The government is a democracy based on universal suffrage, with the Queen of Great Britain as Head of State.

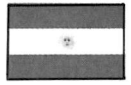

ARGENTINA

Population: 34.77 million
Area: 2,780,400 square kilometres
Capital: Buenos Aires
Language: Spanish
Currency: Peso

As one of the largest and richest countries in South America, Argentina has the potential to become a dominant influence in that region. Internal political troubles, however, have held back the massive growth which is still possible. Military rule was replaced by civilian government in December 1983. A new constitution was adopted in 1994. Argentina has the task of bringing together in harmony the mixed population. The largest ethnic groups are the native Indian peoples, the descendants of Spanish settlers, and more recent European settlers. Sunflower oil and wheat are both produced in quantity, but the largest exports are beef and lamb. Mining is a major contributor to national wealth, with coal, gold, silver and copper all being worked in quantity.

BAHAMAS

Population: 275,700
Area: 13,939 square kilometres
Capital: Nassau
Language: English
Currency: Bahamian Dollar

There are over 1,700 islands and cays in the Bahamas, but only 700 are of any size, and a mere 22 islands are permanently inhabited. The low-lying coral islands support only a thin soil, a fact which has long hampered a more dynamic economy. The agricultural base of the islands remains sugar cane, though livestock and egg production for local consumption are important. Fishing the shallow tropical waters is a thriving industry and fish farming techniques are boosting the catch. The business community is much larger than might be expected, due to the liberal tax laws which have turned the islands into a tax haven for foreign business people. The balmy climate and open beaches have made the islands a centre for tourism, which brings large quantities of foreign currency into the islands.

BARBADOS

Population: 264,300
Area: 430 square kilometres
Capital: Bridgetown
Language: English
Currency: Barbados Dollar

The trident dominates the flag of Barbados, symbolising the wealth of the sea. This is apt for the island has long depended on the sea for its livelihood. The delectable flying fish of the island's waters are a noted delicacy, and during the season hundreds of boats put out in search of these creatures and the high prices they fetch. Recent tourist promotions have boosted the economy, with outsiders flocking to Barbados in search of the warm sea and wide beaches. The island is densely populated, ranking high in the world's population density league, though most of the people live in the countryside. The traditional sugar cane crop, part of which is turned to rum, remains important to the local economy. The country has a democratic constitution with the Queen of Great Britain as Head of State.

BELIZE

Population: 209,500
Area: 22,963 square kilometres
Capital: Belmopan
Language: English, Spanish
Currency: Belize Dollar

The small country of Belize gained its independence from Britain in 1981. A British military garrison remains, however, to provide protection against Guatemala, which claims Belize for its own. Belize has a democratic government operating under a Prime Minister and a two-chamber legislature. Only the coastal region is heavily populated, with the interior being blanketed in dense forests which are, as yet, unexploited. The mainstay of the economy is agriculture, which accounts for much of the country's exports. Sugar cane is the chief crop, followed by citrus fruits which are processed into juice concentrates for export. Maize, rice and livestock are raised for local consumption, making Belize self-sufficient in food.

BERMUDA

Population: 60,144
Area: 53.3 square kilometres
Capital: Hamilton
Language: English
Currency: Bermuda Dollar

The islands of Bermuda lie on the Western Atlantic some 800 kilometres from the North American coast. Only about twenty of the 150 islands are inhabited, the rest being isolated islets and rocky outcrops. The economy is almost entirely reliant on tourism and insurance for survival. Over half a million tourists come to Bermuda each year to enjoy the balmy climate and excellent swimming waters. Several major insurance companies are based here to take advantage of favourable local laws. The islands are officially a colony of the United Kingdom, with a Governor being appointed by the Crown. However, the democratically elected parliament is free to take what action it wishes in all matters other than foreign affairs, defence and the police. The Governor is responsible for these matters.

▲ *A musician performing at a festival, Bolivia.*

BOLIVIA

Population: 8.07 million
Area: 1,098,581 square kilometres
Capital: Sucre
Language: Spanish, Aymara, Quechua
Currency: Boliviano

Bolivia has been landlocked since it lost its coastline to Chile in 1884, and all exports must leave via other nations, predominantly along the

▲ *Kings Landing Historical Settlement, Canada.*

▼ *English Harbour, Antigua.*

▲ *Normans Cays and Exuma Cays, Bahamas.*

▼ *Village children in Belize.*

▲ *A landscape in southern Chile.*

Below left: *Hawkins Island, Bermuda.*

▼ *The Careenage, Bridgetown, Barbados.*

◄ *Cartago, former capital of Costa Rica.*

▼ *Buenos Aires, Argentina.*

rail link to the Chilean town of Arica. The vast bulk of these exports are minerals, with tin leading the field by a large margin. It is planned to expand the smelting capacity of Bolivia so that more tin ore can be processed before export. Silver and gold are exploited in smaller quantities, as is zinc. The agricultural output includes coffee and potatoes grown in the mountains, together with increasing quantities of sugar cane and cotton in the eastern lowlands. Coca is a traditional crop which has recently boomed as a source of cocaine. The United States is sponsoring a government programme to destroy the coca crop. Bolivia is notoriously unstable politically, having experienced fourteen presidents and a military junta since 1966.

▲ *Rio de Janeiro, Brazil.*

BRAZIL

Population: 155.8 million
Area: 8,547,404 square kilometres
Capital: Brasilia
Language: Portuguese
Currency: Real

The present democratic constitution of Brazil came into being in 1988 after two decades of military rule. The country is the only South American state with Portuguese as the official language, a fact that dates back to a treaty between Spain and Portugal in 1494. The southern and eastern regions are the best developed and it is here that agriculture and industry are most heavily concentrated. Coffee is by far the most important crop,

with vast tonnages produced each year for export. Various other tropical crops such as sugar cane, cotton, cassava and citrus fruits are also important. Industry is based on the exploitation of crops and minerals such as quartz, thorium, zirconium and chromium. The vast Amazon Basin contains the largest rainforest in the world, with an incredible diversity of wildlife. Conservationists throughout the world are concerned as large areas of this forest are felled each year to make way for grazing land and to extract the valuable timber.

CANADA

Population: 29.96 million
Area: 9,970,610 square kilometres
Capital: Ottawa
Language: English, French
Currency: Canadian Dollar

As the second largest country in area in the world, Canada has a surprisingly small population. The reason for this is that the vast majority of Canada's land lies in the harsh northern latitudes, where tundra or boreal forest cover the ground. The population is concentrated in the southern region, where the climate is kinder and agriculture is possible. Wheat production is the basis of the agricultural economy, with nearly 900 million bushels being produced each year. Beef output is almost as important, while market gardening and fur farming are important in certain localities. Vast mineral reserves include nickel, zinc, copper and gold. The industrial scene is highly diversified, with a wide range of products being produced both for internal consumption and for export. Canada is a federal democracy with each of the provinces retaining considerable powers. Demands for provincial independence have been made, particularly by Quebec.

CHILE

Population: 14.66 million
Area: 736,905 square kilometres
Capital: Santiago
Language: Spanish
Currency: Chilean Peso

The long, narrow strip of territory which makes up Chile is defined by the Pacific Ocean on the west and the watershed of the Andes on the east. The mountainous terrain has inhibited both communications and economic development and Chile remains one of the poorer South American states. Nonetheless the nation has some potential. The north has rich mineral deposits and these are being exploited on a large scale. Agriculture is restricted to valleys

and terraced highlands. The most important crops are fruits such as apples, plums and citrus fruits. Chile has had a chequered political history, with military coups and a Marxist government featuring strongly. In 1989 the military regime handed rule over to a democratically-elected civilian government, but retained some powers for itself.

COLOMBIA

Population: 34.5 million
Area: 1,141,748 square kilometres
Capital: Bogota
Language: Spanish
Currency: Colombian Peso

When Colombia won independence from Spain in 1819 it included modern Panama, Venezuela and Ecuador within its frontiers. These states broke away in 1830 and 1903, while an internal revolution stripped the remaining areas of power and centralised it in Bogota. Guerrilla forces remain in the country, as does the potential for political violence. The nation is perhaps best known for its coffee, which remains an important crop. Rubber is also cultivated, but the dominant food crops are potatoes and rice. The coca crop forms the basis of a flourishing cocaine trade and the government is engaged in a bitter struggle with drug barons to stamp out the industry. Minerals are found in abundance in Colombia, with gold and silver being the most important. The country also provides about half of world production of emeralds, which are exported in quantity.

COSTA RICA

Population: 3.37 million
Area: 51,100 square kilometres
Capital: San Jose
Language: Spanish
Currency: Costa Rican Colon

Named 'The Rich Coast' when first discovered by Spain in the 16th century, Costa Rica has continued to support a thriving economy despite periodic disturbances. The nation is unusual in that its constitution forbids the raising of an army for any reason. However, the para-military Civil Guard undertakes many duties usually carried out by the army in other nations. Agriculture forms the basis of the economy, with the traditional crops of coffee and bananas still dominating. A burgeoning industrial sector concentrates on processing local products. Since a civil war in 1948 government has been relatively stable and the constitution of 1949 is still in force.

CUBA

Population: 10.98 million
Area: 110,860 square kilometres
Capital: Havana
Language: Spanish
Currency: Cuban Peso

It is ironic that the Cuban flag is based on that of the United States, with a triangle added to symbolise Freemasonry, for the present regime is openly hostile to the United States and has a Communist system. The present flag dates to 1849 and remained unchanged when Fidel Castro seized power in 1959. Since then Castro has pursued a Marxist-Leninist programme and has lent support to similar movements in Third World nations. Agriculture remains the basis of the Cuban economy, with the traditional sugar cane being the chief crop. Tobacco growing is also important, as is cotton. Fishing is a major export earner, with numerous small craft putting out to fish the surrounding waters. Mining and associated processes make up the bulk of the industrial sector, with iron and nickel leading the production tables.

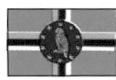

DOMINICA

Population: 74,200
Area: 748.5 square kilometres
Capital: Roseau
Language: English, French Creole
Currency: East Caribbean Dollar

The tiny nation state of Dominica is a democratic republic within the Commonwealth and is one of the poorer Caribbean states. The economy is heavily reliant on agriculture. Bananas and coconuts are the principal crops, both of which are vulnerable to international price fluctuations. The crops are periodically devastated by hurricanes, bringing disaster to the country. Fishing promises to increase significantly and remove the dangerous reliance on agriculture. Tourism is also growing as visitors come to enjoy the sun on the broad sandy beaches of the island. The inland mountains have a diverse wildlife population, including a unique species of parrot, the Sisserou, which features on the national flag.

DOMINICAN REPUBLIC

Population: 7.77 million
Area: 48,442 square kilometres
Capital: Santo Domingo
Language: Spanish
Currency: Peso Oro

The capital city of the Dominican Republic is the oldest European city in the Americas, having been founded by Bartholomew Columbus in 1496. During the bitter colonial struggles of the 18th century the western area of Hispaniola was captured by France, but the eastern section remained under Spanish control and this now forms the Dominican Republic. The nation became independent in 1844, since when it has experienced political instability and periods of occupation by United States troops. The economy remains dependent on sugar cane, with sugar refining the main industry. Sugar accounts for about a quarter of all exports, though coffee and cocoa also earn foreign cash. Minerals being exploited include bauxite, gold and silver.

ECUADOR

Population: 11.7 million
Area: approx 300,000 square kilometres
Capital: Quito
Language: Spanish, Quechua
Currency: Sucre

Perched high in the Andes, the capital of Ecuador, Quito, has witnessed much political instability since independence from Colombia in 1830. The last few decades have seen many changes of government, and confused party loyalties complicate the power structure. There have been continual disputes with Peru over the border territories and this quarrel has occasionally erupted into armed conflict. The discovery of oil in the rainforest region has helped boost the underdeveloped economy but has added fuel to the dispute with Peru. The mountains and coastal regions are the centre of agriculture, much of which is carried out at subsistence level by the Quechua Indians. Foreign currency is earned by the export of coffee, bananas and cocoa.

EL SALVADOR

Population: 5.05 million
Area: 21,041 square kilometres
Capital: San Salvador
Language: Spanish
Currency: Salvadoran Colon

Civil war and acts of terrorism dominated the political scene of El Salvador throughout the 1980s, but by 1992 the Farabundo Marti National Liberation Front (FMLN) guerrillas agreed to demobilize. The country is densely populated, and nearly every piece of fertile land is now under cultivation. Coffee and sugar are the main cash crops for export but large quantities of maize, beans and sorghum are produced for local consumption. There are few mineral resources, hence industry is based on food processing and

▲ A rural scene in Ecuador.

◀ Punta Cana, Dominican Republic.

▶ A diver at Acapulco, Mexico.

▼ Scotts Head Peninsula Dominica.

▼ Women washing clothes, Guatemala.

▲ Cigar maker in Havana, Cuba.

▲ An agricultural scene, Haiti.

▶ Cutting cane, El Salvador.

▲ *A coconut palm plantation, Guyana.*

▲ *Tegucigalpa, capital of Honduras..*

the supply of internal requirements for clothing and other similar items. The interior forests are being exploited for commercial gain, principally for timber and tropical gums. The mixed-blood mestizos form the large majority of the people.

GRENADA

Population: 96,000
Area: 345 square kilometres
Capital: St George's
Language: English, French-African patois
Currency: Eastern Caribbean Dollar

Since independence from Britain in 1974 Grenada has remained within the Commonwealth but has experienced violent changes of government. In 1979 the democratic government was overthrown by a Marxist coup, which was followed by an army takeover in 1983 and an almost immediate invasion by United States troops at the request of neighbouring nations worried by the turn of events. Democracy was soon restored. The economy is based on agriculture and tourism, which together account for almost all foreign earnings. The local agriculture has traditionally specialised in tropical spices, with nutmeg – which features on Grenada's flag – and mace remaining valuable crops.

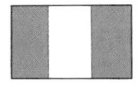

GUATEMALA

Population: 10.62 million
Area: 108,889 square kilometres
Capital: Guatemala City
Language: Spanish, Mayan languages
Currency: Quetzal

As with most Central American states, Guatemala has experienced periods of revolution, civil war and dictatorship. A constitution introduced in 1986 restored democracy and free elections were held in 1990. The ancient Mayan civilisation dominated the region before the arrival of Spanish colonists, and Mayan is still spoken by the Indian population. Most of the people are of Spanish descent or have adopted Spanish culture. The nation relies on agricultural produce for export earnings. Coffee alone accounts for nearly half of exports by value, with cotton, bananas and sugar making up much of the remainder. The bulk of the population is concentrated in the farming regions of the south.

GUYANA

Population: 730,000
Area: 214,969 square kilometres
Capital: Georgetown
Language: English
Currency: Guyana Dollar

The original inhabitants of Guyana, the local Indian tribes now make up barely ten percent of the population and live mainly in the southern highlands. The fertile coastal region is densely populated by the descendants of settlers and slaves of African, Indonesian, European and Chinese racial origins. These racial divides are reflected in the nation's politics, with parties often basing their support on the interests of sections of the population. The wealth of the nation lies in the agriculture of the coastal plain, where sugar cane and rice are grown in large quantities. Tropical fruits are also important crops and much is exported. The exploitation of minerals, particularly bauxite and diamonds, adds to the export drive.

HAITI

Population: 6.76 million
Area: 27,750 square kilometres
Capital: Port-au-Prince
Language: Créole, French
Currency: Gourde

With an economy based on subsistence farming mixed with some cash crops, Haiti is one of the poorest American nations. Haitian coffee commands a high price; however, insufficient farming methods ensure that the business is of only limited profitability. Sugar and rum are also exported, but again without producing dramatic profits. Haiti became the first black-governed republic when the slaves revolted in 1791, and won independence from France in 1804. After periods as a republic, kingdom and empire, Haiti fell under United States occupation before regaining independence in 1934. Between 1957 and 1986 the country was ruled by the notorious Duvalier regime. In 1991 a military junta seized power, but had to stand down in 1994 with the arrival of US troops.

HONDURAS

Population: 5.29 million
Area: 112,088 square kilometres
Capital: Tegucigalpa
Language: Spanish
Currency: Lempira

In 1821 Honduras joined with El Salvador, Guatemala, Costa Rica and Nicaragua to declare independence from Spain. Once colonial rule had been ended, however, the union fell apart and Honduras became fully independent in 1838. Since then the nation has been subject to coups and military rule alternating with periods of democracy, one of which began in 1982. The mountainous interior and continual troubles have combined to ensure that Honduras remains economically backward. The wealth of the nation is derived from two crops, bananas and coffee, which together account for nearly all exports by value. Increasingly heavy catches of lobster and shrimp are beginning to feature in the economy. There is some small-scale mining and industrial activity.

JAMAICA

Population: 2.5 million
Area: 11,425 square kilometres
Capital: Kingston
Language: English
Currency: Jamaican Dollar

Though comparatively wealthy by Caribbean standards, Jamaica has continued to be troubled by a degree of poverty and periodic unemployment. The democracy established on independence in 1962 remains in force. The island nation has a mixed economy better able to withstand international price fluctuations than others in the region. Agriculture is dominated by the traditional Caribbean crops of sugar cane, bananas and citrus fruits, though less usual products such as spices are also to be found. The bulk of exports, however, are created through the mining of bauxite and gypsum. A substantial influence in the local business community, and the island's culture, is tourism. Over a million visitors come to the island each year and pump large quantities of cash into the economy.

▲ *St Elizabeth, Jamaica.*

MEXICO

Population: 91.12 million
Area: 1,967,183 square kilometres
Capital: Mexico City
Language: Spanish
Currency: Mexican Peso

Carved out of Central America by invading Spaniards, Mexico was formerly the territory of the Aztecs and other tribes that had established sophisticated civilisations. Today, the bulk of the population is of mixed blood, though substantial minorities of both

Indians and Spaniards remain. Once notorious for revolutions and bandits, Mexico has preserved its democratic constitution since 1917 and is now a relatively wealthy Central American nation. This wealth is largely based on oil reserves and a booming tourist business. Silver, iron and uranium are also important minerals. Many people live on the land, producing maize, potatoes, fruits and wheat for internal markets.

NICARAGUA

Population: 4.4 million
Area: 130,671 square kilometres
Capital: Managua
Language: Spanish, English
Currency: Cordoba

After being linked with other Central American territories, Nicaragua became completely independent in 1838. Although it has a democratic constitution, a state of civil war existed for many years and civil liberties were much curtailed. The country has remained largely under-developed, with agriculture continuing to employ most of the population. Crops of maize, rice and beans are raised for internal consumption, often by farmers operating at a subsistence level. Coffee, cotton, bananas and sugar make up the bulk of exports, though significant quantities of gold and silver are mined.

PANAMA

Population: 2.33 million
Area: 75,517 square kilometres
Capital: Panama City
Language: Spanish
Currency: Balboa

The Panama Canal has dominated Panamanian history and its economy ever since the nation came into being. Indeed, the province of Panama declared itself independent of Colombia in 1903 because the Colombian government had refused to sanction the construction of the canal, which eventually opened in 1914. The land flanking it was held by the United States, but was returned to Panama in 1979. The late 1980s saw a succession of Presidents as power was manipulated by General Noriega. In 1989 the United States invaded the country and removed Noriega from control. Despite the economic dominance of the canal, food processing and manu-facturing industries are important. Agriculture is restricted due to the lack of fertile ground and provides less than half of the nation's food.

PARAGUAY

Population: 4.9 million
Area: 406,752 square kilometres
Capital: Asuncion
Language: Spanish, Guarani
Currency: Guarani

West of the Paraguay River is a vast region of open grasslands known as the Chaco, where the Guarani ranch cattle. The bulk of the population is of mixed Guarani and Spanish ancestry and inhabits the more fertile southeastern parts of the country. Cassava, maize and beans are produced in large quantities for local consumption, though coffee and tobacco are raised as cash crops. Industry is chiefly concerned with processing agricultural products as the mineral wealth of Paraguay is negligible. There is great potential for hydro-electricity and the largest such complex in the world stands at Itaipu. A 1989 coup overthrew General Stroessner, who had held power since 1956, replacing him with General Rodriguez. In 1992 a new constitution was approved, forbidding the re-election of the President.

PERU

Population: 23.85 million
Area: 1,244,284 square kilometres
Capital: Lima
Language: Spanish, Quechua, Aymara
Currency: Nuevo Sol

Peru is unusual in that the bulk of its population is composed of indigenous Indians, with the Europeans and mixed-ancestry mestizo in the minority. The Indians belong to the Aymara and Quechua tribal groups and generally lead traditional lifestyles in the Andes. The isolated villages and subsistence economy of the Indians have kept them outside the mainstream of Peruvian politics and national life. Along the coastal fringe coffee, cotton and sugar are produced as cash crops. Industrial activity is concentrated around the capital and is composed largely of iron and zinc works. Although there is a democratic constitution, the government of Peru has been notoriously volatile.

ST KITTS AND NEVIS

Population: 43,350
Area: 261.6 square kilometres
Capital: Basseterre
Language: English
Currency: East Caribbean Dollar

The tiny state of St Kitts and Nevis is populated almost entirely by the descendants of African slaves brought to the Caribbean during the 18th century, when sugar cane was the economic mainstay of the area. Sugar remains the major crop on the islands and industry concentrates on sugar refining. Cotton is the secondary crop and livestock is raised for local uses. Tourism is a welcome source of income for many of the citizens. After gaining internal self-government in 1967 the islands became fully independent in 1983. The islands have a democratic constitution and in June 1996 Nevis began legal action to secede from St Kitts.

ST LUCIA

Population: 140,900
Area: 617 square kilometres
Capital: Castries
Language: English, French
Currency: East Caribbean Dollar

When St Lucia was granted self-government in 1967 a competition was launched to design a flag, and the winning entry remains the national flag now that full independence has been achieved. The blue background symbolises the ocean, the black triangle represents the volcanic peak of Mount Gimie and the yellow signifies the sun. Since independence in 1979 St Lucia has struggled to diversify its economy and prevent urban deprivation. Bananas, cocoa and coconuts remain important crops, together with spices, citrus fruits, laundry soap, rum, beverages, electronic assembly and clothing. Tourism is significant, with more people visiting the islands each year than actually live there.

ST VINCENT AND THE GRENADINES

Population: 109,000
Area: 388 square kilometres
Capital: Kingstown
Language: English, French
Currency: East Caribbean Dollar

During the 18th century the sugar plantations of the Caribbean were a rich source of wealth, and they prompted rivalries between European powers. St Vincent was agreed to be neutral territory, but fighting between the British and French soon reached the island, which became a British colony in 1783. The islands achieved independence in 1979, since when the agricultural and tourist industries have continued to flourish. Agriculture is based upon bananas, cocoa, avocado pears and other tropical crops. Tourism attracts over 120,000 visitors each year, who come in search of the balmy climate and broad beaches lapped by warm waters. The constitution allows for a single elected chamber under the Governor General, who acts on behalf of the Queen of Great Britain.

SURINAME

Population: 407,000
Area: 163,820 square kilometres
Capital: Paramaribo
Language: Dutch, Spanish, English
Currency: Suriname Guilder

In 1667 Britain exchanged Suriname for Manhattan in a deal with the Netherlands. Dutch rule continued until 1975, when the nation gained independence. Since that time Suriname has been troubled by volatile politics and ethnic diversity. The major population groups are Indonesians and Creoles, with mixed European and black ancestry, but significant numbers of Chinese, Javanese and blacks form minority communities. The dense inland forests are inhabited by indigenous Indian tribes. Since independence there were several coups before democracy was established in 1988. A military coup in 1990 ousted the government, and there followed a period of instability. The country has a flourishing economy based on mining for bauxite.

TRINIDAD AND TOBAGO

Population: 1.27 million
Area: 5,128 square kilometres
Capital: Port-of-Spain
Language: English
Currency: Trinidad and Tobago Dollar

The two islands which make up this nation were joined administratively by Britain in 1889, but differences remain marked. Tobago has gained the right of limited self-government after agitation against control from Trinidad. The population of Tobago is almost entirely composed of the descendants of African slaves, while Trinidad has a more mixed people. As with other Caribbean islands Trinidad and Tobago produce quantities of cocoa, sugar and other tropical products and enjoys a thriving tourist business. However, the basis of the economy is oil, with major fields existing both on Trinidad and offshore. Un-employment remains high and substantial parts of the population suffer poverty despite government attempts to alleviate the situation.

UNITED STATES OF AMERICA

Population: 265.62 million
Area: 9,809,155 square kilometres
Capital: Washington, D. C.
Language: English
Currency: US Dollar

The United States is a dominant world economic power. All sectors of the economy are highly developed and extremely

▲ *Nevis Peak, St Kitts-Nevis.*

▲ *Washing clothes, Nicaragua.*

▲ *Machu Picchu, Peru.*

▼ *Loading a schooner, St Vincent.*

▼ *Punta del Este, Uruguay.*

▼ *Paramaribo, Suriname.*

▲ *Englishman's Bay, Trinidad and Tobago.*

▼ *The Panama Canal, Panama.*

▲ *Petit Piton and Soufrière, St Lucia.*

▶ *Asuncion, Paraguay.*

productive. Throughout the large area occupied by the nation deposits of a wide range of minerals, including oil, coal and various metals are found. The fertile soils are extensively farmed to produce huge crops; over two billion bushels of wheat alone. Industry is highly developed with high-tech industries leading the world in developing new processes. In other fields, too, the United States leads the industries of the world with a highly diversified range of businesses producing almost every type of goods imaginable. The nation is a democratic federal union of fifty states in which individual states have some rights of self-government, but the most important powers are held by the central administration.

URUGUAY

Population: 3.2 million
Area: 176,215 square kilometres
Capital: Montevideo
Language: Spanish
Currency: Uruguayan Peso

A province of Brazil until it won its independence in 1828 after a brief war, in which Uruguay enjoyed Argentinian support. Uruguay then adopted a flag sharing the same colours and the Sun of May symbol as Argentina. In 1989 democratic elections were held after more than a decade of military intervention in government. The chief wealth of Uruguay is its land, which supports a flourishing pastoral economy. There are about eleven million cattle and twenty-five million sheep grazing on the rich grasslands of Uruguay, together with large numbers of farm animals. The processing of meat and leather are major industries in Uruguay, as is the spinning and weaving of wool. The nation has virtually no mineral resources and only a limited industrial base.

VENEZUELA

Population: 20.41 million
Area: 912,050 square kilometres
Capital: Caracas
Language: Spanish
Currency: Bolivar

The Republic of Venezuela came into being in 1830, when the area broke away from Colombia just nine years after jointly winning independence from Spain. Venezuela is much more heavily dependant on industry than most other South American nations and has large and densely populated cities. Nearly ninety percent of the population lives in towns, far more than in neighbouring states. Vast oil reserves have been discovered and are being exploited. More established is the mining of bauxite, which supports an aluminium smelting business. Iron ore similarly forms the basis of a metal working industry. Agriculture has steadily declined in importance, with more than half of those employed in agriculture living at subsistence level.

AUSTRALASIA

*T*he nations of Australasia do not occupy a single continental entity, as do those of Asia, Africa or Europe. Instead they are united by cultural and ethnic traits more closely linked to the human populations than to the geographical limits of that region commonly called Australasia.

Strictly speaking, Australasia consists of the island continent of Australia, New Guinea, the Solomon Islands and possibly New Caledonia and New Zealand, though these latter are separate geological entities. The remaining islands strung across the vast spaces of the Pacific are isolated outcrops of volcanic rock or coral reefs with no geological or geographical connection unifying them.

These far flung islands and islets are, however, united by their human inhabitants. Several centuries ago, the ancestors of Polynesian and Melanesian islanders sailed across the vast, open stretches of the Pacific Ocean from Southeast Asia to colonise the remote islands of the tropical and sub-tropical regions. With them they brought taro, yams and other tropical crops with which to support themselves. Common ties of culture and religion bound these peoples together. Long voyages in open canoes were often undertaken between the various islands, preserving ties of technology and belief.

When European seamen arrived, from the 16th century onwards, they found the islands densely inhabited by peoples so similar that the entire region of Oceania came to be viewed as a cultural entity. European settlers and missionaries radically altered the society and cultures of the islands, though many features of Polynesian society remain even today.

The modern nations of Australasia are clearly divided into cultural and physical regions. The divides between the regions has as much to do with the economies and lifestyles of the peoples as with the physical location of the islands.

Dominating all is the great landmass of Australia. The Australian nation has a mixed culture based on the various immigrant groups, chiefly from Europe. To a much lesser extent Australian culture rests on the indigenous Aboriginal peoples who are now largely restricted to the Outback. The bulk of Australia is covered by arid deserts, where settlements are few and far between. The only populous centres are mining towns thriving on the exploitation of the rich mineral content of the nation's rocks.

Kinder climatic regions around the coasts are more densely populated, with farming communities producing crops according to the prevailing climate. All the major cities are on the coast, centred on the sites of historic ports. Here the population is engaged in industrial and service occupations more akin to developed western economies than to the prevailing culture of Australasia.

Sharing much of the flavour of Australia is New Zealand, with its largely European population and small indigenous element. The economy and lifestyle here is more rural than in Australia, while the temperate climate dictates the crops and livestock which can be produced.

Away from these economic giants of the region, the nations are far smaller and less developed, though the original cultures are more apparent. Nations may be as small as a single island with a population of just 7,000. The largest consist of archipelagoes spread across thousands of square kilometres of ocean, but even these never top one million in population. The cultures of the smaller nations are closely allied to the indigenous peoples. Christianity has generally replaced the violent ceremonies and beliefs of the former religions, and settlers from Europe and elsewhere often form sizeable minorities among the population.

The disparate nations of Australasia form a complex pattern of human adaptation to harsh environments. From the Australian deserts to the open ocean, Australasia is a place of extremes and superlatives. The differing cultures of European settlers and native populations are sometimes blended together and elsewhere stand in stark contrast to each other. But everywhere there is the great Pacific Ocean, dividing the nations and yet uniting them.

▲ *Mount Tasman, New Zealand.*

▶ *A native girl on the beach, Kiribati.*

◀ *The world-famous Opera House, Sydney, Australia.*

AUSTRALIA

Population: 18.3 million
Area: 7,682,300 square kilometres
Capital: Canberra
Language: English
Currency: Australian Dollar

The vast nation continent of Australia was the last major landmass to be discovered by Europeans, remaining largely unknown until the 18th century. Immigration initially from Great Britain but later from the rest of Europe, and most recently from Asia, produced the dominant social profile of modern Australia. The extensive grazing lands support large numbers of sheep and cattle, while the smaller areas of arable land produce wheat, rice and market crops. The large desert regions are rich in mineral deposits. Industry is well developed, with a wide range of consumer goods and engineering equipment being produced. The nation is a federation of six states, with the central government being responsible for the Northern Territory. It came into being on the first day of the 20th century, when former British colonies joined to form the Commonwealth of Australia.

FIJI

Population: 803,500
Area: 18,333 square kilometres
Capital: Suva
Language: English, Fijian, Hindustani
Currency: Fiji Dollar

Britain annexed the 330 islands of Fiji in 1874 and stamped out the endemic tribal warfare. Independence was granted in 1970 and a troubled history has resulted. The population is almost equally divided between native Fijians of Melanesian and Polynesian ancestry and immigrants from India, who arrived during British rule. In 1987 an Indian coalition won power in Parliament. Within months a coup organised by the native Fijians placed the army in power. A new constitution has been imposed, which places political power in the hands of the native Fijians. The economy is based on agriculture, with sugar cane, coconuts and ginger being the primary crops. Industry is concentrated on processing the crops, while mineral wealth is restricted to two small gold mines.

KIRIBATI

Population: 80,000
Area: 717.1 square kilometres
Capital: Tarawa
Language: English, Gilbertese
Currency: Australian Dollar

Although Kiribati is independent it has no currency of its own, and its citizens use the Australian dollar.

The islands are generally small but are spread over an immense area of the Pacific Ocean, being grouped into three coral archipelagos and one volcanic island. The islands voluntarily became British protectorates in 1892 and regained independence in 1979. The democratically-elected government consists of one chamber and a President. The agricultural economy relies almost exclusively on coconuts and copra, which make up over ninety percent of exports by value. The coconut tree grows well in the thin soil and tropical climate of Kiribati. Pigs, chickens and breadfruit are produced for local consumption, as is a local vegetable named *babai*.

MARSHALL ISLANDS

Population: 58,500
Area: 181 square kilometres
Capital: Dalap-Uliga-Darrit
Language: Marshallese, English
Currency: US Dollar

The Marshall Islands, an independent member of the United Nations since 1991, is an archipelago of coral atolls and islands in the Western Pacific. The state is made up of two strings of islands, the eastern and western. The form of government is a republic, headed by a president. Tourism and agriculture sustain the economy.

MICRONESIA

Population: 104,724
Area: 701 square kilometres
Capital: Palikir
Language: English, indigenous languages
Currency: US Dollar

The Federated States of Micronesia, until independence in 1991 better known as the Caroline Islands, had been under U.S. rule since World War II. During their history the islands were controlled by Spain, Germany and Japan. Made up of more than 500 islands in the Western Pacific, the primarily agricultural nation is a member of the United Nations.

NAURU

Population: 8,100
Area: 21.3 square kilometres
Capital: Yaren
Language: Nauruan, English
Currency: Australian Dollar

With a population among the lowest in the world, Nauru does not support its own currency, using instead the Australian dollar. The population is a mix of Polynesians and Melanesians who arrived generations ago and have merged to produce a single racial group. The island fell under German control in 1888, passed to Australia in 1914, and became independent in 1968. The

▲ *An isolated beach, Nauru.*

▶ *A highly-decorated native, Papua New Guinea.*

▲ *Lefaga Beach, Upolu, Western Samoa.*

◀ *Yasur volcano, Vanuatu.*

▼ *Mananuca Islands, Fiji.*

traditional crop of coconuts is widely grown and exported, while vegetables and livestock are kept for local consumption. The nation's wealth, however, depends on phosphates mined on the island. This gives Nauru the highest per capita income in the Pacific islands.

NEW ZEALAND

Population: 3.66 million
Area: 270,534 square kilometres
Capital: Wellington
Language: English, Maori
Currency: New Zealand Dollar

Descendants of European immigrants form the bulk of New Zealand's population, though the native Maori are the largest minority. The exports of New Zealand have traditionally been agricultural and the pattern continues, with chilled meat, live animals, dairy products and wool far outstripping manufactured goods in value. However, industry is of growing importance internally, with iron and steel works and aluminium smelting being the largest heavy industrial works. The government is based on universal suffrage, though some seats in the Assembly are reserved for Maoris and have an exclusively Maori electorate.

PALAU

Population: 18,000
Area: 1,632square kilometres
Capital: Koror
Language: Palauan, English
Currency: US Dollar

This Western Pacific archipelago was acquired by Spain in 1886, but changed hands several times thereafter. A Compact of Free Association with the United States provides financial assistance in return for military facilities. Palau became an independent republic in 1994. Tuna fishing is the main industry and tourism is also a major source of income.

PAPUA NEW GUINEA

Population: 3.85 million
Area: 462,840 square kilometres
Capital: Port Moresby
Language: English, Motu, tribal languages
Currency: Kina

The rugged highlands of New Guinea are divided into isolated, densely forested valleys in which travel is difficult and communications poor. The numerous tribes speak as many as 700 different languages, though the Motu form of pidgin English is a common *lingua franca*. Many of these tribes were untouched by the outside world, having no knowledge of whites until the 1940s, and they still lead traditional lifestyles. Agriculture for export is concentrated around the coasts and produces coffee, copra and cocoa. Gold is mined on a commercial scale and there are large copper reserves on the island of Bougainville.

SAMOA

Population: 163,000
Area: 2,830.8 square kilometres
Capital: Apia
Language: Samoan, English
Currency: Tala

Formerly a German colony governed from 1920 by New Zealand, Samoa became independent in 1962. His Highness Malietoa Tanumafili became head of state for life, but after his death future heads of state are due to be elected. Though now independent, Samoa maintains direct diplomatic links only within the Pacific. Elsewhere New Zealand acts on its behalf. The economy of the island is basically agricultural, with coconuts, bananas and cocoa being the most important crops. Despite the tropical climate and a marked dry season, tourism is only poorly developed. Industry is limited to the processing of agricultural products.

SOLOMON ISLANDS

Population: 349,500
Area: 28,370 square kilometres
Capital: Honiara
Language: English, tribal languages
Currency: Solomon Island Dollar

The Melanesian tribes of the Solomons retained their freedom until Britain declared a protectorate in 1893. The Japanese invaded during World War II, and Britain granted full independence in 1978. The country is governed by a Parliament elected by universal suffrage. The Head of State – the British monarch – is represented by a Governor-General. The islands are predominantly agricultural, with property ownership held collectively by tribes and clans. Cocoa and coconuts are grown for export while yams, taro and sweet potatoes are consumed locally. The large fishing fleet exploits the tuna shoals of the region and the catch is canned before export.

TONGA

Population: 103,000
Area: 748 square kilometres
Capital: Nuku'alofa
Language: Tongan, English
Currency: Pa'anga

The kingdom of Tonga dates back to the early 19th century, when the warlike King Tupou of the Ha'apai conquered all the island tribes. Tupou overthrew the rule of petty chiefs and established a rudimentary democracy before Britain declared a protectorate in 1899. Internal government continued under the royal family and full independence came in 1970. The present constitution is based on that of King Tupou. The Assembly consists of nine chiefs elected by the chiefs, nine representatives elected by the people and eleven privy councillors appointed by the king. The main exports are coconuts, fish and vanilla, while tourism brings in much foreign capital. Industry is virtually non-existent.

TUVALU

Population: 10,090
Area: 24 square kilometres
Capital: Fongafale
Language: Tuvaluan, English
Currency: Australian Dollar

As with other tiny Pacific states, Tuvalu uses the Australian dollar. However, it mints its own coins with unique and attractive designs. A British protectorate from 1892 to 1978, Tuvalu has a Parliament elected by universal suffrage and consisting of just twelve members, four of whom are ministers. There are no political parties and candidates stand as individuals. The nine islands that make up the group are coral atolls with thin soils capable of supporting little other than coconut trees. Coconuts and copra are the main exports, with vegetables being grown for local consumption. The flag is highly symbolic, with the blue field representing the Pacific Ocean, the nine stars the nine islands, and the Union Jack standing for membership of the Commonwealth.

VANUATU

Population: 160,000
Area: 12,190 square kilometres
Capital: Vila
Language: Bislama, English, French
Currency: Vatu

On independence in 1980 the islands changed their name from New Hebrides to Vanuatu. The former name was given by Captain Cook because the rugged mountainous interiors reminded him of the Scottish islands. Power resides in an elected Parliament together with the tribal chiefs who sit in a separate Council. The Council advises primarily on matters of custom and tradition. Coconut, cocoa and coffee, which flourish in the hot, moist climate, are the basis of the economy. A livestock industry based on cattle is becoming established. Tropical crops such as yams and taro are grown for local markets. Industry is limited to processing export crops and freezing the local catch.

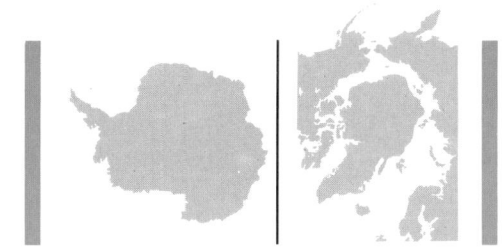

POLAR REGIONS

*T*he polar regions have an image of being blizzard-swept wastes inhabited only by penguins and polar bears. In fact the polar regions are far more than that. It is true that both the North and South Poles are ice-bound throughout the year, but the wildlife of the regions is incredibly varied. In the north polar bears, seals and whales make up the mammal population and the oceans are teeming with fish. The south, which has the advantage of a solid rock continent, is home to a variety of fauna, including penguins.

Both poles have been divided between various nations which maintain scientific bases and conduct research. As the Arctic is open ocean beneath the ice, it is technically not subject to any state. However, those nations that have Arctic coasts maintain various bases, often military, in the area and patrol it regularly.

The political situation of Antarctica is more fraught. Officially, the vast continent is divided between Australia, New Zealand, France, Norway and Britain. Other nations, however, including Chile and Argentina, claim sections of the continent. All these nations, and others, maintain scientific research stations on Antarctica. The population of these outposts varies greatly with the season and from year to year, but there are rarely more than a thousand people on the continent. English is now the recognised scientific language, but each nationality speaks its own language on the continent.

In 1959 the Antarctic Treaty was signed by nations involved on the continent, with an environmental protocol added in 1991. The treaty bans military activity and tightly regulates commercial and scientific activity in Antarctica. It is unlikely that either polar region will ever maintain a sizeable human population but both remain rich in wildlife and environmental interest. It is to be hoped that international co-operation will ensure the continued existence of these great wilderness areas.

▲ An Eskimo in a hunting kayak, northwest Greenland.

▶ As temperatures drop, the sea near Signy Island starts to freeze.

▼ Macaroni penguins on Bird Island, South Georgia.

▲ Heavy-bodied walruses resting on the beaches at Round Island, Alaska.

▼ Probing newly-formed ice in Antarctica.

Shuttle launch

THE
WORLD
FROM
SPACE

Space missions are now so sophisticated and frequent that a constant vigil of the world can be maintained by means of satellites and the hand-held photography of astronauts. To illustrate some of the extraordinary capabilities and practical applications of space-based means of observation, this section brings together many stunning views of the planet. Although the possibility of escaping the confines of Earth's atmosphere was conceived long ago, its realisation brought a perhaps unexpected reaction: a deep sense of awe at our brilliant blue planet, swathed in white clouds, spinning silently through the black void of the solar system. The essence of Earth's incomparable beauty is now revealed on the following pages.

Left: *Satellite image of Phoenix, Arizona*
Below: *The Sinai Peninsula, viewed from the Red Sea, looking northwards to the Mediterranean*

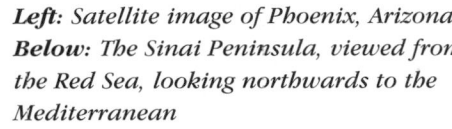

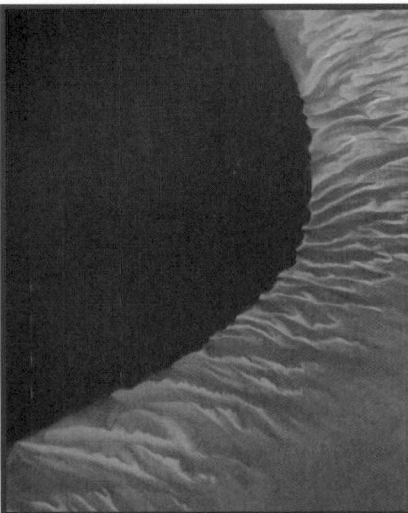

Left: *'Tongue of the Ocean', Bahamas*

INTRODUCTION

An Earth satellite is a man-made object launched into space in either a temporary or permanent orbit around the globe. The idea that an artificial satellite could be placed into orbital flight is far from new. Indeed, it was first proposed in 1687 by Sir Isaac Newton in his book *Philosophiae Naturalis Principia Mathematica*. He suggested that a cannonball fired at sufficient speed from atop a mountain in a direction parallel to the horizon would go all around the world before eventually falling to the ground. Although it would tend to drop in its flight because of gravity, the momentum of the cannonball would result in it descending along a curved path.

In 1957, the first Earth satellite, Sputnik I, was launched into space and abstract theory became practical reality. Over the years, thousands of satellites have been deployed in orbit above the planet for a wide variety of purposes. In broad terms, scientific satellites are used to collect data about the Earth's surface and atmosphere and, turning to the stars, to make astronomical observations. Navigation satellites enable the crews of ships and aircraft, and travellers on land, to determine their position in any kind of weather. Military satellites are used for reconnaissance and surveillance. Communications satellites relay radio and television programmes, telephone and facsimile calls, and other communications data around the globe. Weather satellites transmit information on cloud patterns and measurements of various meteorological conditions that assist in weather forecasting.

Taken together, the Earth is crisscrossed by data-gathering satellites. Many of their applications are now taken for granted. The images that space-based platforms produce, however, can not be disregarded. Pictures derived from satellites have been greatly supplemented with hand-held photography by astronauts, and the result is a profusion of stunning views of the world which draw attention both to its beauty and its fragility. The sight of its cerulean surface, swathed in clouds, is a reminder that the Earth is unique, and is to be both admired and respected.

1. Amid flame and clouds of smoke, and powered by 31,000,000 newtons of energy, the Space Shuttle lifts off. The first manned spacecraft designed for reuse, the orbiter has not only placed satellites into orbit over the Earth, but has also been used in the repair and retrieval of those that have become inoperative.

2

2. Using a nitrogen-propelled Manned Maneuvering Unit, an astronaut floats alone over the azure ocean, seeming as insignificant against the background of Earth beneath as is the planet itself when set against the void of the cosmos above.

1

3

4

5

3. High above the Earth, the cargo bay doors of the Space Shuttle are opened, allowing large payloads – including satellites – to be deployed safely into orbit with the use of the manipulator arm.

4. A hurricane swirls over the Gulf of Mexico, with the eye of the storm passing close to the Yucatan Peninsula. An overlay of the mainland helps make possible a precise identification of its position. Furthermore, by observing hurricanes in colour, cloud temperatures are revealed and meteorologists can determine their height. The tracking of hurricane formation and movement has allowed advance warnings to be made, saving countless lives and reducing damage to property.

5. Tropical Cyclone Litanne passing over the Indian Ocean in mid-March 1994. A few degrees east of Madagascar it was generating a wind speed of 232, gusting to 278, kilometres per hour (144-173 miles per hour). In the western Atlantic and the Caribbean, such storms are designated hurricanes; in the western Pacific, they are termed typhoons; and in western Australia, if the surface winds exceed 117 kilometres (73 miles) per hour, they are called willy-willies.

6. Thunderstorm systems, seen here over the Pacific Ocean with heavy sunglint on its surface, draw water vapour high into the Earth's atmosphere.

6

The Roman Emperor Marcus Aurelius stated about AD 170 that the 'entire Earth is but a point, and the place of our own habitation but a minute corner of it'. Amid the almost incomprehensible reaches of outer space, this planet is, indeed, like a speck of dust upon the seashore. From limited exploration of the Solar System and astronomical observation of the stars, however, it appears that this 'Blue Planet' is special for its distinctive oxygen-rich atmosphere and, beneath protective clouds, the broad expanse of seas and oceans.

The Earth has been called the 'Watery World', and without water it seems that there can be no life, which is partly the reason why it is necessary to protect this natural resource from being contaminated. Mankind lives in precarious balance with the environment. Today, for instance, depletion of the atmosphere's ozone layer through the use of pollutants allows increasing levels of harmful radiation to reach this planet from the sun. That is only one example of why it is now urgent for people to develop a new relationship with the Earth that allows for sustainable development without adverse effects upon ecosystems in which human beings are only one life form among

1. High over Africa, large cumulo-nimbus clouds are accentuated by the low sun angle and the long shadows that result. Agricultural burning, however, makes it impossible for the ground to be seen.

2. A satellite view of forest fires raging amid central Alaska. In the middle of the image are dozens of coloured marks indicating the locations of the fires, with plumes of smoke pouring from them to the south.

3. In the aftermath of the Gulf War, hundreds of burning Kuwaiti oil wells glow red amid the smoke.

5 & 6. Two false-colour composite maps of the world, with data gathered by a polar-orbiting satellite, showing the global effect of the eruption of Mount Pinatubo in the Philippines on 16 June 1991. Volcanic aerosol concentrations are shown as shades of yellow, from brown (lowest) to white (highest). The left image (19-27 June) shows a near normal distribution, with a slight increase over the Indian Ocean. The right picture (8-14 August), however, displays a huge aerosol plume spread around the equator.

4. A composite satellite image showing global vegetation. A time series of such photographs can assist in monitoring important developments, such as the increasing desertification taking place at the southern boundary of the Sahara Desert in Africa.

many. Although today there are numerous initiatives designed to prevent further environmental damage, the scale of the problem is massive and requires a change in the attitudes of governments, businesses and peoples around the globe. Satellite imagery of the environment will be at the forefront of monitoring the outward, physical manifestations of any such inner psychological and spiritual changes.

Centuries ago is was generally believed that the Earth was flat and subsequent, wiser generations smiled at this quaint notion. Until recently, it was thought that the shape of the world was, with the exception of some high mountains and deep valleys, an ellipsoid – that is, a slightly flattened sphere. Then came the space age, and accurate observation of variations in the orbit of the Vanguard I satellite revealed that the world is slightly pear-shaped, the distance between the centre of the Earth and the North Pole being greater than the distance to the South Pole. Observation of the planet from space is able to reveal such basic information which is of

fundamental use to so many, including meteorologists, geologists, farmers, geographers, cartographers, oceanographers, foresters, prospectors, land-use planners, scientists and environmentalists. With the use of imagery that employs both the visible and invisible spectrum, startling pictures are obtained of rivers, lakes, coastlines, seas and oceans; mountains, deserts, plains and cities; forests, scrubland, tundra and glaciers; and a host of other terrains and habitats that exemplify the stupendous diversity of this planet.

Once it was only possible to view the wider world from atop a high mountain. It has been estimated that with a good telescope, and on a clear day, such a method would reveal to the observer only 0.0025 per cent of the whole land surface of the globe, which covers an immense 509,600,000 square kilometres (197,000,000 square miles). Today, satellite imagery is a robust ally to those who wish to monitor the entire Earth: one picture frequently illustrates a point more succinctly than any number of words.

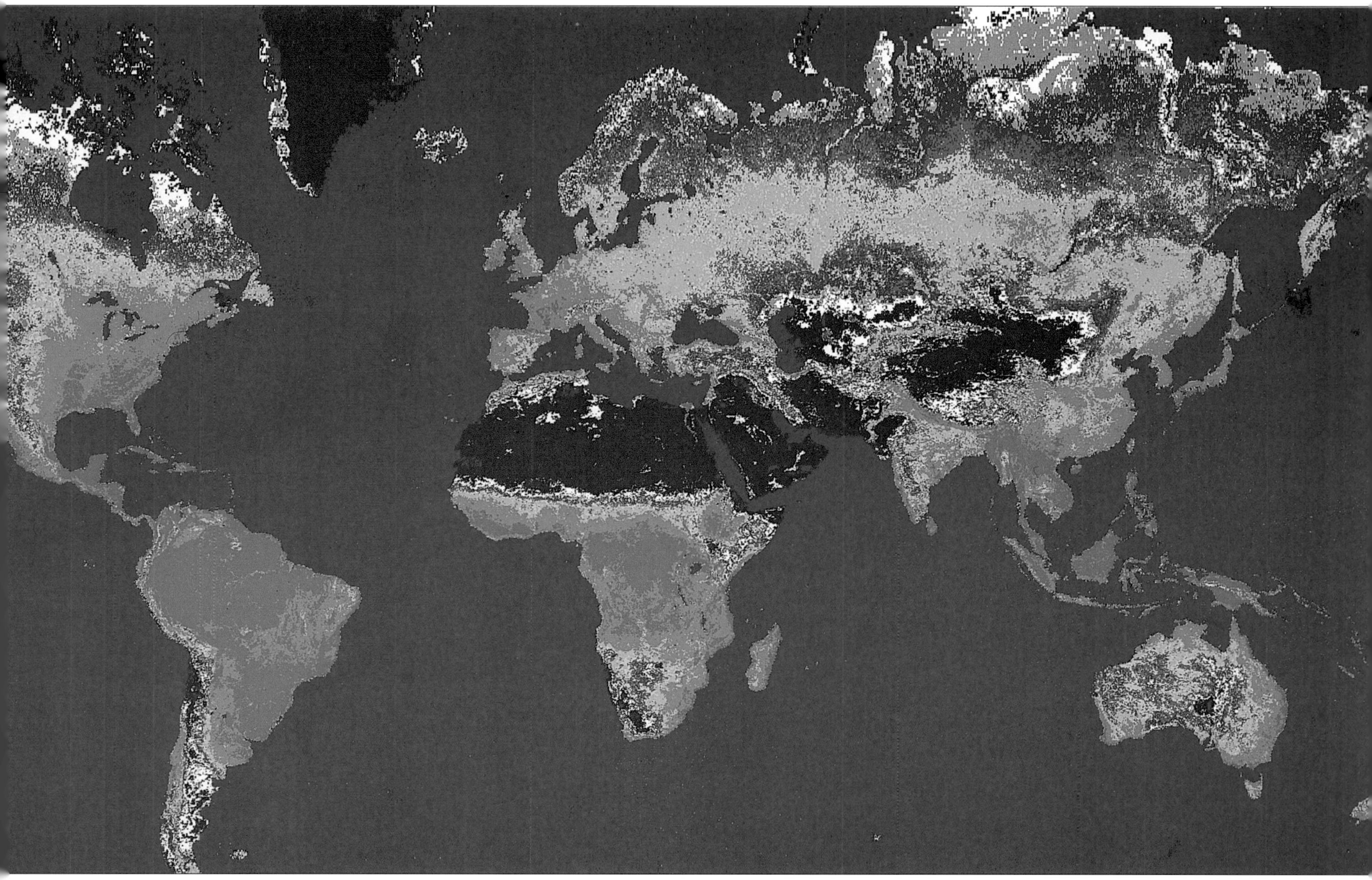

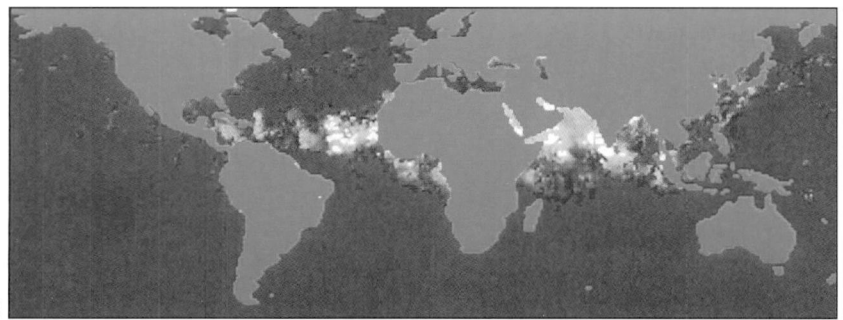

5

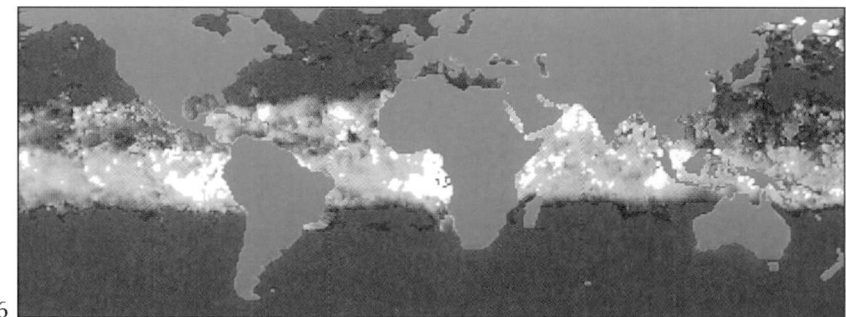

6

Environmental Case Study:
THE OZONE HOLE OVER THE ANTARCTIC

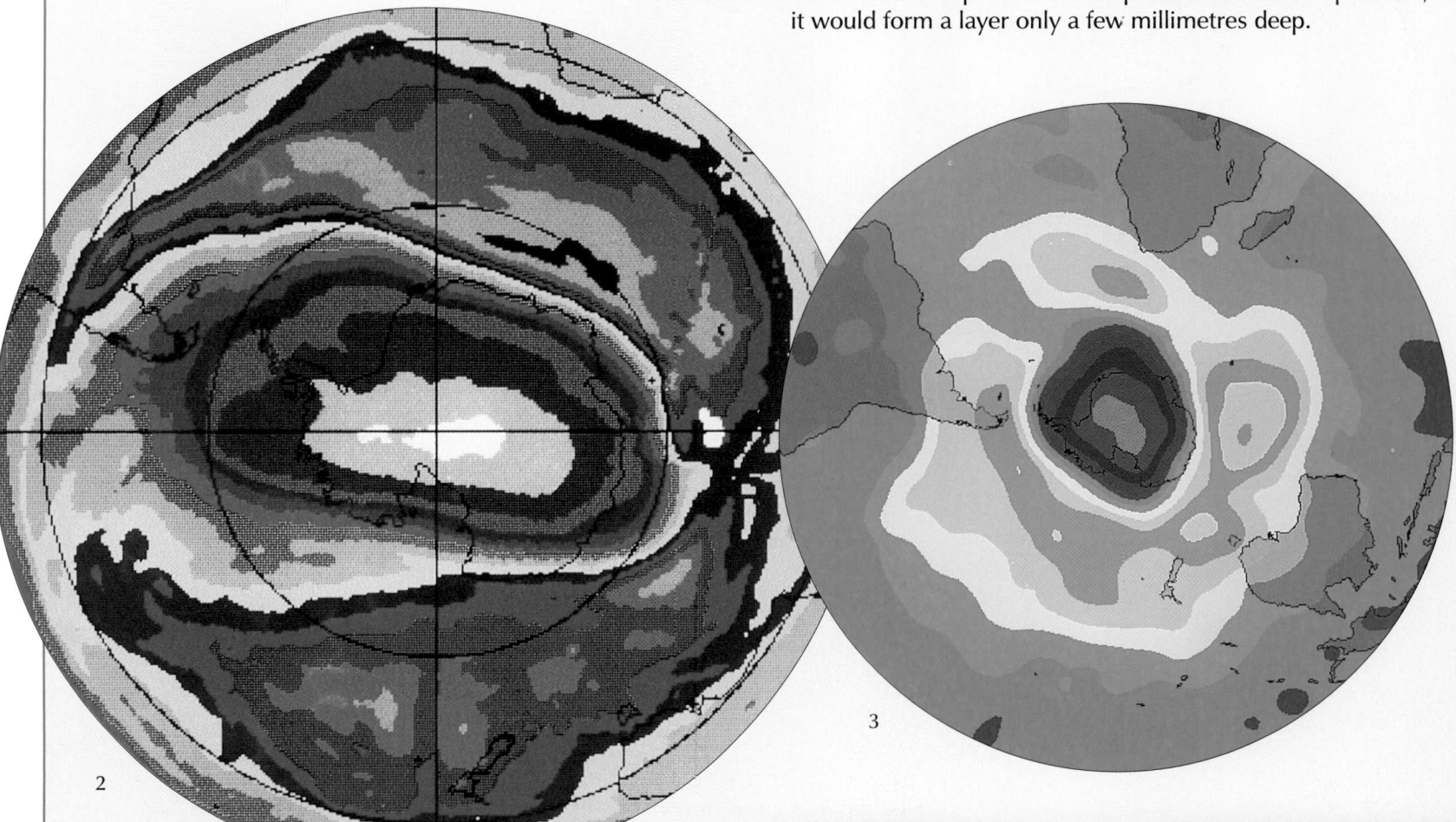

An important environmental concern is the 'hole' in the ozone layer discovered over the continent of Antarctica. Ozone (O_3) occurs naturally in very small amounts in the stratosphere. It absorbs solar ultraviolet radiation, which could otherwise cause severe damage to human and animal life on the Earth's surface. Pollutants in the air, especially nitrogen oxides from car exhausts and chlorofluorocarbons (CFCs), can diffuse into the ozonosphere and accelerate the destruction of ozone. CFCs are used as aerosol propellants, to blow plastic foam, as cleaning agents in the computer industry, and as coolants in refrigerators and air conditioners. Although alternatives are now available, some countries have not yet banned the use of CFCs. The total amount of ozone is quite small in comparison with other, more abundant, gases in the atmosphere. Indeed, if all the ozone in the atmosphere was compressed to sea-level pressure, it would form a layer only a few millimetres deep.

1. A picture of the Antarctic continent from a simulation of space-based imagery.

2. False-colour map of atmospheric ozone over the Southern Hemisphere made from data gathered by the Total Ozone Mapping Spectrometer on the Nimbus 7 satellite. This plot for October 1991 showed the largest 'hole' in the ozone layer ever recorded over a 13-year period. The white centre indicates an ozone concentration value of 110 Dobson Units (DU). A normal value should be around 280 DU.

3. The Antarctic ozone 'hole' in 1996, coloured in blue. Although smaller in area, it is more depleted with the grey centre at less than 100 DU.

4. Global ozone distribution in the upper atmosphere, with a pattern showing the satellite's path.

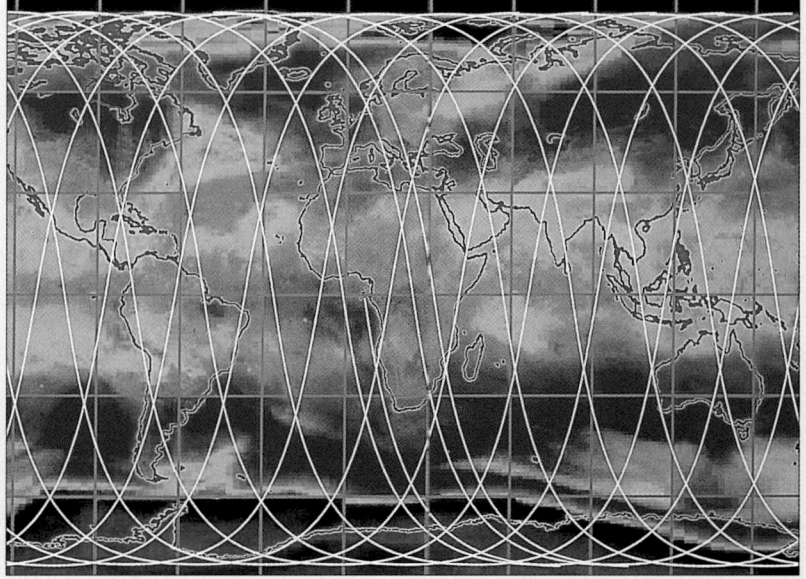

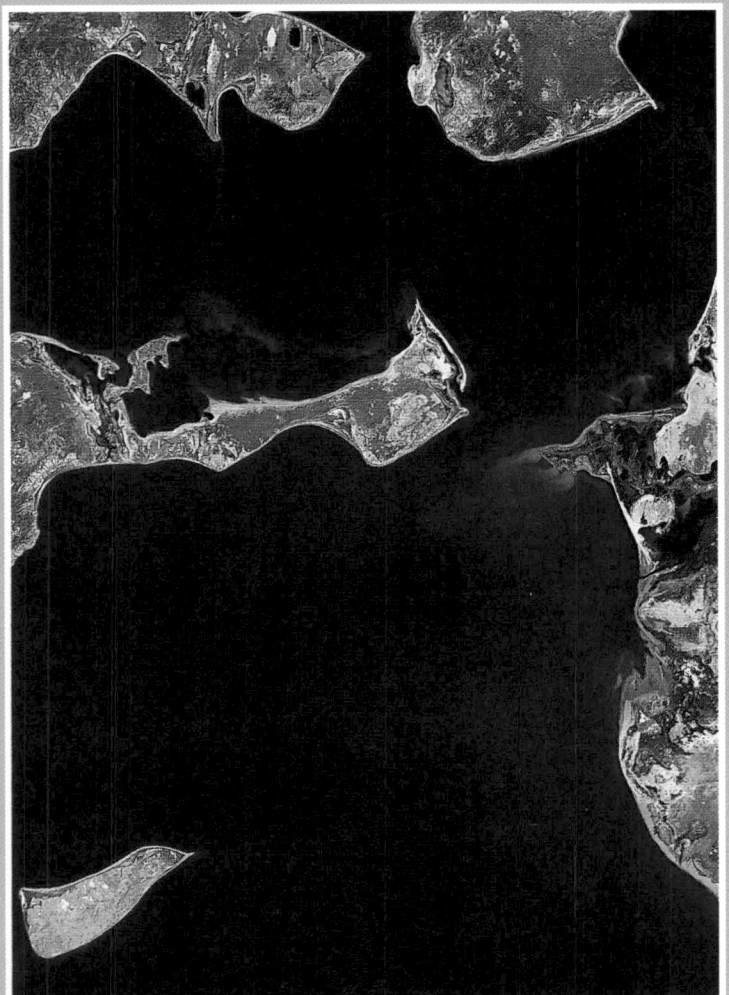

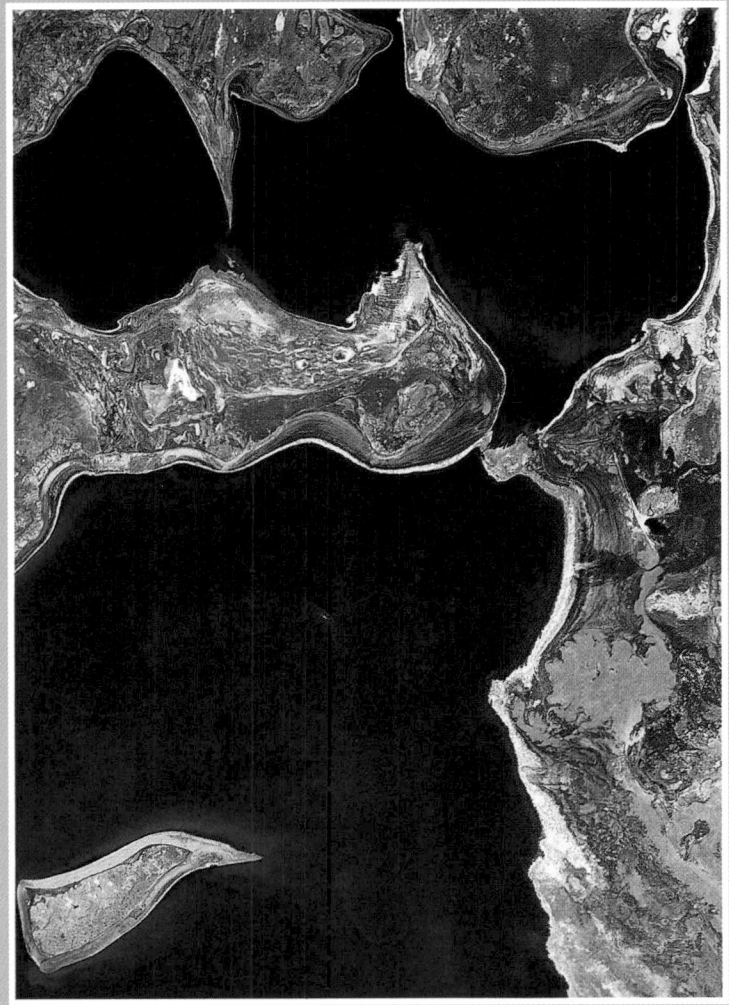

5

6

Environmental Case Study:
THE ARAL SEA

One of the world's largest areas of inland water, the average depth of the Aral Sea is about 21.3 metres (70 feet), although its maximum is over 61 metres (200 feet) off the western shore. The Aral Sea is of considerable interest to scientists and environmentalists because of the remarkable changes it has experienced in area and volume in recent times. This is the result partly of climatic changes but also very much due to human intervention, as the waters of the Syr-Dar'ya and Amu-Dar'ya (dar'ya meaning 'river') were blocked by dams to generate hydroelectricity, or were diverted for agricultural irrigation. Chemicals used by farmers now flow along the rivers and into the Aral Sea, where fish have been dying from poisoning and the increased salinity.

7

5 & 6. These images of Aral'skoye More, the Aral Sea, were taken just over fourteen years apart. The fall in sea level over this short period of time is remarkable. It is ironic that the area derives its name from the Kirgiz Aral-denghiz, or 'Sea of Islands', as Kokaral ceases, at centre, to be one of the three largest islands in the Aral Sea. Instead, it becomes a consid-erable peninsula reaching out to join the eastern shore and, thereby, isolating all the waters to the north. In the southwest, the island of Barsa-Kel'mes

manages to remain, but its coastline is much expanded. Once there were over 1,130 islands of a size of one hectare (2.5 acres) or more scattered across the surface of the Aral Sea. It is now unclear how many will remain as the water levels drops, although others will emerge from the shallow depths, too. The eastern edges of the images show part of the huge delta of the Syr-Dar'ya.

8

7. The Space Shuttle glides silently over Uzbekistan and the southern Aral Sea, as photographed by one of the Mir-18 astronauts aboard the Russian Federation's Mir Space Station. Overflights by satellites and spacecraft allow monitoring of the area over time.

8. Hand-held photography of the Aral Sea taken from the Shuttle as it orbited at an inclination of 58° to the planet. The angle affects the resulting picture, so that the area highlighted appears squashed as compared with the images above.

EUROPE

Europe (4) is the second smallest continent, but it still comprises 10,505,000 square kilometres (4,056,000 square miles) and covers 6.7 per cent of the total land surface of the Earth. Its boundaries are defined by the Arctic Ocean in the north, the Atlantic Ocean in the west and, to the south, the Mediterranean Sea, the Black Sea and the Caucasus Mountains. To the east, its margin is traced by the line of the eastern Ural Mountains, the Emba River, the Caspian Sea, and the Kuma and Manych rivers. Seen from the vantage point of space, however, the political borders of the individual states are invisible: each of the nations shares a common European home.

Sixty per cent of the landmass is less than 180 metres (600 feet) above sea level. In this composite satellite image, however, the snowcapped Alps can be seen stretching from southeastern France, across Switzerland, northern Italy and Liechtenstein to Austria. Further to the east, the Carpathians are also clearly visible. Indented by numerous fiords, bays and seas, continental Europe's highly irregular coastline is some 38,000 kilometres (24,000 miles) long. There are also major islands and archipelagos, including Novaya Zemlya, Iceland, the British Isles, Corsica, Sardinia, Sicily and Crete.

3

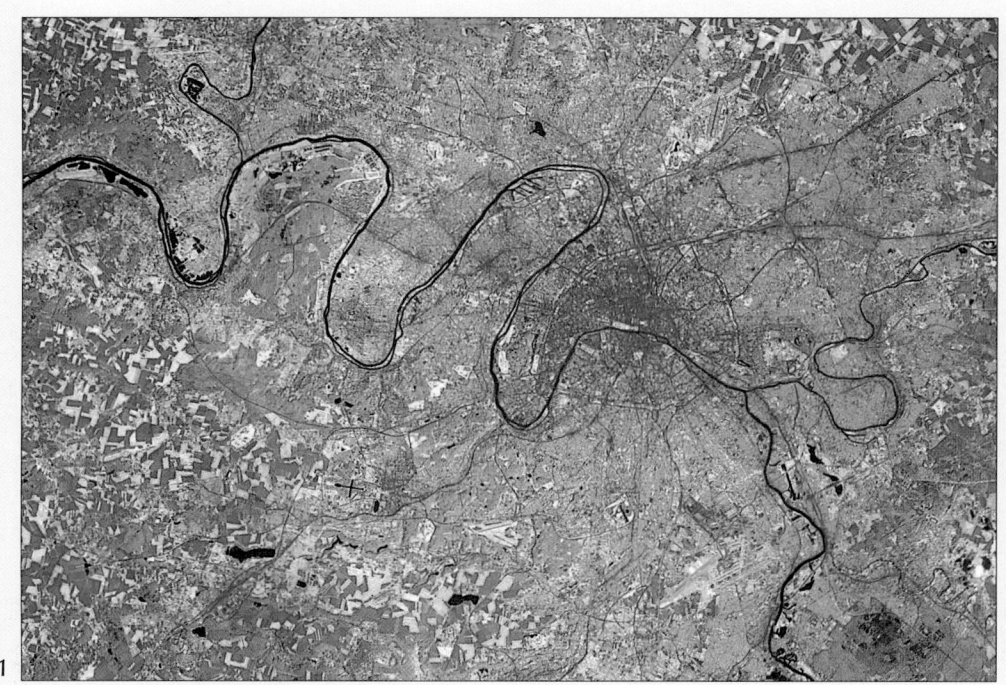

1

1. The distinctive, looping pattern of the Seine as it wends its way through Paris, capital of France and for over two thousand years the country's leading centre of population, economic activity and culture. The Oise River can be seen joining the Seine from the north.

2. Situated between the Black Sea and the Mediterranean Sea, Turkey has a number of rugged mountain ranges, including volcanic cones.

3. Madrid is located in the centre of the Iberian Peninsula on the undulating Central Plateau. At 640 metres (2,100 feet) above sea level, it is one of Europe's highest capital cities.

2

4

The BRITISH ISLES

The British Isles (5), situated off the northwestern coast of Europe, are composed of Ireland, jutting far into the Atlantic Ocean, and the United Kingdom of Great Britain and Northern Ireland, with a number of small island dependencies. The vast majority of the population live in towns or cities. England and Wales are both heavily urbanised, followed by Scotland and then Northern Ireland, with Ireland having the heaviest concentration of people around its capital. This distribution is made clear by a composite image of the British Isles at night (6) derived from weather satellites. The areas with the brightest city lights in England are London and the surrounding Home Counties, as well as the industrialised Midlands, northwest and northeast. Other concentrations occur in southern Wales, in Scotland along a corridor linking Glasgow with Edinburgh, and around Belfast in the north of Ireland and Dublin in the south. At the top right of the image, a number of bright splashes of light can be seen. These are produced by the flares of offshore oil rigs operating in the North Sea.

3. A false-colour image of the Lake District, once home to poet William Wordsworth, in northwest England. The area is enclosed by the Solway Firth (upper left), the snow-covered line of the Pennines (top centre to centre right), and Morecambe Bay (just below centre) with its treacherous, shifting sands. The heart of the Lake District is an uplifted granite dome, also seen veiled in snow. The radiating pattern of lakes, which appear black, is the result of glaciation. Surrounding flat, rich pastureland is shown in red.

3

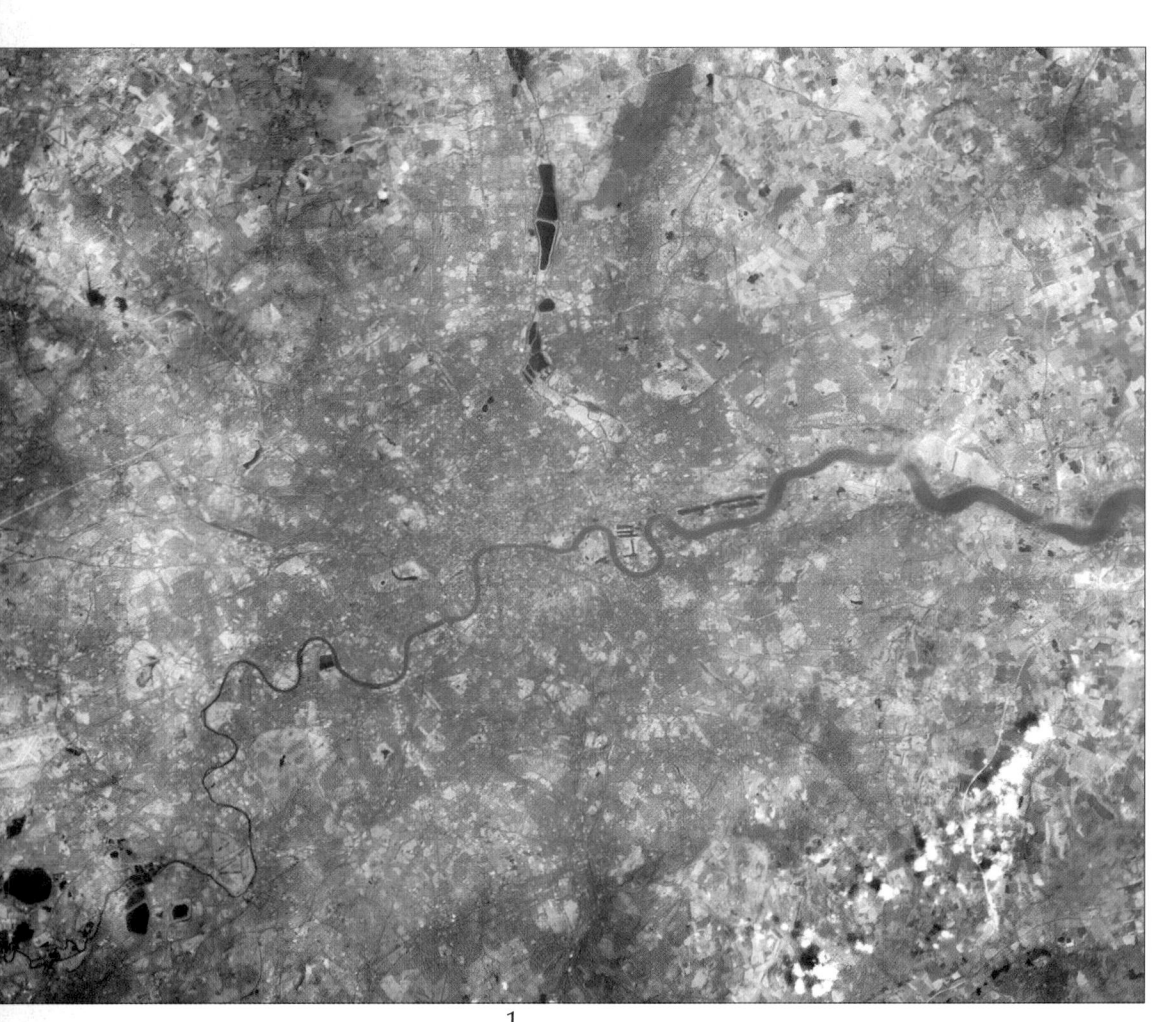

1

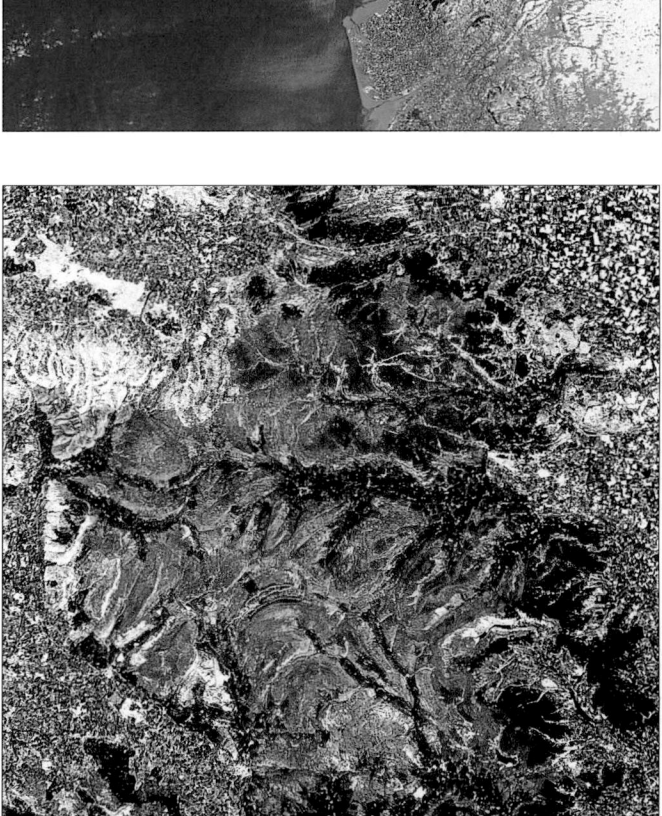

4

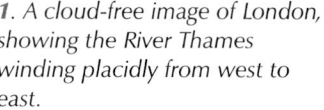

1. A cloud-free image of London, showing the River Thames winding placidly from west to east.

2. A radar image of the south coast of England. Brighton is the white area just upper left of centre with Beachy Head on the far right. The varying colours in the English Channel indicate degrees of surface roughness. In particular, the purple streaks show areas of unusually calm water, possibly the result of oil spills from ships using the Dover Straits.

2

4. A remarkable image of the rugged terrain of the Yorkshire Dales. Only land within the Yorkshire Dales National Park is represented in colour. At least three main river valleys can be discerned: the path of the River Ure is through a large, dark-green valley (Wensleydale) just above centre to centre right; the Wharfe River runs along the 'Y'-shaped valley a little below centre (Wharfedale); and the River Ribble passes through the valley at the lower left of centre, next to a large, pale area which is due to the presence of limestone quarries. The colours in the picture approximate to natural tones, with the mid-brown areas being upland scrub vegetation.

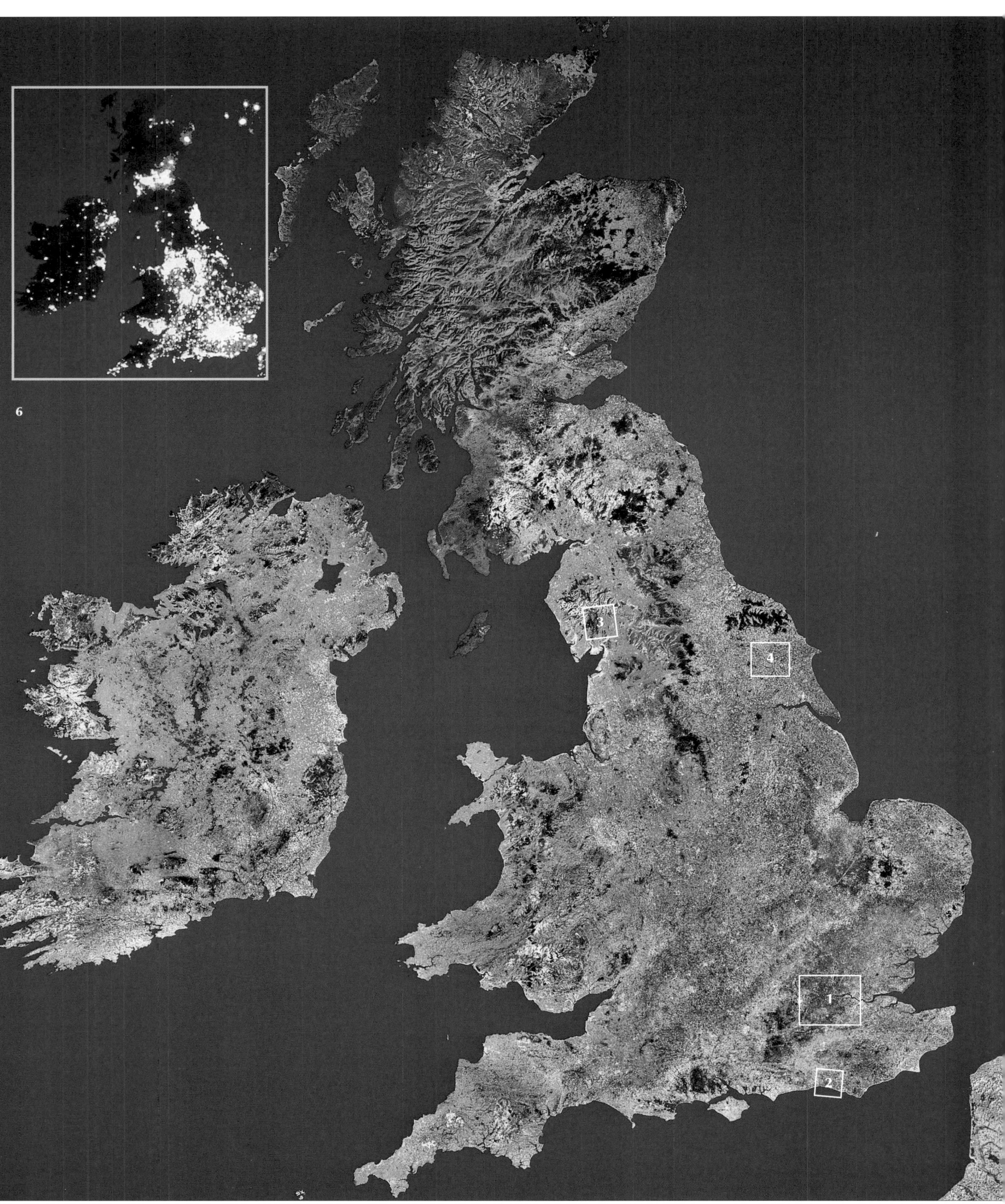

6

5

SCANDINAVIA and the BALTIC

A view of Scandinavia and northern Europe *(opposite page)* compiled from weather satellite data, with the colours approximating to natural tones. At the centre of the picture is the Baltic Sea. Covering an area of 420,000 square kilometres (160,000 square miles), it is the world's largest expanse of brackish water. Historically known as Scandia, modern Scandinavia is generally considered to consist of three countries: Sweden, Norway and Denmark. Sweden can be seen immediately to the left of the Baltic Sea with Norway, displaying its snowcapped mountains and indented coastline, further to the west. The landmass occupied by these two countries is known as the Scandinavian Peninsula, which is about 1,850 kilometres (1,150 miles) long and covers an area of 750,000 square kilometres (289,500 square miles). Much

of its largely mountainous mass formed part of the ancient Baltic Shield, some of which was affected by glaciation during the Pleistocene Epoch. The result is that Sweden benefits from extensive, gently graded slopes while Norway has the majestic heights and its distinctive, deeply dissected fiords. The peninsula and islands of Denmark almost close the south-western end of the Baltic. Some authorities argue that Finland should also be included in the definition of Scandinavia on geological and economic grounds.

To the southeast can be seen the Baltic states of Estonia, Latvia and Lithuania, with the Russian Federation at the eastern edge of the image. In the north lies the strategically important Kola Peninsula, its ice-free ports being vital to Russian naval interests.

In this photograph *(above)*, taken by Space Shuttle astronauts, the beauty of the aurora has been captured using high-speed film. Moonlight floods the sky with its spectral glow, and is reflected from the open ocean and clouds. The aurora is a luminous phenomenon of the upper atmosphere that may be seen primarily in high latitudes. In the Northern Hemisphere it is referred to as the aurora borealis, or northern lights, and in the Southern Hemisphere it is called the aurora australis, or southern lights. It is caused by the interaction of energised particles (electrons and protons) from outside the Earth's atmosphere with atoms of the upper atmosphere, and is most marked at times of intense solar activity. The aurora may change its form quite rapidly, but the bright vertical lines indicate the direction of the magnetic field down which accelerated particles are flowing.

3

CENTRAL EUROPE

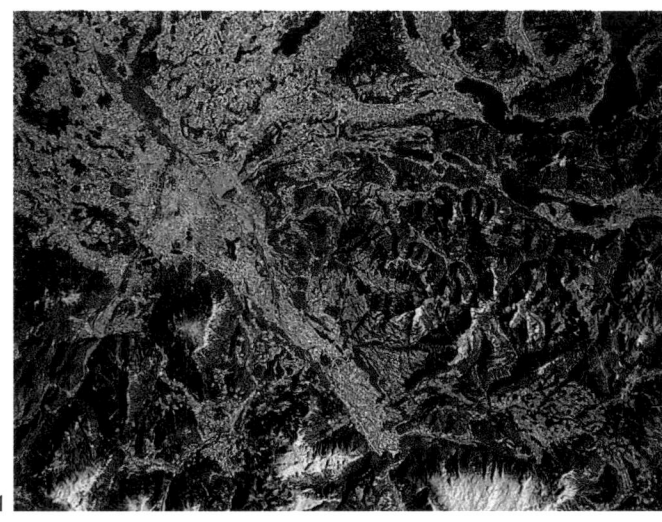

The colours in this satellite view of Central Europe (3) approximate to natural tones and indicate the type of surface cover. For example, at the top centre of the image is Germany, which largely comprises arable land interspersed with forests. Just to the south are the snow-topped Alps of Switzerland and Austria. To the right of the frame are the countries of Eastern Europe, including Poland, the Czech and Slovak Republics, Hungary and the Balkan states. Lying in the Mediterranean Sea, to the left of the Italian peninsula, are the islands of Corsica and Sardinia. To the right of the heel of Italy, across the Strait of Otranto, is Albania and, at the extreme bottom right, northern Greece.

Seen from the Olympian heights of space, Central Europe appears as a single geographical entity. Historically, however, this fertile region has been far from united and marauding armies have plundered their way across its land for untold centuries. In the twentieth century, technological improvements to armaments merely intensified the physical destruction and the human misery which accompanies the scourge of war. Furthermore, for half a century, the land and its people were divided by the 'Iron Curtain' between the Western powers and the Communist Eastern Bloc. Then, as if this was insufficient tragedy, civil war erupted in the Balkans and brought armed conflict to Europe once more. After thousands of years of hostility, a re-vision – a seeing afresh – is required. People must believe that they are united by a common heritage, humanity and hope for lasting peace.

1. Salzburg acts as the north-western gateway to Austria. Situated close to the border with Bavaria, its Alpine landscape and architectural wealth have led to its reputation as one of the world's most beautiful cities. Lying in a level basin on both sides of the Salzach River, it was originally the site of a Celtic settlement and subsequently became the town of Juvavum in Roman times.

2. Toward the left of the image lies Rome, one of Europe's greatest cultural centres as well as being the spiritual and administrative capital of the Roman Catholic Church. The capital of Italy, it is located on the Tiber River 24 kilometres (15 miles) inland from the Tyrrhenian Sea. Surrounding the historic site of the city are the famous seven hills of Rome: the Aventine, Caelian, Capitoline, Esquiline, Palatine, Quirinal and Viminal. The ancient walls of Rome enclose most of the Esquiline and Caelian hills, and all of the other five, but this area only forms some four per cent of the municipality of today. The large lake that can be seen to the northwest of the city is Lago di Bracciano. At the foot of Mont Cavo, to the southeast of the city, are two smaller lakes lying quite close to each other: Lago di Albano and Lago di Nemi. To the east and northeast of Rome is the rugged, mountainous terrain of central Italy, which is highlighted in red.

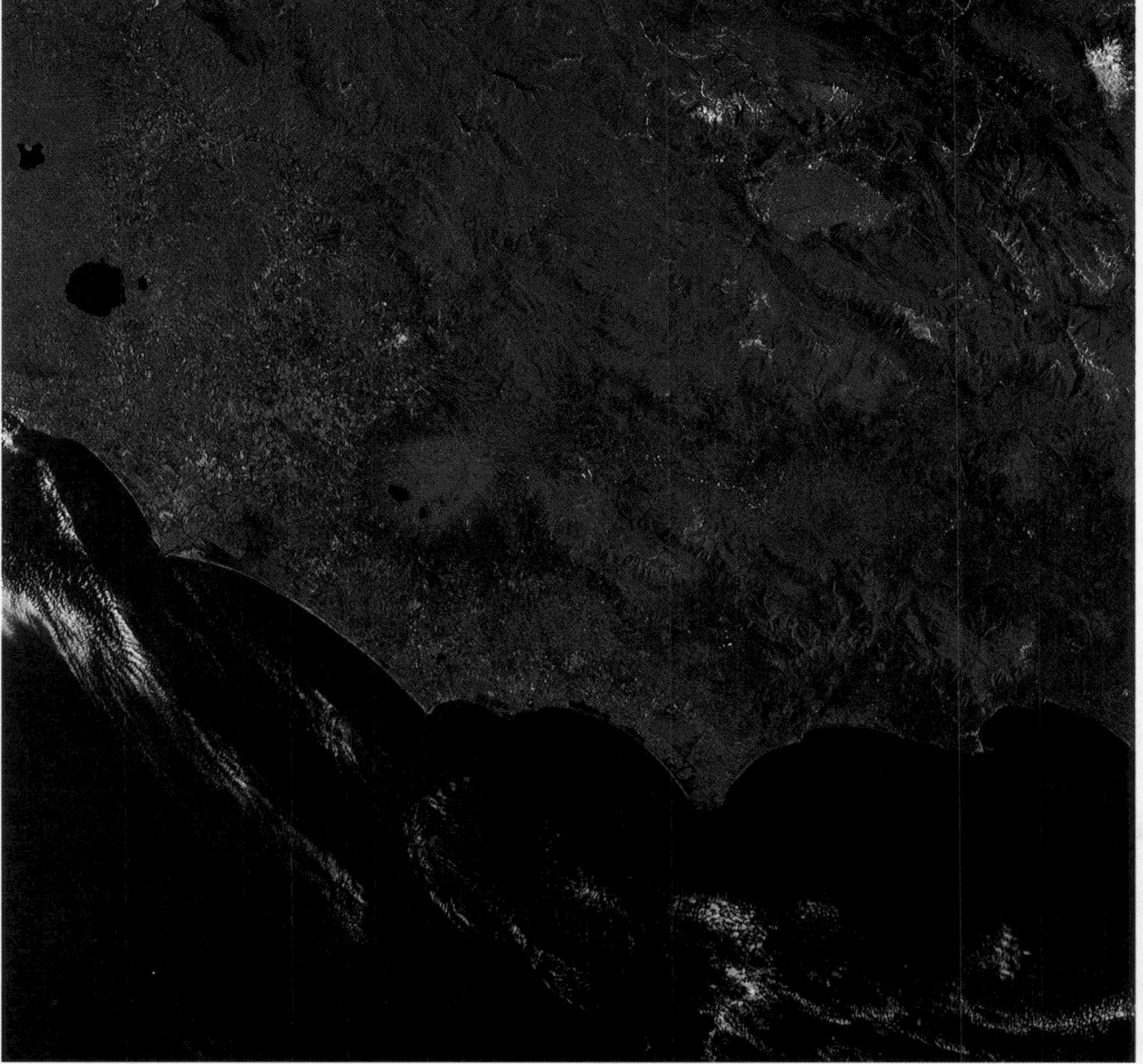

ASIA

Asia is the world's largest and most diverse continent. It covers sixty per cent of the Earth's land area, or approximately 44,614,399 square kilometres (17,225,709 square miles). The mainland of Asia is about 6,400 kilometres (4,000 miles) from north to south and 9,600 kilometres (6,000 miles) from east to west. It is bounded in the north by the Arctic Ocean, in the south by the Indian Ocean and in the east by the Pacific Ocean. In the west, the boundary runs roughly north-south along the eastern Ural Mountains, the Emba River, the Caspian Sea, the Kuma and Manych rivers and the Black, Aegean, Mediterranean and Red seas. The islands of Sri Lanka and Taiwan, and the archipelagos of Indonesia, the Philippines and Japan, are also part of Asia. Although the Russian Federation – the largest country in the world – has its political and administrative capital west of the Urals, within Europe, most of its vast terrain lies to the east in Asia.

The Asian continent contains vast expanses of mountains, and Arctic and desert wasteland. More than ten per cent of the land is arable, although in the southwest of Asia – comprising much of the Middle East – it is scarce. There, and in Central Asia, traditional patterns of pastoral nomadism still persist in some isolated areas. Although higher agricultural yields have been achieved in many Asian states by the increased use of chemical fertilizers and machinery, together with the introduction of new strains of seeds, rapid growth in population has offset much of the gains in food output. Production required to meet domestic demand can usually be achieved, but deficient transportation infrastructure often prevents equitable distribution among poorer rural areas. The major staple food of southern Asia is rice, while wheat is cultivated widely in the southwest of Asia, western India, northern China and Russian Asia. Productivity from livestock in Asia is low because supplies of fodder are generally limited. Fish, however, are a significant source of dietary protein.

Land elevation is very variable, ranging from the heights of Mount Everest at 8,848 metres (29,028 feet) above sea level to the Dead Sea at 400 metres (1,312 feet) below sea level, but mountains and high plateaux predominate. Indeed, approximately sixty-seven per cent of Asia is above 488 metres (1,600 feet), with about twenty per cent above 3,048 metres (10,000 feet). The highest mountains can be grouped into two large belts. The first stretches from the Chukchi Peninsula in the north to the mountains of southern Siberia, while the second is composed of the highest mountain ranges in the world: the South Asian highlands, the Pamirs, the Karakorams, the Himalayas and the Arakan Yoma. Island chains in the east and southeast of Asia are also mainly mountainous and include many volcanoes.

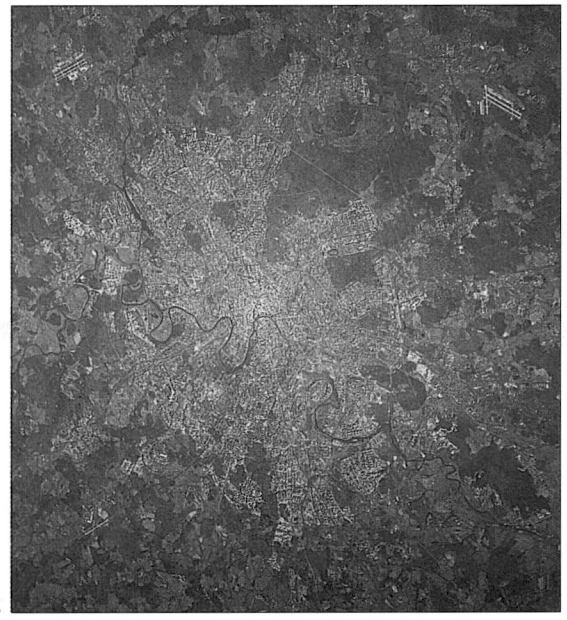

1. A view across the Kamchatka Peninsula in the far east of the Russian Federation. This area is known as a land of ice and fire, and the cluster of volcanoes in the middle distance are active, including Klyuchevskaya Sopka whose summit reaches 4,750 metres (15,580 feet). The region has many geysers and hot springs, and geothermal power is being utilised there.

2. Moscow, capital of the Russian Federation, lies amid the plain of European Russia in the broad and shallow valley of the Moskva River which, in this image, loops its way through the heart of the wheel-shaped city.

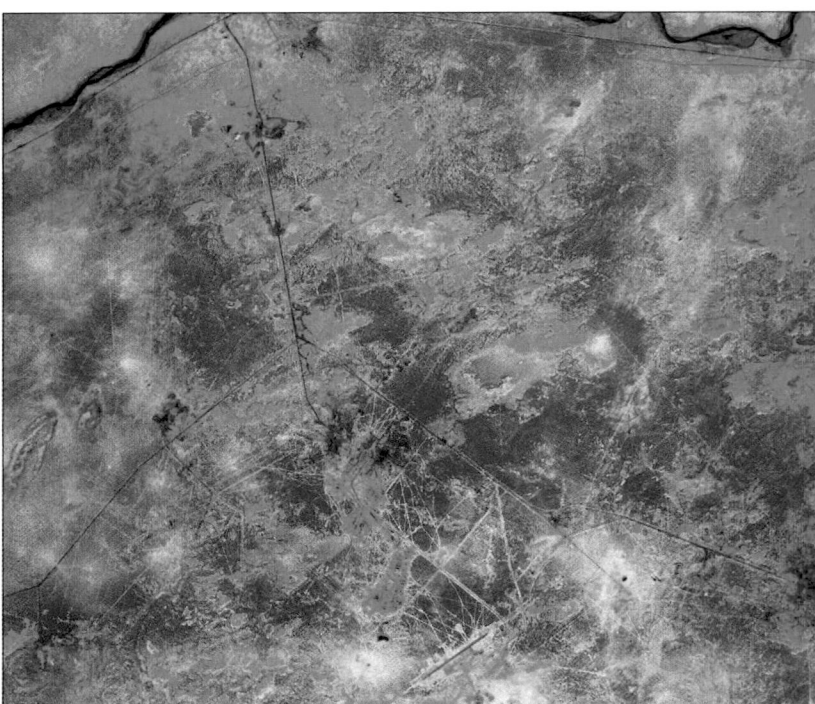

3. Tyuratam, formerly known in Soviet days as Leninsk after the hero of the October Revolution, Lenin.

6. A mosaic of satellite images shows the Black Sea. At top centre is the smaller Sea of Azov and at the bottom left the Sea of Marmara, which separates the European and

Asiatic parts of Turkey. The peninsula just above centre is the Crimea. The thin green line traces the actual coastline of the Black Sea. Any black space between the land and this margin represents missing satellite data.

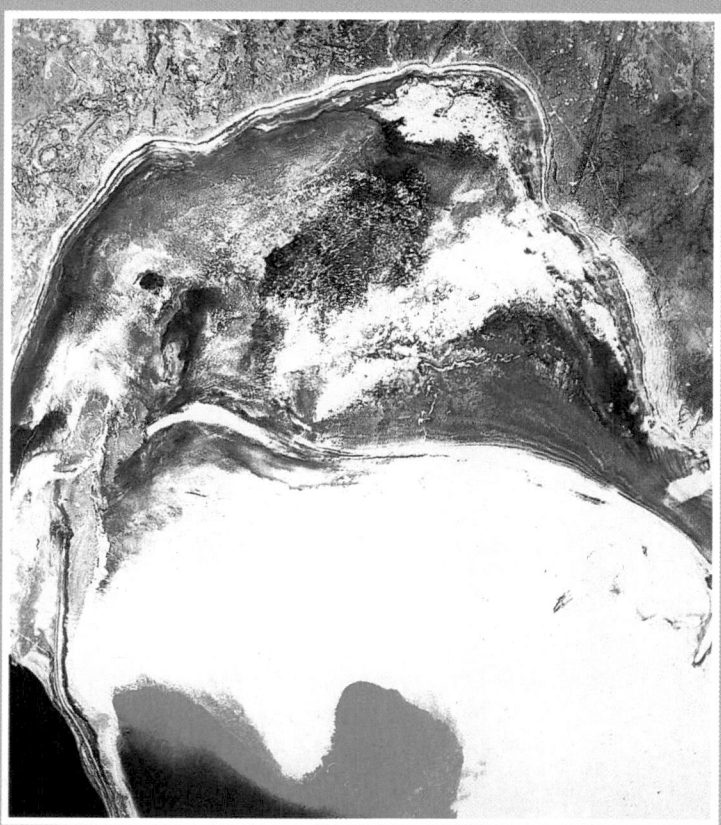

4 & 5. Images taken fifteen years apart show the changing face of the northern half of Zaliv Kara-Bogaz-Gol, an inlet of the eastern Caspian Sea in northwestern Turkmenistan. Although the surface area is some 12,000-13,000 square kilometres (4,600-5,000 square miles), the gulf averages only 10 metres (33 feet) in depth and has a particularly high rate of evaporation. Because of this, it is extremely saline and contains the world's largest deposit of natural marine salts.

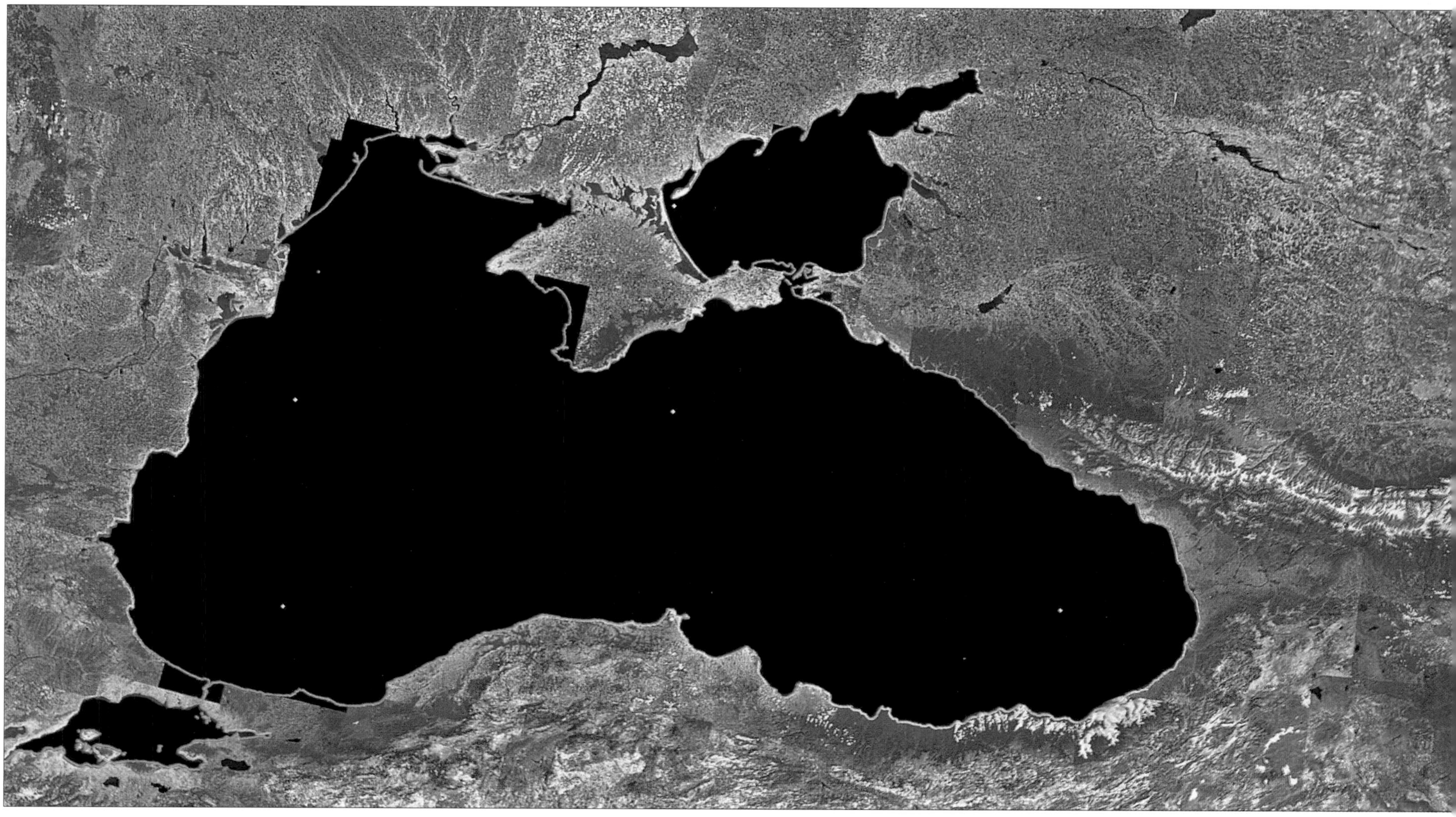

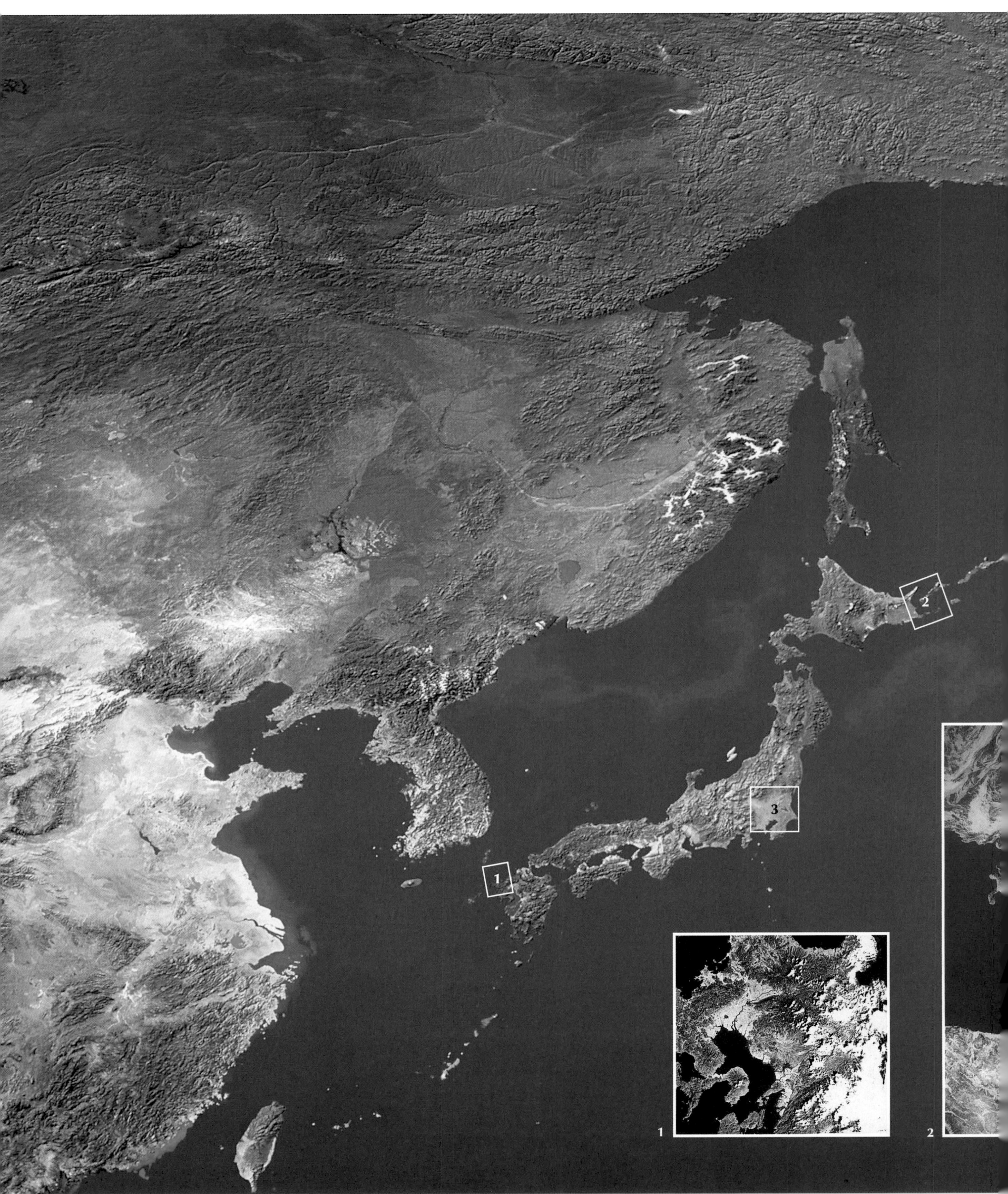

EAST ASIA

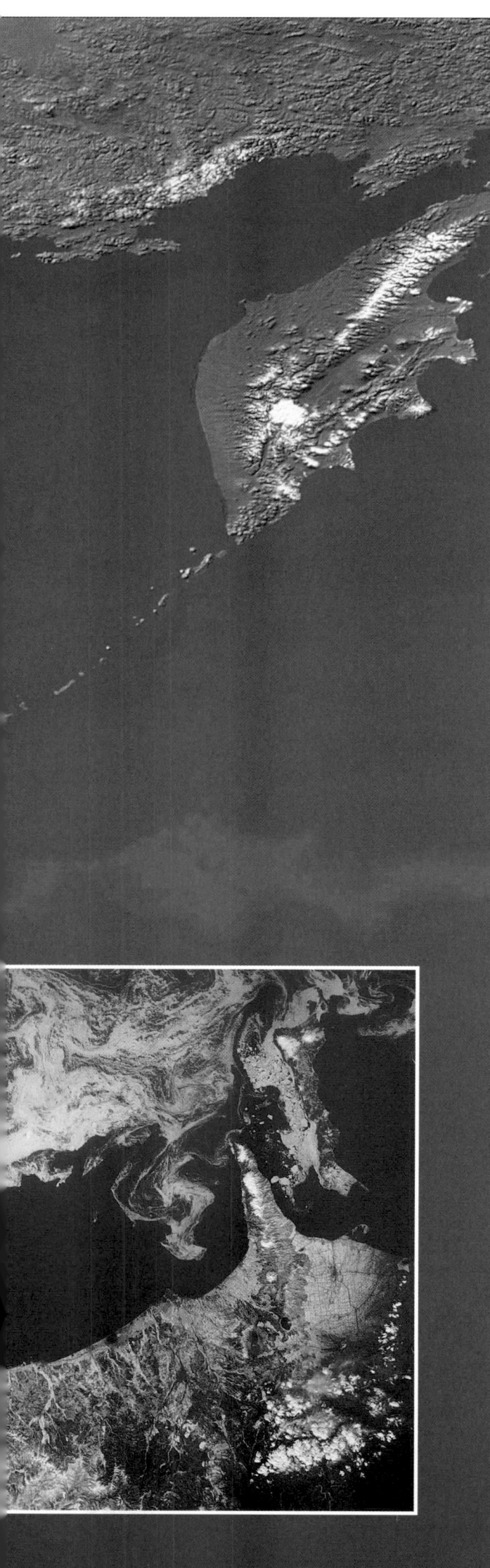

East Asia contains some of the powerhouse economies of the world. The main image (4) on these pages is a good example of how satellite data can be manipulated to provide a clearly intelligible product for the user. The picture has a resolution of one kilometre (0.62 miles) and is a combination of dozens of images acquired by weather satellites from orbits some 826 kilometres (513 miles) above Earth. This regional mosaic was then joined with a high-resolution digital elevation model which, to emphasize relief features, was stretched by a factor of two and simulated sunlight added. The final illustration shows the islands of Japan *(lower centre)* lying in the Pacific Ocean. On the Asian mainland is the far eastern territory of the Russian Federation *(top)*, the Korean Peninsula *(lower centre, left)* and China *(left and lower left)*.

Japan is located within one of the Earth's more active geological zones, with major epicentres lying offshore along faults in the seabed. The country suffers, therefore, from frequent violent volcanic eruptions and almost continuous earthquake activity. Huge waves often accompany the offshore tremors and can cause immense damage along the entire Pacific coast. Politically divided into North and South Korea along the 38th parallel at the end of the Second World War, with Russian troops crossing the common border in the north, the Korean Peninsula is a rugged land with approximately seventy-five per cent of its terrain mountains and uplands. The highly populated People's Republic of China is the third largest country in the world, covering an area of 9,572,900 square kilometres (3,696,100 square miles).

3

1. A colour composite photograph of the north-western part of the island of Kyushu, Japan. Healthy trees, crops and other green plants show up clearly in the infrared spectrum and are shown in bright red. Suburban areas with sparse vegetation are light pink, as along the river valley left of centre. The city of Nagasaki is in the lower left corner and Fukuoka is at top left.

4

2. The northeast coast of Hokkaido, Japan. To the right of the peninsula jutting like a spike into the sea is the island of Kunashir, the southernmost of the Kuril Islands. Sea ice partly occludes the channel between Kunashir and the Japanese mainland, while elsewhere it forms a complex pattern of eddies in response to local water currents and winds.

3. At the bottom centre of the image is Tokyo Bay. At its head, on the western shore, lies Tokyo, capital of Japan. This appears as a large and diffuse patch of blue-grey. To the south, it merges imperceptibly into the port city of Yokohama. Cutting across the centre of the picture is the Tone River, which exits to the Pacific Ocean at Choshi.

SOUTHERN ASIA

Southern Asia is an immense and generally densely populated area dominated by southern China, the Indochina Peninsula, the Malay Archipelago and the Indian subcontinent. For many years, southern China has been at the forefront of economic growth. Special economic zones allowed trade with other powers and, with the return of the financial centre of Hong Kong to Chinese rule, the country is well placed to continue expansion.

The development of Indochina in the twentieth century has been marred by political instability and conflict, including the Vietnam War and the barbarities perpetrated during Khmer Rouge rule in Cambodia-Kampuchea.

The Malay Archipelago, historically referred to as the East Indies, is the largest group of islands in the world, comprising some 7,000 islands of the Philippines and the more than 13,000 islands of Indonesia. The archipelago extends along the equator for more than 6,115 kilometres (3,800 miles) and, at its greatest, measures 3,540 kilometres (2,200 miles) from north to south. Although two of the world's largest cities,

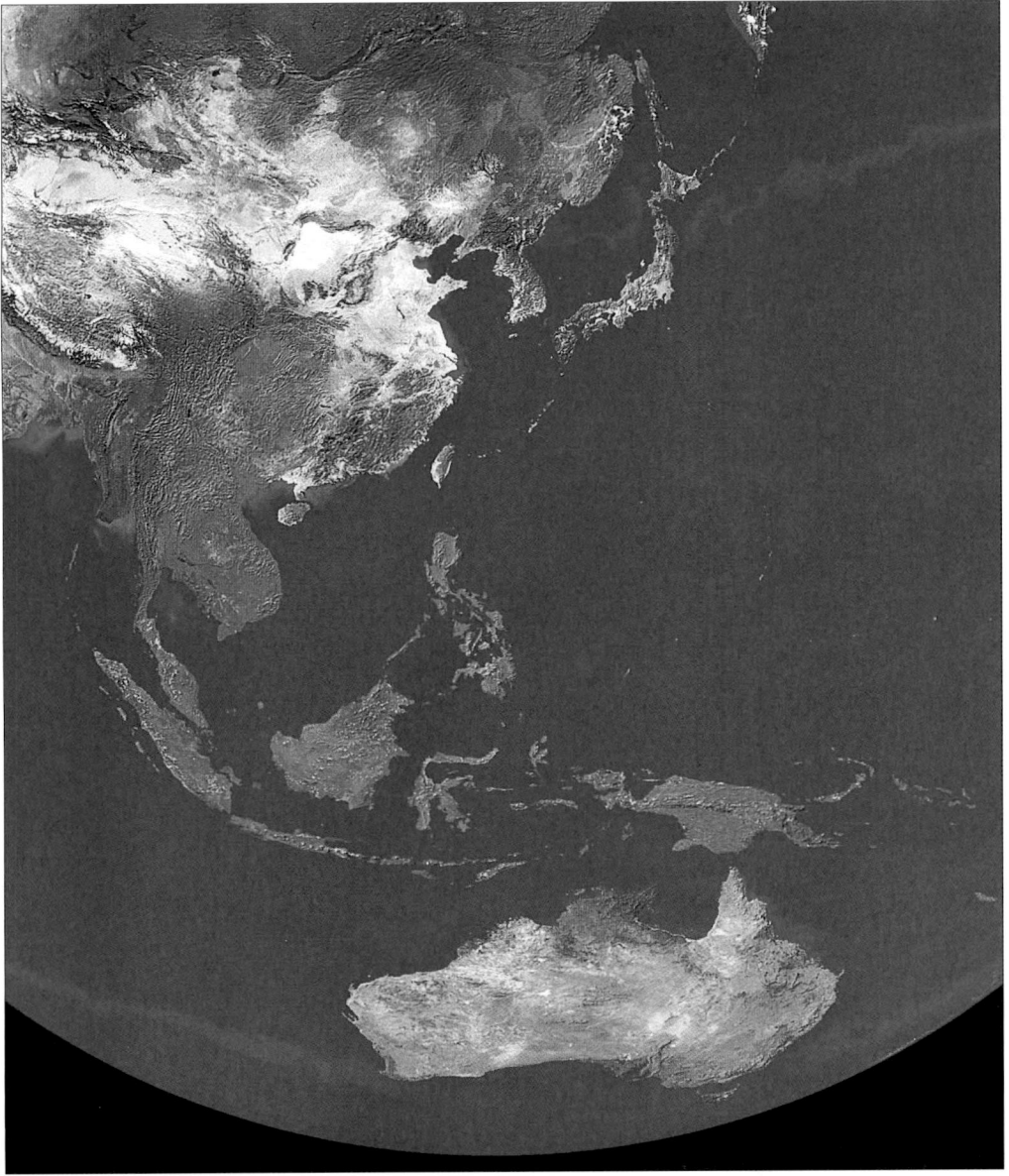

2. Mangrove forests and swamps surround the delta in the Kalimantan region of Indonesia. To the north of the delta, in Sabah, Malaysia, lies a range of volcanoes which were last active more than 100,000 years ago.

3. The city of Bangkok, Thailand, looking west across the Bight of Bangkok, with the deforested hills of the Bilauktaung Range at the top of the image.

4. A west-east view along a volcanic chain in Indonesia, including the eastern half of Java and the islands of Madura, Bali, Lombok and Sumbawa.

1. *Regional mosaic showing southern Asia, and its position in relation to Australasia, at a resolution of one kilometre (0.62 miles). At the top of the image, to the left of centre, can be seen Lake Baikal in the Russian Federation, the largest freshwater lake by volume in the world. To the south are the steppes of Mongolia and the wastes of the Gobi Desert. To the left of the picture are the mountains of Tibet, the Himalayas and, flowing into the Bay of Bengal, the delta of the River Ganges. Just to the left of centre, off the Chinese mainland, is the island of Formosa. Running in an arc to the north are the Ryukyu Islands and Japan, while to the south is the archipelago of the Philippines and then the west-east sweep of islands that form Indonesia.*

5

Jakarta and Manila, are in this region, the economy of the islands is principally rural and agricultural.

The Indian subcontinent is an immense landmass whose fertility has to support over a billion inhabitants. To the northwest and east of India are the Muslim countries of Pakistan and Bangladesh. Amid the Himalayan ranges in the northeast are the mountain states of Nepal and Bhutan. To the south lies the island of Sri Lanka. At the heart of the subcontinent, however, is India itself. A land of the greatest diversity, here may be found snow covered peaks and bleak deserts, fertile plains and tropical jungle. Some seventeen major languages are spoken, together with 22,000 district 'dialects'. With such an assortment of habitats and citizens it can be difficult to see what unites the nation. It has been said, however, that the concept of India does not lie in geographical boundaries, ethnicity, languages, or religions, but rather in the belief that it is one land encompassing the many. So, while a satellite image captures topography, a more subtle reality is also present: all countries are a medley of beauty and spirituality that has to be experienced, and can not be captured on film. One limit of overhead photography is clear: it captures appearances, but not people's hearts.

7

5. A very late formation in geological terms, the Himalayas date from the Miocene period. Formed between 12 and 25 million years ago during the same period of orogenesis that produced the Alps, their comparative youthfulness explains why the mountains have not yet been markedly eroded by the elements. The high and rugged range forms an almost impassable barrier between the Tibetan Plateau to the north and the alluvial plains of the Indian subcontinent to the south.

6. The snow-line along the south face of the Himalayas is at about 3,658 metres (12,000 feet). In this picture, the valley of the Chenab River can be easily seen beneath the snows.

6

7. The Indian subcontinent. In the north is the snow-clad swathe of the Himalayas. In the northwest lies the Indus Valley, coloured a rust-brown, and the striated mountain regions of Pakistan, caused by the Indian tectonic plate pushing remorselessly northward into the continent of Asia. To the east is the Ganges delta in Bangladesh. In the south is the island of Sri Lanka and, to the right, the Andaman Islands may be seen.

105

The MIDDLE EAST

The Middle East is a loose term applied generally to the territory surrounding the eastern and southern shores of the Mediterranean Sea. At its core, however, are the Muslim Arab states, with Israel hemmed in between them. This area has often been described as the cradle of civilization. In ancient times, irrigation by the floodwaters of the River Nile and the Euphrates aided agriculture and, thereby, allowed cultures of great sophistication to flourish. In the present day, vast oil deposits have brought a new wealth to many Middle Eastern countries, lifting their peoples out of poverty and providing all the material trappings of the Western lifestyle. Unfortunately, this region is very prone to dissension and has been subject to seemingly endless warfare in the twentieth century. Where previously there have been confrontations between Arabs and Jews over land, or struggles to obtain control over oil reserves, a glance at the desert terrain – which is so clear in the images on these pages – suggests that a future conflict may involve an even more precious resource: water. Although there is a powerful move towards peaceful settlement of disputes in the Middle East, backed by the world community in the form of the United Nations, there is also a growing tide of Islamic fundamentalism that threatens to sweep back the progress of years in a tide of anti-Jewish and anti-Western feeling.

3

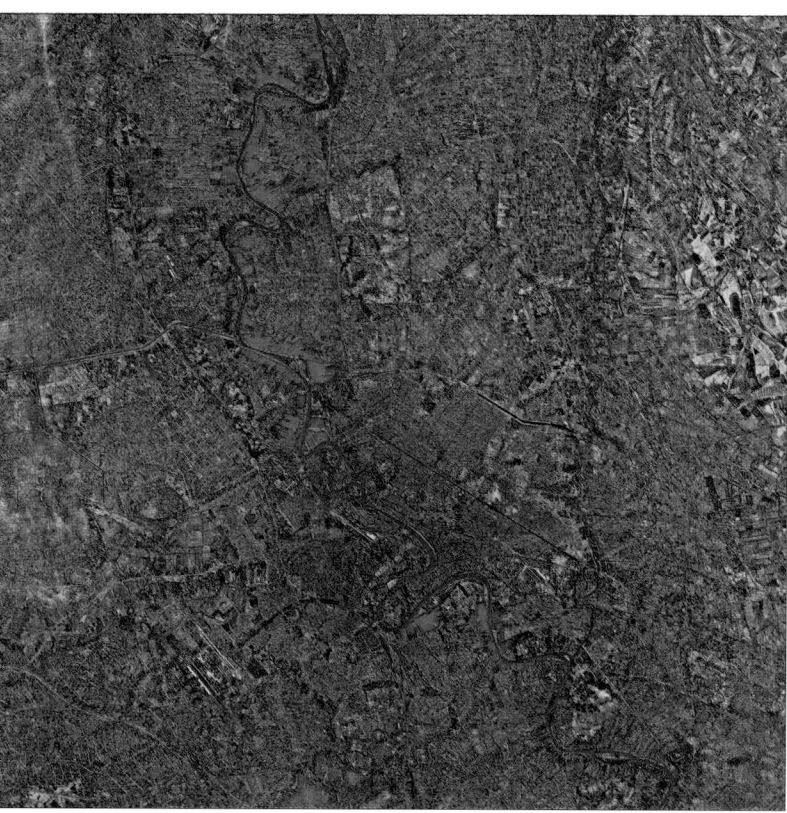

1

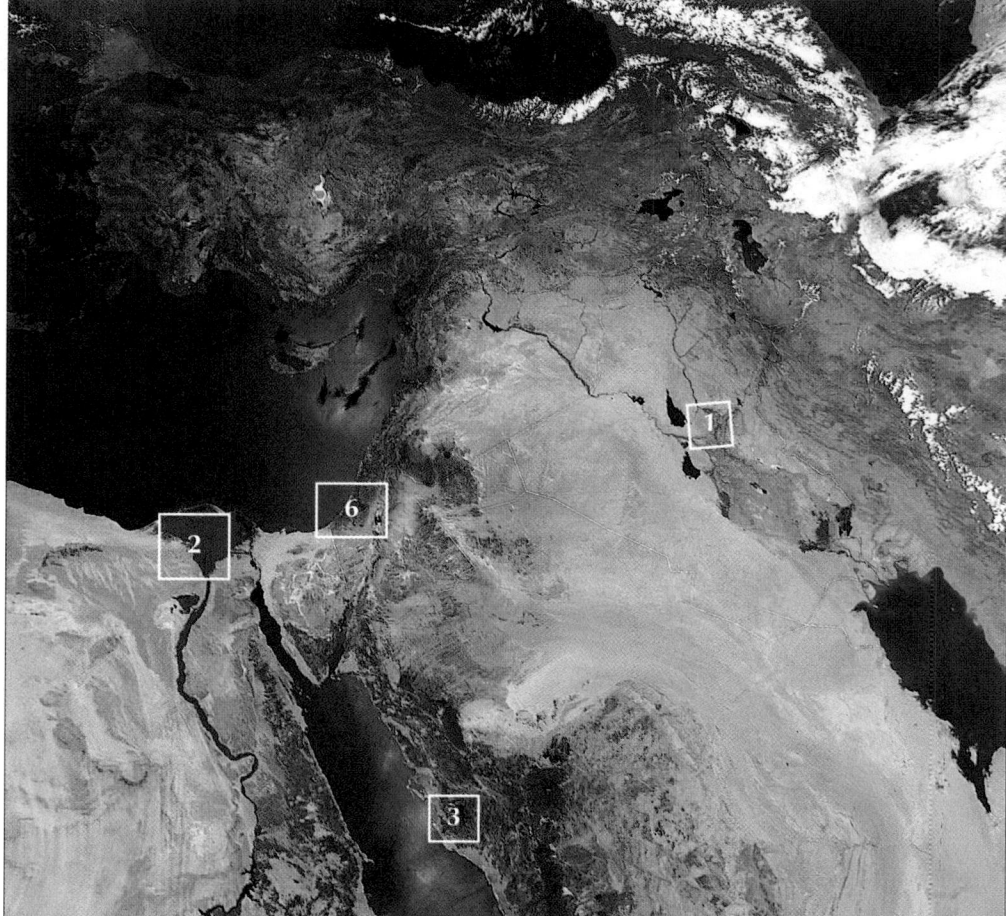

4

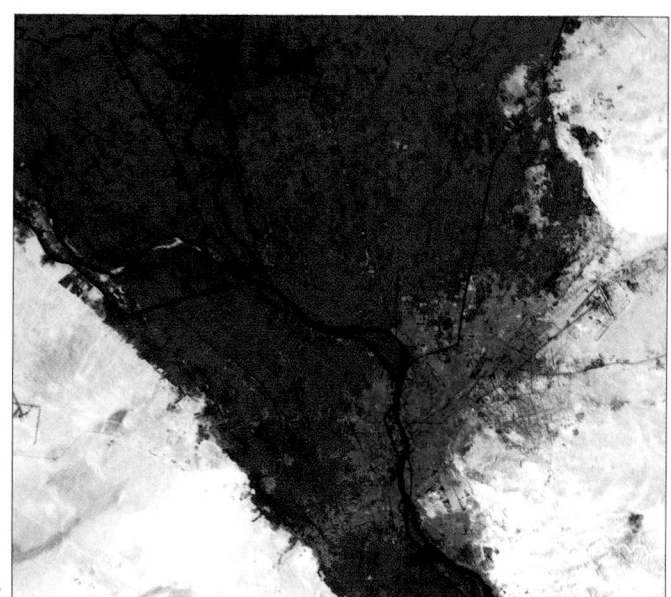

2

1. Baghdad, located on the banks of the Tigris River at the centre of a broad alluvial plain, is the largest city and capital of Iraq. It lies at the intersection of historic trading routes and was the principal city of ancient Mesopotamia.

2. The ancient metropolis of Cairo, Egypt, is located predominantly on the eastern bank of the River Nile. The city is fan-shaped, being widest in the north, where the valley blends into the Nile's delta, but is

wedged in the south between desert escarpments. As the capital of Egypt, Cairo's influence on Middle Eastern affairs is immense.

3. Jiddah on the west coast of the Red Sea. The city takes its name, which means 'ancestress' or 'grandmother', from the reputed tomb of Eve which was located there. A major seaport, it is the gateway to the Islamic holy cities of Mecca and Medina, and is the diplomatic capital of Saudi Arabia.

4. A panoramic view of the Middle East, with an overlay indicating political boundaries. Of particular note is the Nile and its delta, coloured a dark red. The river is bordered by a floodplain of rich alluvial soil. Seeds flourish in the mud left after the annual floodwater subsides, and the Nile has supported continuous human settlement for over 5,000 years. The body of water to the right of the Nile is the Red Sea and, at the far right of the image, lies the Persian Gulf.

5 & 6. These two photographs show the ability of satellite imagery to encompass wide swathes of land or to reveal incredible detail. On the left is an overall view of the Dead Sea, which is shrinking steadily through evaporation. Located between Israel and Jordan, it is the lowest body of water on Earth at approximately 400 metres (1,312 feet) below sea level. At the bottom of the picture is an area coloured light-blue, which has been enlarged in the image shown above. This region at the southern end of the Dead Sea is formed by shallow and murky evaporation flats that may well be completely dry in the space of a few centuries.

AFRICA

The second largest continent, Africa occupies twenty per cent of the Earth's land area, or 30,217,894 square kilometres (11,667,159 square miles). Only about six per cent of Africa is arable. While much of North Africa is desert, nearly a quarter of the continent is forested or wooded. The land is largely composed of a vast rigid block of ancient rocks, forming the huge plateau regions of the African Shield. The average elevation of the continent is about 671 metres (2,200 feet), but the range varies from 5,895 metres (19,340 feet) above sea level at Mount Kilimanjaro, Tanzania, to some 156 metres (512 feet) below sea level at Lake Assal in Djibouti. But perhaps the most striking feature of the terrain is the East African Rift System. This is composed of a western branch – the Great Rift Valley – and the East African Rift Valley. Extending for practically the entire length of the continent, the rift system forms the Red Sea basin, borders the Ethiopian Highlands, includes the extensive volcanic chain of the Virunga Mountains, then exits into the Indian Ocean near the mouth of the Zambezi River in Mozambique. Another major characteristic of Africa that can be easily observed is its hydrology. Two vast rivers basins, the Nile and the Congo, drain almost a quarter of the continent's land area and, at the divide of their watersheds, huge lakes occur.

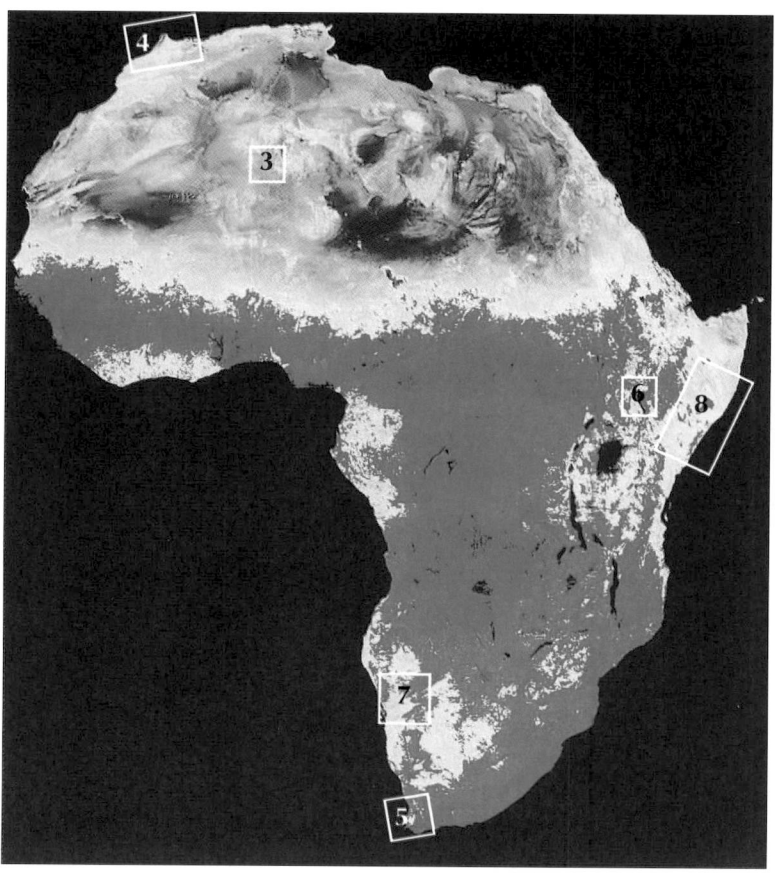

1

1. False-colour image showing distribution of vegetation and variations in ground cover. Sandy desert is seen as deep yellow; rocky desert is red. Two pale yellow areas of scrub and semi-desert, on the south coast of West Africa and on the west coast at centre, are due to extensive destruction of tropical rainforest.

2. The magnificent volcanic Virunga Mountains of east-central Africa, home to the rare mountain gorillas.

3. Sand dune patterns in the Sahara Desert.

4. Looking eastwards, the Straits of Gibraltar and the Mediterranean Sea, separating Europe from North Africa.

5. Cape Town, South Africa, at bottom right of the image.

6. The clear demarcation between the sandy south and the rocky north of the Namib Desert in southwest Africa.

7. Rugged terrain amid the Kenyan uplands.

8. The Somali coastal plain of East Africa, and the Indian Ocean.

2

3

AUSTRALASIA

Australasia covers a vast area of islands dotted across the southwestern Pacific Ocean, and also includes the landmass of the Australian continent and the twin islands of New Zealand to the southeast. To the northwest of Australia, across the Timor and Arafura seas, lies Indonesia. Across the Torres Strait is jungle-clad Papua New Guinea. The Coral Sea Islands Territory is to the northeast, beyond the Great Barrier Reef which lies off Queensland's coast. Further out into the Pacific are a myriad islands piercing the ocean like stars in the night sky. Across the Tasman Sea in the southeast is the 'Land of the Long White Cloud' – New Zealand – and, across Bass Strait, the island of Tasmania. Then, to the south across the Indian Ocean is the massive, frozen landmass of Antarctica.

The heart of Australasia is, of course, the largely arid landmass of Australia itself. This is the smallest continent and also the sixth largest country in the world. It covers an area, including Tasmania, of 7,682,300 square kilometres (2,966,144 square miles). From Cape York Peninsula in the north to Tasmania in the south, it measures about 3,943 kilometres (2,450 miles), and from west to east some 4,345 kilometres (2,700 miles). The continent's relief is generally low with its highest peak, Mount Kosciusko, rising to only 2,230 metres (7,316 feet). The lowest point is at Lake Eyre, 14 metres (46 feet) below sea level. Between the extremely arid southwest of the country and the well-watered coasts lies a wide belt of land with an unreliable average rainfall of some 76 centimetres (30 inches). The country is rich in many mineral resources. In particular, its bauxite and high-grade iron ore reserves are among the largest in the world. Australia's energy resources, too, include huge quantities of high-quality coal, petroleum, natural gas and almost twenty per cent of global reserves of uranium. Although official government policy is to integrate the native Aborigines into the mainstream of Australian life, many remain poorly educated and trained, arrested at the lowest socioeconomic level of society.

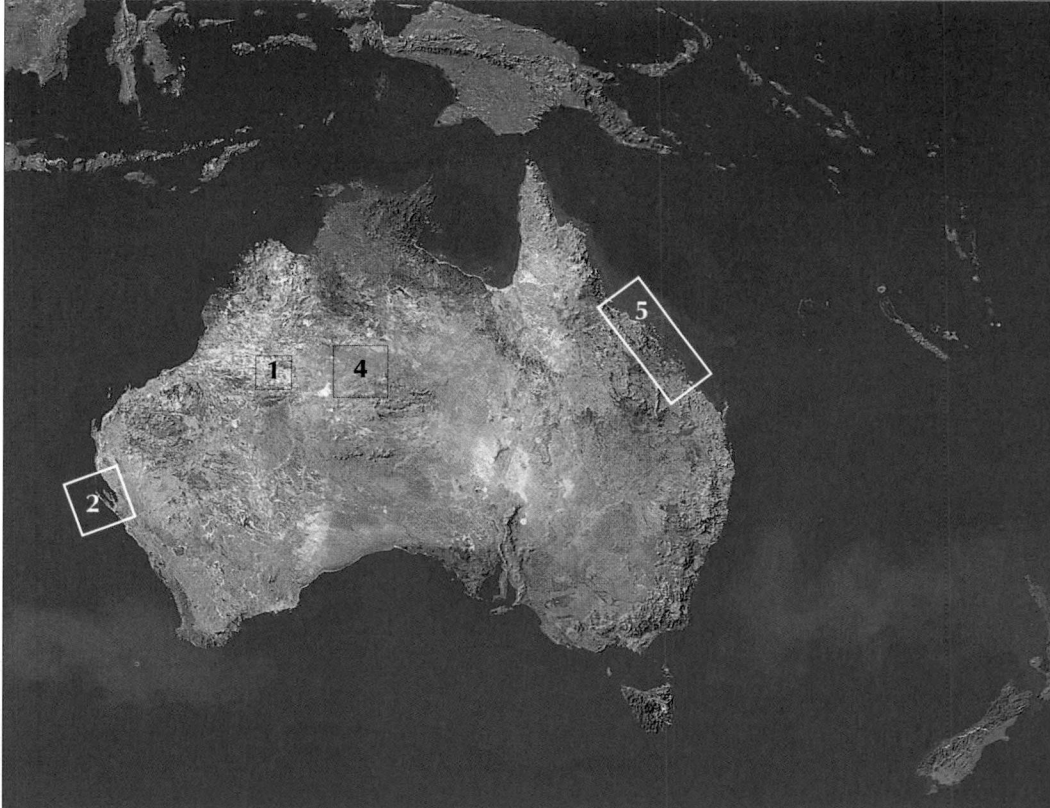

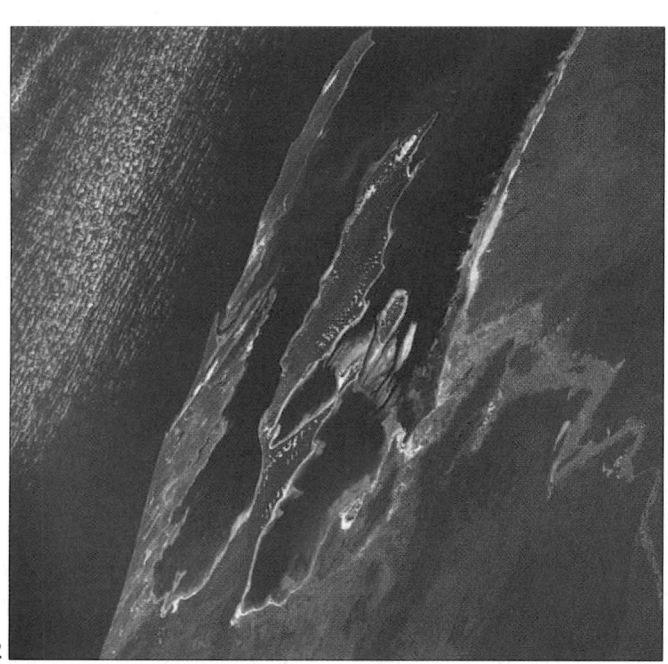

1. Coloured view of the pattern formed by long, dune-like ridges in the Gibson Desert, Western Australia. Recently burnt desert grasses appear in black, while different ages of new growth account for the various colours.

2. Shark Bay, Western Australia, is well known for fine examples of algae reefs, which are most notable in the hypersaline conditions of its south end. On the right, the Wooramel River twists across the landscape.

3. Mosaic of Australasia at a resolution of one kilometre (0.62 miles).

4. View of part of the Sturt Plain, a desert region in the Northern Territory of Australia. Charles Sturt was an explorer who led an expedition north from Adelaide to the edge of the Simpson Desert. The first to penetrate the centre of the continent, his party was finally driven back by heat and scurvy. In the satellite image, long lines of sand dunes, coloured yellow, are seen at left. At the bottom right is part of Lake Woods, a seasonal flood lake 644 kilometres (400 miles) north of Alice Springs.

5. A magnificent view of the northeastern coast of Australia covering the Cooktown, Cairns and Tully region of Queensland. Offshore lies part of the Great Barrier Reef, which extends for more than 2,012 kilometres (1,250 miles) and covers an area of 207,000 square kilometres (80,000 square miles). The Great Barrier Reef actually consists of thousands of individual reefs, shoals and islets. Each has been formed over millions of years from the skeletons and skeletal waste of a mass of marine organisms. Indeed, it has been established that reefs were growing on the continental shelf as early as the Miocene time, more than 25,000,000 years ago. European exploration of the Great Barrier Reef commenced in 1770 when explorer Captain James Cook ran his ship aground upon it. The task of charting channels and passages through such waters has been much simplified by the current use of satellites.

6

6. The Hubble Space Telescope passes over the Australian landmass. Designed to observe far-distant galaxies from high above the optical distortions produced by the Earth's atmosphere, it is clear that the same technology can be used to observe the planet immediately below in the greatest detail. This particular photograph was taken with a fish-eye lens and encompasses much of Western Australia. The twin peninsulas at Shark Bay can be seen at bottom left and, further round the coastline, North West Cape and Exmouth Gulf. Astronaut F Story Musgrave is at the bottom of the frame during a final space walk to service the Hubble Space Telescope.

5

111

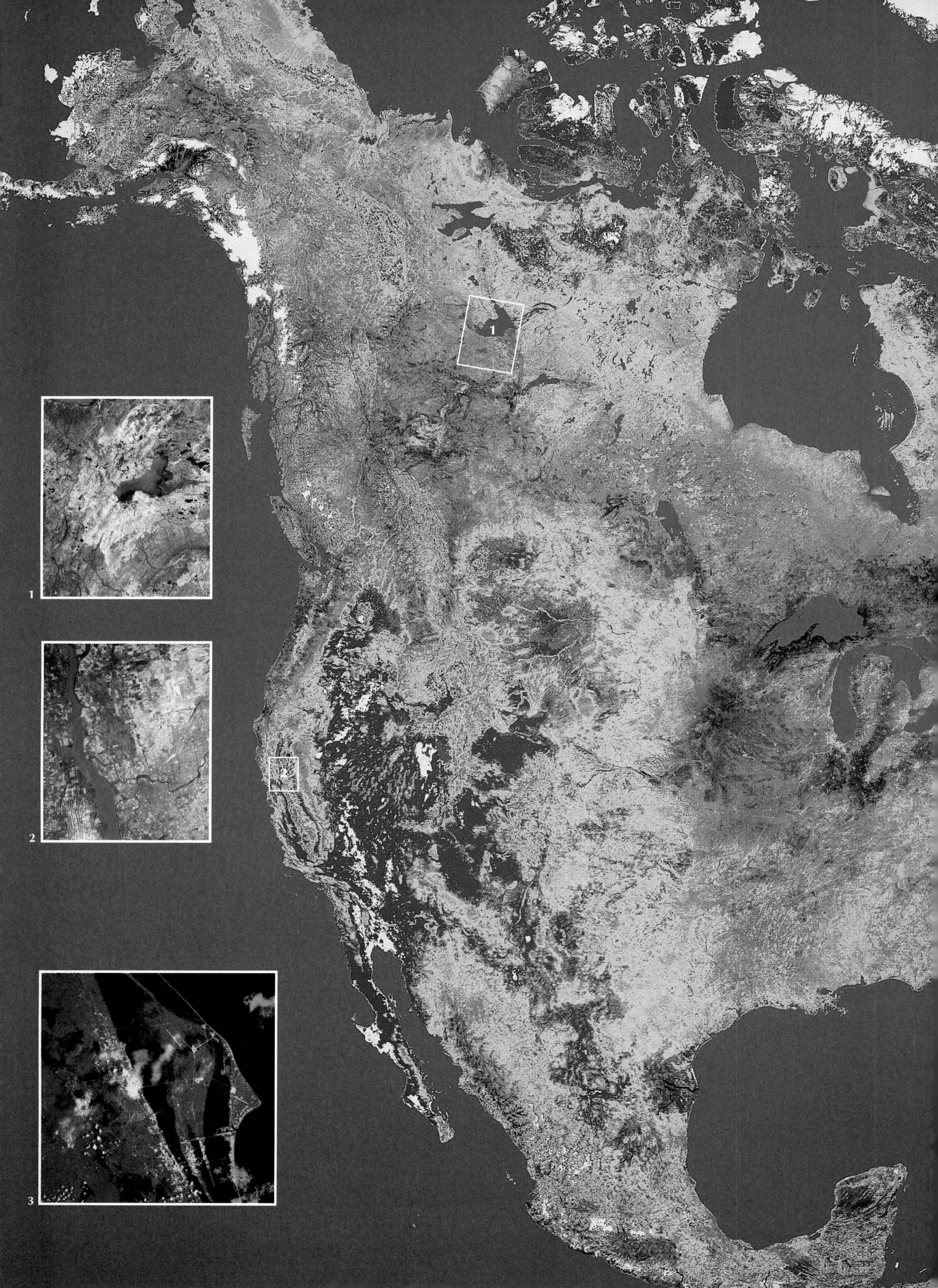

NORTH AMERICA

The North American continent is composed of three major states. Canada, in the north, is the second largest country in the world. Covering 9,970,610 square kilometres (3,849,675 square miles), it occupies forty per cent of North America. Most of Canada's population, however, live within 322 kilometres (200 miles) of the shared border with the United States to the south. Freezing winters and bleak tundra render much of the rest of the land incompatible with large-scale settlement, although some of the native people, the Inuit, continue to live in harmony with their inhospitable surroundings.

The United States comprises forty-eight contiguous states occupying the mid-latitudes of the continent, but also the island state of Hawaii in the mid-Pacific Ocean and the largest state of all, Alaska, in the far northwestern corner of the continent. The total land area is 9,372,571 square kilometres (3,618,770 square miles).

Mexico is a country blessed by an extraordinary physical variety. Covering an area of 1,958,201 square kilometres (756,066 square miles), it is roughly triangular in shape and is situated in the southwestern part of mainland North America.

4

1. Buffalo Lake in Canada's Northwest Territories lies to the south of the massive Great Slave Lake, the fifth largest in North America.

2. The city of Sacramento, capital of California, is situated where the Sacramento and American rivers meet.

3. Cape Canaveral, site of operations for the United States space programme, is a well-preserved national wildlife refuge.

4. The site for Washington, DC, which lies on the Potomac River, was proposed by the first United States president, George Washington. The wide avenues radiating from the Capitol and the White House through a grid of rectangularly drawn streets were part of the original design by French military engineer Pierre-Charles L'Enfant.

5. The North American continent: vast in size, rich in natural resources, diverse in habitats and topography.

5

THE NORTH

Across the continent, in the far north, are lands possessing the harshest environment. Mainland Alaska extends approximately 1,448 kilometres (900 miles) from north to south. From west to east it is about 1,287 kilometres (800 miles) but, when the Aleutian Islands and the southeastern Panhandle are also included, this figure increases to a huge 4,828 kilometres (3,000 miles).

Canada is a massive country. It stretches 4,603 kilometres (2,860 miles) from north to south and almost 5,375 kilometres (3,340 miles) from west to east. Bounded on the south by the United States, it has three oceans – the Pacific, Arctic and Atlantic – at the other cardinal points. Although less than five per cent of Canada's total area is considered to be arable, this still amounts to almost 461,000 square kilometres (178,000 square miles). More than a third of the country is forested. The northern coniferous, or boreal, forest stretches from Alaska to Newfoundland and is one of the largest in the world.

Greenland is the world's largest island, covering 2,175,000 square kilometres (840,000 square miles). Stretching some 2,671 kilometres (1,660 miles) from north to south, and more than 1,046 kilometres (650 miles) from west to east at its widest span, over two-thirds of the country is within the Arctic Circle. Greenland has a deeply indented coastline of 39,315 kilometres (24,430 miles) in length, a distance roughly equivalent to the Earth's circumference at the equator.

3

1

2 4

1. Ottawa, capital of Canada, lies at the confluence of the Gatineau, Ottawa and Rideau rivers, and is named after the Indian tribe which inhabited the region until they fled before the depredations of the Iroquois. The first descriptions of the site of Ottawa were made by the founder of New France, Samuel de Champlain, in 1613.

2. Ice in Hudson Bay, Canada. The bay is named after Henry Hudson who, in 1610, steered his vessel Discovery through these waters, seeking a northwest passage to Asia. For purposes of conservation, the Canadian government decided to declare the whole Hudson Bay Basin a mare clausum, or closed sea, to shipping.

3. At lower centre is the huge mass of the Malaspina Glacier in southern Alaska. To the left of it is Icy Bay and, to the right, Yakutat Bay. Behind the glacier is Mount Saint Elias, which reaches 5,489 metres (18,008 feet). Glaciers occur where snowfall in winter exceeds melting in the summer months, conditions which prevail only in polar regions and high mountain areas. Glacier ice occupies approximately eleven per cent of the land surface of the Earth, almost entirely in Greenland and Antarctica, but it holds about seventy-five per cent of the world's fresh water. There may be anywhere between 70,000 to 200,000 glaciers on the globe.

6. The Finger Lakes of New York. The largest of them (from right to left) are Cayuga, Seneca, the forked lake of Keuka, then Canandaigua to the northwest. These slender bodies of water resulted from glaciers forming in river valleys millions of years ago.

6

5. Bristol Bay and the southwestern coast of Alaska. This land is one of America's last virgin wildernesses and is possessed of a unique natural beauty. Left of lower centre is Hagemeister Island and, beyond Cape Peirce and Cape Newenham, is Kuskokwim Bay. Nunivak Island, separated from the mainland by Etolin Strait, can be seen at the left of the picture. Over the horizon, at the top left of the image, lies the Bering Strait, the common sea border between the territory of the United States and the Russian Federation. A detailed comparison of such photographs over a number of years can provide information about ice drift and an early spring breakup of the coastal ice pack.

4. Greenland, showing numerous indentations. These are fiords carved by glaciers in the last Ice Age. The ice in the centre of Greenland remains some 3,048 metres (10,000 feet) thick.

5

115

USA's NATURAL FEATURES

The continental United States may be classified into five major physiographic regions. These are the North American Cordillera and, within its branches, the Intermontane Plateaux in the west; the Interior Plain across the country's huge middle section; the Appalachian Mountains in the east and southeast; and the Atlantic coastal plain. About twenty per cent of the land is arable. Indeed, the area given over to growing cereal grains alone is approximately the same size as the combined territories of France and Germany. A quarter of the country is rangeland or pastureland, and a further third is covered by forest. Vegetation in Alaska varies from its coastal rainforests to tundra and permafrost along the northern coastal plain. The flora of Hawaii is lush and tropical. The hydrology of the contiguous United States is dominated by the Mississippi River basin, including its major tributaries: the Missouri and Ohio rivers. This river system comprises one of the world's greatest navigable inland waterways. The other major network is shared with Canada in the north and is composed of the St Lawrence River and the Great Lakes. To the west of the Rocky Mountains, most of the rivers are strongly influenced by the arid climate. In the intermontane basins, nearly all of the scanty runoff disappears into interior basins. The Great Salt Lake is the only one of these which holds any large amount of surface water. Leaving to one side lesser coastal streams, only three major rivers systems reach the Pacific Coast: the Colorado, the Columbia and the San Joaquin-Sacramento system of California's Central Valley. All three of these river systems travel for significant distances across dry lands, which supply them with little or no water. Mount McKinley, in the Alaska Range, is the highest peak on the North American continent at 6,194 metres (20,320 feet). Within the conterminous United States, however, that distinction lies in the Sierra Nevada with Mount Whitney at 4,418 metres (14,494 feet). This is a land marked by majesty in its natural features, which invites a corresponding greatness in the people.

1. In 1849, an unfortunate group of people endured a journey through a structural depression in southwestern California: Death Valley was the name they chose to call it. About 225 kilometres (140 miles) long, and from 8-24 kilometres (5-15 miles) wide, it is the hottest and driest part of North America. Any surface water to be found is mostly in saline ponds and marshes. Over a fifty-year period, the average annual rainfall at Furnace Creek was only 42.2 millimetres (1.6 inches). Death Valley also contains the lowest area in the Western Hemisphere at 86 metres (282 feet) below sea level.

1

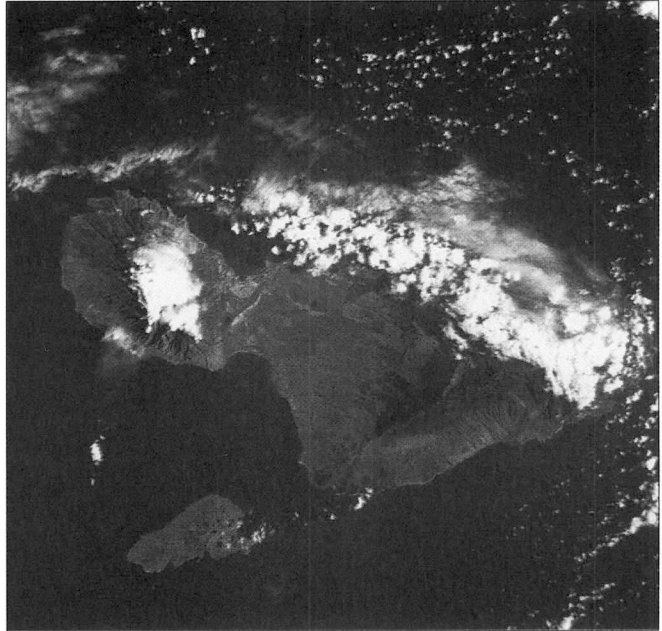

2

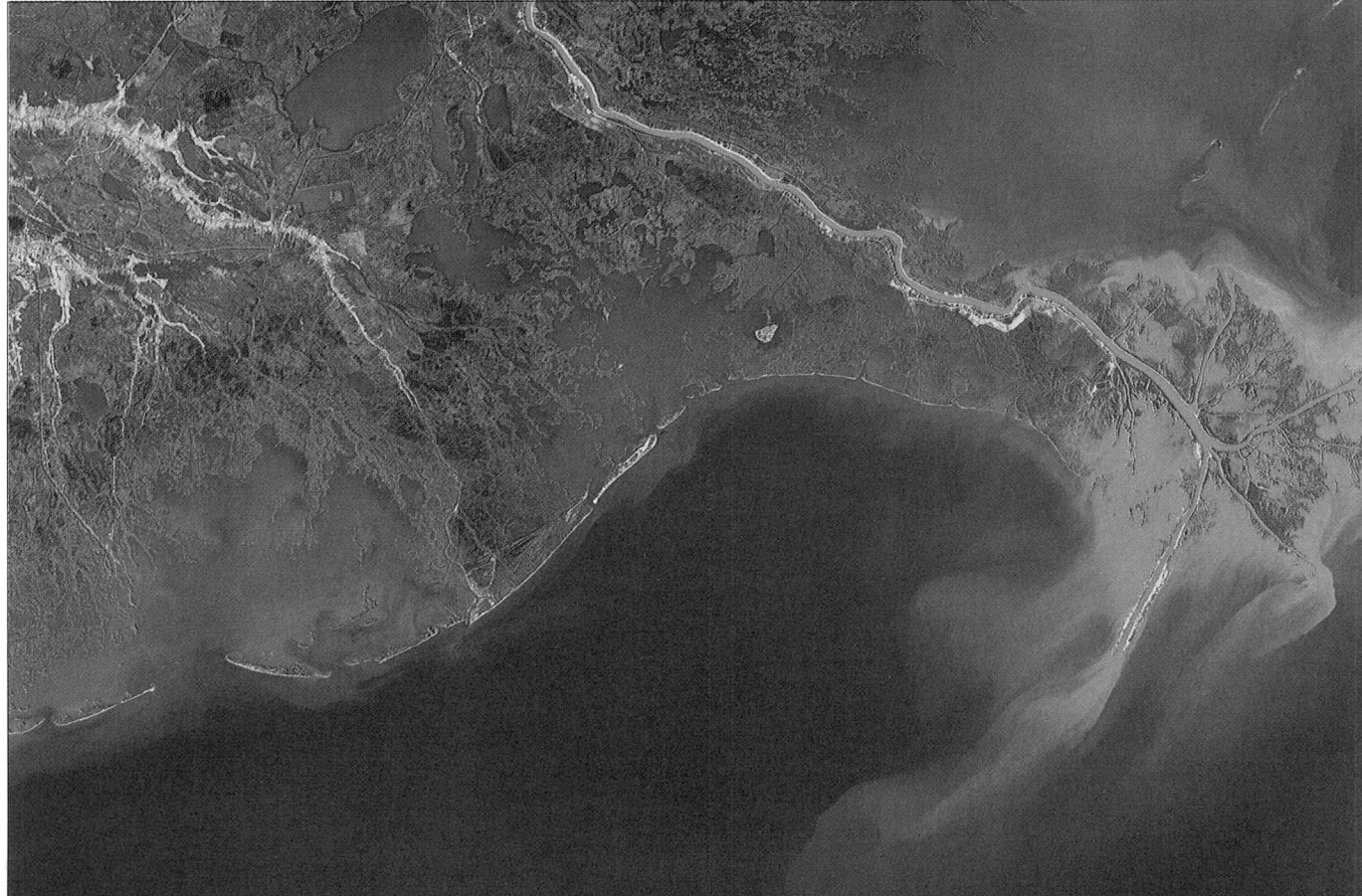

2. The Hawaiian island of Maui, with Kahoolawe across Alalakeiki Channel to the southwest. On the eastern part of the island, cloud cover shrouds Haleakala, the mountain with the world's largest dormant volcanic crater, which measures 32 kilometres (20 miles) in circumference. Away to the northwest, on the isthmus near Kahului, a stream of smoke from burning sugar cane residue is blown towards the area of Hyashi.

3. The Mississippi Delta. Having drained with its major tributaries about one-eighth of the entire continent, the Mississippi empties into the Gulf of Mexico just south of New Orleans. The large body of water to the left of top centre is Lake Salvador.

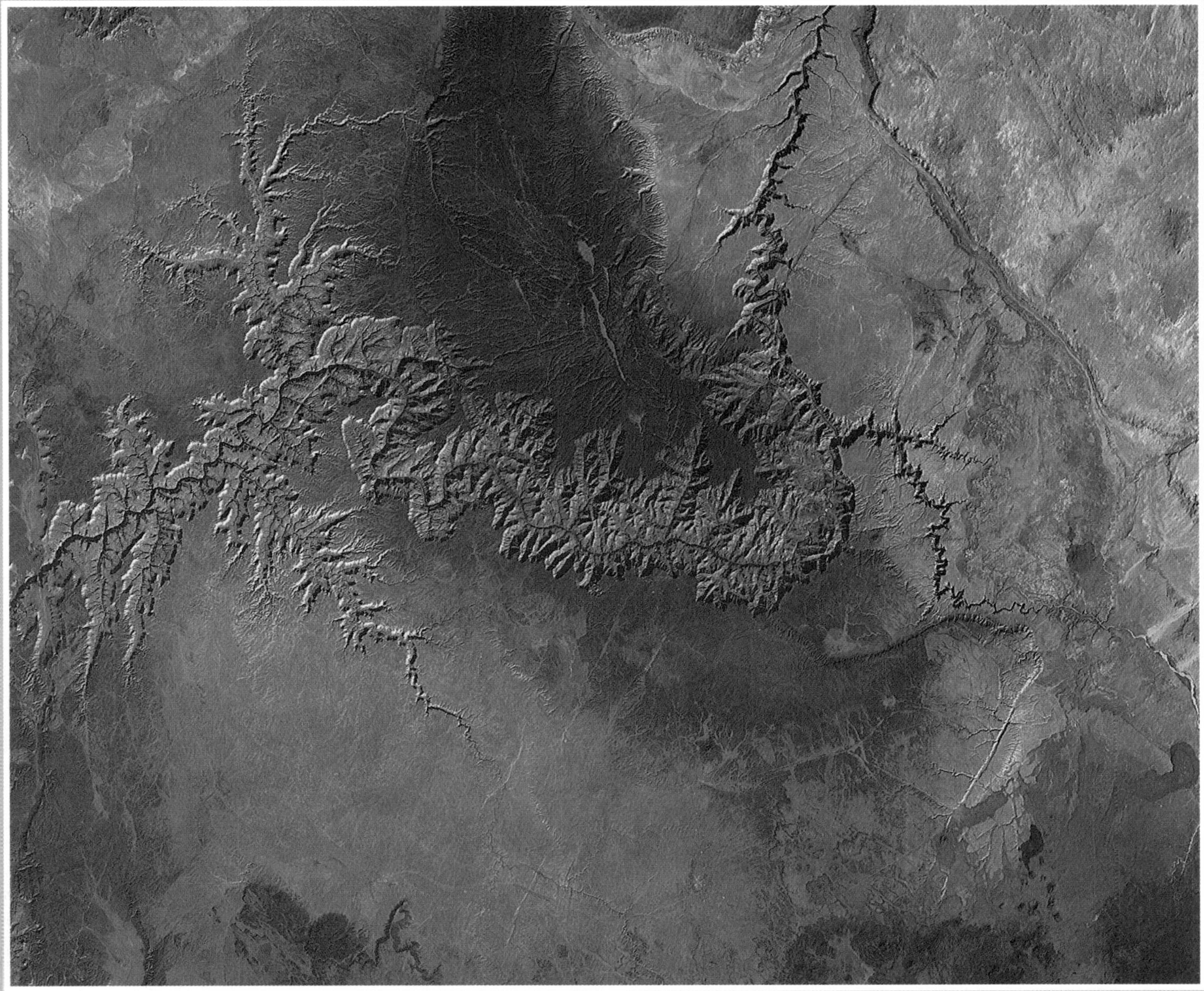

4

4. The Colorado River had to cut through a mile of rock amid the high plateaux of northwestern Arizona to form the Grand Canyon. Contained between the outer walls are a multitude of imposing peaks, buttes, canyons and ravines. Far below, the river plummets 579 metres (1,900 feet) as it passes for 446 kilometres (277 miles) through the immense gorge. This chasm, intricately sculpted by the implacable forces of erosion and time, is indisputably one of the greatest natural wonders of the world.

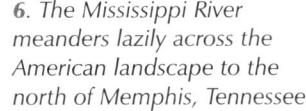

5. A view of California looking northeast over the Salton Sea. San Diego and the Pacific Ocean are at left and a part of the Colorado River is at right. The Salton Sea, despite its name, is a lake at an elevation 71 metres (232 feet) below sea level in Imperial Valley, the pattern of whose fields can be clearly observed at the bottom of the image. The lake is flanked by the Santa Rosa Mountains to the west and the colourfully named Chocolate Mountains to the east.

6. The Mississippi River meanders lazily across the American landscape to the north of Memphis, Tennessee.

6

5

CITIES of the USA

Just a century ago – a mere three generations – the life of the average American citizen was predominantly rural and based upon farming. Today, only about three per cent of the work force is employed in agriculture, which is almost exclusively managed around a mechanistic, chemically fertilized approach to cultivation. The values engendered by the pioneering homesteaders that journeyed across the North American continent in the 1800s may still remain, but the vast majority of the population are now settled in built-up areas. The cities of the United States, therefore, are the modern expression of America. Along the coastlines are some of the great, historical seaports of the country. Fine, natural anchorages allowed early seafarers to cross the Atlantic, and to work their way up the West Coast, in the sure knowledge that a safe haven awaited them. Today, these urban centres have expanded immensely in population and area. Other cities were established along the major rivers, which acted as vital transportation routes before the advent of cars, motorways and rapid technological change allowed civic regions to develop largely unconstrained by factors of terrain. The result is that the modern metropolis eclipses rather than coexists with the natural landscape.

4. Looking northeastward across San Francisco, which lies at the head of the peninsula at lower right. Linking the city with Sausalito to the north is the Golden Gate Bridge.

5. Night-time lighting across America reveals the principal urban centres of population.

6. Boston is a major seaport and the historical, cultural, industrial and commercial centre of New England.

7. The city of Miami. To the west is the Everglades. On the peninsula at bottom right of the image is Miami Beach, south of which is Virginia Key, then Key Biscayne and, at its tip, Cape Florida.

1. A superlative view of New York City. At lower centre, ships sail between Upper and Lower New York Bay under the Verrazano Narrows Bridge; to the left is Staten Island, to the right is Brooklyn. The Hudson River bisects the image from top to bottom. On its lower east bank, at the base of the peninsula, is Manhattan, with the Bronx further to the north.

2. Located on the Salt River, Phoenix occupies a semiarid, saucer-shaped valley, surrounded by mountains and green irrigated fields, in the south central part of Arizona.

3. Des Moines, Iowa, lies in the heart of the Corn Belt, situated midway between the Missouri and Mississippi rivers.

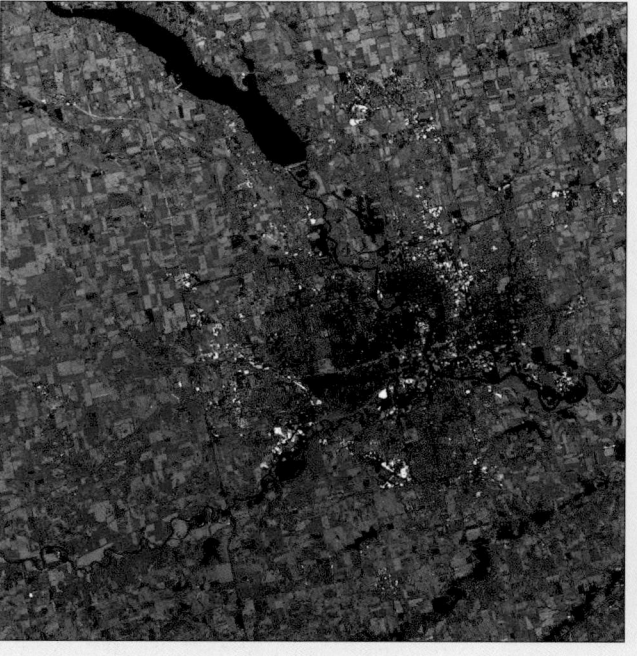

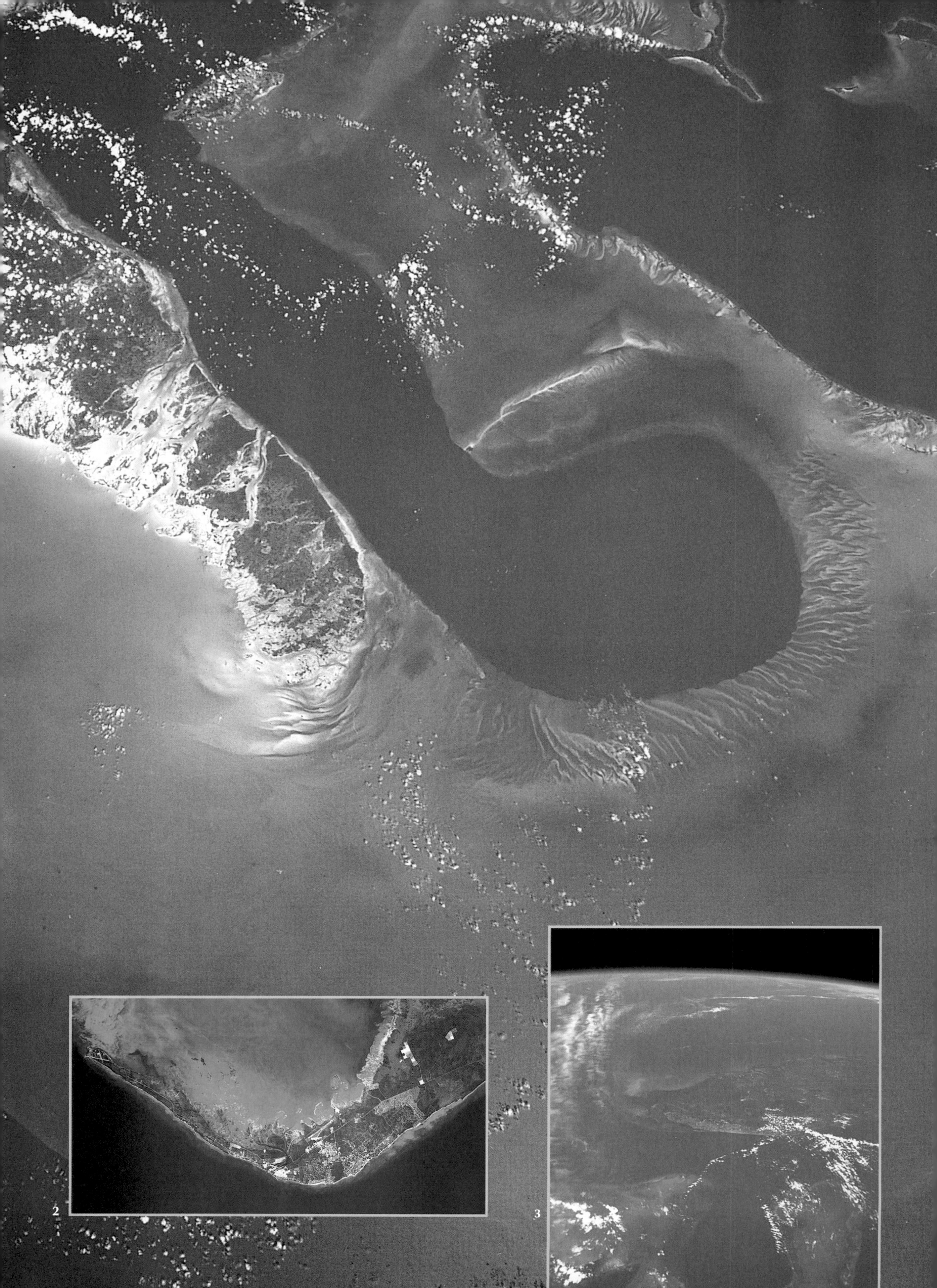

USA and CENTRAL AMERICA

The southeast of the United States contains some of the most sunny and pleasant areas on the continent. Florida, for example, is noted for a balmy environment and beautiful beaches, as well as its famous Everglades.

Not far away to the southeast are the Bahamas, consisting of about seven hundred islands and more than two thousand barren rock formations and cays. Covering about 233,000 square kilometres (90,000 square miles) of ocean in the western Atlantic, the archipelago's total land area is only 13,939 square kilometres (5,382 square miles). The largest of the islands is Andros, 167 kilometres (104 miles) long and 64 kilometres (40 miles) wide. The Bahamas are generally only a few feet above sea level, the highest point being Mount Alvernia on Cat Island at 63 metres (206 feet). The subtropical climate encourages much beautiful flora, including bougainvillea, jasmine, oleander and orchids.

To the west of Florida is the Gulf of Mexico, a huge body of water covering more than 1,300,000 square kilometres (500,000 square miles), with a volume of 2,332,000 cubic kilometres (559,000 cubic miles). The principal rivers draining into the Gulf are the Mississippi and further west the Rio Grande, which marks the frontier between the United States and Mexico before turning northwards into the state of New Mexico at El Paso.

Most of Mexico is occupied by the central Mexican Plateau, which is flanked by two high cordilleras (the Sierra Madre Occidental to the west and the Sierra Madre Oriental to the east), with the Isthmus of Tehuantepec to the south. Half of the country is characterised as predominantly arid, forty per cent semiarid, and less than ten per cent humid.

4

6

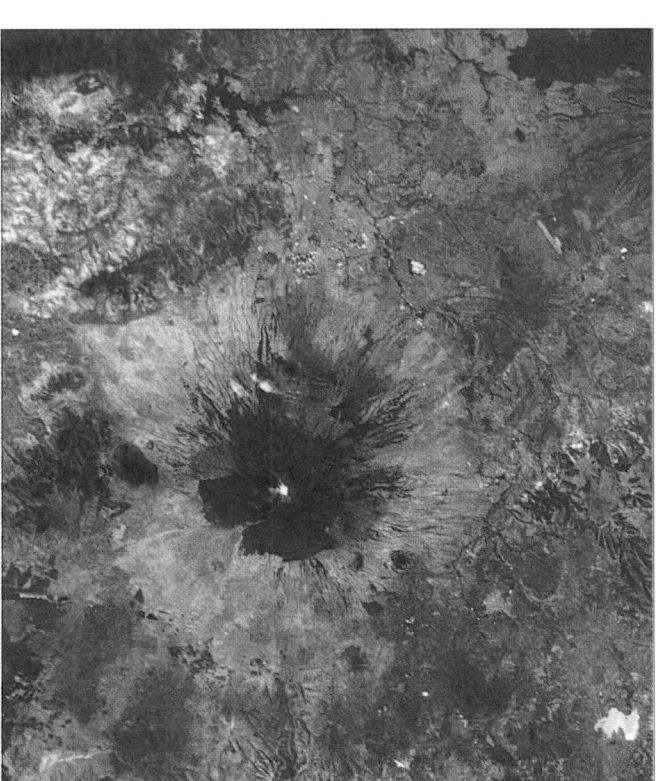

5

1. Southeast of Florida lies the island of Andros in the Bahamas. Undulating waves of sand, built by currents at the bottom of the sea, can be clearly seen and, in particular, the offshore depths known as the 'Tongue of the Ocean'.

2. Freeport City on the southwestern shore of the island of Grand Bahama.

3. Looking westwards across the Florida Peninsula *to the Gulf of Mexico. In the foreground, just right of centre, is Grand Bahama.*

4. New Mexico's Badland, or Malpais, photographed from aboard the Space Shuttle. Flanked by the San Andre Mountains to the west, and the Sacramento Mountains to the east, the Badland is actually a lava flow of the relatively recent geological past. The rattlesnakes in this region have evolved a dark black *colour to adapt to their environment. Also to the west is the Jornada del Muerto (Journey of Death), the old El Paso to Santa Fe wagon trail.*

5. The volcanic Cerro La Malinche rises 4,500 metres (14,766 feet) near Puebla, Mexico.

6. Surrounded by mountains, Mexico City is prone to terrible smogs caused by air pollution.

121

SOUTH AMERICA

The landscape of South America varies from tropical jungles in the north to the cold, dry, rugged regions of the south. In the west, the Andes Mountains tower to the sky, forming a backbone to the continent through the territories of Colombia, Ecuador, Peru, Bolivia, Argentina and Chile. Here the steep slopes are grazed by sure-footed animals such as llamas and are often terraced in order to grow crops such as coffee, wheat and potatoes. By contrast, in the southeast, there are flat and fertile plains – the Pampas – which are grazed by countless cattle, and where farmers can cultivate large crops of barley, maize and wheat.

Great rivers drain the continent, such as the Orinoco and the Parana. But, above all others, it is the Amazon River of Brazil that commands attention. It has been estimated that from twenty to twenty-five per cent of all the water that runs off the Earth's surface is carried by this river. Indeed, the average discharge of 180,000 cubic metres (6,350,000 cubic feet) per second at its mouth is about ten times that of the Mississippi River. This discharge is so great that it turns the ocean from salty to brackish for more than 160 kilometres (100 miles) offshore.

Another awesome natural wonder is the vast Brazilian rainforest, home to perhaps half the living species on Earth. This huge area of trees helps to absorb the increasing levels of atmospheric carbon dioxide that are generated by the combustion of fossil fuels and, in particular, by the use of cars. The reality, however, is that these trees are being felled at an alarming rate. Indeed, one estimate suggests that every minute an area the size of twenty football pitches is being cleared. The destruction of the rainforest has alarmed the world and acts as a powerful symbol of the rapacious nature of unchecked capitalism.

It is clear that fresh ideas and strategies must be considered if humankind is to survive the next millennium. Respect for the living planet, Mother Earth – as well as for its human and animal inhabitants – must be enkindled.

1. Colour composite view of Amazonas, Brazil. The Rio Negro river is the large body of water travelling diagonally across the image from the top left. The Rio Solimoes, at bottom left of centre, flows northeasterly to join the Rio Negro and form the Amazon River at Manaus, seen far right.

The Amazon flows almost 6,437 kilometres (4,000 miles) across northern Brazil, and is the largest river in the world in volume and in the area of its drainage basin. Large freighters can navigate the river as far as Manaus, which lies 1,609 kilometres (1,000 miles) upriver from the Atlantic Ocean.

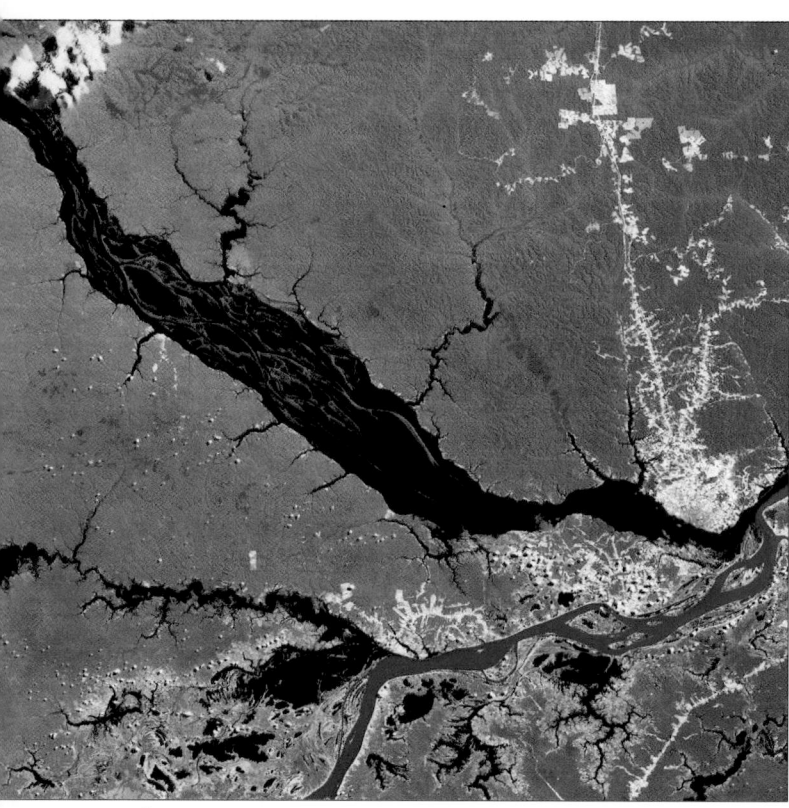

1

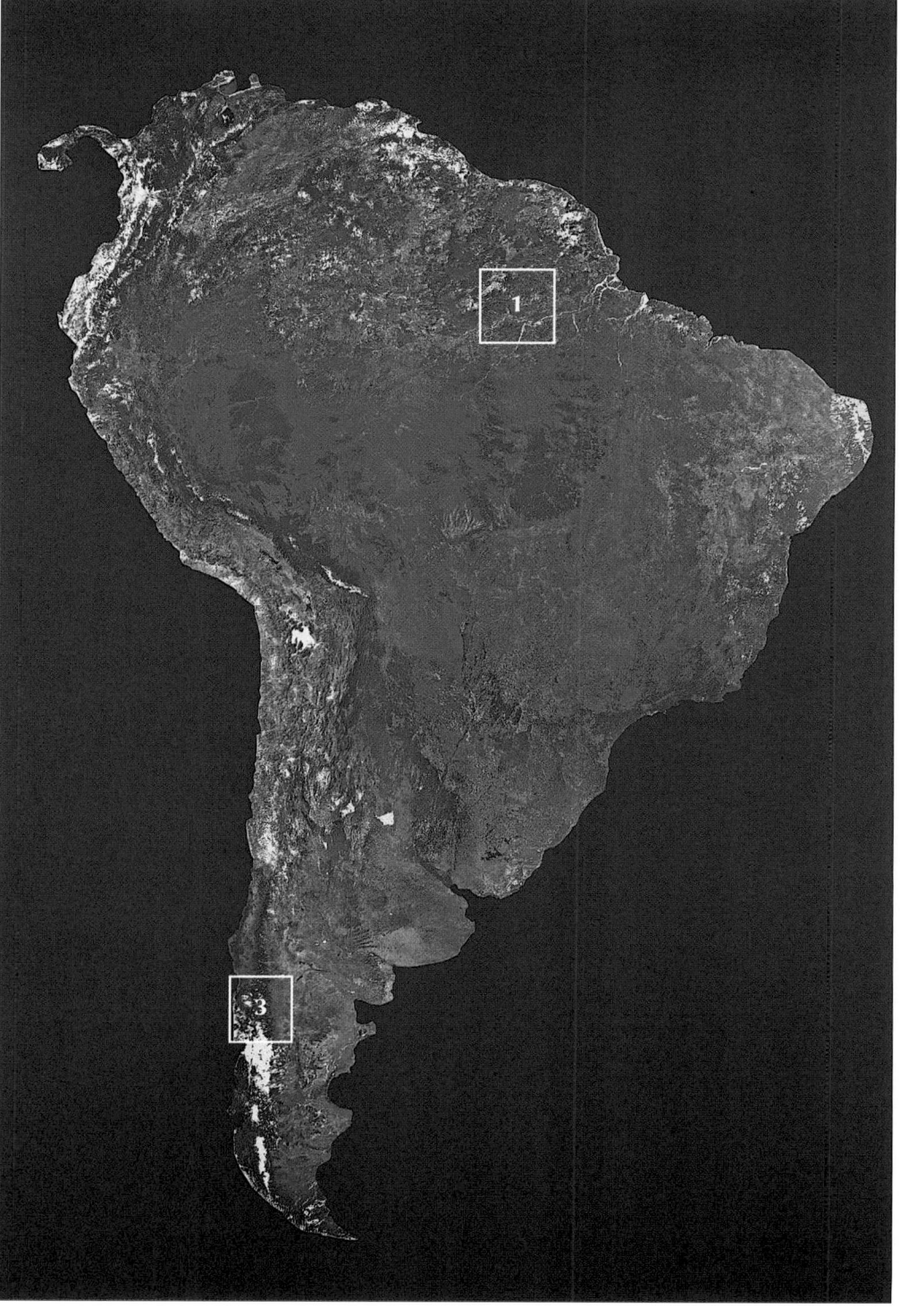

2. South America, home to the world's greatest rainforests.

3. The stark volcanic terrain of the high Andes in northern Chile. In these mountains are hundreds of volcanic edifices (peaks, cinder cones, lava flows, debris fields and eroded calderas), with lakes and dry lake beds (salars) in the basins.

Deeply incised marks on the landscape can be seen where streams cut downwards in their westward passage.

4. Isabela, 966 kilometres (600 miles) west of Ecuador, is the largest of the Galapagos Islands.

2

3

4

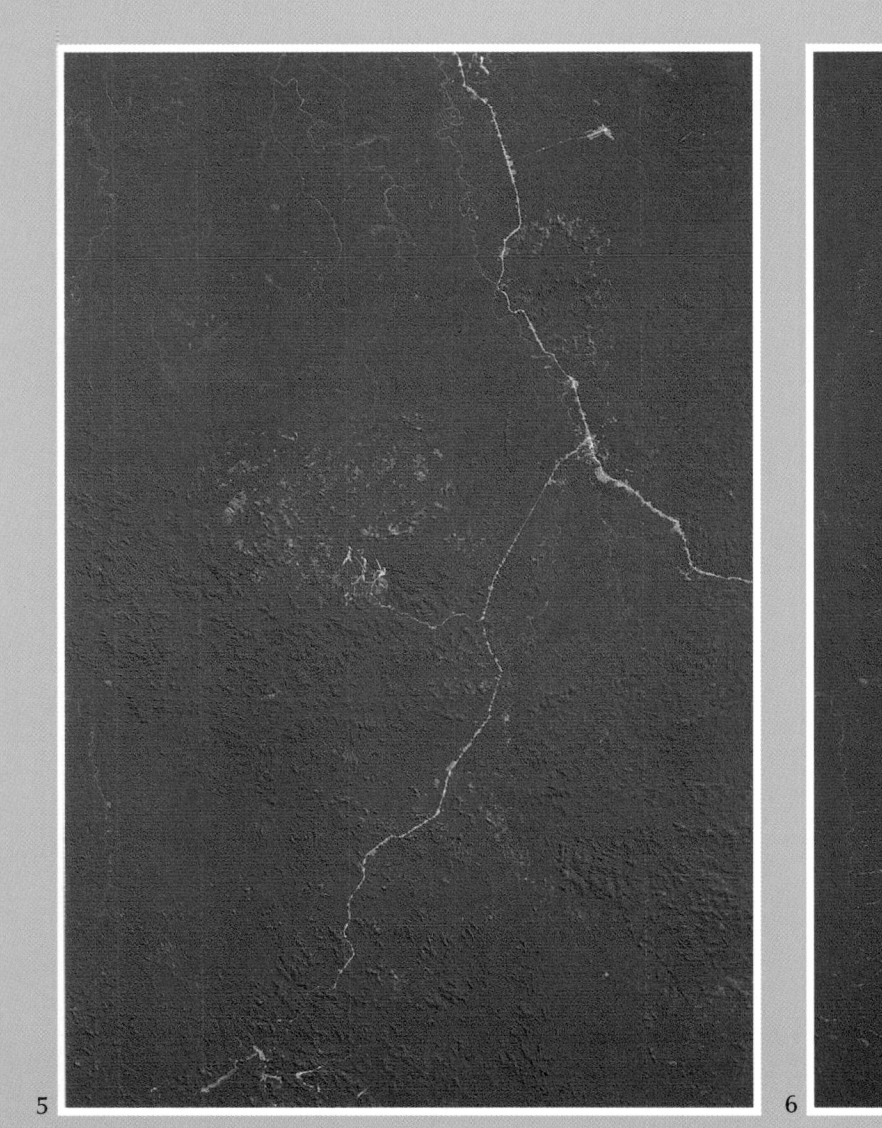

5

6

5 & 6. These remarkable images of the Brazilian rainforest, separated by just eleven years, are eloquent testimony to the disastrous environmental damage that is being executed in South America. Logging, ranching, agricultural, mining and business interests all hope to benefit from the destruction of the luxurious forest that cloaks the Amazon Basin. From these pictures, it is clear that a systematic clearing of vast swathes of rainforest is now going on with incalculable consequences for the Earth as a whole.

The POLAR REGIONS

The Polar regions are among the most inhospitable areas on Earth but, perhaps for that very reason, they still exercise a potent fascination.

The northern polar region is without a landmass beneath it, being formed from the frozen Arctic Ocean. More than 60 per cent of the region is free of ice and three main vegetation zones can be seen: low Arctic tundra, high Arctic tundra and polar desert. Surrounded by continents, the lands of the Arctic are generally low lying or flat, although Greenland and eastern Canada have distinctive highlands with some areas exceeding 2,000 metres (6,561 feet). Besides the Greenland ice sheet, glaciers are restricted to the Canadian Arctic's eastern uplands, and the maritime islands and peninsulas found off northwestern Eurasia.

Antarctica is the fifth in size of the continents, with an area of 14,200,000 square kilometres (5,500,000 square miles) almost wholly covered in ice. The volume of this ice sheet is about 30,000,000 cubic kilometres (7,000,000 cubic miles) and comprises some 90 per cent of the world's glacial ice. While Antarctica's ice contains the potential for vast quantities of fresh water, the continent must still be considered one of the world's great deserts, with very limited precipitation occurring over the polar plateau. The highest point is Vinson Massif, which rises to 5,140 metres (16,864 feet) amid the Sentinel Range.

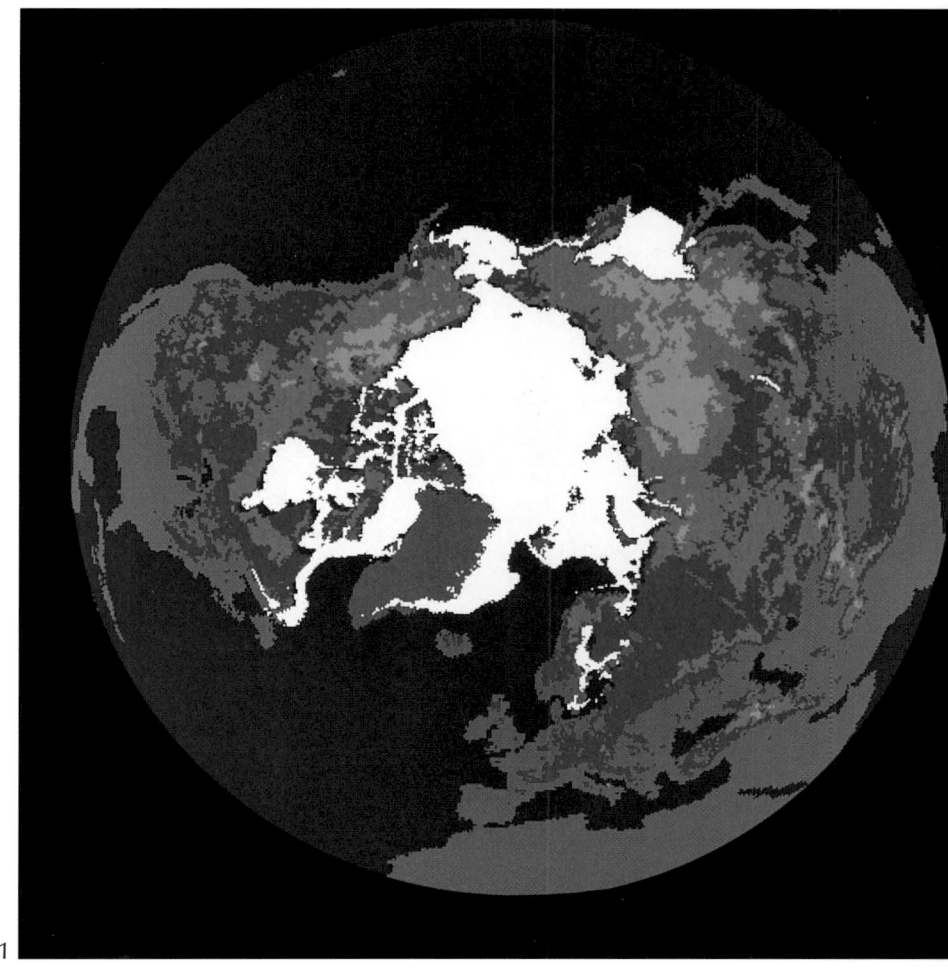

1

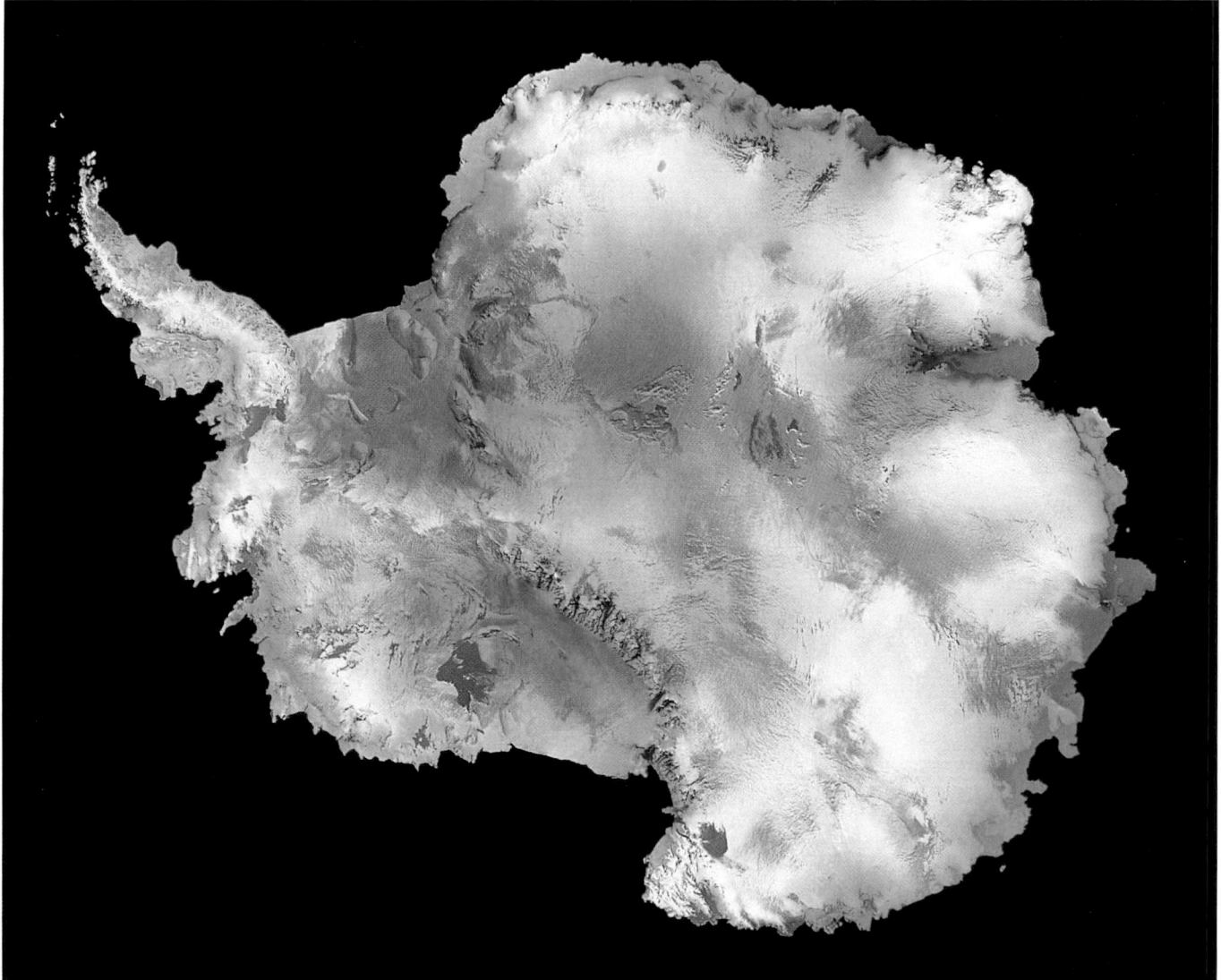

2

1. Image derived from data gathered by a meteorology satellite showing maximum winter distribution of ice and snow cover in the northern polar region. Areas of sea with more than fifty per cent ice are portrayed as white. Snow cover is displayed in shades of blue, ranging from dark blue (up to 10 centimetres, or four inches, depth), to mid-blue (10-20 centimetres, or 4-8 inches, depth) to pale blue (over 20 centimetres, or 8 inches, depth). The deepest snowfalls, therefore, are seen over northern Canada and Siberia in the Russian Federation.

2. An enhanced colour satellite mosaic of Antarctica, aligned with the Greenwich meridian to the top. The colours have been accentuated to show the large-scale structure of the ice cover over the continent, seen here with its permanent ice. The majority of the ice in this picture covers land, with the exception of the Ronne Ice Shelf (brown tint left of centre) and the Ross Ice Shelf (brown tint lower left of centre). Near the centre of the continent, the permanent ice cover is over 3,000 metres (9,844 feet) thick.

MAP LEGEND

SETTLEMENT

For scales larger than 1 inch : 30 miles   Population

	BIRMINGHAM	>1,000,000
	GLASGOW	500,000–1,000,000
	CARDIFF	250,000–500,000
	LIMERICK	50,000–250,000
•	**Dover**	10,000–50,000
•	Lossiemouth	5,000–10,000
○	Church Stretton	<5,000
	CROYDON	London Borough

For scales between 1 inch : 30 miles and 1 inch : 190 miles

	NEW YORK	>5,000,000
	MONTRÉAL	2,500,000–5,000,000
■	**SAN DIEGO**	1,000,000–2,500,000
•	**Hyderabad**	500,000–1,000,000
•	Adelaide	100,000–500,000
○	Key West	<100,000

For scales smaller than 1 inch : 190 miles

■	**LOS ANGELES**	>1,000,000
•	**Maracaibo**	500,000–1,000,000
•	Santa Fe	<500,000

Washington   National capital   **Winnipeg**   State, provincial capital

COMMUNICATIONS

═══════	Highway
░░░░░░░	Highway under construction
───────	Principal road
- - - - - - -	Principal road under construction
───────	Other main road
— — — —	Track, seasonal road
→⊢ ⊣←	Road tunnel
───────	Principal railroad
— — — —	Principal railroad under construction
→⊢ ⊣←	Railroad tunnel
✈	International, main airport

BOUNDARIES

━━━━━	International
▬ ▬ ▬	Undefined, disputed
───────	Internal, state, provincial
— — — —	Armistice, ceasefire line

The representation of a boundary in this atlas does not denote its international recognition and therefore the de facto situation has been depicted.

HYDROGRAPHIC FEATURES

～～～	River, stream
～·～·	Intermittent watercourse
～～～	Waterfall, rapids
～／～	Dam, barrage
╱╱╱	Irrigation, drainage channel
╱╱╱	Canal
～～～	Lake, reservoir
～～～	Intermittent, seasonal lake
～～～	Salt pan, mud flat
∙	Oasis
⣿	Marsh, swamp
～～～	Reef

Depth of sea in meters

Scales larger than 1 inch : 190 miles   Scales smaller than 1 inch : 190 miles

0		0
200		1000
3000		5000

OTHER FEATURES

▲ 3798	Elevation above sea level (meters)
▼ -133	Depression below sea level (meters)
≍	Pass
•—•—■	Oil, gas pipeline with field

ENVIRONMENTAL TYPES

	Permanent ice and snow
	Mountain and moorland
	Tundra
	Coniferous forest
	Deciduous forest
	Tropical forest
	Prairie
	Temperate agriculture
	Mediterranean scrub
	Savannah
	Desert

This representation of the environment and its associated vegetation gives an overview of the landscape. It is not intended to be definitive.

CONVERSION SCALES

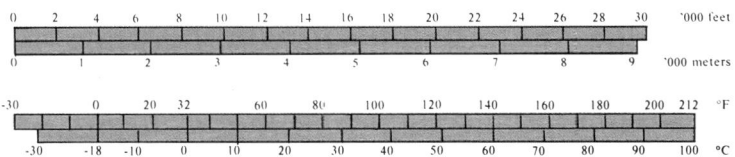

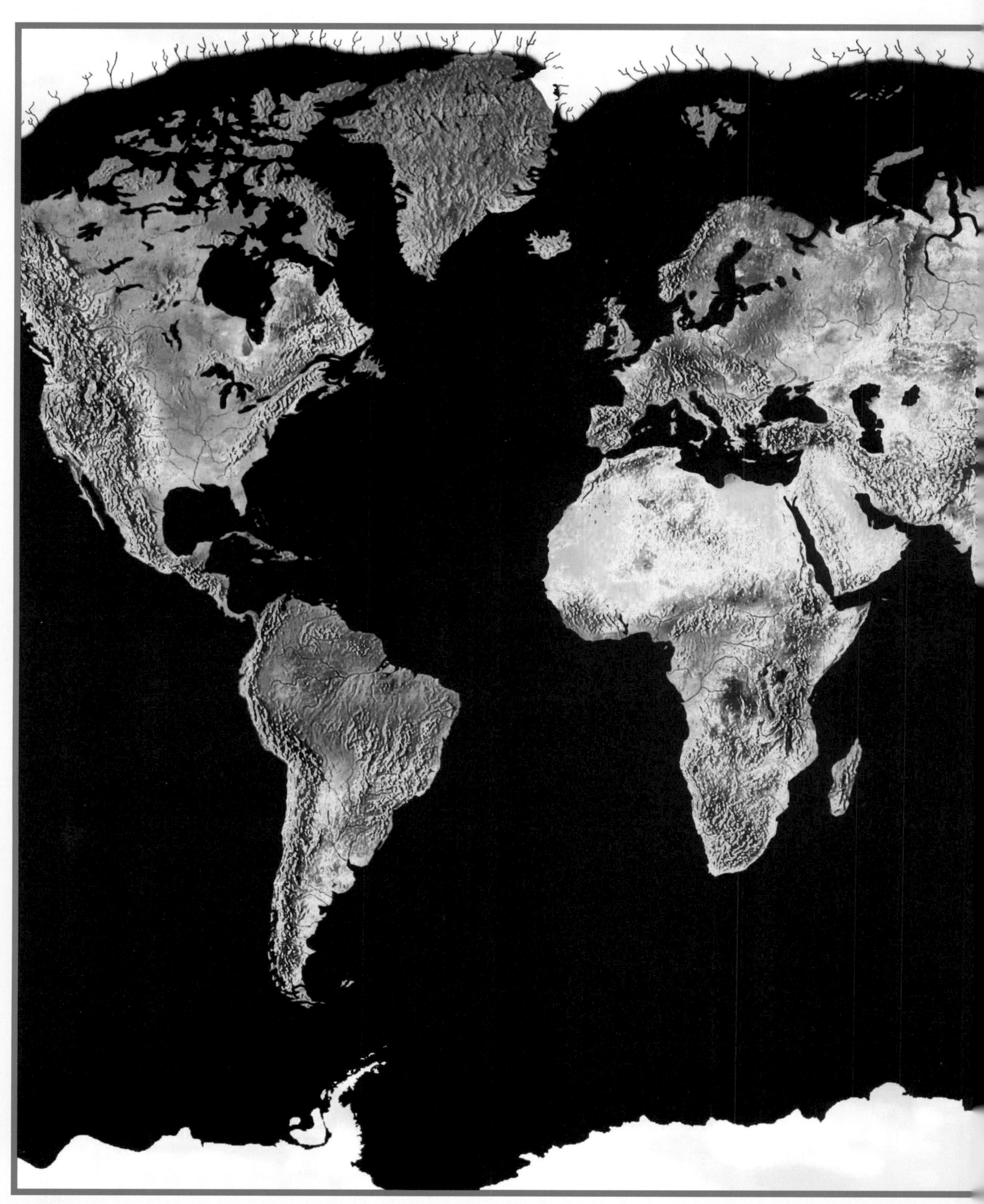

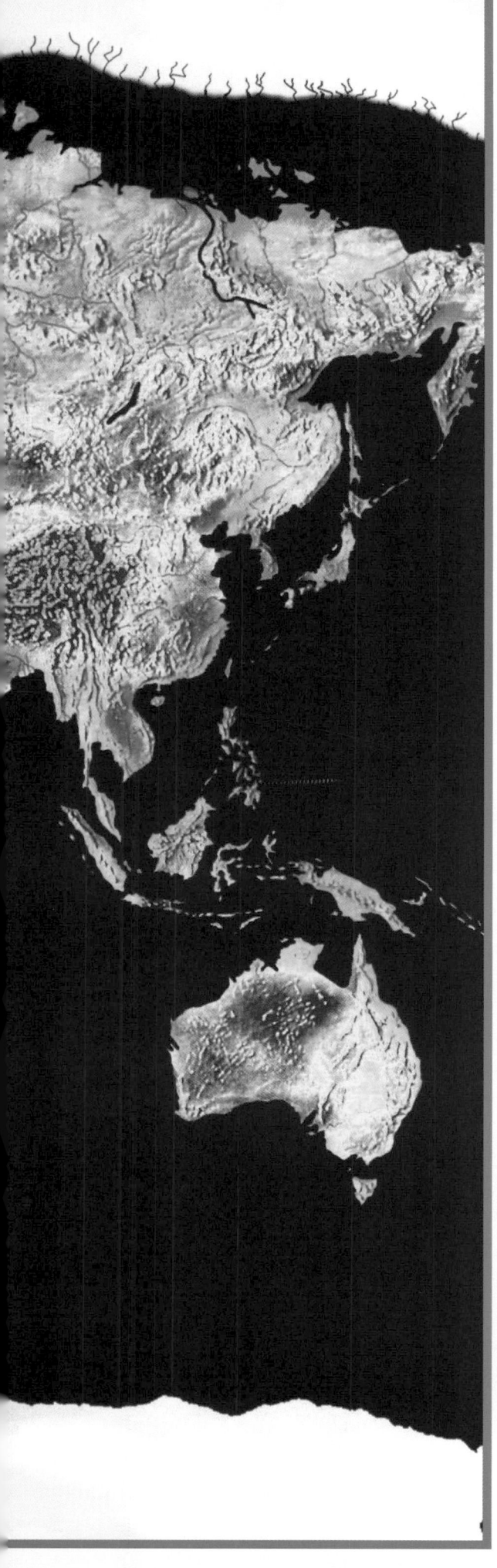

THE
WORLD
IN
MAPS

The oldest known maps were drawn by the Babylonians on clay tablets about 2300 BC. Thereafter, the *Guide to Geography* – written by the Greek mathematician and astronomer Ptolemy (AD 90-168) – influenced cartography for almost a thousand years. During the Middle Ages, religious dogma decreed that the world was a flat disk. Little progress was made, therefore, until the end of the medieval period when worldwide exploration and scientific progress led to improved maps. Aerial photography in the early twentieth century provided another impetus, but the mapping which follows owes much of its accuracy to the current extensive use of satellite imagery. Its clarity, however, is still due to the art of the cartographer.

Mercator Projection

1:85,000,000 (Scale at the Equator)

ARCTIC OCEAN

Zemlya Frantsa-Iosifa
(Russia)

Severnaya Zemlya

Novosibirskiye Ostrova

Karskoye
More
Gory Byrranga
More
Laptevykh
Lyakhovskiye
Ostrova
Vostochno
Sibirskoye
More

Novaya
Zemlya

Ozero Taymyr

Ostrov Vrangelya

Barentsevo
More

Nordkapp
Poluostrov
Yamal
Gydanskiy
Poluostrov
Plato
Putorana
Kolmskaya
Nizmennost

Lappland
Beloye
More
Zapadno
Sibirskaya
Sredne
Sibirskoye
Ploskogor ye
Khrebet Cherskogo
Anadyrskiy
Zaliv

SWEDEN
FINLAND
Ravnina
Arctic Circle
Bering
Sea

Stockholm
Helsingfors
Tallinn
ST. PETERSBURG
RUSSIA
Okhotskoye
More
Aleutian Islands

København
ESTONIA
LATVIA
Riga
MOSKVA
Kuybyshevskoye
Vodokhranilishche
Ozero Baykal
Sakhalin
Bering
Sea

Berlin
LITHUANIA
Vilnius
Minsk
BELARUS
Ulaanbaatar
Kuril'skiye Ostrova

POLAND
Warszawa
Kryïv (Kiev)
UKRAINE
KAZAKHSTAN
MONGOLIA
Gobi
Sakhalin

CZECH
REP.
SLOVAK
REP.
Budapest
MOLDOVA
Prikaspiyskaya
Nizmennost'
Kirgiz
Step'
N KOREA
Pyŏngyang
Sea of
Japan
JAPAN
NORTH
PACIFIC
OCEAN

Black Sea
GEORGIA
Ozero Balkhash
Aral'skoye
More
Tashkent
Alma-Ata
BEIJING
S KOREA
SŎUL
TŌKYŌ

Caspian
Sea
ARMENIA
Baku
AZERBAIJAN
UZBEKISTAN
KYRGYZSTAN
Bishkek
Tian Shan
Tarim
Pendi
CHINA
TIANJIN
Huang
Hai

TURKEY
Ankara
Yerevan
TURKMENISTAN
TAJIKISTAN
Taklimakan
Shamo
SHANGHAI

CYPRUS
Levkosia
Dimashq
Ashgabat
Dushanbe
Hindu Kush
Kūhha
ye Zagros
IRAN
Kābul
AFGHANISTAN
PAKISTAN
Islamabad
Xizang
Gaoyuan
Himalaya
Tropic of Cancer

ISRAEL
Baghdād
Amman
TEHRĀN
Thar
Desert
DELHI
New Delhi
Kathmandu
NEPAL
EVEREST
Tʻai-pei
TAIWAN

LIBYA
EGYPT
EL QĀHIRA
Al Kuwayt
KUW.
Al Manāmah
BAH.
Ad Dawhah
QAT.
Abū Zabī
U.A.E.
KARACHI
INDIA
CALCUTTA
Dhaka
BANG.
Hanoi
HONG KONG

SAUDI
ARABIA
Ar Riyāḍ
Masqaṭ
OMAN
MUMBAI
(Bombay)
Deccan
Bay of
Bengal
MYANMAR
Yangon
LAOS
Viangchan
THAI-
LAND
KRUNG THEP
VIETNAM
CAM.
Phnom Penh
MANILA
Luzon
Marianas Is.
Guam (USA)
Marshall Is.

Red Sea
CHAD
SUDAN
El Khartum
ERITREA
Asmera
San'a
YEMEN
Suquṭrā
(S Yem.)
Arabian
Sea
Lakshadweep
(India)
CHENNAI
(Madras)
Andaman
Islands
(India)
PHILIPPINES
Mindanao
Caroline Islands
Micronesia

ETHIOPIA
Adis Abeba
SOMALIA
Maldives
Malé
Colombo
SRI LANKA
MALAYSIA
Bandar Seri
Begawan
BRU.
Kuala Lumpur
Borneo
Maluku
Tarawa
Gilbert Is.
NAURU
Phoenix Is.

UGANDA
Kampala
KENYA
Nairobi
Muqdisho
MALDIVES
SINGAPORE
Sumatera
Sulawesi
New PAPUA NEW
Guinea GUINEA
Equator

TANZANIA
Dodoma
KILIMANJARO
Victoria
SEYCHELLES
Jawa
JAKARTA
INDONESIA
Laut Arafura
Port Moresby
SOLOMON ISLANDS
Honiara
Santa
Cruz Is.
TUVALU
Fanafuti
Iles Wallice

ANGOLA
ZAMBIA
Lusaka
MALAWI
Lilongwe
INDIAN OCEAN
Java Trench
East Indies
Timor
Laut
Timor
Coral
Sea
VANUATU
Vila
FIJI
Suva
SAMOA
Apia
TONGA
Nuku'alofa

NAMIBIA
Windhoek
ZIMBABWE
Harare
BOTSWANA
Gaborone
MOZAMBIQUE
MADAGASCAR
Antananarivo
MAURITIUS
Réunion
(Fr.)
Port Louis
Nouvelle
Calédonie
(Fr.)
Tropic of Capricorn

SOUTH
AFRICA
Pretoria
Maputo
SWAZILAND
LESOTHO
Maseru
AUSTRALIA
Gt. Victoria Desert
L. Eyre
Gt. Dividing Range
Great Barrier Reef

of Good Hope
C. Leeuwin
Canberra

Tasman Sea
NEW ZEALAND
Wellington
Chatham Is.
(N.Z.)

Tasmania

Prince Edward Is.
(S.A.)
Iles Crozet
(Fr.)
Ile Kerguelen
(Fr.)
Auckland Is.
(N.Z.)
Macquarie Is.
(Aus.)

Heard I.
(Aus.)

Designed and produced by E.S.R.

West of Greenwich   East of Greenwich

© COLOUR LIBRARY BOOKS

1:12,500,000

| 0 | 100 | 200 | 300 | 400 | 500 | 600 | 700 | 800 KILOMETRES |
| 0 | 100 | | 200 | | 300 | | 400 | 500 STATUTE MILES |

Miller Oblated Stereographic Projection

Designed and produced by E.S.R.

Transverse Mercator Projection

1:1,175,000

© COLOUR LIBRARY BOOKS

0 10 20 30 40 50 60 70 80 KILOMETRES

0 10 20 30 40 50 STATUTE MILES

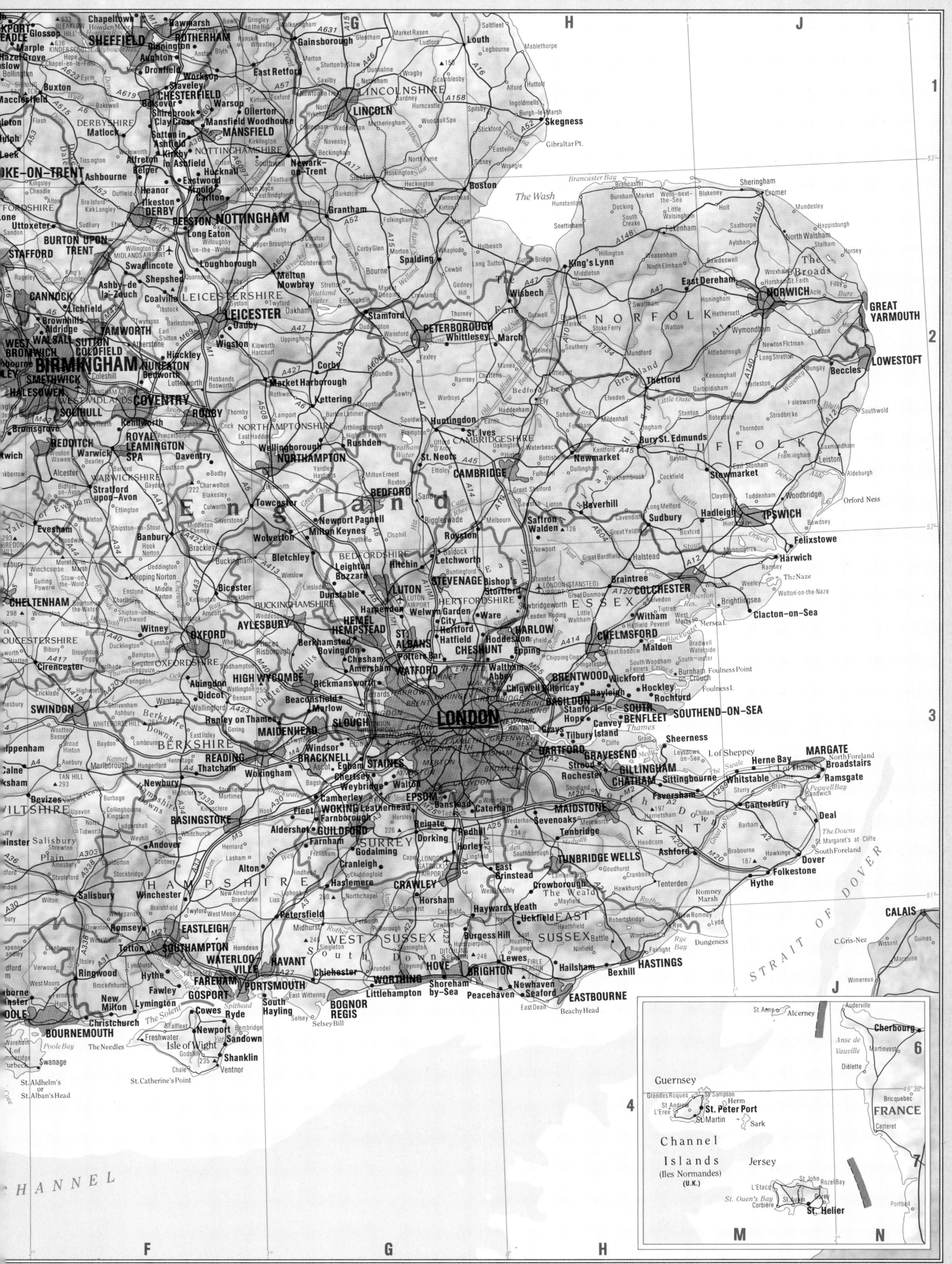

Designed and produced by E.S.R.

West of Greenwich   East of Greenwich

Transverse Mercator Projection

© COLOUR LIBRARY BOOKS

1:1,175,000

0 10 20 30 40 50 60 70 80 KILOMETRES

0 10 20 30 40 50 STATUTE MILES

Designed and produced by E.S.R.

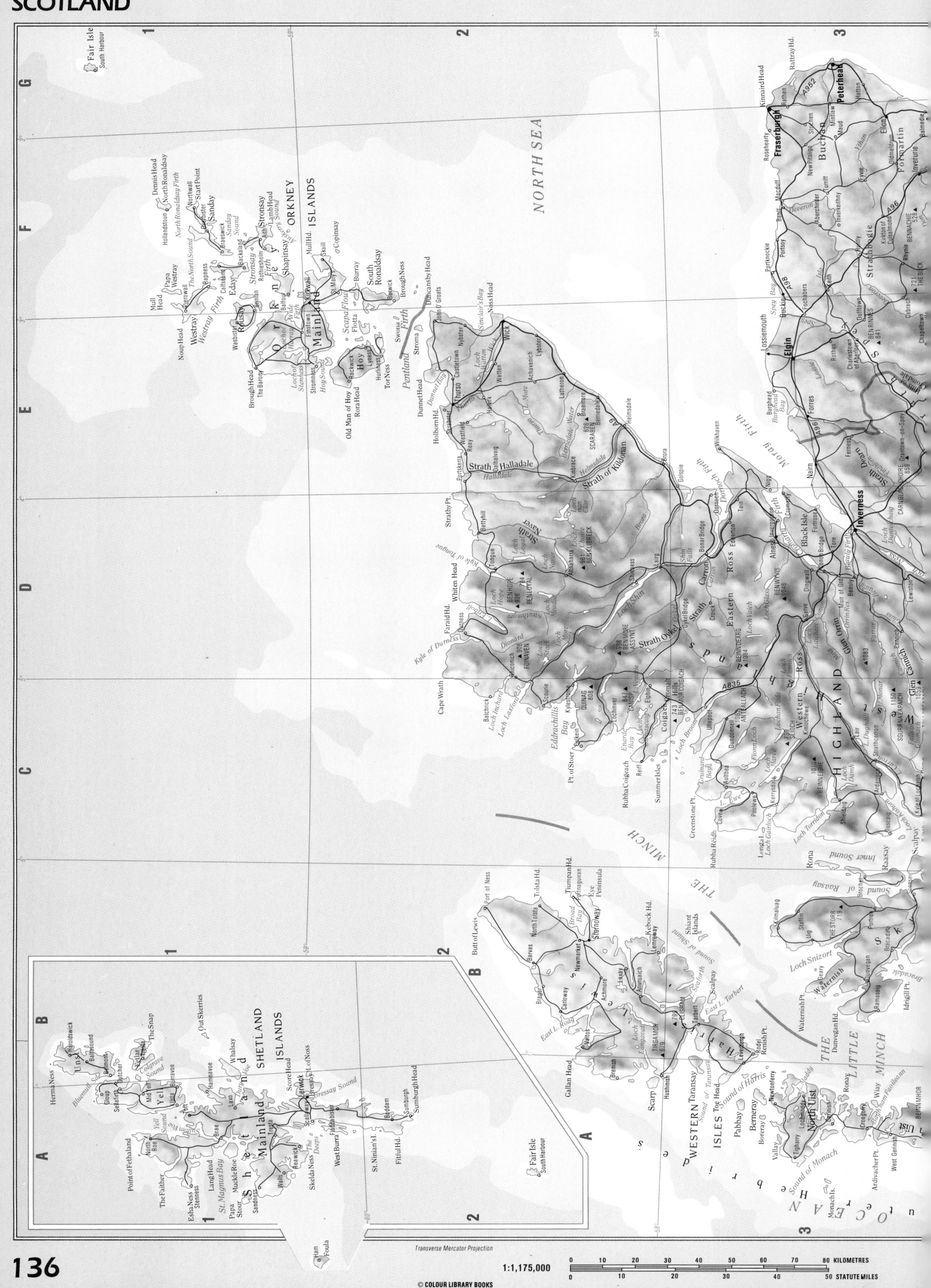

Transverse Mercator Projection

1:1,175,000

| 0 | 10 | 20 | 30 | 40 | 50 | 60 | 70 | 80 KILOMETRES |

| 0 | 10 | 20 | 30 | 40 | 50 STATUTE MILES |

© COLOUR LIBRARY BOOKS

West of Greenwich

Designed and produced by E.S.R.

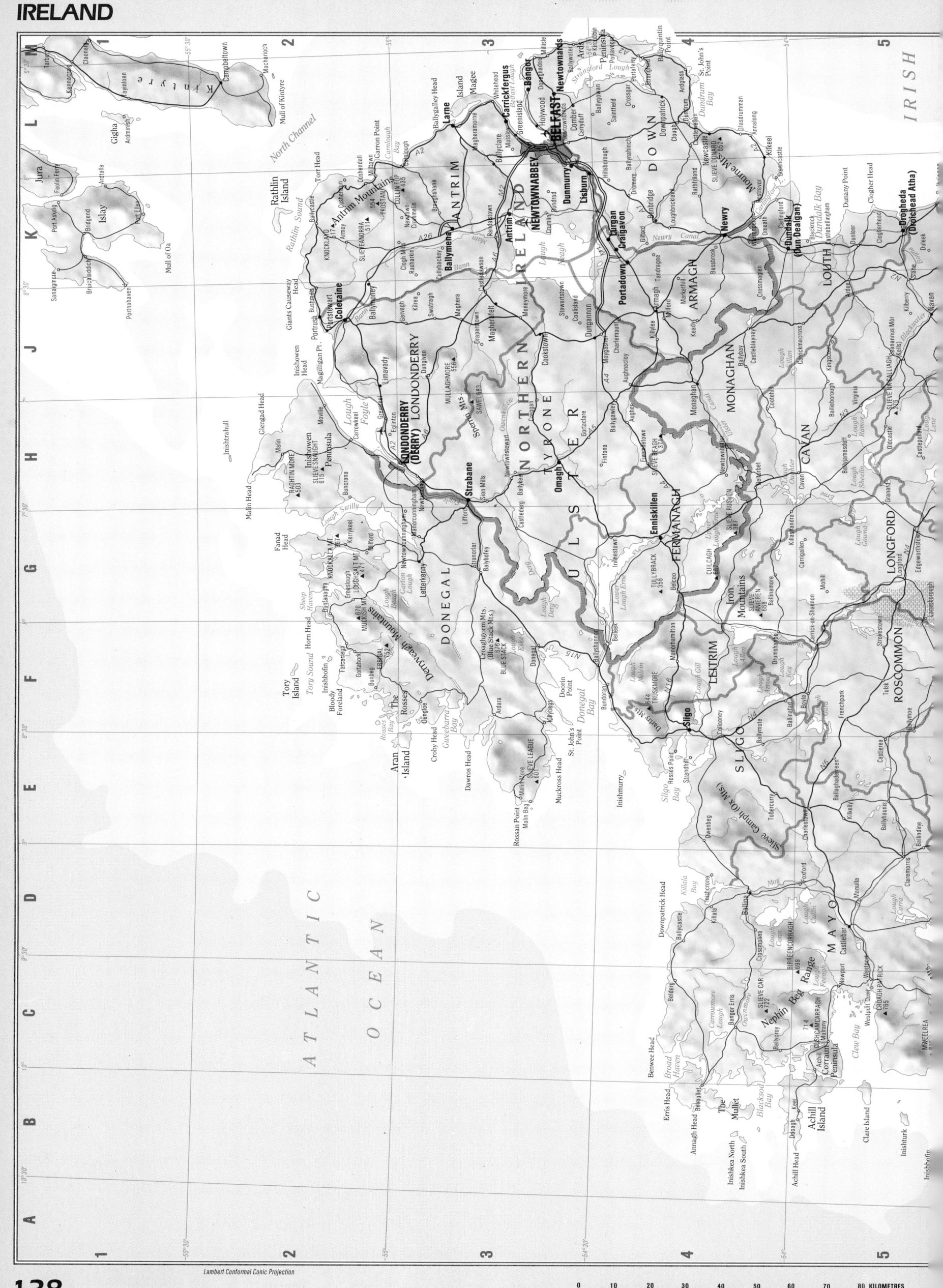

Lambert Conformal Conic Projection

1:1,000,000

© COLOUR LIBRARY BOOKS

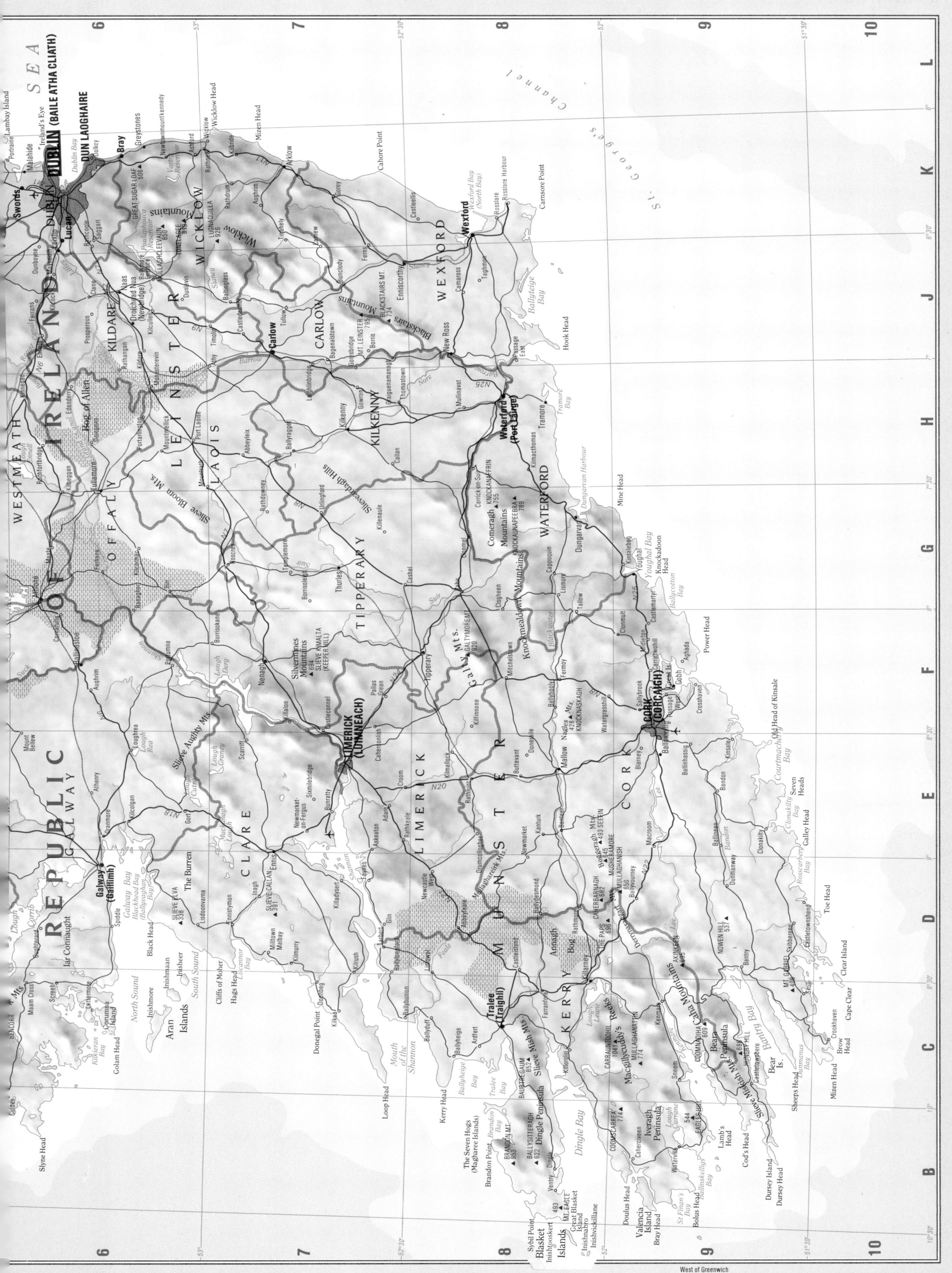

West of Greenwich

Designed and produced by E.S.R.

West of Greenwich

1:5,000,000

© COLOUR LIBRARY BOOKS

East of Greer

| 0 | 50 | 100 | 150 | 200 | 250 | 300 | 350 | 400 KILOMETRES |

| 0 | 50 | 100 | 150 | 200 | 250 STATUTE MI |

Designed and produced by E.S.R.

Miller Oblated Stereographic Projection

SCANDINAVIA AND THE BALTIC

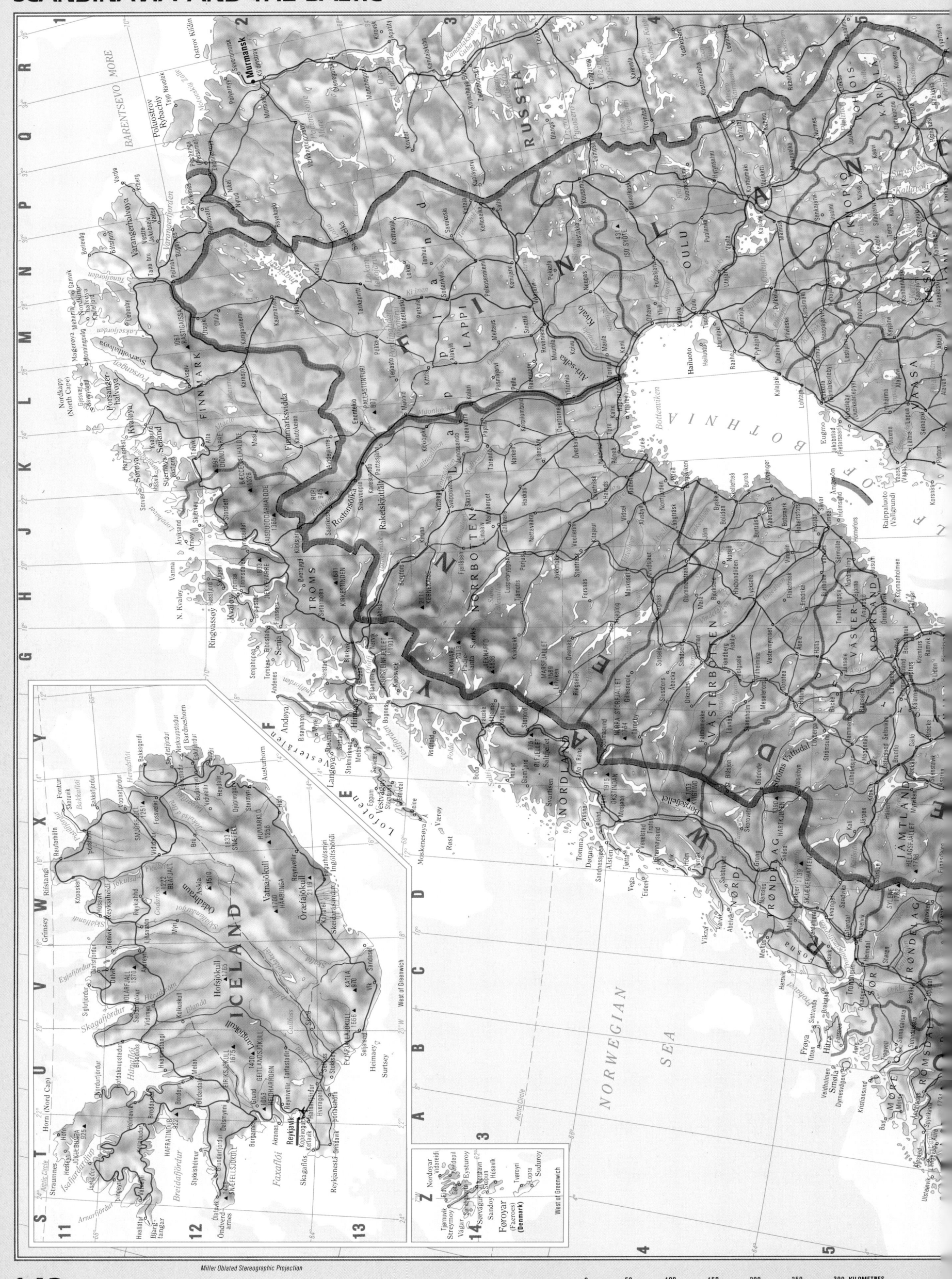

Miller Oblated Stereographic Projection

1:4,500,000

© COLOUR LIBRARY BOOKS

0 50 100 150 200 250 300 KILOMETRES

0 50 100 150 200 STATUTE MILES

East of Greenwich

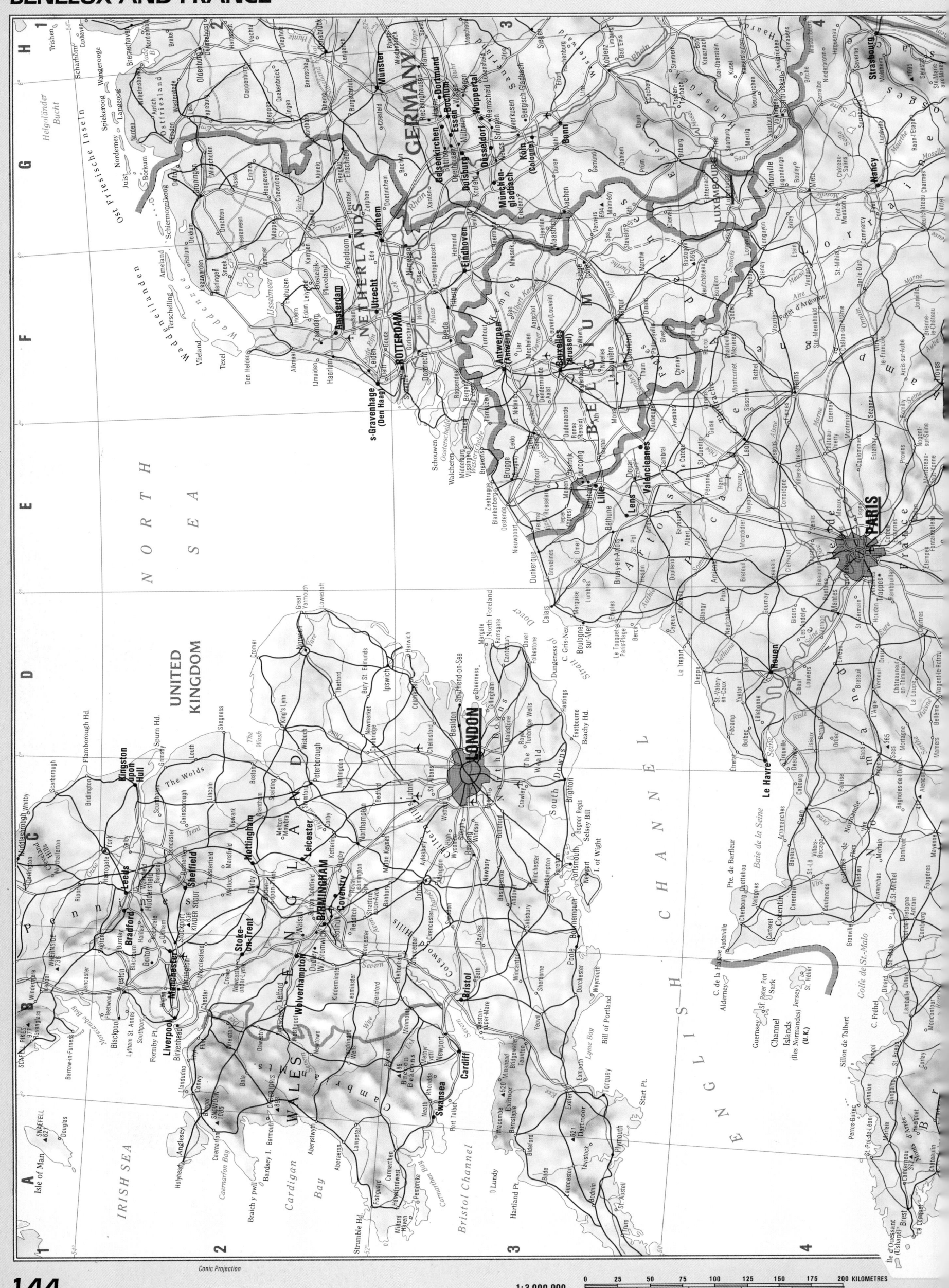

Conic Projection

1:3 000 000

| 0 | 25 | 50 | 75 | 100 | 125 | 150 | 175 | 200 KILOMETRES |

| 0 | 25 | 50 | 75 | 100 | 125 STATUTE MILES |

© COLOUR LIBRARY BOOKS

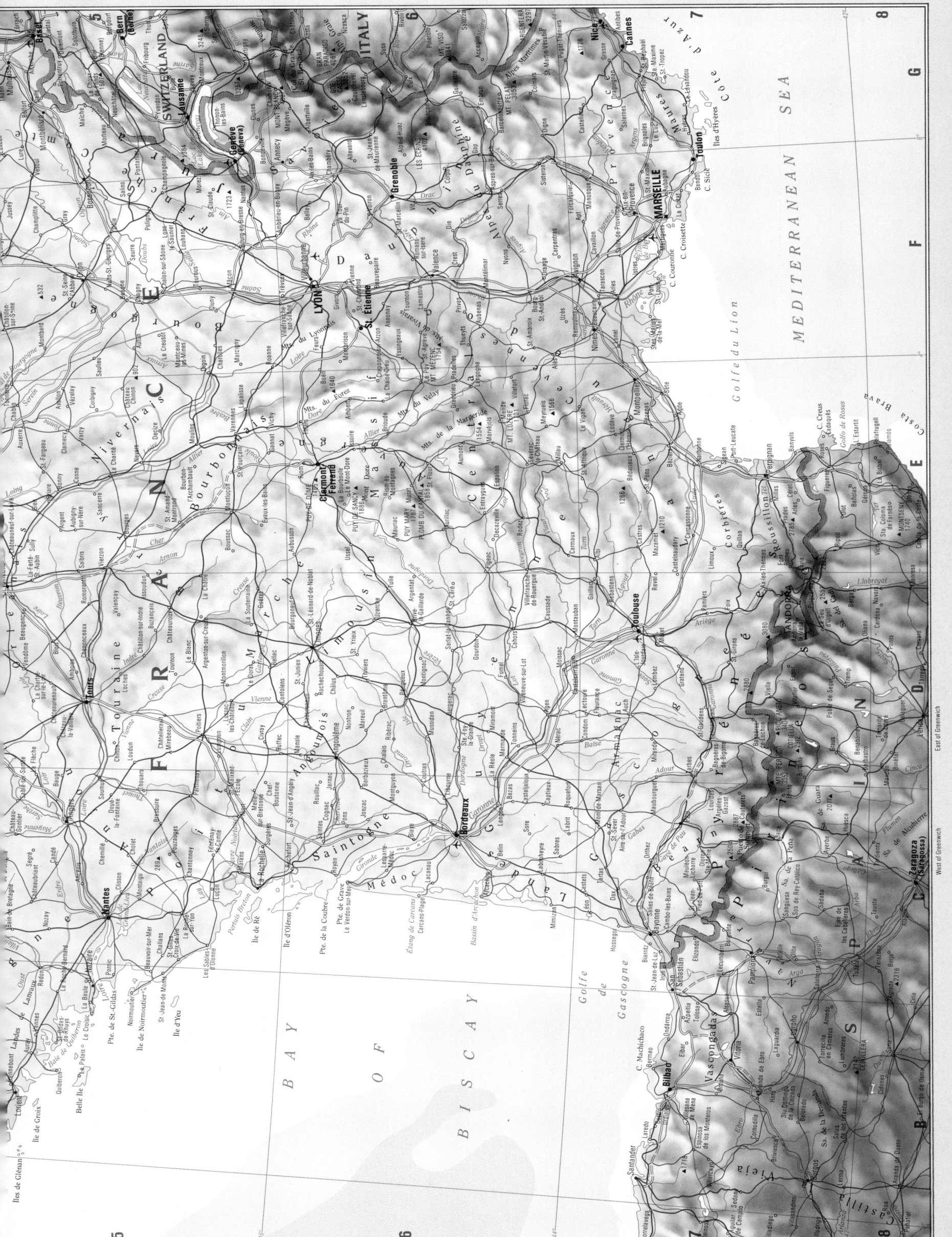

THE IBERIAN PENINSULA

1:3,000,000

Conic Projection

© COLOUR LIBRARY BOOKS

0   25   50   75   100   125   150   175   200 KILOMETRES

0   25   50   75   100   125 STATUTE MILES

F Golfo de Gascuña

Labrit
Roquefort
Castelsarrasin
Montauban
Carmaux
St-Affrique
Le Vigan
Nimes
Avignon
Cavaillon
Apt
Manosque
K

Léon
Castets
Condom
Lectoure
Fleurance
Gaillac
Tarn
St-Pons
Lodève
Hérault
Clermont
Bédarieux
Arles
Beaucaire
Tarascon
Salon-de-Provence
Aix-en-Provence
Provence
Salernes
Draguignan

Mont-de-Marsan
Auch
Isle-Jourdain
1266
Castres
Mazamet
Béziers
Pézenas
Montpellier
Lunel
Ser
St-Maximin
Bagnols
Le Luc
St-Raphaël

F R A N C E
Toulouse
1210
Agde
Sète
Stes-Maries-de-la-Mer
C. Couronne
MARSEILLE
Toulon
Hyères
Iles d'Hyères

Zaragoza (Saragossa)
Barcelona
Hospitalet

1

Golfe du Lion

Golfe de Roses

Costa Brava

2

Costa Dorada

Islas Columbretes

C. Caballeria

Ciudadela
C. de Formentor
Alayor
Menorca (Minorca)
Mahón

Puerto de Pollensa
Alcudia
MAYOR
La Puebla
Artá
Sóller
Inca
Manacor
I. Dragonera
Palma
Lluchmayor
Felanitx
Andraitx
Baia de Palma
Campos del Puerto
Mallorca (Majorca)
C. de Salinas

Golfo de Valencia

Valencia

3

Ibiza (Iviza)
San Juan Bautista
San Antonio Abad
Sta. Eulalia del Rio
Ibiza
Cabrera

Islas Baleares
(Balearic Islands)
(Spain)

San Francisco Javier
Formentera
Pta. Rotja

C. de la Nao
Calpe

M E D I T E R R A N E A N   S E A

Alicante

Murcia
Cartagena
C. de Palos
Costa Blanca

4

El DJAZAÏR (ALGIERS)

Borg El Bahri
Golfe de Bejaia
Jijel
Ziama-Mansouria

Dellys
Tigzirt
Bejaia (Bougie)

A L G E R I A

Massif de l'Ouarsenis

Oran

5

West of Greenwich   East of Greenwich

147

Designed and produced by E.S.R.

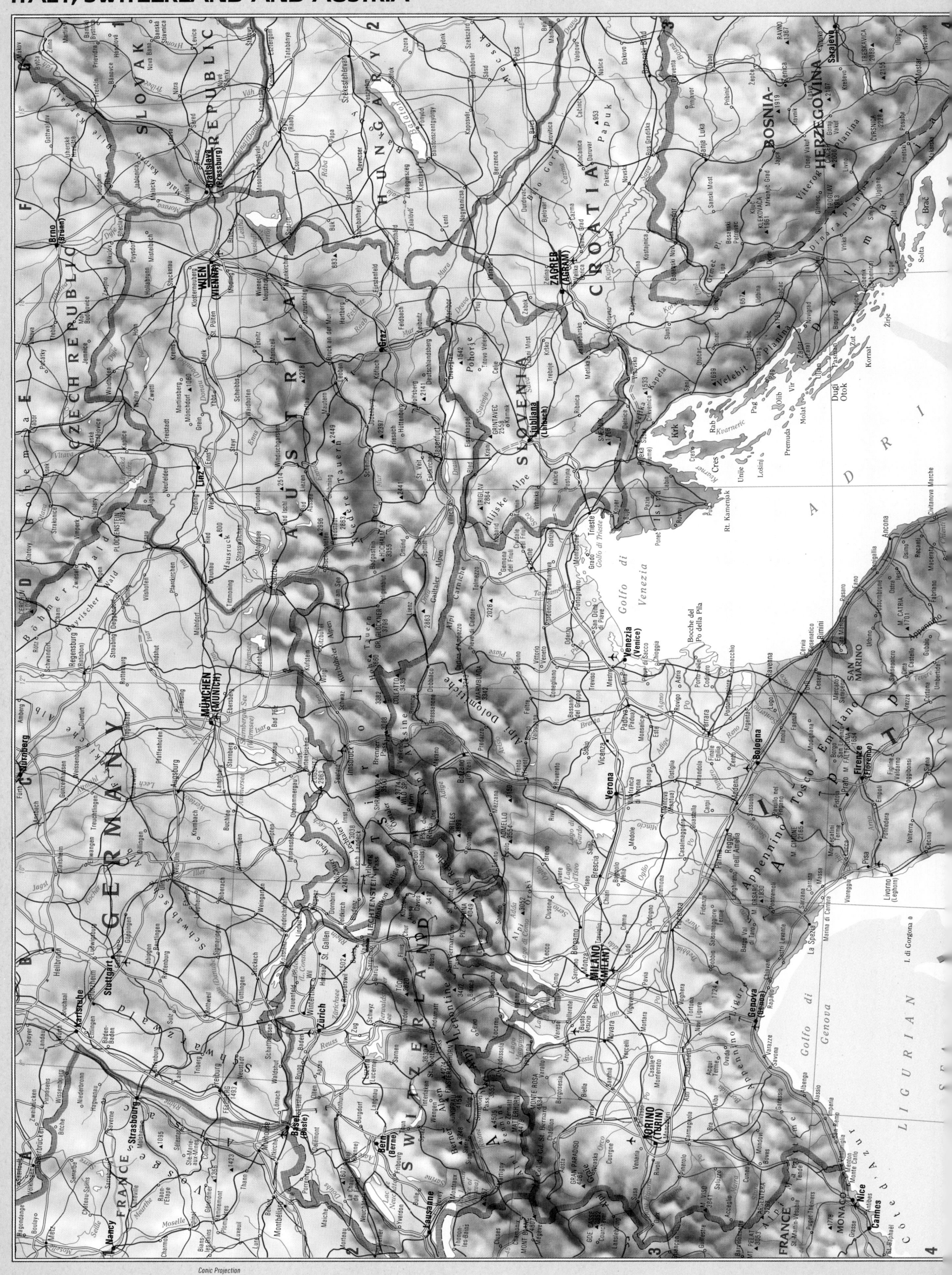

Conic Projection

1:3,000,000

| 0 | 25 | 50 | 75 | 100 | 125 | 150 | 175 | 200 KILOMETRES |

| 0 | 25 | 50 | 75 | 100 | 125 STATUTE MILES |

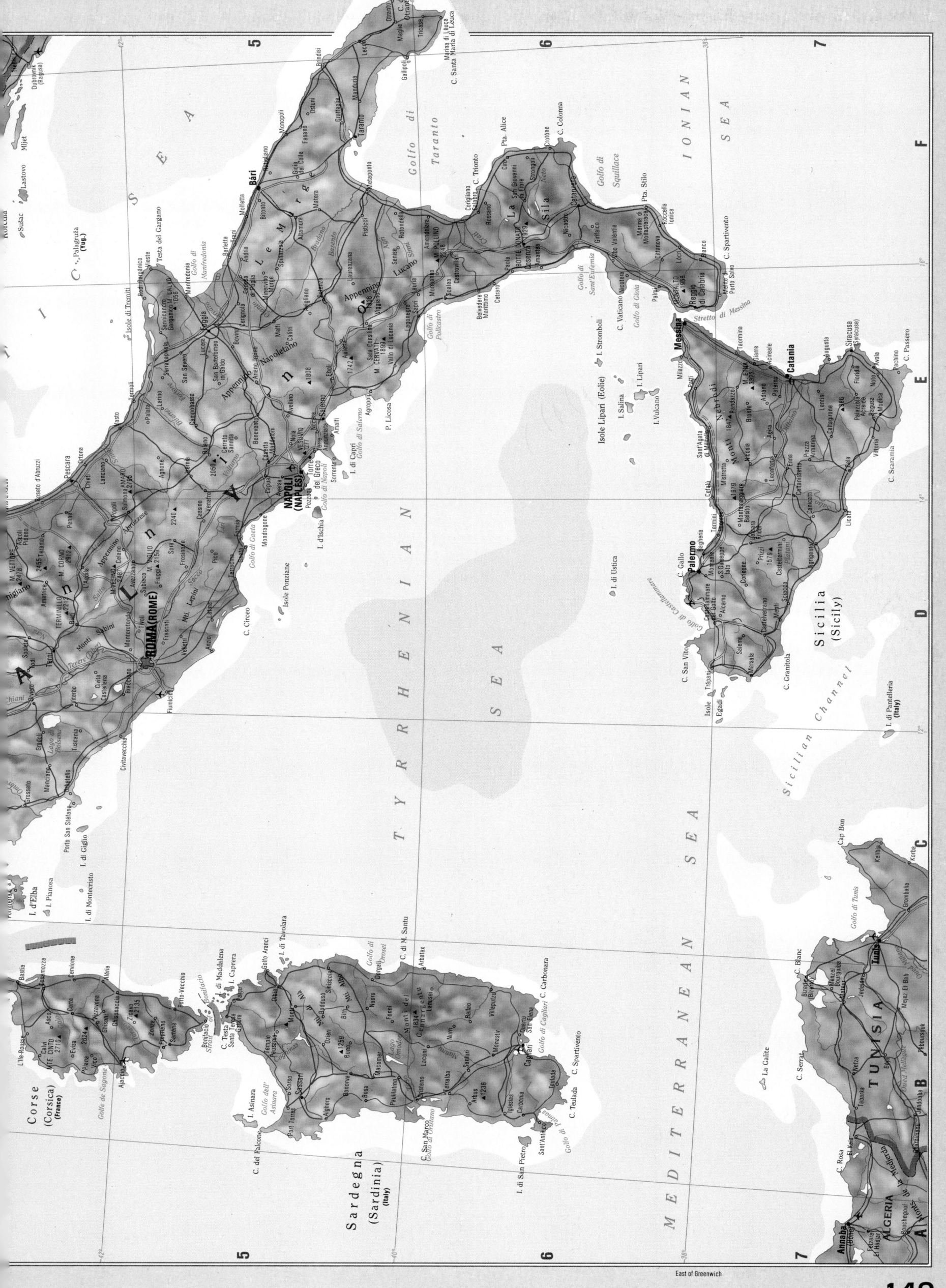

East of Greenwich

Designed and produced by E.S.R.

Conic Projection

1:3,000,000

© COLOUR LIBRARY BOOKS

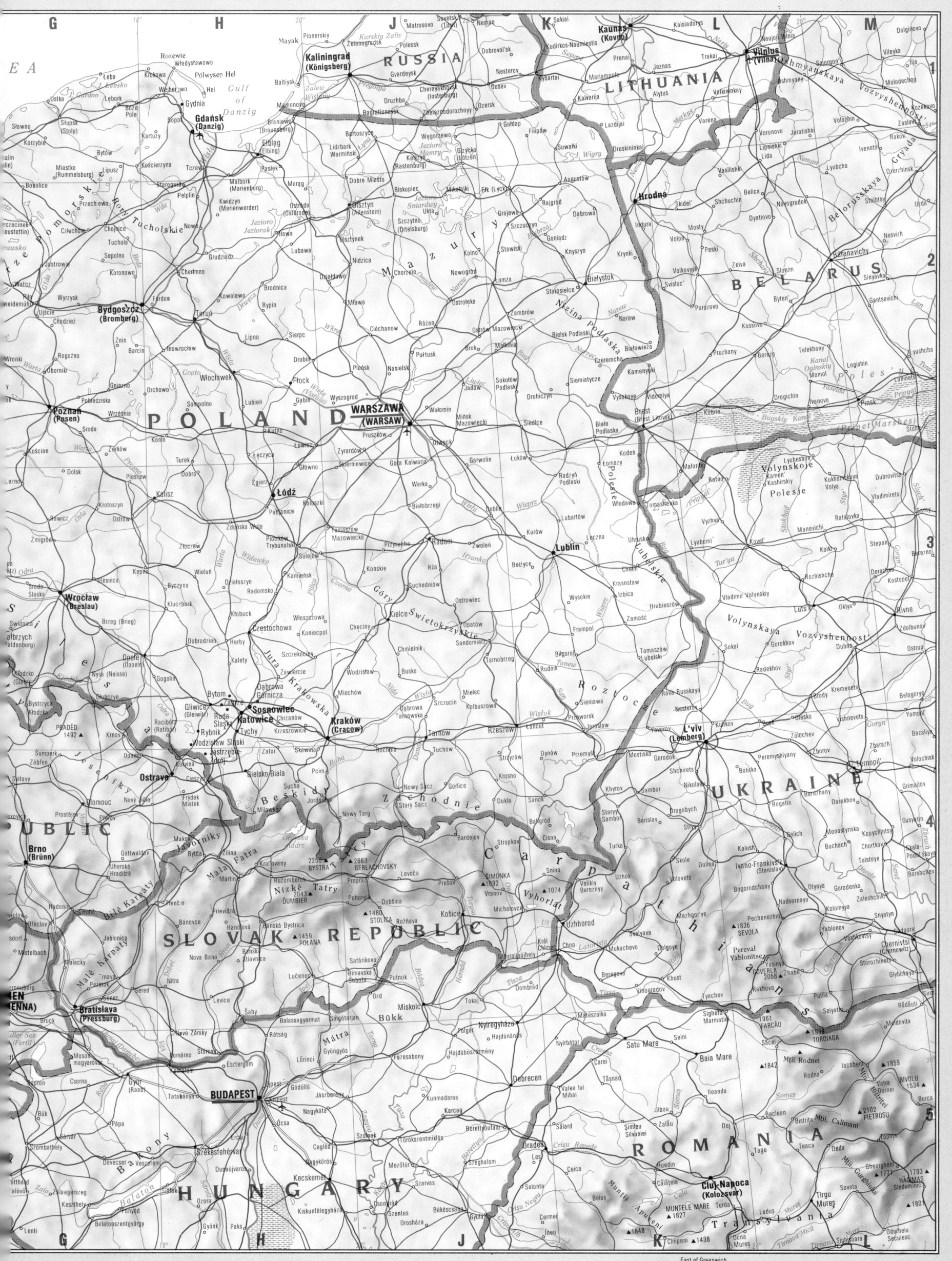

Conic Projection

1:3,000,000

| 0 | 25 | 50 | 75 | 100 | 125 | 150 | 175 | 200 KILOMETRES |
| 0 | | 25 | 50 | | 75 | | 100 | 125 STATUTE MILES |

East of Greenwich

Conic Projection

1:3,000,000

| 0 | 25 | 50 | 75 | 100 | 125 | 150 | 175 | 200 KILOMETRES |

| 0 | 25 | 50 | 75 | 100 | 125 STATUTE MILES |

© COLOUR LIBRARY BOOKS

TURKEY

BLACK SEA

BULGARIA

GREECE

İSTANBUL (CONSTANTINOPLE)

İzmit

BURSA (Brusa)

Balıkesir

Eskişehir

ANKARA

İZMİR (SMYRNA)

Konya

Denizli

Antalya

Mersin (İçel)

Dhodhekánisos (Dodecanese)

Ródhos (Rhodes)

MEDITERRANEAN SEA

CYPRUS

ATTILA LINE

Levkosía (Nicosia)

MT. TROODOS (OLYMPUS)

LEBA

156

Lambert Conformal Conic Projection

1:3,500,000

| 0 | 50 | 100 | 150 | 200 | 250 KILOMETRES |

| 0 | 25 | 50 | 75 | 100 | 125 | 150 STATUTE MILES |

© COLOUR LIBRARY BOOKS

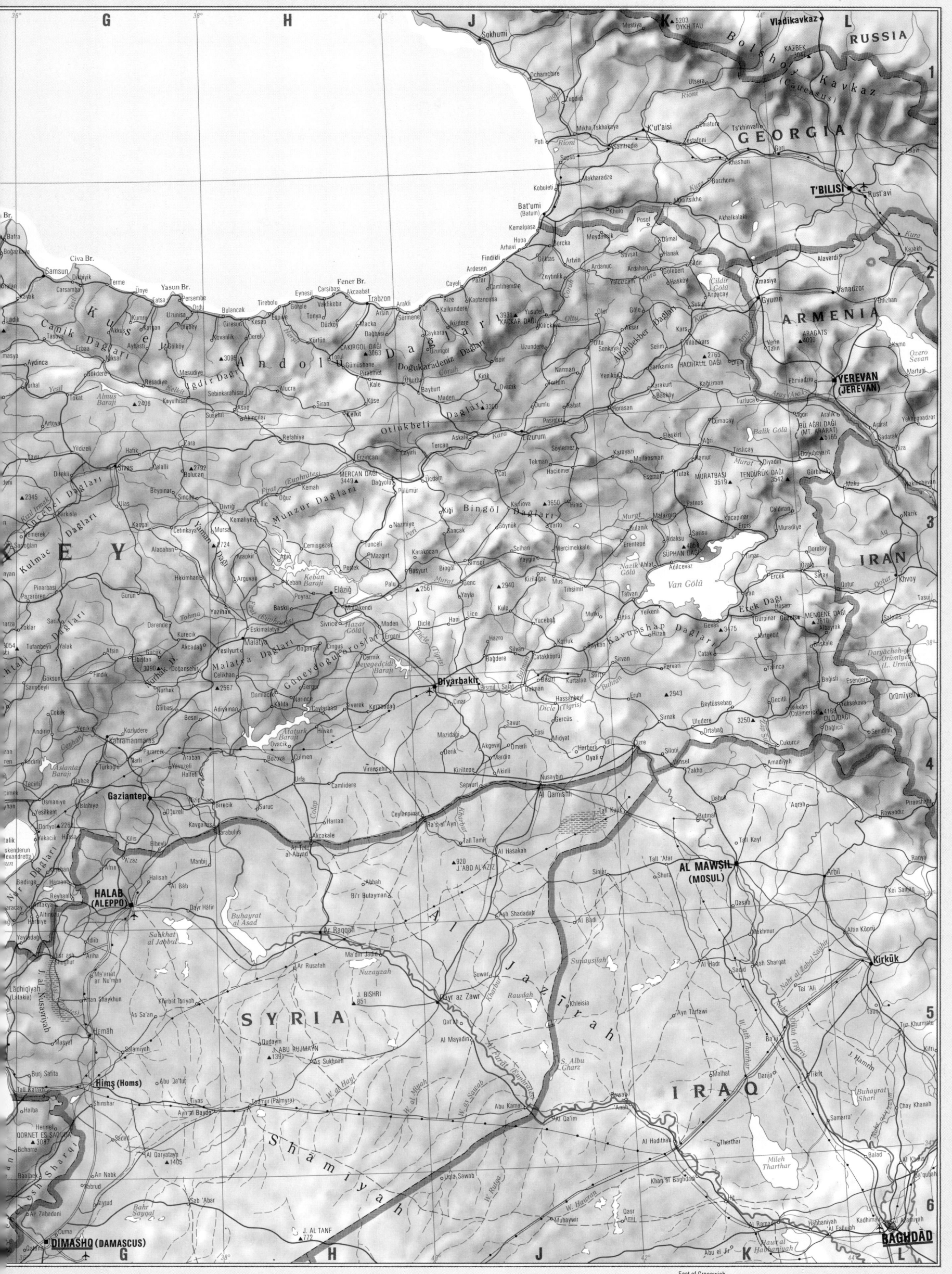

Designed and produced by E.S.R.

East of Greenwich

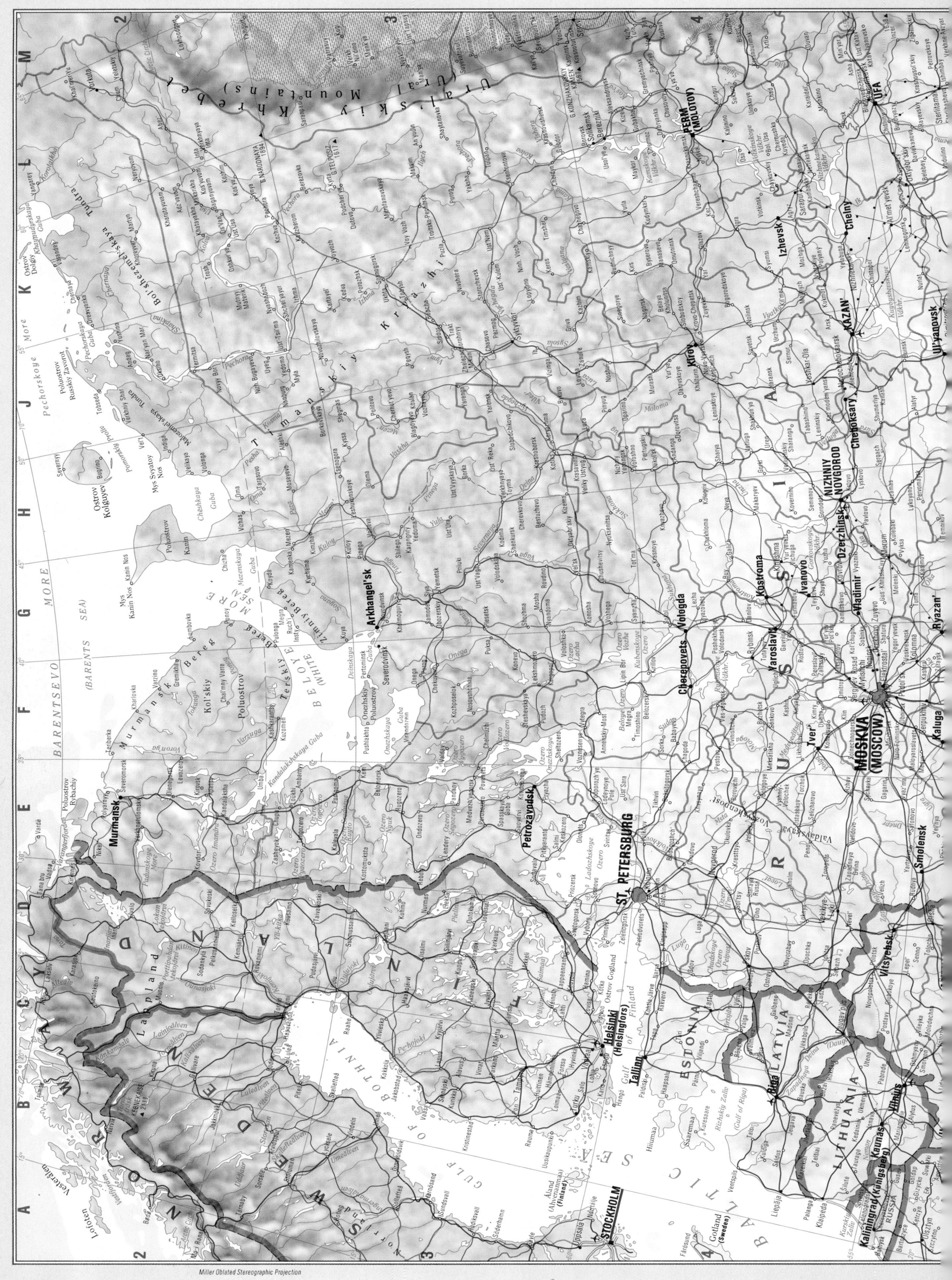

Miller Oblated Stereographic Projection

1:8,000,000

| 0 | 100 | 200 | 300 | 400 | 500 | 600 KILOMETRES |

| 0 | 50 | 100 | 150 | 200 | 250 | 300 | 350 | 400 STATUTE M |

© COLOUR LIBRARY BOOKS

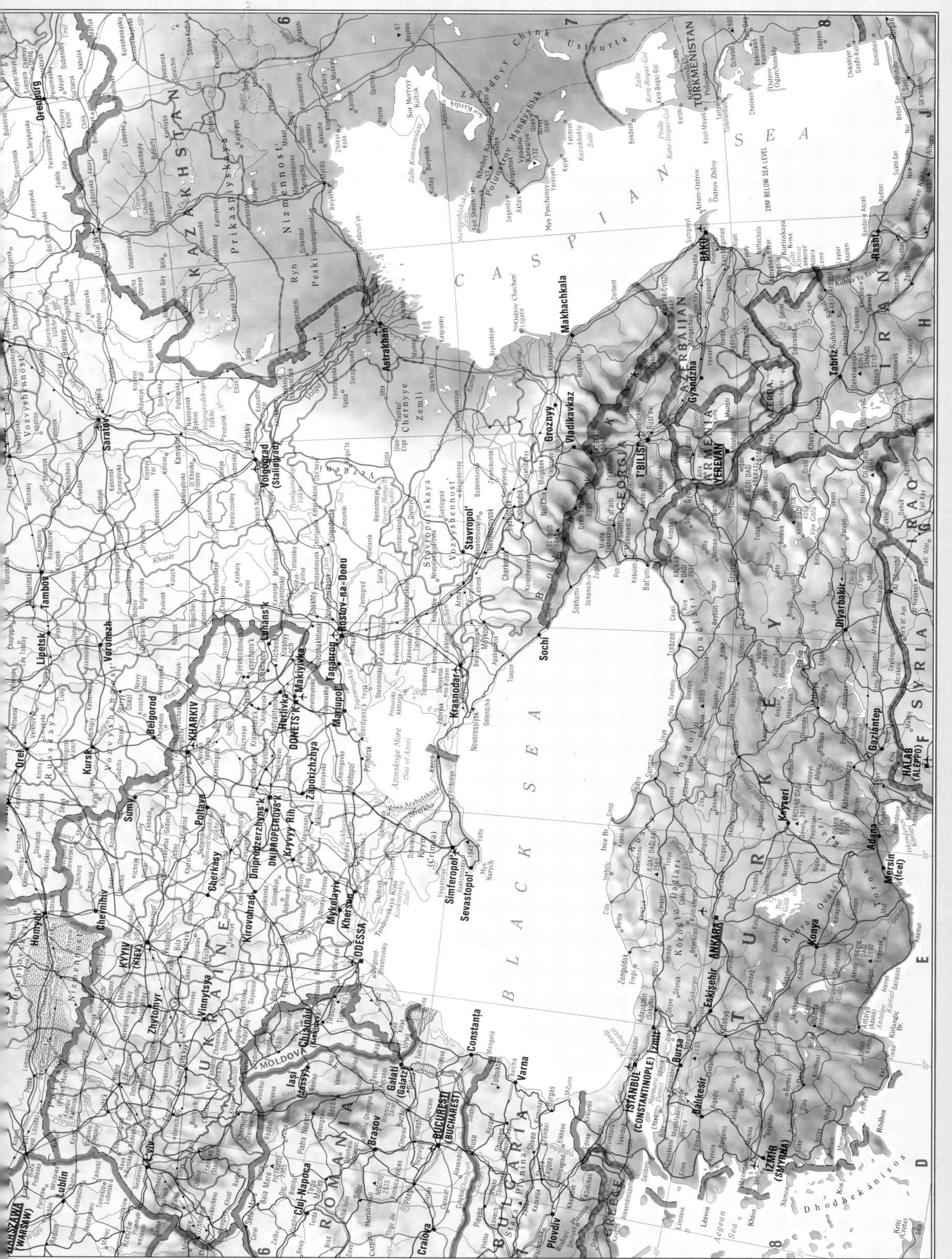

East of Greenwich

159

Designed and produced by E.S.R.

Conic Projection

1:17,000,000

| 0 | 100 | 200 | 300 | 400 | 500 | 600 | 700 | 800 KILOMETRES |

| 0 | 100 | 200 | 300 | 400 | 500 STATUTE MILES |

© COLOUR LIBRARY BOOKS

Severnaya
Zemlya
Ostrov
Bol'shevik

Ostrov Komsomolets

O. Oktyabr'skoy
Revolyutsii

Ostrov
Pioner

Proliv Vil'kitskogo
Ostrov Šokalskogo

Mys Chelyuskin

Poluostrov Taymyr

Gory Byrranga

Ozero
Taymyr

Gory
Putorana

Srednе
Sibirskoye
Ploskogor'ye

MORE
LAPTEVYKH

VOSTOCHNO SIBIRSKOYE
MORE

Novosibirskiye
Ostrova

Ostrova De-Longa

Ostrova
Anzhu

Ostrov
Bennetta

Ostrov
Zhokhova

Ostrov
Vrangelya

Proliv Longa

BERING
SEA

Chukotskiy
Poluostrov

St. Matthew I.
(U.S.A.)

Khrebet Cherskogo

Verkhoyanskiy Khrebet

OKHOTSKOYE
MORE

Sakhalin

Kuril'skiye
Ostrova

Stanovoy Khrebet

Aldanskoye
Nagor'ye

Stanovoye
Nagor'ye

Yablonovyy Khrebet

Khabarovsk

Vladivostok

SEA
OF
JAPAN

Hokkaidō

SAPPORO
Hakodate

Aomori
Akita
Sendai
Fukushima
Niigata
Utsunomiya
HONSHŪ
TOKYO
YOKOHAMA
NAGOYA
KYŌTO
OSAKA
KOBE
Wakayama

Angarsk
Irkutsk
Ulan-Ude
Chita

MONGOLIA

Ulaanbaatar

Gobi

NEI MONGOL ZIZHIQU

BAOTOU
Hohhot
Datong
Zhangjiakou
BEIJING
TANGSHAN
TIANJIN

SHIJIAZHUANG
TAIYUAN
Handan

JINAN
TAI'AN

Manchuria

CHINA

QIQIHAR
HARBIN
Mudanjiang
Baicheng
JILIN
CHANGCHUN
Siping
Liaoyuan
FUSHUN
SHENYANG
ANSHAN
DALIAN

HUANG HAI

QINGDAO

N. KOREA
PYONGYANG

SOUTH
KOREA
SEOUL
INCH'ŎN
TAEGU
PUSAN

KYŪSHŪ
FUKUOKA
NAGASAKI
Kagoshima
Miyazaki

Shikoku
HIROSHIMA

161

MEDITERRANEAN SEA
GREECE
ATHÍNAI
BULGARIA
Khersón
UKRAINE
DONETS'K
Saratov
SAMARA
UFA
YEKATERINBURG
Tyumen
Tobol'sk
Zapadno
Sibirskaya
Ravnina
RUS
ISTANBUL
Bursa
Izmir
Sevastopol'
Rostov-na-Donu
Volgograd
Magnitogorsk
CHELYABINSK
Kurgan
OMSK
Tomsk
Kemerovo
NOVOSIBIRSK
Achinsk
Krasnoyarsk
ANKARA
Konya
Kayseri
BLACK SEA
Sinop
Samsun
Krasnodar
Stavropol'
Sochi
Astrakhan
Brenburg
Orsk
Aktyubinsk
Kokchetav
Petropavlovsk
Akmola
Barnaul
Novokuznetsk
Biysk
TURKEY
Adana
Antalya
CYPRUS
Trabzon
GEORGIA
Batumi
Groznyy
Vladikavkaz
TBILISI
ARMENIA
YEREVAN
AZERBAIJAN
BAKU
CASPIAN SEA
Atyrau
Kirgiz
Step
Turgay
Aktau
Plato
Ustyurt
KAZAKHSTAN
Melkosopochnik
Dzhezkazgan
Kazakhskiy
Karaganda
Semipalatinsk
Ust-Kamenogorsk
B. BELUKA
Ozero Balkhash
Balkhash
Taldy-Kurgan

LIBYA
EL ISKANDARIYA
EGYPT
EL QAHIRA
Asyut
El Minya
Aswan
SUDAN
JIDDAH
Makkah
Bur Sudan
RED SEA
ERITREA
Asmara
ETHIOPIA
ADIS ABEBA
Djibouti
Berbera
SOMALIA
Muqdisho

LEBANON
Bayrut
ISRAEL
TEL AVIV-YAFO
Yerushalayim
Hefa
SYRIA
HALAB
DIMASHQ
Zarqa
JORDAN
Amman
AL MAWSIL
Kirkuk
IRAQ
BAGHDAD
AL BASRAH
AL KUWAYT
KUWAYT
SAUDI
ARABIA
AR RIYAD
Al Madinah
BAHRAIN
QATAR
Dubayy
Abu Zabi
UNITED ARAB
EMIRATES
Ar Rub al Khali
OMAN
REPUBLIC OF YEMEN
San'a
Adan
Gulf of Aden
Hadhramawt
Al Mukalla
Suqutra
(Yemen)

Tabriz
Rasht
TEHRAN
Qom
Hamadan
Bakhtaran
Abadan
Ahvaz
Esfahan
Shiraz
Yazd
IRAN
Dasht-e Kavir
Dasht-e Lut
Kerman
Bandar Abbas
Zahedan
Gulf of Oman
Masqat
Ra's al Hadd

TURKMENISTAN
Ashgabat
MASHHAD
UZBEKISTAN
Bukhara
Samarkand
TASHKENT
Chimkent
Bishkek
ALMA-ATA
KYRGYZSTAN
Dushanbe
TAJIKISTAN
Pamir
AFGHANISTAN
KABUL
Herat
Kandahar
Hindu Kush
Peshawar
Islamabad
Rawalpindi
Quetta
PAKISTAN
Srinagar
FAISALABAD
LAHORE
Amritsar
Multan
Ludhiana
Chandigarh
Karachi
Hyderabad

Yining
Urumqi
XINJIANG
UYGUR
ZIZHIQU
Kashi
Yarkant
Taklimakan Shamo
Kunlun Shan
Altun Shan
XIZANG ZIZHIQU
(TIBET)
Lhasa
NEPAL
Kathmandu
MT EVEREST
BHUTAN
Thimphu

INDIA
DELHI
New Delhi
Meerut
JAIPUR
Agra
KANPUR
LUCKNOW
Bareilly
Gwalior
Jodhpur
Ajmer
Allahabad
Varanasi
Patna
Thar Desert
AHMADABAD
Vadodara
Bhopal
Jabalpur
Jamshedpur
BANGLADESH
DHAKA
Surat
Indore
NAGPUR
Raipur
Khulna
CALCUTTA
CHITTAGONG
MUMBAI
(Bombay)
PUNE
Solapur
Kolhapur
HYDERABAD
Cuttack
Hubli
Vishakhapatnam
BANGALORE
Mangalore
Mysore
Vijayawada
CHENNAI
(Madras)
Calicut
Coimbatore
Tiruchchirappalli
Cochin
Madurai
Trivandrum
C. Comorin
SRI LANKA
Kandy
Colombo
Matara
Dondra Head

ARABIAN SEA
BAY OF BENGAL
Andaman Is.
(India)
Nicobar Is.
(India)
Lakshadweep
(India)
Male
MALDIVES

INDIAN OCEAN
Chagos Archipelago
(U.K.)

Amirante Is.
SEYCHELLES
Victoria
Aldabra Is.
Cosmoledo Is.
Providence
Farquhar Is.
COMOROS
Mayotte
(France)
MADAGASCAR
Antananarivo
Mahajanga
Toamasina

Lambert Azimuthal Equal Area Projection

1:25,000,000

0 200 400 600 800 1000 KILOMETRES
0 100 200 300 400 500 600 STATUTE MILES

© COLOUR LIBRARY BOOKS

Designed and produced by E.S.R.

Miller Oblated Stereographic Projection

1:11,500,000

© COLOUR LIBRARY BOOKS

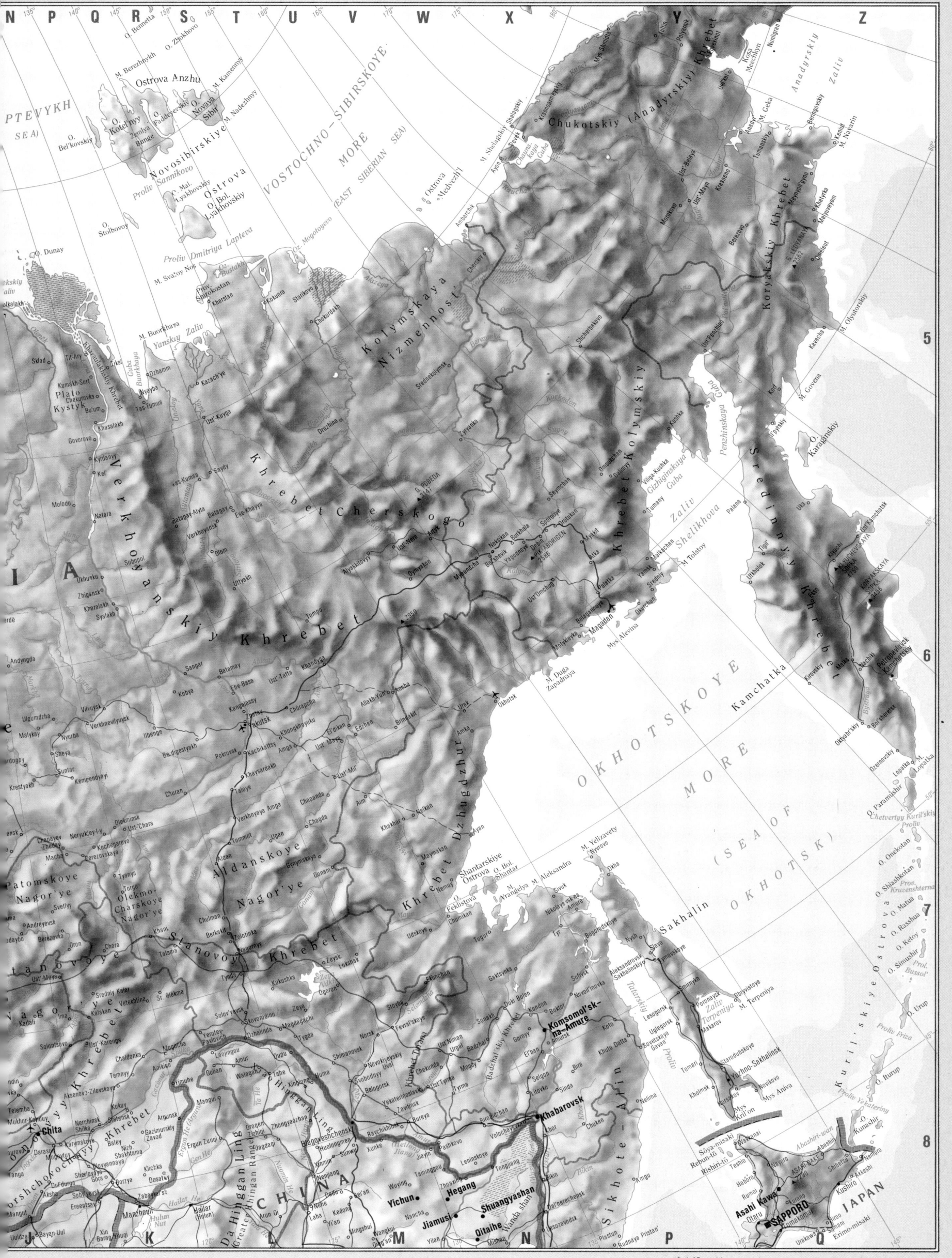

PTEVYKH

(SEA)

PTEVYKH SEA)

O. Dunay

Ostrova Anzhu

M. Berezhnykh

O. Zhokhova

M. Kamenny

Bennetta

Novosibirskiye

O. Kotel'nyy

O. Faddeyevskiy

Zemlya Bunge

O. Novaya Sibir'

Proliv Sannikova

Ostrova Lyakhovskiye

C. Mal. Lyakhovskiy

O. Bol. Lyakhovskiy

Proliv Dmitriya Lapteva

O. Stolbovoy

O. Bel'kovskiy

VOSTOCHNO-SIBIRSKOYE MORE

(EAST SIBERIAN SEA)

Chukotskiy (Anadyrskiy) Khrebet

Koryakskiy Khrebet

Anadyrskiy zaliv

Kolymskaya Nizmennost'

Verkhoyanskiy Khrebet

Khrebet Cherskogo

Khrebet Kolymskiy

Sredinnyy Khrebet

Zaliv Shelikhova

OKHOTSKOYE MORE

(SEA OF OKHOTSK)

Kamchatka

Petropavlovsk-Kamchatskiy

Magadan

Verkhoyanskiy Khrebet

Khrebet Dzhugdzhur

Shantarskiye Ostrova

Sakhalin

Yuzhno-Sakhalinsk

Aldanskoye Nagor'ye

Olekmo-Charskoye Nagor'ye

Patomskoye Nagor'ye

Stanovoye Nagor'ye

Stanovoy Khrebet

Komsomol'sk-na-Amure

Khabarovsk

Sikhote-Alin

Kuril'skiye Ostrova

Chita

Da Hinggan Ling (Greater Hinggan Range)

Xiao Hinggan Ling

CHINA

Yichun

Hegang

Shuangyashan

Jiamusi

Qitaihe

Asahi Kawa

SAPPORO

JAPAN

East of Greenwich

Designed and produced by E.S.R.

165

Miller Oblated Stereographic Projection

1:11,500,000

| 0 | 100 | 200 | 300 | 400 | 500 | 600 | 700 | 800 KILOMETRES |

| 0 | 50 | 100 | 150 | 200 | 250 | 300 | 350 | 400 | 450 | 500 STATUTE MILES |

© COLOUR LIBRARY BOOKS

Designed and produced by E.S.R.

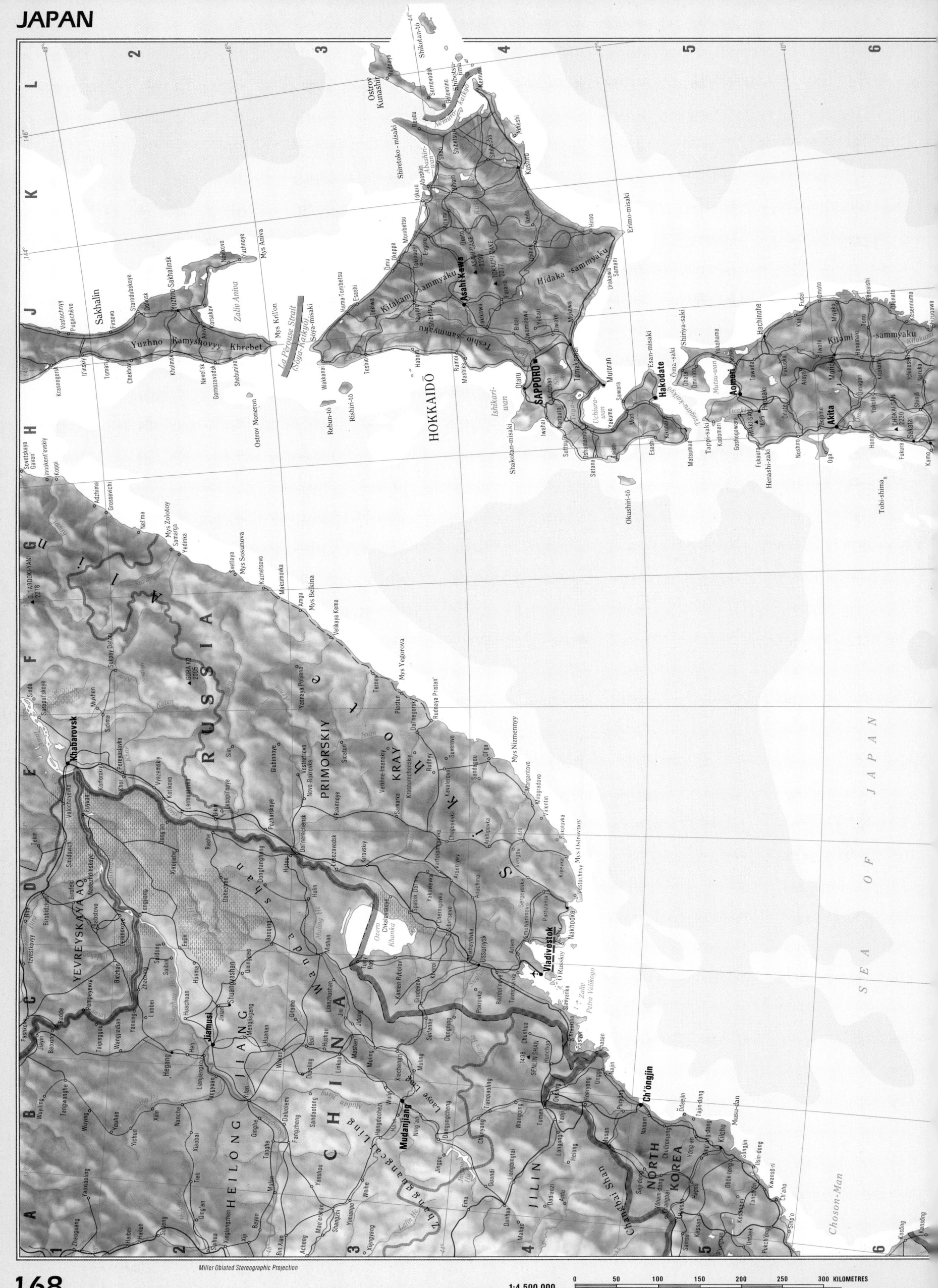

SEA OF JAPAN

RUSSIA

PRIMORSKIY

KRAY

CHINA

HEILONGJIANG

YEVREYSKAYA AO

JILIN

NORTH KOREA

HOKKAIDŌ

Sakhalin

SAPPORO

Hakodate

Aomori

Akita

Asahikawa

Khabarovsk

Vladivostok

Ch'ŏngjin

Jiamusi

Mudanjiang

Hachinohe

La Pérouse Strait
(Sōya-Kaikyō)

Choson-Man

Miller Oblated Stereographic Projection

1:4,500,000

© COLOUR LIBRARY BOOKS

| 0 | 50 | 100 | 150 | 200 | 250 | 300 KILOMETRES |

| 0 | 50 | 100 | 150 | 200 STATUTE MILES |

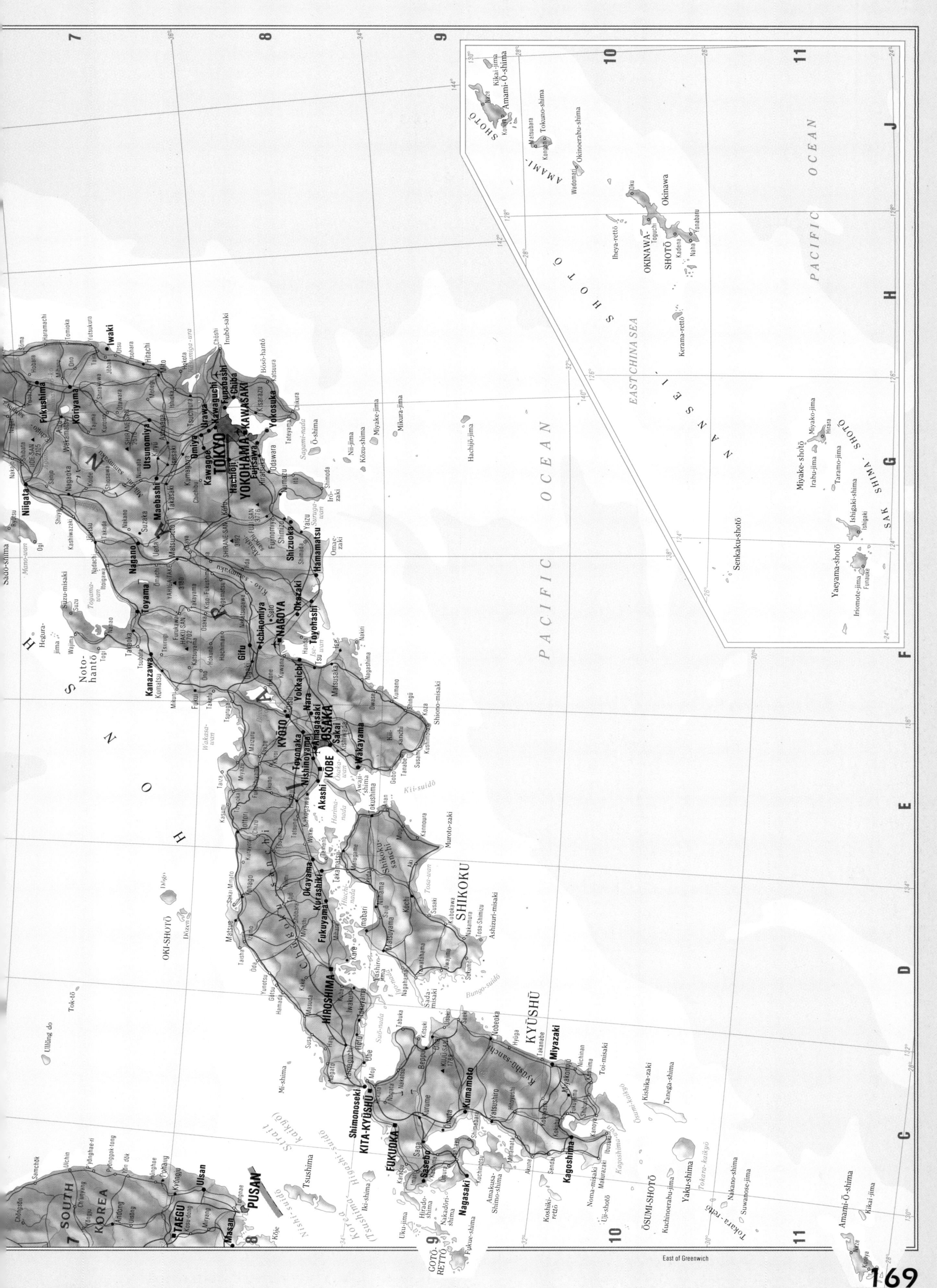

7

8

9

10

11

J

H

G

F

E

D

C

EAST CHINA SEA

NANSEI-SHOTŌ

AMAMI-SHOTŌ

OKINAWA-SHOTŌ

SAKISHIMA-SHOTŌ

PACIFIC   OCEAN

Kikai-jima
Amami-Ō-shima
Tokuno-shima
Okinoerabu-shima
Oku
Okinawa
Iheya-rettō
Kerama-rettō

Miyake-shotō
Miyako-jima
Ishigaki-shima
Yaeyama-shotō
Iriomote-jima

Senkaku-shotō

PACIFIC   OCEAN

Niigata
Fukushima
Kōriyama
Iwaki
TOKYO
YOKOHAMA
KAWASAKI
Yokosuka
Chiba
Utsunomiya
Maebashi
Nagano
Toyama
Kanazawa
Shizuoka
Hamamatsu
NAGOYA
Gifu
Ichinomiya
Okazaki
Toyohashi
Yokkaichi
Nara
KYŌTO
OSAKA
KŌBE
Akashi
Sakai
Amagasaki
Nishinomiya
Toyonaka
Wakayama
HIROSHIMA
Okayama
Kurashiki
Fukuyama
Kure

SHIKOKU

Kōchi
Matsuyama
Tokushima
Takamatsu

KYŪSHŪ

Miyazaki
Kumamoto
FUKUOKA
KITA-KYŪSHŪ
Shimonoseki
Saga
Sasebo
Nagasaki
Kagoshima

GOTŌ-
RETTŌ

ŌSUMI-SHOTŌ
Yaku-shima
Tanega-shima
Amami-Ō-shima
Kikai-jima

OKI-SHOTŌ

*SOUTH
KOREA*

TAEGU
PUSAN
Ulsan
Masan

Tsushima

*Strait
Korea*

H O N S H Ū

Noto-hantō

Sado-shima

Designed and produced by E.S.R.

East of Greenwich

169

SOUTH-EAST ASIA

Mercator Projection

1:12,000,000

© COLOUR LIBRARY BOOKS

0 100 200 300 400 500 600 700 800 KILOMETRES

0 100 200 300 400 500 STATUTE MILES

KAOHSIUNG Pingtung TAIWAN **G**

Bashi Haixia

Itbayat Batan
Basco Is ands
Luzon Batan

Balintang Channel

Babuyan
Calayan Babuyan Islands
Dalupiri Camiguin
Mayraira Point Fuga
Banqui Cape Engaño
Babuyan Chennel San Vincente
Laoag Aparri

Vigan Tuguegarao Palanan Point
Ilagan
San Fernando Bontoc
Tagudin MT. PULOG Casiguran
2929
Bolinao Baguio Palanan Point
Lingayen Cabanatuan
San Jarlos Baler
Dagupan
Angeles Cape San Ildefonso
San Fernando Polillo Islands
Olongapo **Valenzuela** Calagua Islands
MANILA **QUEZON CITY**
Cavite **Pasig** Pandan
Muntinlupa San Pablo Lamon Bay Catanduanes
Lubang Lucena Daet Virac
Islands Batangas Naga
Cape Calavite Calapan Mulanay Legaspi Sorsogon
MT. HALCON Boac Legaspi
Mamburao 2929 Bulan Cape Espiritu Santo
Mindoro SIBUYAN Burias Laoang Oras
Bongabong Romblon Aroroy Masbate Catbalogan
Calamian Busuanga San Jose Tablas Mandaon Calbayog **Samar**
Group Semirara Masbate Catbalogan
Culion Islands Pandan Borongan
Crawford Point Cuyo San Jose Roxas
El Nido Islands de Buenavista Tacloban
Dalanganem Taytay Islands Dao Placer Guiuan
Barton Bayo Point Dumaran **Iloilo** San Ormoc Leyte Gulf
Palawan **Bacolod** Carlos **Leyte**
Dumaguete Dinagat
Babuyan Cadiz Siargao
Puerto Princesa **Negros** Bais Tagbilaran BOHOL
Aborlan Dumaguete Siquijor SEA Surigao
NTALINGAJAN Tubbataha Reefs **Bohol** Cauit Point
2054 Sipalay Oslob Butuan Tandag
Tagolo Point
Dipolog Oroquieta
MT. DALIAK Cagayan de Oro
Bonobono 3560 Iligan Malaybalay Bislig
Liloy Pagadian Mindanao
Zamboanga Ozamiz **Davao**
Cagayan Sulu Malabang Cotabato Datu Piang Tagum
Basilan Moro Lebak Mati
Pangutaran Gulf
Group Jolo Kiamba Cape San Agustin
Sandakan Samales General Santos
Tamag Group
Lahad Datu Tapul Tinaca Point
Group
Sibutu Tawitawi
Sempoma Group

PHILIPPINES

PHILIPPINE SEA

VISAYAN SEA

Linapacan Strait

SIBUYAN SEA

SULU SEA

Moro Gulf

PACIFIC

OCEAN

Ulithi Atoll

Yap Is.

Ngulu Atoll

Palau Babelthuap

Caroline Islands

Sonsorol Is.

Pulo
Anna
Merir

Kepulauan Karakelong Kepulauan Nanusa
Karkaralong Beo Kepulauan
Salebabu Talaud
Sangihe Kaburuang

Kepulauan Sanghe Siau

Tahulandang
Biaro Tobi Helen I.

Tg. Sopi
Morotai
Wayabula Sango
Daruba

SULAWESI

Kepulauan Sanghe

Tg. Arus Tg. Polisan Manado Kikupang
Tolitoli Tondano
Minahassa Peninsula Issimu Belang Loloda G. GAMKUNORO Tg. Lelai
Tg. Margkalihat 2565 Moutong Boroko 7635
Maitong Gorontalo Galela
G. OGOAMAS Jailolo **Halmahera**
Sabargu Marisa Ternate Maba
Tinompo Soa-Siu Segea
Donggala Maidi Weda Patani
Kepulauan Parigi Mafa
Togian Waigeo
Palu G. LOKILALAKI Nartabu Waibeem
Kaluku 3311 Luwuk Kasiruta Cenga Sorong Supiori
Kepulauan Salawati Korido Korim
Mamuju Toli Tataba Bacan Gunedidalem Klamono Biak Bosnik
Sulawesi Banggai Sukon Segef Konda
(Celebes) Bunta Liboho Laiwui Misool Mongge Mogoi Wasian Yapen Serui
G. GANDADWATA Tg. Pemali Kepulauan Ransiki
3016 Peleng Obi Inanwatan Arandai Wasior
Matale Banggai Sanana Babo
Enrekang Mangole Kaimana Waren
Densongi Kepulauan Sula Weri Kwatisore
Parepare Taliabu Dofa Kokas Nabire
Watansopeng Tg. Palpetu Tg. Namaa Wahai Teluk Berau Maki
Kolaka Tg. Namaa Hoti Fakfak Ibonmaro
Majene Kolono Piru Lisabata Bula Adi Modowi
Buru Wasisi Waru Umari Wanapun
Singkang Kolono Namlea **Seram** Karufa Kokenau
Ujung Pandang Wowoni Tifu Ambon (Ceram)
(Makassar) Napabalana Ambon Kepulauan
Kabaena Muna Gorong
Kendari Kepulauan Kepulauan
Wangiwangi Banda Watubela
Kepulauan Kepulauan Kai
Tukangbesi Tayandu
Binongko Kepulauan Kai Besar
Tual Banda Elat
Kepulauan Kai Kecil Wokam
Sabalana Kepulauan Barat Daya Aranlau Aru
Selayar Reblu Pono Kobroor
Kalao Nila Trangan Dobo
Kalaotoa Teun Damar Tg. Weduar
Wetar Romang Larat Doka
Flores Kepulauan Alor Kisar Kepulauan Tg. Ngabordamlu
Tengahdai Moa Babar Tanimbar
Adonara Taramana Ilwaki Selaru
Lomblen Pantar Alor Masela Kepulauan
Solor Maubara Kepulauan Sermata
Kupang Dili Leti Selu
Timor

New Guinea

d'Urville
Bagusa
Ansudu

IRIAN JAYA Pegunungan Van Rees
Genyem Jayapura
Vanimo
Pegunungan Maoke Aitape
PK. JAYA Green River
5030 **PAPUA**
Peg. **PK. YAMIN**
Sudirman 4595 Kubkain
Peg. PK. MANDALA CAPELLA **NEW**
Jayawijaya 4993 **GUINEA**
Agats
Pirimapun Nomad
Tanahmerah
Tg. Dolak Kept
Pulau Jos Sodarso Mappi
(Dolak) Lake
Okaba Murray
Komoran Moreken
Tg. Vals Mari
Merauke

I N D O N E S I A

Teluk
Tomini

Teluk Tolo

LAUT MALUKU

LAUT
HALMAHERA

Selat Jailolo

LAUT SERAM

LAUT BANDA

LAUT
ARAFURA

LAUT
FLORES

LAUT
SAWU

TIMOR SEA

G **H** **J** **K** **L**

East of Greenwich

Designed and produced by E.S.R.

INDIAN SUBCONTINENT

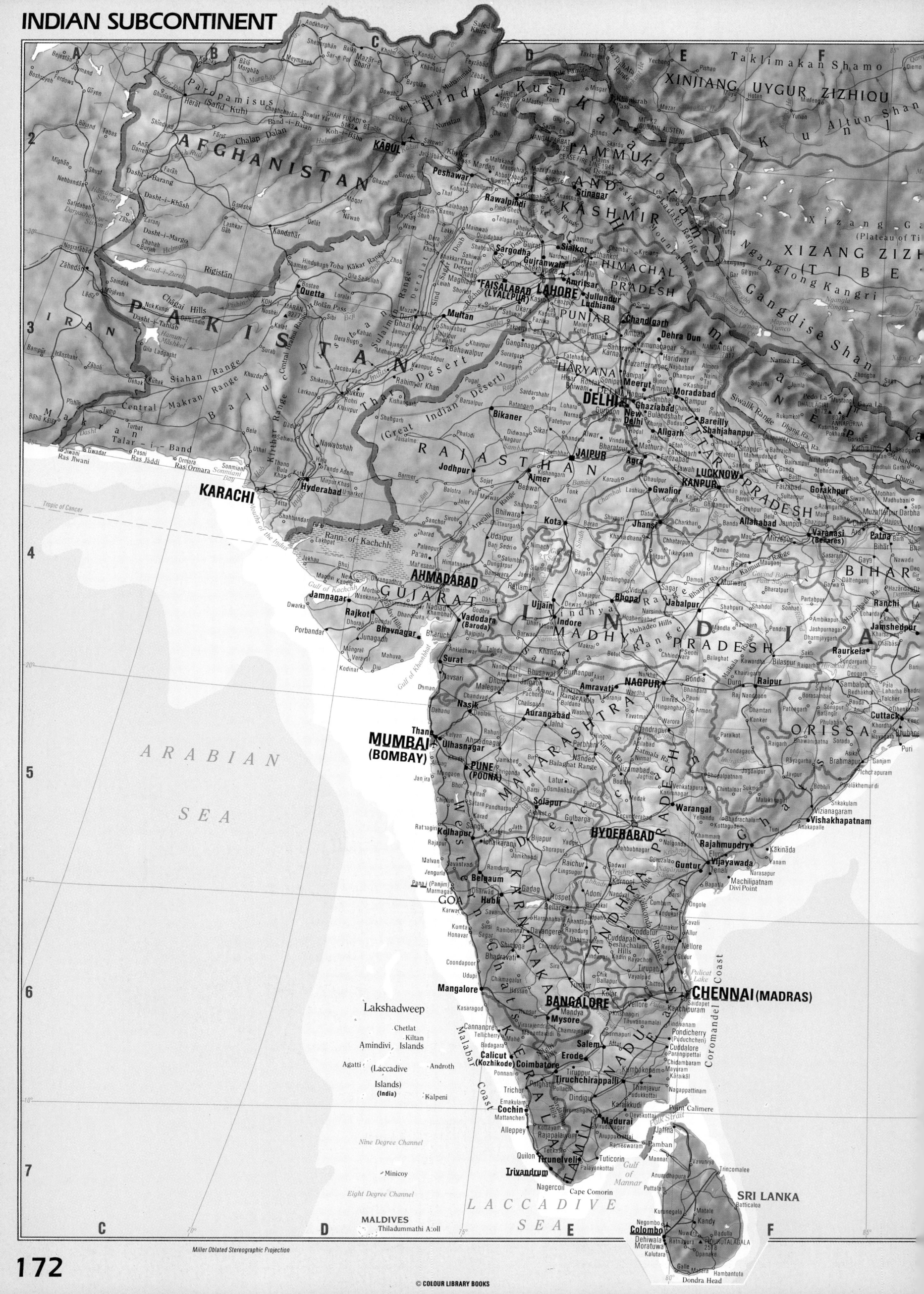

Miller Oblated Stereographic Projection

© COLOUR LIBRARY BOOKS

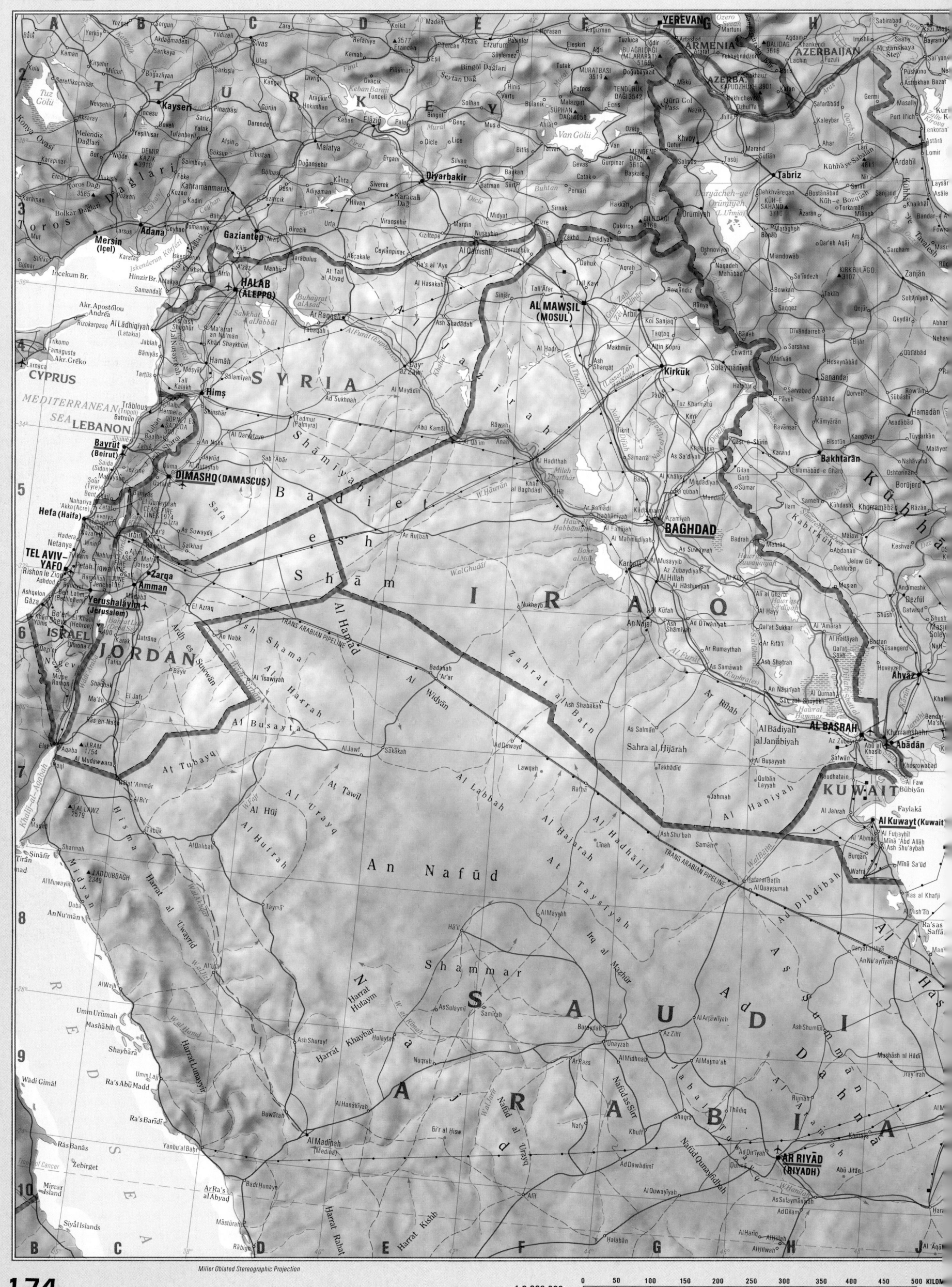

Miller Oblated Stereographic Projection

1:6,000,000

© COLOUR LIBRARY BOOKS

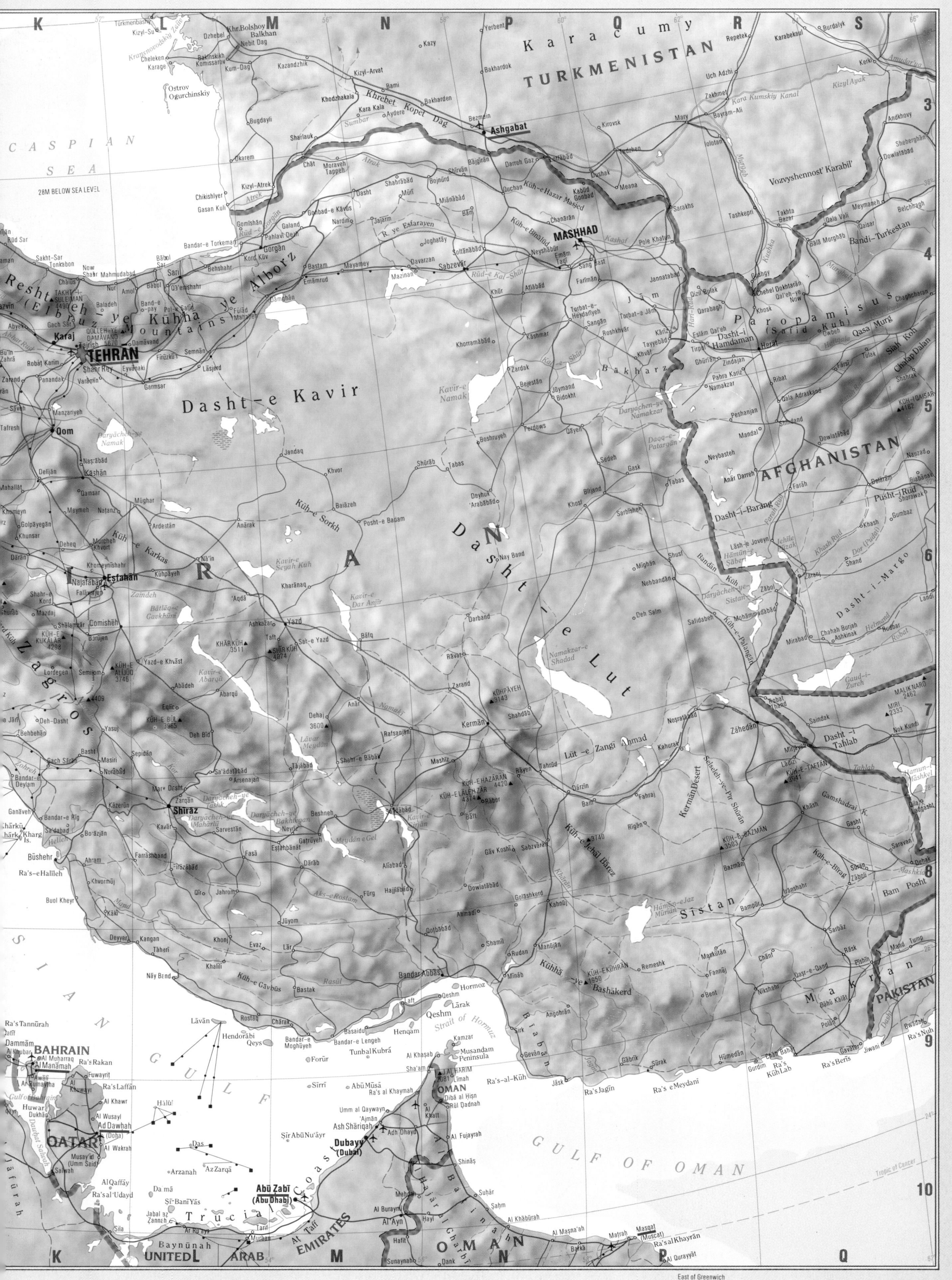

Designed and produced by E.S.R.

East of Greenwich

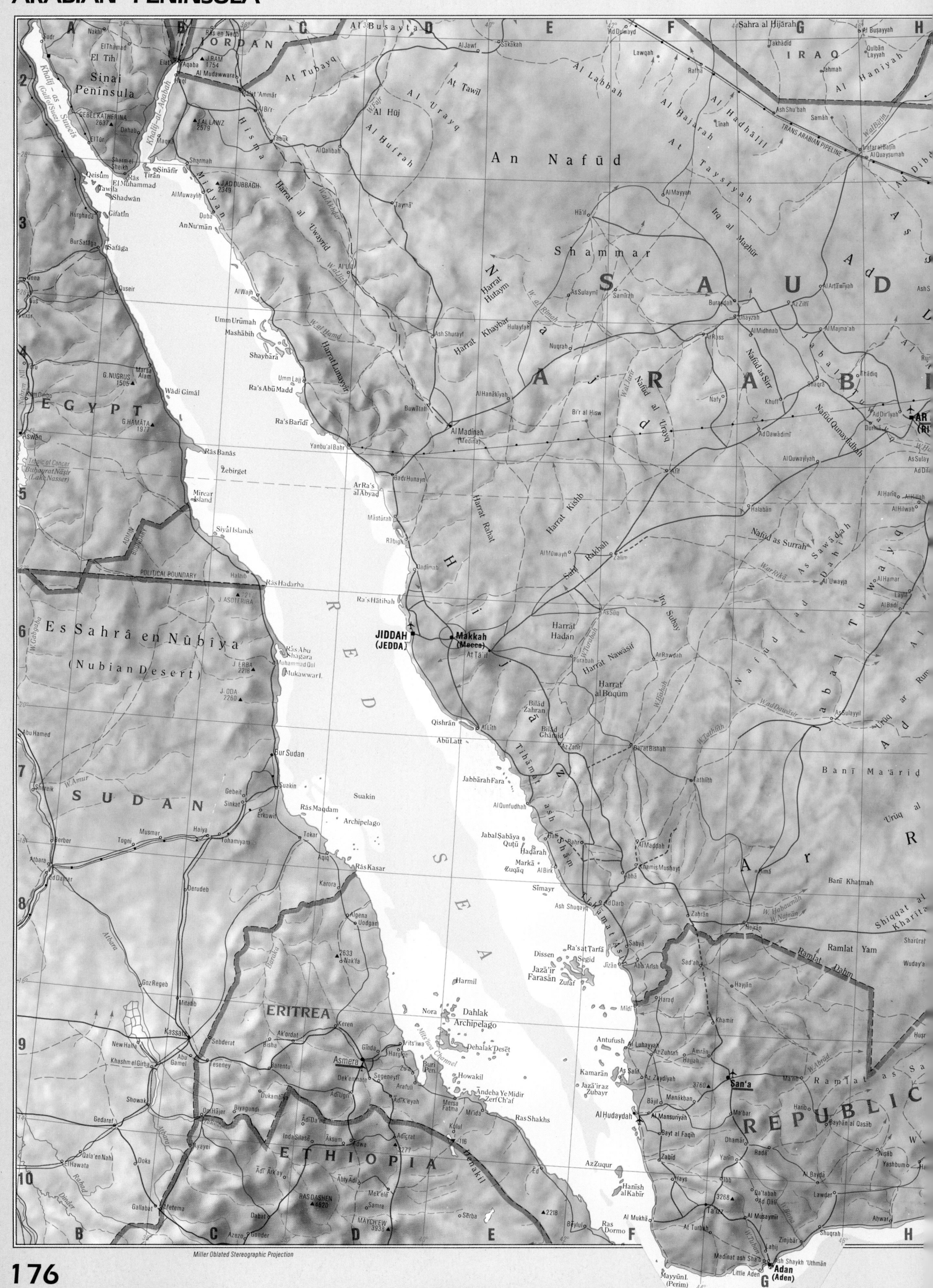

Miller Oblated Stereographic Projection

© COLOUR LIBRARY BOOKS

IT
J
Khorramshahr
Ra's-e
Barkan
Bandar-e
Deylam
MARY Dasht
Zarqan
Shīrāz
Daryācheh-ye
Tashk
Daryācheh-ye
Bakhtegan
Beshneh
Batt
Kūh-e Jebāl Bārez
3740
Rigān
KŪH-E-HAZMĀN
3503
Q

Al Kuwayt (Kuwait)
Al Fuhayhil
Mīnā 'Abd Allāh
Ash Shu'aybah
Mīnā Sa'ūd
Faylakā
Ganāveh
Bandar-e Rīg
Sa'dabad
Borāzjān
Kāzerūn
Būshehr
Kavar
Fasā
Eslahabānāt
Dārāb
Gatrūyeh
Meydān e Gel
Ḥājjiabad
Aliabad
Dowlatābād
Bashākerd
Angohrān
Bazmān
Sīstan
3

Ras al Khafji
Ra'sas
Saffānīyah
Manīfah
Nu'ayrīyah
Jubayl
Abū 'Alī
Al Jubayl
Ahram
Khvormūj
Dalakī
Jahrom
Jūyom
Qīr
Fūrg
Rūdan
Mīnāb
Kahnūj
Remeshk
Fannūj
Bent
Chānf
Nīkshahr
Qa

Ra's az Zawr
Ad Dammām
BAHRAIN
Al Manāmah
Al Muḥarraq
Ra's Rakan
Ra's-e Ḥalīleh
Nāy Band
Rostāū
Chārak
Basaidū
Henqām
Qeshm
Lārak
Strait of Hormuz
Kamzar
Musandam Peninsula
Gevān
Sīrīk
Biaban
Jāsk
Ra's-e Meydānī
4

Maqāsh al Hādī
Uray'irah
Al Mubarraz
Al Hufūf
Buqayq
Ra's Tannūrah
Az Zahrān
Al Khubar
Al Wannān
Al Khuwayr
Al Khawr
Ḥālūl
Sīrrī
Abū Mūsā
Ra's al Khaymah
AL ḤARĪM
JUBLI
Dibā al Ḥisn
Rūʾūs al Jibāl
Rūʾ Qadnah
Ra's-al-Kūh
4

QATAR
Ad Dawḥah (Doha)
Al Wakrah
Das
Arzanah
Az Zarqā
Umm al Qaywayn
'Ajmān
Ash Shāriqah
Adh Dhayd
Al Fujayrah
Shināṣ
Suḥār
OMAN
GULF OF OMAN

Dubayy (Dubai)
Abū Ẓabī (Abu Dhabi)

Ḥawar
Sakhwah
Musay'īd (Umm Saïd)
Al Qaffāy
Ra's al Udayd
Dalmā
Sīr Banī Yās
Jabal az Zannah
Ra's Ḥu'ūs
Al Ḥu'ūs
Ṭarīf
Murban
Al Ṭaff
Al Ayn
Ḥaṣn
Sunaynah
Dānk
Ibrī
Jabal Al Rūwais
J.SHAM
2081
Nazwá
Izki
'Ibrā
Sūr
Ra's al Ḥadd
Tropic of Cancer
Al Hajar ash Sharqī
Maṣqaṭ (Muscat)
Maṭraḥ
Ra's al Khayrān
5

Harad
Al 'Āūlah
Jirwān
Sabkhat al Budū
Sabkhat Maṭṭī
Baynūnah
Ad Dafrah
UNITED ARAB EMIRATES
Al Mariyah
Al Jiwā'
Al Manādir
Adam
Ash Sharqīyah
Ramlat ahl Wahībah
Ra's Jibsh

Al Jawb
Kilākh
Bi'r Fardān
Al 'Ubaylah
Al Kidan
Al Qurayñ
Ar Rimāl
Ummas Samīm
Ramlat Ibn Su'aydān
Ra's an Nuqdah
Dawwah
Maṣīrah
6

As Summān
Aṭ Ṭuwayrifah
Qalamat ar Rakabah
Al Mibrad
Ḥādh Bani Zaynān
Qalamat Fāris
Bi'r Hādī
Ad Dikākah
Al Ḥibāk
Mughshin
Hajmah
Al 'Ajīz
Daqm
Khalīj Maṣīrak
Al Khalūl
Ghubbat Ḥashīsh
Barr al Ḥikmān
Khawr al Maṣīrah
Al Kalban
7

Al Ḥawāya
Umm as Samīm
As Sanām
Al Qa'āmīyāt
Aḍ Ḍila
Jidat al Ḥarāsīs
Al Jawārah
Ra's Madrakah
Ghubbat Sawqirah
8

YEMEN
Minwakh
Al Quzah
Shibām
Tarīm
Al Qaṭn
Ḥawra
Qabr Hūd
Al Mahrah
Hadhramawt
Sanaw
Thamūd
Muday
Ayun Jabal
Qarā
J.Samhān
Zufār
Mirbāt
Thamarīt
Fasad
Dawqah
Muwaffan
Ra's Sawqirah
Ra's Sharbithāt
OMAN

As Sawdā
Al Hallānīyah
Jazā'ir Khuryān Mūryān
Ra's Naws
ARABIAN SEA
8

Al Mukallā
Ghayl Bin Yumayn
Ash Shiḥr
Riyan
Al Ḥuraydah
Ghayl Bā
Wazīr
Say'ūn
Ghayl Bin Yumayn
Itāb
Qishn
Ra's Sharwayn
Sayḥūt
Ḍamqawt
Ra's Fartak
Ghubbat al Qamar
Al Ghaydah
Ḥarūt
Ṭābūt
Raysūt
Ṣalālah
Ṭāqah
Ra's Mirbāṭ
Sadḥ
9

ARABIAN SEA

N
O
P
Qalansīyah
Qādub
Ra's Shu'ab
Ghubah
Ḥadībōh
Ra's Momi
'Abd al Kūrī
Al Ikhwān (The Brothers)
Samḥah
Darsa
Suquṭrā (Socotra) (Yemen)

J   K   L   M

,000,000
0   50   100   150   200   250   300   350   400   450   500 KILOMETRES
0   50   100   150   200   250   300 STATUTE MILES

East of Greenwich

Designed and produced by E.S.R.

177

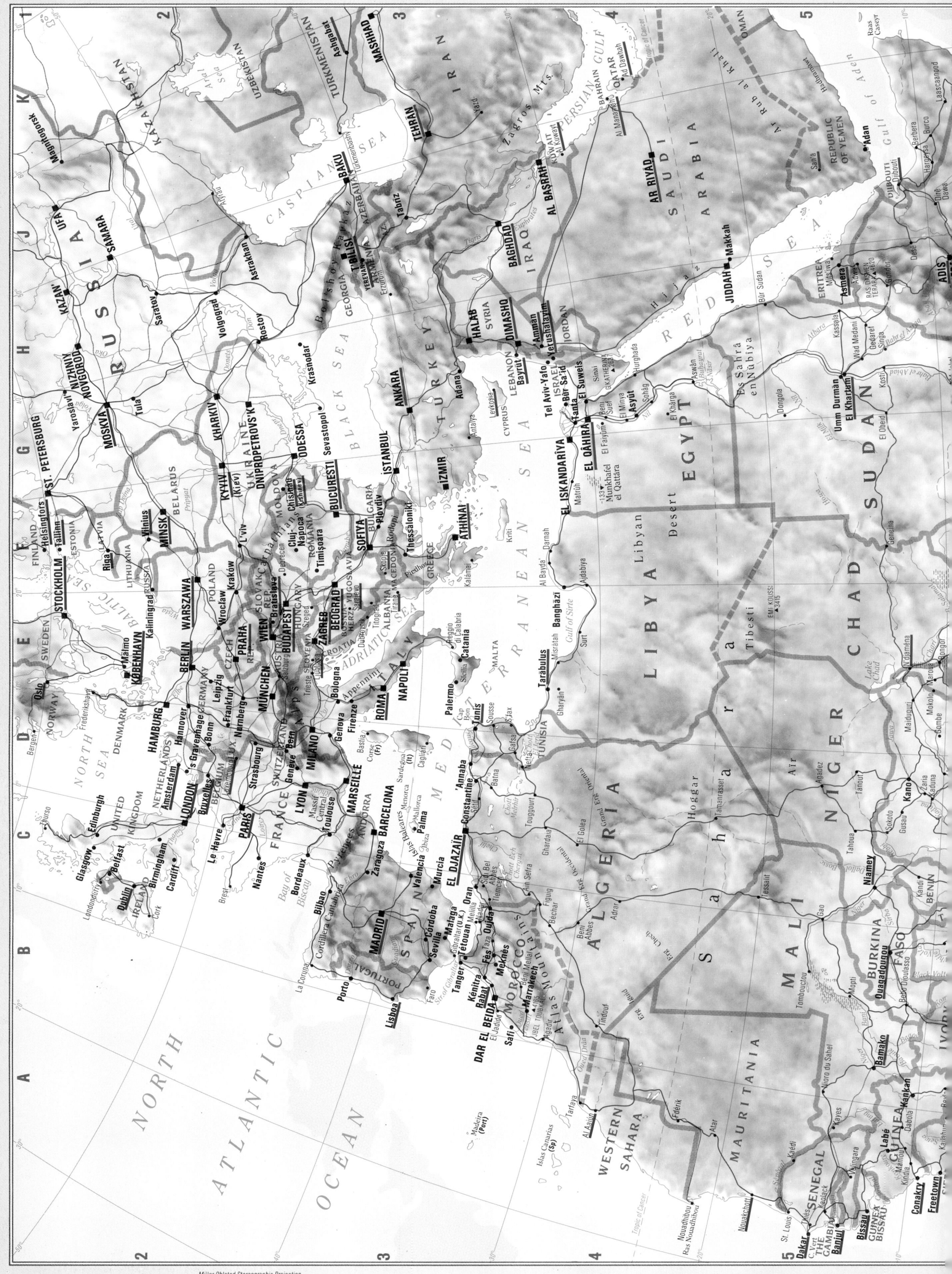

Miller Oblated Stereographic Projection

1:23,000,000

| 0 | 250 | 500 | 750 | 1000 | 1250 | 1500 KILOMETRES |

| 0 | 100 | 200 | 300 | 400 | 500 | 600 | 700 | 800 | 900 | 1000 STATUTE MILES |

© COLOUR LIBRARY BOOKS

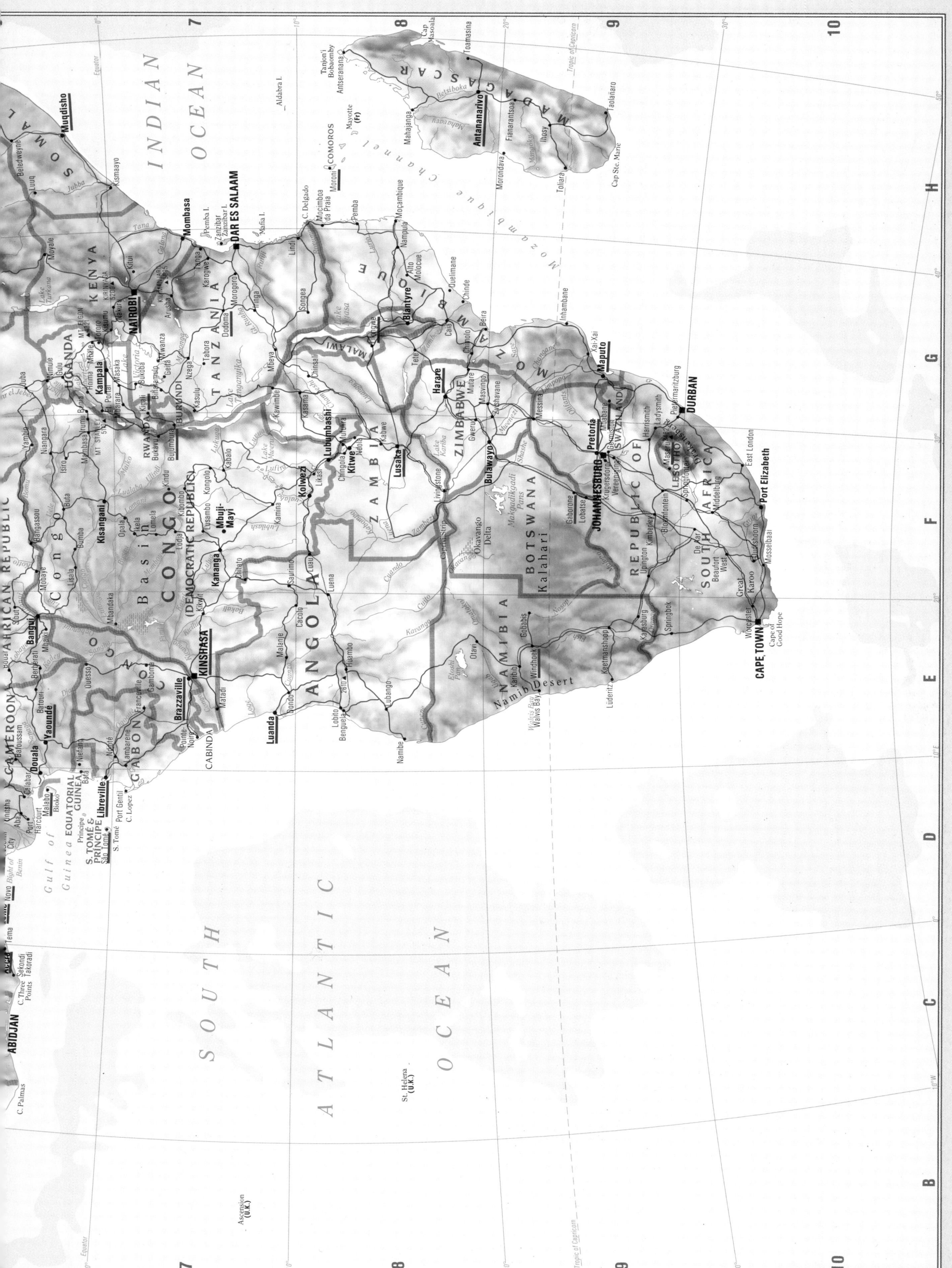

Designed and produced by E.S.R.

A B C D E

SPAIN

Faro
Cádiz
Malaga
Sierra Nevada
Almería

Strait of Gibraltar
Cap Spartel
Gibraltar (U.K.)
Ceuta (Sp.)
Asilah
Tanger
Tétouan
Larache (El Araiche)
Ksar el Kebir
Chaouen
Cap des Trois Fourches
Melilla (Spain)
Oujda
Oran
Mostaganem
Beni Saf
Ghazaouet
Sidi Bel Abbès
Arzew
Mascara
Saïda
Tlemcen
Frenda

Madeira (Portugal)
Funchal

NORTH

ATLANTIC

OCEAN

Ilhas Selvagens (Portugal)

KÉNITRA
Rabat
Salé
Sidi Kacem
Fès
Taza
DAR EL BEIDA (CASABLANCA)
Meknès
Sefrou
El Jadida
Settat
Khemisset
Oulmès
Azrou
Moyen Atlas
Khouribga
Oued Zem
Kasba Tadla
Beni Mellal
ATLAS
Safi
Youssoufia
Essaouira
Oued Tensift
Demnate
MGOUN
El Rachidia (Ksar es Souk)
Kenadsa
Béchar
Marrakech (Marrakesh)
Haut
JEBEL TOUBKAL 4165
Ouarzazate
Figuig
Cap Rhir
Agadir
Taroudannt
Anti-Atlas
Grand Erg Occi
Beni Abbès
Tiznit
Sidi Ifni
Tagounite
Hamada du Dra
Tindouf
Timimoun
Tan-Tan
Oued Drâa
Oued Tigzerte
Ksabi
Tarfaya (Villa Bens)
Cap Juby
Al Aaiún (Laâyoune)
Es Semara
As Saguia al Hamra
ALGE
Adrar

Islas Canarias (Canary Is.) (Spain)
La Palma
Sta. Cruz de la Palma
Lanzarote
Gomera
Sta. Cruz de Tenerife
Fuerteventura
Arrecife
Hierro
Valverde
Tenerife
Puerto del Rosario
Las Palmas
Gran Canaria

Boujdour

Reggane

WESTERN
SAHARA

Bir Moghrein (Fort Trinquet)

Erg Iguidi

C. Barbas

Ad Dakhla (Villa Cisneros)
Baie de Rio de Oro

Tropic of Cancer

Fdérik
Zouérate
Erg Chech
Taoudenni
Tanezrouft

Nouadhibou (Pt. Etienne)
Ras Nouadhibou (C. Blanc)

Makteir

Ouarâne

Irharen

Atar
Chinguetti

Sa h
Tessalit

C. Timiris

El Djouf

MAURITANIA

Aguelhok

Akjoujt

Araouane

MALI

Nouakchott
Beïla

Tidjikdja
Tichitt

Moudjéria

Aouker

L. Faguibine
Tombouctou (Timbuktu)
Gourma-Rharous
Bamba
Bourem

Boutilimit

Tamchaket
Oualata

Ras el Ma
Niger
Gao

Mederdra
Aleg
Kiffa
Aïoun el Atrouss
Néma
Goundam
Niafounké

Senegal
St. Louis
Louga
Dagana
Podor
Bogué
Kaédi
Timbédra
Niono
Moptí
Bandiagara

Kébémer
Diorbivol
Mbout
Bakel
Nioro du Sahel
Nara
Douentza
Ansongo

Tivaouane
Thiès
Linguère
Matam
Sélibabi
Sokolo
Ségou

Cape Vert
Dakar
Diourbel
SENEGAL
Kayes
Djenné
Bani

Mbour
Fatick
Kaffrine
Tambacounda
Béfoulabé
Kati
Bani
Sikasso
Tougan
Yako

THE GAMBIA
Banjul (Bathurst)
Georgetown
Maka
Bassé Santa Su
BAMAKO
Koutiala
BURKINA FASO

C. Roxo
Ziguinchor
GUINEA BISSAU
Kolda
Vélingara
Kédougou
Setadougou
Bafing Makana
Kita
Massigui
Bobo Dioulasso
OUAGADOUGOU

Bissau
Bolama
Arquipelago dos Bijagos
GUINEA
Labé
Siguiri
Banfora
GHANA

Cap Verga
Kankan
Ferkéssédougou

1:9,000,000

Müller Oblated Stereographic Projection
West of Greenwich

KILOMETRES
0 100 200 300 400 500 600
STATUTE MILES
0 50 100 150 200 250 300 350 400

© COLOUR LIBRARY BOOKS

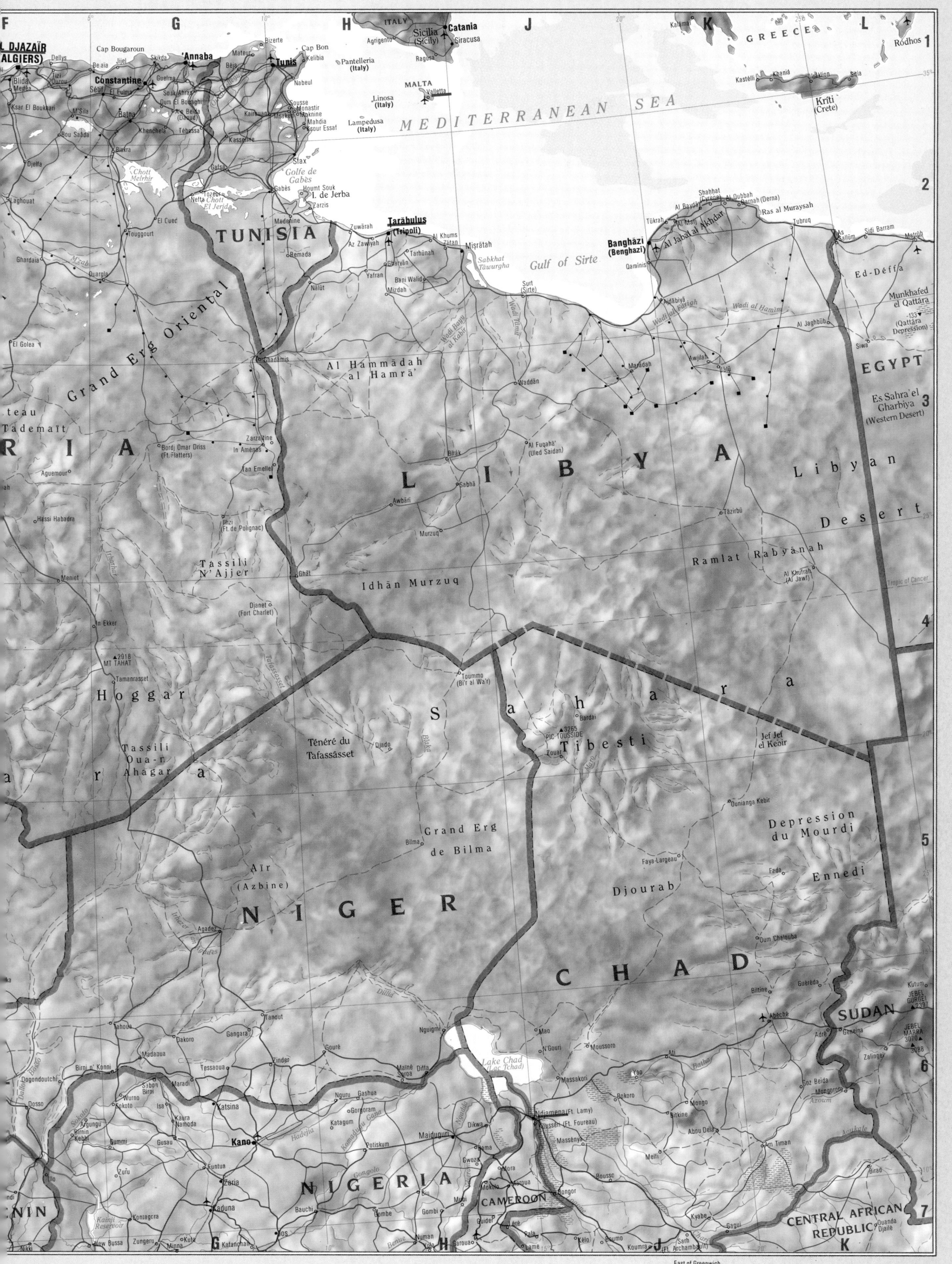

NORTH-EAST AFRICA

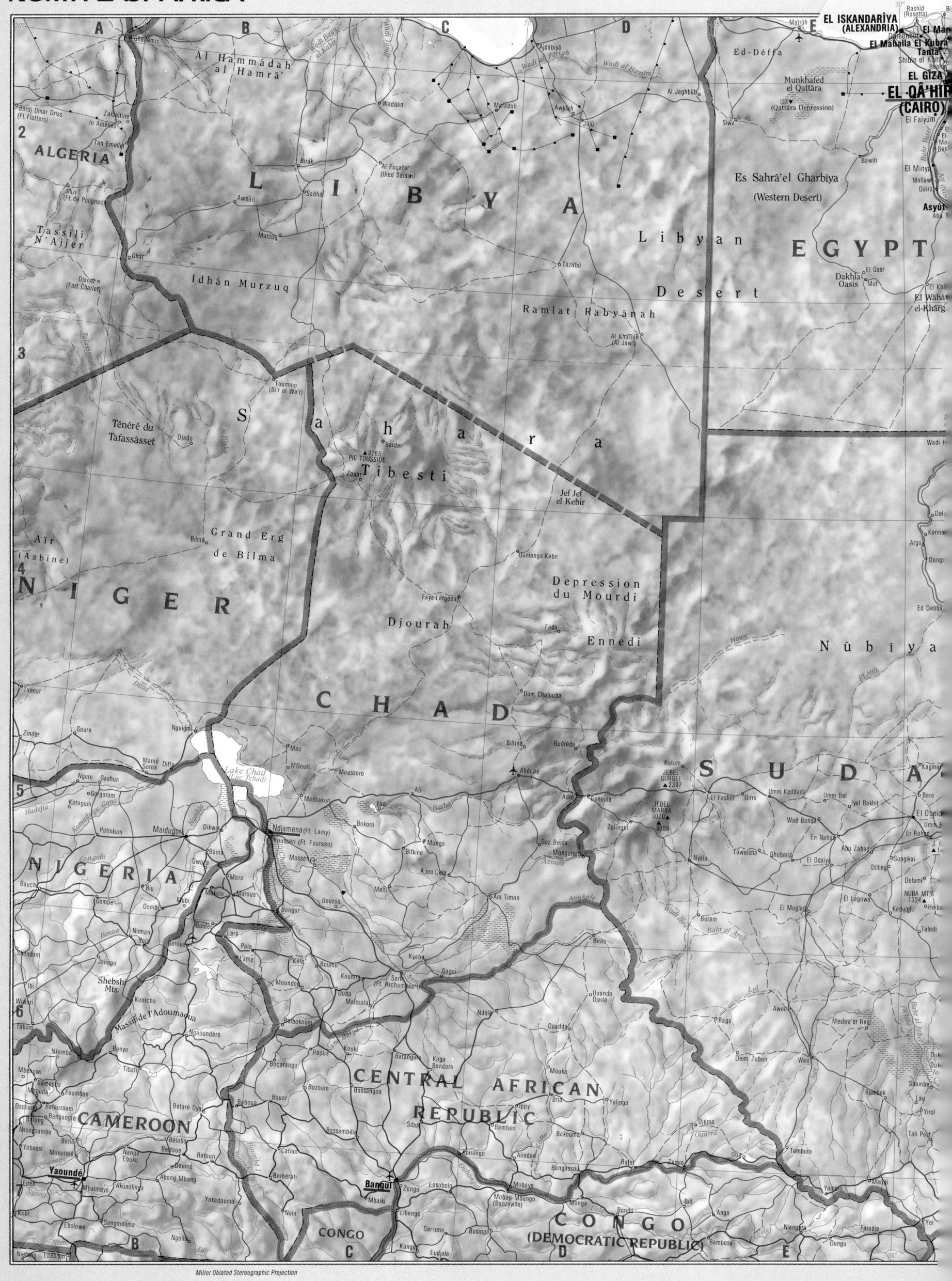

El Iskandarîya (Alexandria)
Rashîd (Rosetta)
El Mahalla El Kubra
Tanta
Shibîn el Kôm
EL GÎZA
EL -QÂ'HIR (CAIRO)
El Faiyûm
El Minya
Mallawi
Asyût

Ed-Défra
Munkhafed el Qattâra
(Qattâra Depression)
Siwa

ALGERIA
Bordj Omar Driss (Ft. Flatters)
In Amenas
Tan Emellel
Zarzaïtine
Illizi (Ft. de Polignac)
Djanet (Fort Charlet)
Tassili N'Ajjer
Ghât

Ghadamis
Al Hammâdah al Hamrâ'
Awbâri
Sabhâ
Murzuq
Idhân Murzuq

LIBYA
Wâddân
Marâdah
Birâk
Al Fuqahâ' (Uled Saïdan)
Tâzirbû

Wadi al Hamîm
Al Jaghbûb
Awjila
Jâlû
Al Jaghbûb

EGYPT
Es Sahrâ'el Gharbîya (Western Desert)
Dakhla Oasis
Mut
El Qasr
El Wâha el-Khârg

Libyan Desert
Ramlat Rabyânah
Al Khufrah (Al Jawf)

Toummo (Bi'r al Wa'r)
Sahara
Tibesti
PIC TOUSSIDE ▲3265
Bardaï
Zouar

Jef Jef el Kebir

Ténéré du Tafassâsset
Djado
Elabo

Aïr (Âzbine)

Grand Erg de Bilma
Bilma

Ounianga Kebir

Depression du Mourdi
Ennedi

Nûbîya

NIGER
Tanout

Faya-Largeau
Djourab
Fada

Oum Chalouba

CHAD

SUDAN

Zinder
Gouré
Nguigmi
Mao
N'Goun
Moussoro
Ati
Biltine
Guéréda
Kutum
JEBEL GURGEI ▲2397
Umm Keddada
El Fasher
Dirra
Umm Bel
Iyal Bakhit
Bara

Maïné Soroa
Diffa
Nguru
Gashua
Gorgoram
Katagum
Hadejia
Potiskum
Maïduguri
Dikwa
Bama
Massakori
Massakori
Bokoro
Mongo
Bitkine
Abéché
Adré
Geneïna
Zalingei
JEBEL MARRA 3070▲ ▲3088
Goz Beida
Mongororo
Nyala
Taweïsha
Ghubeish
El Odaiya
Dilling
NUBA MTS.
Kadugli
Sungikai
El Obeid
Er Rahad

Lake Chad (Lac Tchad)

NIGERIA
Nguru
Gashua
Potiskum
Gombe
Biu
Numan
Mubi
Maroua
Mora
Gwoza
Guide
Lérè
Pala
Bongor
Bousso
Kélo
Moundou
Ndjamena (Ft. Lamy)
Kousséri (Ft. Foureau)
Massénya
Melfi
Am Timan
Mongo
Aï ou Deïa

Shebshi Mts.
Kontcha
Numan
Jalingo
Ibi
Wukari
Takum

Massif de l'Adoumaoua
Ngaoundéré
Banyo
Tibati

Baïbokoum
Moïssala
Sarh (Ft. Archambault)
Ndélé
Ouadda
Raga

CENTRAL AFRICAN REPUBLIC
Bozoum
Bossangoa
Batangafo
Kaga Bandoro
Mouka
Ippy
Bria
Yalinga

CAMEROON
Yaoundé
Mbalmayo
Akonolinga
Abong Mbang
Bertoua
Batouri
Berbérati
Carnot
Bouar
Baboua
Bossembélé
Bangui
Mbaïki

CONGO
CONGO (DEMOCRATIC REPUBLIC)

Miller Oblated Stereographic Projection

1:9,000,000

© COLOUR LIBRARY BOOKS

0 100 200 300 400 500 600 KILOMETRES
0 50 100 150 200 250 300 350 400 STATUTE MILES

Designed and produced by E.S.R.

WESTERN SAHARA

C. Barbas

Nouadhibou
(Pt. Etienne)
Ras Nouadhibou
(C. Blanc)

C. Timiris

Makteir

Ouarâne

MAURITANIA

El Djouf

Sa

h

MALI

Nouakchott Beila

Boutilimit

Mederdra

Aleg

Atar

Akjoujt

Chinguetti

Tidjikdja

Moudjéria

Tichitt

Aoukar

Tamchaket

Araouane

Tombouctou
(Timbuktu)

Niger

Bamba

Bourem

Gourma-
Rharous

St. Louis

Dagana

Podor

Bogué

Kaédi

Louga

Diorbivol

Mbout

Kiffa

Aioun el Atrouss

Oualata

Néma

Ras el Ma

L. Faguibine

Goundam

Gao

Niafounke

Kébemer

Linguère

Matam

Timbédra

Mopti

Bandiagara

Dori

Gourma-

Cape Vert Thiès
Dakar

Tivaouane

Diourbel

Sélibabi

Nioro du Sahel

Nara

Sokolo

Ségou

Djenne

San

Ouahigouya

Yako

Tougan

BURKINA FASO

Mbour Fatick
Founhougne Kaolack

SENEGAL

Kaffrine

Bakel

Kayes

Niono

Bani

Koutiala

Dédougou
Koudougou

Ouagadougou

THE GAMBIA
Banjul
(Bathurst)

Kaolack

Tambacounda

Bafoulabé

Kati

Bamako

Sikasso

Bobo
Dioulasso

Houndé

Léo

Nangrong

Fada N Gou

Tenkodogo

Casamance

Kolda Vélingara

Kédougou

Satadougou

Bafing
Makana

Bougouni

Banfora

Kourémalé

Ziguinchor

C. Roxo

GUINEA
BISSAU

Bissau

Bolama

Arquipelago
dos Bijagos

Labé

Pita

Dalaba

Siguiri

Massigui

Borome

Gaoua

Gaoual

Boké

Telimélé

Dinguiraye

Kouroussa

GUINEA

Kankan

Odienné

Korhogo

Bouna

Cap Verga

Boffa

Mamou

Timbo Dabola

Faranah

1236▲

Boundiali

Kong

Kindia

Dubréka

Conakry

Forécariah

Kabala

Kissidougou

Ferkessédougou

Katiola

Bondoukou

Kumasi

GHANA

Kambia
Port Loko

SIERRA
LEONE

Makeni

Magburaka

Safadu
Guékédou

Beyla

Touba

Séguéla

IVORY COAST

Bouaké

Freetown

Yawri Bay

Sherbro

Meyamba
Shenge

Kenema

Panderu

Wologisi
Mts.

Man

Daloa

Bouaflé

Yamoussoukro

Bonthe

Pujehun

Bo

Nzérékoré
Lola
MTS NIMBA

Zuenoula

Sinfra

Dimbokro

Agboville

Sherbro Island

Tototo

Gbarnga

Buchanan

Zwedru

Buiglo

Soubré

Gagnoa

Abengourou

LIBERIA

Monrovia

Robertsport

Greenville
(Sinoe)

Sasstown

Timbo

Harper

C. Palmas

Tabou

San Pédro

Sassandra

Grand
Lahou

ABIDJAN

Bingerville

Cape Three Points

Accra

ATLANTIC

184

Miller Oblated Stereographic Projection

West of Greenwich

© COLOUR LIBRARY BOOKS

1:9,000,000

| 0 | 100 | 200 | 300 | 400 | 500 | 600 | KILOMETRES |

| 0 | 50 | 100 | 150 | 200 | 250 | 300 | 350 | 400 | STATUTE MILES |

CAPE VERDE

Santo
Antão

Porto Novo

São Vincente

Mindelo

Sal

São Nicolau

São
Tiago

Boa Vista

Maio

Fogo

Praia

Brava

ATLANTIC OCEAN

Equator

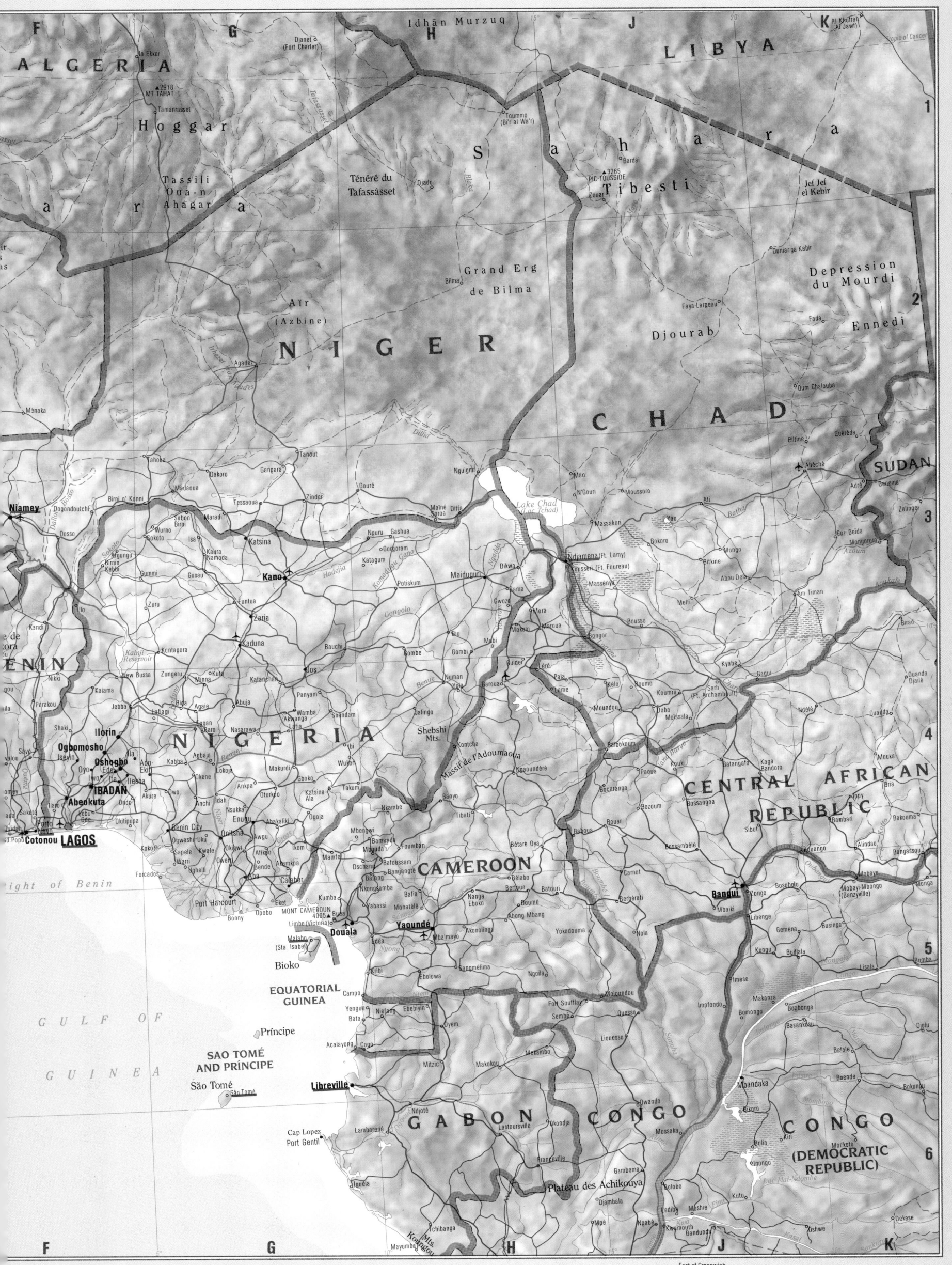

Designed and produced by E.S.R.

Miller Oblated Stereographic Projection

1:9,000,000

| 0 | 100 | 200 | 300 | 400 | 500 | 600 KILOMETRES |

| 0 | 50 | 100 | 150 | 200 | 250 | 300 | 350 | 400 STATUTE MILES |

© COLOUR LIBRARY BOOKS

Miller Oblated Stereographic Projection

1:9,000,000

© COLOUR LIBRARY BOOKS

Designed and produced by E.S.R.

Bonne Projection

1:19,000,000

0   200   400   600   800 KILOMETRES

0   100   200   300   400   500 STATUTE MILES

East of Greenwich

© COLOUR LIBRARY BOOKS

N   P   Q   R   S   T   U   V   W

NAURU

Gilbert Islands (Kiribati)

Banaba

Nonouti
Tabiteuea
Kingsmill Group
Tamana
Onotoa
Arorae

Beru
Nukunau

KIRIBATI

Howland I.
Baker I. (U.S.A.)

Winslow Reef

Equator

1

PACIFIC

Tauu Is.
Nukumanu Is.

Ontong Java Atoll

SOLOMON
ISLANDS
Choiseul
Santa Isabel
New Georgia
Vangunu
Russell Is.
Honiara
Guadalcanal
Malaita
Maramasike
Stewart Is.

OCEAN

Nanumea
Niutao
Nanumanga

Nui
Vaitupu
Nukufetau

Kanton I.
McKean I.
Birnie I.
Nikumaroro
Orona
Manra

Enderbury I.
Rawak

Phoenix Islands (Kiribati)

Carondelet Reef

2

San Cristóbal
Nupani
Tinakula
Swallow Is.
Duff Is.

Rennell I.
Indispensable Reefs

Ndeni
Utupua
Vanikoro Is.
Santa Cruz Is.
Cherry
Tikopia
Mitre

Funafuti
Nukulaelae

TUVALU

Niulakita

Tokelau (N.Z.)
Atafu
Nukunono
Fakaofo

Swains I.

Pukapuka
Nassau

3

Torres Is.
Vot Tandé
Uréparapara
Banks Islands
Vanua Lava
Santa Maria
Méré Lava
Cap Nahoi
Espíritu
Santo
Aoba
Maéwo
Malo
Pentecost I.
Malakula
Ambrym
VANUATU
Épi
Shepherd Is.

Rotuma

Eaglestone Reef

Iles Wallis (Fr.)
Uvea
Futuna
Iles de Horn
Alofi (Fr.)

SAMOA
Savaii
Upolu
Apia
Samoan Is.
Manua
Tau
Pose I.
Tutuila

Suvorov I.

4

Iles Chesterfield (Fr.)

Récifs d'Entrecasteaux
Sable

Iles Bélep
MT. PANIÉ
1628

Ouvéa
Lifou
Thio
Maré
Iles Loyauté (Fr.)

Efaté
Vila
Erromango

Tanna

Aneityum (Anatom)

Vanua Levu
Yasawa Group
Taveuni
Lau Group
Koro
Gau
FIJI
Nadi
Viti Levu
Suva
Kadavu
Lakeba

Niuafo'ou
Tafahi
Niuatoputapu

Late
Vava'u Group
Fonualei
Kao
Tofua
Ha'apai Group
Nomuka

Niue (N.Z.)

Cook Islands (New Zealand)

5

Middleton Reef
Elizabeth Reef

Nouvelle
Calédonie
(France)
Bourail
Nouméa
Île des Pins

Walpole
Matthew
Hunter

Ceva-i-Ra

Vatoa

Tuvana-i-Tholo
Tuvana-i-Ra
Ono-i-Lau

Nuku'alofa
Tongatapu
Group
TONGA
Eua
Ata

Palmerston I.

Minerva Reefs

6

Tropic of Capricorn

Norfolk I.
Philip I. (Aust.)

Lord Howe I.
(Aust.)

Kermadec Is.
(N.Z.)
Raoul
Macauley I.
Curtis I.
L'Esperance Rock

7

TASMAN

SEA

Three Kings Is.
C. Maria van Diemen
Kaitaia
Dargaville
Whangarei
North Cape

Great Barrier I.
Auckland
Manukau
Thames
Hamilton
Tauranga
North Island
Rotorua
Whakatane
New Plymouth
RUAPEHU
2797
Gisborne
East Cape
Mahia Peninsula
Napier
Hawera
Wanganui
Hastings
C. Farewell
Palmerston
North
Motueka
Picton
Masterton
NEW
Westport
Blenheim
Wellington
Cook Strait
South Island
Greymouth
ZEALAND
Hokitika
Kaikoura
Rangiora
MT. COOK
3764
Christchurch
Lyttelton
Cascade Pt.
Ashburton
Southern Alps
Queenstown
Timaru
L. Wakatipu
Oamaru
C. Providence
Alexandra
Dunedin
L. Te Anau
Gore
C. Saunders
Foveaux Strait
Invercargill
Stewart I.
Snares Is.

Chatham Is. (N.Z.)
Pitt I.

8

9

Bounty Is. (N.Z.)

10

Antipodes Is. (N.Z.)

Auckland Is. (N.Z.)

Campbell I. (N.Z.)

11

P   Q   R   S   T   U   V   W   X   Y   Z

West of Greenwich

Designed and produced by E.S.R.

INDIAN

OCEAN

TIMOR SEA

Ashmore Reef

Seringapatum Reef

Scott Reef

C. Bougainville
C. Londonderry

Joseph
Bonaparte
Gulf

Melville I.
Bathurst I.
Beagle Clarence Str. Van Diemen Gulf
C. Van Diemen
Darwin
Batchelor
Butrund
Pine Creek
Edi
Willeroo

Brunswick
Bay
Beegle
Reef

York Sound
Collie
Bay
C. Lévêque

Sunday Str.
Charmley
King Sound

MT. HANN
854

Drysdale
Admiralty Gulf
Wyndham
Kununurra
Auvergne
Goolbah

King Leopold Ranges
MT. ORD
936
Kimberley
MT. LUSH
786
Ord
Turkey Creek
Lake
Argyle
Wave Hill

Dampier
Land
Derby
Yeeda River
Ellendale

Broome
Roebuck Bay

Plateau
Halls Creek
Margaret
River
Christmas Creek

Fitzroy Crossing
McClintock
Range
Antrim
Plateau

Chapman
Fitzroy

NO

TER

Larrey Pt.
Port Hedland
Goldsworthy
De Grey

Eighty Mile Beach
Wallal Downs
Anna Plains

Canning Basin

Great Sandy Desert

Tanami

Exmouth
Rise

Dampier
Archipelago
Barrow I.

Nickol Bay
Dampier
Karratha

Marble Bar

Oakover
Oakover

Throssell Ra.
Broadhurst Ra.

Lake
Waukarlycarly
Lake
Dora

Percival
Lakes

Lake
Tobin

Lake
Wills
Lake White

MT. SINGLETON
844
MT. Doreen
Yuendumu

North West Cape
Onslow
Yarraloola

Fortescue
Mulga Downs

Chichester
Range
Roy Hill

Durak

Lake
Mackay

MT. LEISIER
1005

MT. ZIEL
1511
Macdonnell

Pt. Cloates

Hammersley Range
MT. BROCKMAN
1114
MT. BRUCE
1228
MT. NEWMAN
1228
Newman

Ashburton
Robertson Ra.

WESTERN

Gibson Desert

MT. METHWIN
908

Lake
Hopkins

Lake
Neale
Lake
Amadeus

MT. DEERING
1210

Petermann Ranges

AYERS ROCK
860

Winning Pool
Tyndon

Tropic of Capricorn

Lake
McLeod

Gifford Creek
MT. AUGUSTUS
1106
MT. EGERTON
904
Milgun

Gascoyne
Geographe Ch.

Jimba Jimba
Landor
MT. STEERE
Pearl Hill
MT. FRASER
802
Robinson Ranges

Lake
Disappointment

AUSTRALIA

Lake
Carnegie

Barlow
Range

MT. BURT
663

MT. MORRIS
1255
MT. WO
1514
Musgrave Ranges

Tomkinson
Ranges
MT. ILLBILLE
91

Birksgate Ra.

Carnarvon

Naturaliste Ch.
Shark
Bay

Murchison
Berringarra

Wooramel
Meekatharra

Wiluna
Lake
Way

MT. SHENTON
595

Lake
Rason

Great Victoria Desert

Lake Dey-I
Lake Mauri

Dirk Hartog I.
Edel
Land

Meeberrie

Greenough
Billabalong

Cue
Lake
Austin
Sandstone
Mt. Magnet

Laverton

Lake Carey

Lake Minigwal

Nullarbor

Gold

Bluff Pt.
Ajana
Houtman
Rocks
Geraldton
Dongara

Edah Wagga
Mullewa Wurarga
Marawa Paynes Find
Arrino
Perenjori

Lake Moore

Bonnie Rock

Lake
Barlee

Kalgoorlie

Lake
Ballard

Lake
Rebecca

Lake
Yindarlgooda

Karonie
Zanthus
Rawlinna

Loongana
Forrest

Cook

Deakin

Plain

Vullarbor

Head
of
Bight
Pt.

Yarra
Yarra
Lakes

Wubin
Watheroo
Moora

Southern Cross
Kambalda
Lake Lefroy

Eyre
Madura

Moonpa

Great Australian Bight

Perth
Fremantle
Rockingham
Mandurah

Gingin
Northam
Cunderdin
MT. COOKE
582
Quairading
Beverley
Pingelly
Narrogin
Williams
Wagin

Merredin

Southern Cross

Norseman

The
Johnston
Lakes

Lake Cowan

Balladonia

Rason Ra.

Collie
Bunbury
Harvey
Boyanup
Donnybrook

Kondinin
Lake King
Newdegate
Lake Grace
Lake
Magenta

Bremer Ra.
Lake King
Ravensthorpe
Esperance

C. Pasley

C. Naturaliste
Geographe Bay

Busselton
Collie
Bridgetown
Katanning
Kojonup
Ongerup

Sterling Ra.
BLUFF KNOLL
1110

Esperance Bay

Archipelago of
the Recherche

C. Leeuwin
Augusta
Jardee
Northcliffe
Nornalup
Albany
King George Sound
Pt. Henry

Pt. D'Entrecasteaux
Pt. Nuyts
Tor Bay

Miller Oblated Stereographic Projection

1:10,500,000

0 100 200 300 400 500 600 700 800 KILOMETRES

0 100 200 300 400 500 STATUTE MILES

© COLOUR LIBRARY BOOKS

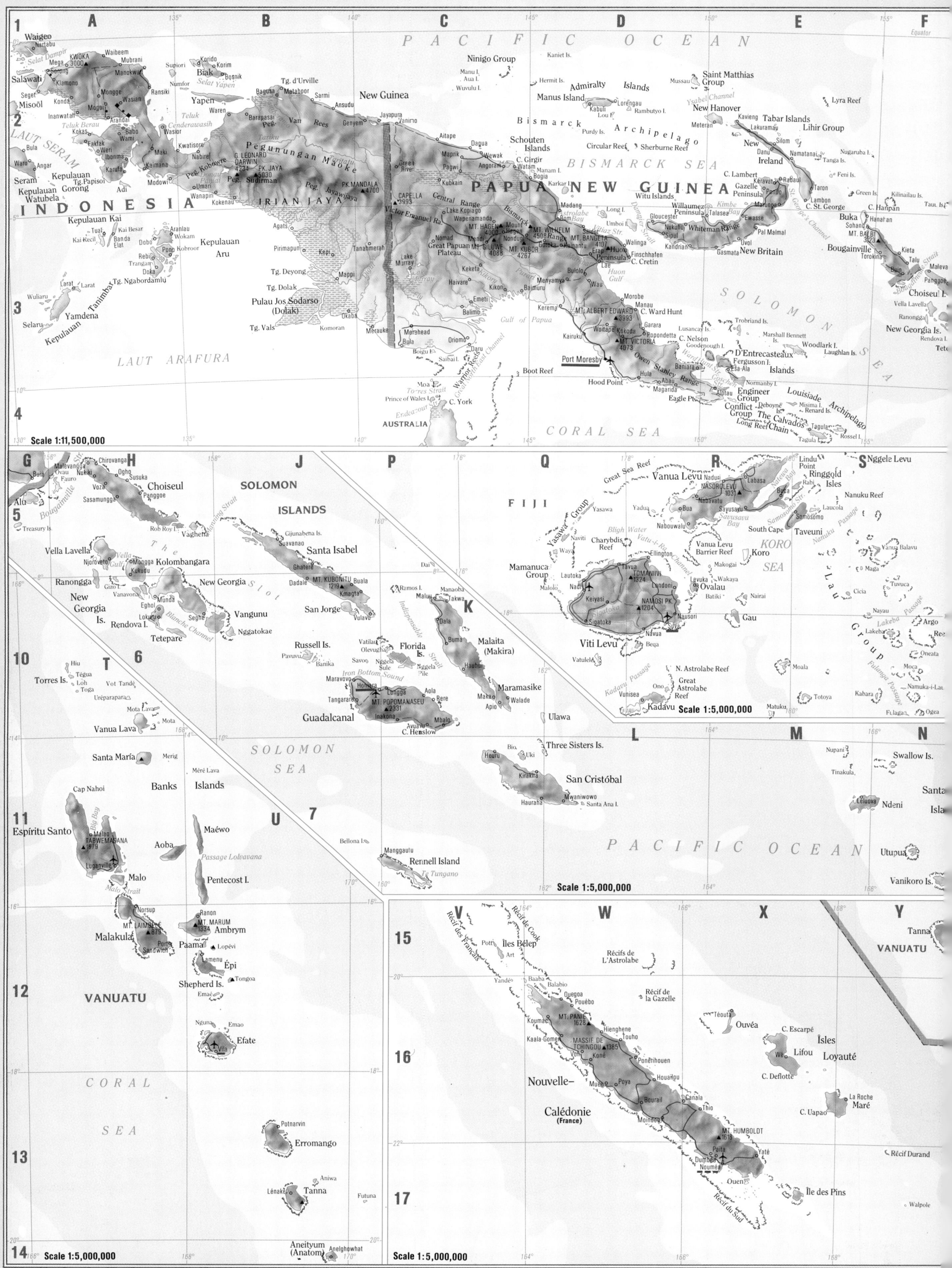

Scale 1:11,500,000

Miller Oblated Stereographic Projection

North Cape
C. Reinga
C. Maria van Diemen
Parengarenga Harbour
North Island
South Island

NEW
ZEALAND

TASMAN SEA

Auckland
Wellington
Christchurch
Dunedin

Southern Alps

PACIFIC OCEAN

Stewart Island

Chatham Islands
Chatham I.
Pitt I.

1:4,500,000

| 0 | 50 | 100 | 150 | 200 | 250 | 300 KILOMETRES |

| 0 | 50 | 100 | 150 | 200 STATUTE MILES |

Designed and produced by E.S.R.

East of Greenwich

Lambert Azimuthal Equal Area Projection

1:20,000,000

© COLOUR LIBRARY BOOKS

0 100 200 300 400 500 600 700 800 900 1000 KILOMETRES

0 100 200 300 400 500 600 STATUTE MILES

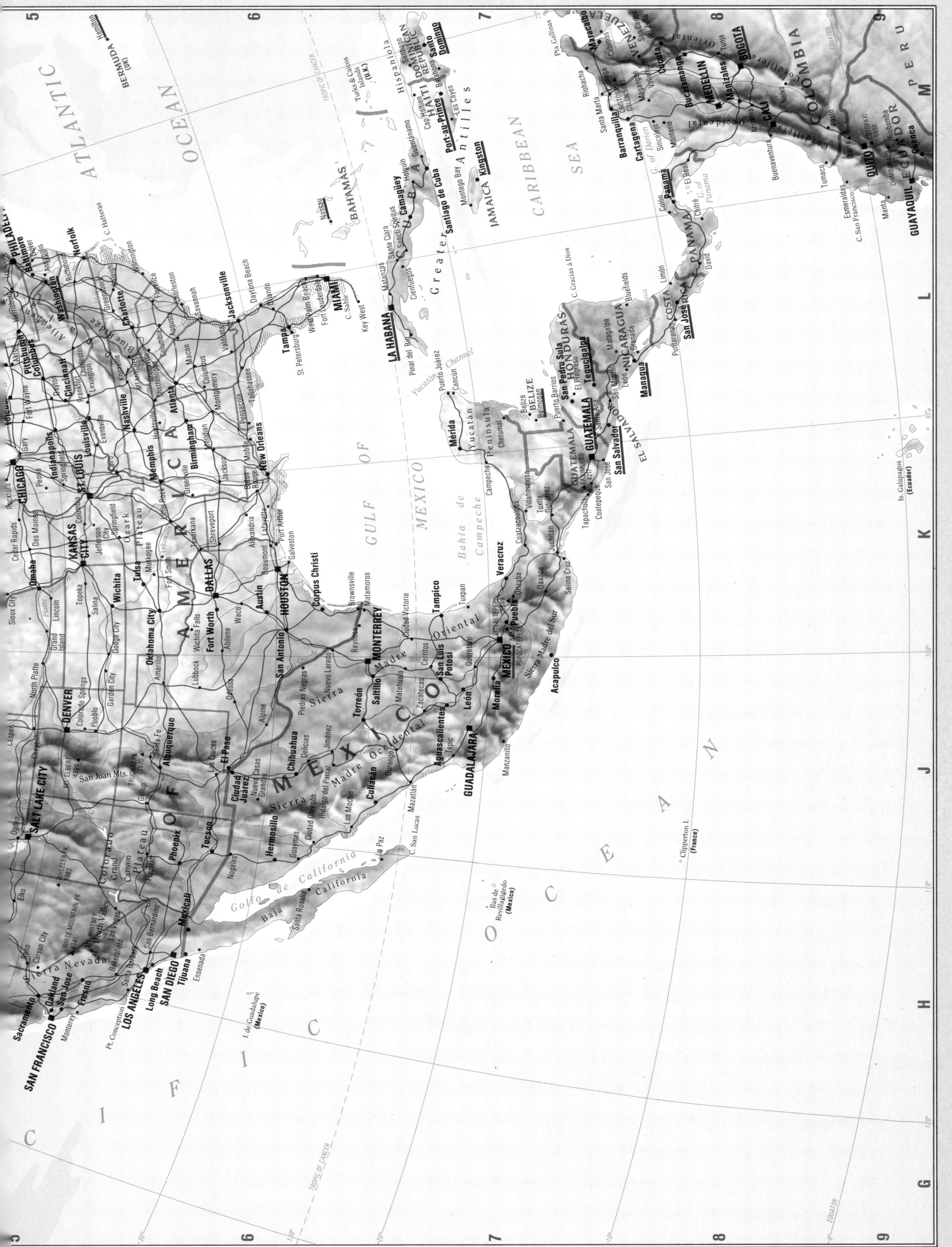

West of Greenwich

ALASKA

Bipolar Oblique Conic Conformal Projection

1:9,000,000

| 0 | 100 | 200 | 300 | 400 | 500 | 600 KILOMETRES |

| 0 | 50 | 100 | 150 | 200 | 250 | 300 | 350 | 400 STATUTE MILES |

© COLOUR LIBRARY BOOKS

1:12,500,000

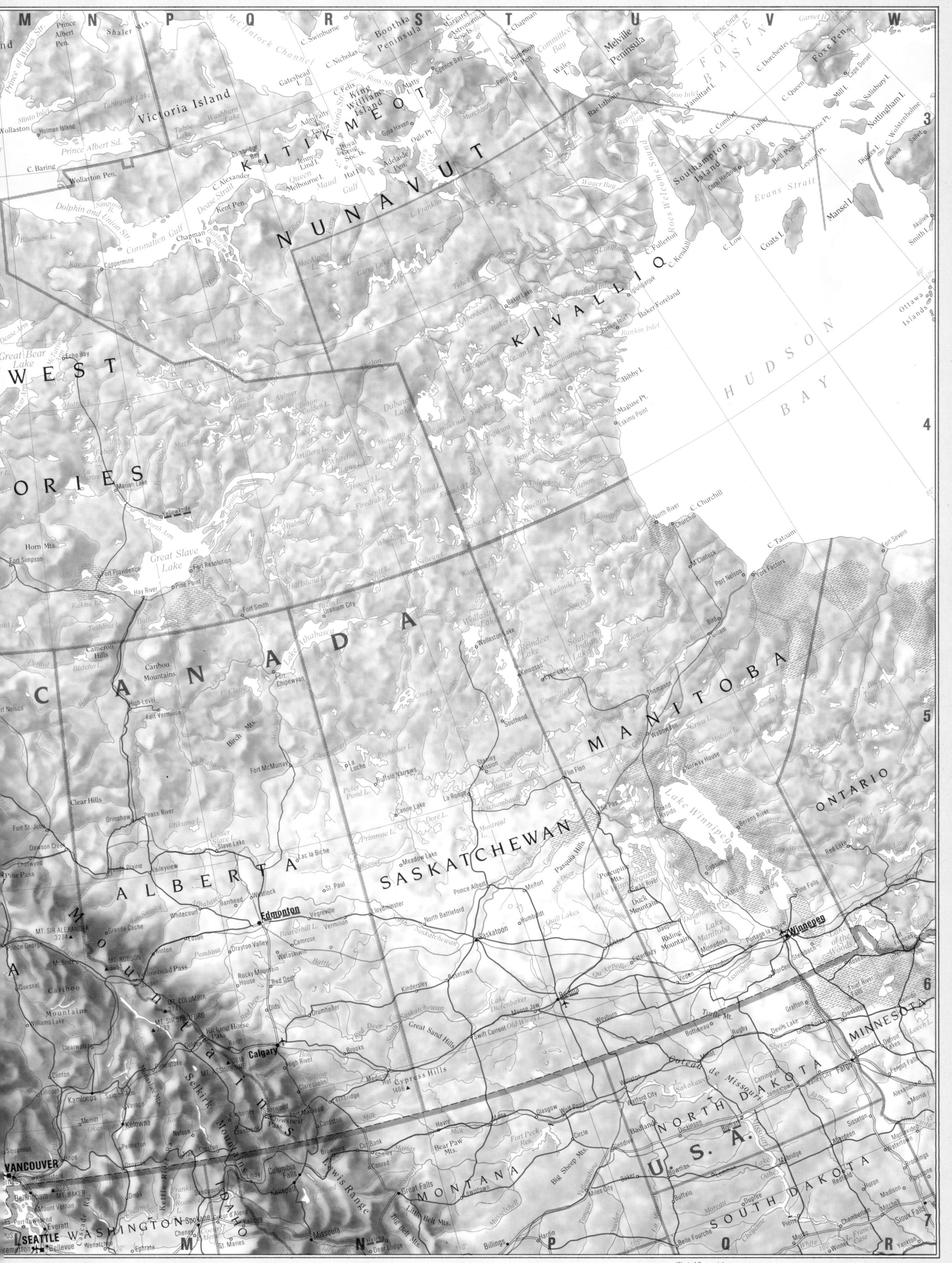

West of Greenwich

Designed and produced by E.S.R.

Bipolar Oblique Conic Conformal Projection

1:9,000,000

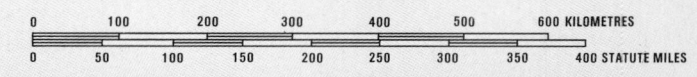

| 0 | 100 | 200 | 300 | 400 | 500 | 600 KILOMETRES |

| 0 | 50 | 100 | 150 | 200 | 250 | 300 | 350 | 400 STATUTE MILES |

© COLOUR LIBRARY BOOKS

West of Greenwich

Designed and produced by E.S.R.

Bipolar Oblique Conic Conformal Projection

1:5,000,000

© COLOUR LIBRARY BOOKS

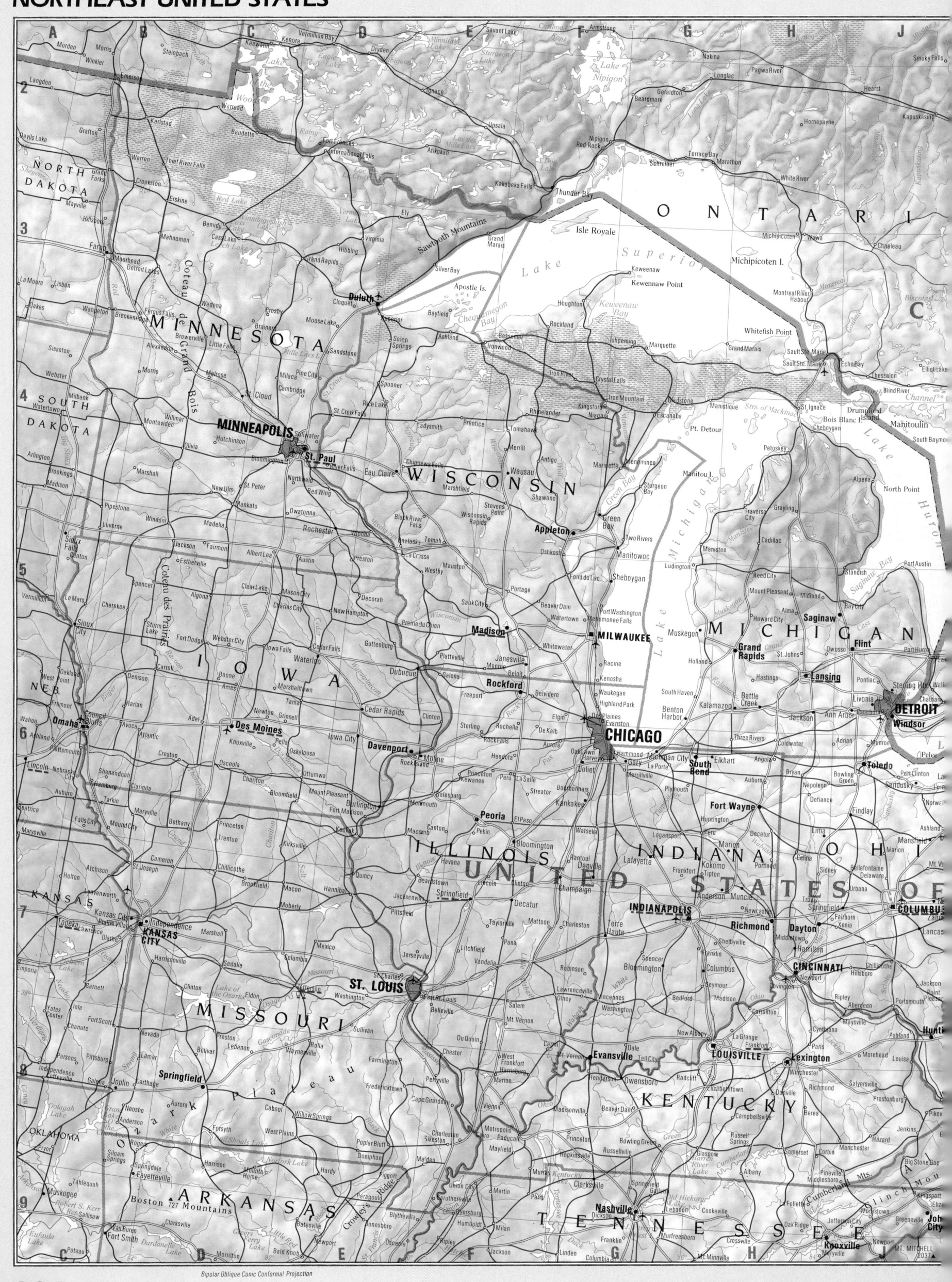

Bipolar Oblique Conic Conformal Projection

© COLOUR LIBRARY BOOKS

1:5,000,000

| 0 | 50 | 100 | 150 | 200 | 250 | 300 | 350 | 400 KILOMETRES |

| 0 | 50 | 100 | 150 | 200 | 250 STATUTE M |

205

© COLOUR LIBRARY BOOKS

1:5,000,000

| 0 | 50 | 100 | 150 | 200 | 250 | 300 | 350 | 400 KILOMETRES |

| 0 | 50 | 100 | 150 | 200 | 250 STATUTE MILES |

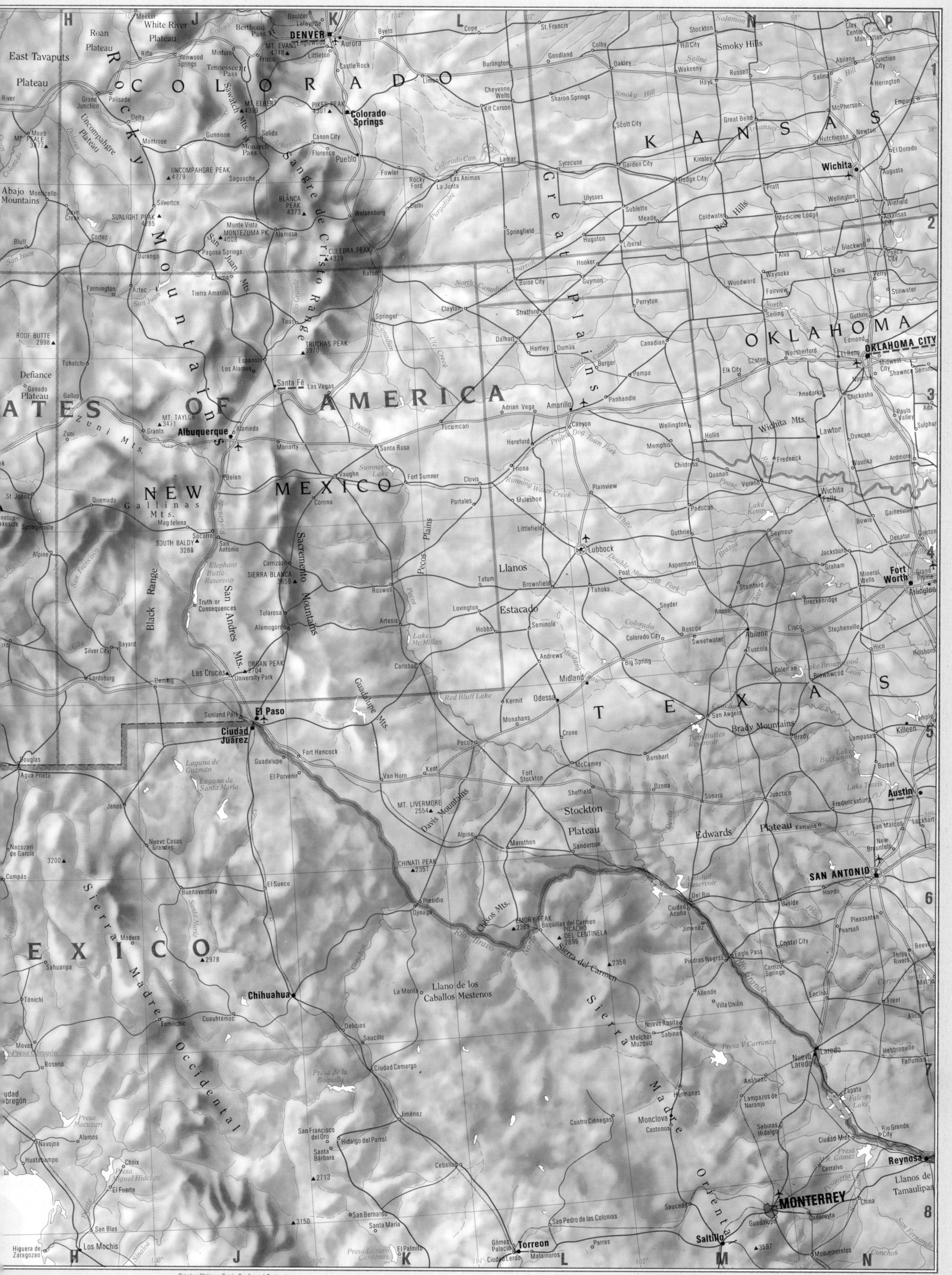

Bipolar Oblique Conic Conformal Projection

West of Greenwich

Designed and produced by E.S.R.

Bipolar Oblique Conic Conformal Projection

1:5,000,000

| 0 | 50 | 100 | 150 | 200 | 250 | 300 | 350 | 400 KILOMETRES |

| 0 | 50 | 100 | 150 | 200 | 250 STATUTE M |

© COLOUR LIBRARY BOOKS

Bipolar Oblique Conic Conformal Projection

1:6,500,000

© COLOUR LIBRARY BOOKS

| 0 | 50 | 100 | 150 | 200 | 250 | 300 | 350 | 400 KILOMETRES |

| 0 | 50 | 100 | 150 | 200 | 250 STATUTE MILES |

GULF OF MEXICO

BAHÍA DE CAMPECHE

CENTRAL AMERICA AND THE CARIBBEAN

Bipolar Oblique Conic Conformal Projection

© COLOUR LIBRARY BOOKS

1:7,000,000

| 0 | 50 | 100 | 150 | 200 | 250 | 300 | 350 | 400 KILOMETRES |

| 0 | 50 | 100 | 150 | 200 | 250 STATUTE MILES |

ATLANTIC

OCEAN

Tropic of Cancer

Puerto Rico Trench

CARIBBEAN SEA

Lesser Antilles

Leeward Islands

Windward Islands

BAHAMAS

Cat I.
San Salvador (Watling I.)
Conception I.
Rum Cay
Long I.
Clarence Town
South Pt.
Crooked I.
Samana Cray
Acklins I.
Mayaguana I.
Abraham's Bay
Hogsty Reef
Little Inagua I.
Great Inagua
Matthew Town
Moa
Baracoa
Guantánamo
Cabo Maisí
Santiago de Cuba

Caicos Is. (U.K.)
Turks I. (U.K.)
Salt Cay

HAITI
PORT-AU-PRINCE
Île de la Tortue
Port-de-Paix
Cap-Haïtien
Monte Cristi
C. Isabela
Puerto Plata
Gonaïves
St Marc
Hinche
Santiago
La Vega
San Francisco de Macoris
Ba. de Escocesa
C. Samaná
Ba. de Samaná
Sabana de la Mar
▲3175 PICO DUARTE
Golfe de la Gonâve
Île de la Gonâve
C. Dame Marie
Dame Marie
Jérémie
Massif de la Hotte
2347
2680 LA SELLE
Les Cayes
Île-à-Vache
Pte.-à-Gravois
Jacmel
San Juan
Barahona
Bani
Pedernales
SANTO DOMINGO
Higüey
La Romana
San Pedros de Macoris
I. Saona
C. Engaño

DOMINICAN REPUBLIC

Isla Beata
Cabo Beata

Antilles

Aguadilla
C. Rojo
Mayagüez
I. Mona

Mona Passage

Arecibo
SAN JUAN
Bayamón
Caguas
CERRO DE PUNTA ▲1338
Ponce
Vieques
Puerto Rico (U.S.A.)

Virgin Islands
St. Thomas (U.S.A.)
Charlotte Amalie
St. John (U.S.A.)
St. Croix (U.S.A.)
Frederiksted

Anegada (U.K.)
Virgin Gorda (U.K.)
Road Town
Tortola (U.K.)

Anguilla (U.K.)
Saint Martin (Fr.)
Sint Maarten (Neth.)
Saba (Neth.)
St Eustatius (Neth.)
Basseterre
ST. KITTS-NEVIS (U.K.)
Montserrat (U.K.)
Plymouth

Barbuda
Antigua
St. John's
ANTIGUA AND BARBUDA

Guadeloupe (France)
La Désirade
Basse Terre
Pointe-à-Pitre
Marie-Galante (France)
Iles des Saintes
I. de Aves (Bird I.) (Ven.)
DOMINICA
Roseau
Marigot

Guadeloupe Passage
Dominica Passage

Martinique Passage
Martinique (France)
Fort-de-France

St. Lucia Channel
ST. LUCIA
Castries

St. Vincent Passage
Kingstown
ST. VINCENT
The Grenadines
Carriacou
GRENADA
St George's

BARBADOS
Bridgetown

Lesser Antilles

Punta Gallinas
Oranjestad
Aruba (Neth.)
Curaçao (Neth.)
Bonaire (Neth.)
Willemstad
Kralendijk
Is. Las Aves (Ven.)
I. Orchila (Ven.)
I. Blanquilla (Ven.)
Is. Los Roques (Ven.)
Isla de Margarita (Ven.)
Los Testigos (Ven.)
Tobago
Scarborough
La Asunción
Porlamar
I. La Tortuga (Ven.)

Bonaire Trench

TRINIDAD AND TOBAGO
Port of Spain
Trinidad
Toco
Río Claro
Galeota Pt.

Punta Estrella
Pto. Estrella
Península de Guajira
Castilletes
Riohacha
Maicao
Carrizal
Santa Marta
Cabo de la Vela
Maracaibo
Cabimas
Sta. Rita
Ciudad Ojeda
Lagunillas
Machiques
La Ceiba
Valera
Trujillo
Bobures
Pueblo Nuevo
Punto Fijo
Amuay
Penín. de Paraguaná
Coro
Churuguara
Capatárida
Dabajuro
San Rafael
Altagracia
Golfo de Venezuela
San Luis
San Felipe
Yaritagua
Barquisimeto
El Tocuyo
Acarigua
Carora
Tinaco
San Carlos
Valencia
Villa de Cura
Maracay
San Juan de los Morros
Pto. Cabello
Golfo Triste
Maiquetía
CARACAS
Guarenas
Los Teques
Cabo Codera
Guasimos
Cumaná
Pto. La Cruz
Barcelona
San Mateo
Anaco
Cantaura
Carúpano
Río Caribe
Penín. de Paria
Guiria
Güiria
Golfo de Paria
Irapa
San Fernando
Pedernales

Serpent's Mouth
Dragon's Mouth
Boca Grande

Cartagena
Turbaco
Calamar
Arjona
Sincelejo
Soledad
ranquilla
PICO CRISTÓBAL COLÓN ▲5775
Ciénaga
Fundación
Valledupar
Robles La Paz
Cabo de la Aguja
Sabanalarga
Plato
Magangué
Mompós
El Banco
Sierra de Perijá
Lago de Maracaibo
El Vigia
Barinas
Mérida
PICO BOLÍVAR ▲5007
Cordillera de Mérida
San Cristóbal
Cúcuta
El Viejo
Rubio
San Antonio del Táchira
Pamplona
Ocaña
La Fría
San Carlos del Zulia
San Silvestre
Guasdualito
Elorza
Arauca
El Samán de Apure
San Fernando de Apure
Mantecal
Bruzual
Calabozo
Las Mercedes
Valle de la Pascua
Zaraza
El Sombrero
Cabruta
Mapire
Caicara
La Urbana
Santa María
La Paragua
CERRO MATO 1863 ▲
CERRO BOLÍVAR 802 ▲
Las Trincheras
El Pao
Ciudad Bolívar
Ciudad Guayana
Upata
Ciudad Piar
Represa Raúl Leoni
Barrancas
San José de Amacuro
Pto. Ordaz
Tucupita
Boca Grande

VENEZUELA

COLOMBIA
Bucaramanga
Barrancabermeja
Simití
Zaragoza
Yarumal
Caucasia
ALTO DE TAMAR 2350 ▲

Serranía de Imataca
Guasipati
El Callao
Tumeremo
San Pedro de las Bocas
El Dorado
Port Kaituma
Kartuni

GUYANA

Designed and produced by E.S.R.

West of Greenwich

213

Bipolar Oblique Conic Conformal Projection

© COLOUR LIBRARY BOOKS

1:16,000,000

| 0 | 100 | 200 | 300 | 400 | 500 | 600 | 700 | 800 KILOMETRES |

| 0 | 100 | 200 | 300 | 400 | 500 STATUTE MILES |

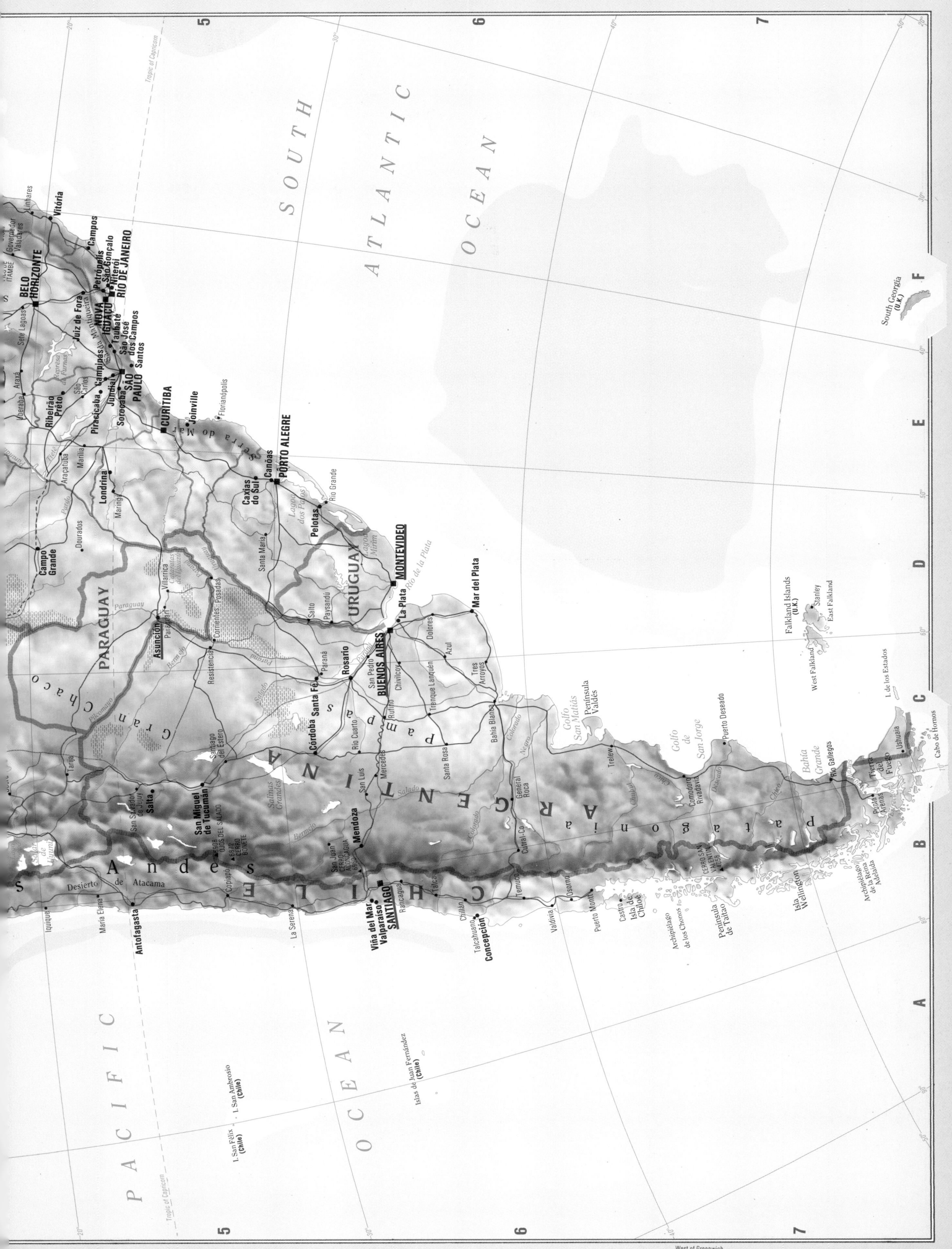

SOUTH

ATLANTIC

OCEAN

PACIFIC

OCEAN

South Georgia
(U.K.)

Vitória
Linhares
Governador Valadares
Itambé
BELO HORIZONTE
Campos
Petrópolis
São Gonçalo
NOVA IGUAÇU
Niterói
RIO DE JANEIRO
Ruiz de Fora
Taubaté
São José dos Campos
Santos
Campinas
Jundiaí
SÃO PAULO
Sorocaba
Piracicaba
CURITIBA
Joinville
Florianópolis
Londrina
Maringá
Caxias do Sul
Canoas
PÔRTO ALEGRE
Rio Grande
Pelotas
Santa Maria
Ribeirão Preto
São Carlos
Aracatuba
Marília
Dourados
Campo Grande

PARAGUAY
Asunción
Paraguay
Gran Chaco
Pilcomayo

URUGUAY
MONTEVIDEO
La Plata
Rio de la Plata
Salto
Paysandú
Rivera

Posadas
Corrientes
Resistencia
Paraná
Santa Fe
Rosario
San Pedro
BUENOS AIRES
Dolores
Azul
Mar del Plata
Chivilcoy
Tres Arroyos
Trenque Lauquen
Bahía Blanca
Santa Rosa
Río Cuarto
Mercedes
San Luis
Córdoba
Santiago del Estero
San Miguel de Tucumán
Salta
San Salvador de Jujuy

ARGENTINA
Mendoza
San Juan
CERRO ACONCAGUA
General Roca
Catral-Co
Temuco
Neuquén

CHILE
SANTIAGO
Valparaíso
Viña del Mar
Rancagua
Talca
Chillán
Concepción
Talcahuano
Valdivia
Osorno
Puerto Montt
Castro
Isla de Chiloé
Archipiélago de los Chonos
Península de Taitao
Isla Wellington
Archipiélago de la Reina Adelaida

Andes
Desierto de Atacama
Antofagasta
María Elena
Iquique
Copiapó
La Serena

Golfo San Matías
Península Valdés
Trelew
Golfo de San Jorge
Puerto Deseado
Comodoro Rivadavia

Patagonia
Bahía Grande
Río Gallegos
Punta Arenas
Tierra del Fuego
Ushuaia
Cabo de Hornos
I. de los Estados

Falkland Islands (U.K.)
West Falkland
East Falkland
Stanley

I. San Félix (Chile)
I. San Ambrosio (Chile)
Islas de Juan Fernández (Chile)

Tropic of Capricorn

West of Greenwich

Designed and produced by E.S.R.

215

Bipolar Oblique Conic Conformal Projection

1:11,000,000

© COLOUR LIBRARY BOOKS

NORTH ATLANTIC OCEAN

Paramaribo · Nieuw Amsterdam · Moengo · Albina
Totness · Groningen · Iracoubo · Sinnamary
Afobakka · Saint Laurent · Kourou
FRENCH · Cayenne · Roura
GUIANA · Kaw
(France) · Cabo Orange
Pontoetoe · Grand Santi · Mana
Orange Geberge · Malavate · Bienvenu · Oiapoque · Cabo Cacipore
Kapiting · Serra · Regina · Punta Grande
Serra Tumucumaque · Serra Lombarda · Amapá
AMAPÁ · Ilha de Maracá
Merirumã · Serra do Navio · Ponta Grossa
Azuari · Pôrto Grande
Macapá

Mouths of the Amazon

Equator 0°

Oriximiná · Óbidos · Chaves · Salinópolis
Óbidos · Almeirim · Ilha Grande · Soure · Curuçá
Juriti · Santarém · do Gurupá · Ilha de Marajó · Igarapé Miri
Belterra · Ponta de Pedras · BELÉM · Ilhas de São João
Prainha · Gurupá · Melgaço · Abaetetuba · São José de Gurupi · Viseu · Turiaçu
Pombal · Cametá · Mojú · Marassumé · Alcântara
Baião · Mocajuba · São Luís · Rosário

PARÁ
Altamira · Tucuruí · Areão · Jacundá
Cachoeira · Serra do Guru · MARANHÃO · Teresina
Carajás · São João do Araguaia · Imperatriz · Barra do Corda · PIAUÍ

BRAZIL · Serra dos Gradaús · Xambioá · TRANS AMAZONIAN HIGHWAY · Balsas

SALVADOR

BAHIA

BRASÍLIA
DISTRITO FEDERAL
Goiânia

GOIÁS

MINAS GERAIS
Uberlândia

MATO GROSSO DO SUL

Designed and produced by E.S.R.

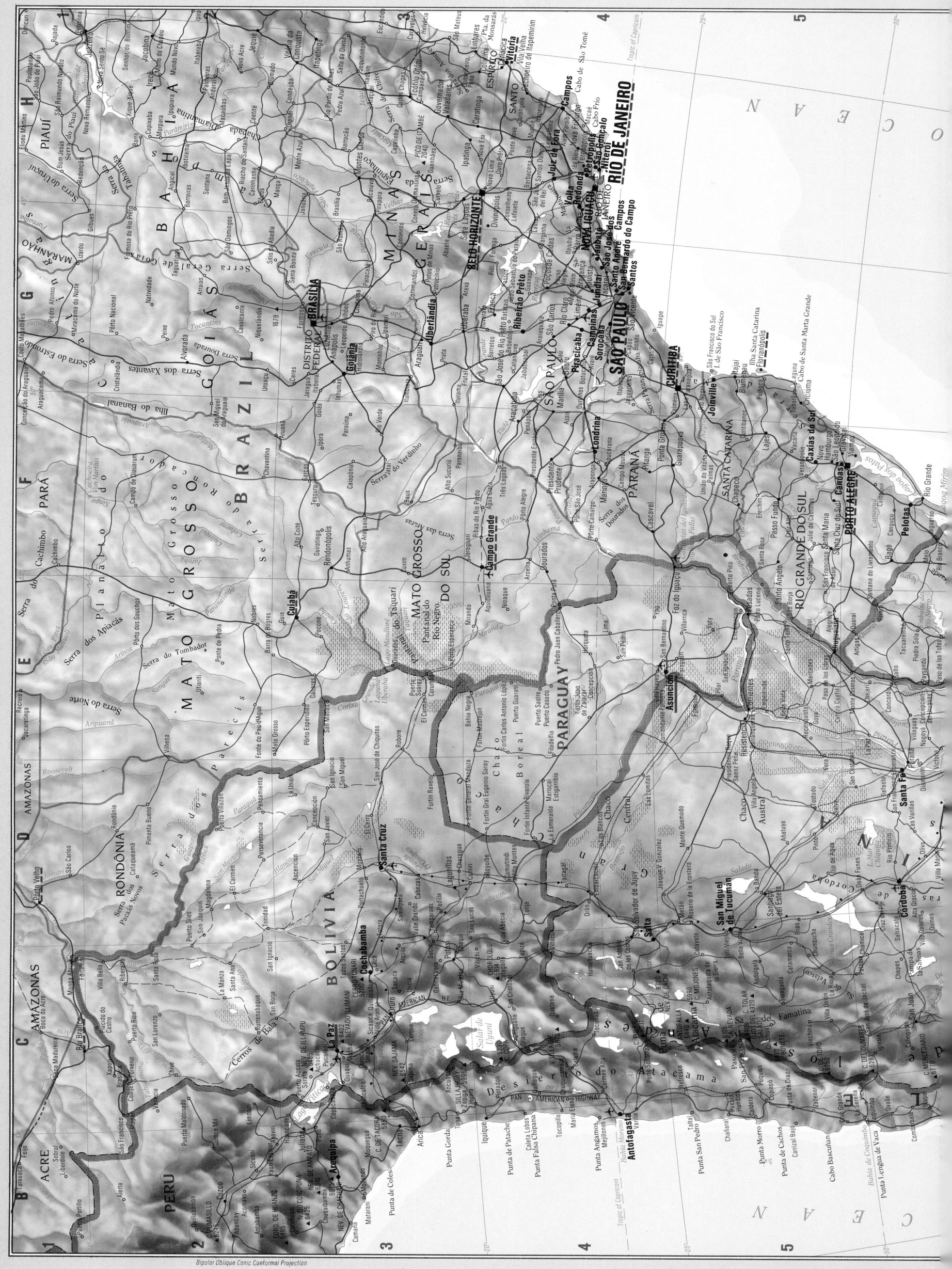

Bipolar Oblique Conic Conformal Projection

1:11,000,000

| 0 | 100 | 200 | 300 | 400 | 500 | 600 | 700 | 800 KILOMETRES |
| 0 | 100 | 200 | 300 | 400 | 500 STATUTE MILES |

© COLOUR LIBRARY BOOKS

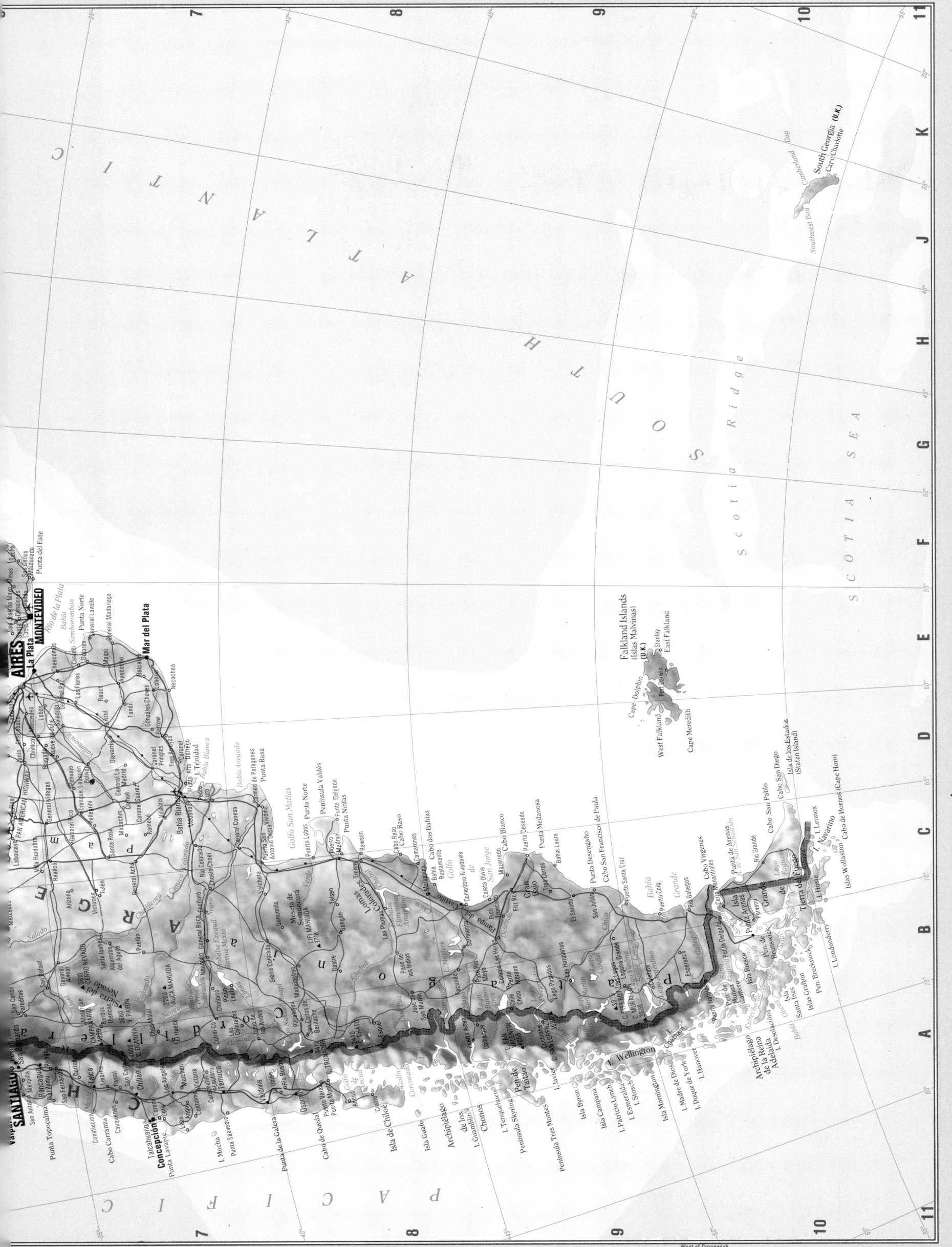

SANTIAGO

Concepción

Montevideo

AIRES

La Plata

MONTEVIDEO

Mar del Plata

PAN AMERICAN HIGHWAY

Bahía Blanca

Golfo San Matías

Península Valdés

Golfo San Jorge

Falkland Islands
(Islas Malvinas)
(U.K.)

Stanley

East Falkland

West Falkland

Cape Dolphin

Port Darwin

Cape Meredith

South Georgia (U.K.)
Cape/Charlotte

Cumberland Bay

Southwest Bay

SCOTIA SEA

Scotia Ridge

SOUTH

ATLANTIC

PACIFIC

Cabo San Diego
Isla de los Estados
(Staten Island)

Cabo de Hornos (Cape Horn)

Tierra del Fuego

Isla de Chiloé

Archipiélago de los Chonos

Península Tres Montes

Golfo de Penas

I. Wellington

Archipiélago de la Reina Adelaida

Punta Arenas

Río Grande

West of Greenwich

219

Designed and produced by E.S.R.

THE ARCTIC

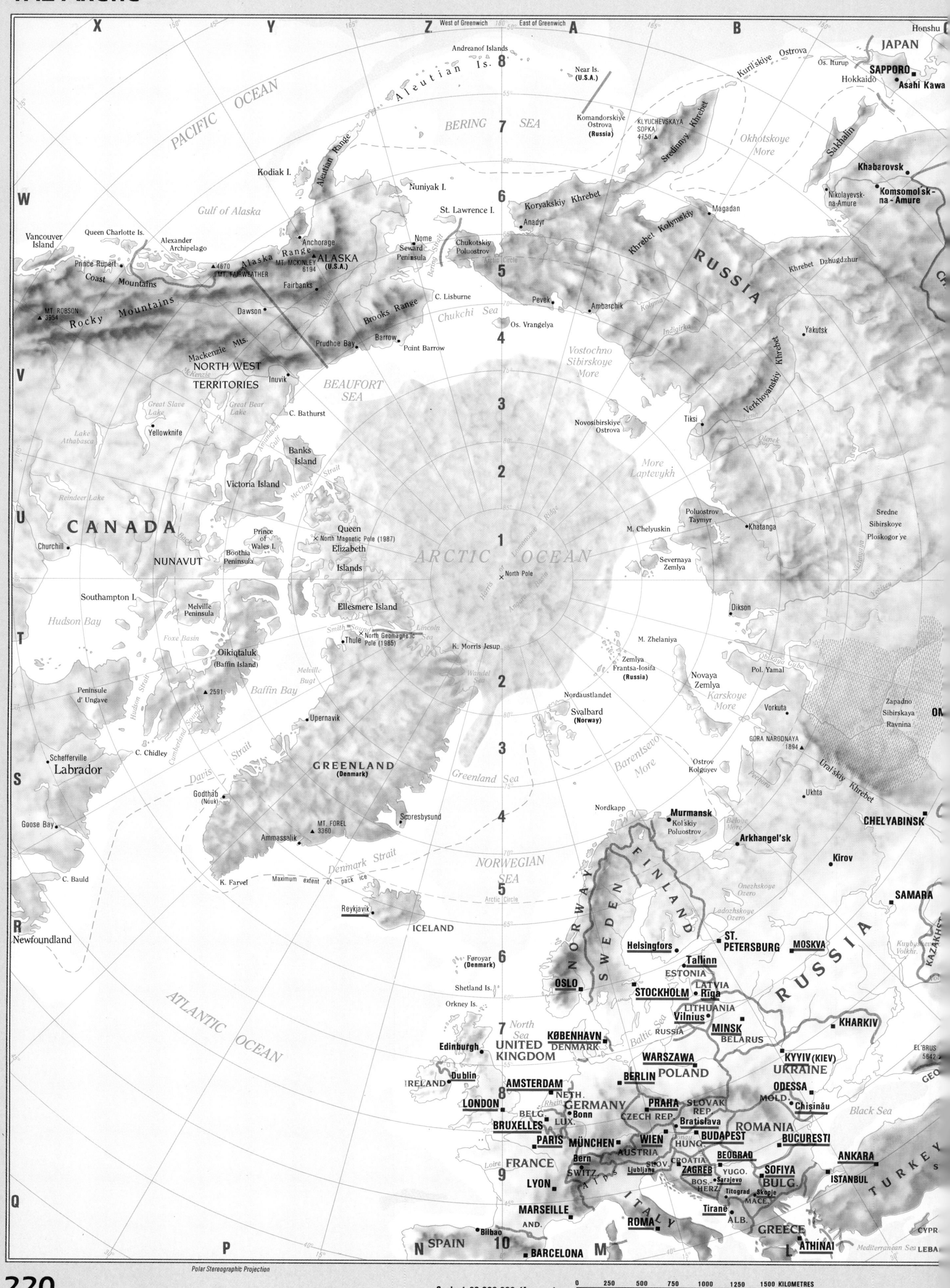

Polar Stereographic Projection

Scale 1:30,000,000 (Approx.)

| 0 | 250 | 500 | 750 | 1000 | 1250 | 1500 KILOMETRES |

| 0 | 250 | 500 | 750 | 1000 STATUTE MILES |

© COLOUR LIBRARY BOOKS

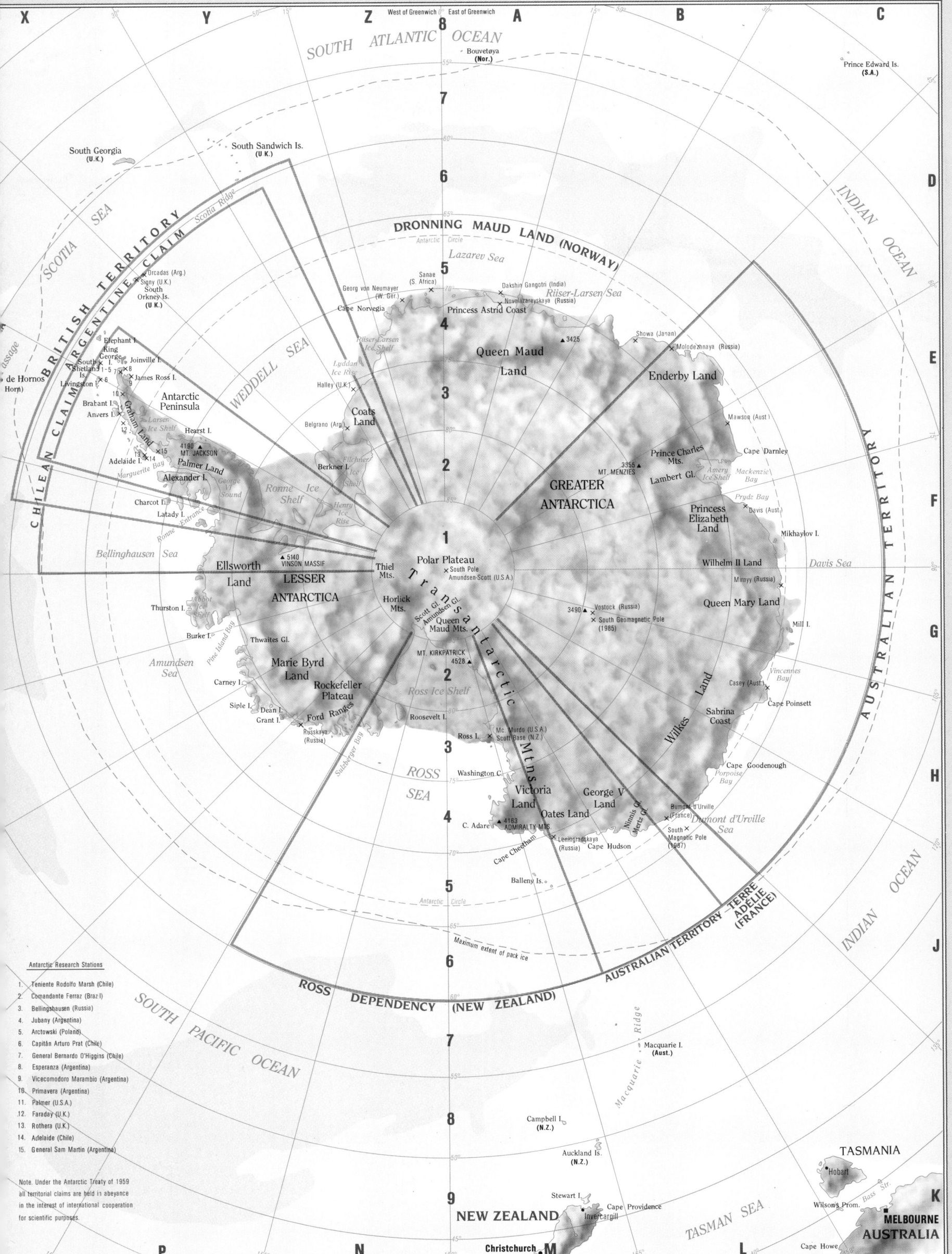

SOUTH ATLANTIC OCEAN

Bouvetøya
(Nor.)

Prince Edward Is.
(S.A.)

INDIAN OCEAN

South Georgia
(U.K.)

South Sandwich Is.
(U.K.)

SCOTIA SEA

Scotia Ridge

DRONNING MAUD LAND (NORWAY)

Antarctic Circle

Lazarev Sea

Georg von Neumayer
(W. Ger.)

Sanae
(S. Africa)

Dakshin Gangotri (India)

Novolazarevskaya (Russia)

Riiser-Larsen Sea

Showa (Japan)

Molodezhnaya (Russia)

Cape Norvegia

Princess Astrid Coast

BRITISH TERRITORY

ARGENTINE CLAIM

Orcadas (Arg.)

Signy (U.K.)
South
Orkney Is.
(U.K.)

Riiser-Larsen
Ice Shelf

3425

Queen Maud
Land

Enderby Land

WEDDELL SEA

Elephant I.
King
George
South 1-5
Shetland 7 8
Is. 6
Livingston

Joinville I.

James Ross I.

Lyddan
Ice Rise

Halley (U.K.)

Mawson (Aust.)

Cape Darnley

de Hornos
Horn)

Brabant I.
Anvers I.

Graham Land

Larsen
Ice Shelf

Hearst I.

Belgrano (Arg.)

Coats
Land

3355
MT. MENZIES

Prince Charles
Mts.

Lambert Gl.

Amery
Ice Shelf

Mackenzie
Bay

CHILEAN CLAIM

Antarctic
Peninsula

4190
MT. JACKSON

Adelaide I.
13
15
14

Palmer Land

Alexander I.

Filchner
Ice
Shelf

Berkner I.

GREATER
ANTARCTICA

Princess
Elizabeth
Land

Prydz Bay

Davis (Aust.)

Charcot I.

Latady I.

Ronne Ice
Shelf

George VI
Sound

Henry
Ice Rise

Mikhaylov I.

Marguerite Bay

Bellinghausen Sea

Ronne Entrance

5140
VINSON MASSIF

Thiel
Mts.

Polar Plateau

South Pole
Amundsen-Scott (U.S.A.)

1

Wilhelm II Land

Davis Sea

Ellsworth
Land

LESSER
ANTARCTICA

Horlick
Mts.

Transantarctic

Scott Gl.
Amundsen Gl.
Queen
Maud Mts.

3490
Vostock (Russia)

South Geomagnetic Pole
(1985)

Queen Mary Land

Mirnyy (Russia)

Mill I.

Abbot
Ice Shelf

Thurston I.

MT. KIRKPATRICK
4528

Vincennes
Bay

Casey (Aust.)

Burke I.

Thwaites Gl.

2

Cape Poinsett

Amundsen
Sea

Marie Byrd
Land

Pine Island Bay

Ross Ice Shelf

Mts.

Wilkes
Land

Sabrina
Coast

Carney I.

Rockefeller
Plateau

Roosevelt I.

Cape Goodenough

Siple I.

Dean I.
Grant I.

Ford Ranges

3

Ross I.

Mc Murdo (U.S.A.)
Scott Base (N.Z.)

Porpoise
Bay

Russkaya
(Russia)

Sulzberger Bay

Washington C.

ROSS
SEA

Victoria
Land

George V
Land

Dumont d'Urville
(France)

Dumont d'Urville
Sea

4

4163
ADMIRALTY MTS.

Oates Land

Nimriz Gl.

Metz Gl.

South
Magnetic Pole
(1987)

C. Adare

Cape Cheetham

Leningradskaya (Russia)

Cape Hudson

Balleny Is.

5

Antarctic Circle

Maximum extent of pack ice

AUSTRALIAN TERRITORY

TERRE
ADÉLIE
(FRANCE)

AUSTRALIAN TERRITORY

INDIAN OCEAN

SOUTH PACIFIC OCEAN

ROSS DEPENDENCY (NEW ZEALAND)

Macquarie Ridge

Macquarie I.
(Aust.)

Campbell I.
(N.Z.)

Auckland Is.
(N.Z.)

TASMANIA

Hobart

Wilson's Prom.

Bass Str.

NEW ZEALAND

Stewart I.

Cape Providence

Invercargill

Christchurch

TASMAN SEA

Cape Howe

MELBOURNE
AUSTRALIA

Antarctic Research Stations

1. Teniente Rodolfo Marsh (Chile)
2. Comandante Ferraz (Brazil)
3. Bellingshausen (Russia)
4. Jubany (Argentina)
5. Arctowski (Poland)
6. Capitán Arturo Prat (Chile)
7. General Bernardo O'Higgins (Chile)
8. Esperanza (Argentina)
9. Vicecomodoro Marambio (Argentina)
10. Primavera (Argentina)
11. Palmer (U.S.A.)
12. Faraday (U.K.)
13. Rothera (U.K.)
14. Adelaide (Chile)
15. General Sam Martin (Argentina)

Note. Under the Antarctic Treaty of 1959
all territorial claims are held in abeyance
in the interest of international cooperation
for scientific purposes.

Polar Stereographic Projection

Designed and produced by E.S.R.

GREENLAND
(Denmark)

Svalbard
(Norway)

Zemlya Frantsa-Iosifa

Severnaya Zemlya

Novosibirskiye Os

Karskoye More

More Laptevykh

Lyakhovskiye Ostrova

Jan Mayen
(Norway)

Nordkapp

Barentsevo More

Novaya Zemlya

Poluostrov Yamal

Gydanskiy Poluostrov

Plato Putorana

Gory Byrranga

Ozero Taymyr

Verkhoyanskiy

Khrebet Chersogo

Koln Nizn

ICELAND

Reykjavik

Denmark Strait

Arctic Circle

Norwegian Sea

Lappland

SWEDEN

FINLAND

Beloye More

Pechora

Uralskiy Khrebet

Zapadno Sibirskaya Ravnina

Sredne Sibirskoye Ploskogor'ye

Okhotskoe More

Sakhalin

Føroyar
(Denmark)

Shetland Is.
(U.K.)

NORWAY

Helsingfors

Oslo Stockholm

Ozero Ladozhskoye

ST. PETERSBURG

Kuybyshevskoye Vodokhranilishche

RUSSIA

Ozero Baykal

NORTH ATLANTIC OCEAN

UNITED KINGDOM

Dublin

IRELAND

LONDON

North Sea

Amsterdam

NETH.

'S-Gravenhage

BEL.

Bruxelles

DENMARK

København

Baltic Sea

ESTONIA

LATVIA

Tallinn

Rīga

LITH.

Vilnius

MOSKVA

POLAND

Berlin

Warszawa

Minsk

BELARUS

GERMANY

Praha

CZECH

SLOVAK

Kyyiv (Kiev)

UKRAINE

Volga

Irtysh

Ob'

Kirgiz Step'

KAZAKHSTAN

Aral'skoye

Ozero Balkhash

Altai

Sayan Min'

Kurl'skiye

ULAN

Ulaanbaatar

MONGOLIA

Gobi

FRANCE

LUX.

PARIS

Bern

SWITZ.

AUST.

Wien

Bratislava

Budapest

HUNG.

ROM.

MOLDOVA

Chişinău
(Kishinev)

Dnieper

Prikaspiyskaya Nizmennost'

Tashkent

Kyzylkum

Bishkek

Alma-Ata

Tyan Shan

Tarim Pendi

N KOREA

Pyŏngyang

Sea of Japan

JAPAN

AND.

CROAT.

Beograd

Bucureşti

YUGO.

BULG.

Black Sea

GEORGIA

El'BRUS

Caspian Sea

UZBEKISTAN

KYRGYZSTAN

Dushanbe

TAJIK.

Taklimakan Shamo

Kunlun Shan

Xizang Gaoyuan

TÖKYÖ

PORTUGAL

Madrid

SPAIN

Roma

BOS. HERZ.

Tirane

ALB.

MACE.

Sofiya

GREECE

Ankara

ARMENIA

Yerevan

AZER.

TURKMENISTAN

Ashgabat

Baku

Hindu Kush

Himalaya

Chang Jiang

BEIJING

TIANJIN

CHINA

S KOREA

SÖUL

Açores
(Port.)

Lisboa

Mediterranean

El Djazair

Tunis

Valletta

MALTA

Athinai

TURKEY

T'bilisi

CYPRUS

LEB.

SYRIA

Dimashq

TEHRAN

Kühhä ye Zagros

IRAN

AFGHANISTAN

Kabul

Islamabad

PAKISTAN

Xining

Huang Hai

SHANGHAI

Madeira
(Port.)

MOROCCO

Atlas Mountains

Tarābulus

Sea

Bayrūt

ISRAEL

Yerushalayim

Baghdād

IRAQ

Thar Desert

New Delhi

DELHI

NEPAL

Kathmandu

EVEREST

BANG.

Tai-pei

TAIWAN

Ilas Canarias
(Sp.)

WESTERN SAHARA

Al Aaiún

Tropic of Cancer

ALGERIA

LIBYA

Hoggar

EGYPT

JOR.

EL QAHIRA

Amman

Al Kuwayt

KUW.

Ar Riyad

Al Manamah

BAH.

QAT.

Ad Dawhah

Abu Zabi

U.A.E.

Masqat

KARACHI

INDIA

CALCUTTA

Dhaka

MYANMAR

Hanoi

HONG KONG

Marianas Is.

Guam (U.S.A.)

Mi

MAURITANIA

Nouakchott

MALI

NIGER

CHAD

Tibesti

El Khartum

SUDAN

ERITREA

San'ā

YEMEN

DJIB.

Asmera

Red Sea

SAUDI ARABIA

OMAN

Arabian Sea

MUMBAI
(Bombay)

Deccan

Bay of Bengal

CHENNAI
(Madras)

Lakshadweep
(India)

Yangon

THAI-LAND

KRUNG THEP

Viangchan

LAOS

CAM.

Phnom Penh

VIETNAM

Luzon

MANILA

PHILIPPINES

Mindanao

Caroline Islands

CAPE VERDE

Praia

Dakar

SEN.

Banjul

THE GAMBIA

GUINEA-BISSAU

Bissau

Conakry

GUINEA

Bamako

BUR. FASO

Ouagadougou

Niamey

BEN.

NIGERIA

N'djaména

CENTRAL AFRICAN REP.

Bangui

ETHIOPIA

Adis Abeba

SOMALIA

Suqutrā
(S. Yem.)

MALDIVES

Colombo

SRI LANKA

Malé

Andaman Islands
(India)

Bandar Seri Begawan

BRU.

MALAYSIA

Kuala Lumpur

SINGAPORE

Borneo

Maluku

Mindanao

SIERRA LEONE

Freetown

Monrovia

LIBERIA

IVORY COAST

Yamoussoukro

GHANA

Accra

Porto Novo

Lomé

TOGO

Lagos

CAMEROON

Yaoundé

Malabo

EQ. GUINEA

Libreville

GABON

CONGO

Brazzaville

Congo Basin

Kinshasa

CONGO
(DEMOCRATIC REPUBLIC)

UGANDA

Kampala

RW.

Kigali

BU.

Bujumbura

KENYA

Nairobi

Dodoma

TANZANIA

KILIMANJARO

Victoria

SEYCHELLES

Sumatera

Jawa

JAKARTA

INDONESIA

Sulawesi

Timor

Laut Timor

Laut Arafura

New Guinea

PAPUA NEW GUINEA

Port

Equator

SÃO TOMÉ AND PRÍNCIPE

Ascension
(U.K.)

Luanda

ANGOLA

ZAMBIA

Lusaka

COMOROS

Moroni

INDIAN OCEAN

St. Helena
(U.K.)

Ilha da Trindade
(Brazil)

SOUTH ATLANTIC OCEAN

Tropic of Capricorn

NAMIBIA

Windhoek

BOTSWANA

Kalahari

Gaborone

Harare

ZIMBABWE

MOZAMBIQUE

Mozambique Channel

MADAGASCAR

Antananarivo

Réunion
(Fr.)

MAURITIUS

Port Louis

AUSTRALIA

Gt. Victoria Desert

Tristan da Cunha
(U.K.)

Gough I.
(U.K.)

Pretoria

Maputo

SWAZILAND

Mbabne

Gaborone

Orange

SOUTH AFRICA

Maseru

LESOTHO

Cape of Good Hope

C. Leeuwin

Canberra

Tasmania

South Sandwich Is.
(U.K.)

Prince Edward Is.
(S.A.)

Iles Crozet
(Fr.)

Ile Kerguelen
(Fr.)

Heard I.
(Aus.)

Mercator Projection

1:85,000,000 (Scale at the Equator)

ARCTIC OCEAN

East of Greenwich | West of Greenwich

G | H | J | K | L | M

stochno
birskoye
More

Ostrov Vrangelya

Chrebet Kolymskiy

*Chucki
Sea*

Pt. Barrow

Brooks Range
ALASKA
(U.S.A.)
Yukon

McKINLEY
6194 ▲
Alaska Range

Bering
Sea

*Anadyrskiy
Zaliv*

Bering Str.

Kodiak I.

Aleutian Islands
Aleutian Trench

Banks
Island

Beaufort Sea

*Amundsen
Gulf*

Victoria Island

Mackenzie Mts.

Great Bear Lake

Back

Great Slave Lake

L. Athabasca

Reindeer Lake

Lincoln
Sea

Queen

Elizabeth

Islands

Ellesmere
Island

*Kane
Basin*

Viscount Melville
Sound

Oikiqtaluk

Baffin Bay

*Foxe
Basin*

Davis Str.

GREENLAND
(Denmark)

Denmark Strait

Arctic Circle

Reykjavik
ICELAND

NORTH
PACIFIC
OCEAN

Vancouver I.

Gulf of Alaska

Rocky Mountains
Columbia

Gt. Salt Lake

SAN FRANCISCO ■

LOS ANGELES ■

Missouri

CANADA

Great
Plains

UNITED STATES
OF
AMERICA

L. Winnipeg

Great
Lakes

Mississippi

St. Lawrence

Ottawa ■

CHICAGO ■

Appalachian Mts.

NEW YORK ■
PHILADELPHIA ■
Washington ■

Hudson Bay

Labrador

Newfoundland

Labrador Sea

Kap Farvel

NORTH
ATLANTIC
OCEAN

Acores
(Port.)

Hawaiian

Islands

HAWAII
(U.S.A.)

Isla de
Guadalupe
(Mex.)

Islas de Revillagigedo
(Mex.)

Rio Grande

MEXICO
CIUDAD DE
MÉXICO ■

Gulf of Mexico

Bermuda .
(U.K.)

BAHAMAS
Nassau ■

La Habana ■
CUBA

West Indies

DOMINICAN REP.
Port au Prince ■ HAITI ■ Santo Domingo ■ Puerto Rico (U.S.A.)
Kingston ■ JAMAICA

Leeward Is.

CAPE
VERDE

Praia ■

Tropic of Cancer

Belmopan ■
BELIZE
HONDURAS
GUATEMALA ■ Tegucigalpa ■
Guatemala ■ EL SALVADOR
San Salvador ■ NICARAGUA
Managua ■
San José ■
COSTA RICA
PANAMÁ

Caribbean Sea

Windward Is.

BARBADOS ■

Caracas ■
Panamá ■
VENEZUELA

TRINIDAD
AND TOBAGO

Marshall Is.

Polynesia

Tarawa ■
NAURU
Gilbert
Is.

MON ISLANDS
niara

Santa
Cruz
Is.

Line Islands

Christmas I.

Phoenix Is.

KIRIBATI

Polynesia

Iles Marquises
(Fr.)

French Polynesia
(Fr.)

Iles Tuamotu

SOUTH
PACIFIC

OCEAN

Islas Galápagos
(Ecuador)

Bogotá ■
COLOMBIA

Quito ■
EQUADOR

PERU

Cordillera

LIMA ■

Georgetown ■
GUY Paramaribo ■
SUR Cayenne ■
FRENCH GUIANA

Orinoco

Napo

Amazonas

Isla Fernando
de Noronha
(Brazil)

Equator

BRAZIL
Planalto do
Mato Grosso

Brasília ■

NUATU Vila ■

VANUATU
nie

FIJI
Suva ■

Fanafuti
TUVALU

Iles
Wallice
(Fr.)
SAMOA
Apia ■ Samoa
(U.S.A.)

TONGA
Nuku'alofa ■

Tonga Trench

Cook Islands
(N.Z.)

Tahiti
*Iles de
la Société*

Iles Gambier

Pitcairn I.
(U.K.) Ducie I.
(U.K.)

Isla de Pascua
(Easter I.)
(Chile)

Paraguai

Cordillera de los Andes

LA PAZ ■
BOLIVIA

Pilcomayo

PARAGUAY

Asunción ■

SÃO PAULO ■

RÍO DE JANEIRO ■

Ilha da Trindade
(Brazil)

Tropic of Capricorn

W ZEALAND
Wellington ■

Chatham Is.
(N.Z.)

Islas Juan
Fernández
(Chile)

Santiago ■
Chile

ACONCAGUA
6960 ▲

URUGUAY
Montevideo ■

BUENOS AIRES ■
ARGENTINA

SOUTH

ATLANTIC

OCEAN

Auckland Is.
(N.Z.)

uan Sea

Kermadec Trench

Patagonia

Falkland Is.
(U.K.)

South Georgia
(U.K.)

acquarie Is.
(Aus.)

Cabo de Hornos

Scotia Sea

South
Sandwich
Is. (U.K.)

G | H | J | K | L | M

Designed and produced by E.S.R.

GLOSSARY AND ABBREVIATIONS

Language abbreviations in glossary

Afr	Afrikaans	*Dut*	Dutch	*I-C*	Indo-Chinese	*Mal*	Malay	*S-C*	Serbo-Croat
Alb	Albanian	*Fin*	Finnish	*Ice*	Icelandic	*Mlg*	Malagasy	*Som*	Somali
Ar	Arabic	*Fr*	French	*Ind*	Indonesian	*Mon*	Mongolian	*Sp*	Spanish
Ber	Berber	*Gae*	Gaelic	*It*	Italian	*Nor*	Norwegian	*Swe*	Swedish
Bul	Bulgarian	*Ger*	German	*Jap*	Japanese	*Per*	Persian	*Th*	Thai
Bur	Burmese	*Gr*	Greek	*Khm*	Khmer	*Pol*	Polish	*Tib*	Tibetan
Ch	Chinese	*Heb*	Hebrew	*Kor*	Korean	*Por*	Portuguese	*Tu*	Turkish
Cz	Czech	*Hin*	Hindi	*Lao*	Laotian	*Rom*	Romanian	*Vt*	Vietnamese
Dan	Danish	*Hun*	Hungarian	*Lat*	Latvian	*Rus*	Russian	*Wel*	Welsh

Glossary

A

Abar (*Ar*) – wells
Abyar (*Ar*) – wells
Adasi (*Tu*) – island
Adrar (*Ber*) – mountains
Ain (*Ar*) – spring, well
Akra (*Gr*) – cape, point
Alb (*Ger*) – mountains
Alpen (*Ger*) – mountains
Alpes (*Fr*) – mountains
Alpi (*It*) – mountains
Alto (*Por*) – high
-alv (*Swe*) – river
-alven (*Swe*) – river
Appenino (*It*) – mountain range
Aqabat (*Ar*) – pass
Archipielago (*Sp*) – archipelago
Arquipielago (*Por*) – archipelago
Arrecife (*Sp*) – reef
Ayia (*Gr*) – saint
Ayios (*Gr*) – saint
Ayn (*Ar*) – spring, well

B

Bab (*Ar*) – strait
Bad (*Ger*) – spa
Badiyah (*Ar*) – desert
Bælt (*Dan*) – strait
Baharu (*Mal*) – new
Bahia (*Sp*) – bay
Bahr (*Ar*) – bay, canal, lake, stream
Bahrat (*Ar*) – lake
Baia (*Por*) – bay
Baie (*Fr*) – bay
Baja (*Sp*) – lower
Ban (*Khm, Lao, Th*) – village
-bana (*Jap*) – cape, point
Banco (*Sp*) – bank
-bandao (*Ch*) – peninsula
Bandar (*Per*) – bay
Baraji (*Tu*) – reservoir
Barqa (*Ar*) – hill
Barragem (*Por*) – reservoir
Bassin (*Fr*) – basin, bay
Batin (*Ar*) – depression
Beinn (*Gae*) – mountain
Beloyy (*Rus*) – white
Ben (*Gae*) – mountain
Bereg (*Rus*) – bank, shore
Berg (*Ger*) – mountain
Berge (*Afr*) – mountains
Bheinn (*Gae*) – mountain
Biar (*Ar*) – wells
Bir (*Ar*) – well
Bi'r (*Ar*) – well
Birkat (*Ar*) – well
Birket (*Ar*) – well
Boca (*Sp*) – river mouth
Bocche (*It*) – mouths, estuary
Bodden (*Ger*) – bay
Bogazi (*Tu*) – strait
Boka (*S-C*) – gulf, inlet
Bol'shoy (*Rus*) – big
Bol'shoye (*Rus*) – big
Bory (*Pol*) – forest
Bratul (*Rom*) – river channel
Bucht (*Ger*) – bay
Bugt (*Dan*) – bay
Buhayrat (*Ar*) – lagoon, lake
Bukit (*Mal*) – hill, mountain
Bukt (*Nor*) – bay
Bulak (*Rus*) – spring
Burnu (*Tu*) – cape, point
Burun (*Tu*) – cape, point
Busen (*Ger*) – bay
Buyuk (*Tu*) – big

C

Cabo (*Por, Sp*) – cape, point
Cachoeira (*Sp*) – waterfall
Cap (*Fr*) – cape, point
Campos (*Sp*) – upland
Cao Nguyen (*Th*) – plateau, tableland
Cataratas (*Sp*) – waterfall
Cayi (*Tu*) – stream
Cayo (*Sp*) – islet, rock
Cerro (*Sp*) – hill
Chaco (*Sp*) – jungle
Chaine (*Fr*) – mountain chain
Chapada (*Por*) – hills
Ch'eng (*Ch*) – town
Chiang (*Ch*) – river
Chiang (*Th*) – town
Chott (*Ar*) – marsh, salt lake
Chute (*Fr*) – waterfall
Cienaga (*Sp*) – marshy lake
Ciudad (*Sp*) – city, town
Co (*Tib*) – lake
Col (*Fr*) – pass
Colinas (*Sp*) – hills
Cordillera (*Sp*) – mountain range
Costa (*Sp*) – coast, shore
Cote (*Fr*) – coast, shore
Coteau (*Fr*) – hill, slope
Coxilha (*Por*) – mountain pasture
Cuchillas (*Sp*) – hills

D

Dag (*Tu*) – mountain
Dagi (*Tu*) – mountain
Daglari (*Tu*) – mountains
-dake (*Jap*) – peak
-dal (*Nor*) – valley
Dao (*Ch*) – island
Darreh (*Per*) – valley
Daryacheh (*Per*) – lake
Dasht (*Per*) – desert
Denizi (*Tu*) – sea
Desierto (*Sp*) – desert
Djebel (*Ar*) – mountain
-djik (*Dut*) – dyke
Do (*Kor, Jap, Vt*) – island
Dolina (*Rus*) – valley
Dolok (*Ind*) – mountain
Dolna (*Bul*) – lower
Dolni (*Cz*) – lower
-dong (*Kor*) – village
-dorp (*Afr*) – village
Dur (*Ar*) – mountains

E

Eiland (*Dut*) – island
Eilanden (*Dut*) – islands
-elva (*Nor*) – river
Embalse (*Sp*) – reservoir
Erg (*Ar*) – sandy desert
Estero (*Sp*) – bay, estuary, inlet
Estrecho (*Sp*) – strait
Etang (*Fr*) – lagoon, pond
Ezers (*Lat*) – lake

F

Feng (*Ch*) – mountain, peak
Fels (*Ger*) – rock
Firth (*Gae*) – estuary
-fjall (*Swe*) – mountain
Fjeld (*Dan*) – mountain
-fjell (*Nor*) – mountain
-floi (*Ice*) – bay
-fjoraur (*Ice*) – fjord
Forde (*Ger*) – inlet
Foret (*Fr*) – forest
-foss (*Ice*) – waterfall

G

-gan (*Jap*) – rock
Gang (*Ch*) – harbour
Ganga (*Hin*) – river
Gata (*Jap*) – inlet, lagoon
Gave (*Fr*) – torrent
Gebel (*Ar*) – mountain
Gebirge (*Ger*) – mountains
Ghat (*Hin*) – range of hills
Ghubbat (*Ar*) – bay
Glen (*Gae*) – valley
Gletscher (*Ger*) – glacier
Gobi (*Mon*) – desert
Golfe (*Fr*) – bay, gulf
Golfo (*It, Sp*) – bay, gulf
Golu (*Tu*) – lake
Gora (*Bul*) – forest
Gora (*Pol, Rus*) – mountain
-gorod (*Rus*) – small town
Gory (*Pol, Rus*) – mountains
Grada (*Rus*) – mountain range
Grad (*Bul, Rus, S-C*) – city, town
Gross (*Ger*) – big
Gryada (*Rus*) – ridge
Guba (*Rus*) – bay
-gunto (*Jap*) – island group
Gunung (*Ind, Mal*) – mountain

H

Hadh (*Ar*) – sand dunes
Hafen (*Ger*) – harbour, port
Haff (*Ger*) – bay, lagoon
Hai (*Ch*) – sea
Haixia (*Ch*) – strait
-holm (*Dan*) – island
Halvo (*Dan*) – peninsula
-hama (*Jap*) – beach
-hamar (*Ice*) – mountain
Hamada (*Ar*) – plateau
Hammadah (*Ar*) – plain, stony desert
Hamun (*Per*) – marsh
-hanto (*Jap*) – peninsula
Harrat (*Ar*) – lava field
Hav (*Swe*) – gulf
Havet (*Nor*) – sea
-havn (*Dan, Nor*) – harbour
Hawr (*Ar*) – lake
He (*Ch*) – river
Heide (*Ger*) – heath, moor
-hisar (*Tu*) – castle
Ho (*Ch*) – river
Hohe (*Ger*) – hills
Horn (*Ger*) – peak, summit
Hu (*Ch*) – lake
-huk (*Swe*) – cape, point

I

Idd (*Ar*) – well
Idhan (*Ar*) – sand dunes
Ile (*Fr*) – island
Iles (*Fr*) – islands
Ilha (*Por*) – island
Ilhas (*Por*) – islands
Insel (*Ger*) – island
Inseln (*Ger*) – islands
Irq (*Ar*) – sand dunes
Irmak (*Tu*) – large river
Isfjord (*Dan*) – glacier
Iskappe (*Dan*) – icecap
Isla (*Sp*) – island
Islas (*Sp*) – islands
Isola (*It*) – island
Isole (*It*) – islands
Istmo (*Sp*) – isthmus

J

Jabal (*Ar*) – mountain
-jarvi (*Fin*) – lake
Jaza'ir (*Ar*) – islands
Jazirat (*Ar*) – island
Jazovir (*Bul*) – reservoir
Jbel (*Ar*) – mountain
Jebel (*Ar*) – mountain
Jezero (*Alb, S-C*) – lake
Jezioro (*Pol*) – lagoon, lake
Jezirat (*Ar*) – island
-jiang (*Ch*) – river
Jibal (*Ar*) – mountain
Jiddat (*Ar*) – gravel plain
-jima (*Jap*) – island
-joki (*Fin*) – river
-jokull (*Ice*) – glacier

K

Kaap (*Afr*) – cape, point
-kai (*Jap*) – bay, sea
-kaikyo (*Jap*) – strait
Kanaal (*Dut*) – canal
Kap (*Ger*) – cape, point
-kapp (*Nor*) – cape, point
Kas (*Khm*) – island
Kavir (*Per*) – desert
-kawa (*Jap*) – river
Kenet (*Alb*) – inlet
Kep (*Alb*) – cape, point
Kepulauan (*Ind*) – archipelago, islands
Kereb (*Ar*) – hill, ridge
Khalij (*Ar*) – bay, gulf
Khawr (*Ar*) – wadi
Khrebet (*Ru*) – mountain range
Kiang (*Ch*) – river
Klein (*Afr, Ger*) – small
Ko (*Th*) – island
-ko (*Jap*) – inlet, lake
Koh (*Khm*) – island
Kolpos (*Gr*) – gulf
Kolymskoye (*Rus*) – mountain range
Korfezi (*Tu*) – bay, gulf
Kosa (*Rus*) – spit
Kotlina (*Cz, Pol*) – basin, depression
Kraj (*Cz, Pol, S-C*) – region
Krasnyy (*Rus*) – red
Kray (*Rus*) – region
Kreis (*Ger*) – district
Kryazh (*Rus*) – mountains
Kucuk (*Tu*) – small
Kuh (*Per*) – mountain
Kuhha (*Per*) – mountains
Kum (*Rus*) – sandy desert
Kyst (*Dan*) – coast
Kyun (*Bur*) – island
Kyunzu (*Bur*) – islands

L

La (*Tib*) – pass
Lac (*Fr*) – lake
Lacul (*Rom*) – lake
Laem (*Th*) – point
Lago (*It, Por, Sp*) – lake
Lagoa (*Por*) – lagoon
Laguna (*Sp*) – lagoon, lake
Lam (*Th*) – stream
Lande (*Fr*) – heath, sandy moor
Laut (*Ind*) – sea
Ling (*Ch*) – mountain range
Liman (*Rus*) – bay, gulf
Limni (*Gr*) – lagoon, lake
Llano (*Sp*) – plain, prairie
Llanos (*Sp*) – plains, prairies

Llyn (*Wel*) – lake
Loch (*Gae*) – lake
Lough (*Gae*) – lake

M

Mae Nam (*Th*) – river
Mala (*S-C*) – small
Malaya (*Rus*) – small
Male (*Cz*) – small
Maloye (*Rus*) – small
Malyy (*Rus*) – small
Mar (*Por, Sp*) – sea
Mare (*It*) – sea
Masirah (*Ar*) – channel
Massif (*Fr*) – mountains
Mato (*Por*) – forest
Meer (*Afr, Dut, Ger*) – lake, sea
Menor (*Por, Sp*) – lesser, smaller
Mer (*Fr*) – sea
Mesa (*Sp*) – tableland
Minami (*Jap*) – south
-misaki (*Jap*) – cape, point
Mont (*Fr*) – mountain
Montagna (*It*) – mountain
Montagne (*Fr*) – mountain
Montagnes (*Fr*) – mountains
Montana (*Sp*) – mountain
Montanas (*Sp*) – mountains
Monte (*It, Por, Sp*) – mountain
Monti (*It*) – mountains
More (*Rus*) – sea
Mull (*Gae*) – cape, point, promontory
Munkhafad (*Ar*) – depression
Muntii (*Rom*) – mountains
Mynydd (*Wel*) – mountain
Mys (*Rus*) – cape, point

N

-nada (*Jap*) – gulf, sea
Nadrz (*Cz*) – reservoir
Nafud (*Ar*) – desert, dune
Nagor'ye (*Rus*) – highland, uplands
Nagy- (*Hun*) – great
Nahr (*Ar*) – river
Namakzar (*Per*) – desert, salt flat
Nei (*Ch*) – inner
Ness (*Gae*) – cape, promontory
Neu (*Ger*) – new
Nevada (*Sp*) – snow capped mountains
Nevado (*Sp*) – mountain
Ngoc (*Vt*) – mountain peak
-nisi (*Gr*) – island
Nisoi (*Gr*) – islands
Nisos (*Gr*) – island
Nizhnyaya (*Rus*) – lower
Nizina (*Pol*) – depression, lowland
Nizmennost' (*Rus*) – lowland
Noord (*Dut*) – north
Nord (*Dan, Fr, Ger*) – north
Norte (*Por, Sp*) – north
Nos (*Bul, Rus*) – point, spit
Nosy (*Mlg*) – island
Nova (*Bul*) – new
Nova (*Cz*) – new
Novaya (*Rus*) – new
Nove (*Cz*) – new
Novi (*Bul*) – new
Nudo (*Sp*) – mountain
Nuruu (*Mon*) – mountain range
Nuur (*Mon*) – lake

O

Ø (*Dan*) – island
Oblast' (*Rus*) – province

Occidental (*Fr, Rom, Sp*) – western
Oki (*Jap*) – bay
-oog (*Ger*) – island
Ojo (*Sp*) – spring
Orasul (*Rom*) – city
Ori (*Gr*) – mountains
Oriental (*Fr, Rom, Sp*) – eastern
Ormos (*Gr*) – bay
Oros (*Gr*) – mountain
Ort (*Ger*) – cape, point
Ostrov (*Rus*) – island
Ostrova (*Rus*) – islands
Otok (*S-C*) – island
Otoki (*S-C*) – islands
Ouadi (*Ar*) – wadi, dry watercourse
Oued (*Ar*) – dry river bed, wadi
Ovasi (*Tu*) – plain
Ozero (*Rus*) – lake

P

Pampa (*Sp*) – plain
Paniai (*Ind*) – lakes
Paso (*Sp*) – pass
Passage (*Fr*) – pass
Passo (*It*) – pass
Pasul (*Rom*) – pass
Pelagos (*Gr*) – sea
Pendi (*Ch*) – basin
Pengunungnan (*Ind*) – mountain range
Peninsola (*It*) – peninsula
Peninsule (*Fr*) – peninsula
Pereval (*Rus*) – pass
Peski (*Rus*) – desert, sands
Phnom (*Khm*) – hill, mountain
Phu (*Vt*) – mountain
Pic (*Fr*) – peak
Picacho (*Sp*) – peak
Pico (*Sp*) – peak
Pik (*Rus*) – peak
Pingyuan (*Ch*) – plain
Pizzo (*It*) – peak
Planalto (*Por*) – plateau
Plana (*S-C, Sp*) – plain
Planina (*Bul, S-C*) – mountains
Plato (*Afr, Bul, Rus*) – plateau
Ploskogor'ye (*Rus*) – plateau
Ploskogorje (*Rus*) – plateau
Poco (*Ind*) – peak

Pohorie (*Cz*) – mountain range
Pointe (*Fr*) – cape, point
Pojezierze (*Pol*) – plateau
Poluostrov (*Rus*) – peninsula
Polwysep (*Pol*) – peninsula
Ponta (*Por*) – cape, point
Presa (*Sp*) – reservoir
Proliv (*Sp*) – strait
Pueblo (*Sp*) – village
Puerto (*Sp*) – harbour, pass
Pulau (*Ind, Mal*) – island
Puna (*Sp*) – desert plateau
Puncak (*Ind*) – peak
Punta (*It, Sp*) – cape, point
Puy (*Fr*) – peak

Q

Qalamat (*Ar*) – well
Qalib (*Ar*) – well
Qararat (*Ar*) – depression
Qolleh (*Per*) – mountain
Qornet (*Ar*) – peak
Qundao (*Ch*) – archipelago

R

Ramlat (*Ar*) – dunes
Ra's (*Ar, Per*) – cape, point
Ras (*Ar*) – cape, point
Rass (*Som*) – cape, point
Ravnina (*Rus*) – plain
Recife (*Por*) – reef
Represa (*Por*) – dam
Reshteh (*Per*) – mountain range
-retto (*Jap*) – island chain
Rijeka (*S-C*) – river
Rio (*Por, Sp*) – river
Riviere (*Fr*) – river
Rt (*S-C*) – cape, point
Rubha (*Gae*) – cape, point
Ruck (*Ger*) – mountain
Rucken (*Ger*) – ridge
Rud (*Per*) – river
Rudohorie (*Cz*) – mountains
Rzeka (*Pol*) – river

S

Sabkhat (*Ar*) – salt flat
Sagar (*Hin*) – lake
Sahara (*Ar*) – desert

Sahl (*Ar*) – plain
Sahra (*Ar*) – desert
Sa'id (*Ar*) – highland
-saki (*Jap*) – cape, point
Salar (*Sp*) – salt pan
Salina (*Sp*) – salt pan
San (*Sp*) – saint
-san (*Jap*) – mountain
-sanchi (*Jap*) – mountainous area
Sankt (*Ger, Swe*) – saint
-sanmyaku (*Jap*) – mountain range
Santa (*Sp*) – saint
Sao (*Por*) – saint
Sar (*Kur*) – mountain
Satu (*Rom*) – village
Sawqirah (*Ar*) – bay
Se (*I-C*) – river
See (*Ger*) – lake
-sehir (*Tu*) – town
Selat (*Ind*) – channel, strait
-selka (*Fin*) – bay
Selva (*Sp*) – forest
Serra (*Por*) – mountain range
Serrania (*Sp*) – mountains
-seto (*Jap*) – channel, strait
Severnaya (*Rus*) – southern
Sfintu (*Rom*) – saint
Shamo (*Ch*) – desert
Shan (*Ch*) – mountains
Shandi (*Ch*) – mountainous area
Shatt (*Ar*) – river mouth, river
-shima (*Jap*) – islands
Shiqqat (*Ar*) – interdune trough
-shoto (*Jap*) – group of islands
Sierra (*Sp*) – mountain range
Sint (*Afr, Dut*) – saint
Slieve (*Gae*) – range of hills
So (*Dan, Nor*) – lake
Soder- (*Swe*) – southern
Sondre (*Dan, Nor*) – southern
Song (*Vt*) – river
Spitze (*Ger*) – peak
Sredne (*Rus*) – middle
Stadt (*Ger*) – town
Stara (*Cz*) – old
Staraya (*Rus*) – old
Stenon (*Gr*) – strait, pass
Step' (*Rus*) – plain, steppe
Strelka (*Rus*) – spit
Stretto (*It*) – strait

-suido (*Jap*) – channel, strait
Sund (*Swe*) – sound, strait
Szent- (*Hun*) – saint

T

-take (*Jap*) – peak
Tall (*Ar*) – hill
Tallat (*Ar*) – hills
Tanggula (*Tib*) – pass
Tanjong (*Ind, Mal*) – cape, point
Tanjon'i (*Mlg*) – cape, point
Tanjung (*Ind, Mal*) – cape, point
Tao (*Ch*) – island
Taraq (*Ar*) – hills
Tassili (*Ber*) – rocky plateau
Tau (*Rus*) – mountains
Taung (*Bur*) – mountain, south
Tekojarvi (*Fin*) – reservoir
Tell (*Ar*) – hill
Teluk (*Ind*) – bay
Tenere (*Fr*) – desert
Terre (*Fr*) – land
Thale (*Th*) – lake
Thamad (*Ar*) – well
Tirat (*Ar*) – canal
Tjarn (*Swe*) – lake
Tso (*Tib*) – lake
Tonle (*Khm*) – lake
Tutul (*Ar*) – hills

U

Ujung (*Ind*) – cape, point
-ura (*Jap*) – inlet
Urayq (*Ar*) – sand ridge
Uruq (*Ar*) – dunes
Ust (*Rus*) – river mouth
Uul (*Mon*) – mountain

V

Valea (*Rom*) – valley
-varos (*Hun*) – town
-varre (*Nor*) – mountain
-vatten (*Swe*) – lake
Vaux (*Fr*) – valleys
Velika (*S-C*) – big
Velikaya (*Rus*) – big
Verkhne (*Rus*) – upper
-vesi (*Fin*) – lake, water
Ville (*Fr*) – town
Vinh (*Vt*) – bay

Virful (*Rom*) – peak
Vodokhranilishche (*Rus*) – reservoir
Volcan (*Sp*) – volcano
Vorota (*Rus*) – strait
Vostochnyy (*Rus*) – eastern
Vozvyshennost' (*Rus*) hills, upland
Vpadina (*Rus*) – depression

W

Wadi (*Ar*) – river, stream
Wahat (*Ar*) – oasis
Wai (*Ch*) – outer
Wald (*Ger*) – forest
Wan (*Ch*) – bay
Wasser (*Ger*) – lake, water
Wenz (*Ar*) – river
Wielka (*Pol*) – big

X

Xan (*Ch*) – strait
Xi (*Ch*) – stream, west
Xia (*Ch*) – gorge, lower
Xian (*Ch*) – county
Xiao (*Ch*) – small
Xu (*Ch*) – island

Y

Yam (*Heb*) – lake
-yama (*Jap*) – mountain
Yarimadasi (*Tu*) – peninsula
Yazovir (*Bul*) – reservoir
Ye (*Bur*) – island
Yoma (*Bur*) – mountain range
Yugo- (*Rus*) – southern
Yuzhnyy (*Rus*) – southern

Z

Zaki (*Jap*) – cape, point
Zalew (*Pol*) – bay, inlet
Zaliv (*Rus*) – bay
-zan (*Jap*) – mountain
Zapadno (*Rus*) – western
Zatoka (*Pol*) – bay
Zee (*Dut*) – sea
Zemiya (*Rus*) – island, land
-zhen (*Ch*) – town

Abbreviations

A

A. – Alp, Alpen, Alpi
Akr. – Akra
And. – Andorra
Arch. – Archipelago
Arr. – Arrecife
Aust. – Australia
Ay. – Ayios

B

B. – Bahia, Baia, Baie, Bay, Bucht, Bukt
Ba. – Bahia
Bang. – Bangladesh
Bah. – Bahrain
Bel. – Belgium
Ben. – Benin
Bg. – Berg
Bhu. – Bhutan
Bk. – Bukit
Bol. – Bol'shoy, Bol'shoye
Bos. – Bosnia-Herzegovina
Br. – Burnu, Burun
Bru. – Brunei
Bt. – Bukit
Bu. – Burundi
Bü. – Büyük
Bulg. – Bulgaria
Bur. Faso – Burkina Faso

C

C. – Cabo, Cap, Cape, Cerro
Cam. – Cambodia
Can. – Canal, Canale
Cga. – Cienaga
Chan. – Channel
Co. – Cerro
Col. – Columbia
Cord. – Cordillera
Cr. – Creek
Czech. – Czech Rep.

D

D. – Dag, Dagi, Daglari, Daryacheh
D.C. – District of Columbia
Den. – Denmark
Djib. – Djibouti

E

E. – East
Eq. – Equatorial
Est. – Estrecho

F

Fd. – Fjord
Fk. – Fork
Fr. – France
Ft. – Fort

G

G. – Golfe, Golfo, Guba, Gulf, Gora, Gunung
Gd. – Grand
Gde – Grande
Geb. – Gebirge
Gen. – General
Geog. – Geographical
Ger. – Germany
Gh. – Ghana
Gl. – Glacier
Gr. – Grande, Gross
Gt. – Great
Guy. – Guyana

H

Har. – Harbor
Hd. – Head
Hung. – Hungary

I

I. – Ile, Ilha, Insel, Isla, Island, Isle, Isola, Isole

Is. – Ilhas, Iles, Islands, Islas, Isles
Isth. – Isthmus

J

J. – Jabal, Jbel, Jebel, Jezioro, Jezero, Jazair
Jor. – Jordan

K

K. – Kap, Kuh, Kuhha, Koh, Kolpos
Kan. – Kanal, Kanaal
Kep. – Kepulauan
Khr. – Khrebet
Kör. – Körfezi
Kuw. – Kuwait

L

L. – Lac, Lacul, Lago, Lake, Limni, Llyn, Loch, Lough
Lag. – Lagoon, Laguna
Leb. – Lebanon
Liech. – Liechtenstein
Lit. – Little
Lux. – Luxembourg

M

M. – Mys
Mal. – Malawi
Mex. – Mexico
Mgne. – Montagne
Mt. – Mont, Mount, Mountain
Mti. – Monti
Mtii. – Muntii
Mts. – Monts, Mounts, Mountains

N

N. – Nord, North, Nos
Neb. – Nebraska
Neth. – Netherlands

Nev. – Nevado
N.H. – New Hampshire
Nizh. – Nizhnyaya
Nizm. – Nizmennost
Nor. – Norway
N.Z. – New Zealand

O

O. – Ost, Ostrov
Os. – Ostova
Oz. – Ozero

P

P. – Point
Pass. – Passage
Penn. – Pennsylvania
Peg. – Peganungan
Pen. – Peninsola, Peninsula, Peninsule
Pk. – Peak, Puncak
Pl. – Planina
Pol. – Poluostrov
Port. – Portugal
Prom. – Promontory
Pt. – Point
Pta. – Ponta, Punta
Pte. – Pointe
Pto. – Puerto, Punto

Q

Qat. – Qatar

R

R. – Reshteh
Ra. – Range
Rep. – Republic
Res. – Reservoir
Rés. – Réservoir
Rom. – Romania
Rw. – Rwanda

S

S. – Shatt, South
Sa. – Serra, Sierra
S.A. – South Africa
Sd. – Sound, Sund
Sp. – Spain
Sprs. – Springs
St. – Saint, Sint
Sta. – Santa
Ste. – Sainte
Str. – Strait
Sur. – Suriname
Switz. – Switzerland

T

Tg. – Tanjong, Tanjung
Tk. – Teluk

U

U.A.E. – United Arab Emirates
U.K. – United Kingdom
U.S.A. – United States of America

V

V. – Volcano
Vdkhr. – Vodokhranilishche
Ven. – Venezuela
Verkh. – Verkhne
Vn. – Volcan
Vol. – Volcan, Volcano

W

W. – Wadi, Wald, West

Y

Y. – Yarimadasi

Z

Zal. – Zaliv

INDEX

The index includes an alphabetical list of all names appearing in the map section of the atlas. Names on the maps and in the index are generally in the local language. For names in languages not written in the Roman alphabet, the officially accepted transliteration system has been used.

Most features are indexed to the largest scale map on which they appear. Extensive features are usually indexed to maps that show the features completely or show them in their relationship to surrounding areas. For extensive regional features, locations are given for the approximate center of the feature, those for linear features are given at the position of the name.

Each entry in the index is located by a page number and an alphanumeric grid reference on that particular page. The grid is defined by letters, positioned at the top and at the bottom of the map spread, and numbers, shown at the sides of the spread. For example, Bandung in Indonesia has the reference 170 D7. It can thus be found on page 170 in the grid square D7.

Where two identical names are referenced to the same page and grid square, it should be noted that they relate to different adjacent features. For example, the name Avon appears twice in the index and in both cases it is referenced to 132 E3. These two entries locate firstly the county of Avon and secondly the River Avon.

Name	Page	Grid
Adda	148	B2
Adda	148	B3
Ad Dakhla	180	B4
Ad Dali	176	G10
Ad Dammam	177	K3
Ad Darb	176	F8
Ad Dawadimi	176	G4
Ad Dawhah	177	K4
Ad Dila	177	K7
Ad Dilam	176	H5
Ad Diriyah	176	H4
Ad Duwaniyah	174	G6
Ad Duwayd	176	F1
Adel	204	C6
Adelaide *Antarctic*	221	V5
Adelaide *Australia*	193	H5
Adelaide *Bahamas*	209	P8
Adelaide Island	221	V5
Adelaide Peninsula	200	G4
Aden	176	G10
Aden, Gulf of	183	J5
Adh Dhayd	177	M4
Adi	194	A2
Adi Ark'ay	176	C10
Adi Dairo	176	D9
Adige	148	C3
Adigrat	176	D9
Adiguzel Baraji	156	C3
Adi Keyah	176	D9
Adilabad	172	E5
Adilcevaz	157	K3
Adin	202	D7
Adirondack Mountains	205	N4
Adis Abeba	183	G6
Adi Ugri	176	D9
Adiyaman	157	H4
Adjud	153	J2
Adjuntas, Presa de las	211	K6
Adka	198	Ac9
Adlington	135	G3
Admello	148	C2
Admiralty Gulf	192	F1
Admiralty Inlet	200	J3
Admiralty Island *Canada*	199	Q2
Admiralty Island *U.S.A.*	198	J4
Admiralty Islands	194	D2
Admund Ringnes Island	200	G2
Ado-Ekiti	185	G4
Adonara	171	G7
Adoni	172	E5
Adorf	150	E3
Adoumaoua, Massif de l'	185	H4
Adour	145	C7
Adra	146	E4
Adrano	149	E7
Adrar	180	E3
Adre	182	D5
Adria	148	D3
Adrian *Michigan*	204	J6
Adrian *Texas*	207	L3
Adriatic Sea	148	E4
Adwa	176	D9
Adwick le Street	135	H3
Adycha	165	P3
Adzhima	168	G1
Adzvavom	158	K2
Aegean Sea	155	H3
Afafura, Laut	171	K7
Afanasevo	158	J4
Affobakka	217	F3
Affric	136	C3
Afghanistan	172	B2
Afgooye	187	J2
Afif	176	F5
Afikpo	185	G4
Afmadow	187	H2
Afognak Island	198	E4
Afon Efyrnwy	132	D2
Afrin	157	G4
Afsin	157	G3
Afyon	156	D3
Agadez	181	G5
Agadir	180	D2
Agadyr	166	C2
Agaie	185	G4
Agalta, Sierra de	212	E7
Agano	169	G7
Agapa *Russia*	164	D2
Agapa *Russia*	164	D2
Agapitovo	164	D3
Agartala	173	H4
Agaruut	167	K3
Agats	194	B3
Agatti	172	D6
Agattu Island	198	Aa9
Agbaja	185	G4
Agboville	184	E4
Agdam	174	H2
Agde	145	E7
Agematsu	169	F8
Agen	145	D6
Aghada	139	P9
Agha Jari	175	J6
Agiabampo, Estero de	210	E4
Agin	157	H3
Agira	149	E7
Aglasun	156	D4
Agnanda	155	F4
Agno	148	C3
Agnone	149	E5
Agout	145	D7
Agra	172	E3
Agram	152	C3
Agreda	147	F2
Agri	149	F5
Agri	157	K3
Agrigento	149	D7
Agrinion	155	F3
Agropoli	149	E5
Agua Clara	218	F4
Aguadas	216	B2
Aguadilla	213	P5
Aguanaval	210	H5
Agua Prieta	207	H5
Aguascalientes	210	H7
Agua, Volcan de	212	B7
Aguelhok	180	F5
Aguemour	181	F3
Aguilar de Campoo	146	D1
Aguilas	147	F4
Aguja, Cabo de la	213	K9
Aguja, Punta	216	A5
Agulhas, Kaap	188	D6
Agusan	171	H4
Ahar	174	H2
Aheim	142	A5
Ahimahasoa	189	J4
Ahipara Bay	195	D1
Ahititi	195	E3
Ahlat	157	K3
Ahmadabad	172	D4
Ahmadi	175	N8
Ahmadnagar	172	D5
Ahmadpur	172	D3
Ahmar Mountains	183	H6
Ahoskie	209	P2
Ahram	175	K7
Ahtari	142	L5
Ahtarinjarvi	142	L5
Ahuachapan	212	C8
Ahvaz	174	J6
Ahvenanmaa	143	H6
Ahwar	176	H10
Aiddejavrre	142	K2
Aidhipsos	155	G3
Aigen	148	D1
Aigues	145	F6
Aiken	209	M4
Ailao Shan	173	K4
Ailsa Craig	137	C5
Aim	165	N5
Aimores, Serra dos	218	H3
Ain	145	F5
Ain Beida	181	G1
Ain Bessem	147	H4
Ain Defla	147	G4
Ain El Hadjel	147	H5
Ain Oulmene	147	J5
Ain Sefra	180	E2
Ainsworth	203	Q6
Aioun el Atrouss	180	D5
Aiquile	218	C3
Air	181	G5
Airbangis	170	B5
Airdrie	137	E5
Aire *France*	144	F4
Aire *U.K.*	135	J3
Airedale	135	H3
Aire-sur-l'Adour	145	C7
Air Force Island	200	M4
Airgin Sum	167	L3
Airi-selka	142	L3
Aisne	144	E4
Aitape	194	C2
Aith	136	F1
Aix-en-Provence	145	F7
Aix-les-Bains	145	F6
Aiyina	155	G4
Aiyinion	155	G2
Aiyion	155	G3
Aizawl	173	H4
Aizpute	143	J8
Aizu-Wakamatsu	169	G7
Ajaccio	149	B5
Ajana	192	C4
Ajanta Range	172	E4
Ajdabiya	181	K2
Ajlun	174	B5
Ajman	177	M4
Ajmer	172	D3
Akaishi-sanchi	169	G8
Akalkot	172	E5
Akamkpa	185	G4
Akaroa Head	195	D5
Akbou	147	J4
Akbulak	159	K5
Akcaabat	157	H2
Akcaakale	157	H4
Akcadag	157	G3
Akcakoca	156	D2
Akcaova	156	C4
Akcay	156	C4
Akchatau	166	C2
Ak Daglari	156	C4
Akdagmadeni	157	F3
Ak Dovurak	164	D6
Akeshir Golu	156	D3
Aketi	185	G4
Akgevir	157	J4
Akhalkalaki	157	K2
Akhaltsikhe	157	K2
Akhdar, Al Jabal al	181	K2
Akhdar, Jabal	177	N5
Akhdar, Wadi	176	C3
Akheloos	155	F3
Akhiok	198	E4
Akhisar	156	B3
Akhmim	183	F2
Akhtubinsk	159	H6
Akhtyrka	159	E5
Aki	169	D9
Akimiski Island	201	K7
Akincilar	157	H2
Akinkeen	139	D9
Akinli	157	J4
Akita	168	H6
Akjoujt	180	C5
Akkavare	142	J3
Akkeshi	168	K4
Akko	174	B5
Akkoy	156	B4
Akkus	157	G2
Aklavik	198	H2
Akmola	164	A6
Akniste	143	L8
Akola	172	E4
Akonolinga	185	H5
Akordat	176	C9
Akoren	156	E4
Akosombo Dam	184	E4
Akot	172	E4
Akpatok Island	201	N5
Akpinar	156	E3
Akqi	166	D3
Akranes	142	T12
Akron	205	K6
Aksar	157	K2
Aksaray	156	E3
Aksay *China*	166	G4
Aksay *Kazakhstan*	159	J5
Aksehir	156	D3
Akseki	156	D4
Aksenovo-Zilovskoye	165	K6
Aks-e Rostam	175	M7
Aksha	165	J6
Akshimrau	159	J7
Aksu *China*	166	E3
Aksu *Turkey*	156	D4
Aksu *Kazakhstan*	159	J5
Aksu-Ayuly	166	C2
Aksu Cayi	156	D4
Aksum	176	D9
Aksumbe	166	B3
Aktau *Kazakhstan*	164	A6
Aktau *Kazakhstan*	159	J7
Akti	155	H2
Aktogay	166	D2
Akulivik	200	L5
Akune	169	C9
Akun Island	198	Ae9
Akure	185	G4
Akureyri	142	V12
Akuse	184	F4
Akutan Island	198	Ae9
Akwanga	185	G4
Akyab	173	H4
Akyatan Golu	156	F4
Akyazi	156	D2
Akyurt	156	E2
Akzhar	166	C3
Al Aaiun	180	C3
Alabama *U.S.A.*	209	J4
Alabama *U.S.A.*	209	J4
Alaca	156	F2
Alacahan	157	G3
Alacam	157	F2
Alacran Daglari	156	C3
Alacran, Arrecife	211	Q6
Alagoas	217	K5
Alagoinhas	217	K6
Alagon *Spain*	146	C2
Alagon *Spain*	147	F2
Al Ahmadi	177	J2
Al Ajaiz	177	N7
Alajarvi	142	K5
Alajuela	212	E9
Alakanuk	198	C3
Alakol, Ozero	166	E2
Alakyla	142	L3
Al Amarah	174	H6
Alameda *California*	206	A2
Alameda *New Mexico*	207	J3
Alamicamba	212	E8
Alamo	206	E2
Alamogordo	207	K4
Ala, Monti di	149	B5
Alamos	207	H7
Alamosa	207	K2
Aland	143	H6
Alands hav	143	M6
Alanya	156	E4
Alaotra, Lake	189	J3
Alapayevsk	164	Ad5
Al Aqulah	177	J5
Alarcon, Embalse de	146	E3
Al Artawiyah	176	G3
Alasehir	156	C3
Al Ashkhirah	177	P6
Alaska	198	E3
Alaska, Gulf of	198	F4
Alaska Peninsula	198	Af8
Alaska Range	198	E3
Alassio	148	B4
Alatna	198	E2
Alatyr	158	H5
Alausi	216	B4
Alavus	142	K5
Al Ayn	177	M4
Alayor	147	J3
Alayskiy Khrebet	166	C4
Al Azamiyah	157	L6
Alazeya	165	S2
Alba	148	B3
Al Bab	157	G4
Albacete	147	F3
Al Badi	176	H5
Al Badi	157	J5
Alba de Tormes	146	D2
Alba Iulia	153	G2
Albak	143	D8
Alba, Mount	195	B6
Albanel, Lake	201	M7
Albania	154	E2
Albano	217	F4
Albany *Australia*	192	D5
Albany *Canada*	201	K7
Albany *Georgia*	209	K5
Albany *Kentucky*	204	H8
Albany *New York*	205	P5
Albany *Oregon*	202	C5
Albarracin	147	F2
Al Basrah	174	H6
Albatross Bay	193	J1
Albatross Point	195	E3
Al Bayda	176	G10
Albayrak	157	L3
Albemarle	209	M3
Albemarle Island	216	A7
Albemarle Sound	209	P2
Albenga	148	B3
Albentosa	147	F2
Alberche	146	D2
Alberga	193	G4
Albergaria-a-Velha	146	B2
Alberique	147	F3
Albert	144	E3
Alberta	199	M5
Albert Edward, Mount	194	D3
Albert Kanaal	144	F3
Albert, Lake	187	F2
Albert Lea	204	D5
Albert Nile	187	F2
Albertville *France*	145	G6
Albertville *Zaire*	187	E4
Albi	145	E7
Albina	217	G2
Al Bir	176	C2
Al Birk	176	E7
Albocacer	147	G2
Albo, Monti	149	B5
Alboran, Isla de	146	E5
Alborg	143	D8
Alborg Bugt	143	D8
Alborz, Reshteh-ye Kuhta ye	175	K3
Albro	193	K3
Albufeira	146	B4
Albu Gharz, Sabkhat	157	J5
Albuquerque	207	J3
Al Buraymi	177	M4
Albury	193	K6
Al Busayyah	174	H6
Al Buzun	177	K9
Alcacer do Sal	146	B3
Alcala de Henares	146	E2
Alcamo	149	D7
Alcanices	146	C2
Alcaniz	147	F2
Alcantara	146	C3
Alcantara	217	J4
Alcantara, Embalse de	146	C3
Alcaraz	146	E3
Alcaraz, Sierra de	146	E3
Alcaudete	146	D4
Alcazar de San Juan	146	E3
Alcester	133	F2
Alchevsk	159	F6
Alcolea del Pinar	146	E2
Alcoutim	147	F3
Alcoy	147	F3
Alcubierre, Sierra de	147	F2
Alcublas	147	F3
Alcudia	147	H3
Aldabra Islands	162	C7
Aldama	211	K6
Aldan *Russia*	165	M5
Aldan *Russia*	165	N4
Aldanskoye Nagorye	165	M5
Alde	133	J2
Aldeburgh	133	J2
Aldeia Nova	146	C4
Alderley Edge	135	G3
Alderney	133	M6
Aldershot	133	G3
Aldridge	133	F2
Aleg	180	C5
Alegrete	218	E5
Aleksandra, Mys	165	P6
Aleksandriya	159	E6
Aleksandrov	158	F4
Aleksandrovac	153	F4
Aleksandrov Gay	159	H5
Aleksandrovsk	158	K4
Aleksandrovskoye	159	G7
Aleksandrovsk-Sakhalinskiy	165	Q6
Aleksandry, Ostrov	160	F1
Alekseyevka *Kazakhstan*	164	A6
Alekseyevka *Russia*	159	F5
Aleksin	158	F5
Alem Paraiba	218	H4
Alencon	144	D4
Alenquer	217	G4
Alentejo	146	C3
Alenuihaha Channel	206	S10
Aleppo	157	G4

Name	Page	Grid
Amuntai	170	F6
Amur *China*	167	N1
Amur *Russia*	165	Q6
Amuri Pass	195	D5
Amursk	165	P6
Amurskaya Oblast	165	M6
Amur, Wadi	183	F4
Amvrakikos Kolpos	155	F3
Amvrosiyevka	159	F6
Anabar	164	J2
Anaco	213	Q10
Anaconda	202	H4
Anadarko	208	C3
Anadyr *Russia*	165	W4
Anadyr *Russia*	165	X4
Anadyrskiy Khrebet	165	W3
Anafi *Greece*	155	H4
Anafi *Greece*	155	H4
Anafjallet	142	E5
Anah	157	J5
Anaheim	206	D4
Anahuac	208	B7
Anakapalle	172	F5
Anaktuvuk	198	E2
Analalava	189	J2
Anambas, Kepulauan	170	D5
Anamur	156	E4
Anamur Burun	156	E4
Anan	169	E9
Ananes	155	H4
Anantapur	172	E6
Anantnag	172	E2
Ananyev	153	K2
Ananyevo	166	D3
Anapolis	218	J3
Anapu	217	G4
Anar	175	M6
Anarak	175	L5
Anar Darreh	175	Q5
Anatuya	218	D5
Anaua	216	E3
Anavilhanas, Arquipielago das	216	E4
A Nazret	183	G6
Anbei	166	H3
Ancenis	145	C5
Ancha	165	P4
Anchi	185	G4
Anchorage	198	F3
Anchor Island	195	A6
Ancohuma, Nevado	218	C3
Ancona	148	D4
Ancrum	137	F4
Ancuabe	189	G2
Ancuaque	218	C3
Ancud	219	B8
Ancud, Golfo de	219	B8
Anda	167	P2
Andalgala	218	C5
Andalsnes	142	B5
Andalucia	146	D4
Andalusia	209	J5
Andaman Islands	173	H6
Andaman Sea	173	J6
Andamarca	216	C6
Andam, Wadi	177	P6
Andanga	158	H4
Andapa	189	J2
Andarai	217	J6
Andeba Ye Midir Zerf Chaf	176	E9
Andeg	158	J2
Andenes	142	G2
Andermatt	148	B2
Anderson *Canada*	198	K2
Anderson *Indiana*	204	H6
Anderson *Missouri*	204	C8
Anderson *S. Carolina*	209	L3
Anderson Bay	193	K7
Andes	216	B2
Andevoranto	189	J3
Andfjorden	142	G2
Andhra Pradesh	172	E5
Andikithira	155	G5
Andimeshk	174	J5
Andimilos	155	H4
Andiparos	155	H4
Andipaxoi	155	F3
Andirin	157	G4
Andizhan	166	C3
Andkhvoy	175	S3
Andoas	216	B4
Andong	169	B7
Andongwei	167	M4
Andorra	146	G1
Andorra la Vella	147	G1
Andover	133	F3
Andoya	142	F2
Andraitx	147	H3
Andrascoggin	205	Q4
Andravidha	155	F4
Andreafsky	198	C3
Andreanof Islands	198	Ac9
Andrews	207	L4
Andreyevka	159	J5
Andreyevo Ivanovka	153	L2
Andreyevsk	165	J5
Andria	149	F5
Andrijevica	152	E4
Andringitra	189	J4
Andros	212	H2
Andros *Greece*	155	H4
Andros *Greece*	155	H4
Androth	172	D6
Andujar	146	D3
Andulo	186	C5
Andyngda	165	K3
Anegada	213	Q5
Anegada, Bahia	219	D8
Aneho	185	F4
Aneityum	194	U13
Anelghowhat	194	U14
Aneto, Pic D'	147	G1
Angamos, Punta	218	B4
Angar	164	E5
Angara	164	E5
Angara Basin	220	A1
Angarsk	164	G6
Ange	142	F5
Angel de la Guarda, Isla	206	F6
Angeles	171	G2
Angel Falls	216	E2
Angelholm	143	E8
Angelino	208	E5
Angellala	193	K4
Angermanalven	142	G5
Angermunde	150	F2
Angers	145	C5
Angeson	142	J5
Angical	218	J6
Angicos	217	K5
Angikuni Lake	199	R3
Anglesey	134	E4
Ango	186	E2
Angoche	189	G3
Angohran	175	N8
Angol	219	B7
Angola	186	C5
Angola *Indiana*	204	H6
Angoram	194	C2
Angostura, Presa de la	211	N9
Angouleme	145	D6
Angoumois	145	D6
Angren	166	B3
Anguila Islands	212	H3
Anguilla	213	R5
Angus, Braes of	137	E4
Anholt	143	D8
Anhua	173	M3
Anhui	173	N2
Anhumas	218	F3
Aniak	198	D3
Anidhros	155	H4
Anina	153	F3
Aniva	168	J2
Aniva, Mys	168	J2
Aniva, Zaliv	168	J2
Aniwa	194	U13
Anjalankoski	143	M6
Anjou	145	C5
Anjouan	189	H2
Anjozorobe	189	J3
Anju	167	P4
Ankacho	164	H4
Ankang	173	L2
Ankara	156	E3
Ankazoabo	189	H4
Ankazobe	189	J3
Ankiliabo	189	H4
Anklam	150	E2
Ankleshwar	172	D4
Ankober	183	G6
Ankpa	185	G4
Anlong	173	L3
Anlu	173	M2
Anna	159	G5
Annaba	181	G1
Annaberg-Buchholz	150	E3
An Nabk *Saudi Arabia*	174	C6
An Nabk *Syria*	174	C4
Anna Creek	193	H4
Annagh Bog	139	D8
Annagh Head	138	B4
Annagh Island	139	C5
An Najaf	174	G6
Annalong	138	L4
Annan *U.K.*	137	E5
Annan *U.K.*	135	F2
Annandale	137	E5
Anna Plains	192	E2
Annapolis	205	M7
Annapurna	172	F3
Ann Arbor	204	J5
An Nasiriyah	174	H6
Ann, Cape	205	Q5
Annecy	145	G6
Annenskiy-Most	158	F3
Annfield Plain	135	H2
An Nhon	173	L6
Anniston	209	K4
Annonay	145	F6
An Nuayriyah	177	J3
An Numan	176	B3
Anosibe an' Ala	189	J3
Ano Viannos	155	H5
Anoyia	155	H5
Anqing	167	M5
Ansbach	150	D4
Anse de Vauville	133	N6
Anserma	216	B2
Anshan	167	N3
Anshun	173	L3
Ansley	203	Q7
Anson	207	N4
Anson Bay	192	G1
Ansongo	180	F5
Anston	135	H3
Anstruther	137	F4
Ansudu	194	B2
Antabamba	216	C6
Antakya	157	G4
Antalaha	189	K2
Antalya	156	D4
Antalya Korfezi	156	D4
Antananarivo	189	J3
Antarctic Peninsula	221	W5
An Teallach	136	C3
Antequera	146	D4
Anti-Atlas	180	D3
Antibes	145	G7
Anticosti Island	201	P8
Antigo	204	F4
Antigua	213	S6
Antigua and Barbuda	213	S6
Antigua Guatemala	212	B7
Antioch	206	B2
Antipayuta	164	B3
Antipodes Islands	191	S11
Antlers	208	E3
Antofagasta	218	B4
Antofagasta de la Sierra	218	C5
Antofalla, Salar de	218	C5
Antofalla, Volcan	218	C5
Antonio, Ponta Santo	217	K7
Antonovo	153	J4
Antrain	144	C4
Antrim *U.K.*	138	K3
Antrim *U.K.*	138	K3
Antrim Mountains	138	K2
Antrim Plateau	192	F2
Antsalova	189	H3
Antseranana	189	J2
Antsirabe	189	J3
Antsohihy	189	J2
Antu	168	B4
Antufush	176	F9
An-tung	167	N7
Antwerp	144	F3
Antwerpen	144	F3
Anuchino	168	D4
Anugul	172	F4
Anundsjo	142	H5
Anupgarh	172	D3
Anuradhapura	172	F7
Anvers Island	221	V6
Anxi	166	H3
Anxious Bay	193	G5
Anyama	184	E4
Anyang	167	L4
Anyemaqen Shan	173	J2
Anyudin	158	K3
Anzhero-Sudzhensk	164	D5
Anzhu, Ostrova	165	Q1
Anzio	149	D5
Aoba	194	T11
Aola	194	K6
Aomori	168	H5
Aosta	148	A3
Aoukale	182	D5
Aouker	180	D5
Apalachee Bay	209	K6
Apalachicola	209	K6
Apaporis	216	D4
Aparri	171	G2
Apatity	142	Q3
Apatzingan	210	H8
Apeldoorn	144	F2
Apia	191	U4
Apiacas, Serra dos	217	F5
Apin-Apin	170	F4
Apio	194	K6
Apizaco	211	K8
Apolda	150	D3
Apollonia	155	H4
Apopka, Lake	209	M6
Apostle Islands	204	E3
Apostolou Andrea, Akra	156	F5
Apostolovo	159	E6
Appennino	148	C4
Appleby-in-Westmorland	135	G2
Appleton	204	F4
Apsheronsk	159	F7
Apt	145	F7
Apucarana	218	F4
Apure	216	D2
Apurimac	216	C6
Apuseni, Muntii	153	G2
Aq	157	L3
Aqaba	174	B7
Aqaba, Gulf of	183	F2
Aqaba, Khalij-al-	176	B2
Aqal	166	D3
Aqda	175	L5
Aqiq	176	D7
Aqrah	157	K4
Aqueda	146	C2
Aquidauana	218	E4
Ara	172	F3
Arababad	175	N5
Araban	157	G4
Arabatskaya Strelkha, Kosa	159	F6
Araba, Wadi	174	B6
Arabelo	216	E3
Arabian Desert	183	F2
Arabian Sea	177	N8
Arab, Shatt al	174	H6
Arac	156	E2
Aracaju	217	K6
Aracati	217	K4
Aracatuba	218	F4
Aracena	146	C4
Aracena, Sierra de	146	C4
Aracuai *Brazil*	218	H3
Aracuai *Brazil*	217	H3
Arad	153	F2
Aradah	177	L5
Arafuli	176	D9
Aragats	157	L2
Aragon	147	F1
Araguacema	217	H5
Aragua de Barcelona	216	E2
Araguaia	217	H5
Araguaine	217	H5
Araguari	217	G3
Araioses	217	J4
Arak	175	J4
Arakamchechen, Ostrov	198	A3
Arakan Yoma	173	H5
Arakhthos	155	F3
Arakli	157	J2
Araks	157	K2
Aral	166	B3
Aral, Al	176	H4
Aranda de Duero	146	E2
Arandai	194	A2
Aran Island	138	E3
Aran Islands	139	C6
Aranjuez	146	E3
Aranlau	194	A3
Araouane	180	E5
Arapahoe	203	Q7
Arapawa Island	195	E4
Arapiraca	217	K5
Arapkir	157	H3
Arapongas	218	F4
Ar'ar	174	E6
Araracuara	216	C4
Araraquara	218	G4
Araras, Serra das *Maranhao, Brazil*	217	H5
Araras, Serra das *Mato Grosso do Sul, Brazil*	218	F3
Ararat	157	L3
Araripe, Chapada do	217	K5
Arar, Wadi	174	E6
Aras	157	K2
Arato	169	H6
Arauca *Colombia*	216	C2
Arauca *Venezuela*	216	D2
Aravalli Range	172	D3
Araxa	218	G3
Araya	168	D5
Araya, Peninsula de	216	E1
Arba	147	F1
Arbatax	149	B6
Arbil	157	L4
Arboga	143	F7
Arboleda, Punta	207	H7
Arborg	199	R5
Arbra	143	G6
Arbroath	137	F4
Arbus	149	B6
Arcachon	145	C6
Arcachon, Bassin d	145	C6
Arcadia	209	M7
Arcata	202	B7
Arc Dome	202	F8
Archidona	146	D4
Arcis-sur-Aube	144	F4
Arco	202	H6
Arcos de la Frontera	146	D4
Arctic Bay	200	J3
Arctic Ocean	220	A1
Arctic Red	198	J2
Arctic Red River	198	J2
Arctowski	221	W6
Arda	153	H5
Ardabil	174	J2
Ardahan	157	K2
Ardalstangen	143	B6
Ardanuc	157	K2
Ardara	138	F3
Ardarroch	136	C3
Ardee	138	J5
Ardennes	144	F3
Ardentinny	137	D4
Ardesen	157	J2
Ardestan	175	L5
Ardfert	139	C8
Ardglass	138	L4
Ardgour	137	C4
Ardh es Suwwan	174	C6
Ardila	146	C3
Ardino	153	H5
Ardivacher Point	136	A3
Ardlussa	137	C4
Ardminish	137	C5
Ardmore	208	D3
Ardnacross Bay	137	C5
Ardnamurchan	137	B4
Ardnamurchan Point	137	B4
Ardnave Point	137	B5
Ardrossan	137	D5
Ards Peninsula	138	L3
Ardtalla	137	B5
Ardvasar	137	C3
Ardvule, Rubha	136	A3
Areao	217	H4
Arecibo	213	P5

Aube 144 F4
Aubenas 145 F6
Aubigny-sur-Nere 145 E5
Aubry Lake 198 K2
Auburn *Australia* 193 L4
Auburn *Alabama* 209 K4
Auburn *California* 206 B1
Auburn *Indiana* 204 H6
Auburn *Maine* 205 Q4
Auburn *Nebraska* 204 C6
Auburn *New York* 205 M5
Aubusson 145 E6
Auca Mahuida 219 C7
Auce 143 K8
Auch 145 D7
Auchavan 137 E4
Auchengray 137 E5
Auchterarder 137 E4
Auckland 195 E2
Auckland Islands 221 M8
Aude 145 E7
Auderville 144 C4
Audierne, Baie 'd 145 A5
Aue 150 E3
Augher 138 H4
Aughnacloy 138 J4
Aughrim *Galway, Ireland* 139 F6
Aughrim *Wicklow, Ireland* 139 K7
Aughton 135 H3
Augsburg 150 D4
Augusta *Australia* 192 D5
Augusta *Georgia* 209 M4
Augusta *Italy* 149 E7
Augusta *Kansas* 208 D2
Augusta *Maine* 205 R4
Augusta *Montana* 202 H4
Augustine Island 198 E4
Augustow 151 K2
Augustus, Mount 192 D3
Auletta 149 E5
Aulia 183 F4
Aulitiving Island 200 N4
Aulne 144 B4
Aultbea 136 C3
Aumont 145 E6
Aupalak 201 N6
Aurangabad 172 E5
Auray 145 B5
Aurdal 143 C6
Aure *Norway* 142 B5
Aure *Norway* 142 C5
Aurich 150 B2
Aurillac 145 E6
Aurkuning 170 E6
Aurora *Colorado* 203 M8
Aurora *Illinois* 204 F6
Aurora *Missouri* 204 D8
Aurora *Nebraska* 203 R7
Au Sable 204 J4
Auskerry Sound 136 F1
Aust-Agder 143 D7
Austin *Minnesota* 204 D5
Austin *Nevada* 206 D1
Austin *Texas* 208 D5
Austin, Lake 192 D4
Australia 190 F6
Australian Capital Territory 193 K6
Austria 148 D2
Austurhorn 142 X12
Autazes 216 F4
Authie 144 D3
Autlan 210 G8
Autun 145 F5
Auvergne *Australia* 192 G2
Auvergne *France* 145 E6
Auxerre 145 E5
Avallon 145 E5
Avanos 156 F3
Avare 218 G4
Avas 155 H2
Avcilar 156 C2
Avebury 133 F3
Aveiro *Portugal* 146 B2
Aveiro *Portugal* 146 B2
Avellino 149 E5
Avelon Peninsula 201 R8
Aversa 149 E5
Aves, Isla de 213 R7
Avesnes 144 E3
Avesta 143 G6
Aveyron 145 E6
Avezzano 149 D4
Avgo 155 H5
Aviemore 137 E3
Aviemore, Lake 195 C6
Avigliano 149 E5
Avignon 145 F7
Avila 146 D2
Avila, Sierra de 146 D2
Aviles 146 D1
Avisio 148 C2
Aviz 146 C3
Avlum 143 C8
Avoca *Australia* 193 J6
Avoca *Iowa* 204 C6
Avola 149 E7
Avon *Devon, U.K.* 132 D4
Avon *Hampshire, U.K.* 133 F4
Avon *U.K.* 132 E3
Avon *U.K.* 132 E3
Avonmouth 132 E3
Avon Park 209 M7
Avon Water 137 D5
Avranches 144 C4

Avrig 153 H3
Avuavu 194 K6
Awaji-shima 169 E8
Awali 177 K3
Awanui 195 D1
Awarik, Uruq al 176 H7
Awarua Point 195 A6
Awa-shima 169 G6
Awash Wenz 183 H5
Awaso 184 E4
Awatere 195 D4
Awbari 181 H3
Aweil 182 E6
Awe, Loch 137 C4
Awful, Mount 195 B6
Awgu 185 G4
Awjilah 181 K2
Axbridge 132 E3
Axe *Dorset, U.K.* 132 E4
Axe *Somerset, U.K.* 132 E3
Axel-Heiberg Island 200 H2
Axim 184 E5
Axios 155 G2
Ax-les-Thermes 145 D7
Axminster 132 D4
Ayabe 169 E8
Ayacucho *Argentina* 219 E7
Ayacucho *Peru* 216 C6
Ayaguz 166 F2
Ayamonte 146 C4
Ayan *Russia* 164 H5
Ayan *Russia* 165 P5
Ayancik 156 F2
Ayas 156 E3
Ayaviri 216 C6
Ayayei 176 C10
Aya-Yenahin 184 E4
Aybasti 157 G2
Aydarkul, Ozero 166 B3
Aydere 175 N2
Aydin 156 B4
Aydinca 157 G2
Aydincik 156 E4
Aydin Daglari 156 C3
Ayerbe 147 F1
Ayers Rock 192 G4
Ayeshka 164 E6
Ayia Anna 155 G3
Ayia Marina 155 J5
Ayios 155 G4
Ayios Andreas 155 G4
Ayios Evstratios 155 H3
Ayios Kirikos 155 J4
Ayios Nikolaos *Greece* 155 F3
Ayios Nikolaos *Greece* 155 H5
Ayios Petros 155 F3
Aykathonisi 155 J4
Aykhal 164 J3
Aylesbury 133 G3
Ayllon 146 E2
Aylmer, Lake 199 P3
Aylsham 133 J2
Ayn al Bayda 157 G5
Ayni 166 B4
Ayn Tarfawi 157 K5
Ayn, Wadi al 177 M5
Ayod 182 F6
Ayon 165 V3
Ayon, Ostrov 165 V3
Ayora 147 F3
Ayr *U.K.* 137 D5
Ayr *U.K.* 137 D5
Ayranci 156 E4
Ayre, Point of 134 E2
Aysgarth 135 H2
Ayshirak 166 C2
Aytos 153 J4
Ayun 177 L8
Ayutthaya 173 K6
Ayvacik 156 B3
Ayvali 156 D4
Azambuja 146 B3
Azamgarh 172 F3
Azaran 174 H3
Azaz 157 G4
Azazga 147 J4
Azbine 181 G5
Azerbaijan 159 H7
Azezo 176 C10
Azogues 216 B4
Azoum 182 D5
Azov, Sea of 159 F6
Azovskoye More 159 F6
Azpeitia 146 E1
Azraq, Bahr el 183 F5
Azrou 180 D2
Aztec 207 H2
Azuaga 146 D3
Azuari 217 G3
Azuero, Peninsula de 212 G11
Azul *Argentina* 219 E7
Azul *Mexico* 211 Q9
Azul, Cordillera 216 B5
Azur, Cote d' 145 G7
Azvaday 156 E2
Az Zabadani 157 G6
Az Zafir 176 E7
Az Zahran 177 K3
Az Zarqa 177 L4
Az Zawiyah 181 H2
Az Zaydiyah 176 F9
Az Zilfi 176 G5
Az Zubaydiyah 174 G5
Az Zubayr 174 H6

Az Zuhrah 176 F9
Az Zuqur 176 F9

B

Baaba 194 W16
Baalbek 157 G5
Baamonde 146 C1
Baardheere 187 H2
Babadag 153 K3
Babaeski 156 B2
Babahoyo 216 B4
Babai Gaxun 167 J3
Baba, Koh-i- 172 C2
Babar 171 H7
Babar, Kepulauan 171 H7
Babayevo 158 F4
Babbacombe Bay 132 D4
Babelthuap 171 J4
Babine Lake 198 K5
Babo 194 A2
Babol 175 L3
Babol Sar 175 L3
Baboua 182 B6
Babruysk 159 D5
Babstovo 168 D1
Babushkin 164 H6
Babuyan *Philippines* 171 F4
Babuyan *Philippines* 171 G2
Babuyan Channel 171 G2
Babuyan Islands 171 G2
Bacabal 217 J4
Bacan 171 H6
Bacau 153 J2
Baccegalhaldde 142 J2
Back 199 R2
Backa 143 E6
Backaland 136 F1
Backa Topola 152 E3
Backe 142 G5
Bac Ninh 173 L4
Bacolod 171 G3
Bacup 135 G3
Badagara 172 E6
Badajoz 146 C3
Badalona 147 H2
Badanah 174 E6
Bad Aussee 148 D2
Badby 133 F2
Bad Doberan 150 D1
Bad Ems 150 B3
Baden 148 B2
Baden-Baden 150 C4
Badenoch 137 D4
Badgastein 148 D2
Bad Homburg 150 C3
Bad Ischl 148 D2
Bad Kissingen 150 D3
Bad Kreuznach 150 B4
Bad Lands 203 N4
Bad Mergentheim 150 C4
Badminton 132 E3
Bad Neustadt 150 D3
Bad Oldesloe 150 D2
Ba Don 173 L5
Badong 173 M2
Badrah 174 G5
Badr Hunayn 176 D5
Bad Segeberg 150 D2
Bad Tolz 150 D5
Badulla 172 F7
Bad Wildungen 150 C3
Badzhal 165 N6
Badzhalskiy Khrebet 165 N6
Bae Can 173 L4
Baena 146 D4
Baeza 216 B4
Bafa Golu 156 B4
Bafang 185 H4
Bafata 184 C3
Baffin 200 H3
Baffin Bay *Canada* 200 N3
Baffin Bay *U.S.A.* 208 D7
Baffin Island 200 L3
Bafia 185 H5
Bafing 180 C6
Bafing Makana 180 C6
Bafoulabe 180 C6
Bafoussam 185 H4
Bafq 175 M6
Bafra 157 F2
Bafra Burun 157 F2
Baft 175 N7
Bafwasende 186 E2
Bagamoya 187 G4
Bagan Datuk 170 C5
Bagansiapiapi 170 C5
Baganyuvam 158 K2
Bagaryak 164 Ad5
Bagdad 206 F3
Bagdere 157 J3
Bage 218 F6
Bagenalstown 139 J7
Baggs 203 L7
Baghdad 157 L6
Bagherhat 173 G4
Bagheria 149 D6
Baghlan 172 C1
Bagh nam Faoileann 136 A3
Bagisli 157 L4
Bagneres-de-Bigorre 145 D7
Bagneres-de-Luchon 145 D7
Bagnoles-de-l'Orne 144 C4

Bagnolo Mella 148 C3
Bagoe 184 D3
Bagrationovsk 151 J1
Bagshot 133 G3
Baguio 171 G2
Bagusa 194 B2
Bahamas 212 J2
Baharampur 173 G4
Bahau 170 C5
Bahaur 170 E6
Bahawalpur 172 D3
Bahce 157 G4
Bahia 217 J6
Bahia Blanca 219 D7
Bahia Bustamante 219 C9
Bahia, Islas de la 212 D6
Bahia Kino 206 G6
Bahia Laura 219 C9
Bahia Negra 218 E4
Bahias, Cabo dos 219 C8
Bahr 176 E7
Bahr, Abu 177 J6
Bahraich 172 F3
Bahrain 177 K3
Bahrain, Gulf of 177 K4
Bahr Sayqal 157 G6
Bahu Kalat 175 Q9
Baia de Maputo 189 F5
Baia Mare 153 G2
Baian, Band-i- 172 C2
Baiao 217 H4
Baiazeh 175 M5
Baibokoum 182 C6
Baicheng *Jilin, China* 167 N2
Baicheng *Xinjiang Uygur Zizhiqu, China* 166 E3
Baie Comeau 205 R2
Baie-du-Poste 201 M7
Baiji 157 K5
Baiju 167 N5
Baikal, Lake 164 H6
Baile Atha Cliath 139 K6
Baile Herculane 153 G3
Bailieborough 138 J5
Baillie Hamilton Island 200 H2
Baillie Island 198 K1
Bailundo 186 C5
Baimuru 194 C3
Bainbridge 209 K5
Bain-de-Bretagne 145 C5
Baing 171 G8
Bains-les-Bains 145 G4
Baird Inlet 198 C3
Baird Mountains 198 C2
Baird Peninsula 200 L4
Bairin Youqi 167 M3
Bairin Zuoqi 167 M3
Bairnsdale 193 K6
Baise 145 D7
Baixingt 167 N3
Baiyanghe 166 F3
Baja 152 E2
Baja, Punta 206 E6
Bajgiran 175 P3
Bajil 176 F9
Bajmok 152 E3
Bakchar 164 C5
Bakel 184 C3
Baker *Chile* 219 B9
Baker *California* 206 E3
Baker *Montana* 203 M4
Baker *Oregon* 202 F5
Baker Foreland 199 S3
Baker Island 191 T1
Baker Lake 199 R3
Baker, Mount 202 D3
Bakersfield 206 C3
Bakewell 135 H3
Bakharden 175 N2
Bakhardok 175 P2
Bakharz 175 P4
Bakhchisaray 159 E7
Bakhmach 159 E5
Bakhta 164 D4
Bakhtaran 174 H4
Bakhtegan, Daryacheh-ye 175 L7
Bakhty 166 F2
Bakinskikh Komissarov 175 M2
Bakir 156 B3
Bakkafjordur 142 X11
Bakkafloi 142 X11
Bakkagerdi 142 Y12
Baklan 156 C4
Bako 183 G6
Bakongan 170 B5
Bakony 152 D2
Bakouma 182 D6
Baku 159 H7
Bakwanga 186 D4
Bala 132 D2
Bala 156 E3
Bala 171 F4
Balabac Strait 170 F4
Balabio 194 W16
Bala, Cerros de 216 D6
Balacita 153 G3
Balad 157 L6
Baladch 175 K3
Balagannoye 165 R5
Balaghat 172 F4
Balaghat Range 172 E5
Balaguer 147 G2
Balaikarangan 170 E5
Balaka 187 F5

Balakhta 164 E5
Balakleya 159 F6
Balakovo 159 H5
Bala Lake 132 D2
Balama 189 G2
Balambangan 171 F4
Bala Morghab 175 R4
Balangir 172 F4
Balashov 159 G5
Balassagyarmat 152 E1
Balaton 152 D2
Balatonszentgyorgy 152 D2
Balazote 146 E3
Balbi, Mount 194 E3
Balboa 212 H10
Balbriggan 138 K5
Balcarce 219 E7
Balchik 153 K4
Balchrick 136 C2
Balclutha 195 B7
Bald Knob 208 G3
Baldock 133 G3
Baleares, Islas 147 H3
Balearic Islands 147 H3
Baleia, Ponta da 217 K7
Baleine, Grande Riviere de la 201 L6
Baleine, Riviere a la 201 N6
Baler 171 G2
Balerno 137 E5
Balestrand 143 B6
Baley 165 K6
Balfes Creek 193 K3
Balfour 136 F1
Balguntay 166 F3
Balhaf 177 J10
Bali 170 F7
Baligrod 151 K4
Balikesir 156 B3
Balik Golu 157 K3
Balikpapan 170 F6
Bali, Laut 170 F7
Balimbing 171 F4
Balimo 194 C3
Balinqiao 167 M3
Balintang Channel 171 G2
Balkashino 164 Ae6
Balkh 172 C1
Balkhash 166 C2
Balkhash, Ozero 166 C2
Balladonia 192 E5
Ballaghaderreen 138 E5
Ballandean 193 L4
Ballangen 142 G2
Ballantrae 137 C5
Ballao 149 B6
Ballarat 193 J6
Ballard, Lake 192 E4
Ballasalla 134 E2
Ballash 172 F4
Ballater 137 E3
Balle 180 D5
Ballenas, Bahia de 206 F7
Ballenas, Canal de las 206 F6
Balleny Islands 221 L5
Ballia 172 F3
Ballina 138 D4
Ballinafad 138 F4
Ballinamore 138 G4
Ballinasloe 139 F6
Ballincollig 139 E9
Ballindine 138 E5
Ballineen 139 E9
Ballinhassig 139 E9
Ballinluig 137 E4
Ballinskelligs Bay 139 B9
Ball Peninsula 200 K5
Ballsh 154 E2
Ballybay 138 J4
Ballybofey 138 G3
Ballybunion 139 C7
Ballycastle *Ireland* 138 D4
Ballycastle *U.K.* 138 K2
Ballyclare 138 L3
Ballycotton Bay 139 G9
Ballycroy 138 C4
Ballydesmond 139 D8
Ballyduff 139 C8
Ballygalley Head 138 L3
Ballygawley 138 H4
Ballygowan 138 L4
Ballyhaunis 138 E5
Ballyheige 139 C8
Ballyheige Bay 139 C8
Ballyhooly 139 F8
Ballyjamesduff 138 H5
Ballykeel 138 H3
Ballylongford 139 D7
Ballymahon 139 G5
Ballymena 138 K3
Ballymoe 138 F5
Ballymoney 138 J2
Ballymore Eustace 139 J6
Ballymote 138 E4
Ballynahinch 138 L4
Ballyquintin Point 138 M4
Ballyragget 139 H7
Ballyshannon 138 F3
Ballysitteragh 139 B8
Ballyteige Bay 139 J8
Ballyvaghan Bay 139 D6
Ballyvourney 139 D9
Ballywater 138 M3
Balmedie 136 F3
Balonne 193 K4
Balotra 172 D3
Balrampur 172 F3
Balranald 193 J5
Bals 153 H3
Balsas *Brazil* 217 H5
Balsas *Mexico* 211 J8
Balsas *Peru* 216 B5
Balsta 143 G7
Balta 159 D6
Baltanas 146 D2
Baltasound 136 A1
Balti 153 J2
Baltic Sea 143 G9
Baltim 182 F1
Baltimore 205 M7
Baltinglass 139 J7
Baluchistan 172 C3
Balurghat 173 G3
Balvicar 137 C4
Balya 156 B3
Balykshi 159 J6
Bam 175 N3
Bam 175 P7
Bama 185 H3
Bamako 180 D6
Bamba 180 E5
Bambari 182 D6
Bamberg *Germany* 150 D4
Bamberg *U.S.A.* 209 M4
Bambesa 186 E2
Bamenda 185 H4
Bami 175 N2
Bamian 172 C2
Bam Posht 175 R8
Bampton 133 F3
Bampur 175 Q8
Banaba 191 Q2
Banadia 213 M11
Banagher 139 G6
Banalia 186 E2
Banam 173 L6
Bananal, Ilha do 217 G6
Ban Aranyaprathet 173 K6
Banas 172 E3
Banas, Ras 176 C5
Bana, Wadi 176 G10
Banaz 156 C3
Banbridge 138 K4
Banbury 133 F2
Banchory 137 F3
Bancroft 205 M4
Banda 172 F3
Banda Aceh 170 B4
Banda Elat 171 J7
Banda, Kepulauan 171 H6
Banda, Laut 171 H7
Bandama Blanc 184 D4
Bandan Kuh 175 Q6
Banda, Punta la 206 D5
Bandar Abbas 175 N8
Bandarbeyla 183 K6
Bandar-e Anzali 174 J3
Bandar-e Deylam 175 K6
Bandar-e Lengeh 175 M8
Bandar e Mashur 174 J6
Bandar-e Moghuyeh 175 M8
Bandar-e Rig 175 K7
Bandar-e Torkeman 175 M3
Bandar Khomeyni 174 J6
Bandar Seri Begawan 170 E5
Bande 146 C1
Band-e-pay 175 L3
Bandiagara 180 E6
Bandirma 156 B2
Bandol 145 F7
Bandon *Ireland* 139 E9
Bandon *Ireland* 139 E9
Bandundu 186 C3
Bandung 170 D7
Baneh 174 G4
Banes 213 K4
Banff *Canada* 202 G2
Banff *U.K.* 136 F3
Banfora 184 E3
Bangalore 172 E6
Bangangte 185 H4
Bangassou 182 D7
Bangeta, Mount 194 D3
Banggai 171 G6
Banggai, Kepulauan 171 G6
Banggi 171 F4
Banghazi 181 K2
Bangka 170 D6
Bangkalan 170 E7
Bangkaru 170 B5
Bangka, Selat 170 D6
Bangko 170 D6
Bangkok 173 K6
Bangkok, Bight of 173 K6
Bangladesh 173 G4
Bangor *Down, U.K.* 138 L3
Bangor *Gwynedd, U.K.* 134 E3
Bangor *U.S.A.* 205 R4
Bangor Erris 138 C4
Bang Saphan Yai 173 J6
Bangui *Central African Rep.* 182 C7
Bangui *Philippines* 171 G2
Bangweulu, Lake 187 E5
Bangweulu Swamps 187 E5
Ban Hat Yai 173 K7
Ban Houei Sai 173 K4
Bani 180 D6
Bani 213 M5
Baniara 194 D3
Banika 194 J6
Bani Khatmah 176 G7
Bani Maarid 176 H7
Bani Walid 181 H2
Baniyas 174 B5
Baniyas 174 B4
Bani Zaynan, Hadh 177 J6
Banja Luka 152 D3
Banjarmasin 170 E6
Banjul 184 B3
Banka Banka 193 G2
Ban Kantang 173 J7
Ban Keng Phao 173 L6
Bankfoot 137 E4
Ban Khemmarat 173 L5
Ban Khok Kloi 173 J7
Banks Island *Australia* 194 C4
Banks Island *British Columbia, Canada* 198 J5
Banks Island *NW.Territories, Canada* 199 L1
Banks Islands 191 Q4
Banks Peninsula 195 D5
Banks, Point 198 E4
Banks Strait 193 K7
Ban Kui Nua 173 J6
Bankura 173 G4
Bankya 153 G4
Ban Mae Sariang 173 J5
Banmauk 173 J4
Ban Me Thuot 173 L6
Bann 138 K3
Ban Nabo 173 L5
Ban Na San 173 J7
Bannockburn 188 E4
Bannu 172 D2
Banolas 147 H1
Banovce 151 H4
Ban Pak Chan 173 J6
Ban Sao 173 K5
Banska Bystrica 151 H4
Banska Stiavnica 151 H4
Bansko 153 G5
Banstead 133 G3
Banswara 172 D4
Bantaeng 171 F7
Ban Takua Pa 173 J7
Ban Tan 173 K6
Banteer 139 E8
Ban Tha Sala 173 J7
Bantry 139 D9
Bantry Bay 139 C9
Banya 153 H4
Banyak, Kepulauan 170 B5
Banyo 185 H4
Banyuls 145 E7
Banyuwangi 170 E7
Banzyville 186 D2
Baoding 167 M4
Baofeng 173 M2
Baoji 173 L2
Baoqing 168 D2
Baoshan 173 J4
Baoting 173 L5
Baotou 167 L3
Baoxing 168 C1
Bapatla 172 F5
Bapaume 144 E3
Baqubah 157 L6
Bar *Ukraine* 153 J1
Bar *Yugoslavia* 157 E1
Bara 182 F5
Baraawe 187 H2
Barabai 170 F6
Bara Banki 172 F3
Barabinsk 164 B5
Barabinskaya Step 164 B6
Baracoa 213 K4
Baraganul 153 J3
Barahona 213 M5
Barail Range 173 H3
Baraka 176 C8
Barakkul 164 Ae6
Baram 170 E5
Baran 172 E3
Baranavichy 151 L2
Barang, Dasht-i- 175 Q5
Barankul 164 Ae6
Baranof Island 198 H4
Baraoltului, Muntii 153 H2
Barapasai 194 B2
Barat Daya, Kepulauan 171 H7
Barbacena 218 H4
Barbados 213 T6
Barbas, Cap 180 B4
Barbastro 147 G1
Barberton *South Africa* 188 F5
Barberton *U.S.A.* 205 K6
Barbezieux 145 C6
Barbuda 213 S6
Barcaldine 193 K3
Barcelona *Spain* 147 H2
Barcelona *Venezuela* 216 E2
Barcelonnette 145 G6
Barcelos *Brazil* 216 E4
Barcelos *Portugal* 146 B2
Barcin 151 G2
Barcoo 193 J3
Barcs 152 D3
Barda 159 H7
Bardai 182 C3
Bardas Blancas 219 C7
Barddhaman 173 G4
Bardejov 151 J4
Bardneshorn 142 Y12
Bardney 135 J3
Bardsey Island 132 C2
Bareilly 172 E3
Barentsevo More 158 F2
Barentsoya 160 D2
Barents Sea 158 F2
Barentu 183 G4
Bareo 170 F5
Barfleur, Point de 144 C4
Barford 133 F2
Bargrennan 137 D5
Barguzinskiy Khrebet 164 H6
Barh 172 G3
Barhaj 172 F3
Barham 133 J3
Bar Harbor 205 R4
Bari 149 F5
Baridi, Ra's 176 C4
Barika 147 J5
Barinas 216 C2
Baring, Cape 199 M1
Baripada 172 G4
Bari Sadri 172 D4
Barisal 173 H4
Barisan, Pegunungan 170 C6
Barito 170 E6
Barka 177 N5
Barkan, Ra's-e 175 J7
Barking 133 H3
Barkley Sound 202 B3
Barkly East 188 E6
Barkly Tableland 193 H2
Barkol 166 F3
Barkston 133 G2
Barle 132 D3
Bar-le-Duc 144 F4
Barlee, Lake 192 D4
Barlestone 133 F2
Barletta 149 F5
Barmby Moor 135 J3
Barmer 172 D3
Barmouth 132 D2
Barnard Castle 135 H2
Barnaul 164 C6
Barnes Ice Cap 200 M3
Barnet 133 G3
Barnhart 207 M5
Barnoldswick 135 G3
Barnsley 135 H3
Barnstaple 132 C3
Barnstaple Bay 132 C3
Baro 185 G4
Baroda 172 D4
Barony, The 136 E1
Barquilla 146 D3
Barquinha 146 B3
Barquisimeto 216 D1
Barra *Brazil* 217 J6
Barra *U.K.* 137 A4
Barra do Bugres 218 E3
Barra do Corda 217 H5
Barra Head 137 A4
Barra Mansa 218 H4
Barranca *Peru* 216 B4
Barranca *Venezuela* 213 L10
Barrancabermeja 216 C2
Barrancas 213 R10
Barrancos 146 C3
Barranqueras 218 E5
Barranquilla 216 C1
Barra, Sound of 137 A3
Barre 205 P4
Barreiras 217 H6
Barreiro 146 B3
Barren Island, Cape 190 L10
Barren Islands 198 E4
Barren River Lake 204 H8
Barretos 218 G4
Barrhead *Canada* 199 N5
Barrhead *U.K.* 137 F4
Barrhill 137 D5
Barrie 205 L4
Barrier, Cape 195 E2
Barriere 202 D2
Barrington Tops 193 L5
Barrocao 218 H3
Barrow *Argentina* 219 D7
Barrow *Ireland* 139 H8
Barrow *U.S.A.* 198 D1
Barrowford 135 G3
Barrow-in-Furness 135 F2
Barrow Islands 192 D3
Barrow, Point 198 D1
Barrow Range 192 F4
Barrow Strait 200 G3
Barry 132 D3
Barry's Bay 205 M4
Barsalpur 172 D3
Barsi 172 E5
Barstow 206 D3
Bar-sur-Aube 144 F4
Bar-sur-Seine 144 F4
Barth 150 E1
Bartica 216 F2
Bartin 156 E2
Bartle Frere, Mount 193 K2
Bartlesville 208 D2
Barton *Philippines* 171 F3
Barton *U.S.A.* 205 P4
Barton-upon-Humber 135 J3
Bartoszyce 151 J1
Barumun 170 C5
Barus 170 B5

Baruun Urt 167 L2
Barvas 136 B2
Barwani 172 D4
Barwon 193 K4
Barysaw 143 Q9
Barysh 159 H5
Basaidu 175 M8
Basankusu 186 C2
Basco 171 G1
Bascunan, Cabo 218 B5
Basel 148 A2
Basento 149 F5
Bashakerd, Kuhha-ye 175 P8
Bashi Haixia 167 N7
Basht 175 K6
Basilan *Philippines* 171 G4
Basilan *Philippines* 171 G4
Basildon 133 H3
Basingstoke 133 F3
Baskale 157 L3
Baskatong, Reservoir 205 N3
Baskil 157 H3
Baskoy 157 K2
Basle 148 A2
Basoko 186 D2
Bassano del Grappa 148 C3
Bassar 184 F4
Bassas da India 189 G4
Bassein 173 H5
Bassenthwaite 135 F2
Bassenthwaite Lake 135 F2
Basse Santa Su 184 C3
Basseterre 213 R6
Basse Terre 213 S6
Bassett 203 Q6
Bassila 185 F4
Bass Strait 193 K6
Bastad 143 E8
Bastak 175 M8
Bastam 175 M3
Basti 172 F3
Bastia 149 B4
Bastogne 144 F4
Bastrop *Louisiana* 208 G4
Bastrop *Texas* 208 D5
Basyurt 157 J3
Bata 185 G5
Batabano, Golfo de 212 F3
Batagay 165 N3
Batagay-Alyta 165 N3
Batakan 170 E6
Bataklik Golu 156 E4
Batala 172 E2
Batalha 146 B3
Batamay 165 M4
Batan 171 G1
Batang 173 J2
Batangafo 182 C6
Batangas 171 G3
Batanghari 170 C6
Batan Islands 171 G1
Batatais 218 G4
Batavia 205 L5
Bataysk 159 F6
Batchelor 192 G1
Batesville 208 G3
Bath *U.K.* 132 E3
Bath *U.S.A.* 205 M5
Batha 182 C5
Bathgate 137 E5
Bathurst *Australia* 193 K5
Bathurst *Canada* 205 T3
Bathurst *Gambia* 184 B3
Bathurst Inlet 199 P2
Bathurst Island 192 G1
Bathurst Islands 200 F2
Batie 184 E4
Batiki 194 R8
Batinah, Al 177 N4
Batin, Wadi al 176 H2
Batiscan 205 P3
Batitoroslar 156 D4
Batlaq-e Gavkhuni 175 L5
Batley 135 H3
Batman *Turkey* 157 J4
Batman *Turkey* 157 J4
Batna 181 G1
Baton Rouge 208 G5
Batouri 185 H5
Batroun 157 F5
Batsfjord 142 N1
Battambang 173 K6
Batticaloa 172 F7
Battle *Canada* 199 N5
Battle *U.K.* 133 H4
Battle Creek 204 H5
Battle Harbour 201 Q7
Battle Mountain 202 F7
Batu 183 G6
Batubetumbang 170 D6
Batum 157 J2
Batumi 157 J2
Batu Pahat 170 C5
Batuputih 171 F5
Baturaja 170 D6
Baturite 217 K4
Baubau 171 G7
Bauchi 185 G3
Bauda 172 F4
Baudette 204 C2
Baudo 216 B2
Baudouinville 187 E4
Bauge 145 C5
Bauhinia Downs 193 K3
Baukau 171 H7
Bauld, Cape 201 Q7
Baumann Fjord 200 J2
Baunie 193 L4
Baurtregaum 139 C8
Bauru 218 G4
Baus 218 F3
Bautzen 150 F3
Bawdeswell 133 J2
Bawdsey 133 J2
Bawean 170 E7
Bawiti 182 E2
Bawku 184 E3
Bawtry 135 H3
Baxley 209 L5
Bayamo 212 J4
Bayamon 213 P5
Bayan 168 A2
Bayan-Aul 164 B6
Bayandalay 167 J3
Bayanday 164 H6
Bayan Harshan 173 J2
Bayanhongor 166 J2
Bayan Mod 167 J3
Bayan Obo 167 K3
Bayano, Laguna 212 H10
Bayan-Ondor 166 H3
Bayantsagaan 166 H3
Bayantsogt 167 K2
Bayan-Uul 167 L2
Bayard *Nebraska* 203 N7
Bayard *New Mexico* 207 H4
Bayat *Turkey* 156 D3
Bayat *Turkey* 156 F2
Bayburt 157 J2
Bay City *Michigan* 204 J5
Bay City *Texas* 208 E6
Baydaratskaya Guba 164 Ae3
Baydhabo 187 H2
Baydon 133 F3
Bayerischer Wald 150 E4
Bayeux 144 C4
Bayfield 204 E3
Bayhan al Qasab 176 G9
Bayindir 156 B3
Bayir 174 C6
Baykadam 166 B3
Baykal 164 G6
Baykalovo 164 Ae5
Baykal, Ozero 164 H6
Baykan 157 J3
Bay-Khak 164 E6
Baykit 164 F4
Baynunah 177 L5
Bayombong 171 G2
Bayona 146 B1
Bayonne 145 C7
Bayo Point 171 G3
Bayram-Ali 175 R3
Bayramic 156 B3
Bayramiy 174 J2
Bayramtepe 156 C2
Bayreuth 150 D4
Bayrut 156 F6
Bay Saint Louis 208 H5
Bayt al Faqih 176 F9
Baytown 208 E6
Bayy al Kabir, Wadi 181 H2
Baza 146 E4
Bazaliya 151 M4
Bazar-Dyuzi 159 H7
Bazaruto, Ilha do 189 G4
Bazas 145 C6
Bazman 175 Q8
Bazman, Kuh-e- 175 Q7
Bcharre 157 F5
Beach 203 N4
Beachy Head 133 H4
Beaconsfield 133 G3
Beadnell Bay 135 H1
Beagh, Lough 138 G2
Beagle Gulf 192 G1
Beagle Reef 192 E2
Beal 137 G5
Bealanana 189 J2
Beaminster 132 E4
Beampingaratra 189 J4
Bear 202 J6
Beara Peninsula 139 C9
Beardmore 204 G2
Beardstown 204 E6
Bear Island *Canada* 201 K7
Bear Island *Ireland* 139 C9
Bear Lake 202 J7
Bearley 133 F2
Bearn 145 C7
Bear Paw Mount 202 K3
Bearsden 137 D5
Beartooth Range 203 K5
Beata, Cabo 213 M6
Beata, Isla 213 M6
Beatrice 203 R7
Beatty 206 D2
Beattyville 205 M2
Beau Basin 189 L7
Beaucaire 145 F7
Beaufort *Malaysia* 170 F4
Beaufort *U.S.A.* 209 M4
Beaufort Sea 198 H1
Beaufort West 188 D6
Beaugency 145 D5
Beauly *U.K.* 136 D3
Beauly *U.K.* 136 D3
Beauly Firth 136 D3
Beaumaris 134 E3
Beaumont *France* 144 E4
Beaumont *California* 206 D4
Beaumont *Texas* 208 E5
Beaune 145 F5
Beaurepaire 145 F6
Beauvais 144 E4
Beauvoir-sur-Mer 145 B5
Beaver *Saskatchewan, Canada* 199 P5
Beaver *Yukon, Canada* 198 K3
Beaver Dam *Kentucky* 204 G8
Beaver Dam *Wisconsin* 204 F5
Beaverhill Lake 199 N5
Beawar 172 D3
Beazley 219 C6
Bebedouro 218 G4
Bebington 135 F3
Beccles 133 J2
Becej 152 F3
Becerrea 146 C1
Bechar 180 E2
Becharof Lake 198 D4
Bechet 153 G4
Beckingham 135 J3
Beckley 205 K8
Beclean 153 H2
Bedale 135 H2
Bedarieux 145 E7
Bede, Point 198 E4
Bedford *U.K.* 133 G2
Bedford *U.S.A.* 204 G7
Bedford Level 133 H2
Bedfordshire 133 G2
Bedlington 135 H1
Bedwas 132 D3
Bedworth 133 F2
Beer Sheva 174 B6
Beeston 133 F2
Beeswing 137 E5
Beeville 208 D6
Befale 186 D2
Befandriana 189 J3
Begejska Kanal 152 F3
Begoml 143 N10
Behbehan 175 K6
Behraamkale 156 B3
Behshahr 175 L3
Beian 167 P2
Beibu Wan 173 L4
Beihai 173 L4
Beijing 167 M4
Beila 180 B5
Beinn a' Ghlo 137 E4
Beinn Bheigier 137 B5
Beinn Dearg *Highland, U.K.* 136 D3
Beinn Dearg *Tayside, U.K.* 137 E4
Beinn Dorain 137 D4
Beinn Eighe 136 C3
Beinn Fhada 136 C3
Beinn Ime 137 D4
Beinn Mhor 136 A3
Beinn na Caillich 137 C3
Beinn Resipol 137 C4
Beinn Sgritheall 137 C3
Beipiao 167 N3
Beira 189 F3
Beirut 156 F6
Bei Shan 166 H3
Beit Lahm 174 B6
Beius 153 G2
Beja 146 C3
Beja 181 G1
Bejaia 181 G1
Bejaia, Golfe de 147 J4
Bejar 146 D2
Bejestan 175 P4
Beji 172 C3
Bekdast 159 J7
Bekescsaba 153 F2
Bekily 189 J4
Bekopaka 189 H3
Bekwai 184 E4
Bela *India* 172 F3
Bela *Pakistan* 172 C3
Belabo 185 H5
Belaga 170 E5
Belang 171 G5
Bela Palanka 153 G4
Belarus 151 L2
Bela Vista 189 F5
Belawan 170 B5
Belaya *Russia* 158 K4
Belaya *Russia* 165 W3
Belaya-Kalitva 159 G6
Belaya Kholunitsa 158 J4
Belayan 170 F5
Belcher Channel 200 G2
Belcher Islands 201 L6
Belchiragh 174 S4
Belchite 147 F2
Belcoo 138 G4
Belderg 138 C4
Belebey 158 J5
Beledweyne 183 J7
Belem 217 H4
Belen *Turkey* 156 E4
Belen *U.S.A.* 207 J3
Belep, Iles 194 V15
Belesar, Embalse de 146 C1
Belev 159 F5
Belfast *New Zealand* 195 D5
Belfast *U.K.* 138 L3
Belfast Lough 138 L3
Belfield 203 N4
Belford 137 G5
Belfort 145 G5
Belgaum 172 D5
Belgium 144 E3
Belgorod 159 F5
Belgorod-Dnestrovskiy 159 E6
Belgrade 152 F3
Belgrano 221 X3
Belica 151 L2
Beli Lom 153 J4
Beli Manastir 152 E3
Belimbing 170 C7
Belin 145 C6
Belinskiy 159 G5
Belinyu 170 D6
Belitsa 153 G5
Belitung 170 D6
Belize 212 C6
Belkina, Mys 168 F3
Belknap, Mount 202 H8
Belkovskiy, Ostrov 165 P1
Bella Bella 198 K5
Bellac 145 D5
Bella Coola 198 K5
Bellaire 208 E6
Bellary 172 E5
Bella Vista *Argentina* 218 C5
Bella Vista *Argentina* 218 E5
Belleek 138 F4
Bellefontaine 204 J6
Belle Fourche *South Dakota* 203 N5
Belle Fourche *Wyoming* 203 M5
Belle Glade 209 M7
Belle Ile 145 B5
Belle Isle 201 Q7
Belleme 144 D4
Belleville *Canada* 205 M4
Belleville *Illinois* 204 F7
Belleville *Kansas* 203 R8
Bellevue *Idaho* 202 G6
Bellevue *Washington* 202 C4
Belley 145 F6
Bellingham *U.K.* 137 F5
Bellingham *U.S.A.* 202 C3
Bellinghausen Sea 221 U5
Bellingshausen 221 W6
Bellinzona 148 B2
Bello 216 B2
Bellona Island 194 J7
Bellona Reefs 191 N6
Bellpuig 147 G2
Bellshill 137 D5
Belluno 148 D2
Bell Ville 218 D6
Belly 202 H3
Belmont 136 A1
Belmonte *Portugal* 146 C2
Belmonte *Spain* 146 E3
Belmopan 212 C6
Belmullet 138 B4
Belogorsk 159 E6
Belogorye 151 M4
Belogradchik 153 G4
Belo Horizonte 218 K4
Beloit 204 F5
Belokorovichi 159 D5
Belomorsk 158 E3
Belorado 146 E1
Belorechensk 159 F7
Beloren 156 E4
Belorusskaya Gryada 151 L2
Belot, Lac 198 K2
Belo-Tsiribihina 189 H3
Belousovka 164 C6
Belovo 164 D6
Beloye More 158 F2
Beloye Ozero 158 F3
Belozersk 158 F4
Belozerskoye 164 Ae5
Belper 135 H3
Belsay 137 G5
Belterra 217 F4
Belton 135 J3
Belturbet 138 H4
Belukha, Gora 166 F2
Belvedere Marittimo 149 E6
Belvidere 204 F5
Belvoir, Vale of 133 G2
Belyando, River 193 K3
Belyayevka 153 L2
Belyy, Ostrov 165 A2
Belyy Yar 164 D5
Belzyce 151 K3
Bemaraha, Plateau du 189 J3
Bembridge 133 F4
Bemidji 204 C3
Benabarre 147 G1
Ben Alder 137 D4
Benalla 193 K6
Benares 172 F3
Benavente 146 D2
Ben Avon 137 E3
Benbaun 139 C5
Ben Chonzie 137 E4
Bencorr 139 C5
Ben Cruachan 137 C4
Bend 202 D5
Bende 185 G4
Bender Qaasim 183 J5
Bendigo 193 J6
Benesov 150 F4
Benevento 149 E5
Bengbu 167 M5
Benghazi 181 K2

Name	Page	Grid
Bengkalis	170	C5
Bengkulu	170	C6
Bengo, Baia do	186	B4
Bengoi	171	J6
Bengtsfors	143	E7
Benguela	186	B5
Benguerua, Ilha	189	G4
Benha	182	F1
Ben Hope	136	D2
Beni *Bolivia*	216	D6
Beni *Zaire*	187	E2
Beni Abbes	180	E2
Benicarlo	147	G2
Benidorm	147	F3
Beni Mazar	182	F2
Beni Mellal	180	D2
Benin	185	F4
Benin, Bight of	185	F4
Benin City	185	G4
Beni Saf	180	E1
Beni Suef	182	F2
Ben Klibreck	136	D2
Ben Lawers	137	D4
Ben Ledi	137	D4
Ben Lomond	137	D4
Ben Loyal	136	D2
Ben Lui	137	D4
Ben Macdui	137	E3
Ben MorCoigach	136	C3
Ben More *Central, U.K.*	137	D4
Ben More *Strathclyde, U.K.*	136	B4
Ben More Assynt	136	D2
Benmore, Lake	195	C6
Bennachie	136	F3
Benn Cleuch	137	E4
Bennetta, Ostrov	165	R1
Bennington	205	P5
Benoni	188	E5
Be, Nosy	189	J2
Ben Rinnes	136	E3
Bensheim	150	C4
Benson *U.K.*	133	F3
Benson *U.K.*	206	G5
Ben Starav	137	C4
Bent	175	P8
Bentinck Island	173	J6
Bent Jbail	174	B5
Bentley	135	H3
Benton	208	F3
Benton Harbor	204	G5
Bentung	170	C5
Benue	185	G4
Ben Venue	137	D4
Ben Vorlich	137	D4
Benwee	138	C5
Benwee Head	138	C4
Ben Wyvis	136	D3
Benxi	167	N3
Beo	171	H5
Beograd	152	F3
Beppu	169	C9
Beqa	194	R9
Berat	154	E2
Berau, Teluk	194	A2
Berber	183	F4
Berbera	183	J5
Berberati	182	C7
Berck	144	D3
Berdichev	159	D6
Berdigestyakh	165	M4
Berdyansk	159	F6
Berea	204	H8
Bereeda	183	K5
Beregovo	159	C6
Berens	199	R5
Berens River	199	R5
Bere Regis	132	E4
Berettyo	153	F2
Berettyoujfalu	153	F2
Bereza	151	L2
Berezhany	151	L4
Berezhnykh, Mys	165	Q1
Berezina	158	D5
Berezino	158	D5
Berezna	159	E5
Berezniki	158	K4
Berezno	151	M3
Berezovka *Russia*	158	K3
Berezovka *Russia*	165	K5
Berezovka *Russia*	165	T3
Berezovka *Ukraine*	159	E6
Berezovo *Russia*	164	Ae4
Berezovo *Russia*	165	W4
Berezovskaya	165	K5
Berg	188	C6
Berga	147	G1
Bergama	156	B3
Bergamo	148	B3
Bergeforsen	142	G5
Bergen *Germany*	150	E1
Bergen *Norway*	143	J6
Bergen op Zoom	144	F3
Bergerac	145	D6
Bergfors	142	H2
Bergisch-Gladbach	150	B3
Bergsviken	142	J4
Berhala, Selat	170	C6
Beringa, Ostrov	161	T4
Bering Glacier	198	G3
Beringovskiy	165	X4
Bering Sea	223	H3
Bering Strait	198	B2
Berislav	159	E6
Beris, Ra's	175	Q9
Berja	146	E4
Berkak	142	C5
Berkakit	165	L5
Berkeley *U.K.*	132	E3
Berkeley *U.S.A.*	206	A2
Berkhamsted	133	G3
Berkner Island	221	W3
Berkovitsa	153	G4
Berkshire	133	F3
Berkshire Downs	133	F3
Berkshire Mountains	205	P5
Berlevag	142	N2
Berlin *Germany*	150	E2
Berlin *U.S.A.*	205	Q4
Bermeja, Sierra	146	D4
Bermejo *Argentina*	218	C6
Bermejo *Argentina*	218	D4
Bermeo	146	E1
Bermillo de Sayago	146	C2
Bermuda	197	N5
Bern	148	A2
Bernau	150	E2
Bernay	144	D4
Bernburg	150	D3
Berne	148	A2
Berner Alpen	148	A2
Berneray *U.K.*	137	A4
Berneray *U.K.*	136	A3
Bernina, Piz	148	B2
Beroroha	189	J4
Berounka	150	E4
Berre, Etang de	145	F7
Berriedale	136	E2
Berriedale Water	136	E2
Berrigan	193	K6
Berringarra	192	D4
Berrouaghia	147	H4
Berry *Australia*	193	L5
Berry *France*	145	E5
Berryessa, Lake	202	C8
Berry Head	132	D4
Berry Islands	212	J1
Bershad	153	K1
Berthoud Pass	203	L8
Bertoua	185	H5
Beru	191	S2
Beruri	216	E4
Berwick	205	M6
Berwick-upon-Tweed	137	F5
Berwyn Mountains	132	D2
Berzence	152	D2
Besalampy	189	H3
Besancon	145	G5
Besar, Kai	171	J7
Besbre	145	E5
Beshneh	175	M7
Besiri	157	J4
Beskidy Zachodnie	151	H4
Beslan	159	G7
Besni	157	G4
Bessarabia	153	K2
Bessarabka	153	K2
Bessbrook	138	K4
Bessemer *Alabama*	209	J4
Bessemer *Winconsin*	204	F3
Bestamak *Kazakhstan*	166	D2
Bestamak *Kazakhstan*	159	K6
Bestobe	164	A6
Bestuzhevo	158	G3
Betafo	189	J3
Betanzos	146	B1
Betare Oya	185	H4
Bethal	188	E5
Bethanie	188	C5
Bethany	204	C6
Bethel	198	C3
Bethel Park	205	L6
Bethesda *U.K.*	134	E3
Bethesda *U.S.A.*	205	M7
Bethlehem *Israel*	174	B6
Bethlehem *South Africa*	188	E5
Bethulie	188	E6
Bethune *France*	144	D4
Bethune *France*	144	E3
Betioky	189	H4
Betpak-Dala	166	B2
Bet-Pak-Data	166	B2
Betroka	189	J4
Betsiamites	205	R2
Betsiboka	189	J3
Bettiah	172	F3
Bettyhill	136	D2
Betul	172	E4
Betwa	172	E4
Betws-y-coed	134	F3
Beuvron	145	D5
Beverley *Australia*	192	D5
Beverley *U.K.*	135	J3
Beverly Hills	206	C3
Bexhill	133	H4
Beykoz	156	C2
Beyla	184	D4
Beylul	176	F10
Beyneu	159	K6
Beypazari	156	D2
Beypinar	157	G3
Beysehir	156	D4
Beysehir Golu	156	D4
Beyton	133	H2
Beytussebap	157	K4
Bezhetsk	158	F4
Beziers	145	E7
Bezmein	175	P2
Bhadgaon	172	G3
Bhadrachalam	172	F5
Bhadrakh	172	G4
Bhadravati	172	E6
Bhagalpur	172	G3
Bhakkar	172	D2
Bhamo	173	J4
Bhandara	172	E4
Bhanrer Range	172	F4
Bharatpur *Pradesh, India*	172	F4
Bharatpur *Rajasthan, India*	172	E3
Bharuch	172	D4
Bhatinda	172	D2
Bhatpara	173	G4
Bhavnagar	172	D4
Bhawanipatna	172	F5
Bhilwara	172	D3
Bhima	172	E5
Bhiwani	172	E3
Bhopal	172	E4
Bhopalpatnam	172	F5
Bhor	172	D5
Bhubaneshwar	172	G4
Bhuj	172	C4
Bhumiphol Dam	173	J5
Bhusawal	172	E4
Bhutan	173	G3
Bia	216	D4
Biaban	175	N8
Biabanak	175	S5
Biak	194	B2
Biala Podlaska	151	K2
Bialobrzegi	151	J3
Bialowieza	151	K2
Bialystok	151	K2
Bianco	149	F6
Biankouma	184	D4
Biaro	171	H5
Biarritz	145	C7
Biasca	148	B2
Biba	182	F2
Bibai	168	H4
Bibala	186	B5
Bibby Island	199	S3
Biberach	150	C4
Bibury	133	F3
Bicester	133	F3
Bicheno	193	K7
Bickle Knob	205	L7
Bida	185	G4
Bidar	172	E5
Biddeford	205	Q5
Biddulph	135	G3
Bidean Nam Bian	137	C4
Bideford	132	C3
Bideford Bay	132	C3
Bidford-on-Avon	133	F2
Bidokht	175	P4
Bidzhan *Russia*	168	C1
Bidzhan *Russia*	168	C2
Biebrza	151	K2
Biel	148	A2
Bielefeld	150	C2
Biella	148	B3
Bielsko-Biala	151	H4
Bielsk Podlaski	151	K2
Bien Hoa	173	L6
Bienne	148	A2
Bienveneu	217	G3
Bienville, Lac	201	M6
Biferno	149	E5
Biga	156	B2
Bigadic	156	C3
Big Bay	194	T11
Big Belt Mountains	202	J4
Big Blue	203	R7
Bigbury Bay	132	D4
Biggar *Canada*	203	K1
Biggar *U.K.*	137	E5
Biggleswade	133	G2
Big Horn	203	K5
Big Horn Mountains	203	L5
Big Island	200	M5
Big Pine	206	C2
Big Piney	203	J6
Big Sheep Mountains	203	L4
Big Sioux	203	R5
Big Snowy Mount	202	K4
Big Spring	207	M4
Big Stone Gap	204	J8
Big Timber	203	J5
Big Trout Lake	199	T4
Bihac	152	C3
Bihar	172	G4
Bihar	172	G3
Biharamulo	187	F3
Bihoro	168	K4
Bihu	167	M6
Bijagos, Arquipelago dos	184	B3
Bijapur	172	E5
Bijar	174	H4
Bijeljina	152	E3
Bijelo Polje	152	E4
Bijie	173	L3
Bijnor	172	E3
Bikaner	172	D3
Bikin *Russia*	168	E2
Bikin *Russia*	168	F2
Bikoro	186	C3
Bilad Bani Bu Ali	177	P5
Bilad Ghamid	176	E6
Bilad Zahran	176	E6
Bilaspur	172	F4
Bila Tserkva	159	E6
Bilauktaung Range	173	J6
Bilbao	146	E1
Bilchir	165	J6
Bilecik	156	C2
Biled	153	F3
Bile Karpaty	151	G4
Bilesha Plain	187	H2
Bilgoraj	151	K3
Bili	186	E2
Bilin	173	J5
Billabalong	192	D4
Billericay	133	H3
Billingham	135	H2
Billings	203	K5
Billingshurst	133	G3
Bilma	181	H5
Bilma, Grand Erg de	181	H5
Biloela	193	L3
Bilo Gora	152	D3
Biloxi	208	H5
Biltine	182	D5
Bilugyun	173	J5
Binalud, Kuh-e	175	P3
Binatang	170	E5
Binder	167	L2
Bindloe Island	216	A7
Bindura	188	F3
Binefar	147	G2
Binga	188	E3
Bingara	193	L4
Bingerville	184	E4
Bingham	205	R4
Binghamton	205	N5
Bingley	135	H3
Bingol	157	J3
Bingol Daglari	157	J3
Binjai *Indonesia*	170	B5
Binjai *Indonesia*	170	D5
Binongko	171	G7
Bintan	170	C5
Bintuhan	170	C6
Bintulu	170	E5
Bin Xian *Heilongjiang, China*	168	A3
Bin Xian *Shaanxi, China*	173	L2
Binyang	173	L4
Bio	194	K7
Biobio	219	B7
Biograd	152	C4
Bioko	185	G5
Bir	172	E5
Bira *Russia*	168	D1
Bira *Russia*	168	D1
Bira *Russia*	165	P7
Birag, Kuh-e	175	Q8
Birak	181	H3
Bir al Hisw	176	E4
Bir al War	181	H4
Birao	182	D5
Biratnagar	173	G3
Bir Butayman	157	H4
Birca	153	G4
Birch Island	202	D2
Birch Mountains	199	N4
Bird	199	S4
Bird Island	213	R7
Birdlip	133	E3
Birdum	193	G2
Birecik	157	G4
Bireun	170	B4
Bir Fardan	177	J5
Bir Ghabalou	147	H4
Bir Hadi	177	K7
Birhan	183	G5
Birikchul	164	D6
Birjand	175	P5
Birkenhead *New Zealand*	195	E2
Birkenhead *U.K.*	135	F3
Birksgate Range	192	F4
Birlad *Romania*	153	J2
Birlad *Romania*	153	J2
Birlestik	166	B2
Birmingham *U.K.*	133	F2
Birmingham *U.S.A.*	209	J4
Bir Moghrein	180	C3
Birnie Island	191	U2
Birnin Kebbi	185	F3
Birni nKonni	181	G6
Birobidzhan	168	D1
Birofeld	168	D1
Birr	139	G6
Bir, Ras el	183	H5
Birreencorragh	138	C5
Birrimbah	192	G2
Birsk	158	K4
Birtle	203	P2
Birtley	135	H2
Biryusa	164	F5
Birzai	143	L8
Biscay, Bay of	145	B6
Bischofshofen	148	D2
Biscotasi Lake	204	J3
Bisert	158	K4
Bisevo	152	D4
Bisha	176	C9
Bishah, Wadi	176	F6
Bishkek	166	C3
Bishnupur	173	G4
Bishop	206	C2
Bishop Auckland	135	H2
Bishop Burton	135	J3
Bishop's Castle	132	D2
Bishops Falls	201	Q8
Bishop's Stortford	133	H3
Bishri, Jbel	157	H5

Biskra 181 G2
Biskupiec 151 J2
Bislig 171 H4
Bismarck Archipelago 194 D2
Bismarck Range 194 D3
Bismark 203 P4
Bismil 157 J4
Bismo 143 C6
Bisotun 174 H4
Bispfors 142 G5
Bissau 184 B3
Bissett 203 S2
Bistcho Lake 199 M4
Bistretu 153 G4
Bistrita *Romania* 153 H2
Bistrita *Romania* 153 J2
Bistritei, Muntii 153 H2
Bitburg 150 B3
Bitche 144 G4
Bitik 159 J5
Bitkine 182 C5
Bitlis 157 K3
Bitola 153 F5
Bitonto 149 F5
Bitterfontein 188 C6
Bitterroot 202 G4
Bitterroot Range 202 G4
Bitti 149 B5
Biu 185 H3
Bivolu 153 H2
Biwa-ko 169 E8
Biyad, Al 176 H5
Biyagundi 176 C9
Biysk 164 D6
Bizerta 149 B7
Bizerte 181 G1
Bjargtangar 142 S12
Bjelovar 152 D3
Bjerkvik 142 L2
Bjorklinge 143 G6
Bjorksele 142 H4
Bjorna 142 H5
Bjorneborg *Finland* 143 J6
Bjorneborg *Sweden* 143 F7
Bjornevatn 142 N2
Bjornoya 160 C2
Bjurholm 142 H5
Bjursas 143 F6
Bla Bheinn 136 B3
Black *Alaska* 198 G2
Black *Arizona* 207 H4
Black *Arkansas* 208 G3
Black *New York* 205 N5
Blackadder Water 137 F5
Blackall 193 K3
Black Bay 204 F2
Black Belt 209 J4
Blackburn 135 G3
Black Canyon City 206 F3
Blackdown Hills 132 D4
Blackfoot 202 H6
Blackford 137 E4
Black Head 139 D6
Blackhead Bay 139 D6
Blackhill 135 H3
Black Hills 203 N5
Black Isle 136 D3
Black Mesa 206 G2
Blackmill 132 D3
Black Mountain 132 D3
Black Mountains 132 D3
Blackpool 135 F3
Black Range 207 J4
Black River Falls 204 E4
Blackrock 138 K5
Black Rock Desert 202 E7
Black Sea 131 P7
Blacksod Bay 138 B4
Blackstairs Mount 139 J7
Blackstairs Mountains 139 J7
Blackthorn 133 F3
Black Volta 184 E4
Black Water 137 E4
Blackwater *Australia* 193 K3
Blackwater *Meath, Ireland* 138 J5
Blackwater *Waterford, Ireland* 139 F8
Blackwater *Essex, U.K.* 133 H3
Blackwater *Hampshire, U.K.* 133 G3
Blackwaterfoot 137 C5
Blackwater Lake 199 L3
Blackwater Reservoir *Highland, U.K.* 137 D4
Blackwater Reservoir *Tayside, U.K.* 137 E4
Blackwell 208 D2
Blackwood 192 D5
Blaenavon 132 D3
Blafjall 142 W12
Blagodarnyy 159 G6
Blagoevgrad 153 G4
Blagoveshchensk *Russia* 158 K4
Blagoveshchensk *Russia* 165 M6
Blagoyevo 158 H3
Blair Atholt 137 E4
Blairgowrie 137 E4
Blaka 181 H4
Blakely 209 K5
Blakeney 133 J2
Blakesley 133 F2
Blanca, Bahia 219 D7
Blanca, Costa 147 F3
Blanca Peak 207 K2
Blanca, Punta 206 E6
Blanca, Sierra 207 K4
Blanc, Cap 149 B7
Blanche Channel 194 H6
Blanche, Lake 193 H4
Blanchland 135 G2
Blanc, Mont 145 G6
Blanco 216 E7
Blanco, Cabo 219 C9
Blanco, Cape 202 B6
Blanda 142 V12
Blandford Forum 133 E4
Blanes 147 H2
Blangy 144 D4
Blankenberge 144 E3
Blanquilla, Isla 216 E1
Blantyre 187 G6
Blarney 139 E9
Blasket Islands 139 A8
Blavet 145 B5
Blaydon 135 H2
Blaye 145 C6
Bleadon 132 E3
Bleaklow Hill 135 H3
Bled 152 C2
Blekinge 143 F8
Bletchley 133 G3
Bleus, Monts 187 F2
Blida 181 F1
Bligh Water 194 R8
Blind River 204 J3
Blisworth 133 G2
Block Island 205 Q6
Bloemfontein 188 E5
Blois 145 D5
Blonduos 142 U12
Bloodvein 203 R2
Bloody Foreland 138 F2
Bloomfield 204 D6
Bloomington *Illinois* 204 F6
Bloomington *Indiana* 204 G7
Bloomington *Minnesota* 204 D4
Bloomsbury 193 K3
Blouberg 188 E4
Blubberhouses 135 H3
Bludenz 148 B2
Bluefield 205 K8
Bluefields 212 F9
Blue Mountain Lake 205 N5
Blue Mountain Peak 212 J5
Blue Mountains 202 E5
Bluemull Sound 136 A1
Bluenose Lake 199 M2
Blue Ridge 209 K3
Blue Ridge Mountains 209 L3
Blue Stack 138 F3
Blue Stack Mountains 138 F3
Bluff *New Zealand* 195 B7
Bluff *U.S.A.* 207 H2
Bluff Knoll 192 D5
Bluff Point 192 C4
Bluff, Punta 206 F6
Blumenau 218 G5
Blunt 203 Q5
Blyth *Northumberland, U.K.* 135 H1
Blyth *Nottinghamshire, U.K.* 135 H3
Blyth *Suffolk, U.K.* 133 J2
Blythe 206 E4
Blythe Bridge 133 E2
Blytheville 208 H3
Bo 184 C4
Boac 171 G3
Boa Fe 216 C5
Boa Vista *Cape Verde* 184 L7
Boa Vista *Amazonas, Brazil* 216 D4
Boa Vista *Roraima, Brazil* 216 E3
Bobai 173 M4
Bobaomby, Tanjoni 189 J2
Bobbili 172 F5
Bobbio 148 B3
Bobo Dioulasso 184 E3
Bobolice 151 G2
Bobr 150 F3
Bobrinets 159 E6
Bobrka 151 L4
Bobrov 159 G5
Bobures 213 M10
Boca del Pao 216 E2
Boca do Acre 216 D5
Boca Grande 216 E2
Bocaiuva 218 H3
Boca Mavaca 216 D3
Bocaranga 182 C6
Boca Raton 209 M7
Bochnia 151 J4
Bocholt 150 B3
Bochum 150 B3
Bodalla 193 L6
Bodaybo 165 J5
Boddam 136 A2
Boden 142 J4
Bodensee 150 C5
Bodhan 172 E5
Bodmin 132 C4
Bodmin Moor 132 C4
Bodo 142 F3
Bodrum 156 B4
Bodva 151 J4
Bodza, Pasul 153 J3
Boen 145 F6
Boende 186 D3
Boffa 184 C3
Bogalusa 208 H5
Bogan 193 K5
Bogaz 156 E2
Bogazkale 156 F2
Bogazkaya 157 F2
Bogazkopru 156 F3
Bogazliyan 156 F3
Bogbonga 186 C2
Bogen 142 L2
Boggeragh Mountains 139 E8
Boghar 147 H5
Bogia 194 D2
Bognes 142 G2
Bognor Regis 133 G4
Bogo 171 G3
Bogodukhov 159 F5
Bogong, Mount 193 K6
Bogor 170 D7
Bogorodchany 151 L4
Bogorodskoye *Russia* 158 J4
Bogorodskoye *Russia* 165 Q6
Bogota 216 C3
Bogotol 164 D5
Bogra 173 G4
Boguchany 164 F5
Boguchar 159 G6
Bogue 180 C5
Bogue Chitto 208 G5
Boguslav 159 E6
Bo Hai 167 K4
Bohemia 150 E4
Bohmer Wald 150 E4
Bohol 171 G4
Bohol Sea 171 G4
Boiano 149 E5
Boigul 194 C3
Boipeba, Ilha 217 K6
Bois Blanc Island 204 H4
Boisdale, Loch 137 A3
Boise *U.S.A.* 202 F6
Boise *U.S.A.* 202 F6
Boise City 207 L2
Bois, Lac des 198 K2
Boissevain 203 P3
Boizenburg 150 D2
Bojana 154 E2
Bojnurd 175 N3
Boka 153 F3
Boka Kotorska 152 E4
Boke 184 C3
Bokhara 193 K4
Boknafjord 143 A7
Bokol 187 G2
Bokoro 182 C5
Boksitogorsk 158 E4
Boktor 165 P6
Bokungu 186 D3
Bolama 184 B3
Bolanos 210 H7
Bolan Pass 172 C3
Bolbec 144 D4
Bolchary 164 Ae5
Bole 184 E4
Boleslawiec 150 F3
Bolgatanga 184 E3
Bolgrad 159 D6
Boli 168 C3
Bolia 186 C3
Boliden 142 J4
Bolinao 171 F2
Bol Irgiz 159 H5
Bolivar 219 D7
Bolivar *Missouri* 204 D8
Bolivar *Tennessee* 208 H3
Bolivar, Cerro 213 R11
Bolivar, Pico 213 M10
Bolivia 218 C3
Boljevac 153 F4
Bolkhov 159 F5
Bollington 135 G3
Bollnas 143 G6
Bollon 193 K4
Bollstabruk 142 G5
Bolmen 143 E8
Bolobo 186 C3
Bologna 148 C3
Bologoye 158 E4
Bolotnoye 164 C5
Boloven, Cao Nguyen 173 L5
Bolsena, Lago di 149 C4
Bolsherechye 164 A5
Bolsheretsk 165 T6
Bolshevik 165 R4
Bolshevik, Ostrov 161 M2
Bolshezemelskaya Tundra 158 K2
Bolshoy Anyuy 165 U3
Bolshoy Atlym 164 Ae4
Bolshoy Balkhan, Khrebet 175 M2
Bolshoy Begichev, Ostrov 164 J2
Bolshoy Chernigovka 159 J5
Bolshoy Kavkaz 157 L1
Bolshoy Kunyak 164 A5
Bolshoy Lyakhovskiy, Ostrov 165 Q2
Bolshoy Murta 164 E5
Bolshoy Pit 164 E5
Bolshoy Porog 164 E3
Bolshoy Shantar, Ostrov 165 P5
Bolshoy Usa 158 K4
Bolshoy Yenisey 164 E6
Bolshoy Yugan 164 A5
Bolsover 135 H3
Boltana 147 G1
Bolt Head 132 D4
Bolton *Greater Manchester, U.K.* 135 G3
Bolton *Northumberland, U.K.* 137 G5
Bolu 156 D2
Bolucan 157 G3
Bolus Head 139 B9
Bolvadin 156 D3
Bolyarovo 153 J4
Bolzano 148 C2
Bom 194 D3
Boma 186 B4
Bombala 193 K6
Bombay (Mumbai) 172 D5
Bomili 186 E2
Bom Jesus 217 J5
Bom Jesus da Lapa 217 J6
Bomlafjord 143 A7
Bomlo 143 A7
Bomongo 186 C2
Bonab 174 H3
Bonaire 213 N8
Bonaire Trench 213 N9
Bona, Mount 198 G3
Bonar Bridge 136 D3
Bonavista 201 R8
Bonavista Bay 201 R8
Bon, Cap 181 H1
Bondo 186 D2
Bondokodi 171 F7
Bondoukou 184 E4
Bone 149 A7
Bo'ness 137 E4
Bonete, Cerro 218 C5
Bone, Teluk 171 G6
Bongabong 171 G3
Bongor 182 C5
Bonham 208 D4
Bonifacio 149 B5
Bonifacio, Strait of 149 B5
Bonn 150 B3
Bonners Ferry 202 F3
Bonnetable 144 D4
Bonneval 144 D4
Bonneville 145 G5
Bonneville Salt Flats 202 H7
Bonnie Rock 192 D5
Bonny *France* 145 E5
Bonny *Nigeria* 185 G5
Bonnyrigg 137 E5
Bono 149 B5
Bonobono 171 F4
Bonorva 149 B5
Bonthe 184 C4
Bontoc 171 G2
Booligal 193 J5
Boologooro 192 C3
Boone *Iowa* 204 D5
Boone *N. Carolina* 209 M2
Booneville *Mississippi* 208 H3
Booneville *New York* 205 N5
Booroorban 193 J5
Boosaaso 183 J5
Boothia, Gulf of 200 J4
Boothia Peninsula 200 H3
Bootle 135 F3
Boot Reefs 194 C3
Bopeechee 193 H4
Boquilla, Presa de la 207 K7
Boquillas del Carmen 207 L6
Bor *Sudan* 182 F6
Bor *Turkey* 156 F4
Bor *Yugoslavia* 153 G3
Boraha, Nosy 189 J3
Borah Peak 202 H5
Boras 143 E8
Borasambar 172 F4
Borazjan 175 K7
Borba 216 F4
Borborema, Planalto da 217 K5
Borca 153 H2
Borcka 157 J2
Bordeaux 145 C6
Borden Island 200 D2
Borden Peninsula 200 K3
Borders 137 F5
Bordertown 193 J6
Bordeyri 142 U12
Bordj-Bou-Arreridj 147 J4
Bordj Bounaama 147 G5
Bordj Omar Driss 181 G3
Borensberg 143 F7
Boreray 136 A3
Borga 143 L6
Borgarnes 142 U12
Borgefjellet 142 E4
Borger 207 M3
Borgholm 143 G8
Borgo San Lorenzo 148 C4
Borgosesia 148 B3
Borgo Val di Taro 148 B3
Borgo Valsugana 148 C2
Borislav 151 K4
Borisoglebsk 159 G5
Borispol 159 E5
Borja 147 F2
Borkovskaya 158 H2
Borkum 150 B2
Borlange 143 F6
Borlu 156 C3
Bormida 148 B3
Bormio 148 C2
Borneo 170 E5
Bornholm 150 F1
Bornholmsgattet 143 F9
Bornova 156 B3
Borohoro Shan 166 E3
Boroko 171 G5
Boromo 184 E3
Boronga Islands 173 H5
Borongan 171 H3

Borovichi 158 E4
Borovlyanka 164 C6
Borovsk 158 K4
Borovskoye 164 Ad6
Borrika 193 J6
Borris 139 J7
Borrisokane 139 F7
Borrisoleigh 139 G7
Borroloola 193 H2
Borrowdale 135 F2
Borshchev 153 J1
Borshchovochnyy Khrebet 165 J6
Borth 132 C2
Borujen 175 K6
Borujerd 174 J5
Borve 137 A4
Borzhomi 157 K2
Borzya 165 K7
Bosa 149 B5
Bosanski Brod 152 E3
Bosanski Novi 152 D3
Bosanski Petrovac 152 D3
Boscastle 132 C4
Bose 173 L4
Bos Gradiska 152 D3
Boshruyeh 175 N5
Bosilegrad 153 G4
Boskovice 151 G4
Bosna 152 E3
Bosnia-Herzegovina 152 D3
Bosnik 194 B2
Bosobolo 186 C2
Boso-hanto 169 H8
Bosphorus 156 C2
Bossambele 182 C6
Bossangoa 182 C6
Bossier City 208 F4
Bostan *Iran* 174 H6
Bostan *Pakistan* 172 C2
Bostanabad 174 H3
Bosten Bagrax Hu 166 F3
Boston *U.K.* 133 G2
Boston *U.S.A.* 205 Q5
Boston Mountains 208 E3
Botesdale 133 J2
Botev 153 H4
Botevgrad 153 G4
Bothel 135 F2
Bothnia, Gulf of 142 J5
Botna 153 K2
Botosani 153 J2
Botsmark 142 J4
Botswana 188 D4
Botte Donato 149 F6
Bottenhavet 143 H6
Bottenviken 142 K4
Bottesford 133 G2
Bottineau 203 P3
Bottisham 133 H2
Bottrop 150 B3
Botucatu 218 G4
Bouafle 184 D4
Bouake 184 D4
Bouar 182 C6
Bouarfa 180 E2
Boucant Bay 193 G1
Bouchegouf 149 A7
Bougainville 194 E3
Bougainville, Cape 192 F1
Bougainville Reef 193 K2
Bougainville Strait 194 J5
Bougaroun, Cap 181 G1
Bougie 147 J4
Bougouni 180 D6
Bougzdul 147 H5
Bouhalloufa 147 G4
Bouillon 144 F4
Bouira 147 H4
Bou Ismail 147 H4
Boujdour 180 C3
Bou Kadir 147 G4
Boulay 144 G4
Boulder 203 M8
Boulder City 206 E3
Boulogne-sur-Mer 144 D3
Boumbe I 182 C7
Boumbe II 182 C7
Boumo 182 C6
Bouna 184 E4
Boundiali 184 D4
Boung Long 173 L6
Boun Tai 173 K4
Bountiful 202 J7
Bounty Islands 191 S11
Bourail 194 W16
Bourbon-l'Archambault 145 E5
Bourbonnais *France* 145 E5
Bourbonnais *U.S.A.* 204 G6
Bourbonne-les-Bains 145 F5
Bourem 180 E5
Bourganeuf 145 D6
Bourg-en-Bresse 145 F5
Bourges 145 E5
Bourgogne 145 F5
Bourgogne, Canal de 145 E5
Bourg-Saint-Andeol 145 F6
Bourke 193 K5
Bourne 133 G2
Bournemouth 133 F4
Bou Saada 181 F1
Boussac 145 E5
Bousso 182 C5
Boutilimit 180 C5
Boves 148 A3
Bovey 132 D4
Bovey Tracy 132 D4
Bovingdon 133 G3
Bovino 149 E5
Bow 202 H2
Bowbells 203 N3
Bowen 193 K3
Bowers Bank 198 Ab9
Bowes 135 G2
Bowfell 135 F2
Bowie 208 D4
Bow Island 202 J3
Bowkan 174 H3
Bowland, Forest of 135 G2
Bowling Green *Kentucky* 204 G8
Bowling Green *Ohio* 204 J6
Bowman 203 N4
Bowman Bay 200 M4
Bowness 135 G2
Bowness-on-Solway 135 F2
Bowraville 193 L5
Boxford 133 H2
Bo Xian 173 N2
Boxing 167 M4
Box Tank 193 J5
Boyabat 156 F2
Boyang 167 M6
Boyarka 164 F2
Boyd Lake 199 Q3
Boyer 204 C6
Boyle 138 F5
Boyne 138 K5
Boynton Beach 209 M7
Boyuibe 218 D4
Bozburun 156 C4
Bozcaada 155 H3
Boz Daglari 156 B3
Bozdogan 156 C4
Bozeman 202 J5
Bozen 148 C2
Boze Pole 151 G1
Bozkir 156 E4
Bozkurt 156 E2
Bozoum 182 C6
Bozova 157 H4
Bozqush, Kuh-e 174 H3
Bozuyuk 156 D3
Bra 148 A3
Brabant Island 221 V6
Brabourne 133 H3
Brac 152 D4
Bracadale 136 B3
Bracadale, Loch 136 B3
Bracciano 149 D4
Bracke 142 F5
Brackley 133 F2
Bracknell 133 G3
Brad 153 G2
Bradano 149 F5
Bradda Head 134 E2
Bradenton 209 L7
Bradford *U.K.* 135 H3
Bradford *U.S.A.* 205 L6
Bradford-on-Avon 132 E3
Bradwell Waterside 133 H3
Brady 207 N5
Brady Mountains 207 N5
Brae 136 A1
Braemar 137 E3
Braemore 136 E2
Braeswick 136 F1
Braga 146 B2
Bragado 219 D7
Braganca 146 C2
Braganca Paulista 218 G4
Bragar 136 B2
Brahman Baria 173 H4
Brahmani 172 G4
Brahmapur 172 F5
Brahmaputra 173 H3
Braidwood 193 K6
Braila 153 J3
Brailsford 133 F2
Brainerd 204 C3
Braintree 133 H3
Braishfield 133 F3
Brake 150 C2
Brakel 150 C3
Brallos 155 G3
Bramdean 133 F3
Bramham 135 H3
Bramming 143 C9
Brampton *Canada* 205 L5
Brampton *U.K.* 135 G2
Bramsche 150 B2
Brancaster 133 H2
Brancaster Bay 133 H2
Branco 216 E3
Branco, Cabo 217 L5
Brandberg 188 B4
Brandbu 143 D6
Brande 143 C9
Brandenburg 150 E2
Brandesburton 135 J3
Brandon *Canada* 203 Q3
Brandon *U.S.A.* 205 P5
Brandon Bay 139 B8
Brandon Mount 139 B8
Brandon Point 139 B8
Brandval 143 E6
Branesti 153 J3
Braniewo 151 H1
Bran, Pasul 153 H3
Brantford 205 K5
Brantley 209 J5
Brantome 145 D6
Brasileia 216 D6
Brasilia *Distrito Federal, Brazil* 218 F3
Brasilia *Minas Gerais, Brazil* 218 H3
Braslav 143 M9
Brasov 153 H3
Brassey Range 171 F5
Brates, Lacul 153 K3
Bratislava 151 G4
Bratsk 164 G5
Bratslav 153 K1
Braunau 148 D1
Braunsberg 151 H1
Braunschweig 150 D2
Braunton 132 C3
Brava 184 L7
Brava, Costa 147 H2
Bravo del Norte, Rio 207 L6
Brawley 206 E4
Bray 139 K6
Bray Head 139 B9
Bray Island 200 L4
Brazil 217 G5
Brazos 208 D5
Brazzaville 186 C3
Brcko 152 E3
Brda 151 G2
Breadalbane 137 D4
Breaksea Sound 195 A6
Brean 132 D3
Brebes 170 D7
Brechfa 132 C3
Brechin 137 F4
Breckenridge *Texas* 208 C4
Breckenridge *Minnesota* 204 B3
Breckland 133 H2
Brecknock, Peninsula 219 B10
Breclav 151 G4
Brecon 132 D3
Brecon Beacons 132 D3
Breda 144 F3
Bredon Hill 133 F3
Bredstedt 150 C1
Breezewood 205 L7
Bregenz 148 B2
Bregovo 153 G3
Breidafjordur 142 T12
Brejo 217 J4
Brekken 142 D5
Brekstad 142 C5
Bremen *U.S.A.* 209 K4
Bremen *Germany* 150 C2
Bremerhaven 150 C2
Bremer Range 192 E5
Bremerton 202 C4
Bremervorde 150 C2
Brendon Hills 132 D3
Brenham 208 D5
Brenig, Llyn 135 F3
Brenish 136 A2
Brenner Pass 148 C2
Breno 148 C3
Brenta 148 C3
Brentford 133 G2
Brentwood *U.K.* 133 H3
Brentwood *U.S.A.* 205 P6
Brescia 148 C3
Breskens 144 E3
Breslau 151 G3
Bressanone 148 C2
Bressay 136 A2
Bressay Sound 136 A2
Bressuire 145 C5
Brest *France* 144 A4
Brest *Belorussia* 151 K2
Brestlitovsk 159 E5
Brest Litovsk 151 K2
Bretagne 144 B4
Bretcu 153 J2
Breteuil *France* 144 D4
Breteuil *France* 144 E4
Breton, Cape 201 Q8
Breton Sound 208 H6
Brett 133 H2
Brett, Cape 195 E1
Breueh 170 B4
Brevoort Island 200 P5
Brewer 205 R4
Brewster 202 E3
Brewton 209 J5
Breznice 150 E4
Brezo, Sierra del 146 D1
Bria 182 D6
Briancon 145 G6
Brianne, Llyn 132 D2
Briare 145 E5
Bribie Island 193 L4
Brichany 153 J1
Bricquebec 133 N7
Bride 134 E2
Bridestowe 132 C4
Bridgend *Mid Glamorgan, U.K.* 132 D3
Bridgend *Strathclyde, U.K.* 137 B5
Bridge of Allan 137 E4
Bridge of Gaur 137 D4
Bridge of Orchy 137 D4
Bridge of Weir 137 D5
Bridgeport *Alabama* 209 K3
Bridgeport *California* 206 C1
Bridgeport *Connecticut* 205 P6
Bridgeport *Nebraska* 203 N7
Bridgeton 205 N7
Bridgetown *Australia* 192 D5
Bridgetown *Barbados* 213 T8
Bridgetown *Canada* 201 N9
Bridgewater 201 P9
Bridgnorth 132 E2
Bridgwater 132 D3
Bridgwater Bay 132 D3
Bridlington 135 J2
Bridlington Bay 135 J2
Bridport 132 E4
Brieg 151 G3
Brienne-le-Chateau 144 F4
Brier Island 205 S4
Briey 144 F4
Brig 148 A2
Brigg 135 J3
Brighouse 135 H3
Brightlingsea 133 J3
Brighton 133 G4
Brignoles 145 G7
Brihuega 146 E2
Brikama 184 B3
Brindakit 165 P4
Brindisi 149 F5
Brinian 136 F1
Brinkley 208 G3
Brioude 145 E6
Brisbane 193 L4
Bristol *U.K.* 132 E3
Bristol *U.S.A* 205 P6
Bristol Bay 198 D4
Bristol Channel 132 D2
Bristol Lake 206 E3
Bristow 208 D3
British Columbia 198 L4
Brits 188 E5
Britstown 188 D6
Brittle, Lake 137 B3
Brive-la-Gaillarde 145 D6
Briviesca 146 E1
Brixham 132 D4
Brlik 166 C3
Brno 151 G4
Broad 209 M3
Broadback 201 L7
Broad Bay 136 B2
Broad Cairn 137 E4
Broad Haven 138 C4
Broad Hinton 133 F3
Broadhurst Range 192 E3
Broad Sound *Australia* 193 K3
Broad Sound *U.K.* 132 B3
Broadstairs 133 J3
Broads, The 133 J2
Broadus 203 M5
Broadway 133 F2
Brochel 136 B3
Brocken 150 D3
Brockenhurst 133 F4
Brock Island 200 D2
Brockman, Mount 192 D3
Brockton 205 Q5
Brod 153 F5
Broddanes 142 U12
Brodeur Peninsula 200 J3
Brodick 137 C5
Brodick Bay 137 C5
Brodnica 151 H2
Brodokalmak 164 Ad5
Brody 159 D5
Brok 151 J2
Broken Bay 193 L5
Broken Bow *Nebraska* 203 Q7
Broken Bow *Oklahoma* 208 E3
Broken Bow Lake 208 E3
Broken Hill *Australia* 193 J5
Broken Hill *Zambia* 187 E5
Bromberg 151 G2
Bromley 133 H3
Bromsgrove 133 E2
Bromyard 132 E2
Bronderslev 143 C8
Bronnoysund 142 E4
Bronte 149 E7
Brookfield 204 D7
Brookhaven 208 G5
Brookings *Oregon* 202 B6
Brookings *S. Dakota* 203 R5
Brookneal 205 L8
Brooks 202 H2
Brooks Range 198 D2
Brooksville 209 L6
Broome 192 E2
Broom, Loch 136 C3
Brora *U.K.* 136 D2
Brora *U.K.* 136 E2
Brosteni 153 G3
Broto 147 F1
Brotton 135 J2
Brou 144 D4
Brough 135 G2
Brough Head 136 E1
Brough Ness 136 F2
Broughshane 138 K3
Broughton 137 E5
Broughton in Furness 135 F2
Broughton Island 200 P4
Broughton Poggs 133 F3
Browerville 204 C3
Brow Head 139 C10
Brownfield 207 L4
Brownhills 133 F2
Browning 202 H3
Brownsville 208 D8
Brownwood 208 C5

C

Carryduff 138 L3
Carsamba 156 E4
Carsamba 157 G2
Carsibasi 157 H2
Carson City 206 C1
Carson Sink 202 E8
Carsphairn 137 D5
Cartagena *Colombia* 216 B1
Cartagena *Spain* 147 F4
Cartago *Colombia* 216 B3
Cartago *Costa Rica* 212 F10
Cartaret 133 N7
Cartaxo 146 B3
Cartaya 146 C4
Carteret 144 C4
Carterton 195 E4
Carthage *Missouri* 204 C8
Carthage *Texas* 208 E4
Cartier Island 190 F4
Cartwright 201 Q7
Caruara 217 K5
Carumbo 186 C4
Carupano 216 E1
Caruthersville 208 H2
Carvoeiro, Cabo 146 B3
Cary 132 E3
Casablanca 180 D2
Casa Grande 206 G4
Casale Monferrato 148 B3
Casalmaggiore 148 C3
Casamance 184 B3
Casanare 216 C2
Casas Ibanez 147 F3
Cascade 202 F5
Cascade Mountains 202 D3
Cascade Point 195 B5
Cascade Range 202 C6
Cascais 146 B3
Cascapedia 205 S2
Cascavel *Ceara, Brazil* 217 K4
Cascavel *Parana, Brazil* 218 F4
Caschuil 218 C5
Caserta 149 E5
Casey 221 H5
Cashel 139 G7
Casiguran 171 G2
Casilda 218 D6
Casma 216 B5
Casnewydd 132 E3
Caspe 147 F2
Casper 203 L6
Caspian Sea 131 S7
Cass 204 J5
Cassamba 186 D5
Casse, Grande 145 G6
Cassiar Mountains 198 J3
Cassinga 186 C6
Cassino 149 D5
Cass Lake *U.S.A.* 204 C3
Cass Lake *U.S.A.* 204 C3
Cassongue 186 B5
Casteljaloux 145 D6
Castellammare del Golfo 149 D6
Castellammare, Golfo di 149 D6
Castellane 145 G7
Castellar de Santiago 146 E3
Castellar de Santisteban 146 E3
Castelli 219 E7
Castellnedd 132 D3
Castellon de la Plana 147 F3
Castellote 147 F2
Castelnaudary 145 D7
Castelo Branco 146 C3
Castelsarrasin 145 D6
Casteltermini 149 D7
Castelvetrano 149 D7
Castets 145 C7
Castilla la Nueva 146 E3
Castilla la Vieja 146 D2
Castilletes 216 C1
Castillo, Pampa del 219 C9
Castillos 219 F6
Castlebar 138 D5
Castlebay 137 A4
Castlebellingham 138 K5
Castleblayney 138 J4
Castle Bolton 135 H2
Castle Carrock 135 G2
Castleconnel 139 F7
Castledawson 138 J3
Castlederg 138 G3
Castledermot 139 J7
Castle Douglas 134 F2
Castleellis 139 K8
Castleford 135 H3
Castleisland 139 D8
Castlemaine 193 J6
Castlemartyr 139 F9
Castlepollard 138 H5
Castlerea 138 E5
Castle Rock 203 M8
Castleside 135 H2
Castleton 135 H3
Castletown *Highland, U.K.* 136 E2
Castletown *Isle of Man, U.K.* 134 E2
Castletownbere 139 C9
Castletownshend 139 D9
Castlewellan 138 L4
Castonos 207 M7
Castor 202 J1
Castres 145 E7
Castries 213 S7
Castro 219 B8
Castro Alves 217 K6
Castro del Rio 146 D4
Castropol 146 C1
Castro Urdiales 146 E1
Castro Verde 146 B4
Castrovillari 149 F6
Castuera 146 D3
Caswell Sound 195 A6
Cat 157 J3
Catacamas 212 E7
Catacaos 216 A5
Cataingan 171 G3
Catak 157 K3
Catakkopru 157 J3
Catalca 156 C2
Cataluna 147 G2
Catalzeytin 156 F2
Catamarca 218 C5
Catanduanes 171 G3
Catanduva 218 G4
Catania 149 E7
Catanzaro 149 F6
Cataqueama 216 E6
Catastrophie, Cape 193 H5
Catatumbo 213 L10
Catbalogan 171 G3
Caterham 133 G3
Catete 186 B4
Cathcart 188 E6
Cat Island 213 K2
Cato 191 N6
Catoche, Cabo 211 R7
Catria, Monte 148 D4
Catrimani *Brazil* 216 E3
Catrimani *Brazil* 216 E3
Catskill 205 P5
Catskill Mountains 205 N5
Catwick Islands 173 L6
Cauca 213 K11
Caucaia 217 K4
Caucasia 213 K11
Caucasus 157 L1
Cauit Point 171 H4
Caulkerbush 135 F1
Caungula 186 C4
Cauquenes 219 B7
Caura 213 Q11
Causapscal 205 S2
Caussade 145 D6
Cauterets 145 C7
Cauto 212 J4
Cauvery 172 E6
Cavado 146 B2
Cavaillon 145 F7
Cavalcante 218 H6
Cavally 184 D4
Cavan *Ireland* 138 H5
Cavan *Ireland* 138 H5
Cavdir 156 C4
Cavendish 133 H2
Cavite 171 G3
Caxias 216 C4
Caxias 217 J4
Caxias do Sul 218 E5
Caxito 186 B4
Cay 156 D3
Cayagzi 156 F2
Caycuma 156 E2
Cayeli 157 J2
Cayenne 217 G3
Cayeux 144 D3
Caygoren Baraji 156 C3
Cayiralan 157 F3
Cayirli 157 H3
Caykara 157 J2
Caylarbasi 157 H4
Cayman Brac 212 H5
Cayman Trench 212 F5
Caynabo 183 J6
Cayuga Lake 205 M5
Cazalla de la Sierra 146 D4
Cazma *Croatia* 152 D3
Cazma *Croatia* 152 D3
Cazombo 186 D5
Cazorla 146 E4
Cea 146 D1
Ceahlau 153 H2
Ceanannus Mor 138 J5
Ceara 217 K5
Ceara-Mirim 217 K5
Ceballos 207 K7
Cebollera 146 E1
Cebu *Philippines* 171 G3
Cebu *Philippines* 171 G3
Cecina 148 C4
Cedar 204 D5
Cedar City 206 F2
Cedar Creek Lake 208 D4
Cedar Falls 204 D5
Cedar Lake 199 Q5
Cedar Rapids 204 E6
Cedartown 209 K3
Cedros, Isla de 206 E6
Ceduna 193 G5
Ceelbuur 183 J7
Ceeldheer 183 J7
Ceerigaabo 183 J5
Cefalu 149 E6
Cega 146 D2
Cegled 152 E2
Ceica 153 G2
Cekerek *Turkey* 157 F2
Cekerek *Turkey* 156 F2
Celalli 157 G3
Celano 149 D4
Celaya 211 J7
Celebes 171 G6
Celebi 156 E3
Celestun 211 P7
Celikhan 157 H3
Celina 204 H6
Celje 152 C2
Celle 150 D2
Celtik 156 D3
Celyn, Llyn 132 D2
Cemaes Head 132 C2
Cemilbey 156 F2
Cemisgezek 157 H3
Cendrawasih, Teluk 171 K6
Cenga 171 H6
Cenrana 171 F6
Center 208 E5
Centinela, Picacho Del 207 L6
Cento 148 C3
Central 137 D4
Central African Republic 182 D6
Central Brahui Range 172 C3
Central, Cordillera *Colombia* 216 B3
Central, Cordillera *Dominican Republic* 213 M5
Central, Cordillera *Peru* 216 B5
Central, Cordillera *Philippines* 171 G2
Central Heights 206 G4
Centralia 202 C4
Central Makran Range 172 B3
Central, Massif 145 E6
Central Range 194 C2
Central Siberian Plateau 164 H3
Cephalonia 155 F3
Cepu 170 E7
Ceram 171 H6
Cercal 146 B4
Cerchov 150 E4
Ceres 218 G3
Ceret 145 E7
Cerignola 149 E5
Cerigo 155 G4
Cerkes 156 E2
Cerkeskoy 156 B2
Cermei 153 F2
Cermik 157 H3
Cerna *Romania* 153 G3
Cerna *Romania* 153 K3
Cerne Abbas 132 E4
Cerralvo 208 C7
Cerralvo, Isla 210 E5
Cerreto Sannita 149 E5
Cerro Azul 216 B6
Cerro de Pasco 216 B6
Cerro Machin 211 L9
Cerro Manantiales 219 C10
Cerros Colorados, Embalse 219 C7
Cervaro 149 E5
Cervati, Monte 149 E6
Cervera 147 G2
Cervera de Pisuerga 146 D1
Cervia 148 D3
Cervione 149 B4
Cesar 213 L9
Cesena 148 D3
Cesenatico 148 D3
Cesis 143 L8
Ceske Budejovice 150 F4
Cesky Brod 150 F3
Cesme 156 B3
Cessnock 193 L5
Cetate 153 G3
Cetinje 152 E4
Cetinkaya 157 G3
Cetraro 149 E6
Ceuta 146 D4
Ceva-i-Ra 191 R6
Cevennes 145 F6
Cevherli 156 F4
Cevio 148 B2
Cevizli 156 D4
Ceyhan *Turkey* 156 F4
Ceyhan *Turkey* 157 F4
Ceylanpinar 157 J4
Chaadayevka 159 H5
Chablis 145 E5
Chacabuco 219 D6
Chachani, Nevado de 218 B3
Chachapoyas 216 B5
Chachoengsao 173 K6
Chaco Austral 218 D5
Chaco Boreal 218 E4
Chaco Central 218 D4
Chad 182 C5
Chad *Russia* 158 K4
Chadan 164 E6
Chadderton 135 G3
Chaddesley Corbett 133 E2
Chadileovu 219 C7
Chad, Lake 182 B5
Chadobets 164 F5
Chadron 203 N6
Chagai Hills 172 B3
Chagda 165 N5
Chaghcharan 175 S4
Chagny 145 F5
Chagoda 158 F4
Chagos Archipelago 162 F7
Chahah Burjah 175 R6
Chah Bahar 175 Q9
Chahbounia 147 H5
Chaho 168 B5
Chahuites 211 M9
Chaibasa 172 G4
Chai Buri 173 K5
Chaiya 173 J7
Chaiyaphum 173 K5
Chajari 218 E6
Chala 216 C7
Chalais 145 D6
Chalap Dalan 172 B2
Chala, Punta 216 B7
Chalatenango 212 C7
Chaldonka 165 K6
Chale 133 F4
Chaleur, Baie de 201 N8
Chaleur Bay 205 T3
Chalhuanca 216 C6
Chalisgaon 172 E4
Challaco 219 C7
Challacombe 132 D3
Challans 145 C5
Challis 202 G5
Chalmny Varre 158 F2
Chalna 173 G4
Chalon-sur-Marne 144 F4
Chalon-sur-Saone 145 F5
Chalus 145 D6
Chalus 175 K3
Cham 150 E4
Chama 207 J2
Chaman 172 C2
Chamba *India* 172 E2
Chamba *Russia* 164 G4
Chambal 172 E3
Chamberlain *Australia* 192 F2
Chamberlain *U.S.A.* 203 Q6
Chambersburg 205 M7
Chambery 145 F6
Chamela 210 G8
Chamical 218 C6
Chamonix 145 G6
Chamouchouane 205 P2
Champagne 144 F4
Champagnole 145 F5
Champaign 204 F6
Champflower 132 D3
Champlaine, Lake 205 P4
Champlitte 145 F5
Champoton 211 P8
Chamrajnagar 172 E6
Chamusca 146 B3
Chanaral 218 B5
Chanaran 175 P3
Chanca 146 C4
Chandalar 198 F2
Chandausi 172 E3
Chandeleur Islands 208 H6
Chandigarh 172 E2
Chandler 201 P8
Chandmani *Mongolia* 166 G2
Chandmani *Mongolia* 166 H2
Chandpur 173 H4
Chandrapur 172 E5
Chandvad 172 D4
Chanf 175 Q8
Changan 173 L2
Changane 189 F4
Changbai 168 B5
Changbai Shan 168 B4
Changchun 167 P3
Changde 173 M3
Chang-hua 167 N7
Chang Jiang 167 M5
Chang, Ko 173 K6
Changle 167 M4
Changling 167 N3
Changma 166 H4
Changnyon 167 P4
Changsan-got 167 N4
Changsha 173 M3
Changshan 167 M6
Changtai 167 M7
Changting 167 M6
Changwu 173 L1
Changxing 167 M5
Changyi 167 M4
Changzhi 167 L4
Changzhou 167 M5
Channel Islands 133 M7
Channel-Port-aux-Basques 201 Q8
Chantada 146 C1
Chanthaburi 173 K6
Chantilly 144 E4
Chantonnay 145 C5
Chantrey Inlet 200 G4
Chanute 208 E2
Chany, Ozero 164 B6
Chao 216 B5
Chao Hu 167 M5
Chao Phraya 173 K5
Chaor He 167 N2
Chaouen 180 D1
Chaoyang *China* 167 N3
Chaoyang *China* 167 N3
Chaozhou 167 M7
Chapadinha 217 J4
Chapala, Laguna de 210 H7
Chapanda 165 N5
Chapayevo 159 J5
Chapayevsk 159 H5
Chapayev-Zheday 165 K4
Chapchachi 159 H6
Chapeco 218 F5
Chapel-en-le-Frith 135 H3
Chapel Hill 209 N3
Chapeltown *Grampian, U.K.* 136 E3

Chugunash 164 D6
Chuguyevka 168 D3
Chukchi Sea 198 B2
Chuken 168 F2
Chukhloma 158 G4
Chukotat 201 L5
Chukotskiy Khrebet 165 W3
Chukotskiy Poluostrov 161 V3
Chulak-Kurgan 166 B3
Chula Vista 206 D4
Chulman 165 L5
Chulmleigh 132 D4
Chulym *Russia* 164 C5
Chulym *Russia* 164 C5
Chum 158 L2
Chumbicha 218 C5
Chumek 166 F2
Chumikan 165 P6
Chumphon 173 J6
Chuna 164 F5
Chunchon 167 P4
Chungju 167 P4
Chunhua 168 C4
Chunoyar 164 F5
Chunya 187 F4
Chunyang 168 B4
Chunyang 169 B7
Chuquibamba 218 B3
Chuquicamata 218 B4
Chur 148 B2
Churan 165 L4
Churapcha 165 N4
Churchill *Canada* 199 S4
Churchill *Canada* 199 S4
Churchill *Newfoundland, Canada* 201 P7
Churchill, Cape 199 S4
Churchill Falls 201 P7
Churchill Peak 198 L4
Church Stretton 132 E2
Churia Ghati Hills 172 G3
Churin 216 B6
Churu 172 D3
Churuguara 216 D1
Chushevitsy 158 G3
Chushul 172 E2
Chusovaya 158 K4
Chusovoy 158 K4
Chust 166 C3
Chute des Passes 205 Q2
Chuuronjang 168 B5
Chuxiong 173 K4
Chu Yang Sin 173 L6
Chwarta 174 G4
Chyulu Range 187 G3
Cianjur 170 D7
Cicekdagi 156 F3
Cicia 194 S8
Cide 156 E2
Cidones 146 E2
Ciechanow 151 J2
Ciego de Avila 212 H4
Cienaga 216 C1
Cienfuegos 212 G3
Cieszyn 151 H4
Cieza 147 F3
Ciftehan 156 F4
Cifteler 156 D3
Cifuentes 146 E2
Cihanbeyli 156 E3
Cijara, Embalse de 146 D3
Cilacap 170 D7
Cildir 157 K2
Cildir Golu 157 K2
Cilo Dagi 157 L4
Cimarron 208 A2
Cimone, Monte 148 C3
Cimpeni 153 G2
Cimpina 153 H3
Cimpulung 153 H3
Cimpuri 153 J2
Cinar 157 J4
Cinaruco 216 D2
Cina, Tanjung 170 C7
Cinca 147 G2
Cincer 152 D4
Cincinnati 204 H7
Cinderford 132 E3
Cine 156 C4
Cingus 157 H3
Cinto, Monte 149 B4
Circeo, Capo 149 D5
Circle *Alaska* 198 G2
Circle *Montana* 203 M4
Circular Reef 194 D2
Cirebon 170 D7
Cirencester 133 F3
Ciri 216 E5
Ciria 147 E2
Ciro 149 F6
Cisco 208 C4
Cislau 153 J3
Cisna 151 K4
Cisneros 216 B2
Cistierna 146 D1
Citac, Nevado 216 C6
Citlaltepetl, Volcan 211 L8
Citta di Castello 148 D4
Cittanova 149 F6
Ciucului, Muntii 153 H2
Ciudad Acuna 207 M6
Ciudad Bolivar 216 E2
Ciudad Camargo 207 K7
Ciudad Cuauhtemoc 211 P10
Ciudad del Carmen 211 P8
Ciudad del Maiz 211 K6
Ciudad de Mexico 211 K8
Ciudadela 147 H3
Ciudad Guayana 216 E2
Ciudad Guzman 210 H8
Ciudad Ixtepec 211 M9
Ciudad Juarez 207 J5
Ciudad Lerdo 207 L8
Ciudad Madero 211 L6
Ciudad Mante 211 K6
Ciudad Mier 208 C7
Ciudad Obregon 207 H7
Ciudad Ojeda 213 M9
Ciudad Piar 213 R11
Ciudad Real 146 E3
Ciudad Rodrigo 146 C2
Ciudad Valles 211 K7
Ciudad Victoria 211 K6
Civa Burun 157 G2
Cividale del Friuli 148 D2
Civita Castellana 149 D4
Civitanova Marche 148 D4
Civitavecchia 149 C4
Civray 145 D5
Civril 156 C3
Cizre 157 K4
Clach Leathad 137 D4
Clacton-on-Sea 133 J3
Cladich 137 C4
Claerwen Reservoir 132 D2
Clain 145 D5
Claire, Lac a lEau 201 M6
Claire, Lake 199 N4
Clamecy 145 E5
Clane 139 J6
Clanton 209 J4
Clanwilliam 188 C6
Claonaig 137 C5
Clare *Australia* 193 H5
Clare *Ireland* 139 D7
Clare Island 138 B5
Claremont 205 P5
Claremorris 138 D5
Clarence *New Zealand* 195 D5
Clarence *New Zealand* 195 D5
Clarence, Cape 200 H3
Clarence Head 200 L2
Clarence Strait *Australia* 192 G1
Clarence Strait *U.S.A.* 198 J4
Clarence Town 213 K3
Clarinda 204 C6
Clarion 205 L6
Clark 203 K5
Clarke River 193 K2
Clark Fork *Montana* 202 H4
Clark Fork *Washington* 202 F3
Clark, Lake 198 E3
Clarksburg 205 K7
Clarksdale 208 G3
Clarks Hill Lake 209 L4
Clarkston 202 F4
Clarksville *Arkansas* 208 F3
Clarksville *Tennessee* 209 J2
Clar, Loch nan 136 D2
Clatteringshaws Loch 137 D5
Claughton 135 G2
Clavering O 200 X3
Claxton 209 M4
Clay Center 203 R8
Clay Cross 135 H3
Claydon 133 J2
Clayton *Georgia* 209 L3
Clayton *New Mexico* 207 L2
Clear, Cape 139 C10
Clearfield *Pennsylvania* 205 L6
Clearfield *Utah* 202 J7
Clear Fork 207 N4
Clear Hills 199 M4
Clear Island 139 D10
Clear Lake *California* 202 C8
Clear Lake *Iowa* 204 D5
Clear Lake Reservoir 202 D7
Clearwater *Canada* 202 G1
Clearwater *Canada* 199 P4
Clearwater *Florida* 209 L7
Clearwater *Idaho* 202 F4
Clearwater Mountains 202 G4
Cleethorpes 135 J3
Clerke Reef 192 D2
Clermont *Australia* 193 K3
Clermont *France* 144 E4
Clermont-Ferrand 145 E6
Clermont-l'Herault 145 E7
Clervaux 144 G3
Cleve 193 H5
Clevedon 132 E3
Cleveland *U.K.* 135 H2
Cleveland *Mississippi* 208 G4
Cleveland *Ohio* 205 K6
Cleveland *Tennessee* 209 K3
Cleveland *Texas* 208 E5
Cleveland, Cape 193 K2
Cleveland Hills 135 H2
Cleveland, Mount 202 H3
Cleveleys 135 F3
Clew Bay 138 C5
Clifden *Ireland* 139 B6
Clifden *New Zealand* 195 A7
Cliffe 133 H3
Cliffs of Moher 139 D7
Clifton 135 G2
Clincha Alta 216 B6
Clinch Mountains 209 L2
Clingmans Dome 209 L3
Clinton *Canada* 202 D2
Clinton *Illinois* 204 F6
Clinton *Iowa* 204 E6
Clinton *Mississippi* 208 G4
Clinton *Missouri* 204 D7
Clinton *N. Carolina* 209 N3
Clinton *Oklahoma* 208 C3
Clinton-Colden Lake 199 P3
Clipperton Island 197 J7
Clisham 136 B3
Clisson 145 C5
Clitheroe 135 G3
Cliza 218 C3
Cloates, Point 192 C3
Clogheen 139 G8
Clogherhead 138 K5
Clogher Head 138 K5
Clogh Mills 138 K3
Clonakilty 139 E9
Clonakilty Bay 139 E9
Cloncurry *Australia* 193 J3
Cloncurry *Australia* 193 J3
Clonmel 139 G8
Clonmult 139 F9
Clophill 133 G2
Cloppenburg 150 C2
Cloquet 204 D3
Cloud Peak 203 L5
Cloudy Bay 195 E4
Clough 138 L4
Cloughton 135 J2
Clovelly 132 C3
Clovis 207 L3
Cloyes 145 D4
Cluanie, Loch 137 C3
Cluj-Napoca 153 G2
Clun 132 E2
Cluny 145 F5
Cluses 145 G5
Clusone 148 B3
Clutha 195 B7
Clwyd *U.K.* 135 F3
Clwyd *U.K.* 135 F3
Clwydian Range 135 F3
Clyde *Canada* 200 N3
Clyde *U.K.* 137 E5
Clydebank 137 D5
Clyde, Firth of 137 D5
Clydesdale 137 E5
Clynnog-fawr 134 E3
Clywedog, Llyn 132 D2
Coa 146 C2
Coachella 206 D4
Coachella Canal 206 E4
Coaldale 206 D2
Coalinga 206 B2
Coalisland 138 J3
Coal River 198 K4
Coalville 133 F2
Coan, Cerro 216 B5
Coari *Brazil* 216 E4
Coari *Brazil* 216 E4
Coast Mountains 202 B2
Coast Range 202 C5
Coatbridge 137 D5
Coaticook 205 Q4
Coats Island 200 K5
Coats Land 221 Y3
Coatzacoalcos *Mexico* 211 M8
Coatzacoalcos *Mexico* 211 M9
Coban 212 B7
Cobar 193 K5
Cobh 139 F9
Cobija 216 D6
Cobourg 205 L5
Cobram 193 K6
Cobue 189 F2
Coburg 150 D3
Coburg Island 200 L2
Cochabamba 218 C3
Cochem 150 B3
Cochin 172 E7
Cochrane *Canada* 202 G2
Cochrane *Chile* 219 B9
Cock Bridge 137 E3
Cockburn 193 J5
Cockburnspath 137 F5
Cockenzie 137 F4
Cockerham 135 G3
Cockermouth 135 F2
Cockfield *Durham, U.K.* 135 H2
Cockfield *Suffolk, U.K.* 133 H2
Coco 212 E7
Cocoa 209 M6
Coco Channel 173 H6
Coco Islands 173 H6
Cocoparra Range 193 K5
Cocos 217 J6
Cocula 210 H7
Codajas 216 E4
Cod, Cape 205 R6
Codera, Cabo 216 D1
Codfish Island 195 A7
Codford 133 E3
Codigoro 148 D3
Cod Island 201 P6
Codo 217 J4
Codogno 148 B3
Cod's Head 139 B9
Coen 193 J1
Coeroeni 217 F3
Coesfeld 150 B3
Coeur d'Alene 202 F4
Coeur d'Alene Lake 202 F4
Coevorden 144 G2
Coffeyville 208 E2
Coffin Bay 193 H5
Coff's Harbour 193 L5
Cogealac 153 K3
Coghinas 149 B5
Cognac 145 C6
Cogo 185 G5
Cogolludo 146 E2
Cohuna 193 J6
Coiba, Isla 212 G11
Coigach 136 C2
Coigeach, Rubha 136 C2
Coihaique 219 B9
Coimbatore 172 E6
Coimbra 146 B2
Coipasa, Salar de 218 C3
Cokak 157 G4
Colac 193 J6
Colap 157 H4
Colatina 218 E3
Colby 203 P8
Colchester 133 H3
Cold Ashton 132 E3
Coldstream 137 F5
Coldwater *Kansas* 207 N2
Coldwater *Michigan* 204 H6
Colebrook 205 Q4
Coleman *Australia* 193 J1
Coleman *U.S.A.* 207 N5
Colemerick 157 K4
Coleraine *Australia* 193 J6
Coleraine *U.K.* 138 J2
Colesberg 188 E6
Coleshill 133 F2
Coles, Punta de 219 B3
Colfax 202 F4
Colgrave Sound 136 B1
Colhue Huapi, Lago 219 C9
Colima 210 H8
Colima, Nevado de 210 H8
Colinas 217 J5
Colintraive 137 C5
Coll 137 C4
Collatto 148 D2
College Park 209 K4
Collie 192 D5
Collier Bay 192 E2
Colliford Lake Reservoir 132 C4
Collingbourne Kingston 133 F3
Collingham 135 J3
Collingwood *Canada* 205 K4
Collingwood *New Zealand* 195 D4
Collins 208 H5
Collin Top 138 K3
Collooney 138 F4
Colmar 144 G4
Colmars 145 G6
Colmenar 146 D4
Colmenar Viejo 146 E2
Colne *Essex, U.K.* 133 H3
Colne *Lancashire, U.K.* 135 G3
Cologne 150 B3
Colombia 216 C3
Colombo 172 E7
Colomoncagua 212 C7
Colon *Cuba* 212 G3
Colon *Panama* 212 H10
Colonia Las Heras 219 C9
Colonna, Capo 149 F6
Colonsay 137 B4
Colorado *Argentina* 219 D7
Colorado *Arizona* 206 E4
Colorado *Texas* 207 M4
Colorado *U.S.A.* 203 L8
Colorado Canal 203 N8
Colorado, Cerro 206 E5
Colorado City 207 M4
Colorado River Aqueduct 206 D4
Colorado Springs 207 K1
Colsterworth 133 G2
Coluene 217 G6
Columbia *Missouri* 204 D7
Columbia *Pennsylvania* 205 M7
Columbia *S. Carolina* 209 M4
Columbia *Tennessee* 209 J3
Columbia *Washington* 202 D5
Columbia, District of 205 M7
Columbia Falls 202 G3
Columbia, Mount 199 M5
Columbine, Cape 188 C6
Columbus *Georgia* 209 K4
Columbus *Indiana* 204 H7
Columbus *Mississippi* 208 H4
Columbus *Montana* 203 K5
Columbus *Nebraska* 203 R7
Columbus *Ohio* 204 J7
Columbus *Texas* 208 D6
Colville *Alaska* 198 D2
Colville *Washington* 202 F3
Colville, Cape 195 E2
Colville Channel 195 E2
Colville Lake 198 K2
Colwyn Bay 134 F3
Comacchio 148 D3
Comana 153 J3
Comandante Ferraz 221 W6
Comandante Fontana 218 E5
Comayagua 212 D7
Combarbala 218 B6
Combe Martin 132 C3
Comber 138 L3
Combermere Bay 173 H5

Name	Page	Grid	Name	Page	Grid	Name	Page	Grid	Name	Page	Grid
Combourg	144	C4	Copa, Cerro	218	C4	Corumba	218	E3	Crewe	135	G3
Comeragh Mountains	139	G8	Cope	203	N8	Corumba	218	G3	Crewkerne	132	E4
Comfort, Cape	200	K4	Copenhagen	143	E9	Corunna	146	B1	Crianlarich	137	D4
Comilla	173	H4	Copiapo	218	B5	Corvallis	202	C5	Criccieth	132	C2
Comitan	211	N9	Copinsay	136	F2	Corve	132	E2	Criciuma	218	G5
Committee Bay	200	J4	Copkoy	156	B2	Corwen	132	D2	Crick	133	F2
Como	148	B3	Copper	198	G3	Cos	155	J4	Crickhowell	132	D3
Comodoro Rivadavia	219	C9	Copper Center	198	F3	Cosamaloapan	211	M8	Cricklade	133	F3
Como, Lago di	148	B3	Coppermine *Canada*	199	M2	Cosamozza	149	B4	Crieff	137	E4
Comorin, Cape	172	E7	Coppermine *Canada*	199	N2	Cosenza	149	F6	Criffel	135	F2
Comoros	189	H2	Copper Mount	202	F2	Cosiguina, Volcan	212	D8	Crikvenica	152	C3
Compiegne	144	E4	Copplestone	132	D4	Cosmoledo Islands	162	C7	Crimea	159	E6
Comporta	146	B3	Copsa Mica	153	H2	Cosne	145	E5	Cristalandia	217	H6
Compostela	210	G7	Coquet	137	G5	Costa, Cordillera de la	213	N9	Cristalina	218	G3
Conakry	184	C4	Coquimbo	218	B5	Costa Rica	212	E9	Cristobal Colon, Pico	216	C1
Conara Junction	193	K7	Coquimbo, Bahia de	218	B5	Costesti	153	H3	Crisu Alb	153	F2
Concarneau	145	B5	Corabia	153	H4	Cotabato	171	G4	Crisu Negru	153	F2
Conceicao do Araguaia	217	H5	Coracora	216	C7	Cotacachi	216	B3	Crisu Repede	153	G2
Concepcion *Bolivia*	218	D3	Coral Harbour	200	K5	Cotagaita	218	C4	Crna Reka	153	F5
Concepcion *Chile*	218	B7	Coral Sea Plateau	193	K2	Cotahuasi	218	B3	Crni Drim	152	E4
Concepcion *Panama*	212	F10	Corantijn	216	F3	Cotentin	144	C4	Croaghgorm Mountains	138	F3
Concepcion *Paraguay*	218	E4	Corbeil-Essonnes	144	E4	Cotiella	147	G1	Croagh Patrick	138	C5
Concepcion del Oro	210	J5	Corbiere	133	M7	Cotonou	185	F4	Croatia	152	C3
Concepcion del Uruguay	218	E6	Corbieres	145	E7	Cotopaxi	216	B4	Crocketford	137	E5
Concepcion, Punta	206	G7	Corbigny	145	E5	Cottage Grove	202	C6	Crockett	208	E5
Conception Bay	201	R8	Corbin	204	H8	Cottbus	150	F3	Croggan	137	C4
Conception Island	213	K3	Corbones	146	D4	Cottingham	135	J3	Crohy Head	138	F3
Conception, Point	206	B3	Corbridge	135	G2	Cottonwood	206	F3	Croick	136	D3
Concho	207	M5	Corby	133	G2	Coubre, Pointe de la	145	C6	Croisette, Cap	145	F7
Conchos *Mexico*	208	C8	Corby Glen	133	G2	Coulommiers	144	E4	Croke, Mount	192	D5
Conchos *Mexico*	207	K6	Corcaigh	139	E9	Coulonge	205	M3	Croker Island	192	G1
Concord *California*	206	A2	Corcovado, Golfo	219	B8	Council Bluffs	204	C6	Cromalt Hills	136	C2
Concord *N. Carolina*	209	M3	Corcubion	146	B1	Coupar Angus	137	E4	Cromar	137	F3
Concord *New Hampshire*	205	Q5	Cordele	209	L5	Courantyne	216	F3	Cromarty	136	D3
Concordia *Argentina*	218	E6	Cordoba *Argentina*	211	L8	Courchevel	145	G6	Cromarty Firth	136	D3
Concordia *U.S.A.*	203	R8	Cordoba *Argentina*	218	D6	Couronne, Cap	145	F7	Cromdale, Hills of	136	E3
Condamine	193	L4	Cordoba *Spain*	146	D4	Courtenay	202	B3	Cromer	133	J2
Condeuba	218	J6	Cordoba, Sierras de	218	D6	Courtmacsherry Bay	139	E9	Cromwell	195	B6
Condolobin	193	K5	Cordova	216	B6	Coutances	144	C4	Crook	135	H2
Condom	145	D7	Cordova	198	F3	Couto Magalhaes	217	H5	Crooked *Canada*	202	D5
Conecuh	209	J5	Corfe	132	D4	Coutras	145	C6	Crooked *U.S.A.*	199	L4
Conegliano	148	D3	Corfu *Greece*	154	E3	Cove	136	C3	Crooked Island	213	K3
Congleton	135	G3	Corfu *Greece*	154	E3	Coventry	133	F2	Crooked Island Passage	213	K3
Congo	186	B3	Coria	146	C2	Covilha	146	C2	Crookham	137	F4
Congo	186	D2	Corigliano Calabro	149	F6	Covington *Kentucky*	204	H7	Crookhaven	139	C10
Congo Basin	179	E6	Corinda	193	H2	Covington *Virginia*	205	L8	Crookston	204	B3
Conisbrough	135	H3	Corinth *Greece*	155	G4	Cowall	137	C4	Croom	139	E7
Coniston	135	F2	Corinth *U.S.A.*	208	H3	Cowan, Lake	192	E5	Crosby *Isle of Man, U.K.*	134	E2
Coniston Water	134	E2	Corinth, Gulf of	155	G3	Cowbit	133	G2	Crosby *Merseyside, U.K.*	135	F3
Connah's Quay	135	F3	Corinto *Brazil*	218	H3	Cowbridge	132	D3	Crosby *U.S.A.*	204	D3
Connaught	138	D5	Corinto *Nicaragua*	212	D8	Cowdenbeath	137	E4	Cross	185	G4
Conneaut	205	K6	Corixa Grande	218	E3	Cowes	133	F4	Crossett	208	G4
Connecticut *U.S.A.*	205	P6	Cork *Ireland*	139	E9	Cowfold	133	G4	Cross Fell	135	G2
Connecticut *U.S.A.*	205	P6	Cork *Ireland*	139	E9	Cowlitz	202	C4	Crossgar	138	L4
Connellsville	205	L6	Corlay	144	B4	Cowra	193	K5	Cross Hands	132	C3
Conn, Lough	138	D4	Corleone	149	D7	Coxim	218	F3	Crosshaven	139	F9
Connors Range	193	K3	Corlu	156	B2	Coxs Bazar	173	H4	Cross Lake	199	R5
Conon	136	D3	Cornafulla	139	F6	Coxwold	135	H2	Crossmaglen	138	J4
Conon Bridge	136	D3	Corner Brook	201	Q8	Cozumel	211	R7	Crossmolina	138	D4
Conrad	202	J3	Cornhill-on-Tweed	137	F4	Cozumel, Isla de	211	R7	Cross Sound	198	H4
Conselheiro Lafaiete	218	H4	Corning	205	M5	Cracow	151	H3	Crossville	209	K3
Conselheiro Pena	218	H3	Corn Islands	212	F8	Cradock	188	D6	Crotone	149	F6
Consett	135	H2	Cornudilla	146	E1	Craig	203	L7	Crouch	133	H3
Con Son	173	L7	Cornwall *U.K.*	132	C4	Craigavon	138	K4	Crowborough	133	H3
Constance, Lake	150	C5	Cornwall *Canada*	205	N4	Craignure	137	C4	Crowle	135	J3
Constancia dos Baetas	216	E5	Cornwallis Island	200	H2	Crail	137	F4	Crowley's Ridge	208	G3
Constanta	153	K3	Cornwall Island	200	H2	Crailsheim	150	D4	Crowsnest Pass	199	N6
Constantina	146	D4	Coro	216	D1	Craiova	153	G3	Croxton Kerrial	133	G2
Constantine	181	G1	Coroata	217	J4	Cramlington	135	H1	Croydon *Australia*	193	J2
Constantine Bay	132	B4	Corocoro	218	C3	Cranborne	133	F4	Croydon *U.K.*	133	G2
Constantine, Cape	198	D4	Coromandel *Brazil*	218	G3	Cranbrook	202	G3	Crozet, Iles	222	C6
Constantinople	156	C2	Coromandel *New Zealand*	195	E2	Crane	207	L5	Crozier Channel	200	G2
Constitucion	219	B7	Coromandel Coast	172	F6	Cranleigh	133	G3	Cruces, Punta	216	B2
Contamana	216	C5	Coromandel Peninsula	195	E2	Cranstown, Kap	200	Q3	Crudgington	132	E2
Contas	217	J6	Corona	207	K3	Craponne-sur-Arzon	145	E6	Crumlin	138	K3
Contratacion	216	C2	Coronado, Bahia de	212	E10	Crasna *Romania*	153	G2	Cruz Alta	218	F5
Contrexeville	144	F4	Coronation Gulf	199	N2	Crasna *Romania*	153	J2	Cruz, Cabo	212	J5
Contulmo	219	B7	Coronel	219	B7	Crater Lake	202	C6	Cruz del Eje	218	C6
Contwoyto Lake	199	N2	Coronel Dorrego	219	D7	Crateus	217	J5	Cruzeiro do Sul	216	C5
Conway *Arkansas*	208	F3	Coronel Pringles	219	D7	Crati	149	F6	Cruz Grande *Chile*	218	B5
Conway *New Hampshire*	205	Q5	Coronel Suarez	219	D7	Crato	217	K5	Cruz Grande *Mexico*	211	K9
Conway *S. Carolina*	209	N4	Corovode	155	F2	Cravo Norte	216	C2	Crymych	132	C3
Conway Bay	134	F3	Corps	145	F6	Crawford	203	N6	Crystal City	207	N6
Conwy	134	F3	Corpus Christi	208	D7	Crawford Point	171	F3	Crystal Falls	204	F3
Coober Pedy	193	G4	Corpus Christi Bay	208	D7	Crawfordville	209	K5	Csongrad	152	F2
Cook	192	G5	Corpus Christi, Lake	208	D6	Crawley	133	G3	Csorna	152	D2
Cook, Cape	202	A2	Corque	218	C3	Crazy Mountains	203	J4	Cuamba	189	G2
Cookeville	209	K2	Corran	137	C4	Creach Bheinn	137	C4	Cuando	186	D6
Cook Inlet	198	E3	Corraun Peninsula	138	C5	Creag Meagaidh	137	D3	Cuangar	186	C6
Cook Islands	223	H5	Corrib, Lough	139	D6	Creagorry	136	A3	Cuango	186	C4
Cook, Mount	195	C5	Corrientes *Argentina*	218	E5	Crediton	132	D4	Cuanza	186	C4
Cook, Recif de	194	W15	Corrientes *Peru*	216	B4	Cree *Canada*	199	P4	Cuatro Cienegas	207	L7
Cookstown	138	J3	Corrientes, Cabo *Colombia*	216	B2	Cree *U.K.*	137	D5	Cuauhtemoc	207	J6
Cook Strait	195	E4	Corrientes, Cabo *Cuba*	212	E4	Cree Lake	199	P4	Cuautla	211	K8
Cooktown	193	K2	Corrientes, Cabo *Mexico*	210	G7	Creeslough	138	G2	Cuba	212	G4
Coolibah	192	G2	Corrigan	208	E5	Creetown	134	E2	Cubango	186	C6
Coolidge	206	G4	Corrigin	192	D5	Creggan	138	H3	Cubara	213	L11
Cooma	193	K6	Corry	205	L6	Creggs	138	F5	Cubuk	156	E2
Coomnadiha	139	C9	Corryvreckan, Gulf of	137	C4	Crema	148	B3	Cuchi	186	C5
Coomscarrea	139	B9	Corse	149	B4	Cremona	148	B3	Cuchilla Grande	218	E6
Coonamble	193	K5	Corse, Cap	148	B4	Crepaja	152	F3	Cuchivero	216	D2
Coondapoor	172	D6	Corsewall Point	137	C5	Creran, Loch	137	C4	Cuchumatanes, Alto	212	B7
Coongan	192	D3	Corsica	149	B4	Cres *Croatia*	152	C3	Cuckfield	133	G3
Coopers Creek	193	H4	Corsicana	208	D4	Cres *Croatia*	152	C3	Cucuta	216	C2
Cooroy	193	L4	Corte	149	B4	Crescent	202	D6	Cuddalore	172	E6
Coosa	209	J4	Cortegana	146	C4	Crescent City	202	B7	Cuddapah	172	E6
Coos Bay *U.S.A.*	202	B6	Cortez	207	H2	Crest	145	F6	Cudgwa	193	K6
Coos Bay *U.S.A.*	202	B6	Cortina d'Ampezzo	148	D2	Creston	204	C6	Cue	192	D4
Cootamundra	193	K5	Cortland	205	M5	Crestview	209	J5	Cuellar	146	D2
Cootehill	138	H4	Cortona	148	C4	Crete	155	H5	Cuenca	216	B4
Copacabana	218	C3	Corubal	184	C3	Cretin, Cape	194	D3	Cuencame	210	H5
			Coruche	146	B3	Creus, Cap	147	H1	Cuenca, Serrania de	146	E2
			Coruh	157	J2	Creuse	145	D5	Cuernavaca	211	K8
			Corum	156	F2	Crevillente	147	F3	Cuero	208	D6

Cuiaba *Brazil*	218 E3	Daly	192 G1

Cuiaba *Brazil* 218 E3
Cuiaba *Brazil* 218 E3
Cuicatlan 211 L9
Cuilcagh 138 G4
Cuillin Hills 136 B3
Cuillin Sound 137 B3
Cuito 186 C6
Cuito Cuanavale 186 C6
Cuitzeo, Laguna de 211 J8
Cuiuni 216 E4
Cukai 170 C5
Cukurca 157 K4
Cu Lao Hon 173 L6
Culbertson 203 M3
Culebra Peak 207 K2
Culebra, Sierra de la 146 C2
Culiacan 210 F5
Culion 171 F3
Culiseui 217 G6
Culkein 136 C2
Cullera 147 F3
Cullin, Lough 138 D5
Cullman 209 J3
Cullybackey 138 K3
Culm 132 D4
Culmen 157 H4
Culpeper 205 L7
Cults 137 F3
Culverden 195 D5
Culworth 133 F2
Culzean Bay 137 D5
Cumacay 157 K3
Cumali 156 B2
Cumana 216 E1
Cumbal, Nevado de 216 B3
Cumberland *Kentucky* 204 H8
Cumberland *W. Virginia* 205 L7
Cumberland Bay 219 J10
Cumberland Mountains 209 K2
Cumberland Peninsula 200 P4
Cumberland Plateau 209 J3
Cumberland Sound 200 N4
Cumbernauld 137 E5
Cumbria 135 G2
Cumbrian Mountains 135 F2
Cumbum 172 E5
Cumina 217 F4
Cummings 202 C8
Cumnock 137 D5
Cumpas 207 H5
Cumra 156 E4
Cunderdin 192 D5
Cunene 186 B6
Cuneo 148 A3
Cunnamulla 193 K4
Cunningham 137 D5
Cuorgne 148 A3
Cupar 137 E4
Cupica 216 B2
Cuprija 153 F4
Cupula, Pico 210 D5
Curacao 213 N8
Curacautin 219 B7
Curaco 219 C7
Curaray 216 B4
Curepipe 189 L7
Curico 219 B7
Curitiba 218 F5
Curitibanos 218 F5
Currais Novos 217 K5
Curralinho 217 H4
Curra, Lough 139 E6
Currane, Lough 139 B9
Currelo 218 H3
Curtici 153 F2
Curtis *Canada* 200 J4
Curtis *U.S.A.* 203 P7
Curtis Channel 193 L3
Curtis Island *Australia* 193 L3
Curtis Island *New Zealand* 191 T8
Curua *Brazil* 217 G4
Curua *Brazil* 217 G5
Curuca 217 G4
Curupira 216 E4
Curupira, Sierra de 216 E3
Curuzu Cuatia 218 E5
Cushcamcarragh 138 C5
Cushendall 138 K2
Cushendun 138 K2
Cusiana 216 C3
Cut Bank 202 H3
Cuthbert 209 K5
Cutral-Co 219 B7
Cuttack 172 G4
Cuvelai 186 C6
Cuxhaven 150 C2
Cuyo Islands 171 G3
Cuyuni 216 F2
Cuzco 216 C6
Cvrsnica 152 D4
Cwmbran 132 D3
Cwmffrwd 132 C3
Cyclades 155 H4
Cynthiana 204 H7
Cypress Hills 203 K3
Cyprus 156 E5
Cyrene 181 K2
Czarna 151 J3
Czech Republic 150 F4
Czeremcha 151 K2
Czernowitz 153 H1
Czerwiensk 150 F2
Czestochowa 151 H3
Czluchow 151 G2

D

Dabakala 184 E4
Daban Shan 173 K1
Daba Shan 173 L2
Dabat 183 G5
Dabeiba 216 B2
Dabie Shan 173 N2
Dabola 184 C3
Daboya 184 E4
Dabrowa 151 K2
Dabrowa Gornicza 151 H3
Dabrowa Tarnowska 151 J3
Dabsan 166 G2
Da Cabreira, Sierra 146 B2
Dacca 173 G4
Dadale 194 J6
Daday 156 E2
Dadianzi 168 B4
Dadu 172 C3
Daeni 153 K3
Daer Reservoir 137 E5
Daet 171 G3
Dafla Hills 173 H3
Dafrah, Ad 177 L5
Dagana 184 B2
Dagardi 156 C3
Dagbasi 157 H2
Dagbeli 156 D4
Dagenham 133 H3
Daggs Sound 195 A6
Daglica 157 L4
Daglingworth 133 E3
Dagongcha 166 H4
Dagua 194 C2
Dagupan 171 G2
Dagyolu 157 H3
Dahab 176 B2
Dahanu 172 D5
Dahezhen 168 D2
Dahi, Nafud ad 176 G5
Da Hinggan Ling 167 N2
Dahlak Archipelago 176 E9
Dahlem 150 B3
Dahme 150 E3
Dahm, Ramlat 176 G8
Dahna, Ad *Saudi Arabia* 176 H6
Dahna, Ad *Saudi Arabia* 176 H4
Dahod 172 D4
Dahra 147 G4
Dahuk 157 K4
Dai 194 K5
Daia 153 J4
Daik 170 D6
Daimiel 146 E3
Daingean 139 H6
Dair, Jebel ed 182 F5
Dairut 182 F2
Daito-jima 163 M4
Dajarra 193 H3
Dakar 184 B3
Dakhla Oasis 182 E2
Dak Kon 173 L6
Dakoro 181 G6
Dakovica 152 F4
Dakovo 152 E3
Dakshin Gangotri 221 A5
Dala 194 K6
Dalaba 184 C3
Dalab, Chalp 175 S5
Dalad Qi 167 K3
Dala-Jarna 143 F6
Dalalven 143 G6
Dalaman 156 C4
Dalandzadgad 167 J3
Dalanganem Islands 171 G3
Dalaoba 166 E3
Da Lat 173 L6
Dalbandin 172 B3
Dalbeattie 134 F2
Dalby 193 L4
Dalch 132 D4
Dale *Norway* 143 A6
Dale *U.S.A.* 204 G7
Dalhalvaig 136 E2
Dalhart 207 L2
Dalhousie 205 S2
Dalhousie, Cape 198 K1
Dali 173 K3
Dalian 167 N4
Dalidag 174 H2
Dalkeith 137 E5
Dalkey 139 K6
Dallas 208 D4
Dalles, The 202 D5
Dall Island 198 J4
Dallol Bosso 181 F6
Dalma 177 L4
Dalmally 137 D4
Dalmatia 152 C3
Dalnaspidal 137 D4
Dalnegorsk 168 E3
Dalnerechensk 168 D3
Daloa 184 D4
Dalou Shan 173 L3
Dalrymple 137 D5
Dalrymple, Mount 193 K3
Dalsmynni 142 U12
Daltenganj 172 F4
Dalton 209 K3
Daluolemi 168 B3
Dalupiri 171 G2
Dalvik 142 V12

Daly 192 G1
Daly Waters 193 G2
Damal 157 K2
Daman 172 D4
Damanhur 182 F1
Damar 171 H7
Damascus 157 G6
Damavand 175 L4
Damba 186 C4
Dame Marie 213 K5
Dame Marie, Cabo 213 K5
Damghan 175 M3
Damh, Loch 136 C3
Damietta 183 F1
Daming 167 M4
Damlacik 157 H4
Damodar 172 G4
Damoh 172 E4
Damongo 184 E4
Dampier 192 D3
Dampier Archipelago 192 D3
Dampier Land 192 E2
Dampier, Selat 171 J6
Dampier Strait 194 D3
Damqawt 177 L8
Da Nang 173 L5
Danau Toba 170 B5
Danba 173 K2
Danbury 205 P6
Danby Lake 206 E3
Dandong 167 N3
Dangchang 173 K2
Dangori 173 J3
Dangrek, Phnom 173 K6
Dangshan 173 N2
Daniel 203 J6
Danilov 158 G4
Danilovgrad 152 E4
Dank 177 N5
Danli 212 D7
Dannenburg 150 D2
Dannevirke 195 F4
Danshui 167 L7
Dansville 205 M5
Danu 194 E2
Danube 151 H5
Danumparai 170 F5
Danville *Illinois* 204 G6
Danville *Kentucky* 204 H8
Danville *Virginia* 205 L8
Dan Xian 173 L5
Dany 193 J6
Danzig, Gulf of 151 H1
Dao 171 G3
Daoud 181 G1
Dao Xian 173 M3
Dapaong 184 F3
Dapiak, Mount 171 G4
Daqing 167 N2
Daqm 177 N7
Daqq-e-Patargan 175 Q5
Dara 174 C5
Darab 175 M7
Darabani 153 J1
Daran 175 K5
Dar Anjir, Kavir-e 175 M5
Darasun 165 J6
Daravica 154 F1
Darband 175 N6
Darbhanga 172 G3
Darby, Cape 198 C3
Dardanelle Lake 208 F3
Dardanelles 155 J2
Dar El Beida 180 D2
Darende 157 G3
Dar Es Salaam 187 G4
Dargaville 195 D1
Darica 156 C2
Darien, Golfo del 216 B2
Darija 157 K5
Darjeeling 173 G3
Darjiling 173 G3
Dar Lac, Cao Nguen 173 L6
Darlag 173 J2
Darling 193 J5
Darling Downs 193 K4
Darling Range 192 D5
Darlington *U.K.* 135 H2
Darlington *U.S.A.* 209 N3
Darmanesti 153 J2
Darmstadt 150 C4
Darnah 181 K2
Darnick 193 J5
Darnley Bay 198 L2
Darnley, Cape 221 E5
Daroca 147 F2
Darokhov 151 L4
Darovskoye 158 H4
Darreh Gaz 175 P3
Darsa 177 N10
Darsi 172 E5
Darsser Ort 150 E1
Dart 132 D4
Dartford 133 H3
Dartmoor 132 D4
Dartmouth *Canada* 201 P9
Dartmouth *U.K.* 132 D4
Darton 135 H3
Darty Mountains 138 F4
Daru 194 C3
Daruba 171 H5
Daruvar 152 D3
Darvel 137 D5

Darvi 166 G2
Darwen 135 G3
Darwin 192 G1
Darwin, Mount 206 C2
Daryacheh-ye Orumiyeh 157 L4
Darzin 175 P7
Das 177 L4
Dashitou 166 F3
Dashizhai 167 N2
Dashkhovuz 160 G5
Dasht *Iran* 175 N3
Dasht *Pakistan* 172 B3
Dashti-oburdon 166 B4
Da, Song 173 K4
Datca 156 B4
Datia 172 E3
Datong 167 L3
Datong Shan 173 J1
Datuk, Tanjung 170 D5
Datu Piang 171 G4
Daugava 143 M8
Daugavpils 143 P9
Daule *Ecuador* 216 B4
Daule *Ecuador* 216 B3
Daun 150 B3
Dauphin 199 Q5
Dauphine 145 F6
Dauphine, Alpes du 145 F6
Dauphin Lake 199 R5
Davangere 172 E6
Davao 171 H4
Davao Gulf 171 H4
Davarzan 175 N3
Dave Creek 207 H2
Davenport 204 E6
Daventry 133 F2
David 212 F10
David-Gorodok 159 D5
Davidson 203 L2
Davidson Mountains 198 G2
Davington 137 E5
Davis *Antarctic* 221 F5
Davis *Australia* 192 E3
Davis *U.S.A.* 206 B1
Davis Mountains 207 K5
Davis Sea 221 F6
Davis Strait 200 P4
Davlekanovo 158 K5
Davos 148 B2
Davulga 156 D3
Dawa 167 N3
Dawasir, Wadi al 176 G6
Dawa Wenz 183 H7
Dawhat Salwah 177 K4
Dawley 132 E2
Dawlish 132 D4
Dawna Range 173 J5
Dawqah 177 M7
Dawros Head 138 E3
Dawson *Australia* 193 K3
Dawson *Canada* 198 H3
Dawson *Georgia* 209 K5
Dawson *N. Dakota* 203 Q4
Dawson Creek 199 L4
Dawson, Mount 202 F2
Dawson Range 198 H3
Dawu 173 M2
Dawusi 173 H1
Dawwah 177 P6
Dax 145 C7
Da Xian 173 L2
Daxue Shan 173 K2
Dayr az Zawr 157 J5
Dayr Hafir 157 G4
Dayton *Ohio* 204 H7
Dayton *Tennessee* 209 K3
Dayton *Washington* 202 F4
Daytona Beach 209 M6
Dayu 173 M3
Da Yunhe 167 M4
Dayville 202 E5
Dazkiri 156 C4
De Aar 188 D6
Dead Sea 174 B6
Deakin 192 F5
Deal 133 J3
Dean 173 N3
Dean *Canada* 198 K5
Dean *U.K.* 135 G3
Dean, Forest of 132 E3
Dean Funes 218 D6
Dean Island 221 R4
Dearborn 204 J5
Dease Arm 199 L2
Dease Inlet 198 D1
Dease Lake 198 J4
Dease Strait 199 P2
Death Valley 206 D2
Deauville 144 D3
Deben 133 J2
Debin 165 S4
Deblin 151 J3
Deboyne Islands 194 E4
Debre Birhan 183 G6
Debrecen 153 F2
Debre Markos 183 G5
Debre Tabor 183 G5
Decatur *Alabama* 209 J3
Decatur *Georgia* 209 K4
Decatur *Illinois* 204 F7
Decatur *Indiana* 204 H6
Decatur *Texas* 208 D4
Decazeville 145 E6
Deccan 172 E5

Name	Page	Ref
Doganhisar	156	D3
Dogankent	156	F4
Dogansehir	157	G3
Doganyol	157	H3
Doganyurt	156	E2
Dog Creek	202	C2
Dogen Co	173	H2
Dog Lake	204	F2
Dogo	169	D7
Dogondoutchi	181	F6
Dogubeyazit	157	L3
Dogukardeniz Daglari	157	J2
Doha	177	K4
Doi Luang	173	K5
Dojran	153	G5
Dojransko Jezero	153	G5
Doka *Indonesia*	194	A3
Doka *Sudan*	176	B10
Dokkum	144	G2
Dokshitsy	143	M9
Dokurcun	156	D2
Dolak	194	B3
Dolak, Tanjung	171	K7
Dolang	132	D2
Dolbeau	205	P2
Dol-de-Bretagne	144	C4
Dole	145	F5
Dolgellau	132	D2
Dolginovo	151	M1
Dolgiy, Ostrov	164	Ac3
Dolgoye	151	K4
Dolina	159	C6
Dolinsk	168	J2
Dolinskaya	159	E6
Dollar	137	E4
Dollar Law	137	E5
Dolni Kralovice	150	F4
Dolok, Tanjung	194	A3
Dolomitiche, Alpi	148	C2
Dolo Odo	183	H7
Dolores *Argentina*	219	E7
Dolores *Uruguay*	219	E6
Dolores *U.S.A.*	202	K8
Dolphin and Union Strait	199	N1
Dolphin, Cape	219	E10
Dolsk	151	G3
Domanic	156	C3
Dombas	143	C5
Dombe	189	F3
Dombe Grande	186	B5
Dombovar	152	E2
Dombrad	153	F1
Dome, Puy de	145	E6
Domett	195	D5
Domfront	144	C4
Dominica	213	S7
Dominical	212	F10
Dominican Republic	213	M5
Dominion, Cape	200	M4
Domo	183	J6
Domodossola	148	B2
Domuya, Cerro	219	B7
Don *Grampian, U.K.*	136	F3
Don *S. Yorkshire, U.K.*	135	H3
Don *Russia*	159	G6
Donaghadee	138	L3
Donaldsville	208	G5
Donau	148	E1
Donauworth	150	D4
Don Benito	146	D3
Doncaster	135	H3
Dondo	186	B4
Dondra Head	172	F7
Donegal *Ireland*	138	F3
Donegal *Ireland*	138	G3
Donegal Bay	138	F3
Donegal Point	139	C7
Donenbay	166	D2
Doneraile	139	E8
Donetsk	159	F6
Dongan *Heilongjiang, China*	168	E2
Dongan *Hunan, China*	173	M3
Dongara	192	C4
Dongbolhai Shan	173	G2
Dongchuan	173	K3
Dongfang	173	L5
Dongfanghong	168	D2
Donggala	171	F6
Dong Hoi	173	L5
Dongjingcheng	168	B3
Dongliu	167	M5
Dongluk	166	F4
Dongning	168	C3
Dongola	182	F4
Dongping	167	M4
Dongshan	167	N5
Dongsheng	167	K4
Dongtai	167	N5
Donguena	186	B6
Dong Ujimqin Qi	167	M2
Dongxi Lian Dao	167	M5
Donington	133	G2
Doniphan	204	E8
Donji Vakuf	152	D3
Donna	142	E3
Donner Pass	202	D8
Donnington	132	E2
Dooagh	138	B5
Doon	137	D5
Doonbeg	139	C7
Doonerak, Mount	198	E2
Doon, Loch	137	D5
Doorin Point	138	F3
Dor	175	R6
Dorada, Costa	147	G2
Dora, Lake	192	E3
Dora Riparia	148	A3
Dorbiljin	166	G2
Dorchester	132	E4
Dorchester, Cape	200	L4
Dordogne	145	C6
Dordrecht	144	F3
Dore	145	E6
Dore Lake	199	P5
Dore, Mont	145	E6
Dorgali	149	B5
Dori	184	E3
Dorking	133	G3
Dormo, Ras	176	F10
Dornbirn	148	B2
Dornie	136	C3
Dornoch	136	D3
Dornoch Firth	136	D3
Dorofeyevskaya	164	C2
Dorohoi	153	J2
Dorotea	142	G4
Dorovitsa	158	H4
Dorset	132	E4
Dortdivan	156	E2
Dortmund	150	B3
Dortyol	157	G4
Doruokha	164	J2
Dorutay	157	L3
Dosatuy	165	K7
Dosso	181	F6
Dossor	159	J6
Dothan	209	K5
Douai	144	E3
Douala	185	G5
Douarnenez	144	A4
Double Mountain Fork	207	M4
Doubs	145	F5
Doubtful Sound	195	A6
Doubtless Bay	195	D1
Doue-la-Fontaine	145	C5
Douentza	180	E5
Douglas *South Africa*	188	D5
Douglas *Isle of Man, U.K.*	134	D2
Douglas *Strathclyde, U.K.*	137	E5
Douglas *Arizona*	207	H5
Douglas *Georgia*	209	L5
Douglas *Wyoming*	203	M6
Doullens	144	E3
Doulus Head	139	B9
Doume	185	H5
Doune	137	D4
Dourada, Serra	217	H6
Dourados *Brazil*	218	E3
Dourados *Brazil*	218	F4
Dourados, Serra dos	218	F4
Douro	146	B2
Dove	135	H3
Dove Dale	135	H3
Dover *U.K.*	133	J3
Dover *Delaware*	205	N7
Dover *New Hampshire*	205	Q5
Dover *Ohio*	205	K6
Dover-Foxcroft	205	R4
Dover, Strait of	133	J4
Dovrefjell	142	C5
Dowa	187	F5
Dowlatabad *Afghanistan*	175	R5
Dowlatabad *Afghanistan*	175	S3
Dowlatabad *Iran*	175	N7
Dowlat Yar	172	C2
Down	138	L4
Downham Market	133	H2
Downpatrick	138	L4
Downpatrick Head	138	D4
Downs, The	133	J3
Downton	133	F4
Dow Rud	174	J5
Dowshi	172	C1
Dozen	169	D7
Draa, Oued	180	D3
Drac	145	F6
Dracevo	153	F5
Drachten	144	G2
Dragalina	153	J3
Dragasani	153	H3
Dragoman	153	G4
Dragonera, Isla	147	H3
Dragon's Mouth	213	S9
Dragsfjard	143	K6
Draguignan	145	G7
Dra, Hamada du	180	D3
Drake	203	P4
Drakensberg	188	E6
Drake Passage	221	V7
Drama	155	H2
Drammen	143	H7
Drangedal	143	C7
Draperstown	138	J3
Dras	172	E2
Drau	148	E2
Drava	152	E3
Dravograd	152	C2
Drawa	150	F2
Drawsko, Jezioro	151	G2
Drayton Valley	199	N5
Dren	153	G4
Drenewydd	132	D2
Dresden	150	E3
Dresvyanka	158	K2
Dreux	144	D4
Drin	155	F2
Drina	152	E3
Drin i zi	154	E1
Drobak	143	H7
Drobin	151	H2
Drogheda	138	K5
Drogichin	151	L2
Drogobych	159	C6
Drohiczyn	151	K2
Droichead Atha	138	K5
Droichead Nua	139	J6
Droitwich	133	E2
Drokiya	153	J1
Drome	145	F6
Dromedary, Cape	193	L6
Dromore	138	K4
Dronfield	135	H3
Dronne	145	D6
Dronning Maud Land	221	Z5
Dropt	145	D6
Drovyanaya	164	A2
Drumcollogher	139	E8
Drumheller	202	H2
Drummond	202	H4
Drummond Islands	204	J3
Drummond Range	193	K3
Drummondville	205	P4
Drummore	134	E2
Drumochter, Pass of	137	D4
Drumshanbo	138	F4
Druridge Bay	135	H1
Druskininkai	151	K1
Druzhba *Kazakhstan*	166	E2
Druzhba *Russia*	151	J1
Druzhina	165	R3
Drvar	152	D3
Drweca	151	H2
Dry	192	G2
Dry Bay *Canada*	201	N6
Dry Bay *U.S.A.*	198	H4
Dryden	204	D2
Drysdale, River	192	F2
Drysdale	185	H4
Duab	174	J4
Dualo	171	G6
Duarte, Pico	213	M5
Duba	176	B3
Dubai	177	M4
Dubawnt Lake	199	Q3
Dubayy	177	M4
Dubbagh, Jambal Ad	176	B3
Dubbo	193	K5
Dubenskiy	159	K5
Dublin *Ireland*	139	K6
Dublin *Ireland*	139	K6
Dublin *U.S.A.*	209	L4
Dublin Bay	139	K6
Dubna	158	F4
Dubno	159	D5
Du Bois	205	L6
Dubois *Idaho*	202	H5
Dubois *Wyoming*	203	K6
Dubossary	159	D6
Dubreka	184	C4
Dubrovitsa	151	M3
Dubrovka *Russia*	159	E5
Dubrovka *Russia*	159	G6
Dubrovnik	152	E4
Dubrovskoye	164	J5
Dubuque	204	E5
Duchang	167	M6
Duchesne *U.S.A.*	203	J7
Duchesne *U.S.A.*	203	J7
Duchess	193	H3
Ducie Island	223	J5
Duck	209	J3
Ducklington	133	F3
Duck Mountain	199	Q5
Duddington	133	G2
Dudinka	164	D3
Dudley	133	E2
Duenas	146	D2
Duero	146	D2
Duffield	133	F2
Duff Islands	194	N6
Dufftown	136	E3
Dufton	135	G2
Duga Zapadnaya, Mys	165	R5
Dughaill, Loch	136	C3
Dugi Otok	152	C3
Duisburg	150	B3
Dukambiya	176	C9
Dukat	153	G4
Duk Fadiat	182	F6
Duk Faiwil	182	F6
Dukhan	177	K4
Duki Bolen	165	P6
Dukla	151	J4
Dukou	173	K3
Dulan	173	J1
Duldurga	165	J6
Duleek	138	K5
Dulgalakh	165	N3
Dullingham	133	H2
Dull Lake	198	C3
Dulnain	136	E3
Dulovo	153	J4
Duluth	204	D3
Duma	157	G6
Dumaguete	171	G4
Dumai	170	C5
Dumaran	171	F3
Dumas *Arkansas*	208	G4
Dumas *Texas*	207	M3
Dumbarton	137	D5
Dumbea	194	X17
Dumbier	151	H4
Dumfries	135	F1
Dumfries and Galloway	137	E5
Dumitresti	153	J3
Dumka	173	G4
Dumlu	157	J2
Dumlupinar	156	C3
Dumoine	205	M3
Dumont d'Urville	221	K5
Dumont d'Urville Sea	221	J6
Dumyat	183	F1
Duna	152	E2
Dunaj	151	H5
Dunajec	151	J3
Dunany Point	138	K5
Dunarea	153	J3
Dunaujvaros	152	E2
Dunav	153	H4
Dunay *Moldova*	153	K3
Dunay *Russia*	168	D4
Dunayevtsy	153	J1
Dunay, Ostrov	165	L2
Dunbar *Australia*	193	J2
Dunbar *U.K.*	137	F4
Dunblane	137	E4
Dunboyne	139	K6
Duncan *Canada*	202	C3
Duncan *U.S.A.*	208	D3
Duncan Passage	173	H6
Duncansby Head	136	E2
Dunchurch	133	F2
Dundaga	143	K8
Dundalk *Ireland*	138	K4
Dundalk *U.S.A.*	205	M7
Dundalk Bay	138	K5
Dundas	200	M2
Dundas, Lake	192	E5
Dundas Peninsula	200	D3
Dundas Strait	192	G1
Dun Dealgan	138	K4
Dundee *South Africa*	188	F5
Dundee *U.K.*	137	F4
Dundonald	137	D5
Dundonnell	136	C3
Dundrennan	134	F2
Dundrod	138	K3
Dundrum	138	L4
Dundrum Bay	138	L4
Dundwa Range	172	F3
Dunecht	137	F3
Dunedin *New Zealand*	195	C6
Dunedin *U.S.A.*	209	L6
Dunfanaghy	138	G2
Dunfermline	137	E4
Dungannon	138	J3
Dungarpur	172	D4
Dungarvan	139	G8
Dungarvan Harbour	139	G8
Dungeness	133	H4
Dungiven	138	J3
Dungloe	138	F3
Dungu	187	E2
Dungun	170	C5
Dunholme	135	J3
Dunhua	168	B4
Dunhuang	166	F3
Dunkeld	193	J6
Dunkerque	144	E3
Dunkirk	205	L5
Dunkur	183	G5
Dunkwa	184	E4
Dun Laoghaire	139	K6
Dunlavin	139	J6
Dunleer	138	K5
Dunmanus Bay	139	C9
Dunmanway	139	D9
Dunmore Town	212	J2
Dunmurry	138	K3
Dunnet Bay	136	E2
Dunnet Head	136	E2
Dunoon	137	D5
Dunragit	134	E2
Duns	137	F4
Dunseith	203	P3
Dunsford	132	D4
Dunstable	133	G3
Dunstan Mountains	195	B6
Dunster	132	D3
Duntelchaig, Loch	136	D3
Duntroon	195	C6
Dunvegan	136	B3
Dunvegan Head	136	B3
Dupang Ling	173	M3
Dupree	203	P5
Duque de York, Isla	219	A10
Du Quoin	204	F7
Duragan	156	F2
Durance	145	F7
Durand, Recif	194	Y17
Durango *Mexico*	210	G5
Durango *U.S.A.*	207	J2
Durankulak	153	K4
Durant	208	D3
Durazno	218	E6
Durazzo	154	E2
Durban	188	F6
Durcal	146	E4
Durdevac	152	D2
Durelj	167	J4
Duren	150	B3
Durg	172	F4
Durgapur *Bangladesh*	173	H3
Durgapur *India*	173	G4
Durham *U.K.*	135	H2

El Sahuaro	206	F5	Ennis *U.S.A.*	208	D4	Escocesa, Bahia de	213	N5	Eure	144	D4
El Salado	219	C9	Enniscorthy	139	J7	Escondido *Brazil*	218	J3	Eureka *California*	202	B7
El Salto	210	G6	Enniskillen	138	G4	Escondido *U.S.A.*	206	D4	Eureka *Montana*	202	G3
El Salvador	212	C8	Ennistymon	139	D7	Escrick	135	H3	Eureka *Nevada*	206	D1
El Sam'an de Apure	213	N11	Enns	148	E1	Escuintla	212	B7	Eureka Sound	200	J2
El Sauzal	206	D5	Enonkoski	142	N5	Ese-Khayya	165	N3	Europa, Ile de l	189	H4
Elsham	135	J3	Enontekio	142	K2	Esemer	157	K3	Europa, Picos de	146	D1
El Socorro	206	F5	Enrekang	171	F6	Esen	156	C4	Europa Point	146	D4
Elster	150	E3	Enschede	144	G2	Esendere	157	L4	Eutaw	209	J4
Elsterwerda	150	E3	Ensenada	206	D5	Esfahan	175	K5	Evans, Lake	201	L7
El Sueco	207	J6	Enshi	173	L2	Esfarayen, Reshteh ye	175	N3	Evans, Mount	203	M8
El Suweis	183	F2	Enstone	133	F3	Eshan	173	K4	Evans Strait	200	K5
El Tambo	216	B4	Entebbe	187	F2	Esha Ness	136	A1	Evanston *Illinois*	204	G5
Eltham	195	E3	Enterprise	209	K5	Esh Sheikh, Jbel	157	G6	Evanston *Wyoming*	202	J7
El Thamad	176	B2	Entinas, Punta de las	146	E4	Esino	148	D4	Evansville	204	G7
El Tigre	213	Q10	Entraygues	145	E6	Esk	137	E5	Evaux-les-Bains	145	E5
El Tih	176	A2	Entrecasteaux, Recifs d'	191	N5	Eskdale	137	E5	Evaz	175	L8
Eltisley	133	G2	Enugu	185	G4	Eske, Lough	138	F3	Evenlode	133	F3
El Tocuyo	213	N10	Enurmino	198	A2	Eskifjordur	142	Y12	Everard, Cape	193	K6
Elton *U.K.*	133	G2	Enz	150	C4	Eskilstuna	143	G7	Everard, Lake	193	G5
Elton *Russia*	159	H6	Eo	146	C1	Eskimalatya	157	H3	Everest, Mount	172	G3
El Tule	211	L9	Eolie	149	E6	Eskimo Lakes	198	J2	Everett	202	C4
El Tur	176	A2	Epano Fellos	155	H4	Eskimo Point	199	S3	Everett Mountains	200	N5
Eluru	172	F5	Epanomi	155	G2	Eskipazar	156	E2	Everglades, The	209	M7
Elvanfoot	137	E5	Epernay	144	E4	Eskishir	156	D3	Evesham	133	F2
Elvas	146	C3	Ephrata	202	E4	Esla	146	D1	Evesham, Vale of	133	F2
Elveden	133	H2	Epi	194	U12	Eslamabad-e Gharb	174	H4	Evigheds Fjord	200	R4
Elverum	143	D6	Epinal	144	G4	Eslam Qaleh	175	Q4	Evisa	149	B4
El Viejo	213	L11	Epping	133	H3	Esme	156	C3	Evje	143	B7
El Vigia	216	C2	Eppynt, Mynydd	132	D2	Esmeralda, Isla	219	A9	Evora	146	C3
Elwy	135	F3	Epsi	157	J4	Esmeraldas	216	B3	Evreux	144	D4
Ely *Cambridgeshire, U.K.*	133	H2	Epsom	133	G3	Espalion	145	E6	Evropos	155	G2
Ely *Mid Glamorgan, U.K.*	132	D3	Eqlid	175	L6	Espanola *Canada*	205	K3	Evros	155	J2
Ely *Minnesota*	204	E3	Equatorial Guinea	185	G5	Espanola *U.S.A.*	207	J3	Evrotas	155	G4
Ely *Nevada*	206	E1	Equeipa	194	D3	Espanola, Isla	216	A7	Evvoia	155	H3
Elze	150	C2	Erap	194	D3	Espenberg, Cape	198	C2	Evvoikos Kolpos	155	G3
Ema	143	M7	Erbaa	157	G2	Esperance	192	E5	Ewasse	194	E3
Emae	194	U12	Erba, Jebel	176	C6	Esperance Bay	192	E5	Ewe, Loch	136	C3
Emamrud	175	M3	Ercek	157	K3	Esperanza *Antarctic*	221	W6	Ewes	137	E5
Emam Taqi	175	P4	Ercis	157	K3	Esperanza *Argentina*	219	B10	Exbourne	132	D4
Eman	143	G8	Ercsi	152	E2	Esperanza *Argentina*	218	D6	Exe	132	D4
Emao	194	U12	Erdek	156	B2	Espiel	146	D3	Exeter	132	D4
Emba	159	K6	Erdemli	156	F4	Espinhaco, Serra da	218	H3	Exford	132	D3
Embarcacion	218	D4	Erdenet	167	J2	Espinho	146	B2	Exmoor	132	D3
Embleton	135	H1	Erdre	145	C5	Espinosa de los Monteros	146	E1	Exmouth	132	D4
Embona	155	J4	Erechim	218	F5	Espirito Santo	218	H3	Exmouth Gulf	192	C3
Embrun	145	G6	Ereenstav	167	M2	Espiritu Santo	194	T11	Exo Hora	155	F4
Embu	187	G3	Eregli *Turkey*	156	D2	Espiritu Santo, Cape	171	H3	Expedition Range	193	K3
Emden	150	B2	Eregli *Turkey*	156	F4	Espiritu Santo, Isla	210	D5	Exploits	201	Q8
Emerald	193	K3	Erek Dagi	157	K3	Espiye	157	H2	Exton	132	D3
Emerald Island	200	D2	Erenhot	167	L3	Espoo	143	N6	Extremadura	146	C3
Emerson	203	R3	Erentepe	157	K3	Esposende	146	B2	Exuma Sound	212	J2
Emet	156	C3	Eresma	146	D2	Espot	147	G1	Eyakit-Terde	165	J3
Emeti	194	C3	Eressos	155	H3	Espungabera	189	F4	Eyam	135	H3
Emi	164	F6	Erfelek	156	F2	Esquel	219	B8	Eyasi, Lake	187	F3
Emigrant Pass	202	F7	Erfurt	150	D3	Es Sahra en Nubiya	176	B6	Eyemouth	137	F4
Emin	166	E2	Ergani	157	H3	Essaouira	180	D2	Eye Peninsula	136	B2
Emine, Nos	153	J4	Ergene	156	B2	Es Semara	180	C3	Eyjafjallajokull	142	U13
Emirdag	156	D3	Ergli	143	L8	Essen	150	B3	Eyjafjordur	142	V11
Emir Dagi	156	D3	Ergun He	165	K6	Essex	133	H3	Eyl	183	J6
Emita	193	K7	Ergun Zuoqi	167	N1	Essex, Punta	216	A7	Eynesil	157	H2
Emmaboda	143	F8	Eriboll, Loch	136	D2	Esslingen	150	C4	Eynsham	133	F3
Emmaste	143	K7	Ericht, Loch	137	D4	Esso	165	T5	Eyre	192	F5
Emmen	144	G2	Ericiyas Dagi	156	F3	Estacado, Llanos	207	L4	Eyre Creek	193	H4
Emory Peak	207	L6	Erie	205	K5	Estados, Isla de los	219	D10	Eyre Mountains	195	B6
Empalme	206	G7	Erie, Lake	205	K5	Estahbanat	175	M7	Eyre North, Lake	193	H4
Empangeni	189	F5	Erikousa	154	E3	Estancia	218	K6	Eyre Peninsula	193	H5
Empedrado	218	E5	Erimanthos	155	F4	Estcourt	188	E5	Eyre South, Lake	193	H4
Empingham	133	G2	Erimo-misaki	168	J5	Este	148	C3	Eysturoy	142	Z14
Empoli	148	C4	Eriskay	137	A3	Esteli	212	D8	Eyvanaki	175	L4
Emporia *Kansas*	208	D1	Erkelenz	150	B3	Estella	147	E1	Ezequil Ramos Mexia,		
Emporia *Virginia*	205	M8	Erkilet	156	F3	Estepona	146	D4	Embalse	219	C7
Ems	150	B2	Erkowit	176	C7	Este, Punta del	219	F6	Ezine	156	B3
Emu	168	B4	Erlandson Lake	201	N6	Esterhazy	203	N2			
Enard Bay	136	C2	Erlangen	150	D4	Esternay	144	E4	**F**		
Encantada, Cerro Del La	206	E5	Erldunda	193	G4	Estes Park	203	M7			
Encarnacion	218	E5	Erme	132	D4	Estevan	203	N3	Faber Lake	199	M3
Enchi	184	E4	Ermelo	188	F5	Estherville	204	C5	Faborg	143	D9
Encinal	208	C6	Ermenak	156	E4	Eston	135	H2	Fabriano	148	D4
Encontrados	216	C2	Ernakulam	172	E7	Estonia	143	L7	Facatativa	216	C3
Encounter Bay	193	H6	Erne	138	H5	Estrela, Sierra da	146	C2	Facundo	219	C9
Endau	170	C5	Erne, Lower Lough	138	G4	Estrella, Punta	206	E5	Fada	182	D4
Ende	171	G7	Erne, Upper Lough	138	G4	Estremadura	146	B3	Fada NGourma	184	F3
Endeavour Strait	193	J1	Erode	172	E6	Estremoz	146	C3	Faddeya, Zaliv	164	H2
Enderbury Island	191	U2	Eromanga	193	J4	Estrondo, Serra do	217	H5	Faddeyevskiy, Ostrov	165	Q1
Enderby Land	221	D5	Er Rachidia	180	E2	Esztergom	152	E2	Faenza	148	C3
Endicott Mountains	198	C2	Er Rahad	182	F5	Etah	172	E3	Faeros	142	Z14
Ene	216	C6	Errego	189	G3	Etain	144	F4	Fafen Shet	183	H6
Enez	156	B2	Errigal	138	F2	Etampes	144	E4	Fagaras	153	H3
Enfield *Ireland*	139	J6	Erris Head	138	B4	Etaples	144	D3	Fagersta	143	F6
Enfield *U.K.*	133	G3	Errochty, Loch	137	D4	Etawah	172	E3	Faget	153	G3
Engano, Cabo	213	N5	Errogie	136	D3	Ethiopia	183	G6	Fagnano, Lago	219	C10
Engano, Cape	171	G2	Erromango	194	U13	Etive, Loch	137	C4	Fagnes	144	F3
Engaru	168	J3	Erseke	155	F2	Etna, Monte	149	E7	Faguibine, Lac	180	E5
Engels	159	H5	Erskine	204	C3	Eton	133	G3	Fagurholsmyri	142	W13
Enggano	170	C7	Ertai	166	G2	Etosha Pan	188	C3	Fahraj	175	P7
Engger Us	167	J3	Eruh	157	K4	Etretat	144	D4	Fairbanks	198	F3
Engineer Group	194	E4	Erwigol	166	F3	Ettington	133	F2	Fairborn	204	J7
Englehart	205	L3	Eryuan	173	J3	Ettlingen	150	C4	Fairfield	206	A1
Englewood	203	M8	Erzen	154	E2	Ettrick	137	E5	Fair Isle	136	A2
English Channel	130	G5	Erzgebirge	150	E3	Ettrick Forest	137	E5	Fairlie	195	C6
Enguera	147	F3	Erzin	164	F6	Etwall	133	F2	Fairlight *Australia*	193	J2
Enguera, Sierra de	147	F3	Erzincan	157	H3	Eu	144	D3	Fairlight *U.K.*	133	H4
Enid	208	D2	Erzurum	157	J3	Eua	191	U6	Fairmont *Minnesota*	204	C5
Enkhuizen	144	F2	Esa-Ala	194	E3	Euboea	155	H3	Fairmont *W. Virginia*	205	K7
Enkoping	143	G7	Esan-misaki	168	H5	Euclid	205	K6	Fair Ness	200	M5
Enna	149	E7	Esashi *Japan*	168	H5	Euclides da Cunha	217	K6	Fairview	208	C2
Ennadai Lake	199	Q3	Esashi *Japan*	168	J3	Eufaula	209	K5	Fairweather, Mount	198	H4
En Nahud	182	E5	Esbjerg	143	C9	Eufaula Lake	208	E3	Faisalabad	172	D2
Ennedi	182	D4	Esbo	143	N6	Eugene	202	C5	Faith	203	N5
Ennell, Lough	139	H6	Escalona	146	D2	Eugenia, Punta	206	E5	Faither, The	136	A1
Ennerdale Water	135	F2	Escambia	209	J5	Eunice	208	F5	Faizabad	172	F3
Enning	203	N5	Escanaba	204	G4	Euphrates	174	G6	Fajr, Wadi	176	D2
Ennis *Ireland*	139	E7	Escarpe, Cape	194	X16	Eupora	208	H4			

249

H

Name	Page	Ref
Halab	174	C3
Halaban	176	G5
Halabja	174	G4
Halaib	183	G3
Halat Ammar	176	C2
Halaveden	143	F7
Halawa *Hawaii*	206	S10
Halawa *Hawaii*	206	T10
Halba	157	G5
Halberstadt	150	D3
Halcon, Mount	171	G3
Halden	143	D7
Haldensleben	150	D2
Halesowen	133	G2
Halesworth	133	J2
Halfeti	157	G4
Halfin, Wadi	177	N6
Halfmoon Bay	195	B7
Halfway	199	L4
Hali	176	E7
Haliburton Highlands	205	L4
Halifax *Canada*	201	P9
Halifax *U.K.*	135	H3
Halifax Bay	193	K2
Halikarnassos	156	B4
Halileh, Ra's-e	175	K7
Halin	168	B3
Halisah	157	G4
Halitpasa	156	B3
Halkapinar	156	F4
Halkett, Cape	198	E1
Halla	142	G5
Halladale	136	E2
Hallanca	216	B5
Halland	143	E8
Hallandsas	143	E8
Halle	150	C3
Hallefors	143	F7
Hallen	142	F5
Halley	221	Y3
Hallingdal	143	C6
Hallingskarvet	143	B6
Hall Peninsula	200	N5
Hallstavik	143	H6
Hallum	144	F2
Halmahera	171	H5
Halmahera, Laut	171	H6
Halmstad	143	E8
Hals	143	D8
Halsinge-skogen	143	F6
Halsingland	143	G6
Halstead	133	H3
Halton Lea Gate	135	G2
Halul	177	L4
Ham *France*	144	E4
Ham *U.K.*	136	A2
Hamada	169	D8
Hamad, Al	174	D6
Hamadan	174	J4
Hamah	174	C4
Hamam	157	G4
Hamamatsu	169	F8
Hamar	143	D6
Hamata, Gebel	176	B4
Hama-Tombetsu	168	J3
Hambantota	172	F7
Hambleton	135	G3
Hamburg *U.S.A.*	204	C6
Hamburg *Germany*	150	D2
Hamdaman, Dasht-i	175	Q4
Hamd, Wadi al	176	C4
Hame	143	L6
Hameln	150	C2
Hamhung	167	P4
Hami	166	F3
Hamilton	193	H3
Hamilton *Bermuda*	197	N5
Hamilton *Canada*	205	L5
Hamilton *New Zealand*	195	E2
Hamilton *U.K.*	137	D5
Hamilton *Alabama*	209	J3
Hamilton *Montana*	202	G4
Hamilton *Ohio*	204	H7
Hamilton Inlet	201	Q7
Hamim, Wadi al	181	K2
Hamina	143	M6
Hamitabat	156	D4
Hamm	150	B2
Hammar, Hawr al	174	H6
Hammarstrand	142	G5
Hammeenlinna	143	L6
Hammerdal	142	F5
Hammerfest	142	K1
Hammersley Range	192	D3
Hammond *Indiana*	204	G6
Hammond *Louisiana*	208	G5
Hammond *Montana*	203	M5
Hamnavoe	136	A1
Hampden	195	C6
Hampshire	133	F3
Hampshire Downs	133	F3
Hampton *Arkansas*	208	F4
Hampton *S. Carolina*	209	M4
Hampton *Virginia*	205	M8
Hamra, Al Hammadah al	181	H3
Hamrange	143	G6
Hamrin, Jebel	157	L5
Hamun-i Mashkel	172	B3
Hamur	157	K3
Hanahan	194	E3
Hanak	157	K2
Hanalei	206	R9
Hanamaki	168	H6
Hancheng	173	M1
Hancock	205	L7
Handa	169	F8
Handan	167	L4
Handeni	187	G4
Handlova	151	H4
Hanford	206	C2
Hangang	167	P4
Hangayn Nuruu	166	H2
Hanggin Houqi	167	K3
Hanggin Qi	167	K4
Hango	143	K7
Hangzhou	167	N5
Hangzhou Wan	167	N5
Hanhongor	167	J3
Hani	157	J3
Hanifah, Wadi	176	H4
Hanish al Kabir	176	F10
Haniyah, Al	174	H7
Han Jiang	167	M7
Hanko	143	K7
Hanksville	206	G1
Hanna	202	H2
Hannah Bay	201	L7
Hannibal	204	E7
Hann, Mount	192	F2
Hannover	150	C2
Hano-bukten	143	F9
Hanoi	173	L4
Hanover *Canada*	205	K4
Hanover *South Africa*	188	D6
Hanover *U.S.A.*	205	P5
Hanover, Isla	219	B10
Hanpan, Cape	194	E2
Han Pijesak	152	E3
Han Shui	173	M2
Hanson Bay	195	F6
Hanstholm	143	C8
Hantay	166	J2
Hanyuan	173	K3
Hanzhong	173	L2
Haparanda	142	L4
Happisburgh	133	J2
Hapsu	168	B5
Hapur	172	E3
Haql	176	B2
Hara	167	K2
Harad *Saudi Arabia*	177	J4
Harad *Yemen*	176	F8
Harads	142	J3
Haramachi	169	H7
Harare	188	F3
Harasis, Jiddat al	177	N7
Harbin	167	P2
Harbiye	157	G4
Harbour Breton	201	Q8
Harby	133	G2
Hardangerfjord	143	B6
Hardanger-Jokulen	143	B6
Hardangervidda	143	B6
Hardin	203	L5
Hardoi	172	F3
Hardy	208	G2
Hare Bay	201	Q7
Harer	183	H6
Harewood	135	H3
Hargeysa	183	H6
Hargigo	176	D9
Har Hu	173	J1
Harib	176	G9
Haridwar	172	E3
Harihari	195	C5
Harima-nada	169	E8
Harim, Jambal Al	177	N4
Hari-Rud	175	S4
Harjedalen	142	E5
Harlan	204	C6
Harlem	203	K3
Harleston	133	J2
Harlingen	144	F2
Harlow	133	H3
Harlowton	203	K4
Harmancik	156	C3
Harmil	176	E8
Harney Basin	202	D6
Harney Lake	202	E6
Harnosand	142	G5
Haro	146	E1
Haro, Cabo	206	G7
Haroldswick	136	A1
Harpanahalli	172	E6
Harpenden	133	G3
Harper	184	D5
Harper Passage	195	C5
Harpstedt	150	C2
Harrah, Ad	174	D6
Harran	157	H4
Harray, Loch of	136	E1
Harricanaw	205	M2
Harrietsham	133	H3
Harrington	135	F2
Harris	136	B3
Harrisburg *Illinois*	204	F8
Harrisburg *Pennsylvania*	205	M6
Harrismith	188	E5
Harrison	208	F2
Harrison Bay	198	E1
Harrisonburg	205	L7
Harrison, Cape	201	Q7
Harrison Lake	202	D3
Harrisonville	204	C7
Harris Ridge	220	A1
Harris, Sound of	136	A3
Harrogate	135	H3
Harrow	133	G3
Harsit	157	H2
Harstad	142	G2
Harsvik	142	D4
Hart	198	H2
Hartbees	188	D5
Hartberg	148	E2
Harteigen	143	B6
Hartford	137	E5
Harthill	137	E5
Hartkjolen	142	E4
Hartland	132	C4
Hartland Point	132	C3
Hartlepool	135	H2
Hartley	207	L3
Hartola	143	M6
Hartsville	209	M3
Hartwell Reservoir	209	L3
Hartz	188	E5
Harut	177	L8
Harvey *Australia*	192	D5
Harvey *U.S.A.*	204	G6
Harwich	133	J3
Haryana	172	E3
Harz	150	D3
Hasan Dagi	156	F3
Hashish, Ghubbat	177	P6
Haskoy	157	K2
Haslemere	133	G3
Haslingden	135	G3
Hassa	157	G4
Hassan	172	E6
Hassankeyf	157	J4
Hassela	143	L5
Hassi Habadra	181	F3
Hassleholm	143	E8
Hastings *Australia*	193	K7
Hastings *New Zealand*	195	F3
Hastings *U.K.*	133	H4
Hastings *Michigan*	204	H5
Hastings *Nebraska*	203	Q7
Hastveda	143	E8
Hasvik	142	K1
Haswell	135	H2
Hatanbulag	167	K3
Hatchie	208	H3
Hatfield *Hertfordshire, U.K.*	133	G3
Hatfield *S. Yorkshire, U.K.*	135	H3
Hatfield Peverel	133	H3
Hatgal	166	J1
Hathras	172	E3
Hatibah, Ra's	176	D6
Ha Tien	173	K6
Ha Tinh	173	L5
Hatip	156	E4
Hat Island	200	G4
Hato	216	A2
Hatohudo	171	H7
Hatskiy	164	D5
Hatteras, Cape	209	Q3
Hattiesburg	208	H5
Hatton	136	G3
Hattras Passage	173	J6
Hatunsaray	156	E4
Hatuoto	171	H6
Haugesund	143	A7
Haughton	133	E2
Hauhui	194	K6
Haukivesi	142	N5
Haukivuori	143	M5
Hauraha	194	K7
Hauraki Gulf	195	E2
Haut Atlas	180	D2
Hauts Plateaux	180	E2
Havana	204	E6
Havant	133	F4
Havasu	206	F3
Havasu, Lake	206	E3
Havel	150	E2
Havelock North	195	F3
Haverfordwest	132	C2
Haverhill *U.K.*	133	H2
Haverhill *U.S.A.*	205	Q5
Havoysund	142	L1
Havran	156	B3
Havre	203	K3
Havre-Saint-Pierre	201	P7
Havsa	156	B2
Havza	157	F2
Hawaii *U.S.A.*	206	R10
Hawaii *U.S.A.*	206	T11
Hawaya, Al	177	J6
Hawea, Lake	195	B6
Hawera	195	E3
Hawes	135	G2
Haweswater Reservoir	135	G2
Hawick	137	F5
Hawke	201	Q7
Hawke Bay	195	F3
Hawke, Cape	193	L5
Hawkesbury	205	N4
Hawkhurst	133	H3
Hawkinge	133	J3
Hawknest Point	213	K2
Hawnby	135	H2
Hawng Luk	173	J4
Hawra	177	J9
Hawran, Wadi	174	E5
Hawsker	135	J2
Hawthorne	206	C1
Haxby	135	H2
Hay *New South Wales, Australia*	193	J5
Hay *Northern Territory, Australia*	193	H3
Hay *Canada*	199	M3
Hayden	203	L7
Hayes	199	R4
Hayes Halvo	200	N2
Hayes, Mount	198	F3
Hayjan	176	G8
Hayl	177	N4
Hayl, Wadi al	157	H5
Haymana	156	E3
Hayrabolu	156	B2
Hay River	199	M3
Hays	176	F10
Hays	203	Q8
Haywards Heath	133	G4
Hazaran, Kuh-e	175	N7
Hazard	204	J8
Hazar Golu	157	H3
Hazaribag	172	G4
Hazaribagh Range	172	F4
Hazar Masjed, Kuh-e	175	P3
Hazel Grove	135	G3
Hazelton *Canada*	198	K4
Hazelton *U.S.A.*	205	N6
Hazen Bay	198	B3
Hazlehurst	208	G5
Hazro	157	J3
Headcorn	133	H3
Head of Bight	192	G5
Healdsburg	206	A1
Healesville	193	K6
Heanor	135	H3
Heard Islands	222	D6
Hearst	204	J2
Hearst Island	221	V5
Heart	203	P4
Heathfield	133	H4
Heathrow	133	G3
Hebbronville	208	C7
Hebden Bridge	135	G3
Hebei	167	M4
Hebel	193	K4
Heber City	202	J7
Hebi	167	L4
Hebrides, Sea of the	137	A4
Hebron *Canada*	201	P6
Hebron *Israel*	174	B6
Hebron *N. Dakota*	203	N4
Hebron *Nebraska*	203	R7
Hecate Strait	198	J5
Hechi	173	L4
Hechuan	173	L2
Heckington	133	G2
Hecla and Griper Bay	200	D2
Hector, Mount	195	E4
Hede	142	E5
Hedland, Port	192	D3
Hedmark	143	D6
Heerenveen	144	F2
Heerlen	144	F3
Hefa	174	B5
Hefei	167	M5
Hefeng	173	M3
Hegang	167	Q2
Hegura-jima	169	F7
Heiban	182	F5
Heide	150	C1
Heidelberg	150	C4
Heidharhorn	142	U12
Heighington	135	H2
Heilbron	188	E5
Heilbronn	150	C4
Heiligenhafen	150	D1
Heiligenstadt	150	D3
Heilong Jiang *China*	168	B2
Heilongjiang *China*	168	D1
Heimaey	142	U13
Heimdal	142	D5
Heinavesi	142	N5
Heinola	143	M6
Heinze Islands	173	J6
Hejing	166	F3
Hekimhan	157	G3
Hel	151	H1
Helagsfjallet	142	E5
Helena *Arkansas*	208	G5
Helena *Montana*	202	J4
Helen Island	171	J5
Helensburgh	137	D4
Helensville	195	E2
Helgoland	150	B1
Helgolander Bucht	168	C2
Heli	148	D2
Heligenblut	148	D2
Helleh	175	K7
Hellin	147	F3
Hell's Mouth	132	C2
Hell-Ville	189	J2
Helmand	175	R6
Helmond	144	F3
Helmsdale *U.K.*	136	E2
Helmsdale *U.K.*	136	E2
Helong	168	B4
Hel, Polwysep	151	H1
Helsingborg	143	E8
Helsingfors	143	L6
Helsingor	143	E8
Helsinki	143	K6
Helston	132	B4
Helvecia	217	K7
Helvellyn	135	F2
Hemel Hempstead	133	G3
Hempstead	208	D5
Hemsworth	135	H3

I

Name	Page	Grid
Jague	218	C5
Jahmah	174	G7
Jahrom	175	L7
Jaicos	217	J5
Jailolo	171	H5
Jailolo, Selat	171	H5
Jaipur	172	E3
Jaisalmer	172	D3
Jajarm	175	N3
Jajce	152	D3
Jajpur	172	G4
Jakarta	170	D7
Jakhau	172	C4
Jakobstad	142	K5
Jakupica	153	F5
Jalaid Qi	167	N2
Jalalabad	172	D2
Jalalpur Pirwala	172	D3
Jalapa *Mexico*	211	L8
Jalapa *Mexico*	211	N9
Jalasjarvi	142	K5
Jalgaon	172	E4
Jalingo	185	H4
Jalna	172	E5
Jalon	147	F2
Jalor	172	D3
Jalostotitlan	210	H7
Jalpa	210	H7
Jalpaiguri	173	G3
Jalpan	211	K7
Jalu	181	K2
Jam	175	Q4
Jamaica	212	J5
Jamaica Channel	213	K5
Jamalpur *Bangladesh*	173	G4
Jamalpur *India*	172	G3
Jamanxim	217	F5
Jamari	216	E5
Jambi	170	C6
James	203	R6
James Bay	201	K7
James Island	216	A7
James Ross, Cape	200	D3
James Ross Island	221	W6
James Ross Strait	200	G4
Jamestown *South Africa*	188	E6
Jamestown *N. Dakota*	203	Q4
Jamestown *New York*	205	L5
Jamjo	143	F8
Jamkhandi	172	E5
Jamkhed	172	E5
Jammerbugten	143	C8
Jammu	172	D2
Jammu and Kashmir	172	E2
Jamnagar	172	D4
Jampur	172	D3
Jamsa	143	L6
Jamshedpur	172	G4
Jamtland	142	F5
Jamuna	173	G3
Janda, Laguna de la	146	D4
Jandaq	175	M4
Jandiatuba	216	D4
Janesville	204	F5
Janjira	172	D5
Jan Mayen	128	F2
Jannatabad	175	Q4
Janos	207	H5
Januaria	218	H3
Janubiyah, Al Badiyah al	174	H6
Jaora	172	E4
Japan	169	G7
Japan, Sea of	168	D6
Japan Trench	222	F3
Japaratuba	217	K6
Japura	216	D4
Japura	174	D3
Jarabulus	174	D3
Jaragua	218	G3
Jaraguari	218	F4
Jarama	146	E2
Jarandilla	146	D2
Jarash	174	B5
Jardee	192	D5
Jardines de la Reina	212	H4
Jari	217	G3
Jarir, Wadi al	176	F4
Jarna	143	G7
Jarnac	145	C6
Jaromer	150	F3
Jaroslaw	151	K3
Jarpen	142	E5
Jarrow	135	H2
Jarruhi	174	J6
Jartai	167	K4
Jarvso	143	G6
Jashpurnagar	172	F4
Jask	175	N9
Jasper *Canada*	199	M5
Jasper *Alabama*	209	J4
Jasper *Florida*	209	L5
Jasper *Texas*	208	F5
Jassy	153	J2
Jastrebarsko	152	C3
Jastrowie	151	G2
Jastrzebie-Zdroj	151	H4
Jaszbereny	152	E2
Jatai	218	F3
Jatapu	216	F4
Jath	172	E5
Jativa	147	F3
Jatoba	217	G6
Jau	216	E4
Jau	218	G4
Jauaperi	216	E4
Jauja	216	B6
Jaunpur	172	F3
Java	170	E7
Java Trench	222	E5
Javier, Isla	219	B9
Javor	152	E3
Javorniky	151	H4
Jawa	170	D7
Jawa, Laut	170	E7
Jawb, Al	177	K5
Jawhar	187	J2
Jawor	151	G3
Jayanca	216	B5
Jaya, Puncak	171	K6
Jayapura	171	L6
Jayawijaya, Pegunungan	171	K6
Jayena	146	E4
Jaypur	172	F5
Jayrud	174	C5
Jazirah, Al	174	E4
Jaz Murian, Hamun-e	175	P8
Jebal Barez, Kuh-e	175	P7
Jebba	185	F4
Jebel, Bahr el	182	F6
Jech Doab	172	D2
Jedburgh	137	F5
Jedeida	149	B7
Jefferson	202	H5
Jefferson City *Missouri*	204	D7
Jefferson City *Tennessee*	209	L2
Jefferson, Mount *Nevada*	202	F8
Jefferson, Mount *Oregon*	202	D5
Jef Jef el Kebir	182	D3
Jehile Puzak	175	Q6
Jekabpils	143	L8
Jeldesa	183	H6
Jelenia Gora	150	F3
Jelgava	143	K8
Jelow Gir	174	H5
Jemaja	170	D5
Jember	170	E7
Jeminay	166	F2
Jemnice	150	F4
Jena	150	D3
Jendouba	149	B7
Jenin	174	B5
Jenkins	204	J8
Jennings	208	F5
Jenny Lind Island	199	Q2
Jens Munk Island	200	L4
Jequie	217	J6
Jequitinhonha *Brazil*	218	H3
Jequitinhonha *Brazil*	218	H3
Jerada	180	E2
Jerba, Ile de	181	H2
Jeremie	213	K5
Jeremoabo	217	K6
Jerevan	157	L2
Jerez	210	H6
Jerez de la Frontera	146	C4
Jericho *Australia*	193	K3
Jericho *Israel*	174	B6
Jerome	202	G6
Jersey	133	M7
Jersey City	205	N6
Jerseyville	204	E7
Jerusalem	174	B6
Jervis Inlet	202	C2
Jeseniky	151	G3
Jessheim	143	D6
Jessore	172	G4
Jesup	209	M5
Jevnaker	143	D6
Jezerce	154	E1
Jeziorak, Jezioro	151	H2
Jeznas	151	L1
Jezzine	174	B5
Jhang Maghiana	172	D2
Jhansi	172	E3
Jhelum *Pakistan*	172	D2
Jhelum *Pakistan*	172	D2
Jialing Jiang	173	L2
Jiamusi	168	C2
Jian	173	N3
Jianchuan	173	I3
Jiande	167	M6
Jiange	173	L2
Jiangjin	173	L3
Jiangjunmiao	166	F3
Jiangmen	173	M4
Jiangsu	167	M5
Jiangxi	173	M3
Jianning	167	M6
Jianou	167	M6
Jianquanzi	166	H3
Jianshi	173	L2
Jiaohe	167	P3
Jiaoling	167	M7
Jiaozuo	173	M1
Jia Xian	167	L4
Jiaxing	167	N5
Jiayin	168	C1
Jiayuguan	166	H4
Jiboia	216	D3
Jibou	153	G2
Jibsh, Ra's	177	P6
Jicatuyo	212	C7
Jiddah	176	D6
Jidong	168	C3
Jiekkevarre	142	H2
Jieknaffo	142	G3
Jiesavrre	142	L2
Jihlava *Czech Rep.*	150	F4
Jihlava *Czech Rep.*	151	G4
Jijel	181	G1
Jijia	153	J2
Jijiga	183	H6
Jijihu	166	F3
Jilava	153	J3
Jilin *China*	167	P3
Jilin *China*	167	P3
Jiloca	147	F2
Jilove	150	F4
Jima	183	G6
Jimba Jimba	192	D4
Jimena de la Frontera	146	D4
Jimenez	207	M6
Jimenez *Mexico*	208	C8
Jimenez *Mexico*	207	K7
Jimo	167	N4
Jinan	167	M4
Jincheng	167	K4
Jingbian	167	K4
Jingchuan	173	L1
Jingdezhen	167	M6
Jinghai	167	M4
Jinghe	166	E3
Jinghong	173	K4
Jingle	167	L4
Jingmen	173	M2
Jingpo	168	B3
Jingpo Hu	168	B4
Jingtai	173	K1
Jingxi	173	L4
Jing Xian	173	L3
Jinhua	167	M6
Jining *Nei Mongol Zizhiqu, China*	167	L3
Jining *Shandong, China*	167	M4
Jinja	187	F2
Jinkou	167	N4
Jinning	173	K4
Jinsha Jiang	173	J3
Jinta	166	H4
Jinxi	167	N3
Jin Xian	167	N4
Jinzhou	167	N3
Jinzhou Wan	167	N4
Jiparana	216	E5
Jipijapa	216	A4
Jiquilpan	210	H8
Jirriiban	183	J6
Jirueque	146	E2
Jirwan	177	K5
Jishou	173	L3
Jisr ash Shughur	174	C4
Jiu	153	G3
Jiujiang	173	N3
Jiuling Shan	173	M3
Jiutai	167	P3
Jiwa , Al	177	M5
Jiwani	172	B3
Jiwani, Ras	172	B4
Jixi *Anhui, China*	167	M5
Jixi *Heilongjiang, China*	167	Q2
Jixian	168	C2
Jizan	176	F8
Jizl, Wadi	176	C3
Jiz, Wadi al	177	K8
Jizan	176	F8
Joao Pessoa	217	L5
Joaquin V. Gonzalez	218	D5
Joban	169	H7
Jodar	146	E4
Jodhpur	172	D3
Joensuu	142	N5
Joetsu	169	G7
Jofane	189	F4
Joffre, Mount	202	G2
Jogeva	143	M7
Joghatay	175	N3
Johannesburg	188	E5
John Day *U.S.A.*	202	D5
John Day *U.S.A.*	202	E5
John H. Kerr Reservoir	209	N2
John O'Groats	136	E2
Johnshaven	137	F4
Johnson City	209	L2
Johnston *U.K.*	132	B3
Johnston *U.S.A.*	209	M4
Johnstone	137	D5
Johnston Lakes, The	192	E5
Johnstown	205	L6
Johor Baharu	170	C5
Joigny	145	E5
Joinville *Brazil*	218	G5
Joinville *France*	144	F4
Joinville Island	221	W6
Jokkmokk	142	H3
Jokulbunga	142	T11
Jokulsa a Bru	142	X12
Jokulsa-a Fjollum	142	W12
Jolfa	174	G2
Joliet	204	G6
Joliette	205	P3
Jolo *Philippines*	171	G4
Jolo *Philippines*	171	G4
Jonava	143	N9
Jonesboro	208	G3
Jones Sound	200	J2
Jonglei Canal	182	F6
Joniskis	143	K8
Jonkoping *Sweden*	143	F8
Jonkoping *Sweden*	143	F8
Jonquiere	205	Q2
Jonzac	145	C6
Joplin	204	C8
Jordan	174	B6
Jordan	174	B5
Jordan *U.S.A.*	203	L4
Jordanow	151	H4
Jordan Valley	202	F6
Jorhat	173	H3
Jorn	142	J4
Jorong	170	E6
Jorpeland	143	B7
Jos	185	G3
Jose de San Martin	219	B8
Joseph Bonaparte Gulf	192	F1
Joseph, Lac	201	N7
Josselin	145	B5
Jos Sodarso, Pulau	171	K7
Jostedalsbreen	143	B6
Jotunheimen	143	C6
Jounie	174	B5
Joutsa	143	M6
Joyces Country	139	C5
J. Percy Priest Lake	209	J2
Juan Aldama	210	H5
Juan de Fuca Strait	202	B3
Juan de Nova	189	H3
Juan Fernandez, Islas de	215	A6
Juanjui	216	B5
Juarez, Sierra	206	D4
Juazeiro	217	J5
Juazeiro do Norte	217	K5
Juba	183	F7
Jubany	221	W6
Jubba	187	F2
Juby, Cap	180	C3
Jucar	147	F3
Juchitan	211	M9
Judenburg	148	E2
Juigalpa	212	E8
Juist	150	B2
Juiz de Fora	218	H4
Juklegga	143	E6
Julia	216	D4
Juliaca	218	B3
Julia Creek	193	J3
Julianhab	196	Q2
Julijske Alpe	152	B2
Julio de Castilhos	218	F5
Jullundur	172	E2
Jumilla	147	F3
Jumla	172	F3
Junagadh	172	D4
Junction	207	N5
Junction City	203	R8
Jundiai	218	G4
Juneau	198	J4
Junee	193	K5
Jungfrau	148	A2
Junggar Pendi	166	F2
Junin	219	D6
Junin de los Andes	219	B7
Junosuando	142	K3
Junsele	142	G5
Jun Xian	173	M2
Jura *France*	145	G5
Jura *U.K.*	137	C5
Jura, Sound of	137	C5
Juratishki	151	L1
Juriti	217	F4
Jurua *Brazil*	216	D4
Jurua *Brazil*	216	D4
Juruena	216	F6
Jussey	145	F5
Jutai *Brazil*	216	D4
Jutai *Brazil*	216	D5
Juterbog	150	E3
Juticalpa	212	D7
Jutland	143	C8
Juuka	142	N5
Juva	143	M6
Juventud, Isla de la	212	F4
Ju Xian	167	M4
Juymand	175	P4
Juyom	175	M7
Juzna Morava	153	F4
Jylland	143	C8
Jyvaskyla	142	L5

K

Name	Page	Grid
Kaala-Gomen	194	W16
Kaamanen	142	M2
Kaavi	142	N5
Kaba	184	C4
Kabaena	171	G7
Kabala	184	C4
Kabale	187	E3
Kabalega Falls	187	F2
Kabalo	186	E4
Kabambare	187	E3
Kabara	194	S9
Kabba	185	G4
Kabinatagami	204	H1
Kabinda	186	D4
Kabirkuh	174	H5
Kabompo	186	D5
Kabongo	186	E4
Kabud Gonbad	175	P3
Kabul *Afghanistan*	172	C2
Kabuli	194	D2
Kaburuang	171	H5
Kabwe	187	E5
Kabyrdak	164	A5
Kachchh, Gulf of	172	C4
Kachchh, Rann of	172	C4
Kachemak Bay	198	E4

Name	Page	Grid	Name	Page	Grid	Name	Page	Grid	Name	Page	Grid
Kirsanov	159	G5	Klodzka *Poland*	151	G3	Kola	142	Q2	Kopaonik	153	F4
Kirsehir	156	F3	Klodzko *Poland*	151	G3	Kolaka	171	G6	Kopasker	142	W11
Kirtgecit	157	K3	Klos	155	F2	Kolar	172	E6	Kopavogur	142	U12
Kirthar Range	172	C3	Klosterneuberg	148	F1	Kolari	142	K3	Koper	152	B3
Kirtlington	133	F3	Klosters	148	B2	Kolarovgrad	153	J4	Kopervik	143	A7
Kirton	135	J3	Klrovskiy	159	H6	Kolasin	152	E4	Kopet Dag, Khrebet	175	N2
Kiruna	142	J3	Kluane	198	H3	Kolay	157	F2	Kopeysk	164	Ad5
Kiryu	169	G7	Kluane Lake	198	H3	Kolberg	150	F1	Koping	143	F7
Kisa	143	F8	Kluczbork	151	H3	Kolbuszowa	151	J3	Kopka	204	F1
Kisamou, Kolpos	155	G5	Klyevka	164	A6	Kolchugino	158	F4	Kopmanholmen	142	H5
Kisangani	186	E2	Klyuchevskaya Sopka	165	U5	Kolda	184	C3	Koppang	143	D6
Kisar	171	H7	Klyuchi	165	U5	Kolding	143	C9	Kopparberg *Sweden*	143	F7
Kisarazu	169	G8	Klyukvinka	164	D5	Kole	186	D3	Kopparberg *Sweden*	143	F6
Kiselevsk	164	D6	Kmagta	194	J6	Kolguyev, Ostrov	158	H2	Koppi *Russia*	168	G1
Kishanganj	173	G3	Kmanjab	188	B3	Kolhapur	172	D5	Koppi *Russia*	168	H1
Kishangarh	172	D3	K2, Mount	172	E1	Kolin	150	F3	Kopru	156	D4
Kishb, Harrat	176	E5	Knapdale	137	C5	Kolki	151	L3	Koprubasi	156	C3
Kishika-zaki	169	C10	Knaresborough	135	H2	Kolkuskull	142	V12	Koprulu	156	E4
Kishiwada	169	E8	Knife	203	N4	Kollabudur	142	T12	Kopruoren	156	C3
Kishorganj	173	H4	Knight Island	198	F3	Koln	150	B3	Kopychintsy	153	H1
Kishorn, Loch	136	C3	Knighton	132	D2	Kolno	151	J2	Kor	175	L6
Kisii	187	F3	Knin	152	D3	Koloa	206	R10	Kora	157	K2
Kiska Island	198	Ab9	Knjazevac	153	G4	Kolobrzeg	150	F1	Korab	152	F5
Kiskunfelegyhaza	152	E2	Knockadoon Head	139	G9	Kologriv	158	G4	Korahe	183	H6
Kiskunhalas	152	E2	Knockalla Mount	138	G2	Kolombangara	194	H5	Koraluk	201	P6
Kislovodsk	159	G7	Knockanaffrin	139	G8	Kolomna	158	F4	Korana	152	C3
Kismaayo	187	H3	Knockaunapeebra	139	G8	Kolono	171	G6	Korba	149	C7
Kiso-Fukushima	169	F8	Knocklayd	138	K2	Koloubara	152	F3	Korbach	150	C3
Kiso-sammyaku	169	F8	Knockmealdown Mountains	139	G8	Kolozsvar	153	G2	Korbu, Gunung	170	C5
Kispest	152	E2	Knocknaskagh	139	F8	Kolpashevo	164	C5	Korce	155	F2
Kissidougou	184	C4	Knottingley	135	H3	Kolpino	158	E4	Korcula	152	D4
Kissimmee	209	M7	Knox, Cape	198	J5	Kolskiy Poluostrov	158	F2	Korda	164	F4
Kisumu	187	F3	Knoxville *Iowa*	204	D6	Koltubanovskiy	159	J5	Kord Kuv	175	M3
Kita	180	D6	Knoxville *Tennessee*	209	L3	Koluszki	151	H3	Korea Bay	167	N4
Kitajaur	142	J3	Knoydart	137	C3	Kolva *Russia*	158	K3	Korea, North	167	P4
Kitakami *Japan*	168	H6	Knud Rasmussen Land	200	P2	Kolva *Russia*	158	K2	Korea, South	167	P4
Kitakami *Japan*	168	H6	Knutholstind	143	C6	Kolwezi	186	E5	Korea Strait	169	B8
Kitakami-sanmyaku	168	J3	Knutsford	135	G3	Kolyma	165	U3	Korennoye	164	H2
Kita-kyushu	169	C9	Knyazhaya Guba	142	Q3	Kolymskaya Nizmennost	165	T3	Korenovsk	159	F6
Kitale	187	G2	Knyazhevo	158	G4	Kolymskiy, Khrebet	165	T4	Korf	165	V4
Kitami	168	J4	Knysna	188	D6	Komadugu Gana	185	H3	Korforskiy	168	E1
Kitami-sammyaku	168	H6	Knyszyn	151	K2	Komandorskiye Ostrova	161	T4	Korgan	157	G2
Kitangari	187	G5	Koba	170	D6	Komarno	151	H5	Korgen	142	E3
Kitay, Ozero	153	K3	Kobarid	152	B2	Komarom	152	E2	Korhogo	184	D4
Kit Carson	207	L1	Kobayashi	169	C10	Komatsu	169	F7	Korido	171	K6
Kitchener	205	K5	Kobberminebugt	200	R5	Komering	170	C6	Korim	171	K6
Kitee	142	P5	Kobelyaki	159	E6	Komodo	171	F7	Korinthiakos Kolpos	155	G3
Kitgum	187	F2	Kobenhavn	143	E9	Komoe	184	E4	Korinthos	155	G4
Kithira *Greece*	155	G4	Koblenz	150	B3	Kom Ombo	183	F3	Koriyama	169	H7
Kithira *Greece*	155	G4	Kobowre, Pegunungan	171	K6	Komoran	171	K7	Korkinitskiy Zaliv	159	E6
Kithnos *Greece*	155	H4	Kobrin	151	L2	Komsomolets, Ostrov	161	L1	Korkodon	165	T4
Kithnos *Greece*	155	H4	Kobroor	171	J7	Komsomolets, Zaliv	159	J6	Korkuteli	156	C4
Kitikmeot	199	N1	Kobuk	198	D2	Komsomolsk	159	E6	Korla	166	F3
Kitimat	198	K5	Kobuleti	157	J2	Komsomolskiy	159	J6	Kormakiti, Akra	156	E5
Kitinen	142	M3	Kobya	165	M4	Komsomolsk-na-Amure	165	P6	Kornat	152	C4
Kitkiojoki	142	K3	Koca *Turkey*	156	B3	Konakovo	158	F4	Koro	194	R8
Kitsuki	169	C9	Koca *Turkey*	156	C3	Koncanica	152	D3	Korocha	159	F5
Kittanning	205	L6	Koca *Turkey*	156	E2	Konch	172	E3	Koroglu Daglari	156	E2
Kittila	142	L3	Kocapinar	157	K3	Konda *Indonesia*	171	J6	Koronia, Limni	155	G2
Kitui	187	G3	Kocarli	156	B4	Konda *Russia*	164	Ae4	Koronowo	151	G2
Kitunda	187	F4	Koceljevo	152	E3	Kondagaon	172	F5	Koros	152	F2
Kitwe	187	E5	Koch Bihar	173	G3	Kondinin	192	D5	Korosten	159	D5
Kitzbuhel	148	D2	Kochechum	164	G3	Kondinskoye	164	Ae5	Korostyshev	159	D5
Kitzbuheler Alpen	148	D2	Kochegarovo	165	K5	Kondoa	187	G3	Korotaikha	158	L2
Kitzingen	150	D4	Kocher	150	C4	Kondon	165	P6	Koryakskaya Sopka	165	U6
Kivalo	142	L3	Kochi	169	D9	Kondoponga	158	E3	Koryanskiy Khrebet	165	Z5
Kivijarvi	142	L5	Koch Island	200	L4	Konduz	172	C1	Koryazhma	158	H3
Kivu, Lake	187	E3	Kochkorka	166	D3	Kone	194	W16	Korzybie	151	G1
Kiyevka	168	D4	Koch Peak	202	J5	Konevo	158	F3	Kos *Greece*	155	J4
Kiyevskoye Vodokhranilishche	159	E5	Kochumdek	164	E4	Kong	184	E4	Kos *Greece*	155	J4
Kiyikoy	156	C2	Koden	151	K3	Kongan	169	J10	Koschagyl	159	J6
Kizel	158	K4	Kodiak	198	E4	Kong Christian den X Land	200	W3	Koscian	151	G2
Kizema	158	H3	Kodiak Island	198	E4	Kong Karls Land	160	D2	Koscierzyna	151	G1
Kizilagac	157	J3	Kodima	158	G3	Kongolo	186	E4	Kosciusco, Mount	193	K6
Kizilcaboluk	156	C4	Kodinar	172	D4	Kongsberg	143	C7	Kosciusko	208	H4
Kizilcadag	156	C4	Kodok	183	F6	Kongsvinger	143	E6	Kose	157	H2
Kizilhisar	156	C4	Kodomari	168	H5	Kong Wilhelms Land	200	X2	Kos Golu	156	B2
Kizilirmak	156	E2	Kodyma	153	L2	Koniecpol	151	H3	Koshiki-retto	169	B10
Kizil Irmak	157	F2	Kofcaz	156	B2	Konigsberg	151	J4	Kosice	151	J4
Kizilkaya	156	D4	Koffiefontein	188	D5	Konigs Wusterhausen	150	E2	Koski	143	K6
Kiziloren	156	E4	Koflach	148	E2	Konin	151	H2	Koslan	158	H3
Kiziltepe	157	J4	Koforidua	184	E4	Konitsa	155	F2	Koslin	151	G1
Kizlyar	159	H7	Kofu	169	G8	Koniya	169	B11	Kosma	158	H2
Kizyl-Arvat	175	N2	Koge	143	E9	Konkamaalv	142	J2	Kosong	168	B6
Kizyl-Atrek	175	M3	Kogilnik	153	K2	Konkoure	184	C3	Kosong-ni	168	B5
Kizyl Ayak	175	S3	Ko, Gora	168	F2	Konnern	150	D3	Kossou, Lac de	184	D4
Kizyl-Su	175	L2	Kohat	172	D2	Konnevesi	142	M5	Kossovo	151	L2
Kjollefjord	142	M1	Kohima	173	H3	Konosha	158	G3	Kostajnica	152	D3
Kjopsvick	142	L2	Koh-i Qaisar	175	S5	Konotop	159	E5	Kosti	183	F5
Kladanj	152	E3	Kohtla-Jarve	143	M7	Konqi He	166	F3	Kostino	164	D3
Kladno	150	F3	Koide	169	G7	Konskie	151	J3	Kostomuksha	142	P4
Kladovo	153	G3	Koi Sanjaq	174	G3	Konstantinovsk	159	G6	Kostopol	151	M3
Klagenfurt	148	E2	Koitere	142	P5	Konstanz	148	B2	Kostroma *Russia*	158	G4
Klaipeda	143	L9	Koivu	142	L3	Konstyantynivka	159	F6	Kostroma *Russia*	158	G4
Klamath *U.S.A.*	202	B7	Koje	169	B8	Kontagora	185	G3	Kostrzyn	150	F2
Klamath *U.S.A.*	202	C7	Kojonup	192	D5	Kontcha	185	H4	Kosu-dong	169	B8
Klamath Falls	202	D6	Kokand	166	B3	Kontiomaki	142	N4	Kosva	158	K4
Klamath Mountains	202	C6	Kokas	171	J6	Kontum	173	L6	Kosyu	158	K2
Klamono	171	J6	Kokchetav	164	Ae6	Kontum, Plateau du	173	L6	Kosyuvom	158	K2
Klaralven	143	J6	Kokemaenjoki	143	K6	Konya	156	E4	Koszalin	151	G1
Klatovy	150	E4	Kokenau	171	K6	Konya Ovasi	156	E3	Kota	172	E3
Klekovaca	152	D3	Kokkola	142	K5	Konzhakovskiy Kamen , Gora	158	K4	Kotaagung	170	C7
Klenak	152	E3	Koko	185	G4	Kootenai	202	G3	Kota Baharu	170	C4
Klerksdorp	188	E5	Kokoda	194	D3	Kootenay	202	F3	Kotabaru *Indonesia*	170	E6
Klichka	165	K7	Kokomo	204	G6	Kootenay Lake	202	F3	Kotabaru *Indonesia*	170	F6
Klimovichi	159	E5	Kokpekty	166	E2				Kota Belud	170	F4
Klin	158	F4	Koksoak	201	N6						
Klinovec	150	E3	Kokstad	188	E6						
Klintsovka	159	H5	Koktas	166	C2						
Klintsy	159	E5	Kokubu	169	C10						
Klisura	153	H4	Kokuora	165	R2						
Kljuc	152	D3	Kokura	169	C9						
Klobuck	151	H3	Kokuy	165	K6						
			Kok-Yangak	166	C3						

Name	Page	Grid
Kotabumi	170	C5
Kota Kinabalu	170	F4
Kotala	142	N3
Kotamubagu	171	G5
Kota Tinggi	170	C5
Kotel	153	J4
Kotelnich	158	H4
Kotelnikovo	159	G6
Kotelnyy, Ostrov	165	P1
Kotikovo	168	E2
Kotka	143	M6
Kot Kapura	172	D2
Kotlas	158	H3
Kotli	172	D2
Kotlik	198	C3
Koto	165	P7
Kotor	152	E4
Kotovo	159	G5
Kotovsk *Russia*	159	G5
Kotovsk *Ukraine*	159	D6
Kotri	172	C3
Kottagudem	172	F5
Kottayam	172	E7
Kotto	182	D6
Kotuy	164	G2
Kotyuzhany	153	K2
Kotzebue	198	C2
Kotzebue Sound	198	C2
Kouango	182	C6
Koudougou	184	E3
Koufonisi	155	J5
Koukajuak, Great Plain of the	200	M4
Kouki	182	C6
Koumac	194	W16
Koumenzi	166	F3
Koumra	182	C6
Koundara	184	C3
Koungou Mountains	186	B3
Kounradskiy	166	D2
Kourou	217	G2
Kouroussa	184	D3
Kousseri	185	J3
Koutiala	180	D6
Kouvola	143	M6
Kova	164	G5
Kovachevo	153	J4
Kovanlik	157	H2
Kovdor	142	P3
Kovdozero, Ozero	142	Q3
Kovel	151	L3
Kovernino	158	G4
Kovero	142	P5
Kovik Bay	201	L5
Kovno	151	K1
Kovrov	158	G4
Kovylkino	158	G5
Kowalewo	151	H2
Kowloon	167	L7
Koycegiz	156	C4
Koyda	158	G2
Koyuk	198	C3
Koyukuk	198	D3
Koyulhisar	157	G2
Koza	169	E9
Kozakli	156	F3
Kozan	157	F4
Kozani	155	F2
Kozekovo	151	M1
Kozelsk	158	F5
Kozhevnikovo	164	B5
Kozhikode	172	E6
Kozhim	158	K2
Kozhposelok	158	F3
Kozhva	158	K2
Kozlu	156	D2
Kozludere	157	G4
Kozluk	157	J3
Kozmodemyansk	158	H4
Kozu-shima	169	G8
Kpalime	184	F4
Krabi	173	J7
Kragero	143	C7
Kragujevac	153	F3
Krakow	151	H3
Krakowska, Jura	151	H3
Kral Chlmec	151	K4
Kralendijk	213	N8
Kraljevo	152	F4
Kralovvany	151	H4
Kralupy	150	F3
Kramatorsk	159	F6
Kramfors	142	G5
Krania	155	F3
Kranidhion	155	G4
Kranj	152	C2
Kranskop	188	F5
Krasavino	158	H3
Krasino	164	Ab2
Kraskino	168	C4
Krasneno	165	X4
Krasnoarmeyesk	164	Ae6
Krasnoarmeyskiy	165	W3
Krasnoborsk	158	H3
Krasnodar	159	F6
Krasnogorsk	168	J1
Krasnograd	159	F6
Krasnokamsk	158	K4
Krasnokutskoye	164	B6
Krasnolesnyy	159	F5
Krasnorechenskiy	168	E3
Krasnoselkup	164	C3
Krasnoslobodsk	158	G5
Krasnoturinsk	164	Ad5
Krasnoufimsk	158	K4
Krasnousolskiy	158	K5
Krasnovishersk	158	K3
Krasnovodskiy Poluostrov	159	J7
Krasnoyarsk	164	E5
Krasnoyarskiy Kray	164	E3
Krasnoye	158	G4
Krasnstaw	151	K3
Krasnyy Chikoy	164	H6
Krasnyye Okny	153	K2
Krasnyy Kholm	159	J5
Krasnyy Kut	159	H5
Krasnyy Luch	159	F6
Krasnyy Yar *Russia*	159	G5
Krasnyy Yar *Russia*	159	H6
Kratie	173	L6
Kraulshavn	200	Q3
Kravanh, Chuor Phnum	173	K6
Krefeld	150	B3
Kremenchugskoye Vodokhranilishche	159	E6
Kremenchuk	159	E6
Kremnets	159	D5
Krems	148	E1
Krenitzin Islands	198	Ae9
Kresevo	152	E4
Kresttsy	158	E4
Kresty	164	D2
Krestyakh	165	K4
Krestyanka	164	C2
Kretinga	143	J9
Kribi	185	G5
Krichev	159	E5
Krichim	153	H4
Krieza	155	H3
Krifovon	155	F3
Krilon, Mys	168	J3
Krios, Akra	155	G5
Krishna	172	E5
Krishnagiri	172	E6
Krishnanagar	173	G4
Kristdala	143	G8
Kristel	147	F5
Kristiansand	143	B7
Kristianstad *Sweden*	143	E8
Kristianstad *Sweden*	143	F8
Kristiansund	142	B5
Kristiinankaupunki	143	J5
Kristinestad	143	J5
Kristinovka	153	K1
Kriti	155	H5
Kritikon Pelagos	155	H5
Kriulyany	153	K2
Kriva Palanka	153	G4
Krivoye Ozero	153	L2
Krk	152	C3
Krnov	151	G3
Krokodil	188	E4
Krokom	142	F5
Krokong	170	E5
Krokowa	151	H1
Krolevets	159	E5
Kromy	159	F5
Kronach	150	D3
Kronanberg	143	F8
Kronshtadt	143	N7
Kroonstad	188	E5
Kropotkin	159	G6
Krosno	151	J4
Krotoszyn	151	G3
Krsko	152	C3
Krugersdorp	188	E5
Krui	170	C7
Kruje	154	E2
Krumbach	150	D4
Krumovgrad	153	H5
Krung Thep	173	K6
Krusenstern, Cape	198	C2
Krusevac	153	F4
Krusevo	153	F5
Krustpils	143	M8
Kruzenshterna, Proliv	165	S7
Kruzof Island	198	H4
Krym	159	E6
Krymsk	159	F7
Krynki	151	K2
Kryry	150	E3
Kryvyy Rih	159	E6
Krzeszowice	151	H3
Ksabi	180	E3
Ksar El Boukhari	181	F1
Ksarel Kebir	180	D2
Ksar es Souk	180	E2
Ksenofontova	155	K3
Ksour Essaf	181	H1
Kstovo	158	G4
Kualakapuas	170	E6
Kuala Kerai	170	C4
Kuala Lipis	170	C5
Kuala Lumpur	170	C5
Kualapembuang	170	E6
Kuala Penyu	170	F4
Kuala Terengganu	170	C4
Kuandian	167	N3
Kuantan	170	C5
Kuba	169	D8
Kuban	159	G6
Kubenskoye Ozero	158	F4
Kubokawa	169	D9
Kubonitu, Mount	194	J6
Kubor, Mount	194	C3
Kubrat	153	J4
Kubuang	170	F5
Kucevo	153	F3
Kuching	170	E5
Kuchinoerabu-jima	169	C10
Kuchinotsu	169	C9
Kuchurgan	153	K2
Kucuk	156	B3
Kucukcekmece	156	C2
Kucuk Kuyu	156	B3
Kudat	170	F4
Kudirkos-Naumiestis	151	K1
Kudus	170	E7
Kudymkar	158	J4
Kufi	156	C3
Kufstein	148	D2
Kugaly	166	D3
Kugi	164	Ad4
Kugmallit Bay	198	J2
Kuhdasht	174	H5
Kuh-e Bul	175	L6
Kuh-e Garbosh	175	K5
Kuh Lab, Ra's	175	Q9
Kuhmo	142	N4
Kuhpayeh *Iran*	175	L5
Kuhpayeh *Iran*	175	N6
Kuhran, Kuh-e	175	P8
Kuh, Ra's-al-	175	N9
Kuito	186	C5
Kuji	168	H5
Kuju-san	169	C9
Kukalar, Kuh-e	175	K6
Kukes	155	F1
Kukhomskaya Volya	151	L3
Kukmor	158	J4
Kukpowruk	198	C2
Kukudu	194	H6
Kukup	170	C5
Kukushka	165	M6
Kula *Turkey*	156	C3
Kula *Yugoslavia*	152	E3
Kulagino	159	J6
Kulakshi	159	K6
Kulal, Mont	187	G2
Kulata	153	G5
Kuldiga	143	N8
Kule	188	D4
Kulebaki	158	G4
Kulgera	193	G4
Kulikov	151	L4
Kulinda *Russia*	164	G4
Kulinda *Russia*	164	H4
Kulmac Daglari	157	G3
Kulmbach	150	D3
Kuloy *Russia*	158	G3
Kuloy *Russia*	158	G2
Kulp	157	J3
Kulsary	159	J6
Kultay	159	J6
Kultuk	164	G6
Kulu	156	E3
Kulu Island	198	J4
Kulul	176	E9
Kulunda	164	B6
Kulundinskoye, Ozero	164	B6
Kulyab	166	B4
Kuma	159	H7
Kumagaya	169	G7
Kumakh-Surt	165	M2
Kumamoto	169	C9
Kumano	169	F9
Kumanovo	153	F4
Kumara	195	C5
Kumasi	184	E4
Kumba	185	G5
Kumbakonam	172	E6
Kum-Dag	175	M2
Kumertau	159	K5
Kuminki	142	L4
Kuminskiy	164	Ae5
Kumkuduk	166	F3
Kumluca	156	D4
Kummerower See	150	E2
Kumnyong	167	P5
Kumon Bum	173	J3
Kumru	157	G2
Kumsong	167	P4
Kumta	172	D6
Kumyr	166	C3
Kunas	166	E3
Kunas Chang	166	E3
Kunashir, Ostrov	168	L3
Kundelungu Mountains	187	E5
Kunduz	172	C1
Kungalv	143	H8
Kungar	158	K4
Kunghit Island	198	J5
Kungrad	131	U7
Kungsor	143	G7
Kungu	186	C2
Kunlun Shan	172	F1
Kunmadaras	152	F2
Kunming	173	K4
Kunsan	167	P4
Kununurra	192	F2
Kunu-ri	167	P4
Kuolayarvi	142	N3
Kuopio *Sweden*	142	M5
Kuopio *Sweden*	142	M5
Kupa	152	C3
Kupang	171	G7
Kuparuk	198	E2
Kupino	164	B6
Kupreanof Island	198	J4
Kupreanof Point	198	Ag8
Kupyansk	159	F6
Kuqa	166	E3
Kura	157	L2
Kurashasayskiy	159	K5
Kurashiki	169	D8
Kurayoshi	169	D8
Kurday	166	D3
Kurdzhali	153	H5
Kure	169	D8
Kure	156	E2
Kurecik	157	G3
Kure Daglari	156	F2
Kuresaare	143	M7
Kureyka	164	D3
Kurgan	164	Ae5
Kurganinsk	159	G7
Kurgan-Tyube	166	B4
Kurikka	142	N4
Kurilskiye Ostrova	165	S7
Kuril Trench	222	G3
Kurkcu	156	E4
Kurlek	164	C5
Kurmuk	183	F5
Kurnool	172	E5
Kuroi	169	E8
Kuroiso	169	G7
Kurow	151	K3
Kursk	159	F5
Kursumlija	153	F4
Kursunlu	156	E2
Kurtalan	157	J4
Kurtamysh	164	Ad6
Kurtun	157	H2
Kuru	143	K6
Kurucasile	156	E2
Kuruman *South Africa*	188	D5
Kuruman *South Africa*	188	D5
Kurume	169	C9
Kurunegala	172	F7
Kurzeme	143	K8
Kusadasi	156	B4
Kusadasi Korfezi	156	B4
Kusel	150	B4
Kusey Andolu Daglari	157	H2
Kushchevskaya	159	F6
Kushima	169	C10
Kushimoto	169	E9
Kushiro	168	K4
Kushka *Russia*	165	U4
Kushmurun	164	Ad6
Kushtia	173	G4
Kushva	158	K4
Kuskokwim	198	C3
Kuskokwim Bay	198	C4
Kuskokwim Mountains	198	D3
Kusma	172	F3
Kussharo-ko	168	K4
Kustanay	164	Ad6
Kustrin	150	F2
Kuta	185	G4
Kutahya	156	C3
Kutaisi	157	K1
Kutchan	168	H4
Kutima	164	H5
Kut, Ko	173	K6
Kutna Hora	150	F4
Kutno	151	H2
Kutu	186	C3
Kutubdia	173	H4
Kutum	182	D5
Kuujjuaq	201	N6
Kuujjuarapik	201	L6
Kuuli-Mayak	159	J7
Kuusamo	142	N4
Kuvango	186	C5
Kuvet	165	X3
Kuwait	174	H7
Kuwait	177	J2
Kuwana	169	F8
Kuya	158	G2
Kuybyshev *Russia*	164	B5
Kuybyshevskoye Vodokhranilishche	158	H4
Kuyeda	158	K4
Kuygan	166	C2
Kuytun	166	F3
Kuyucak	156	C4
Kuyumba	164	F4
Kuyus	164	D6
Kuzino	158	K4
Kuzitrin	198	C2
Kuzmovka	164	E4
Kuznetsk	159	H5
Kuznetsovo	168	G2
Kuzomen	158	F2
Kuzucubelen	156	F4
Kvaloy	142	H2
Kvaloya	142	K1
Kvalsund	142	L1
Kvarner	152	C3
Kvarneric	152	C3
Kvichak Bay	198	D4
Kvidinge	143	E8
Kvigtind	142	E4
Kvikkjokk	142	G3
Kvina	143	B7
Kvorning	143	C8
Kwa	186	C3
Kwale	185	G4
Kwamouth	186	C3
Kwangju	167	P4
Kwango	186	C3
Kwango-ri	168	B5
Kwatisore	171	J6
Kwekwe	188	E3

Name	Page	Ref
Kwidzyn	151	H2
Kwilu	186	C3
Kwoka	171	J6
Kyabe	182	C6
Kyaikto	173	J5
Kyakhta	164	H6
Kyaukpyu	173	H5
Kyaukse	173	J4
Kybartai	151	K1
Kychema	158	G2
Kyeburn	195	C6
Kyelang	172	E2
Kyle	137	D5
Kyleakin	136	C3
Kyle of Lochalsh	136	C3
Kylestrome	136	C2
Kymi	143	M6
Kymijoki	143	M6
Kynuna	193	J3
Kyoga, Lake	187	F2
Kyongju	169	B8
Kyoto	169	E8
Kyrdanyy	165	M3
Kyrgyzstan	166	C3
Kyritz	150	E2
Kyrkheden	143	E6
Kyronjoki	142	K5
Kyrosjarvi	143	K6
Kyrta	158	K3
Kyssa	158	H3
Kystyk, Plato	165	L2
Kyuekh-Bulung	164	J3
Kyurdamir	159	H7
Kyushu	169	C9
Kyushu-sanchi	169	C9
Kyustendil	153	G4
Kyyiv	159	E5
Kyyjarvi	142	L5
Kyyvesi	143	M6
Kyzyk	159	J7
Kyzyl	164	E6
Kyzyldyykan	166	B2
Kyzylkoga	159	J6
Kyzyl-Kommuna	166	B2
Kyzylkum	160	H5
Kzyl-Dzhar	166	B2
Kzyl-Orda	166	B3
Kzyltu	164	A6

L

Name	Page	Ref
La Almunia de Dona Godina	147	F2
Laascaanood	183	J6
Laas Dhuure	183	J5
La Asuncion	216	E1
Laayoune	180	C3
La Baie	205	Q2
La Banda	218	D5
La Baneza	146	D1
La Barca	210	H7
Labasa	194	R8
La Baule	145	B5
Labaz, Ozero	164	F2
Labbah, Al	176	E2
Labe	184	C3
Labe	150	F3
Labelle	205	N3
Laberge, Lake	198	H3
Labi	170	E5
Labin	152	C3
Labinsk	159	G7
Labis	170	C5
La Bisbal	147	H2
Labouheyre	145	C6
Laboulaye	219	D6
La Bourboule	145	E6
Labrador	201	P7
Labrador City	201	N7
Labrador Sea	201	Q6
Labrea	216	E5
Labrit	145	C6
Labuha	171	H6
Labuhan	170	D7
Labuhanbajo	171	F7
Labuhanbilik	170	C5
Labytnangi	164	Ae3
Lac	154	E2
La Calzada de Calatrava	146	E3
Lacanau	145	C6
La Carlota	219	D6
La Carolina	146	E3
La Cava	147	G2
Laccadive Islands	172	D6
Laccadive Sea	172	E7
La Ceiba	212	D7
Lacepede Bay	193	H6
La Chaise-Dieu	145	E6
Lacha, Ozero	158	F3
La Charite	145	E5
La Chartre-sur-le-Loir	145	D5
La Chatre	145	D5
La Chaux-de-Fonds	148	A2
Lachin	174	H2
Lachlan	193	K5
La Chorrera	212	H10
Lachute	205	N4
La Cieneguita	206	G6
La Ciotat	145	F7
Lac la Biche	199	N5
Lac Megantic	205	Q4
La Colorada	206	G6
Laconi	149	B6
Laconia	205	Q5

Name	Page	Ref
La Coruna	146	B1
La Croix, Lac	204	D2
La Crosse	204	E5
La Cruz *Costa Rica*	212	E9
La Cruz *Mexico*	210	F6
Lacul Razelm	153	K3
Ladakh Range	172	E2
Ladder Hills	136	E3
La Desirade	213	S6
Ladik	157	F2
Ladismith	188	D6
Ladiz	175	Q7
Ladozhskoye Ozero	143	P6
Ladybank	137	E4
Ladybower Reservoir	135	H3
Ladybrand	188	E5
Ladysmith *Canada*	202	C3
Ladysmith *South Africa*	188	E5
Ladysmith *U.S.A.*	204	E4
Ladyzhenka	164	Ae6
Ladyzhinka	159	D6
Lae	173	K5
Laem Ngop	173	K6
La Esmeralda *Paraguay*	218	D4
La Esmeralda *Venezuela*	216	D3
La Fayette	209	K3
Lafayette *Colorado*	203	M8
Lafayette *Indiana*	204	G6
Lafayette *Louisiana*	208	F5
La Fe	212	E3
La Ferte-Bernard	144	D4
La-Ferte-Saint-Aubin	145	D5
Laffan, Ra's	177	K4
Lafia	185	G4
Lafiagi	185	G4
La Fleche	145	C5
La Follette	209	K2
La Fria	216	C2
Laft	175	M8
La Fuente de San Esteban	146	C2
La Galite	149	B7
Lagan	143	E8
Lagarfljot	142	X12
Lagen *Norway*	143	C6
Lagen *Norway*	143	D6
Laggan	137	D3
Laggan Bay	137	B5
Laggan, Loch	137	D4
Laghouat	181	F2
Lagny	144	E4
Lagonegro	149	E5
Lago Posadas	219	B9
Lagos *Nigeria*	185	F4
Lagos *Portugal*	146	B4
Lagos de Moreno	210	J7
La Grande *Canada*	201	M7
La Grande *U.S.A.*	202	E5
La Grande 2, Reservoir	201	L7
La Grande 3, Reservoir	201	L7
La Grande 4, Reservoir	201	M7
La Grange *Georgia*	209	K4
La Grange *Kentucky*	204	H7
La Grange *Texas*	208	D6
La Granja	146	D2
La Gran Sabana	216	E2
La Guardia	146	B2
Laguardia	146	E1
La Gudina	146	C1
La Guerche-de-Bretagne	145	C5
Laguna	218	G5
Laguna Grande	219	C9
Lagunillas *Bolivia*	218	D3
Lagunillas *Venezuela*	213	M9
Laha	167	N2
La Habana	212	F3
Lahad Datu	171	F4
Lahave	201	P9
Lahij	176	G10
Lahijan	175	J3
Lahn *Germany*	150	C3
Lahn *Germany*	150	C3
Lahore	172	D2
Lahr	150	B4
Lahti	143	L6
Laibach	152	C2
Laibin	173	L4
Lai Chau	173	K4
L'Aigle	144	D4
Laihia	142	J5
Laimbele, Mount	194	T12
Laina	155	J2
Laingsburg	188	D6
Lainioalven	142	K3
Lair	136	C3
Lairg	136	D2
Lais	170	C6
Laitila	143	J6
Laiwui	171	H6
Laixi	167	N4
Laiyang	167	N4
Laiyuan	167	L4
Laizhou Wan	167	M4
Lajes	218	F5
La Junta	207	L2
Lakatrask	142	J3
Lake Andes	203	Q6
Lakeba	194	S9
Lakeba Passage	194	S9
Lake Cargelligo	193	K5
Lake Charles	208	F5
Lake City *Florida*	209	L5
Lake City *S. Carolina*	209	N4
Lake District	135	F2
Lake Grace	192	D5

Name	Page	Ref
Lake Harbour	200	N5
Lake Havasu City	206	E3
Lake Jackson	208	E6
Lake King	192	D5
Lake Kopiago	194	C3
Lakeland	209	M6
Lake Louise	202	F2
Lake Murray	194	C3
Lakeport	202	C8
Lake Providence	208	G4
Lakeview	202	D6
Lake Wales	209	M7
Lakewood	204	K6
Lakhdaria	147	H4
Lakhpat	172	C4
Lakki	172	D2
Lakonikos Kolpos	155	G4
Laksefjorden	142	M1
Lakselv	142	L1
Lakshadweep	172	D6
Lakuramau	194	E2
Lala Musa	172	D2
Lalaua	189	G2
Laleh Zar, Kuh-e	175	N7
Lalibela	183	G5
La Libertad	212	B6
La Ligua	219	B6
Lalin	146	B1
Lalin	167	P2
La Linea	146	D4
Lalin He	168	A3
Lalitpur	172	E4
Lalla Khedidja	147	J4
La Loche	199	P4
La Loupe	144	D4
La Louviere	144	F3
La Luz	212	E8
Lalyo	182	F7
Lamag	171	F4
La Mancha	146	E3
La Manza	216	D6
Lama, Ozero	164	D3
Lamar *Colorado*	207	L1
Lamar *Missouri*	204	C8
Lamas	216	B5
Lamastre	145	F6
Lamballe	144	B4
Lambarene	186	B3
Lambas	194	R8
Lambay Island	139	K6
Lamberhurst	133	H3
Lambert, Cape	194	E2
Lambert Glacier	221	E4
Lamberts Bay	188	C6
Lamb Head	136	F1
Lambia	155	F4
Lambon	194	E2
Lambourn	133	F3
Lamb's Head	139	B9
Lambton, Cape	198	L1
Lame	182	B6
Lamego	146	C2
Lamenu	194	U12
Lameroo	193	J6
Lamia	155	G3
Lammermuir	137	F5
Lammermuir Hills	137	F5
Lammhult	143	F8
Lammi	143	L6
Lamon Bay	171	G3
Lamont *California*	206	C3
Lamont *Wyoming*	203	L6
La Morita	207	K6
La Moure	203	Q4
Lam Pao Reservoir	173	K5
Lampasas	208	C5
Lampazos de Naranjo	208	B7
Lampedusa	154	B5
Lampeter	132	C2
Lampinou	155	G3
Lampione	154	B5
Lamport	133	G2
Lampsa	142	P4
Lamu	187	H3
Lan	151	M2
Lanai	206	S10
Lanai City	206	S10
Lanark	137	D5
La Nava de Ricomalillo	146	D3
Lanbi Kyun	173	J6
Lancang	173	K4
Lancashire	135	G3
Lancaster *U.K.*	135	G2
Lancaster *Ohio*	204	J7
Lancaster *Pennsylvania*	205	M6
Lancaster *S. Carolina*	209	M3
Lancaster Sound	200	J3
Lanciano	149	E4
Lancut	151	K3
Landau	150	C4
Landeck	148	C2
Lander	203	K6
Landerneau	144	A4
Landes	145	C6
Landi	175	R6
Landor	192	D4
Landrum	209	L3
Landsberg *Poland*	150	F2
Landsberg *Germany*	150	D4
Landsborough	193	J3
Land's End	132	B4
Lands End	200	B2
Landshut	150	E4
Landskrona	143	E9

Name	Page	Ref
Lanesborough	138	G5
Lanett	209	K4
Langa Co	172	F2
Langadhia	155	F4
Langavat, Loch	136	B2
Langdon	203	Q3
Lange Berg	188	C6
Langebergen	188	D5
Langeland	143	D9
Langelmavesi	143	L6
Langeoog	150	B2
Langesund	143	C7
Langevag	142	B5
Langfang	167	M4
Langfjord	142	B5
Lang Head	136	A1
Langhirano	148	C3
Langholm	137	E5
Langjokull	142	U12
Langkawi	173	J7
Langnau	148	A2
Langness Point	134	E2
Langogne	145	E6
Langon	145	C6
Langoya	142	F2
Langport	132	E3
Langres	145	F5
Langsa	170	B5
Langsele	142	G5
Langsett	135	H3
Lang Son	173	L4
Langtoft	135	J2
Langtrask	142	J4
Languedoc	145	E7
Langwathby	135	G2
Langzhong	173	L2
Lannemezan	145	D7
Lannion	144	B4
Lansing	204	H5
Lansjarv	142	K3
Lanslebourg	145	G6
Lanta, Ko	173	J7
Lanusei	149	B6
Lanvaux, Landes de	145	B5
Lanxi	167	P2
Lanzarote	180	C3
Lanzhou	173	K1
Laoag	171	G2
Laoang	171	H3
Lao Cai	173	K4
Laois	139	H7
Laon	144	E4
La Oroya	216	B6
Laos	170	C2
Laoye Ling	168	B3
Laoyemiao	166	F3
Lapa	218	G5
Lapalisse	145	E5
La Palma *Panama*	212	H10
La Palma *Spain*	180	B3
La Palma del Condado	146	C4
La Paragua	216	E2
La Paz *Argentina*	219	C6
La Paz *Argentina*	218	E6
La Paz *Bolivia*	218	C3
La Paz *Mexico*	210	D5
La Pedrera	216	D4
La Piedad	210	H7
La Place	208	G4
La Plant	203	P5
La Plata	219	E6
La Pocatiere	205	R3
La Pola de Gordon	146	D1
La Porte	204	G6
Lapovo	153	F3
Lappajarvi	142	K5
Lappeenranta	143	N6
Lappi	142	M3
Lapseki	156	B2
Laptev Sea	165	M1
Laptevykh, More	165	M1
Lapua	142	K5
La Puebla	147	H3
La Puntilla	216	A4
La Quiaca	218	C4
L'Aquila	149	D4
Lar	175	M8
Larache	180	D1
Larak	175	N8
La Rambla	146	D4
Laramie	203	M7
Laramie Mountains	203	M6
Laranjal	217	F4
Larantuka	171	G7
Larat *Indonesia*	194	A3
Larat *Indonesia*	194	A3
Larba	147	H4
Laredo *Spain*	146	E1
Laredo *U.S.A.*	208	C7
La Reole	145	C6
Largo *U.S.A.*	209	L7
Largo *Venezuela*	213	R10
Largoward	137	F4
Largs	137	D5
Lari	174	H2
Larino	149	E5
La Rioja	218	C5
Larisa	155	G3
Lark	133	H2
Larkana	172	C3
Larkhall	137	F4
Larlomkiny	164	A5
Larne	138	L3
La Robla	146	D1

Name	Pg	Grid	Name	Pg	Grid
La Roche	194	Y16	Lawton	208	C3
La Roche-Bernard	145	B5	Lawu, Gunung	170	E7
La Rochelle	145	C5	Lawz, Jambal Al	176	B2
La Roche-sur-Yon	145	C5	Laxay	136	B2
La Roda	147	E3	Laxford, Loch	136	C2
La Romana	213	N5	Laxo	136	A1
La Ronge	199	P4	Lay	145	C5
Larrey Point	192	D2	Layar, Tanjung	170	F6
Larsen Ice Shelf	221	V5	Layla	176	H5
Larvik	143	D7	Laysar	174	J3
La Salle	204	F6	Lazarevac	152	F3
Las Animas	207	L1	Lazarev Sea	221	A5
Las Aves, Isla	216	D1	Lazaro Cardenas	210	H8
Las Coloradas	219	B7	Lazaro Cardenas, Presa	207	K8
Las Cruces	207	J4	Lazdijai	151	K1
La Selle	213	M5	Lazo	168	D4
La Serena	218	B5	Lead	203	N5
La Seu d'Urgell	147	G1	Leadburn	137	E5
Las Flores	219	E7	Leaden Roding	133	H3
Lasham	133	F3	Leader	203	K2
Lash-e Joveyn	175	Q6	Leader Water	137	F5
Lashkar	172	E3	Leaf	201	M6
Lashkar Gah	172	B2	Leaf Bay	201	N6
Las Horquetas	219	B9	Leane, Lough	139	C8
La Sila	149	F6	Leatherhead	133	G3
Lasjerd	175	L4	Leavenworth *Kansas*	204	C7
Las Lomitas	218	D4	Leavenworth *Washington*	202	D4
Las Marismas	146	C4	Leba	151	G1
Las Mercedes	213	P10	Lebak	171	G4
Laso	143	D8	Lebane	153	F4
La Souterraine	145	D5	Lebanon	174	B4
Las Palmas	180	B3	Lebanon *Missouri*	205	P5
La Spezia	148	B3	Lebanon *Pennsylvania*	209	J2
Las Plumas	219	C8	Lebanon *Tennessee*	204	D8
Lassen Peak	202	D7	Lebanon *Vermont*	205	M6
Last Mountain Lake	203	M2	Lebed	164	D4
Lastoursville	186	B3	Lebedin	159	E5
Lastovo	152	D4	Lebesby	142	M1
Las Trincheras	213	Q11	Le Blanc	145	D5
L'Astrolabe, Recifs de	194	W15	Lebombo Mountains	189	F4
Lasva	152	D3	Lebork	151	G1
Las Varillas	218	D6	Lebrija	146	C4
Las Vegas *Nevada*	206	E2	Lebsko, Jezioro	151	G1
Las Vegas *New Mexico*	207	K3	Lebu	219	B7
Latacunga	216	B4	Lebyazhye	164	B6
Latady Island	221	U4	Le Cateau	144	E3
Latakia	157	F5	Lecce	149	G5
Late	191	U5	Lecco	148	B3
Latefoss	143	B7	Lech *Austria*	148	C2
Latgale	143	M8	Lech *Germany*	150	D4
Latheron	136	E2	Lechang	173	M3
La Tina	216	B4	Lechlade	133	F3
Latina	149	D5	Lechtaler Alpen	148	C2
Latoritsa	151	K4	Leconfield	135	J3
La Tour-du-Pin	145	F6	Le Conquet	144	A4
Latrobe	193	K7	Le Creusot	145	F5
La Tuque	205	P3	Le Croisic	145	B5
Latur	172	E5	Lectoure	145	D7
Latvia	143	K8	Lecumberri	147	F1
Lau *Sudan*	182	F6	Leczna	151	K3
Lau *Sudan*	182	F6	Leczyca	151	H2
Laucola	194	S8	Ledbury	132	E2
Lauder	137	F4	Ledesma	146	D2
Lauderdale	137	F5	Lediba	186	C3
Lauenberg	150	D2	Ledmozero	142	Q4
Laughlan Islands	194	E3	Ledong	173	L5
Lau Group	194	S8	Le Dorat	145	D5
Launceston *Australia*	193	K7	Ledu	173	K1
Launceston *U.K.*	132	C4	Ledyanaya, Gora	165	W4
Launglon Bok Islands	173	J6	Lee	139	E9
La Union *Bolivia*	218	D3	Leech Lake	204	C3
La Union *Chile*	219	B8	Leeds	135	H3
La Union *Colombia*	216	B3	Leedstown	132	B4
La Union *El Salvador*	212	D8	Leek	135	G3
La Union *Mexico*	211	Q9	Leemoore	206	C2
La Union *Spain*	147	F4	Leer	150	B2
Laupheim	150	C4	Leesburg	209	M6
Laura	193	J2	Leesville	208	F5
La Urbana	213	P11	Leeuwarden	144	F2
Laurel *Mississippi*	208	H5	Leeuwin, Cape	192	D5
Laurel *Montana*	203	K5	Leeward Islands	213	R5
Laurencekirk	137	F4	Le Faouet	145	B4
Laurentian Scarp	205	M3	Lefroy, Lake	192	E5
Laurentien, Plateau	201	M7	Leganes	146	E2
Laurenzana	149	E5	Legaspi	171	G3
Lauria	149	E5	Legbourne	135	K3
Laurinburg	209	N3	Leghorn	148	C4
Lausanne	148	A2	Legnago	148	C3
Laut	170	F6	Legnica	151	G3
Lautaro	219	B7	Leh	172	E2
Laut Kecil, Kepulauan	170	F6	Le Havre	144	D4
Lautoka	194	Q8	Leiah	172	D2
Laval *Canada*	205	P4	Leibnitz	148	E2
Laval *France*	145	C4	Leibo	173	K3
Lavan	175	L8	Leicester	133	F2
Lavapie, Punta	219	B7	Leicestershire	133	F2
La Vecilla	146	D1	Leichhardt	193	H2
La Vega	213	M5	Leiden	144	F2
La Venturosa	216	D2	Leie	144	E3
Lavernock Point	132	D3	Leigh *New Zealand*	195	E2
Laverton	192	E4	Leigh *U.K.*	135	G3
Lavina	203	K4	Leigh Creek	193	H5
Lavon, Lake	208	D4	Leighlinbridge	139	J7
Lavras	218	H4	Leighton Buzzard	133	G3
Lawas	170	F5	Leine	150	C3
Lawdar	176	G10	Leinster	139	H6
Lawksawk	173	J4	Leinster, Mount	139	J7
Lawqah	176	F2	Leipzig	150	E3
Lawra	184	E3	Leiria	146	B3
Lawrence *New Zealand*	195	B6	Leirvik	143	A7
Lawrence *Kansas*	204	C7	Leisler, Mount	192	F3
Lawrence *Massachusetts*	205	Q5	Leiston	133	J2
Lawrenceburg	209	J3	Leitha	148	F2
Lawrenceville	204	G7	Leitrim	138	F4

Name	Pg	Grid	Name	Pg	Grid
Leixlip	139	K6	Le Touquet-Paris-Plage	144	D3
Leiyang	173	M3	Le Treport	144	D3
Lek	144	F3	Letsok-aw Kyun	173	J6
Leksand	143	F6	Letterfrack	139	C5
Lekshmozero	158	F3	Letterkenny	138	G3
Leksozero, Ozero	142	P5	Lettermore	139	C6
Leksvik	142	D5	Leuchars	137	F4
Lelai, Tanjung	171	H5	Leuser, Gunung	170	B5
Leland	142	E3	Leuven	144	F3
Le Lavandou	145	G7	Levadhia	155	G3
Le Luc	145	G7	Levan	154	E2
Leluova	194	M7	Levanger	142	D5
Lelysted	144	F2	Levdym	164	Ae4
Leman, Lac	148	A2	Leven, Loch *Highland, U.K.*	137	C4
Le Mans	145	D4	Leven, Loch *Tayside, U.K.*	137	E4
Le Mars	204	B5	Leveque, Cape	192	E2
Lemberg	151	L4	Leverburgh	136	A3
Lemgo	150	C2	Le Verdon-sur-Mer	145	C6
Lemmer	144	F2	Leverkusen	150	B3
Lemmon	203	N5	Levice	151	H4
Lemnos	155	H3	Le Vigan	145	E7
Le Mont-Dore	145	E6	Levin	195	E4
Lempa	212	C8	Levis	205	Q3
Lemreway	136	C2	Levittown	205	N6
Le Murge	149	F5	Levka Ori	155	G5
Lena	165	M2	Levkas *Greece*	155	F3
Lenakel	194	U13	Levkas *Greece*	155	F3
Lene, Lough	138	H5	Levkimmi	154	F3
Lengerich	150	B2	Levkosia	156	E5
Lengshuijiang	173	M3	Levoca	151	J4
Lenhovda	143	F8	Levozero	158	F2
Lenina, Pik	166	C4	Lev Tolstoy	159	F5
Leningradskaya	221	L5	Levuka	194	R8
Leninogorsk	158	J5	Lewannick	132	C4
Leninskiy *Kazakhstan*	158	H4	Lewes	133	H4
Leninskiy *Russia*	166	E2	Lewis	136	B2
Leninsk-Kuznetskiy	164	D6	Lewis, Butt of	136	B2
Leninskoye *Russia*	168	D2	Lewisporte	201	Q8
Leninskoye *Russia*	158	H4	Lewis Range	202	H3
Lenkoran	174	J2	Lewis Smith Lake	209	J3
Lennox, Isla	219	C11	Lewiston *U.K.*	136	D3
Lenoir	209	M3	Lewiston *Maine*	205	Q4
Lens	144	E3	Lewiston *Montana*	202	F4
Lensk	165	J4	Lewistown	203	K4
Lenti	152	D2	Lewisville, Lake	208	D4
Lentini	149	E7	Lexington *Kentucky*	204	H7
Lentura	142	N4	Lexington *N. Carolina*	209	M3
Leo	184	E3	Lexington *Nebraska*	203	Q7
Leoben	148	E2	Lexington *Virginia*	205	L8
Leominster	132	E2	Lexington Park	205	M7
Leon	210	J7	Leyburn	135	H2
Leon	207	N5	Leye	173	L4
Leon *Mexico*	212	D8	Leyland	135	G3
Leon *Nicaragua*	146	D1	Leysdown-on-Sea	133	H3
Leon *Spain*	145	C7	Leyson Point	200	K5
Leonard Darwin, Gunung	171	K6	Leyte	171	G3
Leonforte	149	E7	Leyte Gulf	171	H3
Leonidhion	155	G4	Lezha	158	G4
Leon, Montanas de	146	C1	Lezhe	154	E2
Leopoldina	218	H4	Lezno	151	G3
Leopoldo Bulhoes	218	G3	Lgov	159	F5
Leopoldville	186	C3	Lhasa	173	H3
Leovo	153	K2	Lhaze	173	G3
Le Palais	145	B5	Lhokseumawe	170	B4
Lepaya	143	L8	Liancheng	167	M6
Lepel	143	N9	Liangbingtai	168	B4
Lephepe	188	E4	Liangdang	173	L2
Leping	167	M6	Liangpran, Bukit	170	E5
Lepini, Monti	149	D5	Liangzhen	167	K4
Lepontine, Alpi	148	B2	Lianjiang	173	M4
Lepsy	166	D2	Lianjiangkou	168	C2
Le Puy	145	E6	Lian Xian	173	M3
Lercara Friddi	149	D7	Lianyungang	167	M5
Lere	182	B6	Lianzhushan	168	C3
L'Eree	133	M7	Liaodun	166	F3
Lereh, Tanjung	171	F6	Liao He	167	N3
Lerida	147	G2	Liaoning	167	N3
Lerma	146	E1	Liaoyang	167	N3
Lermontovka	168	E2	Liaoyuan	167	P3
Leros	155	J4	Liapadhes	154	E3
Lerum	143	E8	Liard	199	L3
Lerwick	136	A2	Liban, Jazair	174	B4
Les	153	F2	Liban, Jebel	157	F6
Les Andelys	144	D4	Libano	216	B3
Lesbos	155	J3	Libby	202	G3
Les Cayes	213	L5	Libenge	186	C2
Les Ecrins	145	G6	Liberal	207	M2
Les Escoumins	205	R2	Liberdale	216	C5
Leshan	173	K3	Liberec	150	F3
Leshukonskoye	158	H3	Liberia	184	D4
Lesjofors	143	F7	Liberia *Costa Rica*	212	E9
Leskovac	153	F4	Liberty *New York*	205	N6
Lesnica	152	E3	Liberty *Texas*	208	E5
Lesogorsk	165	Q7	Libobo, Tanjung	171	H6
Lesopilnoye	168	E2	Libourne	145	C6
Lesosibirsk	164	E5	Librazhd	155	F2
Lesotho	188	E5	Libreville	186	A2
Lesozavodsk	168	D3	Librilla	147	F4
Lesparre-Medoc	145	C6	Libya	181	J3
L'Esperance Rock	191	T8	Libyan Desert	182	E3
Les Sables-d'Olonne	145	C5	Libyan Plateau	182	E1
Lesser Antarctica	221	T3	Licata	149	D7
Lesser Antilles	213	Q6	Lice	157	J3
Lesser Slave Lake	199	M4	Lichfield	133	F2
Lesser Zab	174	F4	Lichinga	189	G2
L'Estartit	147	H1	Lichtenburg	188	E5
Lestijarvi	142	L5	Lichtenfels	150	D3
Lesvos	155	J3	Lichuan	167	M6
L'Etacq	133	M7	Licking	204	J7
Letchworth	133	G3	Licosa, Punta	149	E5
Lethbridge	202	H3	Lida	151	L2
Leticia	216	D4	Lidao	167	N4
Leti, Kepulauan	171	H7	Liddel Water	137	F5

Name	Page	Grid
Longhui	173	M3
Long Island *Bahamas*	213	K3
Long Island *Canada*	201	L7
Long Island *New Zealand*	195	A7
Long Island *Papua New Guinea*	194	D3
Long Island *U.S.A.*	205	P6
Long Island Sound	205	P6
Longjiang	167	N2
Longjing	168	B4
Longlac	204	G2
Long Lake	204	G2
Longli	173	L3
Long, Loch	137	D4
Long Melford	133	H2
Longmen	167	L7
Long Mynd, The	132	E2
Longnan	167	L7
Longnawan	170	E5
Longney	132	E3
Long Point *Canada*	205	K5
Long Point *New Zealand*	195	B7
Long Preston	135	G2
Long Range	201	Q8
Long Range Mountains	201	Q7
Longreach	193	J3
Long Reef	194	E4
Longridge	135	G3
Longshan	173	L3
Longsheng	173	M3
Longs Peak	203	M7
Long Stratton	133	J2
Longton	135	G3
Longtown	137	F5
Longuyon	144	F4
Longview *Texas*	208	E4
Longview *Washington*	202	C4
Longwy	144	F4
Longxi	173	K2
Long Xuyen	173	L6
Longyan	167	M6
Longyao	167	L4
Lons-le-Saunier	145	F5
Looe	132	C4
Lookout, Cape	209	P3
Loongana	192	F5
Loop Head	139	C7
Lopatin	159	H7
Lopatino	159	H5
Lopatka	165	T6
Lopatka, Mys	165	T6
Lop Buri	173	K6
Lopevi	194	U12
Lopez, Cap	186	A3
Lop Nur	166	G3
Lopphavet	142	J1
Lopra	142	Z14
Lopydino	158	J3
Lora del Rio	146	D4
Lorain	204	J6
Loralai	172	C2
Lorca	147	F4
Lordegan	175	K6
Lord Howe Island	193	M5
Lordsburg	207	H4
Lore	171	H7
Lorengau	194	D2
Lorentz	171	K7
Lorenzo	216	B3
Loreto *Brazil*	217	H5
Loreto *Colombia*	216	C4
Loreto *Mexico*	206	G7
Lorica	213	K10
Lorient	145	B5
Lorillard	199	S3
Lorinci	152	E2
Lorn	137	C4
Lorne	193	J6
Lorn, Firth of	137	C4
Lorrach	150	B5
Lorraine	144	F4
Los	143	F6
Los Alamos	207	J3
Los Andes	219	B6
Los Angeles *Chile*	219	B7
Los Angeles *U.S.A.*	206	C4
Los Angeles Aqueduct	206	C3
Los Banos	206	B2
Los Blancos	218	D4
Los Filabres, Sierra de	146	E4
Losinj	152	C3
Los Mochis	207	H8
Los Pedraches	146	D3
Los Roques	216	D1
Lossie	136	E3
Lossiemouth	136	E3
Los Teques	216	D1
Los Testigos	213	R9
Lost Trail Pass	202	H5
Lostwithiel	132	C4
Lot	145	D6
Lota	219	B7
Lotfahad	175	P3
Lothian	137	E5
Lotta	142	N2
Lottorp	143	G8
Lo-tung	167	N7
Lotzen	151	J1
Loudeac	144	B4
Loudun	145	D5
Louga	184	B2
Loughborough	133	F2
Loughbrickland	138	K4
Lougheed Island	200	E2
Loughor	132	C3
Loughrea	139	E6
Loughsalt Mount	138	G2
Lough Swilly	138	G2
Louhans	145	F5
Louisa	204	J7
Louisiade Archipelago	194	T10
Louisiana	208	F5
Lou Island	194	D2
Louis Trichardt	188	E4
Louisville *Kentucky*	204	H7
Louisville *Mississippi*	208	H4
Loukhi	142	Q3
Loule	146	B4
Loup	203	Q7
Lourdes	145	C7
Louth *Ireland*	138	K5
Louth *U.K.*	135	K1
Louvain	144	F3
Louviers	144	D4
Lovanger	142	J4
Lovat	158	E4
Lovberga	142	F5
Lovech	153	H4
Loveland	203	M7
Lovell	203	K5
Lovere	148	C3
Loviisa	143	M6
Lovington	207	L4
Lovisa	143	M6
Lovnas	142	F4
Lovosice	150	F3
Lovua	186	D5
Low, Cape	200	J5
Lower Arrow Lake	202	E3
Lower Hut	195	E4
Lowestoft	133	J2
Lowicz	151	H2
Lowther Hills	137	E5
Lowther Island	200	G3
Loyal, Loch	136	D2
Loyaute, Iles	194	X16
Loyma	158	H3
Loyne, Loch	137	C3
Lozarevo	153	J4
Lozere, Mont	145	E6
Loznica	152	E3
Lozovaya	159	F6
Lualaba	186	E3
Luan	173	N2
Luanda	186	B4
Luang Prabang	173	K5
Luangwa	187	F5
Luan He	167	M4
Luanjing	167	K4
Luanping	167	M3
Luanshya	187	E5
Luapula	187	E5
Luarca	146	C1
Luashi	186	D5
Luau	186	D5
Lubalo	186	C4
Lubanas Ezers	142	M8
Lubang Islands	171	G3
Lubango	186	B5
Lubartow	151	K3
Lubawa	151	H2
Lubben	150	E3
Lubbock	207	M4
Lubeck	150	D2
Lubefu	186	D3
Lubenka	159	J5
Lubero	187	E3
Lubie, Jezioro	150	F2
Lubien	151	H2
Lublin	151	K3
Lubny	159	E5
Lubosalma	142	P5
Lubsko	150	F3
Lubtheen	150	D2
Lubudi	186	E4
Lubuklinggau	170	C6
Lubumbashi	187	E5
Lubutu	186	E3
Lucan	139	K6
Lucano, Appennino	149	E5
Lucaya	209	N7
Lucca	148	C4
Lucea	212	H5
Luce Bay	134	E2
Lucedale	208	H5
Lucena *Philippines*	171	G3
Lucena *Spain*	146	D4
Lucena del Cid	147	F2
Lucenec	151	H4
Lucera	149	E5
Lucerne	148	B2
Luchow	150	D2
Luckau	150	E3
Luckenwalde	150	E2
Lucknow	172	F3
Lucon	145	C5
Lucrecia, Cabo	213	K4
Lucusse	186	D5
Luda	167	N4
Ludensheid	150	B3
Luderitz	188	C5
Ludford	135	J3
Ludgvan	132	B4
Ludhiana	172	E2
Ludington	204	G5
Ludlow *U.K.*	132	E2
Ludlow *U.S.A.*	206	D3
Ludogorie	153	J4
Ludus	153	H2
Ludvika	143	F6
Ludwigsburg	150	C4
Ludwigshafen	150	B4
Ludwigslust	150	D2
Ludza	143	M8
Luebo	186	D4
Luena	186	C5
Luepa	216	E2
Lueyang	173	L2
Lufeng	167	M7
Lufkin	208	E5
Luga	143	N7
Lugano	148	B2
Lugano, Lago di	148	B3
Luganville	194	T11
Lugela	189	G3
Lugenda	189	G2
Lugg	132	E2
Lugnaquilla	139	K7
Lugo *Italy*	148	C3
Lugo *Spain*	146	C1
Lugoj	153	F3
Lugovoy	166	C3
Lugton	137	D5
Luhansk	159	F6
Luiana	186	D6
Luichart, Loch	136	D3
Luik	144	F3
Luimneach	139	E7
Luing	137	D4
Luinne Bheinn	137	C3
Luiro	142	M3
Luiza	186	D4
Lujan	219	C6
Lujiang	167	M5
Lukashkin Yar	164	B4
Lukeville	206	F5
Lukovit	153	H4
Lukovo	152	F5
Lukow	151	K3
Lukoyanov	158	G4
Lukulu	186	D5
Lulea	142	K4
Lulealven	142	J3
Luleburgaz	156	B2
Lulo	186	C4
Lulong	167	M4
Lulonga	186	C2
Luluabourg	186	D4
Lulworth Cove	133	E4
Lumbala Nguimbo	186	D5
Lumberton	209	N3
Lumbovka	158	G2
Lumbrales	146	C2
Lumbreras	146	E1
Lumbres	144	E3
Lumijoki	142	L4
Lumphanan	137	F3
Lumsden	195	B6
Lumut, Tanjung	170	D6
Lunan	173	K4
Lunan Bay	137	F4
Lunayyir, Harrat	176	C4
Lunberger Heide	150	C2
Lund	143	E9
Lundar	203	Q2
Lundazi	187	F5
Lundy	132	C3
Lune	135	G2
Luneburg	150	D2
Lunel	145	F7
Luneville	144	G4
Lungga	194	K6
Lungwebungu	186	D5
Luni	172	D3
Luninets	151	M2
Lunsar	184	C2
Lunsemfwa	187	E5
Luntai	166	E3
Luobei	168	C2
Luobuzhuang	166	F4
Luocheng	173	L4
Luodian	173	L3
Luoding	173	M4
Luo He	173	L1
Luohe	173	M2
Luotian	173	N2
Luoyang	173	M2
Luqu	173	K2
Lure	145	G5
Lurgan	138	K4
Lurio *Mozambique*	189	G2
Lurio *Mozambique*	189	H2
Lusaka	187	E6
Lusambo	186	D3
Lusancay Islands	194	E3
Lushi	173	M2
Lush, Mountain	192	F2
Lushoto	187	G3
Lushui	172	F3
Lusignan	145	D5
Lusk	203	M6
Luspebryggan	142	H3
Lussac-les-Chateaux	145	D5
Lut, Bahrat	174	B6
Lut, Dasht-e	175	P6
Lut-e Zangi Ahmad	175	P7
Luthrie	137	E4
Luton	133	G3
Lutong	170	E5
Lutsk	159	D5
Lutterworth	133	F2
Luukkonen	143	N6
Luuq	187	H2
Luverne	204	B5
Luwingu	187	E5
Luwuk	171	G6
Luxembourg	144	F4
Luxembourg	144	G4
Luxeuil	145	G5
Luxi	173	J4
Luxor	183	F2
Luza *Russia*	158	H3
Luza *Russia*	158	H3
Luzern	148	B2
Luzhou	173	L3
Luziania	218	G3
Luzilandia	217	H3
Luzon	171	G2
Luzon Strait	171	G1
Lviv	151	L4
Lvovka	164	B5
Lwowek	151	G2
Lyadova	153	J1
Lyakhovskiye Ostrova	165	Q2
Lyall, Mount	202	G3
Lyallpur	172	D2
Lyapin	158	L3
Lybster	136	E2
Lyck	151	K2
Lycksele	142	H4
Lydd	133	H4
Lyddan Ice Rise	221	Y4
Lydenburg	188	F5
Lydford	132	C4
Lydney	132	E3
Lyell Range	195	D4
Lyman	203	J7
Lyme Bay	132	E4
Lyme Regis	132	E4
Lymington	133	F4
Lymm	135	G3
Lyna	151	J1
Lynchburg	205	L8
Lynd	193	J2
Lyndon	192	D3
Lyne	137	F5
Lyness	136	E2
Lyngdal	143	B7
Lyngseidet	142	J1
Lynher	132	C4
Lynn	205	Q5
Lynn Canal	198	H4
Lynn Lake	199	Q4
Lynton	132	D3
Lynx Lake	199	P3
Lyon *France*	145	F6
Lyon *U.K.*	137	D4
Lyon Inlet	200	K4
Lyon, Loch	137	D4
Lyonnais, Monts du	145	F6
Lyra Reef	194	E2
Lyskovo	158	H4
Lysva	158	K4
Lysychansk	159	F6
Lytham Saint Annes	135	F3
Lythe	135	J2
Lyttelton	195	D5
Lytton	202	D2
Lyubashevka	153	L2
Lyubcha	151	M2
Lyubertsy	158	F4
Lyubeshov	151	L3
Lyubimets	153	J5
Lyuboml	151	L3
Lyubotin	159	F6
Lyudinovo	159	E5
Lyushcha	151	M2

M

Name	Page	Grid
Maaia	189	H2
Maam Cross	139	C6
Maan	174	B6
Maanqiao	166	F3
Maanselka	142	N5
Maanshan	167	M5
Maarianhamina	143	G6
Maarrat an Numan	174	C4
Maas	144	F3
Maaseik	144	F3
Maasin	171	G3
Maastricht	144	F3
Maba	171	H5
Mabalane	189	F4
Mabar	176	G9
Mablethorpe	135	K3
Macachin	219	D7
McAdam	205	S4
Macedonia	153	F5
Macae	218	H4
McAlester	208	E3
McAllen	208	C7
McAllister, Mount	193	K5
MacAlpine Lake	199	Q2
Macapa	217	G3
Macara	216	B4
McArthur	193	H2
Macau	217	K5
Macaubas	218	J6
Macauley Islands	191	T8
McBeth Fjord	200	N4
McBride	199	L5
McCamey	207	L5
McCammon	202	H6
McCarthy	198	G3
Macclesfield	135	G3

Manadir, Al **177** M5
Manado **171** G5
Managua **212** D8
Managua, Laguna de **212** D8
Manakara **189** J4
Manakhah **176** F9
Manambolo **189** H3
Manam Island **194** D2
Mananara *Madagascar* **189** J4
Mananara *Madagascar* **189** J3
Mananjary **189** J4
Manantavadi **172** E6
Manaoba **194** K6
Manapire **216** D2
Manapouri **195** A6
Manapouri, Lake **195** A6
Manas **173** H3
Manau **194** D3
Manaus **216** F4
Manavgat **156** D4
Manbij **174** C3
Mancha Real **146** E4
Manchester *U.K.* **135** G3
Manchester *Connecticut* **205** P6
Manchester *Kentucky* **204** J8
Manchester *New Hampshire,* **205** Q5
Manchester *Tennessee* **209** J3
Mancora **216** A4
Mand **175** K7
Mandab, Bab el **183** H5
Mandal *Afghanistan* **175** Q5
Mandal *Norway* **143** B7
Mandala, Puncak **171** L6
Mandalay **173** J4
Mandalgovi **167** K2
Mandali **174** G5
Mandal-Ovoo **167** J3
Mandan **203** P4
Mandaon **171** G3
Mandar, Teluk **171** F6
Mandasawu, Poco **171** G7
Mandav Hills **172** D4
Mandeville **212** J5
Mandi **172** E2
Mandiore, Lago **218** E3
Mandla **172** F4
Mandoudhion **155** G3
Mandurah **192** D5
Manduria **149** F5
Mandvi **172** C4
Mandya **172** E6
Manea **133** H2
Manevichi **151** L3
Manfredonia **149** E5
Manfredonia, Golfo di **149** F5
Manga **218** J6
Mangakino **195** E3
Mangalia **153** K4
Mangalore **172** D6
Mangaon **172** D5
Mangapehi **195** E3
Manggautu **194** J7
Mangin Range **173** J4
Mangkalihat, Tanjung **171** F5
Manglares, Punta **216** B3
Mangochi **187** G5
Mangoky **189** H4
Mangole **171** H6
Mangonui **195** D1
Mangoro **189** J3
Mangotsfield **132** E3
Mangral **172** D4
Manguari **216** D4
Mangueira, Lagoa **218** F6
Mangui **167** N1
Manguinha, Pontal do **217** K6
Mangut **165** J7
Mangyshlak **159** J7
Mangyshlak, Poluostrov **159** J7
Mangyshlakskiy Zaliv **159** J7
Manhan **166** G2
Manhattan **203** R8
Manhica **189** F5
Manicore **216** E5
Manicouagan **201** N7
Manicouagan, Reservoir **201** N7
Manifah **177** J3
Manika, Plateau de la **186** E4
Manila **171** G3
Manipa, Selat **171** H6
Manipur **173** H4
Manisa **156** B3
Man, Isle of **134** E2
Manistee *U.S.A.* **204** G4
Manistee *U.S.A.* **204** H4
Manistique **204** G4
Manitoba **199** R4
Manitoba, Lake **203** Q2
Manitou Falls **203** T2
Manitou Island **204** G4
Manitoulin **204** J4
Manitowoc **204** G4
Maniwaki **205** N3
Manizales **216** B2
Manja **189** H4
Manjra **172** E5
Mankato **204** C4
Mankono **184** D4
Mankovka **153** L1
Manna **170** C6
Mannar **172** E7
Mannar, Gulf of **172** E7
Mannheim **150** C4
Manning, Cape **200** B2
Manning Strait **194** J5
Manningtree **133** J3
Mannu **149** B6
Manoa Abuna **216** D5
Manokwari **171** J6
Manolas **155** F3
Manonga **187** F3
Manono **187** E4
Manorbier **132** C3
Manorcunningham **138** G3
Manorhamilton **138** F4
Manoron **173** J6
Manosque **145** F7
Manouane, Reservoir **201** M7
Mano-wan **169** G7
Manpojin **167** P3
Manra **191** U2
Manresa **147** G2
Mansa **187** E5
Mansehra **172** D2
Mansel Island **200** L5
Mansfield *U.K.* **135** H3
Mansfield *Louisiana* **208** F5
Mansfield *Ohio* **204** J6
Mansfield *Pennsylvania* **205** M6
Mansfield Woodhouse **135** H3
Mansle **145** D6
Manson Creek **198** L4
Mansoura **147** J4
Manston **133** J3
Mansurlu **157** F4
Manta **216** A4
Mantalingajan, Mount **171** F4
Mantaro **216** B6
Mantecal **216** D2
Mantes **144** D4
Mantiqueira, Serra da **218** G4
Mantova **148** C3
Mantsala **143** L6
Mantta **143** L5
Mantua **148** C3
Mantyharju **143** M6
Manua **191** V4
Manuel **211** K6
Manui **171** G6
Manu Island **194** C2
Manujan **175** N8
Manukau **195** E2
Manukau Harbour **195** E2
Manulla **138** D5
Manus Islands **194** D2
Manya **158** L3
Manyas **156** B2
Manych Gudilo, Ozero **159** G6
Manyoni **187** F4
Manzanares **146** E3
Manzanillo *Cuba* **212** J4
Manzanillo *Mexico* **210** G8
Manzanillo, Punta **216** B2
Manzariyeh **175** K4
Manzhouli **167** M2
Manzini **189** F5
Manzya **164** F5
Mao **182** C5
Maoershan **168** A3
Maoke, Pegunungan **171** K6
Maoming **173** M4
Mapai **189** F4
Mapam Yumco **172** F2
Mapire **213** Q11
Maple Creek **203** K3
Mappi *Indonesia* **171** K7
Mappi *Indonesia* **171** K7
Maprik **194** C2
Mapuera **216** F4
Maputo **189** F5
Maqdam, Ras **176** C7
Maqna **176** B2
Maqueda **146** D2
Maquinchao **219** C8
Maraba **217** H5
Maracaibo **216** C1
Maracaibo, Lago de **216** C2
Maraca, Ilha de **217** G3
Maracay **216** D1
Maradah **181** J3
Maradi **181** G6
Maragheh **174** H3
Marajo, Baia de **217** H4
Marajo, Ilha de **217** H4
Maralal **187** G2
Maramasike **194** K6
Maramba **186** E6
Maran **170** C5
Marand **174** G2
Maranguape **217** K4
Maranhao **217** H5
Maranhao Grande, Cachoeira **217** F4
Maran, Koh-i- **172** C3
Maranon **216** C4
Marans **145** C5
Marari **216** D5
Marasesti **153** J3
Marassume **217** H4
Marateca **146** B3
Marathokambos **155** J4
Marathon *Canada* **204** G2
Marathon *Florida* **209** M8
Marathon *Texas* **207** L5
Marau **170** E6
Marau Point **195** G3
Maravovo **194** J6
Marbella **146** D4
Marble Bar **192** D3
Marble Canyon **206** G2
Marburg **150** C3
Marcelino **216** D4
March **133** H2
Marche *Belgium* **144** F3
Marche *France* **145** D5
Marchena **146** D4
Marchena, Isla **216** A7
Mar Chiquita, Lago **218** D6
Marcigny **145** F5
Marcus Baker, Mount **198** F3
Marcus Island **163** P4
Mardan **172** D2
Mar del Plata **219** E7
Mardin **157** J4
Mare **194** Y16
Mareeba **193** K2
Maree, Loch **136** C3
Mareeq **183** J7
Mareuil **145** D6
Margai Caka **172** G1
Marganets **159** E6
Margaret, Cape **200** H3
Margaret River **192** F2
Margarita, Isla de **216** E1
Margaritovo **168** E4
Margate **133** J3
Margeride, Monts de la **145** E6
Margita **153** F3
Margo, Dasht-i **175** R6
Marguerite **201** N7
Marguerite Bay **221** V5
Mari **194** C3
Maria Elena **218** C4
Maria, Golfo de Ana **212** H4
Maria Madre, Isla **210** F7
Maria Magdalena, Isla **210** F7
Mariampole **151** K1
Marianas Islands **163** N5
Marianas Trench **222** F4
Marian Lake **199** M3
Marianna *Arkansas* **208** G3
Marianna *Florida* **209** K5
Marianske Lazne **150** E4
Marias **202** J3
Marias, Islas **210** F7
Mariato, Punta **212** G11
Maria van Diemen, Cape **195** D1
Mariazell **148** E2
Marib **176** G9
Maribor **152** C2
Maridi **182** E7
Marie Byrd Land **221** S3
Marie Galante **213** S7
Mariehamn **143** H6
Marienbad **150** E4
Marienburg **151** H1
Mariental **188** C4
Marienwerder **151** H2
Mariestad **143** E7
Marietta *Georgia* **209** K4
Marietta *Ohio* **205** K7
Marigot **213** S7
Mariinsk **164** D5
Marina di Carrara **148** C3
Marina di Leuca **149** G6
Marina di Monasterace **149** F6
Marinette **204** G4
Maringa **186** D2
Maringa **218** F4
Marion *Illinois* **204** F8
Marion *Indiana* **204** H6
Marion *Ohio* **204** J6
Marion *S. Carolina* **209** N3
Marion *Virginia* **205** K8
Marion, Lake **209** M4
Marion Reefs **193** L2
Maripa **216** D2
Marisa **171** G5
Mariscal Estigarribia **218** D4
Maritimes, Alpes **145** G6
Maritsa **153** H4
Mariupol **159** F6
Marivan **174** H4
Marjamaa **143** L7
Marjayoun **174** B5
Marka **176** E7
Marka **187** H2
Markam **173** J3
Market Deeping **133** G2
Market Drayton **132** E2
Market Harborough **133** G2
Markethill **138** J4
Market Rasen **135** J3
Market Weighton **135** J3
Markha **165** K4
Markham **194** D3
Marlborough *Australia* **193** K3
Marlborough *Guyana* **216** F2
Marlborough *U.K.* **133** F3
Marlin **208** D5
Marlinton **205** K7
Marlow **133** G3
Marmagao **172** D5
Marmande **145** D6
Marmara *Turkey* **156** B2
Marmara *Turkey* **156** B2
Marmara Denizi **156** C2
Marmaraereglisi **156** B2
Marmara Golu **156** C3
Marmara, Sea of **156** C2
Marmaris **156** C4
Marmblada **148** C2
Marmelos **216** E5
Marne **144** E4
Maro **182** C3
Maroantsetra **189** J3
Marolambo **189** J4
Marondera **189** F3
Maroni **217** G3
Maros **171** F6
Marotiri Islands **195** E1
Maroua **185** H3
Marovoay **189** J3
Marowyne **217** G3
Marple **135** G3
Marquette **204** G3
Marquise **144** D3
Marquises, Iles **223** J5
Marra, Jebel **182** D5
Marrakech **180** D2
Marrakesh **180** D2
Marrak Point **200** R5
Marrawah **193** J7
Marree **193** H4
Marresale **164** Ae3
Marrupa **189** G2
Marsa Alam **176** B4
Marsabit **187** G2
Marsala **149** D7
Marsden *Australia* **193** K5
Marsden *U.K.* **135** H3
Marseille **145** F7
Mar, Serra do **218** G5
Marsfjallet **142** G3
Marshall *Minnesota* **204** C4
Marshall *Missouri* **204** D7
Marshall *Texas* **208** E4
Marshall Bennett Islands **194** E3
Marshall Islands **223** G4
Marshalltown **204** D5
Marshchapel **135** K3
Marshfield **204** E4
Marsh Island **208** G6
Marske-by-the-Sea **135** H2
Marsta **143** G7
Martaban **173** J5
Martaban, Gulf of **173** J5
Martapura **170** E6
Martes, Sierra **147** F3
Marthaguy **193** K5
Martha's Vineyard **205** Q6
Martigny **148** A2
Martigues **145** F7
Martin *Poland* **151** H4
Martin *Spain* **147** F2
Martin *S. Dakota* **203** P6
Martin *Tennessee* **208** H2
Martinavas **133** N6
Martinborough **195** E4
Martinique **213** S7
Martinique Passage **213** S7
Martin Lake **209** K4
Martin Point **198** G1
Martinsberg **148** E1
Martinsville **205** L8
Martock **132** E4
Marton *New Zealand* **195** E4
Marton *U.K.* **135** J3
Martorell **147** G2
Martos **146** E4
Martre, Lac La **199** M3
Martuk **159** K5
Martuni **159** H7
Martyn **158** K2
Martze **216** D4
Marudi **170** E5
Marugame **169** D8
Marum, Mount **194** U12
Marunga **194** E2
Marungu **187** E4
Marv Dasht **175** L7
Marvejols **145** E6
Marvine, Mount **202** J8
Marwar **172** D3
Mary **175** Q3
Maryborough **193** L4
Maryevka **164** Ae6
Maryland **205** M7
Maryport **135** F2
Mary, Puy **145** E6
Marystown **201** Q8
Marysville *California* **206** B1
Marysville *Kansas* **203** R8
Maryvale **193** L4
Maryville *Missouri* **204** C6
Maryville *Tennessee* **209** L3
Marzo, Cabo **212** J11
Masagua **212** B7
Masai Steppe **187** G3
Masaka **187** F3
Masally **174** J2
Masan **169** B8
Masasi **187** G5
Masaya **212** D8
Masbate *Philippines* **171** G3
Masbate *Philippines* **171** G3
Mascara **180** F1
Mascarene Islands **189** L7
Masela **171** H7
Maseru **188** E5
Mashabih **176** C4
Masham **135** H2
Mashan *Guangxi, China* **173** L4
Mashan *Heilongjiang, China* **168** C3
Mashhad **175** P3
Mashike **168** H4
Mashiz **175** N7

Name	Page	Ref
Mashkid	175	R8
Masi	142	K2
Masilah, Wadi al	177	J9
Masi-Manimba	186	C3
Masindi	187	F2
Masirah	177	P6
Masirah, Khalij	177	N7
Masirah, Khawr al	177	P6
Masiri	175	K6
Masisi	187	E3
Masjed Soleyman	174	J6
Mask, Lough	138	D5
Maskutan	175	P8
Maslen Nos	153	J4
Masoala, Cap	189	K3
Mason Bay	195	A7
Mason City	204	D5
Ma, Song	173	K4
Masqat	177	P5
Massa	148	C3
Massachusetts	205	P5
Massachusetts Bay	205	Q5
Massakori	182	C5
Massa Marittima	148	C4
Massangena	189	F4
Massape	217	J4
Massava	164	Ad4
Massenya	182	C5
Massigui	180	D6
Massillon	204	K6
Massinga	189	G4
Massingir	189	F4
Masteksay	159	H6
Masterton	195	E4
Mastikho, Akra	155	J3
Mastuj	172	D1
Masturah	176	D5
Masuda	169	C8
Masulch	174	J3
Masurai, Bukit	170	C6
Masvingo	188	F4
Masyaf	174	C4
Mat	154	F2
Mataboor	171	K6
Mataca	189	G2
Matachel	146	C3
Matad	167	M2
Matadi	186	B4
Matafome	146	B3
Matagalpa	212	E8
Matagami *Ontario, Canada*	205	M2
Matagami *Quebec, Canada*	205	M2
Matagami, Lac	205	M1
Matagorda Bay	208	D6
Matagorda Island	208	D6
Matakana Island	195	F2
Matakaoa Point	195	G2
Matala	186	C5
Matale	172	F7
Matam	184	C2
Matamata	195	E2
Matamoros *Mexico*	208	D8
Matamoros *Mexico*	207	L8
Matane	205	S2
Mata Negra	216	E2
Matanzas	212	G3
Matapan, Cape	155	G4
Matapedia	205	S2
Matara	172	F7
Mataram	170	F7
Matarani	218	B3
Mataranka	192	G1
Mataro	147	H2
Matata	195	F2
Matatiele	188	E6
Mataura *New Zealand*	195	B6
Mataura *New Zealand*	195	B7
Matawai	195	F3
Matay	166	D2
Matcha	166	B4
Matehuala	211	J6
Matera	149	F5
Mateszalka	153	G2
Mateur	181	G1
Matfors	142	G5
Matheson	205	K2
Mathis	208	D6
Mathry	132	B3
Mathura	172	E3
Mati	171	H4
Matlock	135	H3
Mato, Cerro	213	Q11
Mato Grosso	216	F6
Mato Grosso do Sul	218	E3
Mato Grosso, Planalto do	218	E3
Matra	152	E2
Matrah	177	P5
Matrosovo	151	J1
Matruh	182	E1
Matsubara	169	J10
Matsue	169	D8
Ma-tsu Lieh-tao	167	M6
Matsumae	168	H5
Matsumoto	169	F7
Matsusaka	169	F8
Matsuyama	169	D9
Mattagami	201	K8
Mattancheri	172	E7
Mattawa	205	L3
Matterhorn *Switzerland*	148	A3
Matterhorn *U.S.A.*	202	G7
Matthews Peak	187	G2
Matthew Town	213	L4
Matti, Sabkhat	177	K10
Mattoon	204	F7
Matty Island	200	G3
Matua, Ostrov	165	S7
Matuku	216	E2
Maturin	216	E2
Matyushkinskaya	164	B5
Mau	172	F3
Maua	189	G2
Maubara	171	H7
Maubeuge	144	E3
Maubin	173	J5
Maubourguet	145	D7
Mauchline	137	D5
Maud	136	F3
Maues	216	F4
Mauganj	172	F4
Maui	206	S10
Maula	142	L4
Maule	219	B7
Mauleon-Licharre	145	C7
Maumere	171	G7
Maumtrasna	138	C5
Maumturk Mountains	139	C5
Maun	188	D4
Mauna Kea	206	T11
Mauna Loa	206	T11
Maungmagan Islands	173	J6
Maunoir, Lac	198	L2
Maures	145	G7
Mauriac	145	E6
Maurice, Lake	192	G4
Mauritania	180	C5
Mauritius	189	L7
Mauron	144	B4
Mauston	204	E5
Mautern	148	E2
Mavinga	186	D6
Mawbray	135	F2
Mawhai Point	195	G3
Mawlaik	173	H4
Mawson	221	E5
Maxaila	189	F4
Maxmo	142	K5
Maya	165	N5
Mayaguana Island	213	L3
Mayaguana Passage	213	L3
Mayaguez	213	P5
Mayak *China*	166	F2
Mayak *Russia*	151	H1
Mayak *Russia*	159	K5
Mayamey	175	M3
Mayas, Montanas	212	C6
Maybole	137	D5
May, Cape	205	N7
Maychew	176	D10
Maydh	183	J5
Mayenne *France*	144	C4
Mayenne *France*	145	C5
Mayero	164	G3
Mayfaah	177	H9
Mayfield *U.K.*	133	H3
Mayfield *U.S.A.*	204	F8
May, Isle of	137	F4
Maykop	159	G7
Maykor	158	K4
Maymakan *Russia*	165	N5
Maymakan *Russia*	165	P5
Maymyo	173	J4
Mayn	165	W4
Maynooth	139	J6
Mayo *Argentina*	219	B9
Mayo *Canada*	198	H3
Mayo *Ireland*	138	D5
Mayo *Mexico*	210	E4
Mayor Island	195	F2
Mayor, Pic	147	H3
Mayotte	189	J2
May Pen	212	J6
Mayraira Point	171	G2
Mayrata	155	F3
Maysville	204	J7
Mayumba	186	A3
Mayuram	172	E6
Mayville	203	R4
Mayyun Island	176	F10
Mazalat	153	H4
Mazamari	216	C6
Mazamet	145	E7
Mazar	172	E1
Mazar-e Sharif	172	C1
Mazarete	147	E2
Mazarredo	219	C9
Mazarron	147	F4
Mazarsu	166	C3
Mazaruni	216	F2
Mazatenango	212	B7
Mazatlan	210	F6
Mazdaj	175	K5
Mazeikiai	143	K8
Mazgirt	157	H3
Mazhur, Irq al	176	G3
Mazidagi	157	J4
Mazinan	175	N3
Mazirbe	143	K8
Mazury	151	J2
Mbabane	188	F5
Mbaiki	182	C7
Mbala	187	F4
Mbalavu	194	S8
Mbale	187	F2
Mbalmayo	185	H5
Mbalo	194	K6
Mbandaka	186	C2
MBanza Congo	185	B4
Mbanza-Ngungu	186	B4
Mbarara	187	F3
Mbengwi	185	G4
Mbeya	187	F4
Mbouda	185	H4
Mbour	184	B3
Mbout	180	C5
Mbuji-Mayi	186	D4
Mchinji	187	F5
MClintock	199	S4
Meade *Alaska*	198	D1
Meade *Kansas*	207	M2
Meadie, Loch	136	D2
Mead, Lake	206	E2
Meadow Lake	199	P5
Meadville	205	K6
Mealhada	146	B2
Meana	175	Q3
Meath	138	J5
Meaux	144	E4
Mebula	171	G7
Mecca	176	D6
Mechelen	144	F3
Mecheria	180	E2
Mechigmen	198	A2
Mechigmen Zaliv	198	A2
Mecidie	156	B2
Mecitozu	156	F2
Mecklenburger Bucht	150	D1
Mecsek	152	E2
Mecufi	189	H2
Mecula	189	G2
Medak	172	E5
Medan	170	B5
Medanos	219	D7
Medanosa, Punta	219	C9
Medea	181	F1
Medellin	216	B2
Medelpad	142	G5
Medenine	181	H2
Mederdra	180	B5
Medford	202	C6
Medgidia	153	K3
Medicine Bow Mountains	203	L7
Medicine Bow Peak	203	L7
Medicine Hat	203	J3
Medicine Lodge	207	N2
Medina *Saudi Arabia*	176	D4
Medina *N. Dakota*	203	Q4
Medina *New York*	205	L5
Medinaceli	146	E2
Medina del Campo	146	D2
Medina de Rioseco	146	D2
Medina Sidonia	146	D4
Medina Terminal Canal	205	L5
Medinipur	173	G4
Mediterranean Sea	178	D3
Medjerda, Monts de la	149	B7
Medkovets	153	G4
Medoc	145	C6
Medole	148	C3
Medvezhl, Ostrova	165	U2
Medvezhyegorsk	158	E3
Medvyeditsa	158	F4
Medway	133	H3
Medyn	158	F5
Medynskiy Zavorot, Poluostrov	158	K2
Meeberrie	192	D4
Meechkyn, Kosa	165	Y3
Meekatharra	192	D4
Meeker	203	L7
Meerut	172	E3
Meeteetse	203	K5
Mega	171	J6
Megalo Khorio	155	J4
Megalopolis	155	G4
Megara	155	G3
Megeve	145	G6
Megget Reservoir	137	E5
Meghalaya	173	H3
Megion	164	B4
Megisti	156	C4
Megra *Russia*	158	F3
Megra *Russia*	158	G2
Mehamn	142	M1
Mehndawal	172	F3
Mehran	174	H5
Meig	136	D3
Meighen Island	200	G2
Meiktila	173	J4
Meiningen	150	D3
Meira	146	C1
Meissen	150	E3
Mei Xian	167	M7
Mejez El Bab	149	B7
Mejillones	218	B4
Mekambo	186	B2
Mekele	183	G5
Meknes	180	D2
Mekong	173	L6
Mekong, Mouths of the	173	L7
Mela	142	U12
Melaka	170	C5
Melambes	155	H5
Melanesia	222	F4
Melawi	170	E6
Melbourne *Australia*	193	J6
Melbourne *U.S.A.*	209	M6
Melbourne Island	199	Q2
Melbu	142	F2
Melchor Muzquiz	207	M7
Melenki	158	G4
Meleuz	158	K5
Melfi *Chad*	182	C5
Melfi *Italy*	149	E5
Melfort	199	Q5
Melgaco	217	G4
Melhus	142	D4
Melilla	180	E1
Melipilla	219	B6
Melita	203	P3
Melito di Porto Salvo	149	E7
Melitopol	159	F6
Melk	148	E1
Melksham	133	E3
Mellegue, Oued	181	G1
Mellerud	143	E7
Melle-sur-Bretonne	145	C5
Melling	135	G2
Mellish Reef	193	M2
Mellte	132	D3
Melnik	150	F3
Melo	218	F6
Melolo	171	G7
Melozitna	198	E2
Melrhir, Chott	181	G2
Melrose	204	C4
Melsungen	150	C3
Meltaus	142	L3
Melton Mowbray	133	G2
Melun	144	E4
Melut	183	F5
Melvern Lake	204	C7
Melville	203	N2
Melville Bugt	200	P2
Melville, Cape	193	J1
Melville Hills	198	L2
Melville Island *Australia*	192	G1
Melville Island *Canada*	200	D2
Melville, Kap	200	P2
Melville, Lake	201	Q7
Melville Peninsula	200	K4
Melvin, Lough	138	F4
Melykut	152	E2
Melyuveyem	165	W4
Memba	189	H2
Memberamo	171	K6
Memboro	171	F7
Memel	143	L9
Memmingen	150	D4
Mempawah	170	D5
Memphis *Tennessee*	208	H3
Memphis *Texas*	207	M3
Mena	208	E3
Menai Bridge	135	E3
Menaka	181	F5
Mendawai	170	E6
Mende	145	E6
Mendi	194	C3
Mendip Hills	132	E3
Mendocino, Cape	202	B7
Mendoza	218	C6
Menemen	156	B3
Menen	144	E3
Menfi	149	D7
Mengcheng	173	N2
Mengcun	167	M4
Mengen	156	E2
Mengene Dagi	157	L3
Menggala	170	D6
Menghai	173	K4
Mengjiagang	168	C2
Mengjiawan	167	K4
Mengla	173	K4
Mengshan	173	M4
Mengyin	167	M4
Meniet	181	F3
Menihek, Lac	201	N7
Meningie	193	H6
Menkya	158	L3
Menominee *U.S.A.*	204	G4
Menominee *U.S.A.*	204	G4
Menomonee Falls	204	F5
Menongue	186	C5
Menorca	147	J3
Mentawai, Kepulauan	170	B6
Mentawai, Selat	170	B6
Mentok	170	D6
Menton	148	A4
Mentor	205	K6
Menyamya	194	D3
Menzel Bourguiba	149	B7
Meon	133	F4
Meppel	144	G2
Meppen	150	B2
Mequinenza	147	G2
Merabellou, Kolpos	155	H5
Merak	170	D7
Merano	148	C2
Merauke	171	L7
Mercan Dagi	157	H3
Mercato Saraceno	148	D4
Merced	206	B2
Mercedario, Cerro	218	B6
Mercedes *Argentina*	219	C6
Mercedes *Argentina*	219	E6
Mercedes *Argentina*	218	E5
Mercedes *Uruguay*	218	E6
Mercimek	157	F4
Mercimekkale	157	J3
Mercurea	153	G3
Mercury Bay	195	E2
Mercy, Cape	200	P5
Mere	132	E3
Meredith, Cape	219	D10
Meredoua	180	F3

Name	Page	Ref
Mocamedes	186	B6
Mocha, Isla	219	B7
Mochudi	188	E4
Mocimboa da Praia	189	H2
Moctexuma	207	H6
Moctezuma	211	K7
Mocuba	189	G3
Modder	188	E5
Modena *Italy*	148	C3
Modena *U.S.A.*	206	F2
Modesto	206	B2
Modica	149	E7
Modigliana	148	C3
Modling	148	F1
Modowi	171	J6
Moe	193	K6
Moelv	143	D6
Moengo	217	G2
Moffat	137	E5
Moffat Peak	195	B6
Mogadishu	187	J2
Mogadouro	146	C2
Mogdy	165	N6
Mogilev-Podolskiy	159	D6
Mogi-Mirim	218	G4
Mogincual	189	H3
Moglice	155	F2
Mogocha	165	L6
Mogoi	171	J6
Mogok	173	J4
Mogollon Plateau	206	D3
Mogotoyevo, Ozero	165	R2
Mogoyn	166	H2
Mogoytuy	165	J6
Moguer	146	C4
Mohacs	152	E2
Mohaka	195	F3
Mohall	203	P3
Mohammadabad	175	Q6
Mohammadia	180	F1
Mohawk	205	N5
Moheli	189	H2
Mohill	138	G5
Mohoro	187	G4
Moi	143	B7
Moidart	137	C4
Moimenta da Beira	146	C2
Moindou	194	W16
Mointy	166	C2
Mo i Rana	142	F3
Moisie	201	N7
Moissac	145	D6
Moissala	182	C6
Mojave	206	C3
Mojave Desert	206	D3
Moji	169	C9
Mojones, Cerro	218	C5
Moju	217	H4
Mokai	195	E3
Mokelumne	202	D8
Moknine	181	H1
Mokohinau Island	195	E1
Mokokchung	173	H3
Mokolo	185	H3
Mokpo	167	P5
Mokra Gora	152	F4
Molaoi	155	G4
Molat	152	C3
Mold	135	F3
Moldavia	153	J2
Molde	142	B5
Moldova	153	J2
Moldova Noua	153	F3
Moldoveanu	153	H3
Moldovita	153	H2
Mole *Devon, U.K.*	132	D4
Mole *Surrey, U.K.*	133	G3
Molepolole	188	E4
Molfetta	149	F5
Molina de Aragon	147	F2
Molina de Segura	147	F3
Moline	204	E3
Molkom	143	E7
Mollakendi	157	H3
Mollaosman	157	K3
Mollendo	218	B3
Molln	150	D2
Molnlycke	143	E8
Molodechno	151	M1
Molodezhnaya	221	D5
Molodo *Russia*	165	L3
Molodo *Russia*	165	L3
Mologa	158	F4
Molokai	206	S10
Moloma	158	H4
Molotov	158	K4
Moloundou	185	J5
Molsheim	144	G4
Molson Lake	199	R5
Moluccas	171	H6
Moma *Mozambique*	189	R3
Moma *Russia*	165	Q3
Mombasa	187	R3
Mombetsu	168	J3
Momboyo	186	C3
Momi, Ra's	177	P9
Momol	151	L2
Mompos	216	C2
Mon	143	E9
Monach Islands	136	A3
Monach, Sound of	136	A3
Monaco	145	G7
Monadhliath Mountains	137	D3
Monaghan	138	J4
Monahans	207	L5
Mona, Isla	213	P5
Mona Passage	213	N5
Monarch Mount	198	K5
Monarch Pass	203	L8
Monar, Loch	136	C3
Monashe Mountains	202	E2
Monasterevin	139	H6
Monastir *Albania*	153	F5
Monastir *Italy*	149	B6
Monastir *Tunisia*	181	H1
Monastyriska	153	H1
Monatele	185	H5
Moncalieri	148	A3
Moncao	146	B1
Monchdorf	148	E1
Monchegorsk	142	Q3
Monchique	146	B4
Monclova	207	M7
Moncontour	144	B4
Moncton	201	P8
Mondego	146	C2
Mondonedo	146	C1
Mondovi	148	A3
Mondragone	149	D5
Mondsee	148	D2
Monemvasia	155	G4
Moneron, Ostrov	168	H2
Monesterio	146	C3
Moneymore	138	J3
Monfalcone	148	D3
Monforte	146	C3
Monforte de Lemos	146	C1
Monga	186	D2
Mongala	186	D2
Mongalla	183	F6
Mong Cai	173	L4
Mongga	194	H5
Mongge	171	J6
Mong Hang	173	J4
Monghyr	172	G3
Mong Lin	173	K4
Mongo	182	C5
Mongolia	166	G2
Mongororo	182	D5
Mongu	186	D6
Monhhaan	167	L2
Moniaive	137	E5
Monifieth	137	F4
Moniquira	216	C2
Monitor Range	202	F8
Monkira	193	J3
Monkland	132	E2
Monkoto	186	D3
Monmouth *U.K.*	132	E3
Monmouth *U.S.A.*	204	E6
Monnow	132	E3
Mono	185	F4
Mono Lake	206	C2
Monolithos	155	J4
Monopoli	149	F5
Monovar	147	F3
Monreal del Campo	147	F2
Monreale	149	D6
Monroe *Georgia*	209	L4
Monroe *Louisiana*	208	F4
Monroe *Michigan*	204	J6
Monroe *N. Carolina*	209	M3
Monroe *Wisconsin*	204	F5
Monrovia	184	C4
Mons	144	E3
Monsaras, Ponta da	218	J3
Monselice	148	C3
Monserrat	147	F3
Montaigu	145	C5
Montalban	147	F2
Montalbo	146	E3
Montalcino	148	C4
Montalto	149	E6
Montalvo	216	B4
Montamarta	146	D2
Montana	202	K4
Montanchez	146	C3
Montanita	216	B3
Montargis	145	E5
Montauban	145	D6
Montauk Point	205	Q6
Montbard	145	F5
Montbeliard	145	G5
Montblanch	147	G2
Montbrison	145	F6
Montceau-les-Mines	145	F5
Montcornet	144	F4
Mont-de-Marsan	145	C7
Montdidier	144	E4
Monte Alegre	217	G4
Monte Azul	218	H3
Monte Bello	216	B5
Montebello	205	N4
Monte Carlo	148	A4
Monte Caseros	219	E6
Montecatini Terme	148	C4
Monte Cristi	213	M5
Montecristo, Isola di	149	C4
Montego Bay	212	J5
Montelimar	145	F6
Montemaggiore Belsito	149	D7
Montemorelos	208	C8
Montemor-o-Novo	146	B3
Montenegro	152	E4
Montepuez	189	G2
Montepulciano	148	C4
Monte Quemado	218	D5
Montereau-faut-Yonne	144	E4
Monterey	206	B2
Monterey Bay	206	B2
Monteria	216	B2
Montero	218	D3
Monterotondo	149	D4
Monterrey	208	B8
Monte Santu, Capo di	149	B5
Montes Claros	218	E3
Montevideo *Uruguay*	219	E6
Montevideo *U.S.A.*	204	C4
Monte Vista	207	J2
Montezuma Peak	207	J2
Montfort-sur-Meu	144	B4
Montgomery *U.K.*	132	D2
Montgomery *U.S.A.*	209	J4
Montguyon	145	C6
Monti	149	B5
Monticello *Arkansas*	208	G4
Monticello *Florida*	209	L5
Monticello *New York*	205	N6
Monticello *Utah*	207	H2
Montiel, Campo de	146	E3
Montignac	145	D6
Montilla	146	D4
Mont-Joli	205	R2
Mont Laurier	205	N3
Montlucon	145	E5
Montmagny	205	Q3
Montmedy	144	F4
Montmirail	144	E4
Montmorillon	145	D5
Monto	193	L3
Montoro	146	D4
Montpelier	202	J6
Montpellier *France*	145	E7
Montpellier *U.S.A.*	205	P4
Montraux	148	A2
Montreal	204	H3
Montreal	205	P4
Montreal Lake	199	P5
Montreal River Harbour	204	H3
Montrose *U.K.*	137	F4
Montrose *U.S.A.*	207	J1
Mont Saint-Michel	144	C4
Montseny	147	H2
Montserrat	213	R6
Mont Wright	201	N7
Monywa	173	J4
Monza	148	B3
Monzon	147	G2
Moonie	193	K4
Moopna	192	F5
Moora	192	D5
Mooraberree	193	J4
Moorcroft	203	M5
Moore, Lake	192	D4
Moorfoot Hills	137	E5
Moorhead	204	B3
Moorlands	193	H6
Moorlinch	132	E3
Moose	201	K7
Moosehead Lake	205	R4
Moose Jaw	203	M2
Moose Lake *Canada*	199	Q5
Moose Lake *U.S.A.*	204	D3
Moose Mountain Creek	203	N2
Moosonee	201	K7
Mopeia Velha	189	G3
Mopti	180	E6
Moqor	172	C2
Moquequa	218	B3
Mora *Cameroon*	185	H3
Mora *Portugal*	146	B3
Mora *Sweden*	143	F6
Moradabad	172	E3
Moradal, Sierra do	146	C3
Mora de Rubielos	147	F2
Morafenobe	189	H3
Morag	151	H2
Morales	212	C7
Moramanga	189	J3
Moran	203	J6
Morant Cays	212	K6
Morant Point	212	J6
Moratuwa	172	E7
Morava *Czech Rep.*	151	G4
Morava	153	F3
Moraveh Tappeh	175	M3
Morawa	192	D4
Moray Firth	136	E3
Morbi	172	D4
Mor Budejovice	150	F4
Morbylanga	143	G8
Morden	203	Q3
Mordogan	156	B3
Mordovo	159	G5
Moreau	202	N5
Morebattle	137	F5
Morecambe	135	G2
Morecambe Bay	135	E2
Moreda	146	E4
Morehead *Papua New Guinea*	194	C3
Morehead *U.S.A.*	204	J7
Morehead City	209	P3
Morelia	211	J8
Morella	147	F2
More, Loch *U.K.*	136	D2
More, Loch *U.K.*	136	E2
Morena, Sierra	146	D3
Moreno	206	G6
Moreno, Bahia	218	B4
More og Romsdal	142	C5
Moresby Island	198	J5
Mores Island	212	J1
Moreton Bay	193	L4
Moreton-in-Marsh	133	F3
Moreton Island	193	L4
Morez	145	G5
Morgan City	208	G6
Morganton	209	M3
Morgantown	205	L7
Morgongava	143	G7
Mori *China*	166	F3
Mori *Japan*	168	H4
Moriarty	207	K3
Morioka	168	H6
Morlaix	144	B4
Morley	135	H3
Morlunda	143	F8
Mormanno	149	F6
Mornington, Isla	219	A9
Mornington Island	193	H2
Morobe	194	D3
Morocco	180	D2
Morogoro	187	G4
Moro Gulf	171	G4
Morokovo	165	W3
Moroleon	211	J7
Morombe	189	H4
Moron	212	H3
Moron *Mongolia*	166	J2
Moron *Mongolia*	167	L2
Moronade, Cerro des	210	G7
Morondava	189	H4
Moron de la Frontera	146	D4
Moroni	189	H2
Moron Us He	173	H2
Morotai	171	H5
Moroto	187	F2
Morozovsk	159	G6
Morpara	217	J6
Morpeth	135	H1
Morrilton	208	F3
Morrinhos	218	G3
Morrinsville	195	E2
Morris *Canada*	203	R3
Morris *U.S.A.*	204	C4
Morris Jesup, Kap	220	Q2
Morris, Mount	192	G4
Morristown	209	L2
Morro Bay	206	B3
Morro do Chapeu	217	J6
Morro, Punta	219	B5
Morros, Punta	211	P8
Morrosquillo, Golfo de	213	K10
Mors	143	C8
Morshansk	159	G5
Mortagne	144	D4
Mortain	144	C4
Mortara	148	B3
Morteau	145	G5
Morte Bay	132	C3
Mortes	217	G6
Morton *U.K.*	133	G2
Morton *U.S.A.*	202	C4
Morundah	193	K5
Morven *Australia*	193	K4
Morven *U.K.*	137	E3
Morvern	137	C4
Morwell	193	K6
Mosakula	143	L7
Mosby	143	B7
Moscow *U.S.A.*	202	F4
Moscow *Russia*	158	F4
Mosedale	135	F2
Mosel	150	B4
Moselle	144	G4
Moses Lake	202	E4
Moseyevo	158	H2
Mosgiel	195	C6
Mosha	158	G3
Moshchnyy, Ostrov	143	M6
Moshi	187	G3
Mosjoen	142	E4
Moskenesoya	142	E3
Moskosel	142	H4
Moskva	158	F4
Mosonmagyarovar	152	D2
Mosquera	216	B3
Mosquitia	212	E7
Mosquito Lake	199	Q3
Mosquitos, Costa de	212	F8
Mosquitos, Golfo de los	212	G10
Moss	143	D7
Mossaka	186	C3
Mossburn	195	B6
Mosselbaai	188	D6
Mossley	138	L3
Mossman	193	K2
Mossoro	217	K5
Most	150	E3
Mosta	154	C5
Mostaganem	180	F1
Mostar	152	D4
Mostiska	151	K3
Mosty	151	L2
Mostyn	135	F3
Mosul	157	K4
Mosulpo	167	P5
Mota	183	G5
Mota	194	T10
Mota del Cuervo	146	E3
Motala	143	F7
Mota Lava	194	T10
Motegi	169	H7
Motherwell	137	E5
Motihari	172	F3

Motilla del Palancar	147	F3
Motovskiy Zaliv	142	G2
Motril	146	E4
Motueka *New Zealand*	195	D4
Motueka *New Zealand*	195	D4
Motupiko Blenheim	195	D4
Motykleyka	165	R5
Moudhros	155	H3
Moudjeria	180	C5
Mouka	182	D6
Mould Bay	200	C2
Moulins	145	E5
Moulmein	173	J5
Moulouya, Oued	180	E2
Moulton	135	H2
Moultrie	209	L5
Moultrie, Lake	209	M4
Mounda, Akra	155	F3
Mound City	204	C6
Moundou	182	C6
Moung	173	K6
Mountain	198	K2
Mountain Ash	132	D3
Mountain Home *Arkansas*	208	F2
Mountain Home *Idaho*	202	G6
Mountain Village	198	C3
Mount Airy	209	M2
Mount Ararat	157	L3
Mount Bellew	139	E6
Mount Desert Island	205	R4
Mount Doreen	192	G3
Mount Douglas	193	K3
Mount Elba	193	H5
Mount Gambier	193	J6
Mount Hagen	194	C3
Mount Isa	193	H3
Mount Magnet	192	D4
Mountmellick	139	H6
Mount Pleasant *Iowa*	204	E6
Mount Pleasant *Michigan*	204	H5
Mount Pleasant *Texas*	208	E4
Mount Pleasant *Utah*	206	G1
Mountrath	139	H6
Mount's Bay	132	B4
Mount Shasta	202	C7
Mount Thule	200	L3
Mount Vernon *Alabama*	209	H5
Mount Vernon *Illinois*	204	F7
Mount Vernon *Indiana*	204	G8
Mount Vernon *Ohio*	204	J6
Mount Vernon *Washington*	202	C3
Moura *Brazil*	216	E4
Moura *Portugal*	146	C3
Mourdi, Depression du	182	D4
Mourne Mountains	138	K4
Moussoro	182	C5
Moutong	171	G5
Movas	207	H6
Moville	138	H2
Moy	138	D4
Moyale	187	G2
Moyamba	184	C4
Moyen Atlas	180	E2
Moygashel	138	J4
Moyo *Indonesia*	171	F7
Moyo *Uganda*	186	F2
Moyobamba	216	B5
Moyu	172	E1
Mozambique	189	G3
Mozambique Channel	189	H3
Mozhaysk	158	F4
Mozhga	158	J4
Mozyr	159	D5
Mpanda	187	F4
Mpe	186	B3
Mpika	187	F5
Mporokoso	187	F4
Mpraeso	184	E4
Mrakovo	159	K5
M.R. Gomez, Presa	207	N7
Mrkonjic Grad	152	D3
Msaken	181	H1
MSila	147	J5
Msta	158	E4
Mstislav	158	E5
Mtsensk	159	F5
Mtwara	187	G5
Mualo	189	G2
Muang Chiang Rai	173	J5
Muang Khon Kaen	173	K5
Muang Lampang	173	J5
Muang Lamphun	173	J5
Muang Loei	173	K5
Muang Nan	173	K5
Muang Phayao	173	J5
Muang Phetchabun	173	K5
Muang Phichit	173	K5
Muang Phitsanulok	173	K5
Muang Phrae	173	K5
Muanza	189	F3
Muar	170	C5
Muara	170	E4
Muarabungo	170	D6
Muaraenim	170	D6
Muaralesan	171	F5
Muarasiberut	170	B6
Muarasigep	170	B6
Muarasipongi	170	B5
Muaratebo	170	D6
Muarateweh	170	E6
Mubende	187	F2
Mubi	185	H3
Mubrani	171	J6
Mucajai	216	E3
Muchinga Escarpment	187	F5
Much Wenlock	132	E2
Muck	137	B4
Muckanagh Lough	139	E7
Muckish Mount	138	G2
Muckle Roe	136	A1
Muckross Head	138	E3
Muconda	186	D5
Mucuim	216	E5
Mucur	156	F3
Mudanjiang	168	B3
Mudan Jiang	168	B3
Mudanya	156	C2
Mudayy	177	L8
Muddy Gap Pass	203	L6
Mudgee	193	K5
Mudurnu	156	D2
Mueda	189	G2
Muelas	146	D2
Mueo	194	W16
Mufulira	187	E5
Mufu Shan	173	M3
Muganskaya Step	174	J2
Mughar	175	L5
Mughshin	177	M7
Mugi	169	E9
Mugia	146	B1
Mugila, Monts	187	E4
Mugla	156	C4
Muhammad Qol	183	G3
Muhammad, Ras	183	F2
Muhaywir	157	J6
Muhldorf	150	E4
Muhlhausen	150	D3
Muhu	143	K7
Mui Bai Bung	173	K7
Muick	137	E3
Muirkirk	137	D5
Muite	189	G2
Mukachevo	159	C6
Mukah	170	E5
Mukawa	168	H4
Mukawwar	176	C6
Mukdahan	173	K5
Mukden	167	N3
Mukhen	168	F1
Mukhor-Konduy	165	J6
Mukomuko	170	D6
Mukur	159	J6
Mula	147	F3
Mulaly	166	D2
Mulan	168	B3
Mulanay	171	G3
Mulayit Taung	173	J5
Mulchatna	198	D3
Mulchen	219	B7
Mulde	150	E3
Muleshoe	207	L3
Mulga Downs	192	D3
Mulgrave	201	P8
Mulgrave Island	194	C4
Mulhacen	146	E4
Mulheim	150	B3
Mulhouse	145	G5
Muligort	164	Ad4
Muling *China*	168	C3
Muling *China*	168	C3
Muling He	168	D3
Mull	137	C4
Mullaghanattin	139	C9
Mullaghanish	139	D9
Mullaghareirk Mountains	139	D8
Mullaghcleevaun	139	K6
Mullaghmore	138	J3
Muller, Pegunungan	170	E5
Mullet, The	138	B4
Mullewa	192	D4
Mull Head *U.K.*	136	F2
Mull Head *U.K.*	136	F1
Mullinavat	139	H8
Mullingar	139	H5
Mullsjo	143	E8
Mull, Sound of	137	C4
Mulobezi	186	E6
Mulrany	138	C5
Multan	172	D2
Multanovy	164	A4
Multia	142	L5
Mulymya	164	Ad4
Mumbai (Bombay)	172	D5
Mumbles, The	132	C3
Mumbwa	186	E6
Mumra	159	H6
Muna *Indonesia*	171	G7
Muna *Russia*	165	L3
Munayly	159	J6
Munchberg	150	D3
Munchen	150	D4
Munchengladbach	150	B3
Muncie	204	H6
Munda	194	H6
Mundesley	133	J2
Mundford	133	H2
Mundo	147	F3
Mundo Novo	218	J6
Mungbere	187	E2
Munich	150	D4
Muniesa	147	F2
Munkfors	143	E7
Mun, Mae Nam	173	K5
Munoz Gamero, Peninsula de	219	B10
Munster	150	B3
Munster	139	D8
Munsterland	150	B3
Muntenia	153	J3
Muntinlupa	171	G3
Munzur Daglari	157	H3
Muong Khoua	173	K4
Muong Ou Tay	173	K4
Muong Sing	173	K4
Muonio	142	K3
Muoniojoki	142	K3
Muqdisho	187	J2
Muqshin, Wadi	177	M7
Mur	148	E2
Mura	152	D2
Muradiye *Turkey*	156	B3
Muradiye *Turkey*	157	K3
Murallon, Cerro	219	B9
Muranga	187	G3
Murashi	158	H4
Murat *France*	145	E6
Murat *Turkey*	157	J3
Muratbasi	157	K3
Murat Dagi	156	C3
Muratli	156	B2
Muraysah, Ras al	181	K2
Murban	177	L5
Murcheh Khvort	175	K5
Murchison *Australia*	192	C4
Murchison *Canada*	200	H4
Murchison *New Zealand*	195	D4
Murchison Sund	200	M2
Murcia *Spain*	147	F4
Murcia *Spain*	147	F3
Murdo	203	P6
Murdochville	205	T2
Murefte	156	B2
Mures	153	F2
Muret	145	D7
Murfreesboro *N. Carolina*	209	P2
Murfreesboro *Tennessee,*	209	J3
Murgab *Tajikistan*	166	C4
Murgab *Turkmenistan*	175	R3
Muri	175	N3
Muriae	218	H4
Muriege	186	D4
Muritz See	150	E2
Murmansk	158	E2
Murmanskaya Oblast	142	P2
Murmansk Bereg	158	F2
Murmashi	142	Q2
Murnau	150	D5
Murom	158	G4
Muromtsevo	164	B5
Muroran	168	H4
Muros	146	B1
Muroto-zaki	169	E9
Murphy	209	L3
Murra Murra	193	K4
Murray *Australia*	193	H5
Murray *Kentucky*	204	F8
Murray *Utah*	202	J7
Murray Bridge	190	J9
Murray Harbour	201	P8
Murray, Lake *Papua New Guinea*	194	C3
Murray, Lake *U.S.A.*	209	M3
Murraysburg	188	D6
Murree	172	D2
Murrumbidgee	193	K5
Mursal	157	H3
Mursala	170	B5
Murud	170	F5
Murukta	164	G3
Murupara	195	F3
Murwara	172	F4
Murwillumbah	193	L4
Murz	148	E2
Murzuq	181	H3
Murzuq, Idhan	181	H4
Murzzuschlag	148	E2
Mus	157	J3
Musala	153	G4
Musallam, Wadi	177	N5
Musan	168	B4
Musandam Peninsula	177	N3
Musayid	177	K4
Muscat	177	P5
Musgrave Ranges	192	G4
Mushash al Hadi	177	J3
Musheramore	139	D8
Mushie	186	C3
Musi	170	C6
Musian	174	H5
Muskegon *U.S.A.*	204	G5
Muskegon *U.S.A.*	204	H5
Muskingum	204	K7
Muskogee	208	E3
Musmar	183	G4
Musoma	187	F3
Mussau	194	D2
Musselburgh	137	E5
Musselshell	203	K4
Mussende	186	C5
Musserra	186	B4
Mussidan	145	D6
Mussuma	186	D5
Mussy	145	F5
Mustafakemalpasa	156	C2
Mustang	172	F3
Mustang Draw	207	L4
Musters, Lago	219	C9
Mustvee	143	M7
Musu-dan	168	B5
Muswellbrook	193	L5
Mut *Egypt*	182	E2
Mut *Turkey*	156	E4
Muta Ponta do	217	K6
Mutarara	189	G3
Mutare	189	F3
Mutki	157	J3
Mutnyy Materik	158	K2
Mutoko	189	F3
Mutoray	164	G4
Mutsu-wan	168	H5
Muurame	143	L5
Muurola	142	L3
Muwaffaq	177	M7
Muxima	186	B4
Muya	165	J5
Muyunkum, Peski	166	C3
Muzaffarabad	172	D2
Muzaffargarh	172	D2
Muzaffarnagar	172	E3
Muzaffarpur	172	G3
Muzon, Cape	198	J5
Muz Tagh Ata Range	172	E1
Mvuma	188	F3
Mwaniwowo	194	L7
Mwanza	187	F3
Mwaya	187	F4
Mweelrea	138	C5
Mwene Ditu	186	D4
Mwenezi *Zimbabwe*	188	F4
Mwenezi *Zimbabwe*	188	F4
Mwenga	187	E3
Mweru, Lake	187	E4
Mweru Wantipa, Lake	187	E4
Mwinilunga	186	D5
Myakit	165	S4
Myanaung	173	J5
Myanmar	173	J4
Myaundzha	165	R4
Myaungmya	173	H5
Myeik Kyunzu	173	J6
Myingyan	173	J4
Myinmu	173	J4
Myitkyina	173	J3
Myitnge	173	J4
Myittha	173	J4
Mykolayiv	159	E6
Myla	158	J2
Mymensingh	173	H4
Myre	142	F2
Myri	142	W12
Myrtle Beach	209	N4
Myrviken	142	F5
Mysen	143	H7
Mysliborz	150	F2
Mysore	172	E6
Mys Shmidta	165	Y3
My Tho	173	L6
Mytishchi	158	F4
Mzab	181	F2
Mze	150	E4
Mzuzu	187	F5

N

Naalehu	206	T11
Naantali	143	K6
Naas	139	J6
Nabao	146	B3
Nabavatu	194	R8
Naberezhnyye Chelny	158	J4
Nabire	171	K6
Nablus	174	B5
Nabouwalu	194	R8
Naburn	135	H3
Nacala-a-Velha	189	H2
Nacaome	212	D8
Nachiki	165	T6
Nachvak Fjord	201	P6
Nacogdoches	208	E5
Nacozari de Garcia	207	H5
Nadachi	169	G7
Nadezhdinskoye	168	D1
Nadezhnyy, Mys	165	S2
Nadi	194	Q8
Nadiad	172	D4
Nadlac	152	F2
Nador	180	E1
Naduri	194	R8
Nadvornaya	151	L4
Nadym	164	A3
Naft-e Safid	174	J6
Nafud, An	176	E2
Nafy	176	F4
Naga	171	G3
Nagagami	204	H2
Nagahama	169	D9
Naga Hills	173	H3
Nagai	169	G6
Nagaland	173	H3
Nagano	169	G7
Nagaoka	169	G7
Nagappattinam	172	E6
Nagarjuna Sagar	172	E5
Nagasaki	169	B9
Nagashima	169	F8
Nagato	169	C8
Nagaur	172	D3
Nagercoil	172	E7
Nagishot	183	F7
Nagles Mountains	139	F8
Nagornyy	165	L5
Nagorsk	158	J4
Nagoya	169	F8
Nagpur	172	E4
Nagqu	173	H2

Name	Page	Ref
Nags Head	209	Q3
Nagykanizsa	152	D2
Nagykata	152	E2
Nagykoros	152	E2
Naha	169	H10
Nahariya	174	B5
Nahavand	174	J4
Nahe	150	B4
Nahoi, Cap	194	T11
Nahuel Huapi, Lago	219	B8
Naikliu	171	G7
Nailsea	132	E3
Nailsworth	132	E3
Naiman Qi	167	N3
Nain	175	L5
Nain	201	P6
Naini Tal	172	E3
Nairai	194	R8
Nairn	136	E3
Nairobi	187	G3
Najafabad	175	K5
Najd	176	E4
Najibabad	172	E3
Najin	168	C4
N Ajjer, Tassili	181	G3
Najran	176	G8
Najran, Wadi	176	G8
Nakadori-shima	169	B9
Nakajo	169	G6
Nakamura	169	D9
Nakano	169	G7
Nakano-shima	169	B11
Nakatay	164	Ad5
Nakatsu	169	C9
Nakatsugawa	169	F8
Nakfa	183	G4
Nakhichevan	157	L3
Nakhl *Eygpt*	176	A2
Nakhl *Oman*	177	N5
Nakhodka *Russia*	164	B3
Nakhodka *Russia*	168	D4
Nakhon Pathom	173	J6
Nakhon Phanom	173	K5
Nakhon Ratchasima	173	K6
Nakhon Sawan	173	K5
Nakhon Si Thammarat	173	J7
Nakina	201	J7
Nakiri	169	F8
Naknek Lake	198	D4
Nakskov	143	F9
Naktong	167	P4
Nakuru	187	G3
Nakusp	202	F2
Nalchik	159	G7
Nalgonda	172	E5
Nallamala Hills	172	E5
Nallihan	156	D2
Nalut	181	H2
Namaa, Tanjung	171	H6
Namacunde	186	C6
Namacurra	189	G3
Namak, Daryacheh-ye	175	K4
Namaki	175	M6
Namakzar	175	Q5
Namakzar, Daryacheh-ye	175	Q5
Namangan	166	C3
Namapa	189	G2
Namaponda	189	G3
Namarroi	189	G3
Namasagali	187	F2
Namatanai	194	E2
Nambour	193	L4
Nam Can	173	K7
Nam Co	173	H2
Nam Dinh	173	L4
Nametil	189	G3
Namib Desert	188	B4
Namibe	186	B6
Namibia	188	C4
Namlea	171	H6
Namoi	193	L5
Namosi Peak	194	R8
Nampa	202	F6
Nampula	189	G3
Namse La	172	F3
Namsen	142	E4
Namsos	142	D4
Namti	173	J3
Namtok	173	J5
Namuka-i-Lau	194	S9
Namuli	189	G3
Namur	144	F3
Namutoni	188	C3
Namwala	186	E6
Nana Barya	182	C6
Nanaimo	202	C3
Nanam	168	B5
Nanao	169	F7
Nancha	168	B2
Nanchang	167	M6
Nanchong	173	L2
Nancowry	173	H7
Nancy	144	G4
Nanda Devi	172	E2
Nandan	173	L3
Nanded	172	E5
Nandurbar	172	D4
Nandyal	172	E5
Nanfeng	167	M6
Nanga Eboko	185	H5
Nangahpinoh	170	E6
Nanga Parbat	172	D1
Nangatayap	170	E6
Nangong	167	M4
Nan Hai	163	K5
Nanjing	167	M5
Nanking	167	M5
Nan, Mae Nam	173	K5
Nanning	173	L4
Nanortalik	196	Q2
Nanpan Jiang	173	K4
Nanpara	172	F3
Nanping	167	M6
Nansei-shoto	169	H10
Nansen Sound	200	H1
Nanshan Islands	170	E4
Nansha Qundao	170	E4
Nantais, Lac	201	M5
Nantes	145	C5
Nantong	167	N5
Nantua	145	F5
Nantucket Island	205	Q6
Nantucket Sound	205	Q6
Nantwich	135	G3
Nant-y-moch Reservoir	132	D2
Nanuku Passage	194	S8
Nanuku Reef	194	S8
Nanumanga	191	S3
Nanumea	191	S3
Nanusa, Kepulauan	171	H5
Nanyang	173	M2
Nanyuki	187	G2
Nao, Cabo de la	147	G3
Naococane, Lake	201	M7
Naousa	155	G2
Napa	206	A1
Napabalana	171	G6
Napalkovo	164	A2
Napas	164	C5
Nape	173	L5
Napier	195	F3
Naples *Italy*	149	E5
Naples *U.S.A.*	209	M7
Napo	216	C4
Napoleon	204	H6
Napoletano, Appennino	149	E5
Napoli	149	E5
Napoli, Golfo di	149	E5
Naqadeh	174	G3
Nar	133	H2
Nara *Japan*	169	E8
Nara *Mali*	180	D5
Nara *Pakistan*	172	C4
Naracoorte	193	J6
Naran	167	L2
Narasapur	172	F5
Narat	166	E3
Narathiwat	173	K7
Narayanganj	173	H4
Narberth	132	C3
Narbonne	145	E7
Narborough Island	216	A7
Narcea	146	C1
Nardin	175	M3
Narew *Poland*	151	J2
Narew *Poland*	151	K2
Narince	157	H4
Narken	142	K3
Narkher	172	E4
Narli	157	G4
Narmada	172	E4
Narman	157	J2
Narnaul	172	E3
Narodnaya, Gora	164	Ad3
Naro-Fominsk	158	F4
Narowal	172	D2
Narpes	142	J5
Narrabri	193	K5
Narrandera	193	K5
Narrogin	192	D5
Narromine	193	K5
Narsimhapur	172	E4
Narsinghgarh	172	E4
Nart	167	M3
Nartabu	171	J6
Naruko	168	H6
Narva	143	N7
Narvik	142	G2
Naryan Mar	158	J2
Narymskiy Khrebet	166	E2
Naryn *Russia*	164	F6
Naryn *Kyrgyzstan*	166	C3
Naryn *Kyrgyzstan*	166	D3
Nasarawa	185	G4
Naseby	195	C6
Nashua	205	Q5
Nashville	209	J2
Nasice	152	E3
Nasielsk	151	J2
Nasijarvi	143	K6
Nasik	172	D5
Nasir	183	F6
Nasir, Buhayrat	183	F3
Nasorolevu	194	R8
Nasrabad	175	K4
Nass	198	K4
Nassau	209	P8
Nasser, Lake	183	F3
Nassjo	143	F8
Nastapoka Islands	201	L6
Nastved	143	D9
Nata	188	E4
Natagaima	216	B3
Natal *Brazil*	217	K6
Natal *Indonesia*	170	B5
Natanz	175	K5
Natara	165	L3
Natashquan	201	P7
Natchez	208	G5
Natchitoches	208	F5
Natewa Bay	194	R8
National City	206	D4
Natitingou	185	F3
Natividade	217	H6
Natori	169	H6
Natron, Lake	187	G3
Nattavaara	142	J3
Natuna Besar	170	D5
Natuna, Kepulauan	170	D5
Naturaliste, Cape	192	D5
Naturaliste Channel	192	C4
Nauen	150	E2
Naueyi Akmyane	143	K8
Naujoji Vilnia	151	L1
Naul	138	K5
Naumburg	150	D3
Naungpale	173	J5
Nauru	191	Q2
Naurzum	164	Ad6
Nausori	194	R9
Nautanwa	172	F3
Nautla	211	L7
Nauzad	175	S5
Navadwip	173	G4
Navahermosa	146	D3
Naval	171	G3
Navalcarnero	146	D2
Navalmoral de la Mata	146	D3
Navalpino	146	D3
Navan	138	J5
Navarin, Mys	165	X4
Navarino, Isla	219	C11
Navarra	147	F1
Navars	147	G2
Navasota	208	D5
Navassa Island	213	K5
Navax Point	132	B4
Navenby	135	J3
Naver, Loch	136	D2
Navia *Spain*	146	C1
Navia *Spain*	146	C1
Naviti	194	Q8
Navlya	159	E5
Navojoa	207	H7
Navolato	210	F5
Navpaktos	155	F3
Navplion	155	G4
Navrongo	184	E3
Navsari	172	D4
Navua	194	R9
Nawabshah	172	C3
Nawada	172	G4
Nawah	172	C2
Nawasif, Harrat	176	F6
Naws, Ra's	177	M8
Nawton	135	J2
Naxos *Greece*	155	H4
Naxos *Greece*	155	H4
Nayagarh	172	G4
Nayau	194	S8
Nay Band	175	L8
Nay Band	175	N5
Nayoro	168	J3
Nazare	217	K6
Nazareth *Israel*	174	B5
Nazareth *Peru*	216	B5
Nazarovo	164	E5
Nazas	210	G5
Nazca	216	C6
Naze	169	B11
Nazerat	174	B5
Naze, The	133	J3
Nazik	174	G2
Nazik Golu	157	K3
Nazilli	156	C4
Nazmiye	157	H3
Nazwa	177	N5
Nazyvayevsk	164	A5
Ncheu	187	F5
Ndalatando	186	B4
Ndele	182	D6
Ndeni	194	N7
Ndjamena	182	C5
Ndjote	186	B3
Ndola	187	E5
Nea	142	D5
Nea Filippias	155	F3
Neagh, Lough	138	K3
Neah Bay	202	B3
Neale, Lake	192	G3
Nea Moudhania	155	G2
Neapolis *Greece*	155	F2
Neapolis *Greece*	155	H5
Nea Psara	155	G3
Near Islands	198	Aa9
Neath	132	D3
Nebine	193	K4
Nebit Dag	175	M2
Neblina, Pico da	216	D3
Nebraska	203	N7
Nebraska City	204	C6
Nebrodi, Monti	149	E7
Nechako	198	L5
Nechi	213	K11
Neckar	150	C4
Necochea	219	E7
Nedong	173	H3
Nedstrand	143	A7
Needles *Canada*	202	E3
Needles *U.S.A.*	206	E3
Needles Point	195	E2
Needles, The	133	F4
Neepawa	203	Q2
Neergaard Lake	200	L3
Nefedovo	164	A5
Nefta	181	G2
Neftechala	174	J2
Neftegorsk	159	J5
Neftekamsk	158	J4
Nefyn	132	C2
Nefza	149	B7
Negele	183	G6
Negev	174	B6
Negoiu	153	H3
Negombo	172	E7
Negotin	153	G3
Negrais, Cape	173	H5
Negra, Punta	216	A5
Negritos	216	A4
Negro *Argentina*	219	C7
Negro *Amazonas, Brazil*	216	E4
Negro *Santa Catarina, Brazil*	218	F5
Negro *Uruguay*	218	F6
Negros	171	G3
Negru Voda	153	K4
Nehavand	174	J4
Nehbandan	175	Q6
Nehe	167	N2
Nehoiasu	153	J3
Neijiang	173	K3
Nei Mongol Zizhiqu	167	L3
Neisse *Poland*	150	F3
Neisse *Poland*	151	G3
Neiteyugansk	164	A4
Neiva	216	B3
Neixiang	173	M2
Nekemte	183	G6
Neksikan	165	R4
Nekso	143	H9
Nelidovo	158	E4
Neligh	203	Q6
Nelkan	165	P5
Nellore	172	E6
Nelma	168	G2
Nelson *Canada*	202	F3
Nelson *New Zealand*	195	D4
Nelson *U.K.*	135	G3
Nelson, Cape *Australia*	193	J6
Nelson, Cape *Papua New Guinea*	194	D3
Nelson Lagoon	198	Af8
Nelspruit	188	F5
Nema	180	D5
Neman	158	C4
Neman	151	K1
Nemira	153	J2
Nemirov	153	K1
Nemiscau	201	L7
Nemours	144	E4
Nemun	143	J9
Nemuro	168	K4
Nemuro-kaikyo	168	K4
Nemuy	165	P5
Nenagh	139	F7
Nenana	198	F3
Nene	133	G2
Nen Jiang	167	P1
Nenjiang	167	P2
Nenthead	135	G2
Neokhorion	155	F3
Neon Karlovasi	155	J4
Neosho *Kansas*	204	C7
Neosho *Missouri*	204	C8
Nepa *Russia*	164	H5
Nepa *Russia*	164	H5
Nepal	172	F3
Nephi	206	G1
Nephin Beg Range	138	C4
Nera	149	D4
Nerac	145	D6
Nerchinsk	165	K6
Neretva	152	D4
Neriquinha	186	D6
Neris	143	L9
Nermete, Punta	216	A5
Neryuktey-l-y	165	K4
Neryuvom	164	Ad3
Nes	143	C6
Nesbyen	143	C6
Neskaupstadur	142	Y12
Nesna	142	E3
Nesscliffe	132	E2
Ness, Loch	136	D3
Nesterov *Russia*	151	K3
Nesterov *Ukraine*	151	K1
Nesterovo	164	H6
Neston	135	F3
Nestos	155	H2
Nesvizh	151	M2
Netanya	174	B5
Netherlands	144	F2
Neto	149	F6
Nettilling Lake	200	M4
Nettleham	135	J3
Netzahualcoyotl, Presa	211	N9
Neubrandenburg	150	E2
Neuchatel	148	A2
Neuchatel, Lac de	148	A2
Neufchateau *Belgium*	144	F4
Neufchateau *France*	144	F4
Neufchatel	144	D4
Neufelden	148	D1
Neumunster	150	C1
Neunkirchen *Austria*	148	F2
Neunkirchen *Germany*	150	B4

Norresundby 143 C8
Norrfjarden 142 J4
Norristown 205 N6
Norrkoping 143 L7
Norrland 142 F5
Norrtalje 143 H7
Norseman 192 E5
Norsjo 142 M4
Norsk 165 N6
Norsup 194 T12
Norte, Punta *Argentina* 219 D8
Norte, Punta *Argentina* 219 E7
Norte, Serra do 216 F6
Northallerton 135 H2
Northam 192 D5
Northampton *U.K.* 133 G2
Northampton *U.S.A.* 205 P5
Northamptonshire 133 G2
North Andaman 173 H6
North Arm 199 N3
North Astrolabe Reef 194 R9
North Battleford 199 P5
North Bay *Canada* 205 L3
North Bay *Ireland* 139 K8
North Bend 202 B6
North Berwick 137 F4
North Canadian 208 C3
North, Cape 201 P8
North Cape *New Zealand* 195 D1
North Cape *Norway* 142 L1
North Cape *U.S.A.* 198 A3
North Carolina 209 M3
North Cave 135 J3
North Channel *Canada* 204 J3
North Channel *U.K.* 138 L2
Northchapel 133 G3
North Charlton 135 H1
Northcliffe 192 D5
North Dakota 203 P4
North Dorset Downs 132 E4
North Downs 133 H3
Northeast Cape 198 B3
Northeast Providence Channel 212 J2
North Elmham 133 H2
Northern Ireland 138 H3
Northern Sporades 155 H3
Northern Territory 192 G3
North Esk 137 F4
Northfield 204 D4
North Flinders Range 193 H5
North Foreland 133 J3
North Geomagnetic Pole 220 S3
North Henik Lake 199 R3
North Korea 167 P4
North Kyme 135 J3
North Lakhimpur 173 H3
Northleach 133 F3
North Magnetic Pole 220 U3
North Miami Beach 209 M8
North Platte *U.S.A.* 203 N7
North Platte *U.S.A.* 203 P7
North Point *Canada* 201 P8
North Point *U.S.A.* 204 J4
North Pole 220 A1
North River 199 S4
North Roe 136 A1
North Ronaldsay 136 F1
North Ronaldsay Firth 136 F1
North Saskatchewan 199 P5
North Sea 130 H4
North Sentinel 173 H6
North Shields 135 H1
North Shoshone Peak 202 F8
North Sound 139 C6
North Sound, The 136 F1
North Stradbroke Island 193 L4
North Taranaki Bight 195 E3
North Tawton 132 D4
North Thoresby 135 J3
North Tolsta 136 B2
North Tonawanda 205 L5
North Twin Island 201 K7
North Tyne 137 F5
North Uist 136 A3
Northumberland 137 F5
Northumberland Islands 193 L3
Northumberland O 200 M2
Northumberland Strait 201 P8
Northwall 136 F1
North Walsham 133 J2
Northway Junction 198 G3
Northwest Cape 198 A3
North West Cape 192 C3
North West Highlands 136 C3
Northwest Providence Channel 212 H1
Northwest Territories 199 Q2
Northwich 135 G3
North York 205 L5
North Yorkshire 135 H2
Norton *U.K.* 135 J2
Norton *U.S.A.* 203 Q8
Norton Bay 198 C3
Norton Sound 198 C3
Norvegia, Cape 221 Z4
Norwalk 204 J6
Norway 143 C6
Norway House 199 R5
Norwegian Bay 200 H2
Norwegian Sea 142 A3
Norwich *U.K.* 133 J2
Norwich *U.S.A.* 205 Q6
Noshiro 168 G5
Noshul 158 H3
Nosok 164 C2
Nosop 188 D5
Nosovshchina 158 F3
Nosratabad 175 P7
Nossen 150 E3
Noss Head 136 E2
Noss, Island of 136 A2
Nosy-Varika 189 J4
Notec 151 G2
Noto 149 E7
Notodden 143 C7
Noto-hanto 169 F7
Notre Dame Bay 201 Q8
Notre Dame Mountains 201 N8
Nottingham 133 F2
Nottingham Island 200 L5
Nottinghamshire 135 H3
Notukeu Creek 203 L3
Nouadhibou 180 B4
Nouadhibou, Ras 180 B4
Nouakchott 180 B5
Noukloof Mountains 188 C4
Noumea 194 X17
Noup Head 136 E1
Noupoort 188 D6
Nouvelle-Caledonie 194 W16
Nouvelle Caledonie 194 W16
Nouvelle-France, Cap de 200 M5
Novabad 166 C4
Nova Bana 151 H4
Nova Cruz 217 K5
Nova Era 218 H3
Nova Friburgo 218 H4
Nova Iguacu 218 H4
Nova Lima 218 H4
Nova Mambone 189 G4
Novara 148 B3
Nova Remanso 217 J5
Nova Scotia 201 P8
Nova Sento Se 217 J5
Nova Sofala 189 F4
Nova Vanduzi 189 F3
Nova Varos 152 E4
Novaya Kakhovka 159 E6
Novaya Katysh 164 Ae5
Novaya Kazanka 159 H6
Novaya Novatka 164 G5
Novaya Odessa 159 E6
Novaya Sibir , Ostrov 165 R1
Novaya Tevriz 164 B5
Novaya Vodolaga 159 F6
Novaya Zemlya 164 Ab2
Novayo Ushitsa 153 J1
Nove Mesto 150 G4
Nove Zamky 151 H4
Novgorod 158 E4
Novgorod Serverskiy 159 E5
Novigrad 152 C3
Novikovo 168 J2
Novi Ligure 148 B3
Novi Pazar 152 F4
Novi Sad 152 E3
Novo Acre 217 J6
Novoaleksandrovsk 159 G6
Novoalekseyevka 159 K5
Novoanninskiy 159 G5
Novoarchangelsk 153 L1
Novo Aripuana 216 E5
Novobogatinskoye 159 J6
Novocheboksarsh 158 H4
Novocherkassk 159 G6
Novodolinka 164 A6
Novodvinsk 158 G3
Novograd-Volynskiy 159 D5
Novogrudok 151 L2
Novo Hamburgo 218 F5
Novoilinovka 165 P6
Novokazalinsk 166 A2
Novokhopersk 159 G5
Novokiyevskiy Uval 165 M6
Novokocherdyk 164 Ad6
Novokuybyshevsk 159 H5
Novokuznetsk 164 D6
Novolazareyskaya 221 A4
Novoletovye 164 G2
Novo Milosevo 152 F3
Novomitino 164 Ae5
Novomoskovsk *Russia* 158 F5
Novomoskovsk *Ukraine* 159 F6
Novopavlovka 164 H6
Novopokrovskaya 159 G6
Novopolotsk 143 N9
Novo Redondo 186 B5
Novo-Rokrovka 168 E3
Novoromanovo 164 C6
Novorossiysk 159 F7
Novorzhev 143 N8
Novo Sagres 171 H7
Novo Sergeyevka 159 J5
Novoshakhtinsk 159 F6
Novosibirsk 164 C4
Novosibirskiye Ostrova 165 Q1
Novospasskoye 159 H5
Novoukrainka 159 E6
Novo Uzensk 159 H5
Novo-Vyatsk 158 H4
Novoyeniseysk 164 E5
Novozhilovskaya 158 J3
Novozybkov 159 E5
Novska 152 D3
Novy Jicin 151 G4
Novyy 164 H2
Novyy Bor 158 J2
Novyy Bug 159 E6
Novyy Oskol 159 F5
Novyy Port 164 A3
Novyy Uzen 159 J7
Nowbaran 175 J4
Nowe 151 H2
Nowen Hill 139 D9
Nowgong 173 H3
Nowitna 198 E3
Nowograd 150 F2
Nowogrod 151 J2
Nowra 193 L5
Now Shahr 175 K3
Nowshera 172 D2
Nowy Sacz 151 J4
Nowy Targ 151 J4
Noyon *France* 144 E4
Noyon *Mongolia* 166 J3
Nozay 145 C5
Nsanje 187 G6
Nsukka 185 G4
Nsuta 184 E4
Ntem 185 H5
Ntwetwe Pan 188 E4
Nuba, Lake 182 F3
Nuba Mountains 182 F5
Nubian Desert 183 F3
Nubiya 182 E4
Nubiya, Es Sahra en 183 F3
Nudo Coropuna 216 C7
Nueces 208 C6
Nueltin Lake 199 R3
Nueva Florida 213 N10
Nueva Rosita 207 M7
Nueva San Salvador 212 C8
Nueve de Julio 219 D7
Nuevitas 212 J4
Nuevo, Bajo 212 H7
Nuevo Casas Grandes 207 J5
Nuevo Churumuco 210 J8
Nuevo Laredo 208 C7
Nugaruba Islands 194 E2
Nugget Point 195 B7
Nugrus, Gebel 176 B4
Nuhaka 195 F3
Nuh, Ra's 175 R9
Nui 191 S3
Nuits-Saint-Georges 145 F5
Nu Jiang 173 J3
Nukhayb 174 F5
Nukiki 194 H5
Nukualofa 191 T6
Nukufetau 191 S3
Nukuhu 194 D3
Nukulaelae 191 S3
Nukumanu Islands 191 N2
Nukunau 191 S2
Nukunono 191 U3
Nukus 131 U7
Nullarbor 192 G5
Nullarbor Plain 192 F5
Numan 185 H4
Numata 169 G7
Numazu 169 G8
Numedal 143 C6
Numfor 194 B2
Numto 164 A4
Nuneaton 133 F2
Nunivak Islands 196 C2
Nunligran 165 Y4
Nunney 132 E3
Nuomin He 167 N2
Nuoro 149 B5
Nupani 194 M7
Nuqdah, Ra's an 177 P6
Nuqrah 176 E4
Nur 175 K3
Nura 166 C2
Nurabad 175 K6
Nur Daglari 157 G4
Nure 148 B3
Nurek 166 B4
Nurhak 157 G4
Nurhak Dagi 157 G3
Nuristan 172 D1
Nurmes 142 N5
Nurnberg 150 D4
Nurri 149 B6
Nurzec 151 K2
Nusaybin 157 J4
Nusayriyah, Jebel al 157 G5
Nushagak Bay 198 D4
Nu Shan 173 J3
Nushki 172 C3
Nutak 201 P6
Nuugaatsiaq 200 R3
Nuuk 200 R5
Nuupas 142 M3
Nuwara 172 F7
Nuweveldreeks 188 D6
Nuyakuk, Lake 198 D4
Nuyts, Point 192 D6
Nuzayzah 157 H5
Nyahururu 187 G2
Nyainqentanglha Shan 172 G3
Nyaksimvol 164 Ad4
Nyala 182 D5
Nyamboyto 164 C3
Nyandoma 158 G3
Nyang 173 H3
Nyanza 187 E3
Nyasa, Lake 187 F5
Nyashabozh 158 J2
Nyaungu 173 H4
Nyayba 165 N2
Nyborg 143 D9
Nybster 136 E2
Nyeri 187 G3
Nyerol 183 F6
Nyima 173 G2
Nyirbator 153 G2
Nyiregyhaza 153 F2
Nyiru, Mont 187 G2
Nykarleby 142 N4
Nykobing *Denmark* 143 C8
Nykobing *Denmark* 143 D9
Nykoping 143 G7
Nylstroom 188 E4
Nymagee 193 K5
Nymburk 150 F3
Nynashamn 143 G7
Nyngan 193 K5
Nyong 185 H5
Nyons 145 F6
Nyrany 150 E4
Nyrud 142 N2
Nysa 151 G3
Nysh 165 Q6
Nyshott 143 N6
Nystad 143 J6
Nytva 158 K4
Nyuk, Ozero 142 P4
Nyuksenitsa 158 G3
Nyunzu 187 E4
Nyurba 165 K4
Nyurolskiy 164 B5
Nyuya 165 J4
Nyvrovo 165 Q6
Nzambi 186 B3
Nzega 187 F3
Nzerekore 184 D4
Nzeto 186 B4
Nzo 184 D4

O

Oadby 133 F2
Oahe Dam 203 P5
Oahe, Lake 203 P5
Oahu 206 S10
Oakdale 206 B2
Oakengates 132 E2
Oakes 203 Q4
Oakford 132 D4
Oakham 133 G2
Oak Hill 205 K8
Oakington 133 H2
Oakland *California* 206 A2
Oakland *Nebraska* 203 R7
Oak Lawn 204 G6
Oakley 203 P8
Oakover 192 E3
Oakridge 202 C6
Oak Ridge 209 K2
Oak Valley 205 N7
Oamaru 195 C6
Oa, Mull of 137 B5
Oates Land 221 L4
Oa, The 137 B5
Oatlands 193 K7
Oaxaca 211 L9
Ob 164 Ae3
Oban 137 D4
Oberammergau 150 D5
Oberhausen 150 B3
Oberlin 203 P8
Obidos *Brazil* 217 F4
Obidos *Portugal* 146 B3
Obihiro 168 J4
Obi, Kepulauan 171 H6
Obilnoye 159 G6
Obion 208 H2
Obninsk 158 F4
Obo 182 E6
Obock 183 H5
Obok-tong 168 B5
Oborniki 151 G2
Oboyan 159 F5
Obozerskiy 158 G3
Obregon, Presa 207 H6
Obruk 156 E3
Obryvistoye 165 Q7
Observatoire, Caye de l' 191 N6
Obskaya Guba 164 A3
Obuasi 184 E4
Ocala 209 L6
Ocana *Colombia* 216 C2
Ocana *Spain* 146 E3
Occidental, Cordillera *Colombia* 216 B3
Occidental, Cordillera *Peru* 216 B6
Occidental, Grand Erg 180 F2
Oceanside 206 D4
Ocejon, Pic 146 E2
Ochamchire 157 J1
Ochil Hills 137 E4
Ochiltree 137 D5
Ock 133 F3
Ockelbo 143 G6
Ocmulgee 209 L5
Ocna Mures 153 G2
Oconee 209 L4
Ocotlan 210 H7
Ocracoke Island 209 Q3
Ocreza 146 C3
Ocsa 152 E2
Oda 169 D8

Name	Page	Ref
Oda	184	E4
Odadhraun	142	W12
Odaejin	168	B5
Oda, Jebel	183	G3
Odate	168	H5
Odawara	169	G8
Odda	143	B6
Odemira	146	B4
Odemis	156	B3
Odendaalsrus	188	E5
Odense	143	D9
Oder	150	F2
Oderhaff	150	F2
Oderzo	148	D3
Odeshog	143	F7
Odessa *U.S.A.*	207	L5
Odessa *Ukraine*	159	E6
Odesskoye	164	A6
Odienne	184	D4
Odmarden	143	L6
Odorheiu Secuiesc	153	H2
Odra	150	F2
Odzaci	152	E3
Oeiras	217	J5
Oekussi	171	G7
Oelrichs	203	N6
Oena, Wadi	183	F2
Oenpelli Mission	193	G1
Of	157	J2
Ofanto	149	E5
Offaly	139	G6
Offenbach	150	C3
Offenburg	150	B4
Offord D'Arcy	133	G2
Ofidhousa	155	J4
Ofotfjord	142	G2
Ofunato	168	H6
Oga	168	G6
Ogaden	183	H6
Ogaki	169	F8
Ogasawara-shoto	163	N4
Ogbomosho	185	F4
Ogden	202	J7
Ogdensburg	205	N4
Ogea	194	S9
Ogeechee	209	M4
Ogho	194	H5
Ogi	169	G7
Ogilvie Mountains	198	H3
Oginskiy, Kanal	151	L2
Ogle Point	200	G4
Oglethorpe, Mount	209	K3
Oglio	148	C3
Ognon	145	F5
Ogoamas, Gunung	171	G5
Ogoja	185	G4
Ogoki	201	J7
Ogooue	186	B3
Ogoron	165	M6
Ogosta	153	G4
Ograzden	153	G5
Ogre	143	L8
Ogurchinskiy, Ostrov	159	J8
Oguz	157	H3
Oguzeli	157	G4
Ogwashi-Uku	185	G4
Ohai	195	A6
Ohakune	195	E3
Ohata	168	H5
Ohau, Lake	195	B6
O'Higgins, Lago	219	B9
Ohingaiti	195	E3
Ohio *Kentucky*	204	F8
Ohio *U.S.A.*	204	J6
Ohre	150	D2
Ohre	150	E3
Ohrid	153	F5
Ohridska Jezero	152	F5
Ohura	195	E3
Oiapoque *Brazil*	217	G3
Oiapoque *Brazil*	217	G3
Oikiqtaluk	200	L3
Oil City	205	L6
Oise	144	E4
Oita	169	C9
Oituz, Pasul	153	J2
Oiwake	168	H4
Ojinaga	207	K6
Ojo de Agua	218	D5
Ojos del Salado	218	C5
Oka *Russia*	158	G4
Oka *Russia*	164	G6
Okaba	194	B3
Okahandja	188	C4
Okahukura	195	E3
Okaihau	195	D1
Okanagan Lake	202	E3
Okanogan *U.S.A.*	202	E3
Okanogan *U.S.A.*	202	E3
Okara	172	D2
Okarem	175	M2
Okaukuejo	188	C3
Okavango	188	D3
Okavango Delta	188	D3
Okaya	169	G7
Okayama	169	D8
Okazaki	169	F8
Okeechobee, Lake	209	M7
Okehampton	132	C4
Okene	185	G4
Oketo	168	J4
Okha	165	Q6
Okhota	165	Q5
Okhotsk	165	Q5
Okhotskoye More	165	R5
Okhotsk, Sea of	165	R5
Okigwi	185	G4
Okinawa	169	H10
Okinawa-shoto	169	H10
Okinoerabu-shima	169	J10
Oki-shoto	169	D7
Okitipupa	185	F4
Oklahoma	207	N3
Oklahoma City	208	D3
Oklya	151	L3
Okmulgee	208	D3
Okondja	186	B3
Okoppe	168	J3
Oko, Wadi	183	G3
Oksfjord	142	K1
Oksino	158	J2
Okstindan	142	F3
Oktyabrskiy *Russia*	158	G3
Oktyabrskiy *Russia*	158	J5
Oktyabrskiy *Russia*	165	T6
Oktyabrskoye	159	K5
Oktyabrskoy Revolyutsii, Ostrov	161	L2
Oku	169	J10
Okulovka	158	E4
Okurchan	165	S5
Okushiri-to	168	G4
Okwa	188	D4
Olafsfjordur	142	V11
Olafsvik	142	T12
Oland	143	G8
Olanga	142	P3
Olathe	204	C7
Olavarria	219	D7
Olbia	149	B5
Old Bedford River	133	H2
Oldcastle	138	H5
Old Crow	198	H2
Old Deer	136	F3
Oldenburg *Germany*	150	C2
Oldenburg *Germany*	150	D1
Oldham	135	G3
Old Head of Kinsale	139	E9
Old Hickory Lake	209	J2
Oldman	202	H3
Old Man of Coniston	135	F2
Old Man of Hoy	136	E2
Oldmeldrum	136	F3
Old Nene	133	H2
Old Post Point	201	P8
Olds	202	G2
Old Tongy	193	K4
Old Town	205	R4
Old Wives Lake	203	L2
Olean	205	L5
Olekma	165	L5
Olekminsk	165	L4
Olekmo-charskoye Nagorye	165	L5
Olema	158	H3
Olen	143	A7
Olenegorsk	142	Q2
Olenek	165	L2
Olenekskiy Zaliv	165	N2
Oleniy, Ostrov	164	B2
Oleron, Ile d'	145	C6
Olesko	151	L4
Olesnica	151	G3
Olevsk	159	D5
Olevugha	194	K6
Olfjellet	142	F3
Olga	168	E4
Olgiy	166	G2
Olgopol	153	K1
Olhava	142	L4
Oliana	147	G1
Olib	152	C3
Olifants *Namibia*	188	C4
Olifants *South Africa*	188	C6
Olifants *South Africa*	188	F4
Olimbos *Greece*	155	G2
Olimbos *Greece*	155	J5
Olinda	217	L5
Olio	193	J3
Olite	147	F1
Oliva	218	D6
Olivares, Cerro del	218	C5
Olivia	204	C4
Olkhovka	159	G6
Ollague	218	C4
Ollague, Volcan	218	C4
Ollerton	135	H3
Ollila	142	M2
Olmedo	146	D2
Olmos	216	B5
Olney	204	F7
Olofstrom	143	F8
Olom	165	N3
Olomouc	151	G4
Olonets	158	E3
Olongapo	171	G3
Oloron-Sainte-Marie	145	C7
Olot	147	H1
Olovo	152	E3
Olovyannaya	165	K6
Olpe	150	B3
Olsztyn	151	J2
Olsztynek	151	J2
Olt	153	H3
Olten	148	A2
Oltet	153	G3
Oltu *Turkey*	157	J2
Oltu *Turkey*	157	K2
Oltul	153	H3
Olu Deniz	156	C4
Olur	157	K2
Olvera	146	D4
Olympia	202	C4
Olympus *Cyprus*	156	E5
Olympus *Greece*	155	G2
Olympus, Mount	202	C4
Olyutorskiy, Mys	165	W5
Oma *Russia*	158	H2
Oma *Russia*	158	H2
Omachi	169	F7
Omae-zaki	169	G8
Omagari	168	H6
Omagh	138	H3
Omaha	204	C6
Omak	202	E3
Omakau	195	B6
Oman	177	M7
Oman, Gulf of	177	P4
Omarama	195	B6
Omaruru	188	C4
Oma-saki	168	H5
Ombrone	149	C4
Omchali	159	J7
Omdurman	183	F4
Omeath	138	K4
Omeleut	165	W4
Omeo	193	K6
Omerli	157	J4
Omerli Baraji	156	C2
Ometepe, Isla de	212	E9
Om Hajer	176	C9
Ominato	168	H5
Omineca Mountains	198	K4
Omis	152	D4
Omitlan	211	K9
Omiya	169	G8
Ommaney, Cape	198	J4
Ommanney Bay	200	F3
Omnogovi	166	G2
Omodeo, Lago	149	B5
Omolon	165	T3
Omoloy *Russia*	164	H5
Omoloy *Russia*	165	N2
Omono	168	H6
Omoto	168	H6
Omo Wenz	183	G6
Omsk	164	A6
Omsukchan	165	T4
Omu	168	J3
Omulevka	165	S4
Omulew	151	J2
Omura	169	B9
Omuramba Eiseb	188	C4
Omuramba Omatako	188	C4
Omurtag	153	J4
Omuta	169	C9
Omutinskiy	164	Ae5
Omutninsk	158	J4
Onalaska	204	E5
Onan	165	J6
Oncocua	186	B6
Ondaroa	146	E1
Ondava	151	J4
Ondjiva	186	C6
Ondo	185	F4
Ondorhaan	167	L2
Ondorkara	166	F2
Ondozero	158	E3
Ondverdarnes	142	S12
Oneata	194	S9
Onega *Russia*	158	F3
Onega *Russia*	158	F3
One Hundred Mile House	202	D2
Oneida Lake	205	N5
O'Neill	203	Q6
Onekotan, Ostrov	165	S7
Oneonta	205	N5
Onezhskaya Guba	158	F3
Onezhskiy Poluostrov	158	F3
Onezhskoye, Ozero	158	F3
Ongerup	192	D5
Ongole	172	F5
Ongon	167	L2
Ongt Gol	166	J3
Onguday	164	D6
Onich	137	C4
Oni-i-Lau	191	T6
Onilahy	189	H4
Onitsha	185	G4
Onjuul	167	K2
Onkivesi	142	M5
Ono	169	F8
Ono *Fiji*	194	R9
Ono *Japan*	169	H7
Onotoa	191	S2
Onslow	192	D3
Onslow Bay	209	P3
Onsong	168	B4
Ontario *Canada*	201	H7
Ontario *California*	206	D3
Ontario *Oregon*	202	F6
Ontario, Lake	205	M5
Onteniente	147	F3
Ontong Java Atoll	191	N3
Oodnadatta	193	H4
Oolagah Lake	208	E2
Ooldea	192	G5
Oostelijk-Flevoland	144	F2
Oostende	144	E3
Oosterschelde	144	E3
Ootsa Lake	198	K5
Opala	186	D3
Opanake	172	F7
Oparino	158	H4
Opatow	151	J3
Opava	151	G4
Opawica	205	N2
Opelika	209	K4
Opelousas	208	F5
Opheim	203	L3
Ophir, Gunung	170	B5
Opiscoteo, Lake	201	N7
Opobo	185	G5
Opochka	143	N8
Opole	151	G3
Opornyy	159	J6
Oporto	146	B2
Opotiki	195	F3
Opp	209	J5
Oppdal	142	C5
Oppeln	151	G3
Oppland	143	C6
Opua	195	E1
Opunake	195	D3
Oradea	153	F2
Orafajokull	142	W12
Orai	172	E3
Oran	218	D4
Oran	180	E1
Orange *Australia*	193	K5
Orange *France*	145	F6
Orange *Namibia*	188	C5
Orange *U.S.A*	208	F5
Orangeburg	209	M4
Orange, Cabo	217	G3
Orangeville	205	K4
Orange Walk	212	C5
Oranienburg	150	E2
Oranje	188	D5
Oranje Gebergte	217	F3
Oranjemund	216	C1
Oranjestad	216	C1
Oranmore	139	E6
Oras	171	H3
Oravita	153	F3
Oravska nadrz	151	H4
Orawia	195	A7
Orbec	144	D4
Orbetello	149	C4
Orbigo	146	D1
Orbost	193	K6
Orbyhus	143	G6
Orcadas	221	X6
Orcera	146	E3
Orchila, Isla	216	D1
Orchowo	151	G2
Orco	148	A3
Ord	192	F2
Orderville	206	F2
Ord, Mountain	192	F2
Ordu	157	G2
Orduna	146	E1
Ore	137	E4
Orealven	142	H4
Orebro *Sweden*	143	F7
Orebro *Sweden*	143	F7
Oregon	202	D6
Oregon City	202	C5
Orekhovo Zuyevo	158	F4
Orel	159	F5
Orem	202	J7
Oren	156	B4
Orenburg	159	K5
Orencik	156	C3
Orense	146	C1
Orestias	155	J2
Oreti	195	B6
Orford Ness	133	J2
Organ Peak	207	J4
Orgaz	146	E3
Orgeyev	159	D6
Orgiva	146	E4
Orgon Tal	167	L3
Orhaneli	156	C3
Orhangazi	156	C2
Orhon Gol	167	K2
Oriental, Cordillera *Colombia*	216	C2
Oriental, Cordillera *Peru*	216	B5
Oriental, Grand Erg	181	G2
Orihuela	147	F3
Orinoco	216	E2
Oriomo	194	H5
Oris	148	C2
Orissa	172	F4
Oristano	149	B6
Oristano, Golfo di	149	B6
Orivesi *Hame, Finland*	143	L6
Orivesi *Pohjois-karjala, Finland*	142	N5
Oriximina	217	F4
Orizaba	211	L8
Orizare	153	J4
Orje	143	D7
Orjen	152	E4
Orkanger	142	C5
Orkelljunga	143	E8
Orkla	142	C5
Orkney	136	E1
Orkney Islands	136	F1
Orla	151	G3
Orlando	209	M6
Orleanais	145	D5
Orleans	145	D5
Ormara	172	B3
Ormara, Ras	172	B3
Ormoc	171	G3
Ormond Island	200	K4

Name	Page	Grid
Ormos	155	H4
Ormskirk	135	G3
Ornain	144	F4
Orne	144	C4
Ornskoldsvik	142	H5
Oro	210	G4
Orobi, Alpi	148	B3
Orocue	216	C3
Orofino	202	F4
Oromocto	205	S4
Oron	165	K5
Orona	191	U2
Oronsay	137	B5
Oronsay, Passage of	137	B5
Orontes	157	G5
Oropesa	146	D3
Oroqen Zizhiqi	167	N1
Oroquieta	171	G4
Orosei, Golfo di	149	B5
Oroshaza	152	F2
Orotukan	165	S4
Oroville *California*	202	D8
Oroville *Washington*	202	E3
Oroville, Lake	202	D8
Orrin Reservoir	136	D3
Orsa	143	F6
Orsa Finnmark	143	F6
Orsaro, Monte	148	C3
Orsha	158	E5
Orsta	142	B5
Orta	156	E2
Ortabag	157	K4
Ortaca	156	C4
Ortakoy *Turkey*	156	F2
Ortakoy *Turkey*	156	F3
Ortatoroslar	156	F4
Ortega	216	B3
Ortegal, Cabo	146	C1
Ortelsburg	151	J2
Orthez	145	C7
Ortigueira	146	C1
Ortiz	213	P10
Ortles	148	C2
Ortona	149	E4
Orto-Tokoy	166	D3
Orumiyeh	157	L4
Orumiyeh, Daryacheh-ye	174	G3
Oruro	218	C3
Orvieto	149	D4
Orwell	133	J3
Oryakhovo	153	G4
Os	142	D5
Osa	158	K4
Osage	204	D7
Osaka *Japan*	169	E8
Osaka *Japan*	169	F8
Osaka-wan	169	E8
Osa, Peninsula de	212	F10
Osceola *Arkansas*	208	H3
Osceola *Iowa*	204	D6
Osh	166	B3
Oshamambe	168	H4
Oshawa	205	L5
O-shima	169	G8
Oshkosh	204	F4
Oshkurya	164	Ac3
Oshmarino	164	C2
Oshmyanskaya Vozvyshennost	151	M1
Oshmyany	151	L1
Oshnoviyeh	174	G3
Oshogbo	185	F4
Oshtoran Kuh	174	J5
Oshtorinan	174	J4
Oshwe	186	C3
Osijek	152	E3
Osimo	148	D4
Osinniki	164	D6
Osipovichi	159	D5
Oskaloosa	204	D6
Oskamull	137	B4
Oskara, Mys	164	F1
Oskarshamn	143	G8
Oskarstrom	143	E8
Oskoba	164	G4
Oskol	159	F5
Oslo *Norway*	143	D7
Oslo *Norway*	143	D7
Oslob	171	G4
Oslofjorden	143	H7
Osmanabad	172	E5
Osmancik	156	F2
Osmaneli	156	C2
Osmaniye	157	G4
Osmington	132	E4
Osmino	143	N7
Osmo	143	G7
Osnabruck	150	C2
Osogovska Planina	153	G4
Osorno *Chile*	219	B8
Osorno *Spain*	146	D1
Osoyro	143	A6
Osprey Reef	193	K1
Oss	144	F3
Ossa	155	G3
Ossa, Mount	190	L10
Ossett	135	H3
Ossian, Loch	137	D4
Ossokmanuan Lake	201	P7
Ostashkov	158	E4
Ostavall	142	F5
Ostby	143	E6
Oste	150	C2
Osterburken	150	C4

Name	Page	Grid
Osterdalalven	143	E6
Osterdalen	143	D5
Ostergotland	143	F7
Osterode	151	H2
Ostersund	142	F5
Ostfold	143	D7
Ost Friesische Inseln	150	B2
Ostfriesland	150	B2
Osthammar	143	H6
Ostiglia	148	C3
Ostra	148	D4
Ostrava	151	H4
Ostroda	151	H2
Ostrog	159	D5
Ostrogozhsk	159	F5
Ostroleka	151	J2
Ostrov	143	N8
Ostrovnoy, Mys	168	D4
Ostrow	151	G3
Ostrowiec	151	J3
Ostrow Mazowiecki	151	J2
Ostuni	149	F5
Osum	155	F2
Osum	153	H4
Osumi-kaikyo	169	C10
Osumi-shoto	169	C10
Osuna	146	D4
OsVan	158	K2
Oswaldtwistle	135	G3
Oswego	205	M5
Oswestry	132	D2
Otaki	195	E4
Otaru	168	H4
Otava	150	E4
Otavi	188	C3
Otawara	169	G7
Otchinjau	186	B6
Otelec	153	F3
Otelu Rosu	153	G3
Otematata	195	C6
Othe, Foret d'	145	E4
Othonoi	154	E3
Othris	155	G3
Oti	184	F4
Otira	195	C5
Otis	203	N7
Otish, Monts	201	M7
Otjiwarongo	188	C4
Otley	135	H3
Otlukbeli Daglari	157	J2
Otnes	143	D6
Otocac	152	C3
Otorohanga	195	E3
Otoskwin	201	H7
Otra	143	B7
Otranto	149	G5
Otranto, Capo d	149	G5
Otranto, Strait of	154	E2
Otsu	169	E8
Otsu	169	H7
Otta *Norway*	143	C6
Otta *Norway*	143	C6
Ottawa *Canada*	205	L3
Ottawa *Canada*	205	N4
Ottawa Islands	201	K6
Otter	132	D4
Otterburn	137	F5
Otter Rapids	205	K1
Otterup	143	D9
Ottery	132	C4
Ottery Saint Mary	132	D4
Ottumwa	204	D6
Oturkpo	185	G4
Otway, Bahia	219	B10
Otway, Cape	193	J6
Otway, Seno	219	B10
Otwock	151	J2
Otynya	151	L4
Otztaler Alpen	148	C2
Ouachita	208	F4
Ouachita, Lake	208	F3
Ouachita Mountains	208	E3
Ouadda	182	D6
Ouagadougou	184	E3
Ouahigouya	184	E3
Oualata	180	D5
Oua-n Ahagar, Tassili	181	G4
Ouanda Djaile	182	D6
Ouarane	180	D4
Ouargla	181	G2
Ouarra	182	E6
Ouarsenis, Massif de l'	147	G5
Ouarzazate	180	D2
Ouatoais	205	M4
Oubangui	186	C3
Oudenaarde	144	E3
Oude Rijn	144	F2
Oudtshoorn	188	D6
Oued Zem	180	D2
Oueme	185	F4
Ouen	194	X17
Ouessant, Ile d'	144	A4
Ouesso	186	C2
Ouezzane	180	D2
Oughterard	139	D6
Oughter, Lough	138	H4
Ouidah	185	F4
Oujda	180	E2
Oulainen	142	L4
Oulmes	180	D2
Oulu *Finland*	142	L4
Oulu *Finland*	142	M4
Oulujarvi	142	M4
Oulujoki	142	M4

Name	Page	Grid
Oulx	148	A3
Oum Chalouba	182	D4
Oum El Bouaghi	181	G1
Oum er Rbia, Oued	180	D2
Ou, Nam	173	K4
Ounasjoki	142	L3
Oundle	133	G2
Ounianga Kebir	182	D4
Oupu	167	P1
Ouricuri	217	J5
Ourinhos	218	G4
Ouro Preto	218	H4
Ourthe	144	F3
Ouse *Australia*	193	K7
Ouse *U.K.*	135	H3
Oust	145	B5
Outardes, Reservoir	201	N7
Outer Hebrides	136	A3
Outokumpu	142	N5
Out Skerries	136	B1
Outwell	133	H2
Ouvea	194	X16
Ouyen	193	J6
Ovacik *Turkey*	157	H4
Ovacik *Turkey*	157	J2
Ovada	148	B3
Ovalau Batiki	194	R8
Ovalle	218	B6
Ovau	194	H5
Ovejo	146	D3
Oven	195	X17
Overbister	136	F1
Overbygd	142	H2
Overkalix	142	K3
Overnas	142	G3
Overtornea	142	K3
Oviedo	146	D1
Ovinishche	158	F4
Ovre Ardal	143	B6
Ovruch	159	D5
Owahanga	195	F4
Owaka	195	B7
Owando	186	C3
Owase	169	F8
Owatonna	204	D4
Owbeh	175	R4
Owel, Lough	138	H5
Owenbeg	138	E4
Owenkillew	138	H3
Owenmore	138	C4
Owens	206	C2
Owensboro	204	G8
Owens Lake	206	D2
Owen Sound	205	K4
Owen Stanley Range	194	D3
Owerri	185	G4
Owo	185	G4
Owosso	204	H5
Owyhee *Nevada*	202	F7
Owyhee *Oregon*	202	F6
Oxbow	203	N3
Oxelosund	143	G7
Oxenholme	135	G2
Oxenhope	135	H3
Oxford *New Zealand*	195	D5
Oxford *U.K.*	133	F3
Oxford *U.S.A.*	208	H3
Oxfordshire	133	F3
Ox Mountains	138	E4
Oxnard	206	C3
Oxton	135	H3
Oyaca	156	E3
Oyali	157	J4
Oyapock	217	G3
Oyem	186	B2
Oykel	136	D3
Oykel Bridge	136	D3
Oymyakon	165	Q4
Oyo	185	F4
Ozalp	157	L3
Ozamiz	171	G4
Ozark Plateau	204	D8
Ozarks, Lake of the	204	D7
Ozd	152	F1
Ozernovskiy	165	T6
Ozernoye	164	A5
Ozersk	151	K1
Ozhogina	165	R3
Ozieri	149	B5
Ozinki	159	H5
Ozona	207	M5
Ozora	152	E2
Ozyurt	156	F3

P

Name	Page	Grid
Paama	194	U12
Paarl	188	C6
Pabbay *U.K.*	136	A3
Pabbay *U.K.*	137	A4
Pabellon de Arteaga	210	H6
Pabjanice	151	H3
Pabna	172	G4
Pabrade	143	L9
Pacaas Novos, Serra dos	216	E6
Pacaraima, Sierra	216	E3
Pacasmayo	216	B5
Pachino	149	E7
Pachora	172	E4
Pachuca	211	K7
Pacifica	206	A2
Pacific Ocean	167	P7
Pacific Ocean, North	223	H3

Name	Page	Grid
Pacific Ocean, South	223	J5
Pacitan	170	E7
Packwood	202	D4
Padang *Indonesia*	170	C6
Padang *Indonesia*	170	C5
Padangpanjang	170	D6
Padangsidimpuan	170	B5
Padasjoki	143	L6
Padauiri	216	E3
Paderborn	150	C3
Pades	153	G3
Padiham	135	G3
Padilla *Bolivia*	218	D3
Padilla *Mexico*	211	K5
Padina	153	J3
Padje-Ianta	142	G3
Padloping Island	200	P4
Padova	148	C3
Padrao, Pointa do	186	B4
Padron	146	B1
Padstow	132	C4
Padstow Bay	132	C4
Padua	148	C3
Paducah *Kentucky*	204	F8
Paducah *Texas*	207	M4
Padunskoye More	142	P2
Paekariki	195	E4
Paengnyong-do	167	N4
Paeroa	195	E2
Pag *Croatia*	152	C3
Pag *Croatia*	152	C3
Pagadian	171	G4
Pagasitikos Kolpos	155	G3
Pagatan	170	F6
Page	206	G2
Pagosa Springs	207	J2
Pagwa River	204	H2
Pagwi	194	C2
Pahala	206	T11
Pahang	170	C5
Pahia Point	195	A7
Pahiatua	195	E4
Pahlavi Dezh	175	M3
Pahoa	206	T11
Pahokee	209	M7
Pahra Kariz	175	Q4
Paia	206	S10
Paide	143	L7
Paignton	132	D4
Paijanne	143	L6
Pailolo Chan	206	S10
Paimpol	144	B4
Painswick	133	E3
Painted Desert	206	G2
Paisley	137	D5
Paita	216	A5
Paita	194	X17
Paittasjarvi	142	K2
Pajala	142	K3
Pakaraima Mountains	216	E2
Pakistan	172	C3
Pak Lay	173	K5
Pakokku	173	H4
Pakpattan	172	D2
Pakrac	152	D3
Paks	152	E2
Pakse	173	L5
Pala	182	B6
Palabuhanratu	170	D7
Palafrugell	147	H2
Palagruza	152	D4
Palaiokastron	155	J5
Palaiokhora	155	G5
Pala Laharha	172	G4
Palamos	147	H2
Palana	165	T5
Palanan Point	171	G2
Palanga	143	J9
Palangan, Kuh-e-	175	Q6
Palangkaraya	170	E6
Palanpur	172	D4
Palapye	188	E4
Palar	172	E6
Palata	149	E5
Palatka *U.S.A.*	209	M6
Palatka *Russia*	165	S4
Palau	149	B5
Palau Islands	171	J4
Palawan	171	F4
Palawan Passage	171	F4
Palayankottai	172	E7
Palazzola Acreide	149	E7
Paldiski	143	L7
Palembang	170	C6
Palena, Lago	219	B8
Palencia	146	D1
Palermo	149	D6
Palestine	208	E5
Paletwa	173	H4
Palghat	172	E6
Palgrave Point	188	B4
Palhoca	218	G5
Pali	172	D3
Palisade	207	H1
Palit, Kep i	154	E2
Palkane	143	L6
Palk Strait	172	E7
Pallaresa	147	G1
Pallas Green	139	F7
Pallasovka	159	H5
Pallastunturi	142	K2
Palliser Bay	195	E4
Palliser, Cape	195	E4
Palma *Mozambique*	189	H2

Penas, Cabode 146 C1
Penasco, Puerto 206 F5
Pena, Sierra de la 147 F1
Pencader 132 C3
Pencaitland 137 F5
Pendalofon 155 F2
Pendembu 184 C4
Pendine 132 C3
Pendleton 202 E5
Pend Oreille Lake 202 F3
Pendra 172 F4
Penedo 218 K6
Penfro 132 C3
Penganga 172 E5
Pengkou 167 M6
Pengze 167 M5
Peniche 146 B3
Penicuik 137 E5
Peniscola 147 G2
Penistone 135 H3
Penitentes, Serra do 217 H5
Penmaenmawr 134 F3
Penmarch, Pointe de 145 A5
Penne 149 D4
Penner 172 E6
Penneshaw 193 H6
Pennine, Alpi 148 A2
Pennines 135 G2
Pennsylvania 205 L6
Penny Highlands 200 N4
Peno 158 E4
Penobscot 205 R4
Penobscot Bay 205 R4
Penonome 212 G10
Penrith 135 G2
Penryn 132 B4
Pensacola 209 J5
Pensamiento 216 E6
Pentecost Island 194 U11
Pentire Head 132 C4
Pentland Firth 136 E2
Pentland Hills 137 E5
Pen-y-ghent 135 G2
Penza 159 H5
Penzance 132 B4
Penzhina 165 V4
Penzhinskaya Guba 165 U4
Peoria 204 F6
Peqin 154 E2
Perak 170 C5
Perama 155 F3
Percival Lakes 192 E3
Perdido, Monte 147 G1
Peregrebnoye 164 Ae4
Pereira 216 B3
Perelazovskiy 159 G6
Perello 147 G2
Peremyshlyany 151 L4
Perenjori 192 D4
PereslavlZalesskiy 158 F4
Perevolotskiy 159 J5
Pereyaslavka 168 E2
Pergamino 219 D6
Pergamum 156 B3
Perhojoki 142 K5
Peri 157 J3
Peribonca 201 M8
Peribonca 205 Q2
Perigueux 145 D6
Perija, Sierra de 216 C2
Perim 176 F10
Peris 153 J3
Peristrema 156 F3
Perito Moreno 219 B9
Peritoro 217 J4
Perlas, Punta de 212 F8
Perlez 152 F3
Perm 158 K4
Pernambuca 217 K5
Pernik 153 G4
Peronne 144 E4
Perote 211 L8
Perote, Cofre de 211 L8
Perouse Strait, La 168 J3
Perpignan 145 E7
Perran Bay 132 B4
Perranporth 132 B4
Perros-Guirec 144 B4
Perry *Canada* 199 Q2
Perry *Florida* 209 L5
Perry *Oklahoma* 208 D2
Perryton 207 M2
Perryville *Alaska* 198 D4
Perryville *Missouri* 204 F8
Persembe 157 G2
Perseverancia 216 E6
Persian Gulf 177 K3
Pertek 157 H3
Perth *Australia* 192 D5
Perth *Canada* 205 M4
Perth *U.K.* 137 E4
Perth-Andover 205 S3
Pertominsk 158 F3
Pertugskiy 158 H4
Pertuis Breton 145 C5
Peru 216 B5
Peru *Illinois* 204 F6
Peru *Indiana* 204 G6
Peru-Chile Trench 223 L5
Perugia 148 D4
Perushtitsa 153 H4
Pervari 157 K4
Pervomaskiy 159 K5
Pervomaysk *Russia* 158 G5
Pervomaysk *Ukraine* 159 E6
Pervouralsk 164 Ac5
Pesaro 148 D4
Pescara 149 E4
Peschanyy, Mys 159 J7
Pesha 158 H2
Peshanjan 175 Q5
Peshawar 172 D2
Peshkopi 155 F2
Peski *Belarus* 151 L2
Peski *Kazakhstan* 164 Ae6
Pesqueira *Brazil* 217 K5
Pesqueria *Mexico* 207 N8
Pestovo 158 F4
Petah Tiqwa 174 B5
Petajavesi 142 L5
Petalcalco, Bahia 210 H9
Petalioi 155 H4
Petalion, Kolpos 155 H4
Petaluma 206 A1
Petatlan 211 J9
Petauke 187 F5
Peterborough *Australia* 193 H5
Peterborough *Canada* 205 L4
Peterborough *U.K.* 133 G2
Peterhead 136 G3
Peterlee 135 H2
Petermann Ranges 192 F3
Peter Pond Lake 199 P4
Petersburg *Alaska* 198 J4
Petersburg *Virginia* 205 M8
Petersfield 133 G3
Peterstow 132 E3
Petite Kabylie 147 J4
Petite Miquelon 201 Q8
Petit Mecatina, Riviere du 201 P7
Petitot 199 L4
Petkula 142 M3
Peto 211 Q7
Petoskey 204 H4
Petra Velikogo, Zaliv 168 C4
Petre Bay 195 F6
Petrila 153 G3
Petrodvorets 143 N7
Petrolandia 217 K5
Petrolina *Amazonas, Brazil* 216 D4
Petrolina *Pernambuco, Brazil* 217 J5
Petropavlovsk 164 Ae6
Petropavlovsk-Kamchatskiy 165 T6
Petropolis 218 H4
Petrovac 152 E4
Petrovsk 159 H5
Petrovskoye 158 K5
Petrovsk-Zabaykalskiy 164 H6
Petrozavodsk 158 E3
Petsamo 142 P2
Petteril 135 G2
Petukhovo 164 Ae5
Petworth 133 G4
Peureula 170 B5
Pevek 165 W3
Pewsey, Vale of 132 F3
Peza 158 H2
Pezenas 145 E7
Pezinok 151 G4
Pezmog 158 J3
Pfaffenhofen 150 D4
Pfarrkirchen 150 E4
Pforzheim 150 C4
Phalaborwa 188 F4
Phalodi 172 D3
Phaltan 172 D5
Phangan, Ko 173 K6
Phangnga 173 J7
Phan Rang 173 L6
Phan Thiet 173 L6
Phatthalung 173 K7
Phenix City 209 K4
Phet Buri 173 J6
Phetchabun, Thiu Khao 173 K5
Philadelphia *Mississippi* 208 H4
Philadelphia *Pennsylvania* 205 N6
Philip 203 P5
Philip Island 191 Q7
Philippeville 144 F3
Philippines 171 G2
Philippine Sea 171 G1
Philipstown 188 D6
Phillipsburg 203 Q8
Philpots Island 200 L2
Phnom Penh 173 K6
Phoenix 206 F4
Phoenix Islands 191 U2
Phong Saly 173 K4
Phong Tho 173 K4
Phu Cuong 173 L6
Phu Dien Chau 173 L5
Phuket 173 J7
Phuket, Ko 173 J7
Phulabani 172 F4
Phu Ly 173 L4
Phuoc Le 173 L6
Phu Tho 173 L4
Phyajoki 142 L4
Piacenza 148 B3
Piana 149 B4
Pianosa, Isola 149 C4
Piatra Neamt 153 J2
Piaui 217 J5
Piaui, Serra do 217 J5
Piave 148 D3
Piaya 170 F7
Piazza Armerina 149 E7
Pibor 183 F6
Pibor Post 183 F6
Pic 204 G2
Picardie 144 E4
Picayune 208 H5
Pichilemu 219 B6
Pickering 135 J2
Pickering, Vale of 135 J2
Pickle Lake 201 J7
Pico 149 D5
Picos 217 J5
Pico Truncado 219 C9
Picton 195 E4
Picun-Leufu 219 C7
Pidalion, Akra 156 F5
Pidurutalagala 172 F7
Piedecuesta 216 C2
Piedrabuena 146 D3
Piedrahita 146 D2
Piedralaves 146 D2
Piedras Negras 207 M6
Piedra Sola 218 E6
Pielavesi 142 M5
Pielinen 142 N5
Pierowall 136 F1
Pierre 203 P5
Pietarsaari 142 K5
Pietermaritzburg 188 F5
Pietersburg 188 E4
Pietrosu 153 H2
Pieve di Cadore 148 D2
Pigadhia 155 J5
Piggott 208 G2
Pihtipudas 142 L5
Pijijiapan 211 N10
Pikes Peak 203 M8
Pikeville 204 J8
Pikhtovka 164 C5
Pila 151 G2
Pilar 218 E5
Pilaya 218 D4
Pilcaniyeu 219 B8
Pilcomayo 218 D4
Pili 155 J4
Pilibhit 172 E3
Pilica 151 H3
Pilion 155 G3
Pilos 155 F4
Pilot Point 198 D4
Pilsen 150 E4
Pimenta Bueno 216 E6
Pimentel 217 G4
Pina 147 F2
Pinang *Malaysia* 170 C4
Pinang *Malaysia* 170 C4
Pinarbasi *Turkey* 156 E2
Pinarbasi *Turkey* 157 G3
Pinar del Rio 212 F3
Pinarhisar 156 B2
Pinawa 203 S2
Pincher Creek 202 H3
Pindare 217 H4
Pindhos Oros 155 F3
Pindi Gheb 172 D2
Pine Bluff 208 F3
Pine Bluffs 203 M7
Pine City 204 D4
Pine Creek 192 G1
Pine Creek Lake 208 E3
Pinedale 203 K6
Pine Falls 199 R5
Pinega *Russia* 158 G3
Pinega *Russia* 158 G3
Pine Island Bay 221 T4
Pine Pass 199 L5
Pine Point 199 N3
Pine Ridge 203 N6
Pinerolo 148 A3
Pines, Lake O' the 208 E4
Pinetop-Lakeside 207 H3
Pineville 204 J8
Pingbian 173 K4
Pingdingshan 173 M2
Pingelly 192 D5
Pingeyri 142 T12
Pingguo 173 L4
Pingjiang 173 M3
Ping, Mae Nam 173 J5
Pingquan 173 L1
Pingtan Dao 167 M6
Ping-tung 167 N7
Pingwu 173 K2
Pingxiang *Guangxi, China* 173 L4
Pingxiang *Jiangxi, China* 173 M3
Pingyang 167 N6
Pingyao 167 L4
Pingyi 167 M4
Pingyin 167 M4
Pinhao 146 C2
Pinhel 146 C2
Pini 170 B5
Pinios *Greece* 155 F4
Pinios *Greece* 155 F3
Pinnes, Akra 155 H2
Pinos, Point 206 B2
Pinotepa Nacional 211 L9
Pinrang 171 F6
Pins, Ile des 194 X17
Pinsk 151 M2
Pintados 218 C4
Pinta, Isla 216 A7
Pinto 218 D5
Pinyug 158 H3
Pioche 206 E2
Piombino 149 C4
Pioner, Ostrov 161 L2
Pionerskiy *Russia* 164 Ad4
Pionerskiy *Russia* 151 J1
Piotrkow Trybunalski 151 H3
Piove di Sacco 148 D3
Piperi 155 H3
Pipestone 204 B5
Pipmudcan, Reservoir 205 Q2
Piracicaba 218 G4
Piracuruca 217 J4
Piraeus 155 G4
Pirahmet 157 H2
Piraievs 155 G4
Piranhas *Amazonas, Brazil* 216 E5
Piranhas *Sergipe, Brazil* 217 K5
Piranshahr 157 L4
Pirapora 218 H3
Pirara 216 F3
Pirgos *Greece* 155 F4
Pirgos *Greece* 155 H5
Pirimapun 194 B3
Pirineos 147 F1
Pirin Planina 153 G5
Piripiri 217 J4
Pirmasens 150 B4
Pirna 150 E3
Piro do Rio 218 G3
Pirot 153 G4
Pir Panjal Range 172 D2
Piru 171 H6
Piryatin 159 E5
Piryi 155 H3
Pisa 148 C4
Pisco 216 B6
Piscopi 155 J4
Pisek 150 F4
Pishan 172 E1
Pishin 175 Q8
Pishin-Lora 172 C3
Pistayarvi, Ozero 142 P4
Pisticci 149 F5
Pistilfjordur 142 X11
Pistoia 148 C4
Pisuerga 146 D1
Pit 202 D7
Pita 184 C3
Pitanga 218 E4
Pitcairn Island 223 J5
Pitea 142 J4
Pitealven 142 H4
Pitesti 153 H3
Pithiviers 144 E4
Pitkyaranta 158 E3
Pitlochry 137 E4
Pitlyar 164 Ae3
Pitt Island *Canada* 198 K5
Pitt Island *New Zealand* 195 F7
Pittsburg 204 C8
Pittsburgh 205 K6
Pittsfield 204 E7
Pitt Strait 195 F7
Piui 218 G4
Piura 216 A5
Pjorsa 142 N2
Pjorsa 142 V12
Placentia Bay 201 Q8
Placer 171 G3
Placerville 206 B1
Placido do Castro 216 D6
Plackoviea 153 G5
Plainview 207 M3
Plaka 155 H2
Plakenska Planina 153 F5
Plampang 171 F7
Plana 150 E4
Planeta Rica 213 K10
Plankinton 203 Q6
Plant City 209 L7
Plaquemine 208 G5
Plasencia 146 C2
Plastun 168 F3
Platani 149 D7
Plata, Rio de la 219 E6
Plati 155 G2
Plato 216 C2
Platte 203 R7
Platteville 204 E5
Plattling 150 E4
Plattsburgh 205 P4
Plattsmouth 204 C6
Plauen 150 E3
Plav 152 E4
Playa Azul 210 H8
Pleasanton 208 C6
Pleihari 170 E6
Pleiku 173 L6
Plenty, Bay of 195 F2
Plentywood 203 M3
Plesetsk 158 G3
Plessisville 205 Q3
Pleszew 151 G3
Pletipi Lake 201 M7
Pleven 153 H4
Plitra 155 G4
Pljevlja 152 E4
Plock 151 H2
Plockenstein 150 E4
Ploermel 145 B5
Ploiesti 153 J3
Plomb du Cantal 145 E6
Plombieres 145 G5
Ploner See 150 D1
Plonsk 151 J2
Ploty 150 F2

Rebrovo **153** G4
Rebun-to **168** H3
Recanati **148** D4
Recea **153** G3
Recherche, Archipelago of the **192** E5
Rechitsa **159** E5
Rechna Doab **172** D2
Recife **217** L5
Recklinghausen **150** B3
Recknitz **150** E2
Reconquista **218** E5
Recreio **216** F5
Red *Canada* **203** R2
Red *U.S.A.* **208** F5
Redalen **143** D6
Red Bay **201** Q7
Redbird **203** M6
Red Bluff **202** C7
Red Bluff Lake **207** L5
Redcar **135** H2
Redcliffe **193** L4
Red Cloud **203** Q7
Red Deer *Canada* **202** G2
Red Deer *Canada* **202** H1
Red Deer *Canada* **203** J2
Red Deer *Saskatchewan, Canada* **199** Q5
Redding **202** C7
Redditch **133** F2
Redencao **217** J5
Redfield **203** Q5
Redhakhol **172** F4
Redhill **133** G3
Red Hills **207** N2
Red Lake *Canada* **203** S2
Red Lake *Canada* **203** T2
Red Lake *U.S.A.* **204** C3
Red Lake *U.S.A.* **203** R4
Red Lodge **203** K5
Redmond **202** D5
Redon **145** B5
Redondela **146** B1
Redondo **146** C3
Red Rock **204** F2
Redruth **132** B4
Red Sea **183** G3
Red Tank **193** K5
Red Wharf Bay **134** E3
Red Wing **204** D4
Redwood City **206** A2
Reed City **204** H5
Reedsport **202** B6
Ree, Lough **138** G5
Reetton **195** C5
Refahiye **157** H3
Refresco **218** C5
Rega **150** F2
Regen **150** E4
Regensburg **150** E4
Reggane **180** F3
Reggio di Calabria **149** E6
Reggio nell Amelia **148** C3
Regina *Brazil* **217** G3
Regina *Canada* **203** M2
Reguengos de Monsaraz **146** C3
Rehna **150** D2
Rehoboth **188** C4
Rehoboth Beach **205** N7
Rehovot **174** B6
Reidh, Rubha **136** C3
Reidsville **209** N2
Reiff **136** C2
Reigate **133** G3
Reighton **135** J2
Re, Ile de **145** C5
Reims **144** F4
Reina Adelaida, Archipielago de la **219** B10
Reindeer Lake **199** Q4
Reine **142** E3
Reinga, Cape **195** D1
Reinheimen **142** B5
Reinosa **146** D1
Reitz **188** E5
Relizane **180** F1
Remada **181** H2
Rembang **170** E7
Remeshk **175** P8
Remiremont **145** G4
Remontnoye **159** G6
Remoulins **145** F7
Remscheid **150** B3
Rena *Norway* **143** D6
Rena *Norway* **143** D6
Renaix **144** E3
Renard Islands **194** E4
Rendova Island **194** H6
Rendsburg **150** C1
Renfrew *Canada* **205** M4
Renfrew *U.K.* **137** D5
Rengat **170** D6
Rengo **219** B6
Renish Point **136** B3
Renk **183** F5
Renmark **193** J5
Renmin **167** P2
Rennell Island **194** K7
Rennes **144** C4
Reno *Italy* **148** C3
Reno *U.S.A.* **202** E8
Reo **171** G7
Repetek **175** R2
Repolovo **164** Ae4
Republican **203** R7
Repulse Bay *Australia* **193** K3
Repulse Bay *Canada* **200** J4
Requena *Peru* **216** C5
Requena *Spain* **147** F3
Rere **194** K6
Resadiye *Turkey* **156** B4
Resadiye *Turkey* **157** G2
Resen **153** F5
Resia, Passo de **148** C2
Resistencia **218** E5
Resita **153** F3
Resolution Island *Canada* **201** P5
Resolution Island *New Zealand* **195** A6
Resolution Lake **201** P6
Restigouche **205** S3
Retalhuleu **212** B7
Rethel **144** F4
Rethimnon **155** H5
Retiche, Alpi **148** C2
Retsag **152** E2
Retuerta de Bullaque **146** D3
Reunion **189** L7
Reus **147** G2
Reuss **148** B2
Reut **153** J2
Reutlingen **150** C4
Revel **145** D7
Revelstoke **202** E2
Reventador, Volcan **216** B4
Revillagigedo Island **198** J5
Revillagigedo, Islas **210** D8
Rewa **172** F4
Rewari **172** E3
Rexburg **202** J6
Reyes, Point **202** C9
Reyhanli **157** G4
Rey, Isla del **212** H10
Reykjaheidi **142** W12
Reykjahhd **142** W12
Reykjanesta **142** T13
Reykjavik **142** U12
Reynivellir *Iceland* **142** U12
Reynivellir *Iceland* **142** W12
Reynosa **208** C7
Rezekne **143** M8
Rhatikon Pratigau **148** B2
Rhayader **132** D2
Rheda-Wiedenbruck **150** C3
Rhee **133** G2
Rhein **150** B3
Rheine **150** B2
Rhewl **135** F3
Rhiconich **136** D2
Rhine **144** G4
Rhinelander **204** F4
Rhino Camp **187** F2
Rhir, Cap **180** D2
Rho **148** B3
Rhode Island **205** Q6
Rhodes **155** J4
Rhodopi Planina **153** G4
Rhondda **132** D3
Rhone **145** F7
Rhoose **132** D3
Rhosneigr **135** E3
Rhuddlan **135** F3
Rhum **137** B3
Rhum, Sound of **137** B4
Rhydaman **132** C3
Rhyl **135** F3
Rhynie **136** F3
Riachao do Jacuipe **218** K6
Riacho de Santana **218** J6
Riano **146** D1
Riansares **146** E3
Riau, Kepulauan **170** C5
Riaza **146** E2
Ribadeo **146** C1
Ribadesella **146** D1
Ribas do Rio Pardo **218** F4
Ribat **175** R5
Ribatejo **146** B3
Ribble **135** G2
Ribe **143** C9
Ribeirao Preto **218** G4
Ribeiro do Pombal **217** K6
Riberac **145** D6
Riberalta **216** D6
Ribnica **152** C3
Ribnitz-Damgarten **150** E1
Riccall **135** H3
Rice Lake *Canada* **205** L4
Rice Lake *U.S.A.* **204** E4
Richard Collinson Inlet **199** N1
Richards Island **198** H2
Richardson **208** D4
Richardson Mountains **198** H2
Richelieu **205** P4
Richfield **206** F1
Richland **202** E4
Richlands **205** K8
Richmond *Australia* **193** J3
Richmond *New Zealand* **195** D4
Richmond *South Africa* **188** D6
Richmond *Greater London, U.K.* **133** G3
Richmond *North Yorkshire, U.K.* **135** H2
Richmond *Indiana* **204** H7
Richmond *Kentucky* **204** H8
Richmond *Virginia* **205** M8
Richmond Range **195** D4
Rickmansworth **133** G3
Ricla **147** F2
Ricobayo, Embalse de **146** D2
Ridgecrest **206** D3
Ridgeland **209** M4
Ridgway **205** L6
Riding Mountain **203** P2
Ridsdale **137** F5
Ried **148** D1
Rienza **148** C2
Riesa **150** E3
Riesco, Isla **219** B10
Rietfontein **188** D4
Rieti **149** D4
Rifle **203** L8
Rifstangi **142** W11
Riga **143** L8
Riga, Gulf of **143** K8
Rigan **175** P7
Rigistan **172** B2
Rigolet **201** Q7
Rihab, Ar **174** G6
Rihand **172** F4
Riiser-Larsen Sea **221** B5
Rijeka **152** C3
Rika **151** K4
Rika, Wadi al **176** G5
Rimah, Wadi al **176** E3
Rimal, Ar **177** L6
Rimavska Sobota **151** J4
Rimbo **143** H7
Rimini **148** D3
Rimna **153** J3
Rimnicu Sarat **153** J3
Rimnicu Vilcea **153** H3
Rimouski **205** R2
Rinca **171** F7
Rinchinlhumbe **166** H1
Ringe **143** D9
Ringebu **143** D6
Ringgold Isles **194** S8
Ringkobing **143** C8
Ringkobing Fjord **143** C9
Ringmer **133** H4
Ringselet **142** L3
Ringvassoy **142** H2
Ringwood **133** F4
Rinia **155** H4
Rinjani, Gunung **170** F7
Rinns Point **137** B5
Riobamba **216** B4
Rio Branco *Brazil* **216** D5
Rio Branco *Uruguay* **218** F6
Rio Bravo **208** D8
Rio Bueno **219** B8
Rio Caribe **216** E1
Rio Claro **216** E1
Rio Colorado **219** D7
Rio Cuarto **218** D6
Rio de Janeiro *Brazil* **218** H4
Rio de Janeiro *Brazil* **218** H4
Rio de Oro, Baie de **180** B4
Rio Gallegos **219** C10
Rio Grande *Argentina* **219** C10
Rio Grande *Brazil* **218** F6
Rio Grande *U.S.A.* **210** H6
Rio Grande City **208** C7
Rio Grande de Santiago **210** G7
Rio Grande do Norte **217** K5
Rio Grande do Sul **218** F5
Riohacha **216** C1
Rio Hato **212** G10
Rio Lagartos **211** Q7
Riom **145** E6
Riom-es-Montagnes **145** E6
Rio Mulatos **218** C3
Rionegro **216** C2
Rio Negro *Brazil* **218** G5
Rio Negro *Spain* **146** C1
Rio Negro, Embalse del **218** E6
Rio Negro, Pantanal do **218** E3
Rioni **157** J1
Rio Pardo de Minas **218** H3
Rio Primero **218** D6
Rio Sao Goncalo **218** H4
Riosucio *Colombia* **216** B2
Riosucio *Colombia* **216** B2
Rio Verde **218** F3
Ripley *Ohio* **204** J7
Ripley *Tennessee* **208** H3
Ripley *W. Virginia* **205** K7
Ripoll **147** H1
Ripon **135** H2
Ripponden **135** H3
Risca **132** D3
Rishiri-to **168** H3
Rishon le Zion **174** B6
Risle **144** D4
Risor **143** C7
Risoyhamn **142** F2
Ritchie's Archipelago **173** H6
Ritter, Mount **202** E9
Ritzville **202** E4
Riva **148** C3
Rivas **212** E9
Rivera **218** E6
River Falls **204** D4
Riverina **193** K5
Riversdale **188** D6
Riverside **206** D4
Riverton *Australia* **193** H5
Riverton *Canada* **203** R2
Riverton *New Zealand* **195** B7
Riverton *U.S.A.* **203** K6
Riviere-du-Loup **205** R3
Rivne **159** D5
Rivoli **148** A3
Riwaka **195** D4
Riwoqe **173** J2
Riyan **177** J9
Rize **157** J2
Rizhskiy Zaliv **143** K8
Rizokarpaso **156** F5
Rjukan **143** C7
Rjuven **143** B7
Roa **146** E2
Road Town **213** Q5
Roan Fell **137** F5
Roanne **145** F5
Roanoke *N. Carolina* **209** P2
Roanoke *Virginia* **205** L8
Roanoke Rapids **209** P2
Roan Plateau **203** K8
Robat **175** R6
Robat Karim **175** K4
Robat Thand **175** Q7
Robel **150** E2
Robert Brown, Cape **200** K4
Roberton **137** E5
Robertsbridge **133** H4
Robertsfors **142** J4
Robert S. Kerr Reservoir **208** E3
Robertson Range **192** E3
Robertsport **184** C4
Roberval **205** P2
Robinson **204** G7
Robinson Ranges **192** D4
Robleda **146** C2
Robledollano **146** D3
Robles La Paz **216** C1
Roblin **203** P2
Robore **218** E3
Rob Roy Island **194** H5
Robson, Mount **199** M5
Roca, Cabo da **146** B3
Roca Partida, Isla **210** C8
Roca Partida, Punta **211** M8
Roccella Ionica **149** F6
Rocha **219** F6
Rocha da Gale, Barragem **146** C4
Rochdale **135** G3
Rochechouart **145** D6
Rochefort **145** C6
Rochelle **204** F6
Rochester *Kent, U.K.* **133** H3
Rochester *Northumberland, U.K.* **137** F5
Rochester *New Hamshire* **205** Q5
Rochester *New York* **205** M5
Rochester *Wisconsin* **204** D4
Rochford **133** H3
Rochfortbridge **139** H6
Rock **204** F5
Rockefeller Plateau **221** R3
Rock Falls **204** F6
Rockford **204** F5
Rockglen **203** L3
Rockhampton **193** L3
Rockingham *Australia* **192** D5
Rockingham *U.S.A.* **209** N3
Rockingham Bay **193** K2
Rock Island **204** E6
Rockland *Maine* **205** R4
Rockland *Michigan* **204** F3
Rock Springs *Montana* **203** L4
Rock Springs *Wyoming* **203** K7
Rockwood **205** R4
Rocky Ford **207** L1
Rocky Mount **209** P3
Rocky Mountain House **199** N5
Rocky Mountains **196** G3
Rocroi **144** F4
Rodberg **143** C6
Rodby **143** D9
Rodeby **143** F8
Rodel **136** B3
Roden **132** E2
Rodez **145** E6
Rodhos *Greece* **155** J4
Rodhos *Greece* **155** K4
Rodi Garganico **149** E5
Roding **133** H3
Rodinga **193** G3
Rodna **153** H2
Rodnei, Muntii **153** H2
Rodney, Cape *New Zealand* **195** E2
Rodney, Cape *U.S.A.* **198** B3
Rodonit, Kep i **154** E2
Rodosto **156** B2
Roebuck Bay **192** E2
Roermond **144** F3
Roeselare **144** E3
Roes Welcome Sound **200** J5
Rogachev **159** E5
Rogaland **143** B7
Rogatin **151** L4
Rogers **208** E2
Rogers, Mount **205** K8
Roggeveld Berge **188** D6
Rogliano **148** B4
Rognan **142** F3
Rogozno **151** G2
Rohri **172** C3
Rohtak **172** E3
Rois Bheinn **137** C3
Rojas **219** D6
Rojo, Cabo *Mexico* **211** L7
Rojo, Cabo *U.S.A.* **213** P6
Rokan **170** C5

Saginaw Bay 204 J5
Sagiz *Kazakhstan* 159 J6
Sagiz *Kazakhstan* 159 J6
Sagiz *Kazakhstan* 159 J6
Sagkaya 157 F4
Saglek Bay 201 P6
Sagone, Golfe de 149 B4
Sagres 146 B4
Saguache 207 J1
Sagua la Grande 212 G3
Saguenay 201 M8
Sagunto 147 F3
Sahagun 146 D1
Sahand, Kuh-e 174 H3
Sahara 178 C4
Saharanpur 172 E3
Sahin 156 B2
Sahiwal *Pakistan* 172 D2
Sahiwal *Pakistan* 172 D2
Sahm 177 N4
Sahra al Hijarah 174 G6
Sahuaripa 207 H6
Sahuayo 210 H7
Sa Huynh 173 L6
Sahy 151 H4
Saibai Island 194 C3
Saicla 174 B5
Saida *Algeria* 180 F2
Saida *Lebanon* 156 F6
Saidabad 175 M7
Saidapet 172 F6
Saidor 194 D3
Saidpur 173 G3
Saigon 173 L6
Saijo 169 D9
Saimaa 143 M6
Saimbeyli 157 G3
Saindak 175 Q7
Saindezh 174 H3
Saint Abb's Head 137 B5
Saint-Affrique 145 E7
Saint-Agathe-des-Monts 205 N3
Saint Agnes *U.K.* 132 B4
Saint Agnes *U.K.* 132 K5
Saint-Agreve 145 F6
Saint Albans *U.K.* 133 G3
Saint Albans *Vermont* 205 P4
Saint Albans *W. Virginia* 204 K7
Saint Alban's Head 133 E4
Saint Aldhelm's 133 E4
Saint-Amand-Montrond 145 E5
Saint-Ambroix 145 F6
Saint Andre, Cap 189 H3
Saint Andrew 133 M7
Saint Andrews *New Zealand* 195 C6
Saint Andrews *U.K.* 137 F4
Saint Andrews Bay 137 F4
Saint-Anne-des-Monts 205 S2
Saint Annes 133 M6
Saint Ann's Bay 212 J5
Saint Ann's Head 132 B3
Saint Anthony *Canada* 201 Q7
Saint Anthony *U.S.A.* 202 J6
Saint Arnaud 195 D4
Saint Asaph 135 F3
Saint Aubin 133 M7
Saint Augustin 201 Q7
Saint Augustine 209 M6
Saint Augustin Saguenay 201 Q7
Saint Austell 132 C4
Saint Austell Bay 132 C4
Saint Bees 135 F2
Saint Bees Head 135 F2
Saint Benoit 189 L7
Saint Blazey 132 C4
Saint Brides 132 B3
Saint Brides Bay 132 B3
Saint-Brieuc 144 B4
Saint-Calais 145 D5
Saint Catherines 205 L5
Saint Catherines Island 209 M5
Saint Catherine's Point 133 F4
Saint-Cere 145 D6
Saint-Chamond 145 F6
Saint Charles 204 E7
Saint Clair, Lake 204 J5
Saint-Claude 145 F5
Saint Clears 132 C3
Saint Cloud *Florida* 209 M6
Saint Cloud *Minnesota* 204 C4
Saint Columb Major 132 C4
Saint Croix *Canada* 205 S4
Saint Croix *Minnesota* 204 D4
Saint Croix *U.S.A.* 213 Q6
Saint Croix Falls 204 D4
Saint David's 132 B3
Saint David's Head 132 B3
Saint-Denis 144 E4
Saint Denis 189 L7
Sainte-Foy-la-Grande 145 D6
Saint Elias, Mount 198 G3
Saint Elias Mountains 198 H3
Sainte-Marie 189 J3
Sainte-Marie-aux-Mines 144 G4
Sainte Marie, Cap 189 J5
Sainte-Maxime 145 G7
Sainte-Menehould 144 F4
Sainte Nazaire 145 B5
Saintes 145 C6
Saintes, Iles des 213 S7
Saintes-Maries-de-la-Mer 145 F7
Saint Etienne 145 F6
Saint Eustatius 213 R6
Saint-Fargeau 145 E5
Saintfield 138 L4
Saint Finan's Bay 139 B9
Saint-Florent, Golfe de 149 B4
Saint-Florentin 145 E4
Saint-Flour 145 E6
Saint Francis *Canada* 205 P4
Saint Francis *Arkansas* 208 G3
Saint Francis *Kansas* 203 P8
Saint Francis, Cape 188 D6
Saint Gallen 148 B2
Saint-Gaudens 145 D7
Saint George *Australia* 193 K4
Saint George *U.S.A.* 206 F2
Saint George, Cape *Canada* 201 Q8
Saint George, Cape *Papua New Guinea* 194 E2
Saint George Head 193 L6
Saint George Island *Alaska* 198 Ae8
Saint George Island *Florida* 209 K6
Saint Georges 205 Q3
Saint George's 213 S8
Saint Georges Bay 201 Q8
Saint George's Channel *Papua New Guinea* 194 E2
Saint George's Channel *U.K.* 132 B3
Saint-Germain 144 D4
Saint-Gildas-de-Rhuys 145 B5
Saint-Gilles-Croix-de-Vie 145 C5
Saint-Girons 145 D7
Saint Gotthard Pass 148 B2
Saint Govan's Head 132 C3
Saint Helena 179 C8
Saint Helena Bay 188 C6
Saint Helens *Australia* 193 K7
Saint Helens *U.K.* 135 G3
Saint Helens, Mount 202 C4
Saint Helens Point 193 K7
Saint Helier 133 M4
Saint Ignace 204 H4
Saint Ignatius 202 G4
Saint Ives *Cambridgeshire, U.K.* 133 G2
Saint Ives *Cornwall, U.K.* 132 B4
Saint Ives Bay 132 B4
Saint James, Cape 198 J5
Saint-Jean-d'Angely 145 C6
Saint-Jean-de-Luz 145 C7
Saint-Jean-de-Maurienne 145 G6
Saint-Jean-de-Monts 145 B5
Saint-Jean, Lac 205 P2
Saint-Jean-Pied-de-Port 145 C7
Saint-Jean-Sur-Richelieu 205 P4
Saint Jerome 205 P4
Saint John *Canada* 201 N8
Saint John *Canada* 201 N8
Saint John *U.K.* 133 M7
Saint John *U.S.A.* 213 Q5
Saint John Bay 201 Q7
Saint John's *Antigua* 213 S6
Saint Johns *Canada* 201 R8
Saint Johns *Arizona* 207 H3
Saint Johns *Florida* 209 M6
Saint Johns *Michigan* 204 H5
Saint Johnsbury 205 Q4
Saint John's Point *Ireland* 138 F3
Saint John's Point *U.K.* 138 L4
Saint Joseph *Arkansas* 208 G5
Saint Joseph *Missouri* 204 C7
Saint Joseph Island 208 D7
Saint-Junien 145 D6
Saint Just 132 B4
Saint Keverne 132 B4
Saint Kitts-Nevis 213 R6
Saint Laurent 217 G2
Saint Lawrence *Australia* 193 K3
Saint Lawrence *Canada* 201 N8
Saint Lawrence *Canada* 201 Q8
Saint Lawrence, Gulf of 201 P8
Saint Lawrence Island 198 B3
Saint Lawrence Seaway 205 N4
Saint Leonard 205 S3
Saint-Leonard-de-Noblat 145 D6
Saint Lewis 201 Q7
Saint Lo 144 C4
Saint Louis *Minnesota* 204 D3
Saint Louis *Missouri* 204 E7
Saint Louis *Senegal* 184 B2
Saint Lucia 213 S8
Saint Lucia, Cape 189 F5
Saint Lucia Channel 213 S7
Saint Lucia, Lake 189 F5
Saint Magnus Bay 136 A1
Saint-Maixent-l'Ecole 145 C5
Saint Malo 144 B4
Saint-Malo, Golfe de 144 C4
Saint Marc 213 L5
Saint-Marcellin 145 F6
Saint Margaret's-at-Cliffe 133 J3
Saint Maries 202 F4
Saint Martin *France* 213 R5
Saint Martin *U.K.* 133 M7
Saint Martin, Lake 203 Q2
Saint Martin's 132 L5
Saint-Martin-Vesubie 145 G6
Saint Mary Peak 193 H5
Saint Marys *Australia* 193 K7
Saint Mary's *Cornwall, U.K.* 132 L5
Saint Mary's *Orkney Islands, U.K.* 136 F2
Saint Marys *Florida* 209 M5
Saint Marys *Pennsylvania* 205 L6
Saint Mary's Loch 137 E5
Saint Matthias Group 194 D2
Saint-Maurice 201 M8
Saint Maurice 205 P3
Saint Mawes 132 B4
Saint-Maximin 145 F7
Saint Michael 198 C3
Saint-Mihiel 144 F4
Saint Monance 137 F4
Saint Moritz 148 B2
Saint Neots 133 G2
Saint Niklaas 144 F3
Saint Ninian's Island 136 A2
Saintogne 145 C6
Saint Omer 144 E3
Saint Pamphile 205 R3
Saint Pascal 205 R3
Saint Paul *Alberta, Canada* 199 N5
Saint Paul *Quebec, Canada* 201 Q7
Saint Paul *Liberia* 184 C4
Saint Paul *U.S.A.* 204 D4
Saint Paul Island 198 Ad8
Saint Peter 204 D4
Saint Peter Port 133 M7
Saint Petersburg *U.S.A.* 209 L7
Saint Petersburg *Russia* 158 E4
Saint Pierre *Canada* 201 Q8
Saint Pierre *France* 189 L7
Saint Pierre Bank 201 Q8
Saint Pol 144 E3
Saint-Pol-de-Leon 144 B4
Saint Polten 148 E1
Saint-Pons 145 E7
Saint-Pourcain 145 E5
Saint Queens Bay 133 M7
Saint-Quentin 144 E4
Saint-Raphael 145 G7
Saint Sampson 133 M7
Saint Sebastian Bay 188 D6
Saint-Seine-l'Abbaye 145 F5
Saint-Sever 145 C7
Saint Simeon 205 R3
Saint Stephen *Canada* 205 S4
Saint Stephen *U.S.A.* 209 N4
Saint Thomas *Canada* 205 K5
Saint Thomas *U.S.A.* 213 Q5
Saint-Tropez 145 G7
Saint-Valery-en-Caux 144 D4
Saint Veit 148 E2
Saint Vincent 213 S6
Saint Vincent, Gulf of 193 H6
Saint Vincent Island 209 K6
Saint Vincent Passage 213 S8
Saint Vith 144 G3
Saint-Yrieix 145 D6
Sajama 218 C3
Sajama, Nevado de 218 C3
Saji-dong 168 B5
Sajir, Ra's 177 L8
Sak 188 D6
Sakai 169 E8
Sakai-Minato 169 D8
Sakakah 176 E2
Sakakawea, Lake 203 P4
Sakami 201 L7
Sakami, Lake 201 L7
Sakania 187 E5
Sakarya *Turkey* 156 D2
Sakarya *Turkey* 156 D2
Sakata 168 G6
Sakete 185 F4
Sakhalin 165 Q6
Sakht-Sar 175 K3
Sakiai 151 K1
Sakmara 159 K5
Sakon Nakhon 173 K5
Sak-shima-shoto 169 G11
Sakti 172 F4
Sal *Cape Verde* 184 L7
Sal *Russia* 159 G6
Sala 143 G7
Salaberry-De-Valleyfield 205 N4
Salaca 143 L8
Salacgriva 143 L8
Sala Consilina 149 E5
Saladillo 219 E7
Salado *Argentina* 219 C6
Salado *Argentina* 218 D5
Salaga 184 E4
Salalah 177 M8
Salama 212 B7
Salamanca *Mexico* 211 J7
Salamanca *Spain* 146 D2
Salamanca *U.S.A.* 205 L5
Salamina 216 B2
Salamis 155 G4
Salamiyah 157 G5
Salard 153 G2
Salas 153 G3
Salas de los Infantes 146 E1
Salat 157 J4
Salavat 158 K5
Salawati 171 J6
Salba 164 E6
Salbris 145 E5
Salcha 198 F3
Salcia 153 H4
Salcombe 132 D4
Salda Golu 156 C4
Saldana 146 D1
Saldanha 188 C6
Saldus 143 K8
Sale 180 D2
Sale *Australia* 193 K6
Sale *U.K.* 135 G3
Salebabu 171 H5
Salekhard 164 Ae3
Salem *India* 172 E6
Salem *Illinois* 204 F7
Salem *Oregon* 202 C5
Salemi 149 D7
Salen *Highland, U.K.* 137 C4
Salen *Strathclyde, U.K.* 137 C4
Salernes 145 G7
Salerno 149 E5
Salerno, Golfo di 149 E5
Salford 135 G3
Salgotarjan 152 E1
Salgueiro 217 K5
Salida 207 J1
Salies-de-Bearn 145 C7
Salihli 156 C3
Salima 187 F5
Salina *Kansas* 203 R8
Salina *Utah* 206 G1
Salina, Isola 149 E6
Salinas *Ecuador* 216 A4
Salinas *U.S.A.* 206 B2
Salinas, Cabo de 147 H3
Salinas Grandes 218 C4
Salinas O'Lachay, Punta de 216 B6
Salinas, Pampa de la 218 C6
Saline 203 Q8
Salinopolis 217 H4
Salins 145 F5
Salisbury *Maryland* 205 N7
Salisbury *N. Carolina* 209 M3
Salisbury *U.K.* 133 F3
Salisbury *Zimbabwe* 188 F3
Salisbury Island 200 L5
Salisbury Plain 132 F3
Saliste 153 G3
Salkhad 174 C5
Salla 142 N3
Sallisaw 208 E3
Sallvit 200 L5
Sallybrook 139 F9
Salmas 157 L3
Salmi 158 E3
Salmon *Canada* 199 L5
Salmon *U.S.A.* 202 F5
Salmon *U.S.A.* 202 H5
Salmon Arm 202 E2
Salmon Falls Creek 202 G6
Salmon River Mountains 202 G5
Salo 148 C3
Salo 143 K6
Salon-de-Provence 145 F7
Saloniki 155 G2
Salonta 153 F2
Salor 146 C3
Sal, Punta 212 D7
Salsacate 219 C6
Salsbruket 142 H4
Salsipuedes, Punta 206 D4
Salsk 159 G6
Salso 149 D7
Salsomaggiore Terme 148 B3
Salt *Jordan* 174 B5
Salt *Kentucky* 204 H8
Salt *Missouri* 204 D7
Salt *Oklahoma* 208 D2
Salta 218 C4
Saltash 132 C4
Saltburn-by-the-Sea 135 J2
Salt Cay 213 M4
Saltcoats 137 D5
Saltfjellet 142 F3
Saltfjord 142 F3
Saltfleet 135 K3
Saltillo 207 M8
Salt Lake City 202 J7
Salto *Italy* 149 D4
Salto *Uruguay* 218 E6
Salto da Divisa 218 G3
Salton Sea 206 E4
Saltpond 184 E4
Saluda *U.S.A.* 209 L3
Saluda *U.S.A.* 209 M3
Salumbar 172 D4
Saluzzo 148 A3
Salvador 217 K6
Salvatierra 211 J7
Salwah 177 K4
Salween 173 J5
Salyany 174 J2
Salyersville 204 J8
Salzach 148 D2
Salzburg 148 D2
Salzgitter 150 D2
Salzwedel 150 D2
Samah 176 G2
Samaipata 218 D3
Samak, Tanjung 170 D6
Samales Group 171 G4
Samana, Bahia de 213 N5
Samana, Cabo 213 N5
Samana Cay 213 L3
Samandag 157 F4
Samani 168 J4
Samanli Daglari 156 D2
Samanskoye 166 C2
Samar 171 H3
Samara 159 J5
Samarga *Russia* 168 G2
Samarga *Russia* 168 G2
Samariapo 216 D2
Samarina 155 F2
Samarinda 171 F6
Samarka 168 E3
Samarkand 166 B4
Samarra 157 K5
Samarskoye 166 F2

Sambah 177 N10
Sambaliung 171 F5
Sambalpur 172 F4
Sambar, Tanjung 170 E6
Sambas 170 D5
Sambava 189 K2
Sambhal 172 E3
Sambhar 172 E3
Sambhar Lake 172 D3
Samboja 171 F6
Sambor 159 C6
Samborombon, Bahia 219 E7
Sambre 144 F3
Samchok 169 B7
Samhan, Jabal 177 M8
Sami 155 F3
Samirah 176 F3
Sam Neua 173 K4
Samoded 158 G3
Samos 155 J4
Samosomo Strait 194 R8
Samothraki *Greece* 154 E3
Samothraki *Greece* 155 H2
Samothraki *Greece* 155 H2
Samoylovka 159 G5
Sampit *Indonesia* 170 E6
Sampit *Indonesia* 170 E6
Sam Rayburn Lake 208 E5
Samre 176 D10
Samrong 173 K6
Samso 143 D9
Samsu 168 A5
Samsun 157 G2
Samtredia 157 K1
Samui, Ko 173 K6
Samut Prakan 173 K6
San *Mali* 180 E6
San *Poland* 151 K3
Sana 152 D3
Sana 176 G9
Sanae 221 Z4
Sanaga 185 H5
San Agustin 216 B3
San Agustin, Cape 171 H4
Sanaigmore 137 B5
Sanak Island 198 Af9
Sanam, As 177 K6
San Ambrosio, Isla 215 B5
Sanana 171 H6
Sanandaj 174 H4
San Andreas 206 B1
San Andres, Isla de 212 G8
San Andres Mountains 207 J4
San Andres Tuxtla 211 M8
San Angelo 207 M5
San Antonio *Chile* 219 B6
San Antonio *New Mexico* 207 J4
San Antonio *Texas* 208 C6
San Antonio *Texas* 208 D6
San Antonio Abad 147 G3
San Antonio, Cabo 212 E4
San Antonio de Caparo 216 C2
San Antonio de los Cobres 218 C4
San Antonio Nuevo 212 C6
San Antonio, Punta 206 E6
Sanaw 177 K8
San Bartolomeo in Galdo 149 E5
San Benedetto del Tronto 149 D4
San Benedicto, Isla 210 D8
San Benito 208 D7
San Bernardino *Paraguay* 218 E5
San Bernardino *U.S.A.* 206 D3
San Bernardino Mountains 206 D3
San Bernardino Pass 148 B2
San Bernardo *Chile* 219 B6
San Bernardo *Mexico* 207 K7
San Bernardo do Campo 218 G4
San Blas 207 H7
San Blas, Cape 209 K6
San Blas, Punta 216 B2
San Borja 216 D6
San Borjas, Sierra de 206 F6
Sancak 157 J3
San Carlos *Argentina* 219 C6
San Carlos *Chile* 219 B7
San Carlos *Colombia* 216 D3
San Carlos *Nicaragua* 212 E9
San Carlos *Philippines* 171 G3
San Carlos *Philippines* 171 G2
San Carlos *Uruguay* 219 F6
San Carlos *U.S.A.* 206 G4
San Carlos *Venezuela* 216 D2
San Carlos de Bariloche 219 B8
San Carlos de la Rapita 147 G2
San Carlos del Zulia 216 C2
San Carlos Lake 206 G4
Sancerre 145 E5
Sanchakou 166 D4
Sanchor 172 D4
San Clemente 146 E3
San Clemente Island 206 C4
San Cristobal *Argentina* 218 D6
San Cristobal *Bolivia* 218 C4
San Cristobal *Solomon Is.* 194 L7
San Cristobal *Venezuela* 216 C2
San Cristobal, Bahia de 206 E7
San Cristobal de las Casas 211 N9
San Cristobal, Isla 216 A7
Sancti Spiritus 212 H4
Sancy, Puy de 145 E6
Sandagou 168 E4
Sanda Island 137 C5
Sandakan 171 F4
Sandanski 153 G5
Sandaohumiao 167 J4
Sandaotong 168 B3
Sandarne 143 G6
Sandasel 142 V13
Sanday 136 F1
Sanday Sound 136 F1
Sandbach 135 G3
Sandefjord 143 D7
Sanderson 207 L5
Sandhead 134 E2
Sand Hills 203 N6
San Diego 206 D4
San Diego, Cabo 219 C10
Sandikli 156 D3
Sandila 172 F3
Sandnes 143 A7
Sandness 136 A1
Sandnessjoen 142 E3
Sandoa 186 D4
Sandomierz 151 J3
Sandon 133 E2
San Dona di Piave 148 D3
Sandoway 173 H5
Sandown 133 F4
Sandoy 142 Z14
Sandpoint 202 F3
Sandray 137 A4
Sandsele 142 G4
Sandstone *Australia* 192 D4
Sandstone *U.S.A.* 204 D3
Sandusky *U.S.A.* 204 J6
Sandvig 150 F1
Sandvika 142 E5
Sandviken 143 G6
Sandwich 133 J3
Sandy 133 G2
Sandy Cape 193 L3
Sandy Lake 199 S5
Sandy Point 173 H6
San Esteban, Isla de 206 F6
San Felipe *Chile* 219 B6
San Felipe *Mexico* 206 E5
San Felipe *Mexico* 211 J7
San Felipe *Venezuela* 216 D1
San Felix, Isla 215 A5
San Fermin, Punta 206 E5
San Fernando *Chile* 219 B6
San Fernando *Mexico* 208 C8
San Fernando *Mexico* 208 C8
San Fernando *Philippines* 171 G2
San Fernando *Spain* 146 C4
San Fernando *Trinidad and Tobago* 213 S9
San Fernando de Apure 216 D2
San Fernando de Atabapo 216 D3
Sanford *Florida* 209 M6
Sanford *Maine* 205 Q5
Sanford *N. Carolina* 209 N3
Sanford, Mount 198 G3
San Francisco *Argentina* 218 D6
San Francisco *California* 206 A2
San Francisco *New Mexico* 207 H4
San Francisco, Cabo de 216 A3
San Francisco de Assis 218 E5
San Francisco del Oro 207 K7
San Francisco de Macoris 213 M5
San Francisco de Paula, Cabo 219 C9
San Francisco Javier 147 G3
San Francisco, Paso de 218 C5
San Gabriel, Punta 206 F6
Sangan 175 P4
Sangar 165 M4
Sang Bast 175 P3
Sangeang 171 F7
Sanggau 170 E5
Sangha 186 C2
Sangihe 171 H5
Sangihe, Kepulauan 171 H5
San Gil 216 C2
San Giovanni in Fiore 149 F6
Sangkhla Buri 173 J6
Sangli 172 D5
Sangmelima 185 H5
Sangonera 147 F4
San Gorgonio Peak 206 D3
Sangowo 171 H5
Sangre de Cristo Range 207 K1
Sangro 149 E4
Sangue 217 F6
Sanguesa 147 F1
San Guiseppe Iato 149 D7
San Hipolito, Punta 206 F7
Sanibel Island 209 L7
San Ignacio *Bolivia* 218 D3
San Ignacio *Bolivia* 216 D6
San Ignacio *Mexico* 206 F7
San Ignacio *Paraguay* 218 E5
Sanikiluaq 201 L6
San Ildefonso, Cape 171 G2
San Javier 218 D3
Sanjbod 174 J3
Sanjo 169 G7
San Joaquin *Bolivia* 216 E6
San Joaquin *U.S.A.* 206 B2
San Joaquin Valley 206 B2
San Jorge *Colombia* 213 K10
San Jorge *Solomon Is.* 194 J6
San Jorge, Bahia de 206 F5
San Jorge, Golfo de *Argentina* 219 C9
San Jorge, Golfo de *Spain* 147 G2
San Jose *Costa Rica* 212 E10
San Jose *Philippines* 171 G3
San Jose *Spain* 147 E4
San Jose *California* 206 B2
San Jose *New Mexico* 207 J3
San Jose de Amacuro 216 E2
San Jose de Buenavista 171 G3
San Jose de Chiquitos 218 D3
San Jose de Gracia 206 F7
San Jose de Jachal 219 C6
San Jose del Cabo 210 E6
San Jose de Mayo 219 E6
San Jose, Isla 210 D5
San Juan 211 M8
San Juan *Argentina* 218 C6
San Juan *Argentina* 218 C6
San Juan *Dominican Republic* 213 M5
San Juan *Mexico* 207 N8
San Juan *Nicaragua* 212 E8
San Juan *Peru* 216 B7
San Juan *Puerto Rico* 213 P5
San Juan *Utah* 207 H2
San Juan Bautista 147 G3
San Juan Bautista, Cabo 206 F6
San Juan del Norte 212 F9
San Juan del Norte, Bahia de 212 F9
San Juan de los Morros 216 D2
San Juan del Rio 211 K7
San Juanico, Punta 206 F7
San Juan Islands 202 C3
San Juan Mountains 207 J2
San Julian 219 C9
Sankt Blasjon 142 F4
Sankuru 186 D3
San Lazaro, Cabo 210 C5
San Lazaro, Sierra de 210 E6
San Lorenzo 216 D6
San Lorenzo, Cabo 216 A4
San Lorenzo, Cerro 219 B9
San Lorenzo de El Escorial 146 D2
San Lorenzo de la Parrilla 146 E3
San Lorenzo, Isla 206 F6
Sanlucar de Barrameda 146 C4
Sanlucar la Mayor 146 C4
San Lucas *Bolivia* 218 C4
San Lucas *Mexico* 210 E6
San Lucas, Cabo 210 E6
San Luis 212 C6
San Luis *Argentina* 219 C6
San Luis *Venezuela* 213 N9
San Luis Obispo 206 B3
San Luis Potosi 211 J6
San Luis Rio Colorado 206 E4
Sanluri 149 B6
San Manuel 206 G4
San Marco, Capo 149 B6
San Marcos *Mexico* 211 K9
San Marcos *U.S.A.* 208 D6
San Marcos, Island 206 F7
San Marino 148 D4
San Marino 148 D4
San Martin *Bolivia* 216 E6
San Martin *Colombia* 216 C3
San Martin de Valdeiglesias 146 D2
San Martin, Lago 219 B9
San Mateo 216 E2
San Matias 218 E3
San Matias, Golfo 219 D8
Sanmenxia 173 M2
San Miguel *Bolivia* 218 D3
San Miguel *Bolivia* 218 D3
San Miguel *El Salvador* 212 C8
San Miguel de Allende 211 J7
San Miguel de Tucuman 218 C5
San Miguel do Araguaia 217 G6
San Miguel Island 206 B3
San Miguelito 212 H10
Sanming 167 M6
Sannicandro Garganico 149 E5
San Nicolas 218 D6
San Nicolas, Bahia de 216 B7
San Nicolas Island 206 C4
Sannikova, Proliv 165 Q2
Sanok 151 K4
San Pablo 171 G3
San Pablo, Cabo 219 C10
San Pablo de Loreto 216 C4
San Pablo, Punta 206 E7
San Pedro 184 D5
San Pedro *Argentina* 219 E6
San Pedro *Mexico* 210 D6
San Pedro *Paraguay* 218 E4
San Pedro *U.S.A.* 206 G4
San Pedro Channel 206 C4
San Pedro de las Colonias 207 L8
San Pedro de Lloc 216 B5
San Pedro Martir, Sierra 206 E5
San Pedro, Punta 218 B5
San Pedros 210 G6
San Pedros de Macoris 213 N5
San Pedro, Sierra de 146 C3
San Pedro Sula 212 C7
San Pietro, Isola di 149 B6
Sanquhar 137 E5
San Quintin, Bahia de 206 E5
San Rafael *Argentina* 219 C6
San Rafael *Colombia* 216 C1
San Rafael *U.S.A.* 206 A2
San Remo 148 A4
San Salvador *Bahamas* 213 K2
San Salvador *El Salvador* 212 C8
San Salvador de Jujuy 218 C4
San Salvador, Isla 216 A7
San Sebastian 147 F1
San Sebastian Bahia de 219 C10
San Sebastiao, Ponta 189 G4
Sansepolcro 148 D4
San Severo 149 E5
San Silvestre 213 M10
Sanski Most 152 D3
Santa Ana *Bolivia* 216 D6
Santa Ana *El Salvador* 212 C7
Santa Ana *Mexico* 206 G5
Santa Ana *U.S.A.* 206 D4
Santa Ana Island 194 L7
Santa Barbara 206 C3
Santa Barbara *Honduras* 212 C7
Santa Barbara *Mexico* 207 K7
Santa Barbara Channel 206 B3
Santa Catalina, Gulf of 206 D4
Santa Catalina, Isla 210 D5
Santa Catalina Island 206 C4
Santa Catarina 218 F5
Santa Catarina, Ilha 218 G5
Santa Clara 212 H3
Santa Coloma de Farnes 147 H2
Santa Coloma de Gramanet 147 H2
Santa Comba Dao 146 B2
Santa Comba de Rossas 146 C2
Santa Cruz *Argentina* 219 B10
Santa Cruz *Bolivia* 218 D3
Santa Cruz *U.S.A.* 206 A2
Santa Cruz de la Palma 180 B3
Santa Cruz de Moya 147 F3
Santa Cruz de Tenerife 180 B3
Santa Cruz do Sul 218 F5
Santa Cruz, Isla *Ecuador* 216 A7
Santa Cruz, Isla *Mexico* 210 D5
Santa Cruz Island 206 C3
Santa Cruz Islands 194 N7
Santa Elena 216 E3
Santa Elena, Cabo 212 E9
Santa Eulalia del Rio 147 G3
Santafe 146 E4
Santa Fe *Argentina* 218 D6
Santa Fe *Panama* 212 G10
Santa Fe *U.S.A.* 207 K3
Sant Agata di Militello 149 E6
Santai *Sichuan, China* 173 L2
Santai *Xinjiang Uygur Zizhiqu, China* 166 E3
Santa Ines, Isla 219 B10
Santa Isabel *Argentina* 219 C7
Santa Isabel *Equatorial Guinea* 185 G5
Santa Isabel *Solomon Is.* 194 J5
Santa Lucia 219 E6
Santa Lucia Range 206 B2
Santa Luzia 217 K5
Santa Margarita, Isla 210 D5
Santa Maria *Brazil* 218 F5
Santa Maria *Mexico* 207 J6
Santa Maria *Mexico* 207 K8
Santa Maria *U.S.A.* 206 B3
Santa Maria *Vanuatu* 194 T11
Santa Maria *Venezuela* 213 P11
Santa Maria, Cabo de *Mozambique* 189 F5
Santa Maria, Cabo de *Portugal* 146 C4
Santa Maria di Leuca, Capo 149 G6
Santa Maria, Isla 216 A7
Santa Maria, Laguna de 207 J5
Santa Marta 216 C1
Santa Marta, Cabo de 186 B5
Santa Marta Grande, Cabo de 218 G5
Santa Maura 155 F3
Santa Monica 206 C3
Santan 171 F6
Santana 217 J6
Santana do Ipanema 217 K5
Santana do Livramento 218 E6
Santander *Colombia* 216 B3
Santander *Spain* 146 E1
Sant Antioco 149 B6
Santarem *Brazil* 217 G4
Santarem *Spain* 146 B3
Santaren Channel 212 H3
Santa Rita 216 C1
Santa Rosa *Argentina* 219 C6
Santa Rosa *Argentina* 219 D7
Santa Rosa *Bolivia* 216 D6
Santa Rosa *Brazil* 218 F5
Santa Rosa *California* 206 A1
Santa Rosa *New Mexico* 207 K3
Santa Rosa de Cabal 216 B3
Santa Rosa de Copan 212 C7
Santa Rosa Island 206 B4
Santa Rosalia 206 F7
Santa Rosa Range 202 F7
Santa Teresa Gallura 149 B5
Santa Vitoria do Palmar 219 F6
Santa Ynez 206 B3
Santee 209 M4
Santerno 148 C3
Sant Eufemia, Golfo di 149 F6
Santhia 148 B3
Santiago *Brazil* 218 F5
Santiago *Chile* 219 B6
Santiago *Dominican Republic* 213 M5
Santiago *Panama* 212 G10
Santiago *Peru* 216 B4
Santiago, Cerro 212 G10
Santiago de Chuco 216 B5
Santiago de Compostela 146 B1
Santiago de Cuba 213 K4
Santiago del Estero 218 D5
Santiago do Cacem 146 B3
Santiago Ixcuintla 210 G7
Santiago Papasquiaro 210 G5
San Tiburcio 210 J5
Santo Amaro 217 K6
Santo Andre 218 G4
Santo Angelo 218 F5

Name	Page	Grid
Shibotsu-jima	168	L4
Shibushi	169	C10
Shickshock Mountains	205	S2
Shiel Bridge	136	C3
Shieldaig	136	C3
Shiel, Loch	137	C4
Shihan, Wadi	177	L8
Shihezi	166	F3
Shiikh	183	J6
Shijiazhuang	167	L4
Shikarpur	172	C3
Shikoku	169	D9
Shikoku-sanchi	169	D9
Shikong	167	K4
Shikotan-to	168	L4
Shikotsu-ko	168	H4
Shildon	135	H2
Shilega	158	G3
Shiliguri	173	G3
Shilka *Russia*	165	K6
Shilka *Russia*	165	L6
Shillingstone	132	E4
Shillong	173	H3
Shilovo	158	G5
Shimabara	169	C9
Shimada	169	G8
Shimanovsk	165	M6
Shimian	173	K3
Shimizu	169	G8
Shimoda	169	G8
Shimoga	172	E6
Shimonoseki	169	C9
Shinano	169	G7
Shinas	177	N4
Shindand	175	R5
Shin Falls	136	D3
Shingu	169	E9
Shinjo	168	H6
Shinness	136	D2
Shinshar	157	G5
Shinyanga	187	F3
Shiogama	169	H6
Shiono-misaki	169	E9
Shiosawa	169	G7
Shiping	173	K4
Shipley	135	H3
Shippensburg	205	M6
Shippigan Island	201	P8
Shipston-on-Stour	133	F2
Shipton	135	H2
Shipton-under-Wychwood	133	F3
Shipunovo	164	C6
Shirakawa	169	H7
Shirane-san *Japan*	169	G8
Shirane-san *Japan*	169	G7
Shiraz	175	L7
Shire	187	F6
Shirebrook	135	H3
Shiretoko-misaki	168	K3
Shiriya-saki	168	H5
Shir Kuh	175	M6
Shirten Holoy Gobi	166	H3
Shirvan	175	N3
Shishaldin Volcano	198	Af9
Shivpuri	172	E3
Shivwits Plateau	206	F2
Shiwan Dashan	173	L4
Shiyan	173	M2
Shizhu	173	L3
Shizugawa	168	H6
Shizuishan	167	K4
Shizuoka	169	G8
Shkoder	154	E1
Shkumbin	154	E2
Shmidta, Ostrov	161	L1
Shobara	169	D8
Shokalskogo, Ostrov	164	A2
Shorapur	172	E5
Shorawak	175	S6
Shoreham-by-Sea	133	G4
Shorkot	172	D2
Shoshone	202	G6
Shoshone Mountains	202	F8
Shoshoni	203	K6
Shostka	159	E5
Shouguang	167	M4
Shouning	167	M6
Showa	221	C5
Showak	176	B9
Shozhma	158	G3
Shpikov	153	K1
Shpola	159	E6
Shrankogl	148	C2
Shreveport	208	F4
Shrewsbury	132	E2
Shrewton	133	F3
Shrigonda	172	D5
Shropshire	132	E2
Shrule	139	D5
Shuab, Ra's	177	P9
Shuanghezhen	167	P3
Shuangliao	167	N3
Shuangyashan	167	Q2
Shubar-Kuduk	159	K6
Shubra el-Khema	182	F1
Shucheng	167	M5
Shuga	164	B6
Shuicheng	173	K3
Shuikou	167	M6
Shujaabad	172	D3
Shulan	167	P3
Shumagin Islands	198	Af9
Shumen	153	J4
Shumerlya	158	H4
Shungnak	198	D2
Shuqrah	176	G10
Shura	157	K4
Shurab	175	K5
Shurab	175	N5
Shusf	175	Q6
Shush	174	J5
Shushenskoye	164	E6
Shushtar	174	J5
Shuswap Lake	202	E2
Shuya	158	G4
Shuya	169	G7
Shwebo	173	J4
Shwegyin	173	J5
Shweli	173	J4
Shyok	172	E2
Siahan Range	172	B3
Siah Koh	175	S5
Sialkot	172	D2
Siargao	171	H4
Siau	171	H5
Siauliai	143	K9
Sibenik	152	C4
Siberut	170	B6
Siberut, Selat	170	B6
Sibi	172	C3
Sibirskaya Nizmennost	164	G2
Sibirtsevo	168	D3
Sibiryakovo, Ostrov	164	B2
Sibiti	186	B3
Sibiu	153	H3
Sibolga	170	B5
Sibsagar	173	H3
Sibsey	135	K3
Sibu	170	E5
Sibut	182	C6
Sibutu	171	F5
Sibutu Passage	171	F5
Sibuyan	171	G3
Sibuyan Sea	171	G3
Sicasica	218	C3
Sichuan	173	K2
Sichuan Pendi	173	L3
Sicie, Cap	145	F7
Sicilia	149	D7
Sicilian Channel	149	C7
Sicily	149	D7
Sicuani	216	C6
Sidatun	168	E3
Sideby	143	J5
Sidheros, Akra	155	J5
Sidhirokastron	155	G2
Sidi Akacha	147	G4
Sidi Barram	182	E1
Sidi Bel Abbes	180	E1
Sidi Ifni	180	C3
Sidi Kacem	180	D2
Sidima	168	E1
Sidlaw Hills	137	E4
Sidmouth	132	D4
Sidmouth, Cape	193	J1
Sidney *Canada*	202	C3
Sidney *Montana*	203	M4
Sidney *Ohio*	204	H6
Sidon	174	B5
Sidorovsk	164	C3
Siedlce	151	K2
Siegen	150	C3
Siemiatycze	151	K2
Siem Reap	173	K6
Siena	148	C4
Sieniawa	151	K3
Sierpc	151	H2
Sierra Colorada	219	C8
Sierra Leone	184	C4
Sierra Vista	207	G5
Sierre	148	A2
Sifnos	155	H4
Sifton Pass	198	K4
Sigatoka *Fiji*	194	Q8
Sigatoka *Fiji*	194	Q9
Sigean	145	E7
Sighetu Marmatiei	153	G2
Sighisoara	153	H2
Sigli	170	B4
Siglufjordur	142	V11
Sigmaringen	150	C4
Signy	221	W6
Sigovo	164	D4
Sigtuna	143	G7
Siguenza	146	E2
Siguiri	184	D3
Sigulda	143	L8
Siikajoki	142	L4
Siikavuopio	142	J2
Siilinjarvi	142	M5
Siin	168	E2
Siipyy	143	J5
Siirt	157	J4
Sikar	172	E3
Sikasso	180	D6
Sikeston	204	F8
Sikhote Alin	168	E3
Sikinos	155	H4
Sikkim	173	G3
Sil	146	C1
Sila	177	K4
Silchar	173	H4
Sile	156	C2
Silesia	151	G3
Silgarhi	172	F3
Silifke	156	E4
Siligir	164	J3
Siling Co	173	G2
Silistra	153	J3
Silivri	156	C2
Siljan	143	F6
Silkeborg	143	C8
Sillajhuay	218	C3
Sillan, Lough	138	J4
Sillon de Talbert	144	B4
Siloam Springs	208	E2
Silom	194	E2
Silopi	157	K4
Silovayakha	158	L2
Silsbee	208	E5
Silute	143	J9
Silvan	157	J3
Silver Bay	204	E3
Silver City	207	H4
Silvermines Mountains	139	F7
Silver Spring	205	M7
Silverstone	133	F2
Silverton *U.K.*	132	D4
Silverton *U.S.A.*	207	J2
Simanggang	170	E5
Simard, Lac	205	L3
Simareh Karkheh	174	H5
Simav *Turkey*	156	C3
Simav *Turkey*	156	C2
Simayr	176	E8
Simcoe	205	K5
Simcoe, Lake	205	L4
Simeonovgrad	153	H4
Simeulue	170	B5
Simferopol	159	E7
Simi	155	J4
Simiti	216	C2
Simitli	153	G5
Simla	172	E2
Simleu Silvaniei	153	G2
Simmern	150	B3
Simojarvi	142	M3
Simojoki	142	L4
Simonka	151	J4
Simplicio Mendes	217	J5
Simplon Pass	148	B2
Simpson Bay	199	N2
Simpson Desert	193	H3
Simpson Peninsula	200	J4
Simrishamn	143	F9
Simsor	157	J3
Simushir, Ostrov	165	S7
Sinabang	170	B5
Sinabung	170	B5
Sinac	152	C3
Sinafir	176	B3
Sinaia	153	H3
Sinai Peninsula	183	F2
Sinaloa	210	F4
Sinanaj	154	E2
Sinaxtla	211	L9
Sincan *Turkey*	156	E3
Sincan *Turkey*	157	G3
Since	213	K10
Sincelejo	216	B2
Sinclair's Bay	136	E2
Sind	172	E3
Sinda	168	F1
Sindal	143	D8
Sindangbarang	170	D7
Sindel	153	J4
Sindhuli Garhi	172	G3
Sindirgi	156	C3
Sindominic	153	H2
Sindor	158	J3
Sind Sagar Doab	172	D2
Sinegorye	158	J4
Sinelnikovo	159	F6
Sines	146	B4
Sines, Cabo de	146	B4
Sinetta	142	L3
Sinfra	184	D4
Singa	183	F5
Singapore	170	C5
Singaraja	170	F7
Sing Buri	173	K6
Singida	187	F3
Singitikos, Kolpos	155	G2
Singkang	171	G6
Singkawang	170	D5
Singkep	170	C6
Singleton	133	G4
Singleton, Mount	192	G3
Singosan	167	P4
Siniatsikon	155	F2
Siniscola	149	B5
Sinj	152	D4
Sinjai	171	G7
Sinjajevina	152	E4
Sinjar	157	J4
Sinkat	183	G4
Sinnamary	217	G2
Sinnes	143	B7
Sinni	149	F5
Sinnicolau Mare	152	F2
Sinoe	184	D4
Sinoe, Lacul	153	K3
Sinop	156	F2
Sinpo	168	B5
Sinpung-dong	168	B5
Sintang	170	E5
Sint Maarten	213	R5
Sinton	208	D6
Sintra	146	B3
Sinu	216	B2
Sinuiju	167	N4
Sinyavka	151	M2
Sinyaya	143	N8
Siocon	171	G4
Siofok	152	E2
Sion	148	A2
Sionascaig, Loch	136	C2
Sion Mills	138	H3
Sioule	145	E5
Sioux City	204	B5
Sioux Falls	203	R6
Sioux Lookout	199	S5
Sipalay	171	G4
Siping	167	N3
Sip Song Chau Thai	173	K4
Sipul	194	D3
Sipura	170	B6
Siquia	212	E8
Siquijor	171	G4
Sira *India*	172	E6
Sira *Norway*	143	B7
Sir Abu Nuayr	177	M4
Siracusa	149	E7
Sirajganj	173	G4
Sir Alexander, Mount	199	M5
Siran	157	H2
Sir Bani Yas	177	L4
Sir Edward Pellew Group	193	H2
Siret *Romania*	153	J2
Siret *Romania*	153	J2
Sirhan, Wadi	174	D6
Siri Kit Dam	173	K5
Sirik, Tanjung	170	E5
Sir James McBrien, Mount	198	R3
Sirjan, Kavir-e	175	L6
Sirk	175	N8
Sirna	155	J4
Sirnal	157	K4
Sirohi	172	D4
Siros *Greece*	155	H4
Siros *Greece*	155	H4
Sirri	175	M9
Sirr, Nafud as	176	G4
Sirsa	172	D3
Sir Sanford, Mount	202	F2
Sirsi	172	D6
Sirte	181	J2
Sirte, Gulf of	181	J2
Sirvan	157	K3
Sisak	152	D3
Sisaket	173	K5
Sisophon	173	K6
Sisseton	203	R5
Sissonne	144	E4
Sistan	175	P8
Sistan, Daryacheh-ye-	175	Q6
Sisteron	145	F6
Sistig-Khem	164	F6
Sistranda	142	C5
Sitamau	172	E4
Sitapur	172	F3
Sitges	147	G2
Sithonia	155	G2
Sitia	155	J5
Sitian	166	F3
Sitidgi Lake	198	J2
Sitio da Abadia	218	H6
Sitka	198	H4
Sittang	173	J5
Sittingbourne	133	H3
Sittwe	173	H4
Situbondo	170	E7
Siuri	173	G4
Siuruanjoki	142	M4
Sivas	157	G3
Sivasli	156	C3
Siverek	157	H4
Siverskiy	143	P7
Sivrice	157	H3
Sivrihisar	156	D3
Sivrihisar Daglari	156	D3
Sivuk	165	Q6
Siwa	182	E2
Siwalik Range	172	F3
Siwan	172	F3
Si Xian	167	M5
Sixmilebridge	139	E7
Sixpenny Handley	133	E4
Siya	158	G3
Siyal Islands	176	C5
Sizin	164	F6
Sjælland	143	D9
Sjorup	143	C8
Skadarsko Jezero	154	E1
Skadovsk	159	E6
Skafta	142	V13
Skagafjordur	142	V12
Skagaflos	142	T12
Skagen	143	D8
Skagerrak	143	C8
Skagit	202	D3
Skagway	198	H4
Skaill	136	F2
Skala-Podolskaya	153	J1
Skanderborg	143	C8
Skanor	143	E9
Skansholm	142	G4
Skara	143	E7
Skaraborg	143	E7
Skarbak	143	C9
Skard	142	V12
Skardu	172	E1
Skarnes	143	D6
Skattkarr	143	E7
Skaudvile	143	K9

Skaulo	142	J3	Slobodskoy	158	J4	Soderala	143	G6	Sonipat	172	E3
Skawina	151	H4	Slobodzeya	153	K2	Soderhamn	143	G6	Sonkajarvi	142	M5
Skeena	198	K5	Slobozia *Romania*	153	H3	Soderkoping	143	G7	Sonkovo	158	N4
Skeena Mountains	198	K4	Slobozia *Romania*	153	J3	Sodermanland	143	G7	Son La	173	K4
Skegness	135	K1	Slonim	151	L2	Sodertalje	143	G7	Sonmiani	172	C3
Skeidararsandur	142	W13	Slot, The	194	J6	Sodra Ratansbyn	142	F5	Sonmiani Bay	172	C3
Skelda Ness	136	A2	Slough	133	G3	Soe	171	G7	Sonoita	206	F5
Skelleftea	142	J4	Slovak Republic	150	H4	Soest	150	C3	Sonora	206	G6
Skelleftealven	142	H4	Slovenia	152	C2	Sofia *Bulgaria*	153	G4	Sonoran Desert	206	F4
Skelmersdale	135	G3	Slovyansk	159	F6	Sofia *Madagascar*	189	J3	Sonsonate	212	C8
Skelton	135	J2	Sluch	152	C3	Sofiya	153	G4	Son Tay	173	L4
Skerpioenpunt	188	D5	Slunj	152	C3	Sofiysk	165	P6	Sooghemeghat	198	B3
Skerries	138	K5	Slupsk	151	G1	Sogamoso *Colombia*	216	C2	Sopi, Tanjung	171	H5
Skerries, The	134	E3	Slussfors	142	G4	Sogamoso *Colombia*	216	C2	Sopot	151	H1
Skhiza	155	F4	Slutsk	159	D5	Sogndalsfjora	143	B6	Sopron	152	D2
Ski	143	D7	Slyne Head	139	B6	Sognefjorden	143	A6	Sopur	172	D2
Skiathos	155	G3	Slyudyanka	164	G6	Sogn og Fjordan	143	B6	Sor	146	B3
Skibbereen	139	D9	Smaland	143	F8	Sogod	171	G3	Sora	149	D5
Skiddaw	135	F2	Smallwood Reservoir	201	P7	Sogut *Turkey*	156	C4	Sorada	172	F5
Skidegate	198	J5	Smcanli	156	D3	Sogut *Turkey*	156	D2	Soraker	142	G5
Skidel	151	L2	Smederevo	153	F3	Sogutlu	156	D2	Sorata	218	C3
Skien	143	C7	Smela	159	E6	Sog Xian	173	H2	Sorbas	147	E4
Skierniewice	151	J3	Smethwick	133	E2	Sohag	183	F2	Sore	145	C6
Skiftet Kihti	143	J6	Smidovich	168	D1	Sohano	194	E3	Sorel	205	P3
Skikda	181	G1	Smiltene	143	M8	Sohela	172	F4	Sorgun	156	F3
Skipton	135	G3	Smirnykh	165	Q7	Sohuksan	167	P5	Soria	146	E2
Skiropoula	155	H3	Smith Arm	198	L2	Soissons	144	E4	Sorisdale	137	B4
Skiros *Greece*	155	H3	Smith Bay *Canada*	200	L2	Sojat	172	D3	Sorka	158	F4
Skiros *Greece*	155	H3	Smith Bay *U.S.A.*	198	E1	Sojotan Point	171	G4	Sorkh, Kuh-e	175	M5
Skive	143	C8	Smithfield *N. Carolina*	209	N3	Sokal	151	L3	Sormjole	142	J5
Skjakerhatten	142	E4	Smithfield *Utah*	202	J7	Soke	156	B4	Sorocaba	218	G4
Skjalfandafljot	142	W12	Smith Island	201	L5	Sokhumi	159	G7	Sorochinsk	159	J5
Skjalfandi	142	W11	Smith Mount Lake	205	L8	Soko Banja	153	F4	Soroki	159	D6
Skjern	143	C9	Smiths Falls	205	N4	Sokode	184	F4	Sorong	171	J6
Skjervoy	142	J1	Smith Sound	200	M2	Sokol	158	G4	Sorot	143	N7
Sklad	165	L2	Smithton	193	K7	Sokolo	180	D6	Soroti	187	F2
Skoghall	143	E7	Smjorfjoll	142	X12	Sokolovka	168	D4	Soroya	142	K1
Skole	151	K4	Smoky	199	M4	Sokolow Podlaski	151	K2	Soroysundet	142	K1
Skomer Island	133	B3	Smoky Cape	193	L5	Sokoto *Nigeria*	185	F3	Sorraia	146	B3
Skopelos *Greece*	155	G3	Smoky Falls	201	K7	Sokoto *Nigeria*	185	G3	Sorrento	149	E5
Skopelos *Greece*	155	G3	Smoky Hill	203	R8	Sola	151	H4	Sorsele	142	G4
Skopelos Kaloyeroi	155	H3	Smoky Hills	203	Q8	Solander Island	195	A7	Sorso	149	B5
Skopin	159	F5	Smola	142	C5	Solapur	172	E5	Sorsogon	171	G3
Skopje	153	F4	Smolenka	159	H5	Sol, Costa del	146	D4	Sortavala	143	P6
Skopun	142	Z14	Smolensk	158	E5	Soledad	213	K9	Sortland	142	F2
Skorodum	164	A5	Smolikas	155	F2	Soledade	216	D5	Sor-Trondelag	142	D6
Skorovatn	142	E4	Smolyan	153	H5	Solen	143	D6	Sorvagsvatn	142	Z14
Skoruvik	142	X11	Smolyaninovo	168	D4	Solent, The	132	F4	Sorvagur	142	Z14
Skovde	143	E7	Smooth Rock Falls	205	K2	Solhan	157	J3	Sorvar	142	K1
Skovorodino	165	L6	Smorgon	151	M1	Soligorsk	159	D5	Sorvattnet	143	E5
Skowhegan	205	R4	Smotrich	153	J1	Solihull	133	F2	Sos del Rey-Catolico	147	F1
Skreia	143	D6	Smyrna	156	B3	Solikamsk	158	K4	Sosnogorsk	158	J3
Skudenshavn	143	D6	Snaefell	134	E2	Sollletsk	159	J5	Sosnovka	164	H6
Skulgam	142	H2	Snafell	142	X12	Solimoes	216	E4	Sosnovo	143	P6
Skull	139	C9	Snafellsjokull	142	T12	Solingen	150	B3	Sosnovo-Ozerskoye	165	J6
Skulyany	153	J2	Snaith	135	H3	Solleftea	142	G5	Sosnowiec	151	H3
Skuodas	143	J8	Snake	202	E4	Soller	147	H3	Sosunova, Mys	168	G2
Skutec	150	F4	Snake Range	202	G8	Solnechnogorsk	158	F4	Sosva	164	Ad5
Skutskar	143	G6	Snake River Plain	202	H6	Solo	170	E7	Sotik	187	G3
Skvira	159	D6	Snap Point	212	J3	Solobkovtsy	153	J1	Sotra	143	A6
Skwierzyna	150	F2	Snap, The	136	B1	Solok	170	D6	Sotuelamos	146	E3
Skye	136	B3	Snares Islands	191	Q11	Solomon	203	Q8	Soubre	184	D4
Skyring, Peninsula	219	B9	Snasa	142	E4	Solomon Islands	194	J5	Soudan	193	H3
Skyring, Seno	219	B10	Snasavatn	142	E4	Solon Springs	204	E3	Souflion	155	J2
Slagelse	143	D9	Sndre Isortoq	200	R4	Solontsovo	165	K6	Souk Ahras	181	G1
Slagnas	142	H4	Sndre Strmfjord	200	R4	Solor, Kepulauan	171	G7	Soumntam	147	J4
Slamannan	137	E5	Sndre Sund	200	Q3	Solothurn	148	A2	Sour	174	B5
Slamet, Gunung	170	D7	Sneek	144	F2	Solotobe	166	B3	Sour al Ghozlane	147	H4
Slane	138	J5	Sneem	139	C9	Solovyevsk	165	L6	Soure	217	H4
Slaney	139	J8	Snettisham	133	H2	Solta	152	D4	Souris *Manitoba, Canada*	203	P3
Slany	150	F3	Snezka	150	F3	Soltanabad	175	P3	Souris *Prince Edward Island,*		
Slapin, Loch	137	B3	Sneznik	152	C3	Soltaniyeh	174	J3	*Canada*	201	P8
Slatina	153	H3	Sniardwy, Jezioro	151	J2	Soltau	150	C2	Sousse	181	H1
Slave	199	N4	Snina	151	K4	Soltsy	158	E4	South Africa, Republic of	188	D6
Slave Lake	199	N4	Snizort, Loch	136	B3	Solvesborg	143	F8	Southampton *U.K.*	133	F4
Slavgorod *Russia*	164	*B6*	Snodland	133	H3	Solway Firth	135	F2	Southampton *U.S.A.*	205	P6
Slavgorod *Ukraine*	159	F6	Snohetta	142	C5	Solwezi	186	E5	Southampton Island	200	K5
Slavo	165	Q6	Snoqualmie Pass	202	D4	Soma	156	B3	Southampton Water	133	F4
Slavyanka	168	C4	Snoul	173	L6	Soma	169	H7	South Andaman	173	H6
Slavyansk-na-Kubani	159	F6	Snowdon	134	E3	Somalia	183	J6	South Baldy	207	J4
Slawno	151	G1	Snowtown	193	H5	Sombor	152	E3	South Baymouth	204	J4
Slawoborze	150	F2	Snowville	202	H7	Sombrerete	210	H6	South Bend *Indiana*	204	G6
Slea	135	J3	Snowy, Mount	202	G3	Sombrero Channel	173	H7	South Bend *Washington*	202	C4
Sleaford	133	G2	Snug Corner	213	L3	Somerset *Kentucky*	204	H8	South Benfleet	133	H3
Sleat, Sound of	137	C3	Snyatyn	153	H1	Somerset *Pennsylvania*	205	L6	Southborough	133	H3
Sleetmute	198	D3	Snyder	207	M4	Somerset *U.K.*	132	D3	South Boston	205	L8
Sleights	135	J2	Soalala	189	J3	Somerset East	188	E6	South Canadian	208	D3
Slidell	208	H5	Soalara	189	H4	Somerset Island	200	H3	South Cape *Fiji*	194	R8
Slieve Anieren	138	G4	Soan Kundo	167	P5	Somerton	132	E3	South Cape *U.S.A.*	206	T11
Slieveanorra	138	K2	Soa Pan	188	E4	Somerville Reservoir	208	D5	South Carolina	209	M3
Slieveardagh Hills	139	G7	Soar	133	F2	Somes	153	G2	South China Sea	167	L7
Slieve Aughty Mountains	139	E6	Soa-Siu	171	H5	Somes Point	195	F6	South Creake	133	H2
Slieve Beagh	138	H4	Soavinandriana	189	J3	Somme	144	D3	South Dakota	203	N5
Slieve Bloom Mountains	139	G6	Soay	137	B3	Sommerda	150	D3	South Dorset Downs	132	E4
Slieve Callan	139	D7	Soay Sound	137	B3	Somosomo	194	S8	South Downs	133	G4
Slieve Car	138	C4	Sobat	183	F6	Sompolno	151	H2	Southeast Cape	198	B3
Slieve Donard	138	L4	Sobinka	158	F4	Somport, Puerto de	147	F1	South East Cape	193	K6
Slieve Elva	139	D6	Sobopol	165	M3	Somuncura, Meseta de	219	C8	Southend	199	Q4
Slieve Gamph	138	E4	Sobradinho, Barragem de	217	J5	Son	172	F4	Southend-on-Sea	133	H3
Slieve Kimalta	139	F7	Sobrado	217	G5	Sonakh	165	P6	Southern Alps	195	C5
Slieve League	138	E3	Sobral *Acre, Brazil*	216	C5	Sonapur	172	F4	Southern Cross	192	D5
Slieve Mish Mountains	139	C8	Sobral *Ceara, Brazil*	217	J4	Sonara	207	M5	Southern Indian Lake	199	R4
Slieve Miskish	138	C9	Sobv'yevsk	165	K7	Sonderborg	143	C9	Southern Pine Hills	208	H5
Slieve Na Calliagh	138	H5	Soca	152	B2	Sondre Strmfjord	200	R4	Southern Pines	209	N3
Slieve Rushen	138	G4	Socha	216	C2	Sondrio	148	B2	Southern Uplands	137	E5
Slieve Snaght	138	H2	Sochi	159	F7	Songea	187	G5	Southery	133	H2
Sligo *Ireland*	138	E4	Societe, Iles de la	223	H5	Songhua	168	B2	South Esk	137	E4
Sligo *Ireland*	138	F4	Socorro *Colombia*	216	C2	Songhua Jiang	167	P2	South Foreland	133	J3
Sligo Bay	138	E4	Socorro *U.S.A.*	207	J4	Songjin	168	B5	South Forty Foot Drain	133	G2
Slioch	136	C3	Socorro, Isla	210	D8	Songkhla	173	K7	South Geomagnetic Pole	221	H3
Slipper Island	195	E2	Socotra	177	P10	Songololo	186	B4	South Georgia	219	J10
Sliven	153	J4	Soda Lake	206	D3	Sonhat	172	F4	South Glamorgan	132	D3
Slobodchikovo	158	H3	Sodankyla	142	M3	Sonid-Youqi	167	L3	South Harbour	136	A2
Slobodka	153	K2	Soda Springs	202	J6	Sonid Zuoqi	167	L3			

Taganrog	159	F6
Taganrogskiy Zaliv	159	F6
Tagbilaran	171	G4
Taghmon	139	J8
Tagliamento	148	D3
Tagolo Point	171	G4
Tagounite	180	D3
Tagu	153	H2
Taguatinga	218	H6
Tagudin	171	G2
Tagula	194	E4
Tagula Island	194	E4
Tagum	171	H4
Tagus	146	C3
Tahan, Gunung	170	C5
Tahat, Mont	181	G4
Ta He	167	N1
Tahe	167	N1
Taheri	175	L8
Tahiryuak Lake	199	N1
Tahiti	223	J5
Tahlab, Dasht-i-	172	B3
Tahlequah	208	E3
Tahoe Lake *Canada*	199	P1
Tahoe, Lake *U.S.A.*	202	E8
Tahoka	207	M4
Tahoua	181	G6
Tahrud	175	N7
Tahta	182	F2
Tahtali Daglari	157	G3
Tahuamanu	216	D6
Tahulandang	171	H5
Taian	167	M4
Taibai Shan	173	L2
Taibus Qi	167	M3
Tai-chung	167	N7
Taier	195	C6
Taieri	195	C6
Taigu	167	L4
Taihape	195	E3
Taihe *Anhui, China*	173	N2
Taihe *Jiangxi, China*	173	M3
Tai Hu	167	N5
Taimba	164	F4
Tain	136	D3
Tai-nan	167	N7
Tainaron, Akra	155	G4
Taining	167	M6
Taipale	142	N5
Tai-pei	167	N6
Taiping	170	C5
Taipingbao	166	J4
Taipinggou	168	C1
Taira	169	H7
Taisei	168	G4
Taisha	169	D8
Taitao, Peninsula de	219	B9
Tai-tung	167	N7
Taivalkoski	142	N4
Taiwan	167	N7
Taiwan Haixia	167	M7
Taiyetos Oros	155	G4
Taiyuan	167	L4
Taiza	169	E8
Taizhou	167	M5
Taizz	176	G10
Tajabad	175	M6
Tajikistan	166	B4
Tajima	169	G7
Tajin-dong	168	B5
Tajito	206	F5
Tajo	146	D3
Tajrish	175	K4
Tajumuclo, Volcan de	212	B7
Tajuna	146	E2
Tak	173	J5
Takab	174	H3
Takada	169	G7
Takaka	195	D4
Takamatsu	169	E8
Takanabe	169	C9
Takaoka	169	F7
Takapuna	195	E2
Takasaki	169	G7
Takatshwane	188	D4
Takaungu	187	G4
Takayama	169	F7
Takefu	169	F8
Takengon	170	B5
Takeo	173	K6
Takestan	175	J3
Takhadid	174	G7
Takhi-i-Suleiman	175	K3
Takhta Bazar	175	R4
Takhtabrod	164	Ae6
Takikawa	168	H4
Takinoue	168	J3
Taklimakan Shamo	172	F1
Taku	198	J4
Takum	185	G4
Takwa	194	K6
Talagang	172	D2
Talamanca, Cordillera de	212	F10
Talangbetutu	170	C6
Talara	216	A4
Talar-i-Band	172	B3
Talas	166	C3
Talasea	194	E3
Talaton	132	D4
Talaud, Kepulauan	171	H5
Talavera de la Reina	146	D3
Talayuelas	147	F3
Talbot Inlet	200	L2
Talca	219	B7

Talcahuano	219	B7
Talcher	172	G4
Taldy-Kurgan	166	D2
Talgarth	132	D3
Taliabu	171	G6
Talihina	208	E3
Tali Post	182	F6
Talisay	171	G3
Talitsa	164	Ad5
Taliwang	171	F7
Talkeetna	198	E3
Talkeetna Mountains	198	F3
Talladega	209	J4
Tall Afar	157	K4
Tallahassee	209	K5
Tallinn	143	L7
Tall Kalakh	157	G5
Tall Kayf	157	K4
Tall Kujik	157	K4
Tallow	139	F8
Tall Tamir	157	J4
Talmenka	164	C6
Talnoye	159	E6
Taloda	172	D4
Talodi	182	F5
Talok	171	F5
Talovka	164	E5
Taloye	165	M4
Talsi	143	K8
Taltal	218	B5
Taltson	199	N3
Talu	194	F3
Taluma	165	L5
Talvik	142	K1
Tama	204	D6
Tamabo Range	170	F5
Tamale	184	E4
Tamames	146	C2
Tamana	191	S2
Tamano	169	D8
Tamanrasset *Algeria*	180	F4
Tamanrasset *Algeria*	181	G4
Tamar *Australia*	193	K7
Tamar *U.K.*	132	C4
Tamar, Alto de	213	K11
Tamarite de Litera	147	G2
Tamatave	189	J3
Tamaulipas, Llanos de	208	C8
Tamazunchale	211	K7
Tambacounda	184	C3
Tambangsawah	170	C6
Tambelan, Kepulauan	170	D5
Tambey	164	A2
Tambo	193	K3
Tambora, Gunung	171	F7
Tamboril	217	J4
Tambov	159	G5
Tambre	146	B1
Tambura	182	E6
Tamchaket	180	C5
Tame	216	C2
Tamega	146	C2
Tamiahua, Laguna de	211	L7
Tamil Nadu	172	E6
Tamis	152	F3
Tamit, Wadi	181	J2
Tammerfors	143	M6
Tammisaari	143	K6
Tampa	209	L7
Tampa Bay	209	L7
Tampere	143	M6
Tampico	211	L6
Tamsagbulag	167	M2
Tamuin	211	K7
Tamworth *Australia*	193	L5
Tamworth *U.K.*	133	F2
Tana *Chile*	218	C3
Tana *Kenya*	187	H3
Tana *Norway*	142	M1
Tanabe	169	E9
Tana bru	142	N2
Tanafjorden	142	N1
Tana Hayk	183	G5
Tanahbala	170	36
Tanahgrogot	170	F6
Tanahjampea	171	G7
Tanahmasa	170	36
Tanahmerah	194	C3
Tanah Merah	170	C4
Tanami	192	F3
Tanana	198	E2
Tananarive	189	J3
Tanchon	168	B5
Tandag	171	H4
Tandek	171	F4
Tandil	219	E7
Tando Adam	172	C3
Tandragee	138	K4
Taneatua	195	F3
Tanega-shima	169	C10
Tan Emellel	181	G3
Tanen Tong Dan	173	J5
Tanew	151	K3
Tanezrouft	180	E4
Tanf, Jbel al	157	H6
Tanga *Tanzania*	187	G4
Tanga *Russia*	165	J6
Tanga Islands	194	E2
Tanganyika, Lake	187	F4
Tangarare	194	J6
Tanger	180	D1
Tanggula Shan	173	G2
Tanggula Shankou	173	H2
Tangra Yumco	172	G2

Tangshan	167	M4
Tangwang He	168	B2
Tangwanghe	168	B1
Tangyuan	168	B2
Tan Hill	133	F3
Tanhua	142	M3
Taniantaweng Shan	173	J2
Tanimbar, Kepulauan	194	A3
Tanjung	170	F6
Tanjungbalai	170	B5
Tanjungkarang Telukbetung	170	D7
Tanjungpandan	170	D6
Tanjungpura	170	B5
Tanjungredeb	171	F5
Tanjungselor	171	F5
Tankapirtti	142	M2
Tankovo	164	D4
Tankse	172	E2
Tanlovo	164	A3
Tanna	194	U13
Tannu Ola	164	E6
Tannurah, Ra's	177	K3
Tanout	181	G6
Tan-shui	167	N6
Tanta	182	F1
Tan-Tan	180	C3
Tantoyuca	211	K7
Tanumshede	143	D7
Tanzania	187	G4
Tacan	167	N2
Tao He	173	K2
Tao, Ko	173	J6
Taclanaro	189	J5
Taormina	149	E7
Taos	207	K2
Taoudenni	180	E4
Taourirt	180	E2
Tapa	143	L7
Tapachula	211	N10
Tapah	170	C5
Tapajos	217	F4
Tapaktuan	170	B5
Tapan	170	D6
Tapanahoni	217	F3
Tapaua	216	D5
Taperoa	217	K6
Tappahannock	205	M8
Tappi-saki	168	H5
Tapsuy	158	L3
Tapti	172	D4
Tapuaenuku	195	D4
Tapul Group	171	G4
Taqah	177	M8
Taqtaq	174	G4
Taquari	218	E3
Taquari, Pantanal do	218	E3
Tara	164	A5
Tarabulus	181	H2
Taradale	195	F3
Tara, Hill of	138	J5
Tarakan	171	F5
Tarakli	156	D2
Tarakliya	153	K3
Taramana	171	G7
Taramo-jima	169	G11
Taran	164	A2
Tarancon	146	E2
Taransay	136	A3
Taransay, Sound of	136	A3
Taranto	149	F5
Taranto, Golfo di	149	F5
Tarapoto	216	B5
Tararua Range	195	E4
Tarascon	145	F7
Tarasovo	158	H2
Tarauaca *Brazil*	216	C5
Tarauaca *Brazil*	216	C5
Taravo	149	B5
Tarazona	147	F2
Tarazona de la Mancha	147	F3
Tarbagatay, Khrebet	166	E2
Tarbert *Ireland*	139	D7
Tarbert *Strathclyde, U.K.*	137	C5
Tarbert *Western Isles, U.K.*	136	B3
Tarbes	145	D7
Tarbet	137	D4
Tarbolton	137	D5
Tarboro	209	P3
Tarcaului, Muntii	153	J2
Tarcoola	193	G5
Tardienta	147	F2
Tardoki-yani, Gora	168	F1
Taree	193	L5
Tarendo	142	K3
Tareya	164	E2
Tarfa, Ra's at	176	F8
Tarfa, Wadi el	183	F2
Tarfaya	180	C3
Tarfside	137	F4
Targhee Pass	202	J5
Tarhunah	181	H2
Tarif	177	L4
Tarifa	146	D4
Tarija	218	D4
Tariku	194	B2
Tarim	177	J8
Tarim Basin	166	E3
Tarim He	166	E3
Tarim Pendi	166	E3
Taritatu	194	B2
Tarkasale	164	A3
Tarkastad	188	E6
Tarkhankut, Mys	159	E6
Tarkio	204	C6

Tarkwa	184	E4
Tarlac	171	G2
Tarlak	166	E3
Tarleton	135	G3
Tarma	216	B6
Tarn	145	D7
Tarna	152	F2
Tarnaby	142	F4
Tarnobrzeg	151	J3
Tarnow	151	J4
Tarnsjo	143	G6
Taro	148	B3
Taron	194	E2
Taroom	193	K4
Taroudannt	180	D2
Tarporley	135	G3
Tarragona	147	G2
Tarrasa	147	H2
Tarrega	147	G2
Tarsus	156	F4
Tartagal	218	D4
Tartas	145	C7
Tartu	143	P7
Tartung	170	B5
Tartus	174	B4
Tartus	157	F5
Tarutino	153	K2
Tarzout	147	G4
Tasci	157	F3
Tashakta	166	F2
Tashigang	173	H3
Tashk, Daryacheh-ye	175	L7
Tashkent	166	B3
Tashkepri	175	R3
Tashla	159	J5
Tashtagol	164	D6
Tasikmalaya	170	D7
Tasiujaq	201	N6
Taskesken	166	E2
Taskopru	156	F2
Tas-Kumsa	165	N3
Taslicay	157	K3
Tasman Bay	195	D4
Tasmania	193	K7
Tasman Mountains	195	D4
Tasnad	153	G2
Tasova	157	G2
Tas-Tumus	165	N2
Tasty	166	B3
Tasucu	156	E4
Tasuj	157	L3
Tataba	171	G6
Tatabanya	152	E2
Tatarbunary	153	K3
Tatarka	164	B6
Tatarsk	164	B5
Tataurovo	165	J6
Tateyama	169	G8
Tathlina Lake	199	M3
Tathlith	176	F7
Tathlith, Wadi	176	F6
Tatnam, Cape	199	S4
Tatry	151	H4
Tatsinskiy	159	G6
Tatsuno	169	E8
Tatta	172	C4
Tatum	207	L4
Tatvan	157	K3
Tau	191	V4
Tauari	217	F4
Taubate	218	G4
Tauchik	159	J7
Taumarunui	195	E3
Taung-gyi	173	J4
Taungnyo Range	173	J5
Taunton *U.K.*	132	D3
Taunton *U.S.A.*	205	Q6
Taunus	150	C3
Taupo	195	F3
Taupo, Lake	195	E3
Tauq	174	G4
Tauq	157	L5
Taurage	143	K9
Tauranga	195	F2
Tauroa Point	195	D1
Taurus	156	E4
Tauste	147	F2
Tauu Islands	194	F2
Tavalesh, Kuhha-ye	174	J3
Tavana-i-Tholo	191	T6
Tavas	156	C4
Tavda *Russia*	164	Ad5
Tavda *Russia*	164	Ae5
Taverner Bay	200	M4
Taveuni	194	S8
Tavira	146	C4
Tavistock	132	C4
Tavolara, Isola di	149	B5
Tavoy	173	J6
Tavrichanka	168	C4
Tavsanli	156	C3
Tavua	194	Q8
Tavuna-i-Ra	191	T6
Tavy	132	C4
Taw	132	D4
Tawakoni, Lake	208	E4
Tawau	171	F5
Tawe	132	D3
Taweisha	182	E5
Tawila	176	A3
Tawil, At	176	D2
Tawitawi Group	171	G4
Ta-wu	167	N7
Tawurgha, Sabkhat	181	J2

Till	137	F5	Tiverton	132	D4	Tomah	204	E4	Torngat Mountains	201	P6
Tillaberi	180	F6	Tivoli	149	D5	Tomahawk	204	F4	Tornio	142	L4
Tillanchang	173	H7	Tiwi	177	P5	Tomakomai	168	H4	Toro, Cerro de	218	C5
Tillicoultry	137	E4	Tiyas	157	G5	Tomani	170	F5	Toroiaga	153	H2
Tilomar	171	H7	Tizimin	211	Q7	Tomaniivi	194	R8	Torokina	194	F3
Tilos	155	J4	Tizi Ouzou	181	F1	Tomar *Portugal*	146	B3	Torokszentmiklos	152	F2
Tilsit	151	J1	Tiznit	180	D3	Tomar *Kazakhstan*	166	D2	Toronaios, Kolpos	155	G2
Tilt	137	E4	Tjamotis	142	H3	Tomari	168	J2	Toronto	205	L5
Timanskiy Kryazh	158	H3	Tjornuvik	142	Z14	Tomarza	157	F3	Toropets	158	E4
Timar	157	K3	Tjotta	142	E4	Tomasevo	152	E4	Tororo	187	F2
Timaru	195	C6	Tlaltenango	210	H7	Tomashevka	151	K3	Toros Dagi	156	F4
Timashevsk	159	F6	Tlapa	211	K9	Tomashevka	151	K3	Toros Daglari	156	E4
Timbakion	155	H5	Tlapehuala	211	J8	Tomaszow Lubelski	151	K3	Torpoint	132	C4
Timbedra	180	D5	Tlaxiaco	211	L9	Tomaszow Mazowiecka	151	J3	Torquay	132	D4
Timbo *Guinea*	184	C3	Tlemcen	180	E2	Tombador, Serra do	216	F6	Torrance	206	C4
Timbo *Liberia*	184	D4	Toad River	198	K4	Tombe	183	F6	Torrao	146	B3
Timbuktu	180	E5	Toamasina	189	J3	Tombigbee	209	H5	Torre Annunziata	149	E5
Timfristos	155	F3	Tobago	213	S9	Tomboco	186	B4	Torre Baja	147	F2
Timimoun	180	F3	Toba Kakar Ranges	172	C2	Tombouctou	180	E5	Torreblanca	147	G2
Timiris, Cap	180	B5	Tobercurry	138	E4	Tombua	186	B6	Torrecilla en Cameros	146	E1
Timis	153	G3	Tobermory *Canada*	205	K4	Tomelilla	143	E9	Torre del Greco	149	E5
Timisoara	153	F3	Tobermory *U.K.*	137	B4	Tomelloso	146	E3	Torrelaguna	146	E2
Timkapaul	164	Ad4	Toberonochy	137	C4	Tomini, Teluk	171	G6	Torrelavega	146	D1
Timmernabben	143	G8	Tobi	171	J5	Tomioka	169	H7	Torremolinos	146	D4
Timmins	205	K2	Tobin Lake	192	F3	Tomkinson Ranges	192	F4	Torrens Creek	193	K3
Timok	153	G3	Tobi-shima	163	G6	Tomma	142	E3	Torrens, Lake	193	H5
Timolin	139	J7	Toboali	170	D6	Tommot	165	M5	Torrente	147	F3
Timor	171	H7	Tobol	164	Ae5	Tomo	216	D2	Torreon	207	L8
Timor, Laut	171	H7	Tobolsk	164	Ae5	Tomochic	207	J6	Torres Island	194	T10
Timoshino	158	F3	Tobseda	158	J2	Tompa	164	H5	Torres Novas	146	B3
Timsher	158	J3	Tobysh	158	J3	Tompo	165	P4	Torres Strait	194	C4
Tinaca Point	171	H4	Tocache Nuevo	216	B5	Tomsk	164	D5	Torres Vedras	146	B3
Tinaco	213	N10	Tocantins	217	H4	Tonbridge	133	H3	Torrevieja	147	F4
Tinahely	139	K7	Toccoa	209	L3	Tondano	171	G5	Torr Head	138	K2
Tinakula	194	M7	Toco	213	S9	Tonder	150	C1	Torridge	132	C4
Tindivanam	172	E6	Toconao	218	C4	Tone	132	E3	Torridon, Loch	136	C3
Tindouf	180	D3	Tocopilla	218	B4	Tonelagee	139	K6	Torrijos	146	D3
Tineo	146	C1	Tocuyo	213	N9	Tonga	191	U6	Torrington *Connecticut*	205	P6
Tinglev	143	C9	Todeli	171	G6	Tonga *Sudan*	182	F6	Torrington *Wyoming*	203	M6
Tingo Maria	216	B5	Todi	148	B2	Tongariro	195	E3	Torrox	146	E4
Tingsryd	143	F8	Todi	149	D4	Tongatapu	191	U6	Torsas	143	F8
Tingvoll	142	C5	Todmorden	135	G3	Tongatapu Group	191	T6	Torsby	143	E6
Tinhare, Ilha de	217	K6	Todog	166	E3	Tonga Trench	223	H5	Torshavn	142	Z14
Tinogasta	218	C5	Todos os Santos, Baia de	217	K6	Tongcheng	173	M3	Torsken	142	L2
Tinompo	171	G5	Todos Santos *Bolivia*	218	C3	Tongchuan	173	L1	Tortkuduk	164	A6
Tinos *Greece*	155	H4	Todos Santos *Mexico*	210	D6	Tongdao	173	L3	Tortola	213	Q5
Tinos *Greece*	155	H4	Todos Santos, Bahia de	206	D5	Tonggu	173	M3	Tortona	148	B3
Tintinara	193	J6	Toe Head *Ireland*	139	D10	Tongguan	173	M2	Tortosa	147	G2
Tinto *Spain*	146	C4	Toe Head *U.K.*	136	A3	Tonghai	173	K4	Tortosa, Cabo de	147	G2
Tinto *U.K.*	137	E5	Toetoes Bay	195	B7	Tonghe	168	B2	Tortue, Ile de la	213	L4
Tinto Hills	137	E5	Tofino	202	B3	Tonghua	167	P3	Tortuga, Isla	206	G7
Tinwald	195	C5	Toft	136	A1	Tongjiang	168	D2	Tortuga, Isla la	216	D1
Tiomilaskogen	143	E6	Tofte	143	D7	Tongking, Gulf of	173	L5	Tortum	157	J2
Tipaza	147	H4	Tofua	191	T5	Tongliao	167	N3	Torul	157	H2
Tipitapa	212	D8	Toga	194	T10	Tongling	167	M5	Torun	151	H2
Tippecanoe	204	G6	Togi	169	F7	Tonglu	167	M6	Tory Island	138	F2
Tipperary *Ireland*	139	F8	Togiak	198	C4	Tongnae	169	B8	Torysa	151	J4
Tipperary *Ireland*	139	G7	Togian, Kepulauan	171	G6	Tongoa	194	U12	Tory Sound	138	F2
Tipton	204	H6	Togni	176	B7	Tongren	173	L3	Torzhok	158	F4
Tiptree	133	H3	Togo	184	F4	Tongtianheyan	173	H2	Torzym	150	F2
Tiquicheo	211	J8	Togtoh	167	L3	Tongue *U.K.*	136	D2	Tosa-shimizu	169	D9
Tiracambu, Serra do	217	H4	Toguchi	169	H10	Tongue *U.S.A.*	203	L5	Tosa-wan	169	D9
Tiran	176	B3	Togur	164	C5	Tongue, Kyle of	136	D2	Toscaig	136	C3
Tirana	154	E2	Tohamiyam	183	G4	Tongue of the Ocean	212	J2	Tosco-Emiliano, Appennino	148	C3
Tirane	154	E2	Tohatchi	207	H3	Tong Xian	167	M4	Tostado	218	D5
Tirano	148	C2	Tohma	157	G3	Tongxin	173	L1	Tosya	156	F2
Tiraspol	159	D6	Toi-misaki	169	C10	Tongyu	167	N3	Totana	147	F4
Tire	156	B3	Tojo	169	D8	Tongzi	173	L3	Totes	144	D4
Tirebolu	157	H2	Tok	198	G3	Tonichi	207	H6	Totma	158	G4
Tiree	137	C4	Tokachi	168	J4	Tonk	172	E3	Totnes	132	D4
Tirga Mor	136	B3	Tokachi-Dake	168	J4	Tonkabon	175	K3	Totness	217	F2
Tirgoviste	153	H3	Tokaj	153	F1	Tonle Sap	173	K6	Totora	218	C3
Tirgu Bujor	153	J3	Tokanui	195	B7	Tonneins	145	D6	Totota	184	C4
Tirgu Carbunesti	153	G3	Tokar	183	G4	Tonnerre	145	E5	Totoya	194	S9
Tirgu Frumos	153	J2	Tokara-kaikyo	169	C10	Tono	168	H6	Totton	133	F4
Tirgu Jiu	153	G3	Tokara-retto	169	B11	Tonopah	206	D2	Tottori	169	E8
Tirgu Mures	153	H2	Tokat	157	G2	Tonosi	212	G11	Touba	184	D4
Tirgu Neamt	153	J2	Tokelau	191	U3	Tonsberg	143	D7	Toubkal, Jebel	180	D2
Tirgu Ocna	153	J2	Tokiwa	168	J3	Tonstad	143	B7	Tougan	184	E3
Tirich Mir	172	D1	Tokke	143	C7	Tonya	157	H2	Touggourt	181	G2
Tirnava Mare	153	H2	Toklar	157	G3	Tooele	202	H7	Touho Ouegoa	194	W16
Tirnava Mica	153	H2	Tokmak	166	D3	Toowoomba	193	L4	Toul	144	F4
Tirnavos	155	G3	Tokolon	164	H5	Topeka	204	C7	Toulon	145	F7
Tirol	148	C2	Tokoro	168	K3	Toplane	154	E1	Toulouse	145	D7
Tirpul	175	Q4	Tokoroa	195	E3	Toplica	153	F4	Toummo	181	H4
Tirso	149	B6	Toksun	166	F3	Toplita	153	H2	Toumodi	184	D4
Tirua Point	195	E3	Tok-to	169	C7	Topocalma, Punta	218	B6	Toungoo	173	J5
Tiruchchirappalli	172	E6	Toktogul	166	C3	Topola	152	F3	Touraine	145	D5
Tirumangalam	172	E7	Tokuno-shima	169	J10	Topolcani	153	F5	Tourcoing	144	E3
Tirunelveli	172	E7	Tokushima	169	E8	Topoli	159	J6	Tournai	144	E3
Tirupati	172	E6	Tokuyama	169	C8	Topolkki	143	N6	Tournon *France*	145	D5
Tiruppur	172	E6	Tokyo	169	G8	Topolovgrad	153	J4	Tournon *France*	145	F6
Tiruvannamalai	172	E6	Tolar, Cerro	218	C5	Topozero, Ozero	142	P4	Tournus	145	F5
Tisa	152	F3	Tolbonuur	166	G2	Toppenish	202	D4	Touros	217	K5
Tisisat Falls	183	G5	Tolbukhin	153	J4	Toprakli	156	F3	Tours	145	D5
Tissa	151	K4	Toledo *Spain*	146	D3	Toraka Vestale	189	H3	Tousside, Pic	182	C3
Tissington	135	H3	Toledo *U.S.A.*	204	J6	Tora-Khem	164	F6	Touws River	188	D6
Tista	173	G3	Toledo Bend Reservoir	208	F5	Torbali	156	B3	Tovarkovskiy	159	F5
Tisza	152	F2	Toledo, Montes de	146	D3	Torbat-e-Heydariyeh	175	P4	Towada	168	H5
Tit-Ary	165	M2	Tolentino	148	D4	Torbat-e Jam	175	Q4	Towanda	205	M6
Titchfield	133	F4	Toliara	189	H4	Tor Bay *Australia*	192	D5	Towcester	133	G2
Titicaca, Lago	218	C3	Tolitoli	171	G5	Tor Bay *U.K.*	132	D4	Tower Island	216	B7
Titograd	152	E4	Tolka	164	C4	Tordesillas	146	D2	Towie	136	F3
Titova Mitrovica	153	F4	Tolmezzo	148	D2	Tore	136	D3	Townsend	202	J4
Titovo Uzice	152	E4	Tolmin	152	B2	Tore	142	K4	Townshend Island	193	L3
Titovo Velenje	152	C2	Tolochin	158	D5	Torfastadir	142	U12	Townsville	193	K2
Titov Veles	153	F5	Tolosa	147	E1	Torgau	150	E3	Towson	205	M7
Titran	142	C5	Tolo, Teluk	171	G6	Torgo	165	K5	Toxkan He	166	D3
Tittmoning	150	E4	Tolsta Head	136	B2	Torhout	144	E3	Toya-ko	168	H4
Titu	153	H3	Tolstoye	153	H1	Torino	148	A3	Toyama	169	F7
Titusville	209	M6	Tolstoy, Mys	165	T5	Torkaman	174	H3	Toyama-wan	169	F7
Tiumpan Head	136	B2	Toluca	211	K8	Tormes	146	D2	Toyohashi	169	F8
Tivaouane	184	B2	Toluca, Nevado de	211	K8	Tornealven	142	K3	Toyonaka	169	E8
Tiveden	143	F7	Tolyatti	159	H5	Tor Ness	136	E2	Toyooka	169	E8
						Torne-trask	142	H2			

V

Vigan 171 G2
Vigevano 148 B3
Viggiano 149 E5
Vigia 217 G4
Viglio, Monte 149 D5
Vigo 146 B1
Vigrestad 143 A7
Viiala 143 K6
Vijayawada 172 F5
Vijose 154 E2
Vik 142 E4
Vik 142 V13
Vikajarvi 142 M3
Vikersund 143 D7
Vikhorevka 164 G5
Vikna 142 D4
Viksoyri 143 B6
Vila 194 U12
Viladikars 157 K2
Vila Franca 146 B3
Vilaine 145 C5
Vilaller 147 G1
Vilanculos 189 G4
Vila Nova 217 F4
Vila Nova de Famalicao 146 B2
Vila Pouca de Aguiar 146 C2
Vila Real 146 C2
Vila Real de Santo Antonio 146 C4
Vila Velha 218 H4
Vila Velha de Rodao 146 C3
Vila Vicosa 146 C3
Viled 158 H3
Vileyka 151 M1
Vilhelmina 142 G4
Vilhena 216 E6
Viliga-Kushka 165 T4
Viljandi 143 L7
Vilkitskogo, Proliv 161 M2
Vilkovo 153 K3
Villa Abecia 218 C4
Villa Angela 218 D5
Villa Aroma 218 C3
Villa Bella 216 D6
Villa Bens 180 C3
Villablino 146 C1
Villacarrillo 146 E3
Villacastin 146 D2
Villach 148 D2
Villa Cisneros 180 B4
Villa Constitucion 218 D6
Villa de Cura 216 D2
Villadiego 146 D1
Villa Dolores 219 C6
Villafranca del Bierzo 146 C1
Villafranca de los Barros 146 C3
Villafranca del Penedes 147 G2
Villafranca di Verona 148 C3
Villaguay 218 E6
Villa Hayes 218 E5
Villahermosa 211 N9
Villa Huidobro 219 D6
Villa Iris 219 D7
Villajoyosa 147 F3
Villalba 146 C1
Villalon de Campos 146 D1
Villalpando 146 D2
Villa Maria 218 D6
Villamayor de Santiago 146 E3
Villa Montes 218 D4
Villanueva 210 H6
Villanueva de Cordoba 146 D3
Villanueva del Fresno 146 C3
Villanueva de los Castillejos 146 C4
Villanueva de los Infantes 146 E3
Villanueva y Geltru 147 G2
Villaputzu 149 B6
Villarcayo 146 E1
Villarejo 146 E2
Villarrica 218 E5
Villarrobledo 146 E3
Villasandino 146 D1
Villa Union *Argentina* 218 C5
Villa Union *Mexico* 207 M6
Villavicencio 216 C3
Villaviciosa 146 D1
Villazon 218 C4
Villedieu 144 C4
Villefort 145 E6
Villefranche-de-Rouergue 145 E6
Villefranche-sur-Saone 145 F6
Villena 147 F3
Villeneuve-sur-Lot 145 D6
Villeneuve-sur-Yonne 145 E4
Ville Platte 208 F5
Villers-Bocage 144 C4
Villers-Cotterets 144 E4
Villeurbanne 145 F6
Villodrigo 146 D1
Vilna 151 L1
Vilnius 151 L1
Vilnya 151 L1
Vilshofen 150 E4
Vilyuy 165 M4
Vilyuysk 165 L4
Vilyuyskoye Plato 164 H3
Vimmerby 143 F8
Vimperk 150 E4
Vina del Mar 219 B6
Vinaroz 147 G2
Vinas 143 F6
Vincennes 204 G7
Vincennes Bay 221 H5
Vinchina 218 C5

Vindelalven 142 J4
Vindeln 142 H4
Vindhya Range 172 E4
Vineland 205 N7
Vinga 153 F3
Vinh 173 L5
Vinh Loi 173 L7
Vinh Long 173 L6
Vinh Yen 173 L4
Vinica 153 G5
Vinkovci 152 E3
Vinnytsya 159 D6
Vinogradov 151 K4
Vipiteno 148 C2
Vir 152 C3
Virac 171 G3
Viramgam 172 D4
Virandozero 158 F3
Viransehir 157 H4
Virarajendrapet 172 E6
Virden 203 P3
Vire *France* 144 C4
Vire *France* 144 C4
Virfurile 153 G2
Virgenes, Cabo 219 C10
Virgin 206 E2
Virgin Gorda 213 Q5
Virginia *Ireland* 138 H5
Virginia *Minnesota* 204 D3
Virginia *U.S.A.* 205 L8
Virginia Beach 205 N8
Virginia Falls 198 L3
Virgin Islands 213 Q5
Virmasvesi 142 M5
Virovitica 152 D3
Virrat 143 K5
Virudunagar 172 E7
Vis 152 D4
Visalia 206 C2
Visayan Sea 171 G3
Visby 143 H8
Viscount Melville Sound 200 M3
Visegrad 152 E4
Viseu *Brazil* 217 H4
Viseu *Portugal* 146 C2
Vishakhapatnam 172 F5
Vishera 158 K3
Vishnevets 151 L4
Vislanda 143 F8
Visoko 152 E4
Viso, Monte 148 A3
Vista 206 D4
Vistonis, Limni 155 H2
Vit 153 H4
Vitava 150 F4
Viterbo 149 D4
Viterog Planina 152 D3
Vitiaz Strait 194 C3
Vitichi 218 C4
Vitigudino 146 C2
Viti Levu 194 Q9
Vitim *Russia* 165 J5
Vitim *Russia* 165 J5
Vitina 155 G4
Vitoria 146 E1
Vitoria 218 H4
Vitoria da Conquista 217 J6
Vitoria de Santa Antao 217 K5
Vitre 144 C4
Vitry-le-Francois 144 F4
Vitsyebsk 158 E4
Vittangi 142 J3
Vittel 144 F4
Vittoria 149 E7
Vittorio Veneto 148 D3
Vivarais, Monts du 145 F6
Viver 147 F3
Vivero 146 C1
Vivi *Russia* 164 F4
Vivi *Russia* 164 F4
Vizcaino, Desierto de 206 F7
Vizcaino, Sierra 206 F7
Vize 156 B2
Vizhas 158 H2
Vizianagaram 172 F5
Vizinga 158 J3
Vizzavona 149 B4
Vladicin Han 153 G4
Vladikavkaz 157 L1
Vladimir 158 G4
Vladimirets 151 M3
Vladimirovka 159 J5
Vladimir Volynskiy 151 L3
Vladivostok 168 C4
Vlakherna 155 G4
Vlasenica 152 E3
Vlieland 144 F2
Vlissingen 144 E3
Vlore 154 E2
Vodice 152 C4
Vodlozero, Ozero 158 F3
Vogan 185 J4
Voghera 148 B3
Voh 194 W16
Vohemar 189 J2
Vohilava 189 J4
Vohimarina 189 J2
Vohipeno 189 J4
Voi 187 G3
Voiron 145 F6
Vojens 143 C9
Vojmsjon 142 G4
Vojnic 152 C3
Volary 150 E4

Volborg 203 M5
Volchansk 159 F5
Volda 142 B5
Volga 159 H6
Volgodonsk 159 G6
Volgograd 159 G6
Volgogradskoye Vodokhranilishche 159 H6
Volgsele 142 G4
Volissos 155 H3
Volkhov *Russia* 158 E4
Volkhov *Russia* 158 E4
Volklingen 150 B4
Volkovysk 151 L2
Volksrust 188 E5
Volnovakha 159 F6
Volochankao 164 E2
Volochayevka 168 E1
Volochisk 151 M4
Volodskaya 158 G3
Vologda 158 F4
Volokon 164 H5
Volonga 158 H2
Volos 155 G3
Voloshka 158 F3
Volovets 151 K4
Volozhin 151 M1
Volpa 151 L2
Volsk 159 H5
Volta 184 F4
Volta, Lake 184 E4
Volta Redonda 218 H4
Volterra 148 C4
Volteva 158 G3
Volturno 149 E5
Volvi, Limni 155 G2
Volynskaya Vozvyshennost 151 L3
Volynskoje Polesje 151 L3
Volzhskiy 159 G6
Von Martius, Cachoeira 217 G6
Vopnafjordur 142 X12
Voras Oros 155 F2
Vordingborg 143 D9
Voriai Sporadhes 155 H3
Vorkuta 158 L2
Vormsi 142 K7
Voronezh 159 F5
Voronovo 151 L1
Vorontsovo 143 N8
Voronya 158 F2
Voroshno 158 H4
Vortsjarv 143 M7
Voru 143 M8
Vosges 144 G4
Voskresensk 158 F4
Voss *Norway* 143 B6
Voss *Norway* 143 B6
Vostochno-Sibirskoye More 165 T2
Vostochnyy *Russia* 168 D4
Vostochnyy *Russia* 168 J1
Vostok 221 H3
Vostretsovo 168 E3
Votice 150 F4
Votkinsk 158 J4
Votkinskoye Vodokhranilishche 158 K4
Vot Tande 194 T10
Vouga 146 C2
Vouziers 144 F4
Vowchurch 132 E2
Voxnan *Sweden* 143 F6
Voxnan *Sweden* 143 F6
Voynitsa 142 P4
Voy Vozh 158 J3
Voyvozh 158 K3
Voza 194 H5
Vozhayel 158 H3
Vozhe, Ozero 158 G3
Vozhega 158 G3
Voznesensk 159 E6
Voznesenye 158 F3
Vozvyshennost Karabil 175 R3
Vrancei, Muntii 153 J3
Vrangelya, Mys 165 P6
Vrangelya, Ostrov 161 U2
Vranje 153 F4
Vranov 151 J4
Vratsa 153 G4
Vrbas 152 D3
Vrbovsko 152 C3
Vrede 188 E5
Vrhnika 152 C3
Vrindavan 172 E3
Vrlika 152 D4
Vrondadhes 155 J3
Vrsac 153 F3
Vrsacki Kanal 153 F3
Vryburg 188 D5
Vryheid 188 F5
Vucitrn 153 F4
Vukovar 152 E3
Vulavu 194 J6
Vulcan 153 G3
Vulcano, Isola 149 E6
Vung Tau 173 L6
Vunisea 194 R9
Vuokatti 142 N4
Vuollerim 142 J3
Vyartsilya 142 P5
Vyatka 158 J4
Vyatskiye Polyany 158 J4
Vyazemskiy 168 E2
Vyazma 158 E4
Vyazniki 158 G4

Vyborg 143 N6
Vychegda 158 H3
Vydrino 164 F5
Vygoda 153 L2
Vygozero, Ozero 158 F3
Vyhorlat 151 K4
Vyksa 158 G4
Vym 158 J3
Vyrnwy 132 D2
Vyshniy-Volochek 158 E4
Vysokoye 151 K2
Vytegra 158 F3
Vyzhva 151 L3

W

Wa 184 E3
Waal 144 F3
Waat 183 F6
Wabana 201 R8
Wabasca 199 N4
Wabash 204 G7
Wabe Gestro Wenz 183 H6
Wabe Shabele Wenz 183 H6
Wabigoon Lake 204 D2
Wabowden 199 R4
Wabush 201 N7
Waccasassa Bay 209 L6
Waco 208 D5
Wad Banda 182 E5
Waddan 181 J3
Waddeneilanden 144 F2
Waddenzee 144 F2
Waddesdon 133 G3
Waddington, Mount 198 K5
Wadebridge 132 C4
Wadena 204 C3
Wadi Gimal 176 B4
Wadi Halfa 182 F3
Wad Medani 183 F5
Wadomari 169 J10
Wad Rawa 183 F4
Wafra 177 H2
Wager Bay 200 J4
Wagga Wagga 193 K6
Wagin 192 D5
Wahai 171 H6
Waharoa 195 E2
Wahiawa 206 R10
Wahibah, Ramlat ahl 177 P6
Wahidi 176 H9
Wahoo 203 R7
Wahpeton 203 R4
Waialua 206 R10
Waianae 206 R10
Waiau *New Zealand* 195 A6
Waiau *New zealand* 195 D5
Waiau *New Zealand* 195 D5
Waibeem 171 J6
Waidhofen *Austria* 148 E2
Waidhofen *Austria* 148 E1
Waigeo 171 J6
Waiheke Island 195 E2
Waihi 195 E2
Waikabubak 171 F7
Waikato 195 E3
Waikerie 193 H5
Waikouaiti 195 C6
Wailuku 206 S10
Waimakariri 195 D5
Waimamaku 195 D1
Waimate 195 C6
Wainganga 172 E4
Waingapu 171 G7
Waini Point 216 F2
Wainwright 198 D1
Waiotapu 195 F3
Waiouru 195 E3
Waipa 195 E2
Waipahi 195 B7
Waipara 195 D5
Waipawa 195 F3
Waipiro 195 G3
Waipu 195 E1
Waipukurau 195 F3
Wairau 195 D4
Wairau Valley 195 D4
Wairio 195 B7
Wairoa 195 F3
Waitaki 195 C6
Waitangi 195 F6
Waitara 195 E3
Waitoa 195 E2
Waiuku 195 E2
Wajima 169 F7
Wajir 187 H2
Wakasa-wan 169 E8
Waka, Tanjung 171 H6
Wakatipu, Lake 195 B6
Wakaya 194 R8
Wakayama 169 E8
Wake 169 E8
Wakeeny 203 Q8
Wakefield 135 H3
Wakkanai 168 H3
Wakool *Australia* 193 J6
Wakool *Australia* 193 J6
Waku Kungo 186 C5
Walachia 153 H3
Walade 194 K6
Walagan 167 N1
Walbrzych 151 G3
Walcha 193 L5

Walcheren 144 E3
Walcz 151 G2
Waldenburg 151 G3
Waldon 132 C4
Waldron 208 E3
Waldshut 150 C5
Wales 198 A2
Wales Island 200 J4
Walgett 193 K4
Walikale 187 E3
Walinga 194 D3
Walker 202 E8
Walkeringham 135 J3
Walker Lake 202 E8
Wallace 209 P3
Wallaceburg 204 J5
Wallal Downs 192 E2
Wallasey 135 F3
Walla Walla 202 E4
Walldurn 150 C4
Wallhallow 193 H2
Wallingford 133 F3
Wallis, Iles 191 T4
Wallowa 202 F5
Walls 136 A1
Wallsend 135 H2
Walney, Island of 135 F2
Walpole 194 Y17
Walsall 133 F2
Walsenburg 207 K2
Walsingham, Cape 200 P4
Walsrode 150 C2
Walterboro 209 M4
Walter F. George Reservoir 209 K5
Waltham Abbey 133 H3
Walton 133 G3
Walvis Bay 188 B4
Wama 186 C5
Wamba *Nigeria* 185 G4
Wamba *Zaire* 186 C4
Wami 194 A2
Wana 172 C2
Wanaaring 193 J4
Wanaka 195 B6
Wanaka, Lake 195 B6
Wanapiri 171 K6
Wanapitei 204 K3
Wanda Shan 168 C3
Wandel Sea 220 P2
Wandingzhen 173 J4
Wanganui *New Zealand* 195 E3
Wanganui *New Zealand* 195 E3
Wangaratta 193 K6
Wangary 193 H5
Wangerooge 150 B2
Wangiwangi 171 G7
Wangjiadian 168 C2
Wangkui 167 P2
Wang, Mae Nam 173 J5
Wangqing 168 B4
Wanie-Rukula 186 E2
Wankaner 172 D4
Wankie 188 E3
Wanlaweyn 187 H2
Wanquan 167 L3
Wantage 133 F3
Wanxian 173 L2
Wanyuan 173 L2
Wanzai 173 M3
Wapenamanda 194 C3
Wapsipinicon 204 E5
Warangal 172 E5
Waratah Bay 193 K6
Warboys 133 G2
Warbreccan 193 J3
Warburg 150 C3
Warburton 193 H4
Ward 195 E4
Wardha 172 E4
Ward Hunt, Cape 194 D3
Ward Hunt Strait 194 E3
Ware *Canada* 198 K4
Ware *U.K.* 133 G3
Ware *U.S.A.* 205 P5
Wareham 133 E4
Waren *Germany* 150 E2
Waren *Indonesia* 171 K6
Warka 151 J3
Wark Forest 137 F5
Warkworth 195 E2
Warlingham 133 G3
Warmbad 188 C5
Warminster 133 E3
Warm Springs 206 D1
Warner Robins 209 L4
Warnow 150 D2
Warora 172 E4
Warracknabeal 193 J6
Warrego 193 K5
Warren *Minnesota* 204 B2
Warren *Ohio* 205 K6
Warren *Pennsylvania* 205 L6
Warrenpoint 138 K4
Warrenton *South Africa* 188 D5
Warrenton *U.S.A.* 205 M7
Warri 185 G4
Warrina 193 H4
Warrington *U.K.* 135 G3
Warrington *U.S.A.* 209 J5
Warrior Reefs 194 C3
Warrnambool 193 J6
Warroad 204 C2
Warsaw 151 J2
Warshiikh 187 J2
Warsop 135 H3
Warszawa 151 J2
Warta 151 G2
Waru 171 J6
Warwick *Australia* 193 L4
Warwick *U.K.* 133 F2
Warwick *U.S.A.* 205 Q6
Warwick Channel 193 H1
Warwickshire 133 F2
Wasbister 136 E1
Wasco 206 C3
Wasdale Head 135 F2
Washburn Lake 199 P1
Washim 172 E4
Washington *U.K.* 135 H2
Washington *District of Columbia* 205 M7
Washington *Georgia* 209 L4
Washington *Indiana* 204 G7
Washington *Missouri* 204 E7
Washington *N. Carolina* 209 P3
Washington *Pennsylvania* 205 K6
Washington *U.S.A.* 202 D4
Washington Cape 221 M4
Washington Land 200 N1
Washington, Mount 205 Q4
Wash, The 133 H2
Wasian 171 J6
Wasior 171 J6
Wasisi 171 H6
Waskaganish 201 L7
Waspan 212 E7
Wast Water 135 F2
Watam 194 C2
Watampone 171 G6
Watansoppeng 171 F6
Watchet 132 D3
Waterbeach 133 H2
Waterbury 205 P6
Wateree 209 M3
Waterford *Ireland* 139 G8
Waterford *Ireland* 139 H8
Watergrasshill 139 F8
Waterloo *Belgium* 144 F3
Waterloo *U.S.A.* 204 D5
Waterlooville 133 F4
Waternish 136 B3
Waternish Point 136 B3
Waterside 137 D5
Watertown *New York* 205 N4
Watertown *S. Dakota* 203 R5
Watertown *Wisconsin* 204 F5
Waterville *Ireland* 139 B9
Waterville *U.S.A.* 205 R4
Watford 133 G3
Watford City 203 N4
Watheroo 192 D5
Watkaremoana, Lake 195 F3
Watling Island 213 K2
Watlington 133 F3
Watroa 195 F3
Watsa 187 E2
Watseka 204 G6
Watson 203 M1
Watson Lake 198 K3
Watsonville 206 B2
Watten 136 E2
Watten, Loch 136 E2
Watton 133 H2
Watubela, Kepulauan 171 J6
Wau *Papua New Guinea* 194 D3
Wau *Sudan* 182 E6
Wauchope 193 G3
Waukarlycarly, Lake 192 E3
Waukegan 204 G5
Waurika 208 D3
Wausau 204 F4
Wave Hill 192 G2
Waveney 133 J2
Waverly 205 M5
Wavre 144 F3
Wawa 204 H3
Waxahachie 208 D4
Waya 194 Q8
Wayabula 171 H5
Waycross 209 L5
Way, Lake 192 E4
Waynesboro *Georgia* 209 L4
Waynesboro *Mississippi* 208 H5
Waynesboro *Pennsylvania* 205 M7
Waynesburg 205 K7
Waynesville *Missouri* 204 D8
Waynesville *Tennessee* 209 L3
Waynoka 208 C2
Wda 151 H2
We 170 B4
Wé 194 X16
Weald, The 133 H3
Wear 135 H2
Weardale 135 H2
Weasenham 133 H2
Weatherall Bay 200 E2
Weatherford 208 C3
Weaver 135 G3
Webi Shabeelle 183 J7
Webster 203 R5
Webster City 204 D5
Weda 171 H5
Weddell Sea 221 W4
Wedel 150 C2
Weduar, Tanjung 171 J7
Weeley 133 J3
Weemelah 193 K4
Wegorzewo 151 J1
Wegorzyno 150 F2
Weichang 167 M3
Weiden 150 E4
Weifang 167 M4
Weihai 167 N4
Weihe 168 B3
Wei He 173 L2
Weilu 167 L3
Weimar 150 D3
Weinan 173 L2
Weingarten 150 C5
Weiser 202 F5
Weissenburg 150 D4
Weissenfels 150 D3
Weiss Lake 209 K3
Weitra 148 E1
Weixin 173 K3
Wejherowo 151 H1
Welch 205 K8
Welcome Kop 188 C6
Welda 150 E3
Weldiya 183 G5
Welkom 188 E5
Welland 133 G2
Wellesley Islands 193 H2
Wellingborough 133 G2
Wellington *New Zealand* 195 E4
Wellington *South Africa* 188 C6
Wellington *Shropshire, U.K.* 132 E2
Wellington *Somerset, U.K.* 132 D4
Wellington *Kansas* 208 D2
Wellington *Texas* 207 M3
Wellington Channel 200 H2
Wellington, Isla 219 B9
Wells *U.K.* 132 E3
Wells *U.S.A.* 202 G7
Wellsford 195 E2
Wells-next-the-Sea 133 H2
Welney 133 H2
Wels 148 D1
Welshpool 132 D2
Welwyn Garden City 133 G3
Wemindji 201 L7
Wenasaga 203 T2
Wenatchee 202 D4
Wenchang 173 M5
Wenchuan 173 K2
Wendover 202 G7
Wengen 148 A2
Wenling 167 N6
Wenlock Edge 132 E2
Wenshan 173 K4
Wensleydale 135 H2
Wensu 166 E3
Wen Xian 173 K2
Wenzhou 167 N6
Wepener 188 E5
Weri 171 J6
Wernigerode 150 D3
Werra 150 D3
Werris Creek 193 L5
Wertach 150 D4
Weser 150 C2
Weslaco 208 D7
Wessel Islands 193 H1
West Auckland 135 H2
West Bay 208 H6
West Bengal 173 G4
West Branch Susquehanna 205 M6
West Bromwich 133 E2
Westbrook 205 Q5
West Burra 136 A2
Westbury 133 E3
Westbury-sub-Mendip 132 E3
Westby 204 E5
West Calder 137 E5
West End 209 N7
Westerdale 135 J2
Westerham 133 H3
Westerland 150 C1
Western Australia 192 E3
Western Desert 183 E2
Western Ghats 172 D5
Western Isles 136 A3
Westernport 205 L7
Western Ross 136 C3
Western Sahara 180 C4
Western Samoa 191 U4
Westerschelde 144 E3
Westerstede 150 B2
Westerwald 150 B3
West Falkland 219 E10
Westfield *U.K.* 136 E2
Westfield *Massachusetts* 205 P5
Westfield *New York* 205 L5
West Frankfort 204 F8
Westgate 135 G2
West Gerinish 136 A3
West Glamorgan 132 D3
West Glen 133 G2
West Harptree 132 E3
West Heslerton 135 J2
West Hoathly 133 G3
West Indies 128 D4
West Kilbride 137 D5
West Kirby 135 F3
West Linton 137 E5
Westlock 199 N5
Westmeath 139 G6
West Memphis 208 G3
West Meon 133 F3
West Mersea 133 H3
West Midlands 133 F2
West Moors 133 F4
Westmoreland 193 H2
Weston 205 K7
Weston-Super-Mare 132 E3
West Palm Beach 209 M7
West Plains 204 E8
West Point *Mississippi* 208 H4
West Point *Nebraska* 203 R7
Westport *Ireland* 138 C5
Westport *New Zealand* 195 C4
Westport Quay 138 C5
Westray 136 F1
Westray Firth 136 E1
West Road 198 L5
West Sussex 133 G4
West Tavaputs Plateau 202 J8
West Virginia 205 K7
West Wellow 133 F4
West Wyalong 193 K5
West Yellowstone 202 J5
West Yorkshire 135 H3
Wetar 171 H7
Wetar, Selat 171 H7
Wetaskiwin 199 N5
Wetherby 135 H3
Wewahitchka 209 K5
Wewak 194 C2
Wexford *Ireland* 139 J8
Wexford *Ireland* 139 K8
Wexford Bay 139 K8
Wey 133 G3
Weybridge 133 G3
Weyburn 203 N3
Weyhill 133 F3
Weymouth 132 E4
Weymouth Bay *Australia* 193 J1
Weymouth Bay *U.K.* 132 E4
Whakataki 195 F4
Whakatane 195 F2
Whalsay 136 A1
Whanganui Inlet 195 D4
Whangaparaoa 195 G2
Whangarei 195 E1
Whangaruru Harbour 195 D1
Whaplode 133 G2
Wharanui 195 E4
Wharfe 135 H2
Wharfedale 135 H3
Wharton 208 D6
Whataroa 195 C5
Wheatland 203 M6
Wheatley *Nottinghamshire, U.K.* 135 J3
Wheatley *Oxfordshire, U.K.* 133 F3
Wheeler Peak 202 G8
Wheeling 205 K6
Whernside 135 G2
Whidbey, Point 193 H5
Whitburn *Lothian, U.K.* 137 E5
Whitburn *Tyne and Wear, U.K.* 135 H2
Whitby 135 J2
Whitchurch *Avon, U.K.* 132 E3
Whitchurch *Hampshire, U.K.* 133 F3
Whitchurch *Shropshire, U.K.* 132 E2
White *Canada* 198 G3
White *Arkansas* 208 G3
White *Indiana* 204 G7
White *Missouri* 204 D8
White *S. Dakota* 203 P6
White *Texas* 207 M4
Whiteadder Reservoir 137 F5
White Bay 201 Q7
Whitecourt 199 M5
Whitefish 202 G3
Whitefish Lake 199 P3
Whitefish Point 204 H3
White Gull Lake 201 P6
Whitehall 205 P5
White Handkerchief, Cape 201 P6
Whitehaven 135 F2
Whitehead 138 L3
Whitehorse 198 H3
Whitehorse Hill 133 F3
White Island 195 F2
White, Lake 192 F3
White Lake 208 F6
Whiteman Range 194 E3
White Mountains 198 F2
White Mount Peak 202 E9
Whitemouth 204 B2
Whiten Head 136 D2
Whiteparish 133 F3
White Pass 198 H4
White River 204 H2
White River Plateau 203 L8
White Salmon 202 D5
White Sea 158 F2
White Sulphur Springs 202 J4
White Volta 184 E4
Whitewater 204 F5
Whitewood 203 N2
Whitfield Moor 135 G2
Whithorn 134 E2
Whiting Bay 137 C5
Whitley Bay 135 H1
Whitmore 132 E2
Whitney, Mount 206 C2
Whitney-on-Wye 132 D2
Whitsand Bay 132 C4
Whitstable 133 J3
Whittlesey 133 G2
Whitton 135 J3
Whittonstall 135 H2
Whitworth 135 G3

301